FIFTH EDITION

Marketing Communications
Integrating offline and online with social media

PR Smith & Ze Zook

KoganPage

LONDON PHILADELPHIA NEW DELHI

39.50

Publisher's note

Every possible effort has been made to ensure that the information contained in this book is accurate at the time of going to press, and the publishers and authors cannot accept responsibility for any errors or omissions, however caused. No responsibility for loss or damage occasioned to any person acting, or refraining from action, as a result of the material in this publication can be accepted by the editor, the publisher or any of the authors.

First published by Kogan Page Limited in 1993
Second edition published in 1998
Third edition published in 2002
Fourth edition published in 2004
Fifth edition published in 2011
Reprinted 2012

120 Pentonville Road
London N1 9JN
United Kingdom
www.koganpage.com

1518 Walnut Street, Suite 1100
Philadelphia PA 19102
USA

4737/23 Ansari Road
Daryaganj
New Delhi 110002
India

© P R Smith 1993, 1998, 2002, 2004, 2011

The right of P R Smith and Z Zook to be identified as the authors of this work has been asserted by them in accordance with the Copyright, Designs and Patents Act 1988.

ISBN   978 0 7494 6193 5
E-ISBN 978 0 7494 6194 2

British Library Cataloguing-in-Publication Data

A CIP record for this book is available from the British Library.

Library of Congress Cataloging-in-Publication Data

Smith, P. R. (Paul Russell), 1957-
   Marketing communications : integrating offline and online with social media / Paul R Smith, Ze Zook.
– 5th ed.
      p. cm.
   Includes index.
   ISBN 978-0-7494-6193-5 – ISBN 978-0-7494-6194-2   1. Communication in marketing.
I. Zook, Ze.   II. Title.
   HF5415.123.S65 2011
   658.8'02–dc22

                                                        2010045798

Typeset by Graphicraft Ltd, Hong Kong
Print production managed by Jellyfish
Printed and bound in Great Britain by Ashford Colour Press

Marketing Communications

Dedicated to the memory of Chris Berry

Chris had the courage of his convictions
and was champion of the underdog.
He was generous in every conceivable way
– the kindest man I ever knew.
A genius in writing, teaching and marketing,
a gentleman and a true friend.
There'll never again be anyone quite like
Christopher Granville Berry.

PAUL SMITH

CONTENTS

FOREWORD

Marketing, and Marketing Communications in particular, has changed forever. And it has all happened since the last edition of this book – the 4th edition – written way back in 2005. What's changed? Two things essentially: first, Social Media arrived and changed the communications model, the budget allocation, workflows and even the definition of media, communications and customer experience as they morphed together.

Second, marketing standards have slipped backwards as customer service got sloppier; whether due to arduous automated telephone queuing systems, sloppy websites or de-motivated staff suffering incessant corporate culls.

The good news is that marketers are now effectively presented with a major opportunity to be outstanding by just doing the basics right. In fact, they can become world-class players if they layer on top some creativity, disciplined processes and constant improvement.

Marketers have also got the opportunity of getting back into the boardroom as social media positions marketing at the centre of the business; listening to customers, extending the brand experience and reaching out and collaborating with stakeholders in previously entirely unimaginable ways, compared with just a few years ago. Social Media – if fully integrated – draws marketers into Product Portfolio Planning; New Product Development; Customer Engagement; Customer Relationship Management; Lifetime Values.

In fact, social media has created a new Marketing Utopia – listening and engaging and effectively inviting customers to shape the future of the business (explored in Chapter 1). This requires new skills, which have been explored throughout the book. This 5th edition also has a subtle theme of creativity integrated throughout. Creativity – with structured processes and workflows behind it, combined with Social Media – can deliver significant results. Do alert us about any examples of creative marketing that delivers results offline or online at www.Facebook.com/PRSmithMarketing.

What's new in this 5th edition?

Emerging creative marketing talent, Ze Zook, has co-authored this edition, which incorporates new chapters on Branding, Relationship Marketing and of course, Social Media (and websites). In Part 2, the ten communications tools all have online and social media integrated with the offline communications tools. In addition to the complete set of new mini cases, KAM (Key Account Management) has been added to the Sales Management chapter, Rational Emotional dichotomy to the Advertising chapter, and New Laws/ Regulations and emerging ethics in the Changing Communications Environment.

There is also a swathe of online support materials including video clips on www.PRSmith.org.

ACKNOWLEDGEMENTS

Special thanks to Jonathon Taylor, co-author on previous editions.

Kristina Allen, ion interactive

Warren Allot, Photographer

Zaid Al-Zaidy, Saint Digital

Jeremy Baker

Riccardo Benzo, Managing Expectations

Michael Bland, Author

Sarah Botterill, European Interactive Advertising Association

Adrian Brady, Eulogy

JoAnna Brandi, The Customer Care Coach®

Alan Briefel, StratCom

Scott Brinker, ion international

Ged Carroll, Ruder Finn

Dr Dave Chaffey, Smart Insights

Mary Pat Clark, Pew Research Center

Alistair Clay, Plan UK

Amelia Collins, Photographer

Keith Curley, Muzu.TV

Jenny Ellery, Saatchi **mailto: jenny.ellery@saatchi.co.uk** & Saatchi

Annie Fong, Mischief PR

Stuart Fowkes, Oxfam

Rob Gotlieb, Muzu.TV

Jonathan Grant, Grenadier Advertising

Gavin Grimes, McBoom

Craig Hannah Econsultancy

Dr Hansen, Hansen

Chloe Haynes, Cadbury

Neil Hegarty, BMP Optimum

John Horsley, Ace-A-metric.com **http://ace-a-metric.com/**

Martin Hutchins, Cambridge Professional Academy

Peter 'Magic' Johnston, MediaZoo Studios

Nigel Jones, Herdman Jones Associates Ltd

Isobel Kerr-Newell, SweeneyVesty

Gary Leyden, Vrising

Chris Lake, Econsultancy **mailto:chris@econsultancy.com**

Mike Langford, BT

Basil Long, Kroner Consultants

Jez Lysaght, HD&M Creative

Toby Marsden, Survival International

Steve Martin, M&C Saatchi Sport & Entertainment

Ian Maynard, Northstar Research Partners

Davy McDonald, davymac.com

Paul McFarland, Goldhawk

Gerry McGovern, Gerry McGovern

Sharon McLaughlin, McLaughlin Gibson Communications

Claire Mitchell, Natural History Museum

Ian Morton, Happy Tuesdays

Jorian Murray, DDB London

Orson Nava, Director/ Content Producer

Julia O'Brien, Moonshine Media

Brian O'Neill, Freshideas.ie Ltd

Paul O'Sullivan, Dublin Institute of Technology

Marie Page, Musicademy.com

Hina Patel, Creating Results From Vision Ltd

Alexandra Phelan, Paddy Power

Ben Queenborough, Photographer

Suresh Raj, Borkowski

Charles Randall, SAS Solutions

Mark Read, Photographer

Josh Rex, This Is Open

Kevin Roberts, Saatchi & Saatchi

Dennis Sandler, PACE University

Heather Sewell, ICE

Adam Sharp, CleverTouch

Joel Simon, Flickerpix Animations Ltd

Graeme Slattery, Slattery Communications

Merlin Stone, The Customer Framework

Rex Sweetman, Muscutt Sweetman

Dr Peter Tan, World Financial Group

Jamie Tosh, Kick4change

Jon Twomey, Student Support Group

Neil Verlander, Friends of the Earth

Gian Walker, Network Co-op Ltd

Steve Wellington, Havavision Records

Ze's particular thanks: I dedicate this work to my wife, Revital and daughter, Nessa, for their patience and understanding and to my mother and father for their acceptance and nourishment of my being.

Paul's particular thanks to Aran, Cian and Lily and the ever patient, lovely, Beverley. And lastly, a very special thanks to Owen Palmer (RIP) who gave me my first break in UK Academia and never ceased to inspire and encourage me even long after he had retired.

ABOUT THE AUTHORS

PR Smith

Paul is a marketing consultant, best-selling business author and inspirational speaker. Paul has helped hundreds of businesses to boost their results with better marketing, including innovative start-ups such as 'short game golf' in China and established blue chip companies like IBM in the United States. He integrates social media with all marketing activities. He manages the social media for a start-up renewable energy company who have achieved market capitalization of over US $500 million in 18 months. He also advises UK Trade & Investment and Business Links. Paul's books, DVDs and renowned SOSTAC® Planning system are used in over 60 countries. The Chartered Institute of Marketing (CIM) describe Paul's best-selling *Marketing Communications* as a "Marketing Major". His eMarketing eXcellence book is CIM's recommended text. His *Great Answers To Tough Marketing Questions* is translated into seven languages and his Strategic Marketing Communications breaks new ground. A Fellow of CIM, Paul's own personal passion is his social media campaign to get sportsmanship back on the agenda with an inspirational book and blog called **www. GreatMomentsOfSportsmanship.com**. Paul enjoys public speaking, and whether conferences, workshops, webinars or virtual events, his presentations are engaging, entertaining and carefully structured to embed immediate improvements. Visit **www.PRSmith.org** or **www.Facebook.com/PRSmithMarketing**.

Ze Zook

Ze Zook is an up and coming integrated marketing author, lecturer and consultant specializing in the creative industries. He has worked with ballet, film and music, working with sponsors such as Sainsbury's and The Prince's Trust. He has also worked with PR Smith for over 20 years on projects ranging from an award-winning, innovative, 3 screen PR Training video to the Chartered Institute of Marketing's online eLearning programmes developed with PR Smith's eLearning company to writing and researching innovative marketing projects. Having started as a video/digital media producer and photographer, Ze developed a unique creative perspective on integrated marketing. He helps creative businesses to fulfil both their missions and their business goals, and he has written on media and digital marketing for Cambridge Marketing College. His consultancy, lecturing and writing, harness creativity in a fast-changing digital age. Visit **http:// www.linkedin.com/in/zzook**.

HOW TO USE THIS BOOK

This book should not be read from cover to cover but rather it should be used as a reference when addressing a particular aspect of marketing communications. The integrated nature of the subject does, however, refer the reader to other chapters and sections that are relevant to the particular area of interest. The anecdotal style, examples, case studies, questions, key points and sections have been carefully structured so that the reader can dip into an area of interest, absorb the information and cross-refer if required. This allows the reader to extract specific answers quickly and easily. This book is designed to entertain as well as inform and so it is hoped that when dipping into a particular area, the reader will be lured into reading more.

Part 1 (see Figure 0.1) introduces new marketing communications (largely driven by social media), branding, customer relationship management, buyer behaviour and communications theory. Part 1 continues to build a background to marketing communications by looking at what information market research can and cannot provide, how to work with agencies and consultancies of all types, understanding the media, moving with the changing business environment, international marketing and ultimately shows how to write a marketing communications plan using the simple SOSTAC® Planning System.

Part 2 covers specific marketing communication tools that marketing professionals have to manage at some time or other. These include selling and sales management (and Key Account Management), advertising, PR, sponsorship, sales promotion, direct mail, exhibitions (all online and offline), packaging, and finally, websites that work and social media that wins.

The case studies at the end of each chapter in Part 2 have been carefully selected to show a range of different types and sizes of organizations using various communications tools across a range of different industries and markets. Materials are drawn from both small organizations with small budgets and larger businesses with multi-billion dollar budgets.

This book should prove useful to anyone interested, or working, in marketing.

The reader will discover that all of the communication tools can and should integrate with each other, as shown in Figure 0.2 and explained at the end of Chapter 1.

It is therefore sometimes difficult to separate and categorize an activity as being one type of tool or another. For example, direct marketing and sales promotions should probably be called 'direct promotions' since they both more than likely involve each other. The chapters are not listed in order of importance. Selling and sales management is not always included in a marketing communications budget but the sales force is a potent form of communication and generally they (or the sales manager) report to the marketing manager. In fact it has been put to the top of the list because all the other chapters thereafter tend to lead into each other.

The successful application of the marketing communications mix is helped by an understanding of communication theory and buyer behaviour theory. Marketing research can provide some practical and specific answers to the questions that the theories generate. This provides the building blocks for the marketing communications plan, which draws upon an understanding of how agencies operate and how different media work. The details of the plan are worked out within the sometimes complex, but always integrated, web of the marketing communications mix (see Figure 0.2). The changing marketing communications environment and international opportunities/threats constantly affect the whole marketing communications mix. The world has moved on since the 4th edition.

Different organizations allocate the same communication tools to different departments/budgets, eg exhibitions may be seen to be part of public relations, although the sales team will man the stand and benefit from extra sales. Sponsorship is considered by some to be an extension of advertising, while others consider it to be part of PR. And no one is too sure about whose budget covers the website. Regardless of classifications, ownership and responsibilities, each tool must integrate with many others.

We are always looking to update the material within the book and our readers are invited to contact us with any ideas, suggestions and contributions to the next edition. As our subject of marketing communications is ever changing, we are keen to keep the content fresh and lively. Please post your examples of excellent marketing communications to us at **www.Facebook.com/PRSmithMarketing**.

All lecturers who use this fifth edition can obtain instructor support materials from Kogan Page. Visit **http://www.koganpage.com/ resources/books/marketingcommunications** and use the password MC0389.

FIGURE 0.1   Part One: Background to the communications process

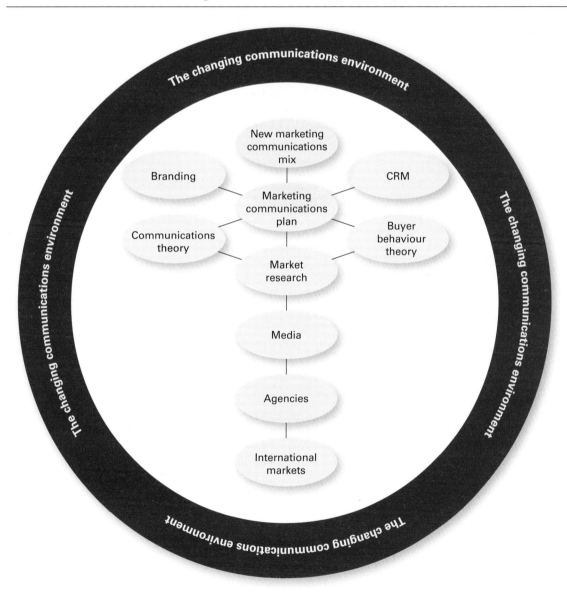

FIGURE 0.2   Part Two: The marketing communications mix

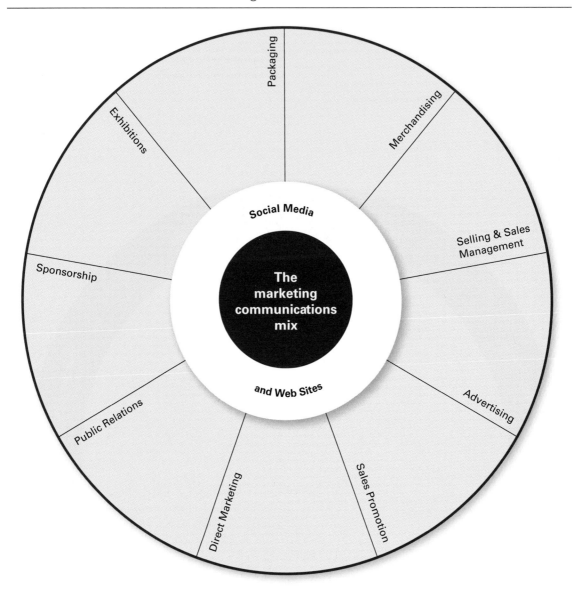

PART ONE
Communications Background and Theories

01
New marketing communications

LEARNING OBJECTIVES

By the end of this chapter you will be able to:

- Understand why this is the beginning of a new era in marketing
- Grasp the importance of social media
- Consider applying the ladder of engagement
- Present a case for the marketing director to sit on the board

The revolution has started

A new marketing era, long overdue, was heralded in when social media emerged as a real game changer. Social media put customers back at the centre of the organization and gave marketers a new set of tools to listen to them and to encourage them to engage with the brand. A golden opportunity has emerged as organizations realize the possibilities of engaging with customers in new ways so they can become partners driving the business forward. The ladder of engagement makes it easy to nurture customers up to higher levels of involvement.

'Joined-up marketing' brings the old 'outbound marketing' (eg advertising, direct mail, telemarketing, etc, sending out messages) together with inbound marketing (where social media brings conversations to the organization). Integrating inbound and outbound with online and offline communications delivers higher impact and more cost-effective 'joined-up marketing'.

Marketing communications have to be integrated for two reasons. Firstly, unintegrated databases cause many problems and complications, as there is no single picture of the customer. Secondly, as communications morph into customer experiences, all communications need to be integrated to deliver a consistent experience.

Amidst hyper-competition this ladder helps to build a ring fence of protection around the precious customer. It also encourages customers, and even non-customers, to collaborate and create anything from better promotions to better processes to better products. This marketing utopia is the beginning of a new creative age in marketing. It is also a new era of collaborative co-creation, which moves marketing into a strategic position and earns its seat at the board.

There is a golden opportunity for marketers to create stronger brands and sustainable competitive advantage and ultimately to build better businesses (or organizations). There has never been a better time to be involved in marketing.

The colouring department is dead

A lot of 'old' marketing has had too much emphasis on just marketing communications. This is a weakness. Once upon a time this worked, as customers had far fewer communication channels and therefore it was easier to get a customer's attention if marketers had the budget. And the big budget brands often announced 'as seen on TV' on their packaging, at point-of-sale and in their press advertisements. Being on TV gave the brand a level of credibility, perhaps because customers unconsciously assumed that being on TV meant that the company was a big company and big companies were trustworthy. Or perhaps customers trusted TV and the authorities that regulate the advertisements that are allowed on TV.

This may have led to communications strategies that told customers about product benefits. Today, marketing strategies ask 'How will customers engage with us and each other?' This leads to the bigger question 'What kind of customer experience are marketers creating?' This in turn brings marketers back to the quintessential marketing question: 'How do we help customers?' This is, for example, the ultimate reason why any company has a website. Yet many, if not most, marketers answer this question incorrectly. Ask around and see. In fact, helping customers is the only reason a company exists, as American guru Peter Drucker used to say.

These kinds of questions move marketers beyond communications, into customer experiences, customer relations, new product development processes, service processes and, of course, brand evaluation, which affects market capitalization. This, ultimately, invites marketers back into the boardroom, hopefully speaking the language of the board. Social media and the ladder of engagement, in particular, have opened the door to the boardroom for marketers.

The colouring department

'Not so long ago I was invited into a major global bank and given the brief: "To stop the board from referring to the marketing department as the colouring department."'

P R Smith

When real marketing percolates up through the organization, real competitive advantage emerges. Consider National Semiconductor in the United States. They make chips for mobiles and DVD players. Their target market was design engineers and purchasing agents. Their enlightened CEO asked that quintessential marketing question: 'How can the website help engineers more?' A truly inquisitive mind forced them to understand how design engineers work and whether any online tools could help. They explored customer scenarios and discovered that the design process of choosing a part was to create a design, analyse the design, build a prototype, test, etc.

Now the engineer logs on and is prompted to specify the overall parameters and key components. The system auto-generates possible designs and technical specs, parts list, prices and cost benefit analysis. Engineers refine it and share it with colleagues. They test and refine it. Result engineers can do in two hours what previously took two months. By the end of the first year they had 31,000 visitors generating 3,000 orders or referrals every day. One integrated socket with Nokia was worth 40 million units. This site helps customers so well that it creates sustainable competitive advantage whilst delivering a highly engaging brand experience. The change was made in 2000.

It is time for marketing to move beyond communications, permeate the boardroom and help to build more sustainable businesses amidst a rapidly changing marketplace.

Why marketing was marginalized

'And seeing marketing as a series of distinct activities has been the reason that marketing has become more marginalised over the last 15 years because it has been positioned as managing communications rather than managing the whole business orientation.'

Jenkinson (2004)

Communications morphing with experiences

Marketing communications are morphing with customer experiences and product development and distribution, as the impact of digital media is hugely enhanced by social media. This has not gone unnoticed by the world's best marketers. Take Unilever, which moved its digital marketing out of the media mix and into the marketing mix in 2007 (*WARC*, 2007). It realized that its digital budget was part of the overall marketing mix, rather than part of its media spend/marketing communications mix 'in recognition that successful digital campaigns are based more on producing engaging content than paying for media time and space' (*Financial Times*, 25 June 2007). Engaging content enhances the customer experience.

The search for added value is now relentless, whether through new features or more likely through enhanced web experiences, social media sharing or simply the addition of features to a product or service never dreamt possible before the arrival of the iPhone apps, eg Gibson Guitar's app includes a guitar tuner, a metronome and a chord chart, all of which are extremely useful for any guitarist. Kraft's iFood Assistant delivers recipes and a feature that creates a shopping list that automatically includes the ingredients for the chosen recipes. It even identifies the locations of nearby grocery stores and which aisles stock the items.

In fact Kraft Foods' continued creative approach seems to have scored a hit for its Lacta chocolate bar in Greece by showing a long form of a long-form ad – a 27-minute branded-entertainment film about love, made by many customers (see 'The ladder of engagement', page 18).

Nike's search to help customers led it to the Nike+ – a joint venture with Apple's iPod that enables joggers to access a jogging community website, log their runs and connect with and compare to other joggers by using their iPods (or their iPhones) and a Nike+ branded transmitter that can be fitted into some specially designed Nike shoes or attached to other running shoes. This is a far cry from just marketing communications, but it is all about helping customers and strengthening the brand and growing revenues. Word-of-mouth marketing has become an 'over-riding industry preoccupation for marketers as it provides a good measure of success (if customers endorse brands to their peers). Nike's initiative has generated impressive results with Nike's director of digital and content claiming "97 per cent of Nike+ users said they would recommend the service to a friend. That figure is unheard of"' (Grande, 2007).

Think of '4Es instead of 4Ps' (Rothery, 2008) from the old marketing mix. A product is an experience (including online), place becomes everyplace, price becomes exchange and promotion becomes evangelism. Alternatively, promotion is morphing with product as communications seek to engage customers with experiences.

Marketing's antithesis

All of the above is the 'antithesis of the "compared to Brand X" or "now 10 per cent better" approaches' (Beck, 2010). Although it does mean some 'show and tell' communications, it heavily depends on discovering what current customers really like about the product or service and how else the company could help the customer, and then ensuring every other contact point consistently reflects these highly relevant added values, whereas marketing used to be largely about creating messages for a passive audience with little choice and less empowerment, where the most active element was the decision whether to notice or ignore an advertisement. The once passive audience has been unshackled and empowered by technology. As marketers stalk rapidly changing markets, they face a brave new world, one that has changed for ever, offering new opportunities to those who seize them.

Social media opens up new channels of communication that give marketers direct access to customers and opinion formers. Web 2.0, and soon Web 3.0, facilitates a dialogue; some call it a 'trialogue' (Earls, 2002), as opinion formers and customers and the brand owners engage in conversations. Some of these conversations are within the brand's official online space, and some occur way beyond the brand's space and are just amongst customers without any corporate influence.

> ### What will happen?
>
> 'What will happen when consumer experiences [created by consumers] are much more interesting and accurate than anything an organization's marketers upload?'
>
> Hoffman (2009)

Utopia?

The more enlightened companies build information architecture and business processes around social media: processes that pick up comments about the brand wherever they occur; systems that respond (sometimes auto-responses and sometimes individual human responses); and systems that categorize the discussions. The dialogue generates valuable feedback that is often quicker and cheaper than focus groups. This research needs to be fed to the right people in marketing. Social media allows us to learn a lot more about customers very quickly – if the systems and processes are in place. The key is to use this information to make better decisions.

Other levels of engagement invite customers as stakeholders to engage at a higher level by creating user-generated content or fully blown collaborative co-creation to deliver new products and solutions. See page 19 for more.

Social media is more than just communications; it is a new way of working that requires new information flows. They affect more than just communications, but feed into new product development, distribution channels and even pricing.

Marketing is being forced out of the communications silo and back into full-blown marketing courtesy of social media. This new opportunity to excel as marketers is increased by the decline of marketing, and customer service in particular.

The customer service time bomb

Continual culling of employees and general cost cutting combined with sloppy marketing execution has put marketers on the cusp of a customer revolution. Many organizations' efforts to continuously cut costs and cull employees have finally delivered a threshold of inefficiency, leaving in their wake an overburdened, over-anxious and, frankly, less caring staff. Customer surveys reveal that many customers are angry, irritated, impatient and ready to switch to another brand as soon as something better becomes available. In a word, they are dissatisfied. This is a real marketing problem, or opportunity, depending which way the CEO and CMO see it.

We have gone backwards in marketing. Look around. You will see falling satisfaction scores, sloppy websites, telephone queues, customer service people who can't answer questions and others who simply don't really care. Have salespeople lost their vocation, their passion and their deep product knowledge? How many bad experiences do customers suffer whilst seeking service from a utility, a phone company or a bank either on the phone or on a website? Why are there so many sloppy websites?

The manager's online banking system: a foreign country he rarely visited

'Recently, I had problems with online banking. After lots of frustration with technical support, I rang my bank manager. In the past, whenever I had a problem he had been extremely helpful and made sure it was resolved immediately. This time around, things were different. "I'm not technical," he told me. He began to talk about his bank's online banking service as if it were a foreign country he had rarely visited. He was behaving like a typical senior manager when it came to IT. He wanted to wash his hands of responsibility. It was not his domain. IT, it seems, is not the responsibility of senior managers or CEOs. They have much more important things to do, obviously.'

McGovern (2010)

Look at the stats. Look at the surveys – even the UK National Customer Satisfaction Index shows falling satisfaction scores amongst the top-performing brands.

One recent customer service conference speaker showed falling customer satisfaction scores across a range of industries. When asked if this meant that we were getting worse at marketing, the speaker said 'No, it's the customers' rising expectations combined with lower tolerance levels that have changed.' So it is the customers' fault?

'I was at a conference recently where a speaker asked an audience of some 600 intranet professionals to raise their hands if their organizations used SAP. About 60 percent of the audience put their hands up. Then the speaker asked the audience: "How many of you like using SAP?" Not a single hand went up. Not one.'

McGovern (2010)

Lower tolerance levels: perhaps customers have simply become angrier. And, if so, why so? Perhaps anxiety is on the rise. Don't customers like endless automated telephone queuing systems, robotic

rerouteing or, if they are lucky, after queuing and rerouting getting to speak to someone whom they cannot understand, or to someone who cannot solve the problem, who then puts them back into a queuing system? We have gone backwards in marketing.

How many people have had bad experiences online with websites that are confusing, have dead ends or just don't work, sites that waste precious time and cause irritation? And all the time advertising budgets are wasted driving customers to these sites. Why are there so many sloppy websites? They forget the basics – regular usability testing. This is basic stuff, which many brands are ignoring. Check the website to see it works all right on-screen and across different browsers also.

Harvard's Ram Charan and business CEO Larry Bossidy wrote a book called *Execution: The discipline of getting things done* (2002), where they claimed that the ability to execute better than the competition was the last source of real sustainable competitive advantage. Even though it was written in 2002, it is now more appropriate than ever before as major organizations damage their brands day after day with dead-end websites and atrocious, systemized but sloppy customer care. It is relatively easy to be better than most if the basics are executed professionally.

So have companies got worse at marketing? If yes, this creates a huge opportunity for those organizations that know how to listen to their customers, continually improve and stay relevant.

There are no secrets

'The networked market knows more than companies do about their own products. And whether the news is good or bad, they tell everyone.'

Levine *et al* (2000)

Accelerated change and hyper-competition

We are experiencing accelerated change. Take accelerated brand creation. Once upon a time it took two generations to build a major brand; now it takes just a year or two if you get it right. Look at Amazon, Facebook and Hotmail. Once upon a time it took several generations to acquire 50 million users. Facebook did it in less than one (in fact Facebook acquired 100 million in one year). This simply could never have happened 10 years ago. Radio took almost 40 years to reach 50 million users, while TV took 13 years, the Internet four years, the iPod three years, Facebook one year and the iPhone less than a year to get 100 million users.

And now we've got accelerated brand power as global boundaries fall. Perhaps a seminal moment in marketing occurred when the *Financial Times* journalist Winston Fletcher acknowledged the power of the brand and ergo the power and importance of marketing when he asked: 'What gives brands their power to influence, if not quite control, people's purchasing decisions and thus their power to influence, if not quite control, modern economies?'

And then China's President Hu visited the United States. His first appointment was with a brand, Microsoft, and his second appointment was with President Bush.

Another seminal moment occurred in 2000, as for the first time 50 per cent of the world's largest economic entities were companies (brands) and not countries.

Global boundaries are falling; the Iron Curtain has been swept aside, the Berlin Wall torn down and the Chinese gates flung open partly by political movement, partly by aggressive businesses seeking growth overseas and partly by the internet giving instant global access driven by customers who are ready to buy from anywhere in the world whenever they want.

And, all the time, category-less competitors quietly step across old borders.

Once upon a time, supermarkets sold groceries and petrol stations sold petrol. Now petrol stations sell DVDs, fresh coffee, groceries, gambling and a lot more, while grocery stores sell petrol, garden furniture, car insurance and soon legal advice (including DIY divorce kits), as well as groceries. Powerful category-less brands take more 'share of wallet'. Customers trust some brands sufficiently to try other products from the same brand name. The Tesco brand is so strong it could probably sell customers anything (as long as it meets reasonable quality standards). This is 'share of wallet'. Growth for most US companies was forecasted to come from share of wallet rather than growth from finding new

customers. Enlightened boardrooms understand the power of the brand, its access to 'share of wallet' and its impact on the balance sheet.

Combine category-less, fast-moving competitors with borderless markets and you get hyper-competition. No market or business is safe.

The need to wholeheartedly adapt to and embrace change is akin to the need for frogs to stay out of the kitchen. If you take a frog and put it into a boiling pot of water, it will jump out somewhat blistered, but it will survive. If, on the other hand, you put a frog in a cold pan of water and slowly raise the temperature it will boil to death.

Business is similar. No one will change your environment so rapidly that you have to change your behaviour immediately. It just changes continually.

Amidst this hyper-competition some CEOs wake up in the middle of the night in a cold sweat worried about their value chain and wondering who is unpicking the lock on their value chain. Teams of analysts and MBAs from Boston to Beijing analyse industry after industry, sector by sector, to find businesses with a weak link in their value chain that would benefit from a third-party supplier fulfilling a piece of the value chain. Most CEOs know some parts of their value chain, whether production, logistics or after-sales, are more profitable than other parts. When they get an offer to replace the weakest link with a higher-quality link (or service) at lower cost and seamlessly linked by web technology, many CEOs find this a very attractive proposition.

> 'We have only two sources of competitive advantage: the ability to learn more about our customers faster than the competition; the ability to turn that learning into action faster than the competition.'
>
> Former GE CEO Jack Welch

As the company moves from a value chain to a seamlessly connected value network, CEOs are forced to consider the most basic of questions: 'What business are we in?' This can only be answered by asking a very basic question: 'What do customers want now and in the future and what is our sustainable competitive advantage (SCA)?'

When I ask CEOs what is their SCA, I usually get answers that include patents, product differentiation, cost efficiencies, and sometimes distribution channels. Most of these can be, and are being, attacked. Two major sources of SCA, if managed carefully, are the brand and customer relationships – inseparable, you may say.

However, many companies damage these two critical assets. Sloppy customer service and negative customer relationship management (CRM) destroy brands. (See Chapters 2, 3 and 21.) Despite the importance of CRM, many companies are still sitting on a customer service time bomb. And it's ticking. Those who ignore it will be left behind, in the same way that those who ignore the golden opportunity presented by social media will also be left behind. Those who embrace it, seize the opportunity, develop rigorous processes around the new technologies and continually strive to find and satisfy customer needs will survive and thrive.

Who are the survivors?

'It is not the strongest of the species that survives, nor the most intelligent that survives. It is the one that is the most adaptable to change.'

Charles Darwin

Social media – the biggest change since the industrial revolution

'Social Media is the biggest change since the industrial revolution.' *Business Week* said this as far back as 2005. A month later the *Economist* magazine went further and simply said: 'companies that don't understand digital communities will die'. Social media has now become the centre of many marketing strategies.

Customers have discovered a whole new way to find out about products and services. Product review sites, ratings, discussion groups, Facebook petitions, blogs, mobile price comparison applications (apps), YouTube demonstrations (positive and negative videos) and Flickr photos: these are social media tools. And customers, not companies, are controlling the flow of marketing information as they shut out interruption marketing and use, instead, social media to find products, ratings and reviews.

Outbound marketing (the old interruption marketing model of advertising, direct mail and telesales) has suffered as audiences switch channels or fast-forward through TV ads, turn on ad blockers on their browsers, stop e-mails with aggressive spam blockers and use caller ID to bar unwanted phone calls. Some outbound marketing does get through but not as much as a few years ago.

While channels fragment (eg TV has approximately 500 channels, while 20 years ago it had five channels), the sources of trust are shifting. Which of these has the biggest influence on your customers: *The Times*, BBC, Sky or Google?

Social media has arrived and customers love it. Social media gives customers control. Marketing has been democratized courtesy of the internet and social media. And within the mass of customers lie the new opinion formers and opinion leaders: bloggers and twitterers. Marketers have a choice: join the conversation or fail to communicate.

Old mass communications interruption models like TV advertising have simply got to be a lot more creative to cut through the clutter and grab the eye of the busy consumer. They also use social media to spread the message (if the content is good enough). Any social media content has not only to be more creative but also highly relevant to the target audience. Suddenly the marketing of a refrigerator has become so creative that it becomes compulsive viewing. And all of this amidst the white heat of hyper-competition.

Social media is not just a marketing tool. It is, effectively, a new way of running a business. It requires a new company culture, which in turn requires company-wide support, systems and incentives. It requires a new mindset: more listening, less shouting. Think relationships and not just sales or transactional marketing. Hasn't this been said before? Yes, it has. It is basic old-school marketing, except that social media allows marketers to listen to customers more easily and more cost-effectively. Social media also relies on a 'sharing' culture, which means sharing information and being helpful. This, in turn, nurtures relationships, which again is the essence of good marketing – developing and strengthening relationships. Social media is not about making short-term sales. It is about sharing and listening and channelling information into systems that alert certain staff to negative discussions, positive discussions, suggestions, complaints, and ideas for new products, new ads, new promotions and new discussions.

Harnessing all these conversations requires new skill sets and new organizational structures. In turn this helps marketers to create a marketing utopia where customers drive the business while marketers lend a helping hand.

There is a new opportunity to use these new technologies to improve marketing in a radically different way – in fact, one so profound that social media has delivered a marketing utopia.

Marketing utopia has arrived

Why social media works

Social media fulfils a fundamental human need: to communicate. We are social animals. We like to communicate with each other. Social media facilitates this by helping us to communicate more easily, to more people, whenever we want. That is why social networks like Myspace, Facebook, YouTube and blogs are so successful. Social media is huge because it simply lets customers communicate with each other and organizations communicate with customers (this includes listening).

This new business environment allows marketers to listen to customers and opinion formers (and other stakeholders), channel their feedback into suggestions and new product ideas, and even test out new concepts and brand names, while all the time engaging customers, developing higher levels of customer loyalty and nurturing brand ambassadors. It's a marketer's utopia.

Web 2.0 is a participatory platform. Organizations that tap into that willingness to participate can do very well. Think beyond the old one-way communications and even beyond a basic dialogue between customer and brand and instead consider a trialogue amongst customers, opinion formers and the brand. Brands can reinterpret themselves as facilitators.

Think about creating branded content, services, and even applications and widgets that give real benefits to customers (and that boost their engagement with the brand). Think about social networks. Become part of them. Exist inside them. Create a profile. Embrace these social platforms, whether photo sharing, music sharing, video sharing, or interest sharing platforms such as bookmarking.

Enabling rating of content and online services – services such as Delicious and comments on blogs – supports this.

Think engagement. Marketers are searching not only for ways to connect brands to customers, but also for ways to connect those customers to each other – with the brand simply facilitating the discussion. The brand can be a place where the community can congregate and discuss and collaborate.

From customer feedback, to product ratings, recommendations and discussions, through to prosumers (customers who help to create, or produce, the next product): this is collaborative co-creation (see 'The ladder of engagement', page 18, for more). Customers are encouraged to be part of an organization's product/service design system and production system. Many customers feel their favourite brand is engaging with them, and they feel some reciprocity as the organization demonstrates that it is listening and consequently taking action. This inherently deepens brand loyalty, purchasing and advocacy.

Many customers like to have a meaningful input into the products and services they consume. Some don't, but many influential ones do. Getting private previews or input into shaping what is yet to come creates a sense of being an insider as opposed to being just another external customer sitting on a 'customer service time bomb'.

> 'If you're paying attention, you get the answers to questions you didn't even think to ask.'
> Schlack (2008)

Social media makes it easy for both customers and organizations to communicate with each other. They allow everyone to get to know each other better, understand each other's needs and issues, nurture relationships and collaborate, sometimes in highly destructive ways and sometimes in highly creative ways.

How social media works

Consider the basics – blogs, Twitter, YouTube, Flickr, Wikipedia, Google Maps, Google Earth, virtual worlds and augmented reality (AR). All of these help to spread or share useful information with potentially vast online audiences. By posting articles and comments on to blogs, photographs on to Flickr and videos on to YouTube, you allow other people to see your messages and, if they like them, share them with their friends, who in turn can share them with their friends' networks. Social media simply widens an organization's net by spreading its branded content (and web links) out to a potentially vast audience.

These social assets are picked up by search engines when people search for certain phrases. Search engines like Google do a universal search, which now includes websites, videos, photos and a lot more, so broadening an organization's social assets simply widens an organization's net, which may consequently catch more prospects who are searching for specific terms if these terms or key phrases have been added as tags (or labels) to the various assets.

All social media can be optimized, eg blogs and websites can be optimized (search engine optimization – SEO) so that critical key phrases are used in the copy, headings, links to other pages or other sites (this is called 'anchor text'), page title tags (labels), photo tags (labels) and video tags (labels). Most importantly, Google also measures key phrase frequency of use, recency of postings and, of course, inbound links. These inbound links from venerable sites improve Google rankings, as Google treats it as a vote of confidence in the site if venerable organizations are linking to the site.

The website and/or blog can become a unique platform of expertise or entertainment or whatever the desired goal. It may also become a hub of discussions on whatever subscribers want. When other relevant bloggers link to a blog it widens the net again.

Multiple social bookmarking facilities on the blog allow readers to bookmark it (or make it a favourite), post it to their own Facebook profile or send the link via e-mail to a friend. It is just one click away. Then other people look at their network members' bookmarks to see what their network of friends or business colleagues are reading and recommending. The net widens.

Simultaneously, an RSS feed automatically feeds the new blog posts directly into a person's RSS reader, so instead of having to visit 10 favourite websites the person can get all the updates from the reader.

Twitter is the hugely popular 140-character micro-blogging network. It is a river of short messages usually with links to interesting content on a blog, a website or YouTube. The twitterer's messages (tweets) appear in the stream of messages (or updates) shared by the network of followers. Just like Facebook and LinkedIn, Twitter allows networks to see who is saying what (or doing what).

Your tweets can also be found if key phrases that are being searched for also appear in the tweet. Organizations search and track all Twitter conversations for references to their brands, companies and staff – particularly during conference time, when twitterers tweet comments about companies.

The 'retweet' facility allows twitterers to pass someone else's tweet to their own network of followers with just one click of a button. Certain messages can spread like wildfire on Twitter. Twitter can widen an organization's net. It can also be used for customer service, as is proved by easyJet, which finds it to be a useful tool to give quick responses. The Irish Bus Company (Bus Eireann) sells thousands of euros' worth of special-offer bus tickets every week to its network of mostly students. Dell says Twitter has helped to sell millions of dollars of kit. See Chapter 21 for more.

Videos can be posted on all the current popular video-sharing sites, including YouTube, via a video aggregator called TubeMogul, and photos can be posted on Flickr. YouTube and Flickr can be seamlessly embedded in the blog or website, so they appear on the website but also appear in YouTube if someone searches for certain keywords. Each of these social platform attracts its own audience towards key phrases and similar videos, photos or audios. All of these assets are publicly searchable, so once again tagging (labelling) is critical. It is easy to create your own channel on YouTube. Social bookmarking, sharing and favourites extend videos' reach even further into the net.

Wikipedia is a growing fountain of knowledge. Over time organizations can build their own profile by adding relevant factual articles (complete with links). This further spreads the net and may embrace other experts to participate in collaborating on certain articles.

Google Maps and Google Earth complete the net at this stage. Office locations, addresses, phone numbers, directions and web addresses can all be uploaded into Google Earth and Google Maps. Photographs of buildings can be added. Videos can be uploaded also. All of this can be shared with peers and visitors. Data created in Google Earth are also available in Google Maps. Again this spreads your net by extending your presence.

If the locations have visually interesting material for different audiences, visitors can view offices, factories, stores, building sites or any projects in 360-degree virtual reality photos from different viewpoints (and, if relevant, with time-lapse photos showing development stages). All data are tagged (labelled) and linked so that the net widens while the visitor experience is enhanced (eg each office and/or project can have a map for directions, a photograph of the building to recognize it, a video tour in advance or a greeting from the MD, or anything that brings it to life and helps the user, plus spreads the net). Three-dimensional models (eg turbines on a wind farm) can also be added. Although data can be seen in both, the Google Earth display is much richer (3D aspects can be shown) than that in Google Maps. All Google Maps display can have a button 'View this in Google Earth'. If someone has not got Google Earth installed it will still show the core data and displays as shown in Google Maps.

Virtual reality

Marketing adaptability requires an inquisitive mind and some experimentation to find what works and what doesn't. Although somewhat criticized, virtual worlds are worth exploring. One of the most popular virtual worlds, Second Life, is reported to be having a 'second life' as its population starts to grow again. Massively multiplayer online games (MMOGs) are forecasted by their owners to reach 1 billion customers in less than 10 years. As initial suggestions are that Web 3.0 will be more 3D and virtual world orientated, it is worth exploring virtual worlds. They cannot be ignored. In 2007, the author held a parallel launch of Northern Ireland's creative digital hub in Second Life. The Minister for Enterprise's avatar addressed a virtual audience (of avatars), with the virtual world presentation simultaneously beamed into the 'real-world' audience in Belfast.

More and more customer service avatars (interactive cartoon characters) are appearing on websites, particularly in the customer care sectors, where they offer themselves as 'your assistant'. Virtual immersion in a non-real world has been around for some time and has crept into people's living rooms in the form of Wii games. These popular virtual

FIGURE 1.1   The real-world presentation

FIGURE 1.2
The virtual-world presentation

games convert a living room instantaneously into a gymnasium, a tennis court, a boxing ring, a dance studio, a keep-fit studio or even a golf course, and players play happily in their virtual worlds. It will become a lot more sophisticated. Have a look at the GE Renewables Smart Grid website, which allows viewers to blow at their PCs and make the virtual turbines turn faster.

The University of Tokyo already has perfect virtual rain that looks like and probably feels like water dropping on to a surface. It may well be that Web 3.0, the semantic web, may combine virtual worlds with intelligent systems, creating whole new opportunities for those who embrace the technology.

Augmented reality allows users to see additional information, eg text or photographs, by pointing a mobile phone and reading any hyper-data posted, eg a building site might contain AR information on the site and what it will look like when finished. Through use of AR software like Layar or other apps from the iStore, the horizon expands as augmented reality emerges.

To summarize, it is not surprising that social media has grown so quickly (the Facebook population now equals that of the fourth-largest country in the world), because social media taps into something deep inside us all – the need to communicate, talk, share and be part of a community. This is fundamental to us as social animals, and satisfies a deep need that is profoundly embedded into our genetic structure. The old push marketing model (of interrupting audiences and pushing ads at them) with 'sell, sell, sell' is being replaced by 'listen, listen, listen' to the conversations and 'share, share, share'.

It is easy to see why social media is now so powerful. The next section reveals why and also proves the power of social media by explaining the maths behind it.

Social networks – herds or individuals?

Consider a target audience of 20 people. Here's how Lilley (2007) calculates how many messages can spread around depending on what media is being used.

Broadcast network is based on a 'one to many' model (eg old TV advertising). It is called a Sarnoff network (after David Sarnoff, the broadcasting legend). A hypothetical Sarnoff network with 20 viewers has a score of 20. The network score is simply the number of nodes (audience members) $\boxed{= 20}$

Telephone and e-mail network is based on a 'many to each other' model. It is called a Metcalf network (after Bob Metcalf, one of the inventors of the Ethernet). This communications model allows everyone to contact each other. Because everyone can call each other, the total possible number of calls or e-mails is 20 squared, or 400. This is potentially much more powerful for communicating messages among people than a Sarnoff network. The network score is node to the power of 2 or 20^2 $\boxed{= 400}$

Social network is an 'immensely more powerful category of network' based on a 'many belong to numerous networks' model. It is called a Reed network (after David Reed, who observed that people in social situations belong to more than just one network). The possible value of a Reed network is 2 to the power of the number of nodes on the network. Take the same group of 20 people in a social situation, whether virtual or real. A Reed network generates a score of 2 the power of the node. This generates a network score of 2^{20} $\boxed{= 1,000,000}$

Moving from a broadcast network to a telephone/e-mail network, even if only 10 per cent of the people pass the message (maybe a special offer, or perhaps a criticism), it still means that 40 messages will be sent around. This is twice as powerful as the TV network, which only had a possible total of 20 messages being received. Moving on to the Reed network (social media network), if 10 per cent spread the message, that generates 100,000 possible messages that can be received. Or, even if only one-tenth of 1 per cent pass the message on, it would still generate 1,000 messages, which is 50 times more powerful than the old TV model with just 20 messages.

Now consider just one social network, LinkedIn, which is sometimes referred to as Facebook for businesspeople. It is a powerful tool. Once registered (which is free), businesspeople start connecting with other businesspeople, effectively building their own networks. If an individual has 170 connections (contacts), LinkedIn calculates how the individual becomes part of a network of approximately 3 million people. Figure 1.3 shows how LinkedIn calculates the size of anyone's network. The maths in the table is taken directly from LinkedIn.

Networks, herds or individuals

Group behaviour is well documented in social studies. Marketers understand the natural impulse to follow the crowd. Some sociologists believe humans are just copying machines, basically. Because humans are social animals, a large percentage of an individual's brainpower is devoted to interacting with others, watching their behaviour and wondering what they think of us. We carry this legacy with us every time we buy a particular brand of washing powder or choose what movie to watch in the cinema. We have learnt or evolved to be animals that are good at copying.

FIGURE 1.3   Your network of trusted professionals

You have 170 connections and are at the centre of your network. Your connections can introduce you to 2,727,600+ professionals – here's how your network breaks down:

1 Your connections   170
Your trusted friends and colleagues

2 Two degrees away   32,900+
Friends of friends; each connected to one of your connections

3 Three degrees away   2,694,600+
Reach these users through a friend and one of their friends

Total users you can contact through an introduction   2,727,600+

> ### Think caveman
>
> If everyone is running away you don't ask why; you just run. Copying means you don't have to learn everything from scratch, and you can defend or protect yourself more easily because you react to things more quickly, so it makes sense from a survival viewpoint.

In the 1960s the sales of domestic air conditioning were followed and mapped for years. Findings showed that the best way to predict who would buy air conditioning came down to whether a person's neighbour had it. People had to see it to be likely to copy it.

The Mexican wave – why? Because everyone in the crowd can see everyone else and is aware of the group behaviour. The Mexican wave cannot be re-created in a shopping centre, because people can't see each other, nor can they see the group behaviour.

Facebook, on the other hand, is like a digital version of the Mexican wave, because people can see what all their friends are doing. They can not only see if their friends are online but also what their friends are currently doing and what they have been up to in the past. If someone gets an invite to Facebook and joins, that person in turn sends invites to his or her friends. Wherever the herd moves next, people follow. The internet just manifests or provides the mechanics for what we are naturally programmed to do.

If someone stands staring at the sky and pointing, that person is bound to get strange looks from passers-by, but get six or seven people standing together staring and pointing at the invisible spaceship and the crowd will swell.

Harnessing the knowledge of the herd has greater potential when it comes to building brand loyalty.

Social media cultural shift

Organizations that are not looking out for and listening to online conversations about their brand are missing a major opportunity. If someone attacks a brand there is an opportunity to address any criticisms and rectify the issues before rumours spread out of control. Conversations cannot be controlled like advertising messages, but organizations can feed accurate information as well as being seen to listen and care. In addition to collecting crucial feedback, ideas and public comments from the marketplace, marketers are provided with a welcome platform to get their message across if it is relevant. This also grows a brand's presence wherever the market congregates online. Ignoring these conversations leaves an organization on the outside and soon to be replaced by another brand that does want to be a part of the conversation.

Social media provides a platform to:

● reach out to increasingly difficult-to-contact customers;

- help customers by sharing expertise (and therefore branding) with audiences rather than trying to use it for direct sales;
- listen to the vocal elements within a market.

This requires a cultural and organizational shift and more of a listening and sharing culture than a selling culture. It requires a real customer orientation, which drives the marketing utopia. After the listening and sharing, relationships can blossom. After this warm awareness and affection, all things being equal, sales will eventually follow when the customer is ready (as opposed to when the organization wants to sell).

Develop a systematic listening team and a system to use the information

Who monitors what? Who compiles the analysis and the reports? Who responds to comments on blogs and in group discussions on LinkedIn? Who analyses the comments, complaints, suggestions, worries, issues and opportunities? What happens to all this highly useful information? What systems channel which information to whom? If embarking on the highest level of customer engagement, collaborative co-creation (see page 19), who manages the channelling of new ideas into new product development processes? Who handles the responses back to the original contributor? These are some of the questions that need to be addressed. More and more organizations are using third-party organizations or their software to scan for any online comments, discussions or tweets regarding their brand, their company, their customers or their competitors.

Develop knowledge assets (which can be used to lure traffic)

Most organizations have a lot of assets already, assuming colleagues speak at conferences, do interviews, write white papers, commission market research or even answer customer e-mails and develop answers to frequently asked questions (FAQs). Even writing a book review is a knowledge asset, if it is written by an expert or perhaps the CEO. These are knowledge assets that can be repackaged and offered to customers. Record all the organization's speeches on video. Knowledge assets include videos, PowerPoint presentations, decks, articles, blog posts, commissioned research, white papers, e-books, expert insights and helpful customer tips.

Sometimes these knowledge assets are buried in customer e-mail responses, which can be categorized and used to generate FAQs for your website and also can be used as the '10 most popular questions', '10 questions you've got to answer', '10 reasons why' or '10 things you've got to know'. These can be converted into quizzes with multiple answers, or self-assessment widgets.

These knowledge assets can be used as 'link bait' or as a lure to entice an audience of Twitter followers or members of a discussion on a blog or on LinkedIn to visit your website. Other lures that work are provocative questions or statements or a discussion topic supported by a reasoned argument generated over 2,000 carefully thought-out responses. These responses are engaging with individuals and their brands.

How do we share? How do we collaborate?

'Open source technology – we need to drive Twitter and all these other open source tools deeper inside the organization – drive use of said collaboration technology inside the firewall – social cast, yammer etc.'

Brogan (2009)

The social media process – 10 steps

1 *Start monitoring and listening.* A social media audit establishes an organization's reputation (and your competitors' reputations). Develop a comprehensive monitoring strategy to discover:

   - the issues: what can have an impact on your brand;

   - the influencers in your marketplace;

   - the platforms or places where your customers (and influencers) congregate (the influential networks, including blogs, discussion groups and other social networks);

– the opinions customers have about your product, your company and the competition.

If your brand or industry discussions are focused on one or two platforms, this makes it easier to concentrate your efforts.

2 *Set priorities and goals, and don't try to cover all social media outlets.* It is not possible to engage in all conversations everywhere. Pick the more important ones initially. Not all online conversations have the same impact. Identify the more important ones. Learn when and when not to engage. Have clearly defined objectives and know exactly what you are trying to achieve with social media (eg reposition the company, develop relationships, establish the brand as credible, grow awareness, etc).

3 *Agree key messages.* Have crystal-clear messages. Be ready to engage with the target audience in a meaningful way (give them what's relevant and important to them). What topics and key phrases does the organization want to be associated with? Prepare canned messages for a range of issues or situations so that they can be tailored easily. Show the team how to create links, back-links and retweets. Share guidelines for what is and is not appropriate.

4 *Develop good content – help and share.* Your content has to be valuable; otherwise you're just shouting or 'making noise'. You have to be prepared to help and share good content. Do not sell primarily. Sales may follow good content. Social media is not a direct marketing tool. Share articles, presentations and videos that are relevant – these can be yours or someone else's (as long you credit them and link to them). Only add comments to other discussions if you are being helpful and relevant.

> 'The more valuable your content, the more valuable you become, the more your audience will grow.'
>
> Source unknown

5 *Recruit and train the team of spokespeople.* Whether a blog or a Twitter account or a YouTube channel, you need to identify who is in the team, ie who has permission to write a blog post or a tweet or upload a video. Who handles responses? Is it certain people for certain issues? Is it one spokesperson or several? Equally, who monitors what? Who reports to whom? Once you have your team trained, brief the rest of the organization. Share the strategy with the whole organization.

6 *Commit time and resources.* You need a consistent stream of useful content. Don't just dabble. This requires clear briefings, training and motivation, which in turn requires resources. Monitoring requires resources also, whether you use an outside agency or do it in-house. Once you start proving the value of social media, you should find it easier to allocate resources to it.

7 *Constantly promote social media.* Just as all organizations now promote their websites in everything they do, so too should social media be promoted. Announce your Twitter handle (name), Facebook page or LinkedIn profile at every opportunity. Add it to all the company's e-mail signatures and collateral. Announce it at conferences and news releases. Add the details to slides, news releases and the letterhead. List it on your website. Post all presentations on your social media sites. In fact, all offline communications should be integrated with social media, eg Twitter, blog and Facebook announcements about an upcoming conference. Videos and photos of the event and speeches can be uploaded to YouTube and Flickr respectively.

8 *Integrate online and offline events.* The online social media team or consultancy needs to work more closely with the offline team, as it needs to know what marketing events are happening in advance. As the website is a conduit, it can get more bang for its buck if it is integrated, eg brief video production companies and photographers as to what formats and style are needed for web use. A shared schedule of events or an outline

plan to allow integration and leverage of various marketing assets on to social media platforms (like ads, promotions, videos, etc) is essential.

9 *Plan for success.* Although it may take some time to build up your networks and followers, be prepared for a sudden influx of comments, visitors and enquiries. This is a nice problem to have. However, if the organization cannot handle the incoming web traffic with its comments and enquiries, it could end up generating a lot of negative PR. Develop credibility before raising visibility.

10 *Measure, measure, measure.* Don't play Russian roulette by (up)loading your message, pushing or spinning it out and then closing your eyes and hoping for the best. Watch the analytics. See if traffic has spikes as a result of any particular posting.

What posts generate a buzz? One new discussion on an e-marketing group in LinkedIn generated over 2,000 responses. It was called 'Social media is crap', and had a detailed post of why the person felt it didn't work. Watch what generates visitors, conversions and good comments (as opposed to negative comments).

How do you measure social media? Some companies use a formula (the PR industry has used formulas for years) to generate a score each week on editorial coverage, allowing for brand name mentions, whether they are positive, negative or neutral, and the importance of the outlet to the brand.

Although 'sentiment tracking' is in its infancy, marketing professionals need to spend time monitoring (and acting upon) what is being said about their brands, their people, their organization and their industry across blogs, micro-blogs (Twitter), forums, social networks and online news media.

Not everything comes down to ROI

'What's the ROI for putting on your pants every morning? But it's still important to your business.'
Scott Monty,
Digital Communications Manager, Ford

Social media is not for the pure mercenary business. They are for organizations that are truly customer orientated. Social media, for them, is a godsend. Customers segment themselves into interest groups that generate more inside information in the minds of customers than any focus group ever could, because everyone shares information, tips, suggestions, ideas, examples, and details of what upsets them and what excites them. Social media helps to build relationships with customers and prospects rather than shouting and broadcasting messages at them.

Finally, remember to have an exit strategy if, for example, participation rates are too low and therefore do not justify the resources required. How would you stop a blog or a discussion? What reason would you give? Where would you send the group? Some brands transfer their audiences to other relevant sites or groups.

The ladder of engagement

Customer engagement creates stronger brands and more advocates

Marketers who understand and influence customer engagement better than their competitors are more likely to develop stronger brands and more loyal customers. Engaged customers are more likely to become brand zealots. Therefore it is important to identify engaged customers and start a brand ambassador programme to further strengthen the relationship and energize their word of mouth.

The ideal customer, or most valuable customer, does not have to be someone who buys a lot. The ideal customer could be an influencer who is a small irregular buyer but who posts ratings and reviews, as the reviews could influence another 100 people.

Identifying engaged customers

Monitoring the quantity and frequency of blog posts, comments, forum discussions, reviews and profile updates helps to identify opportunities and also acts as an early warning system to any future problems. Consider targeting brand evangelists rather than just purchasers. Some companies ask customers to give a product rating or even post a product review as a standard part of their after-sales contact strategy. This way the more engaged customers identify themselves by their own self-selection.

A customer who doesn't care about the product is likely to be less committed or less emotionally attached to the brand. On the other hand, a customer who is engaging is likely to be more emotionally connected to the brand. Marketers need to know about the sentiment, opinion and affinity a person has towards a brand. This is often expressed through repeat visits, purchases, product ratings, reviews, blogs, discussion forums and, ultimately, their likelihood to recommend a friend.

Product reviewers want to engage more

'70% of customers who left reviews for products wanted to help improve those products and they purchased more products, more often than non-reviewers did.'

Aarons, Edwards and Lanier (2009)

Is customer engagement measured? Does this identify the engaged customers and use their feedback to improve your promotion and products? It is possible to increase some customers' level of engagement by moving them up from giving a product rating, to writing a product review, to joining a discussion, to suggesting ideas, to screening ideas, to testing ideas and eventually to buying the ideas when they become products or services. Many of these will become brand champions, evangelists or brand ambassadors. This is why moving some customers up the 'ladder of engagement' is valuable.

The ladder of engagement

Moving customers up the ladder of engagement creates brand loyalty, unleashes brand zealots, and can help improve an organization's processes, products and services. This can also create sustainable competitive advantage for an organization as customers become more engaged and more loyal to the brand that they feel a part of.

The lower half of the ladder encourages customers to engage via product ratings, reviews and discussions. The upper half of the ladder is user-generated content (UGC), which encourages customers to become co-creators of content for the organization. This is sometimes referred to as crowd-sourcing. The highest level of co-creation occurs when customers co-create the products that they subsequently buy (see examples in 'Collaborative co-creation' below).

Not everyone will rise to the top of the ladder. In fact, Nielsen suggest only 1 per cent of website visitors will; 90 per cent lurk, 9 per cent occasionally contribute and 1 per cent regularly contribute. They call it the 90–9–1 rule. But those 1 per cent are important: hence the importance of identifying engaged customers.

While moving customers and other stakeholders up the ladder of engagement strengthens brand loyalty and boosts sales, it does require careful planning, systems and resources. This is a long-term strategic decision.

Beginning of a beautiful relationship

Remember the second visit to a website is the beginning of a relationship. Therefore it is always worth asking the question: What is a brand doing to bring relevant visitors back to the site?

At the highest end of the ladder, the virtual circle completes itself. It is a self-fulfilling system. As the

FIGURE 1.4
Strategic ladder of engagement

Collaborative Co-Creation → Products / Processes ↑ / Brands ↑ / Ads ↑ / Ideas ↑

Discussions ↑
Reviews ↑
Ratings ⌟

FIGURE 1.5   Collaborative co-creation

Collaborative co-creation
Now consider the higher levels of engagement, a kind of marketing nirvana – when customers help an organization to create products, promotions and advertisements. This is collaborative co-creation. There are many levels of co-creation, including ideas, product concepts, product screening, product components, product upgrades and updates, and even complete products, as well as creating advertisements, brand names and, ultimately, the products themselves.

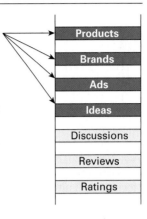

customers create the product, they create their own demand. However cutting-edge this is, it does require basic business skills of systems of communications, registration, processing, feedback, rewarding and putting into action. So back to basics – developing systems that work requires careful planning and rigorous testing. Here are some examples of how companies use the different steps on the ladder of engagement.

Ratings and reviews: Amazon

Amazon will try to engage customers by asking for a product rating, which takes just a few seconds. They then invite you to write a product review, which takes a few minutes. As mentioned, some companies make ratings and reviewing a standard part of their after-sales contact strategy. Customers value reviews from their peers. This shows that consumers are able to apply their own filters and, effectively, rate the ratings. There is a hierarchy of trust online, which starts with personal friends.

Discussions – ask and answer: the Home Depot

One level of discussions is 'ask and answer', where customers throw out questions and other customers answer them. US DIY chain the Home Depot invites customers to ask DIY questions and eventually get other customers to answer the questions. Issues of liability for any careless advice obviously need to be addressed, and real experts may be preferred to casual customer experts.

Discussions – passionate stories: great sporting moments

Another level of discussions is where customers discuss the product or, in the case of the sporting book, they passionately discuss sporting stories. They also reveal themselves as potential brand ambassadors. Those who do engage in discussions are usually passionate about the brand or product.

Collaborative co-creation

Ideas

Dell's Ideastorm (**www.ideastorm.com**) generates ideas on how to improve the business and uses systemized suggestion boxes. Customers, and even non-customers, can suggest new products and features, as well as better ways of running the business, eg improvements in their processes. Dell have earned $10 million from the early stages of Ideastorm. This may seem tiny to a company of Dell's size but, remember, this is brand engagement, a form of brand promotion to the brand zealots, and it also contributes something to the bottom line.

TV advertisement

Co-creating ads is more common in the United States, where customers are asked to generate ads. In 2008, Chrysler's Tahoe supplied graphics, music, photos and video clips and asked its audience to make an ad. The best one would be shown during the Superbowl, the most sought-after TV spot in

FIGURE 1.6   Collaborative co-creation: products

Collaborative co-creation: products
Now consider the highest level of engagement, the marketing nirvana or the marketing utopia mentioned earlier, where customers co-create products.

This is when customers actually create an organization's products and services.

This is where social media facilitates an atmosphere and systems where customer ideas flourish and the next generation of product modifications or new products is created by the customers for the customers. This is a real marketing orientation model.

Products
Brands
Ads
Ideas
Discussions
Reviews
Ratings

the world. It generated a huge response. It also discovered some user-generated discontent (UGD), with several negative ads posted on YouTube. It took the brave decision to allow both positive and negative ads to be created – a classic double-sided argument, which generated more discussions and a lot of press coverage. By the time the Superbowl came, the PR surrounding the user-generated ad campaign had boosted anticipation of the ads, and an enthralled audience watched with great intrigue.

More recently, Kraft Foods in Greece scored a hit with a user-generated 27-minute long-form ad for its Lacta chocolate bar. The crowd sourced the story and the casting, and some of the crowd even appeared as extras. The Love in Action campaign started using traditional TV advertisements to invite people to send in their love stories. Thirteen hundred love stories and one month later (it took a month to sift through the stories), the winning story was selected. Online polls voted for and selected the cast (full screen tests were put up online), the characters' names and even their costumes. Updates were posted on Facebook and Kraft's blog, which was followed by over 11,000 registered voters and 20,000 fans and eventually watched over 150,000 times. It created such a buzz that Greece's leading TV station, MEGA Channel, offered to screen it free of charge on 14 February as part of its Valentine's Day programming, which attracted a 12 per cent share of viewers and was seen by more than 335,000 people. Lacta sales are also up in a declining market (Hall, 2010). For a full case study on

collaborative advertising see the T-Mobile case (Case study 13.1).

Brand names

Co-creation can go way beyond ads and promotions; it can even generate brand names, if the basic systems are in place. Boeing created a buzz around the launch of the new 787, the Dreamliner, by inviting input from potential customers and passengers online. Indeed it was the community that named the aircraft the Dreamliner, with some 500,000 votes cast online from 160 countries (O'Dea, 2008).

Products and services

Some say that UGC has been used offline for many years now. MTV has been getting users to screen or research products through user text votes, and reality TV has been using the UGC formula for far too long in my opinion. *The X Factor* attracts UGC to create new product concepts, new product screening and new product testing. Why is UGC so successful?

Back to the online world, Peugeot invited their online audience to submit new product concepts, ie submit car designs. This attracted 4 million page views. Peugeot built a demonstration model of the winning design to exhibit at marketing events. It also partnered with software developers to put it into a video game.

Another online company where users generate the complete product is Constant Comedy.com, an online comedy site where users upload their jokes on video. Audiences watch them and then vote them on or off. The best ones are voted to the top, and new careers take off.

Take product variations and product components. *Great Moments of Sportsmanship* is a book about sportsmanship. Customers send in their sportsmanship stories for further discussion in the blog and possible inclusion in the next edition. The goal is to have future editions totally user generated. In addition, more UGC is added as YouTube videos that match the stories in the book are added to the site.

In the area of careers, there is a highly engaging UGC company whose product is 100 per cent user generated. Called pods4jobs, it is an online careers advice site with a difference – videos only and all created by the target market, ie mostly teenagers interviewing people at work, revealing a 'warts and all' insight into different careers. Here, kids interview their parents, aunts, uncles, grandparents, neighbours or anyone who has a career. Students shoot their own video, upload it and, if it is accepted, get a certificate of achievement.

And they are not alone. Another very important collaborative co-creation project is the Myelin Repair Foundation (MRF), which is a closed group of researchers from five universities who aim to develop a drug that will treat multiple sclerosis (MS) in 10 years. After a couple of years they have identified 10 targets and three therapeutic candidates, developed 11 tools to study myelin, and published nearly 20 scientific articles. Half of any royalties go back into the foundation to finance future projects. An IP agreement allows MRF to license discoveries to pharmaceutical companies.

Occasionally B2B is mixed with B2C, as in the case of the InnoCentive site, which allows 180,000 freelance scientists, engineers, entrepreneurs, students and academics to work on problems posed by industry, creating and selling solutions in return for cash rewards. Major players, including P&G, are involved.

One outstanding UGC website is called Threadless.com, whose loyal community of graphic designers, artists and generally creative people send in designs for new T-shirts. The community votes for the best one; they then produce it and sell it back to the community. The retail trade has spotted these high-quality and unusual T-shirts and now orders significant quantities of their limited-edition, high-quality products.

Remember, UGC is not always B2C, as almost always many of the best online examples are actually B2B. Consider MMOGs, where dozens, hundreds and even thousands of players around the world participate in an online game. Now imagine dozens, hundreds and even thousands of scientists collaborating on and creating new products. The Atlas particle detector, which measures subatomic particles in high-energy physics, involved 2,000 scientists disaggregated across 165 working groups who then found a successful solution online. IBM has adopted Linux for some of its computer products and systems. Linux is continually improved by a huge global community of software developers, mostly non IBM-ers. Sun Microsystem developed the Solaris operating system with a global community of software developers. Some call it 'crowdsourcing'; others call it 'open innovation'.

It is interesting to note that Apple netted some $1 billion in app sales in the first year, and shares 70 per cent of revenues with the 125,000-strong developer community in the iPhone developer programme (Kennedy, 2009).

IBM also uses open innovation for its Big Green Innovations unit. Likewise, P&G revamped its innovation model by adopting open innovation a few years ago. From Intel to Xerox, NASA to Novell and Vodafone to Virgin, more and more organizations are unleashing the collective brainpower of people outside their organization. Offline, LEGO have been collaborating with customers for years, asking children to suggest, create and screen new product ideas. They then financially reward 'those whose ideas go to market'.

Successful UGC and even the lower levels of engagement are dependent on a vibrant, responsive audience and one of marketing's often forgotten fundamentals – systems and processes that work, and basic marketing principles of testing interfaces and back-office systems. Usability testing is a prerequisite.

UGC is in search results

'25% of search results for the world's top 20 largest brands are links to user-generated content.'
Qualman (2009)

Remember, websites are fun, but back office means business.

All of these UGC systems draw from the basics of perfect marketing processes and the passionate attention to detail required if user-generated systems are to work successfully.

Ask: 'How well are we measuring the engagement of our different online audiences and then closing the loop by using the data to identify the advocates and deliver more relevant communications?'

Collaborative co-creation has been extended into management. Results to date are inconclusive as to how successful this can be. Consider MyFootball-Club.co.uk, which is a group of approximately 50,000 football-obsessed internet users who pooled resources and bought a minor English football club. Members paid £35 and acquired a majority stake in Ebbsfleet United, which plays five divisions below the premiership. Members vote on transfers, player selection and all major decisions affecting the club. Since then it has won the FA Trophy at Wembley – the club's greatest achievement since it was founded in 1890. Now it is aiming for promotion to the football league proper. This has been done before. In June 2006, minor league baseball team Schaumburg Flyers from Chicago let fans co-manage the second half of the season by voting via the website on managerial moves such as setting up the roster. It flopped, going from a 31–17 record in the first half of the season to the 15–33 worst record in the league. A similar thing was also done pre-internet, way back in 1951, when the St Louis Browns major league baseball team gave control to the fans by issuing 'yes' and 'no' placards. Although it was a publicity stunt, the Grandstand Managers' Day involved thousands of fans directing the club to a 5–3 win over Philadelphia Athletics. Now that's engagement.

FIGURE 1.7   *On the Air*

'We've moved from "The Attention Economy (push)" to "The Attraction Economy (pull)" to "The Participation Economy (share)".'

Roberts (2010)

The race is on

Cut through the clutter

Amidst the hyper-competition and a vast sea of communications, whether outbound, inbound, online or offline, the race is on to somehow break through the clutter, engage with customers (and other stakeholders) and ultimately nurture lifetime loyalty. Once a real dialogue is established and is used to continually improve and service the customers' continually changing needs, a platform of loyalty begins to emerge. This builds a wall against other competitors. In many ways, the first organizations that get it right are likely to prevail and win in the longer term as they strengthen customer relationships and secure loyalty.

The social media revolution started quietly long ago. The race is on to win and keep customers

BBC Radio Northern Ireland take UGC to a new level

Co-creation and user-generated content have been around for a long time, as is the case with radio show phone-ins, whereby the audience's input and opinions are a key part of the programme. However, BBC Radio Northern Ireland took it to a new level a few years ago when they felt that the audience input was so funny that they should make an animated TV show from it. They even kept, with permission, the callers' actual voices and dubbed them into the animation. Called *On the Air* by FlickrPix, some of the series is still on YouTube.

before the competition does. Customers' attention has to be attracted and then engaged in meaningful, helpful, added-value ways that some of us would never have even dreamt of 10 years ago. Marketers have to add new ways to engage customers and move them up the ladder of engagement.

Attracting attention and generating website traffic is dependent on being creative enough to catch the attention and then being relevant when using communications tools, including social media and the more traditional web tools ('tradigital tools').

Be there, be relevant and be creative

A brand needs to be wherever its customers are. Be wherever customers might have a need. Find out what they really want and give it to them. Find out where customers go (offline and online) and when they go there. Be creative with messages and media.

Find creative partnerships that take the brand's message and products to its target audience in a completely different environment (wherever the target market is) and perhaps just when they need help (as they leave a venue or as they start a search). Be where customers go online and offline. There may be ways of reaching them through collaborative partnerships with parallel non-competitive suppliers both offline and online. Field marketing or the slightly more elaborate experiential marketing partnerships may occur, eg a rugby book sold at the grounds of a rugby stadium, or new iPods being sold at a concert. And help customers tell their friends about you.

Be relevant to their needs – if a brand gives customers useful, relevant information at just the right time, it strengthens the brand relationship. Being creative always helps. But being relevant is even more important, as customers only want and listen to whatever is relevant to their needs. Constant monitoring of their changing needs is critical. Whether it is at the lowest levels of interaction, ie product ratings, reviewing products or creating user-generated content, engagement helps to keep customer attention and to nurture stronger relationships.

Be creative. Experiment with different media, different messages, and live demonstrations in different places, videoed on camera and posted to YouTube. Use permanent media (buildings, walls and gates, or laser your logo on to the moon) and

product placement (in other productions). Think hard about what would make someone buy a brand, and then see if this reason can be translated into a stunningly creative message. Test it and try it.

Open and integrate your new toolkit

Traffic is also generated by the traditional collection of 11 communications tools (see Table 1.1), which include what the US marketers consider to be the Big 5 tools: advertising, PR (plus sponsorship), sales promotion, direct mail and the sales force. There are also the three 3D tools, which include packaging, point-of-sale (merchandising), and exhibitions and conferences, and finally the 2Ws – your website and the most potent of all communications tools, word of mouth. Social media has catapulted the power of word of mouth. All 11 tools are replicated online.

The creative age is here

Creativity and marketing will help to break through the clutter of noise and hyper-competition that is out there. As Kevin Roberts (2009), CEO Saatchi & Saatchi Worldwide, said, this is the dawning of a new creative age in marketing. In fact, it is the dawning of a new age of creativity both inside and outside the whole organization – as witnessed by the collaborative co-creation models already discussed. Even advertisements are going to have to be a lot more creative. User-generated long-form ads are here, and so is the one-second ad. As Eric Schmidt, CEO Google, said: 'Despite this need for creativity in business, many organizations feel uncomfortable with acknowledging and unleashing the power of creativity' Manyika (2008) Harvard Business School professor John Kao (1997) summed this up when he said 'I know: In many business people's lexicon, "creativity" is right up there with "nice" in the mushy-word category. Such people had better revise their lexicons.' Look at the more successful companies out there: they nurture creativity. It is not accidental. The importance of creativity is recognized, encouraged and nurtured. Listen to what some of these organizations say:

● 'Either you'll learn to acquire and cultivate [creative people] or you'll be eaten alive' (Leon Royer, Executive Director, 3M).

TABLE 1.1   Communications tools

Offline tools	Online outbound tools
1. Advertising	Interactive TV ads Pay-per-click ads and banner ads Intelligent media units
2. PR	Online optimized PR Viral marketing
3. Sponsorship	Online sponsorship – communities, pages, sites, events
4. Sales promotion	Incentives and calls to action online in e-mails and websites
5. Direct mail	Opt-in e-mail (viral marketing)
6. Sales force	Affiliate marketing Digital body language (on a website)
7. Packaging	Pack images on the website
8. Point of sale	Website – your online POS; particularly calls to action; product photos and product users' photos
9. Retail store design or commercial offices	Website – design, online value proposition (OVP), search engine optimization (SEO)
10. Exhibitions and conferences	Virtual exhibitions, virtual worlds like Second Life
11. Word of mouth	Social media – inbound marketing *Blogs:* Microblogs (eg Twitter) *Social networking sites:* Facebook MySpace LinkedIn *Social content sites:* YouTube Flickr Wikis *Social recommendation sites:* Digg StumbleUpon *Social bookmarking sites:* Delicious Article marketing Google Maps Google Earth Virtual worlds

- 'My job is to listen to, search for, think of, and spread ideas, to expose people to good ideas and role models' (Jack Welch, former CEO, GE).

- 'The first step in the creative process is "hiring the best of the best". This is how HP maintains an environment that "crackles with creativity and intellectual spirit"' (Mary Patterson, former Director of Corporate Engineering, Hewlett-Packard).

- 'To make money in a disinflationary period takes real innovation and creativity at all levels of the corporation' (Michael Fradette, Manufacturing Consultant, Deloitte & Touche).

The reality is that creativity is hard work. And managing creativity is, as Kao (1997) says:

if anything, even harder work. It has nothing to do with finding a nice safe place for people to goof off. Managing creativity is much more difficult. It means finding an appropriate place for people to contend and collaborate – even if they don't particularly want to. It means scrounging from always-limited resources. It means controlling the uncontrollable, or at least unpredictable, process. Creativity, for many, is a blood sport.

But, as Albert Einstein said, 'Anyone who has never made a mistake has never tried anything new.'

Creativity will fuel growth in the future

'The search for value has led companies to seek efficiency through: downsizing; rationalizing; right-sizing approaches that eventually result in a diminishing level of return. But what will fuel growth in the future? Growth will come through mastering the skills of creativity and making creativity actionable.'

John Kao, Harvard Business School

Former President of McKinsey's Japan and highly respected author Kenichi Ohmae, in an interview with the author, was asked if he could sense if a company was going to be successful. Was there something he could smell or sense when he was in an organization that suggested this company was going to be a winner? He said 'yes' and went on to explain that, 'if a company is not afraid to ask questions, if everyone asks questions from the CEO down to the office boy, if they ask questions like "Why do we do it this way?" then this company will succeed' (Ohmae, 1996). So the inquisitive mind is an essential ingredient for future success. This is echoed by Susan Greenfield of the University of Oxford when speaking at the Third European Futurists Convention in Lucerne in 2007. She confirmed the need for creativity and the need to challenge old dogma: 'So creativity, this eureka connection (neuronal connection) that triggers a new insight in yourself and others, is all about forging connections and so providing environments that will foster a challenging of dogma, of old stale connections, a forging of new ones that trigger even more connections that give a meaning and an insight to both yourself and others' (Greenfield, 2007).

Edison – a genius who combined creativity with marketing

The United States' greatest inventor, Thomas Edison, was a creative genius, but it was not until he discovered some of the principles of marketing that he found increased success. One of his first inventions was, although much needed, a flop. In 1869, he created and patented an electronic vote recorder, which tallied the votes in the Massachusetts state legislature faster than the chamber's old hand-tab system. 'To Edison's astonishment, it flopped. Edison had not taken into account legislators' habits. They don't like to vote quickly and efficiently. They do like to lobby their fellow legislators as voting takes place. Edison had a great idea, but he completely misunderstood the needs of his customers' (Caldicott, 2010). He learnt from his failure the relationship between invention and marketing. Edison learnt that marketing and invention must be integrated. 'Anything that won't sell, I don't want to invent,' he said. 'Its sale is proof of utility, and utility is success.' He realized he needed to put the customers' needs first and tailor his thinking accordingly, despite any temptation to invent for invention's sake. His change of mindset led to tremendous success (Caldicott, 2010).

Edison made market research a fundamental part of the creative process:

He literally went to homes and places of work and analyzed what people did in order to gain

Creativity + marketing = success

'Anything that won't sell, I don't want to invent,' said Thomas Edison, best known for the light bulb. He was a prolific inventor, registering an extraordinary 1,093 US patents and 1,293 international patents. The six industries he pioneered between 1873 and 1905 – and their offshoots – are estimated to be worth more than $1 trillion today. He was one of the world's first market researchers.

Caldicott (2010)

insight to invent products that could help them do it better and faster. He looked first for unmet needs and then applied science and creativity to fill them. The first example of Edison's success using a 'needs-first' approach to invention is one we seldom associate with him: Document duplication. Post-Civil War newspaper accounts of the re-building of the South and the tremendous demand it created for insurance policies led him to think that the insurance business could use some efficiencies. Edison got permission from insurance agents to watch their clerks at work. He saw that most of their day was spent hand-copying documents for each party to the insurance sale instead of selling insurance. Edison realized that if he could invent something that would save both the insurance clerks' and agents' time writing, they could all make more money.

Caldicott (2010)

But customers do not understand their own needs – particularly innovations

However valuable market research is, significant creative leaps can sometimes be too difficult for customers to grasp. Therefore negative customer feedback for discontinuous innovations (significant innovations) can sometimes be misleading. In some cases, 'Listening too much to customer input is a recipe for a disaster' (Christensen, 2003). 'If I'd listened to my customers, I would have invented a faster horse,' said Henry Ford. Whoever could have imagined that a device created for engineers to communicate with each other would one day become a global necessity for all young people – text messaging? Whoever could have imagined that one day people would walk around with record players or DVD players on their heads (headphones)? Whoever could have imagined a nation seemingly talking loudly to themselves (hands-free mobile phones)? Here are some classic quotations that demonstrate how not just customers but even experts in their field could not see the benefit of a significant innovation that subsequently went on to become a massive global success:

- 'This "telephone" has too many shortcomings to be seriously considered as a means of communication. The device is inherently of no value to us' (Western Union, internal memo, 1876).

- 'The wireless music box has no imaginable commercial value. Who would pay for a message sent to nobody in particular?' (David Sarnoff's associates in response to his urgings for investment in the radio in the 1920s).

- 'Who the hell wants to hear actors talk?' (Harry M. Warner, Warner Bros, 1927).

- 'TV will never be a serious competitor to radio because people must sit and keep their eyes glued on a screen. The average American family doesn't have time for it' (*New York Times*, 1939).

- 'I think there is a world market for maybe five computers' (Thomas Watson, Chairman of IBM, 1943).

- 'There is no demand for guitar bands' (Decca Records turning down the Beatles, 1962).

- 'There is no reason for any individuals to have a computer in their home' (Ken Olsen, President, Chairman and Founder of Digital Equipment Corp, 1977).

Looking back on it, there are many innovations in common use now, the need for which simply did not exist 5 or 10 years ago. This applies to both B2C and B2B markets. 'Customers want to know what to do with their call centres, how to integrate them with the internet, issues of security, what mobility means, what sort of networks they should have... These business needs simply did not exist 10 years ago' (Garvey, 2002).

As organizations, and marketers in particular, embrace creative thinking, new solutions will emerge and contribute to continued success once we learn to think 'outside the box'.

For organizations seeking to define creativity and inspire it, perhaps Susan Greenfield's (2007) definition may help:

> It's seeing one thing in terms of something else. That eureka moment. You don't have to be a brilliant novelist or painter or musician... it can be about some private matter. It can be about economics. It can be while you are reading a novel, you suddenly make a connection that suddenly gives you an insight that no one else has had. Someone defined science as 'seeing what everyone else can see but thinking what no one else has thought'.
>
> Doesn't it feel great when you have that eureka moment. My own view is that this could be what we should be aiming for, because this gives you both individuality and a sense of fulfilment, and, incidentally, it is useful to society.

Enter the boardroom

The missed opportunity

Marketers can and should demonstrate to any board of directors how marketing can create two sources of sustainable competitive advantage by creating two assets – one on the balance sheet, the other off the balance sheet. Brands appear as an asset on the balance sheet, and a well-maintained, integrated customer database does not appear as an asset on the balance sheet.

A well-integrated website helps to grow a database of customers and prospects, as well as boosting a brand's value as more and more relevant 'services' and 'sizzle' are added to the customer experience. Well-managed databases create a mini-monopoly of customers and prospects, and can be used with a variety of channels to communicate intimately with customers (e-mail, snail mail, telephone calls and personal visits). Although the value of a database can be quantified by estimating lifetime values, it still does not appear on the balance sheet.

Marketers missed their chance to enter the boardroom when the web first emerged in the early 1990s. The internet, and websites in particular, presented a whole new way for businesses to exploit the 5Ss (sell more, serve better, save money, speak

with customers, and sizzle or create some magic around the brand by doing things that simply could not be done offline). Three of these Ss will attract the ears of the financial director and the CEO: sell, save and sizzle.

'Sell' means revenue, and any promise to boost revenues is taken seriously. 'Save' is of interest, and any proposal that offers to make 99 per cent savings will demand attention, as there is no other aspect of business that can attain such massive savings as that of well-designed, self-service websites. Some financial directors and CEOs will appreciate the importance of brands on the balance sheet, in fact the necessity to have them on the balance sheet if in an acquisition or merger situation. Hence brands, and 'sizzle' that enhances a brand's value, will be of renewed interest to the CEO and CFO.

However, the moment was missed by marketers, and it seems that websites became the responsibility of other departments, eg IT, corporate PR and sales. The benefits were diluted and the cohesive marketing argument lost.

One other opportunity was missed also. As businesses move from the linear value chain to the web-linked value network, boards have to ask themselves 'What business are we in?' Whilst the web created a golden opportunity to re-evaluate brands (what added value they could give and ultimately what they represent), the internet created a golden opportunity to re-evaluate 'What business are we in?' As businesses outsourced chunks of the value chain, the business effectively became a 'box of contracts'.

The opportunity knocks twice

More than 10 years later, the opportunity for marketers to get back in the boardroom appears as social media changes all the business models and sweep aside the old thinking about marketing just being the 'colouring department'. The biggest change since the industrial revolution falls into the marketer's court. As all marketers are becoming experts in social media, it follows that this expertise is required in the boardroom as businesses revamp their organizational cultures and change their modus operandi.

A McKinsey survey (2009) supported this by reporting that marketing and sales and IT derive most benefits from social media (as opposed to procurement and finance). In their words, 'Social media engages customers, deepens relations, generates extra sales, faster time to market, better NPD [new product development] and lowers the cost of doing business.'

Social media and the opportunity it gives organizations to create sustainable competitive advantages cannot be left to IT departments or production departments, as these by definition are production orientated. Social media is driven by the marketplace and is therefore the centre of a marketing-driven business.

So social media, the ladder of engagement, integrated marketing and creativity offer marketers another golden opportunity to get back into the boardroom and influence the strategic directions of a business in such a way that the business becomes a truly market-orientated business, primed and ready to satisfy customers and enjoy continued success.

Nightmare on Banking Street – the author's own experience

I hadn't physically visited a bank in years. However, when I was doing a favour for a friend, I walked into a well-known high street branch in London on a Saturday afternoon to be greeted almost immediately by a friendly-faced customer service clerk, who pleasantly informed me that the queue in front of me would take 40 minutes. I thought I had stepped into a time warp. What amazed me was that other customers seemed prepared to queue.

Was it always like this? Then I thought about online banking and also about lovely shiny ATMs that cannot make your day any worse, whilst standing in the rain, trying to block prying eyes and hidden cameras from stealing your pin numbers, whilst hoping the muggers around the corner have not spotted you yet. Fear has increased in many people's lives.

But that's out there on the street. What about in the comfort of your own home? I received two letters recently – both from high street banks.

One told me that my account had received a certain sum of money, it had been credited to me at a certain exchange rate and I had been charged a certain amount of commission charges. Now I never accept money unless I know who is giving it to me and why. The letter didn't tell me, so I had to find out. I made a call, met a robot, queued, gave an account number, answered a string of security questions and eventually, after eight minutes, got the answer. My whole point is: Why couldn't the system generate this information for me? Didn't anyone think that customers might like to know where money is coming from? Did they test it?

I opened the statement from the second bank and it told me some good news. I had overpaid them and was now in credit to the tune of £12. I looked at the letter. It was a 'notice of variation'. What is a notice of variation? Now, I know this is anecdotal evidence, but is this good customer service? Is this good marketing? Is it getting better or worse? Is there an opportunity to be outstandingly good?

Key points from Chapter 1

- This is the beginning of a new era in marketing amidst hyper-competition.

- Social media is here to stay.

- The ladder of engagement can create competitive advantage.

- There is an opportunity for marketers to take a seat on the board and drive a marketing culture.

References and further reading

Aarons, C, Edwards, A and Lanier, X (2009) Turning blogs and user-generated content into search engine results, *Marketing Vox and Nielsen BuzzMetrics SES Magazine*, 8 June

Beck, S (2010) Make your product work for your brand: Why what you're selling has become your primary advertising channel, *Financial Times*, 4 May

Bird, Drayton (2008) *Commonsense Direct and Digital Marketing*, 5th edn, Kogan Page, London

Brogan, C (2009) The serendipity engine, **www.delicious.com/chrisbrogan/casestudy**

Caldicott, S (2010) Invention and marketing: Joined at the hip, *Media Week*, 28 April

Chaffey, D and Smith, P R (2008) *eMarketing eXcellence*, 3rd edn, Butterworth-Heinemann, Oxford

Charan, R and Bossidy, L (2002) *Execution: The discipline of getting things done*, Crown Business, New York

Christensen, C (2003) *The Innovator's Dilemma*, Harper Business Essentials, New York

Earls, M (2002) *Welcome to the Creative Age: Bananas, business and the death of marketing*, Wiley, Chichester

Fletcher, W (2010) author, lecturer and former chairman of the Royal Institution in conversation with PR Smith

Garvey, D (2002) BT Ignite, *Marketing Business*, March

Grande, C (2007) Cannes diary: Six of the best by Carlos Grande, *Financial Times*, 24 June

Greenfield, S (2007) The future of brain – the brain of the future, Third European Futurists Convention, Lucerne

Hall, E (2010) In Greece, Kraft scores a hit for Lacta chocolate with crowdsourced film, *Advertising Age*, 24 March

Hoffman, D (2009) Managing beyond Web 2.0, *McKinsey Quarterly*, July

Jenkinson, A (2004) The bigger picture, *Marketing Business*, March

Kao, J (1997) *Jamming: The art and discipline of business creativity*, HarperCollins, New York

Kennedy, J (2009) App-fab, *Marketing Age*, November

Levine, R *et al* (2000) *The Cluetrain Manifesto*, FT.com, London

Lilley, A (2007) Why Web 2.0 adds up to a revolution for our industry, *Media Guardian*, 1 October

Manyika, J (2008) Google's view on the future of business: An interview with CEO Eric Schmidt, *The McKinsey Quarterly*, September

McGovern, G (2010) Time is (still) money: Increasing employee productivity (Part 1), 9 May, **www.gerrymcgovern.com**

McKinsey (2009) How companies are benefiting from Web 2.0: McKinsey Global Survey Results, National Customer Satisfaction Scores, Technology Office, *McKinsey Quarterly*, September

O'Dea, A (2008) Innovation, *Marketing Age*, September/October

Ohmae, K (1996) Video interview with P R Smith, *The Marketing CDs*, P R Smith

Qualman, E (2009) Statistics show social media is bigger than you think, Socialnomics [Online] **http://socialnomics.net/2009/08/11/statistics-show-social-media-is-bigger-than-you-think/**

Roberts, K (2009) in conversation with PR Smith, The Worshipful Company of Marketors, The Great Hall at Barts, St Bartholomew's Great Hall, 17 November

Roberts, K (2010) Video interview with P R Smith, **www.prsmith.org**

Rothery, G (2008) The matchmaker, *Marketing Age*, November/December

Ryan, D and Jones, C (2009) *Understanding Digital Marketing*, Kogan Page, London

Safco, L and Brake, D (2009) *The Social Media Bible*, Wiley, Hoboken, NJ

Schlack, W (2008) Open for innovation, *Business & Leadership*, [Online] **http://www.businessandleadership.com/marketing/item/11417-open-for-innovation**

Scott, D (2009) *The New Rules of Marketing and PR*, Wiley, Hoboken, NJ

WARC (2007) Unilever changes online focus, 25 June

Further information

Advertising Association
7th Floor North
Artillery House
11–19 Artillery Row
London SW1P 1RT
Tel: +44 (0)20 7340 1100
www.adassoc.org.uk

Chartered Institute of Marketing
Moor Hall
Cookham
Maidenhead
Berkshire SL6 9QH
Tel: +44 (0)1628 427120
Fax: +44 (0)1628 427499
www.cim.co.uk

CIPR
52–53 Russell Square
London WC1B 4HP
Tel: +44 (0)20 7631 6900
www.cipr.co.uk

Communications Advertising and Marketing
Education Foundation Limited (CAM Foundation)
Moor Hall
Cookham
Maidenhead
Berkshire SL6 9QH
Tel: +44 (0)1628 427120
Fax: +44 (0)1628 427158
www.camfoundation.com

Incorporated Society of British Advertisers
ISBA Langham House
1b Portland Place
London W1B 1PN
Tel: +44 (0)20 7291 9020
Fax: +44 (0)20 7291 9030
www.isba.org.uk

Institute of Promotional Marketing Ltd
70 Margaret Street
London W1W 8SS
Tel: +44 (0)20 7291 7730
Fax: +44 (0)20 7291 7731
www.isp.org.uk

International Organization for Standardization (ISO)
1 ch de la Voie-Creuse
Case postale 56 CH-1211
Geneva 20
Switzerland
Tel: +41 22 749 01 11
Fax: +41 22 733 34 30
www.iso.org

Marketing Society
1 Park Road
Teddington
Middlesex TW11 0AR
Tel: +44 (0)20 8973 1700
Fax: +44 (0)20 8973 1701
www.marketing-society.org.uk

Public Relations Consultants Association
Willow House
Willow Place
London SW1P 1JH
Tel: +44 (0)20 7233 6026
Fax: +44 (0)20 7828 4797
www.prca.org.uk

02
Branding

LEARNING OBJECTIVES

By the end of this chapter you will be able to:

- Appreciate the importance of branding and why it is a strategic issue
- List the stages in building a brand process
- Avoid the classical branding mistakes
- Understand why brands need to be maintained

Introduction to branding

What is a brand?

A brand is an intangible, legally protectable, valuable asset. It is how a company or product is perceived by customers (or the target audience). It is the image, associations and inherent value customers put on your product and services. Brands include intangible attributes and values. For a brand to be successful, its components have to be coherent, appropriate, and appealing to consumers. A brand is a promise to the customer. A brand also embraces vision, values and personality (see 'Brand components' below). A brand is far more than just a logo or a name (this is just brand identity). It is the complete customer experience (the integrated sum of all the marketing mix and the communications mix from products to customer service, from packaging to advertising, from rumour to discussion). The last two components are less controllable, from a brand management perspective, but they are nevertheless influenceable, as good brand management participates wholeheartedly in social media also. So a brand is everything a customer (or stakeholder) sees, feels and experiences about a product or service (or organization). A brand is the 'magical' difference between many competing products and services.

A (favourable) consensus of subjectivity

'Because brand reputations exist only in the minds of their observers – and all observers are different... the strongest brands are those that enjoy what's been called "a (favourable) consensus of subjectivity". And that's when their brand managers, in the widest sense of that phrase, should be most warmly congratulated. They didn't build those brands themselves; but they fed such enticing titbits to their audience that their audience gratefully did the rest.'

Millward Brown Optimor BrandZ survey (2010)

The power of branding

How do brands become so powerful that they control economies, determine corporate takeovers, or make customers pay almost 1,000 per cent price premiums? How do brands become the most valuable asset in a company, which determine the whole financial value of a company and drive corporate takeovers? How do brands create sustainable competitive advantage? What makes people all around the world hand over their hard-earned cash for the same brand whether in Taiwan or Tokyo, Kashmir or Carlisle? Today, the power of branding is such that brands defend organizations from competitors, nurture customer relationships, and boost sales, profits and balance sheet assets.

Company benefits from branding

Brands create sustainable competitive advantage from hyper-competition, boost relationships, boost sales, boost profits and boost balance sheets. Why would any managers not nurture their brand very carefully? The truth is that many do not (see 'The customer service time bomb', Chapter 1). However, consider these individual benefits of nurturing strong brands.

Brands create sustainable competitive advantage

Brands will be, for many organizations, the critical success factor in the hyper-competitive 21st-century marketplace. Strong brands create sustainable competitive advantage. For the first time in the history of business, the most powerful barriers to competition are no longer controlled by companies but by customers. The old barriers are falling. Factories and even access to finance are not as powerful barriers as the barriers erected inside customers' minds. Only a few chosen winners are allowed inside. These are the successful brands with which customers have relationships. Successful brands build differentiators.

The CEO of one of the world's greatest brands, Coca-Cola, reputedly once said: 'They can take everything we have, our machinery, our plants, our distribution – as long as they don't take our brand – and we will be able to rebuild our organization in six months.'

For many years now more people in Britain have trusted top brands than trust the church. In fact Heinz and Nescafé are trusted more than the church, the police and Members of Parliament (Croft [1998], in Reynolds, Cuthbertson and Bell, 2004). How come British people give their credit card details over the internet to an unknown, invisible American on the other side of the Atlantic? How come Americans pour down their throats water from someone they don't know from an unknown source in France? Brand trust in Amazon and Evian is strong.

Brands control people and brands control economies

'What gives brands their power to influence – if not quite control – people's purchasing decisions and thus their power to influence – if not quite control – modern economies?'

Winston Fletcher (2010)

Brands differentiate a company's products or services and help them to stand out from a crowd. Brands are often the primary source of competitive advantage and a company's most valuable strategic asset. All markets tend towards commodities (as patents run out and the competition catches up and copies others). Brands protect and defend a business from competition, as they differentiate the product by adding perceived value. This creates barriers to entry for potential new competitors that are constantly tempted to enter the new borderless and category-less market space.

Some years ago it was suggested that two-thirds of the stock market capitalization of US companies was attributable to intellectual assets (brands,

Chinese president visits a brand before visiting the president

When visiting the United States, President Hu Jintao of China chose Microsoft's Bill Gates as his first visit, followed the next day by a visit to US President Bush. The *International Herald Tribune* headline read 'Chinese president's itinerary for U.S. visit: Gates first, Bush later'.

Yeong and Yu (2006)

patents and know-how). That's a massive $4.5 trillion. One-third of global wealth is accounted for by brands (Clifton, 2004).

Brands boost relationships

Brands create (mostly unconscious) relationships between the user and the brand. Brands add a subtle meaning to the act of consumption. We allow these brands into our homes and offices and into our lives because they generally mean something to us all. They represent something. At the heart of any successful brand proposition there is a human dimension. That's why brands have personality, values and associations. Brands used to be just a seal of quality. Today brands have emotional connections that differentiate them. Brands provide reassurance to customers and differentiation from competitors. Brands save customers time by being easily recognizable and providing a reassuring sense of order in an increasingly destabilized and chaotic world. Brands inspire loyalty, trust and continuity. Brands are built upon a platform of reliable quality. As in any relationship, a brand's promise must never be broken.

Brands are even used to pigeonhole people: 'He drives a Porsche and drinks Pimm's.' A person's entire life can be effectively categorized by his or her use of brands. Some brands are even definitive, eg 'He is the Rolls-Royce of hosts.'

'Coca-Cola sells more because our love of a particular brand is as important as our love of a flavour.'

Ronay (2004)

Brands boost sales

Brands help customers by making their purchasing process easier. Brands are easier to recognize and to associate with quality; it is easier to understand their benefits, and they are less risky than unknown commodities. Brands encourage repeat purchases and brand relationships, which in turn boost sales. Strong brands are easily recognizable and build single-minded awareness, ensuring they have a greater chance of being included in the customer's 'considered set' of possible purchases or, better still, 'preferred purchases'. Brands build relationships and inspire loyalty, trust and most importantly continuity, providing a reassuring sense of order in an increasingly chaotic, insecure and fast-changing world. Established brands also provide a platform from which to launch other products under the same brand names, thereby increasing share of wallet.

Brands boost profits

Brands, rightly or wrongly, can command premium prices, which results in increased profits, which consequently allows more money to be spent on better (relevant and tested) communications with clearer messages – which continually strengthens the brand. For example, in the same store, Coca-Cola charges a price premium of almost 1,000 per cent with its 2-litre bottle priced at £1.25 (compared to Asda's 2-litre bottle at £0.15). Incidentally, Coca-Cola knows the long-term power of its brand and invests in it accordingly (eg investing $65 million in 12 years' Olympic sponsorship until 2012). Profits are also boosted by repeat purchase customers, who generate on average five times more profits than sales to new customers. In online sales, this figure rises to 10 times more profitability (Eltvedt and Flores, 2005). Strong brands also boost margins, as strong brands increase bargaining power with the trade.

Brands boost balance sheets

As well as affecting politics and economics, brands affect company valuations. Brands can indicate future profit trends and assist decisions and investor relations. Today, brands are recognized as assets, and more companies are putting brand values on to their balance sheets. Below is a list of brand values taken from the Millward Brown Optimor BrandZ survey (2010), which reveals the world's first $100 billion brand – Google.

Google	$114 billion
IBM	$87 billion
Apple	$83 billion
Microsoft	$76 billion
Coca-Cola	$70 billion
McDonald's	$66 billion
Marlboro	$57 billion
China Mobile	$53 billion
GE	$45 billion
Vodafone	$44 billion

There are now seven Chinese brands in the world's top 100 brands. The best known in the West is probably Baidu, the Chinese search engine. Samsung and Baidu are the fastest-growing brands (Millward Brown Optimor, 2010).

There is no doubt that brands add value to the balance sheet, grow the value of the business (market capitalization) and therefore boost the sale price of a business if looking to exit.

New accounting rules worldwide require companies to value their intangible assets – such as brands – on their balance sheets when they are acquired (IAS 38). When these assets are judged to have an indefinite life, which is often the case with a brand, they will be subject to annual review for impairment. This means that the difference between the price paid and the current value will be calculated. Any resulting write-downs can often have major implications as seen in 2002 when AOL Time Warner (formerly known as) had to write off $54 billion for the value lost when AOL acquired Time Warner at the end of the dotcom boom in 2000.

You have the factory and staff; I'll have the brand

'If we split the business tomorrow, you kept all the factories and staff and I kept the brand name, within two years I would be a multimillionaire and you would be bankrupt.'

CEO, Quaker Foods

Customers benefit from brands

So we know how brands help businesses, but how do they help customers? What do they do for customers? Brands save customers time, reduce their perceived risk and fulfil their aspirations. Now consider each benefit.

Brands save customers time

Brands help customers' busy lives by saving them time through helping them to find goods and services quickly. Imagine trying to buy books or DVDs on the internet if you couldn't remember the name of

Amazon or CD WOW. Or it could be beans in the supermarket or mortgages on the high street. Unilever's chairman, Niall FitzGerald, calls a brand 'a storehouse of trust which matters more and more as choices multiply' and we face what David Ogilvy once called 'the misery of choice'. People want to simplify their lives, simplify their decision making and get on with the rest of their busy lives.

Brands reduce perceived risk

A strong brand is an implicit guarantee or promise of consistent quality, image and style. A brand is built on trust. Customers trust the promise made in the advertisement and on the pack. Customers form relationships with brands. Brands, in turn, provide a reassuring sense of order. Brands provide a safe and trusted option. Would you buy from someone you didn't know? Customers would prefer to reduce the amount of time and energy involved in decision making. That's one of the reasons why brand extensions are valuable. The brand is an implicit guarantee or promise. Customers trust the promise made in the advertisement and on the pack.

Brands satisfy aspirations

Brands give status and recognition. Brands reflect aspirations, images and associations that are carefully gleaned from in-depth customer motivation research. This is compounded by our search for identity and beliefs. 'In an irreligious world, brands provide us with beliefs', says Wally Olins of Wolff Olins. Some brands unconsciously create a sense of belonging from their cultish quality. In a way, buying and consuming brands actually defines who we are. Brands signal our affiliations. 'You are what you shop.' Brands reflect aspirations and act as a badge of self-image or desired self-image.

Do brands fill the vacuum left by the decline of organized religion?

'In the developed world, they [brands] are seen by some to have expanded into the vacuum left by the decline of organized religion.'

Economist (2001)

Consider the magic marketing formula: identify needs; reflect them; deliver/satisfy them. Remember, brands need to continually do this. Think about what needs Coca-Cola advertising reflects. It reflects people's own aspirations, so that when they buy a can or a case of Coca-Cola they actually buy a slice of their own aspirations (and a product whose promise of refreshing cola is consistently delivered anywhere in the world).

Business disadvantages of weak brands

If a product or service does not have a single strong unifying brand, its presence becomes diluted, seen differently by different people. A diluted brand is less recognizable, therefore less known, therefore less trusted and ultimately a more risky purchase. Without a strong unified brand, products and services become buried in a busy world of other, stronger brands. If a product or service has no real strong brand, it may be symptomatic that the management team are themselves not sure of what the brand really is, what it is really good at, what distinguishes it, what needs it meets and what emotions it connects with. Without a strong brand most of the marketing efforts fragment, splinter and disappear.

No brand, no cattle

The term 'brand' comes from the old Norse verb *brandr*, which meant to burn, which eventually became a noun and adjective in medieval English. The noun *brand* meant flame, fire or torch, and *brand* the adjective meant burning, hence 'brand hot'. Animals were marked with red-hot branding irons as a mark of ownership and an easy way to identify particular cattle.

So strong brands beat weak brands. But, despite creating protection against competition and boosting relationships, sales, profits and balance sheets, brands are continually damaged and weakened. Why do so many marketers allow so many brands to press their own self-destruct button? Read on.

Brand self-destruction

The brand relationship is always fragile. Constant sloppy service or a single moment of disaster, such as contamination or a misplaced word (eg Ratners; see 'Uncontrollable publicity – any publicity is good publicity?', Chapter 14), can destroy the customer's trust. And customers are changing. They're becoming more demanding.

Not only do they talk back, but they now shout back and even bite back if brands break their promise. Today's customers have unlocked 'brand control' from marketers and set up their own brand discussions. Although they are still time pressed and information fatigued, they have found a new energy, fuelled by Web 2.0, which allows them to fulfil their age-old desire to communicate about what interests or concerns them. Customers now have a platform to raise their voices, and some of them can't stop shouting!

Customers have been abused by businesses that dump sloppy service on them, again and again. Surveys reveal that marketers have, in fact, got worse at marketing over the last 10 years. And customers are angry. They are also impatient. The clock is ticking. We are sitting on a customer service time bomb. Sloppy marketing and self-destructing brands go hand in hand.

Lousy marketing

Surprisingly, we've got worse at marketing. We are in an era of declining marketing skills, measured by falling customer satisfaction scores in market after market. Meanwhile automated customer service telephone queuing systems and unworkable websites continue to insult and frustrate customers. Robotic answer machines with self-service menus dump all the work on the information-fatigued, time-poor customer. Add websites that don't work, with dead ends, error messages, complicated navigation and, if you have the patience to struggle through all of that, electronic shopping carts that crash. The customer service time bomb is ticking (see Chapter 1 for more). Some angry customers publicize their feelings on the many blogs and hate sites attacking brands. These can fuel an exponential spreading of negative word of mouth (or 'word of mouse').

Angry customers

Research shows that today's customers are less tolerant of bad service, with 80 per cent of consumers saying they will never go back to an organization after a bad customer experience, up from 68 per cent in 2006 (Harris Interactive, 2006). Add in customers who talk back and who talk to each other via Web 2.0 social media facilities. The goal posts have moved for many marketers. Social network sites facilitate customer discussions about all sorts of brand-related content, eg Coca-Cola never asked for rockets, but it just happened that customers discovered that mixing Coke and Mentos mints caused an explosive reaction and they started posting videos of this phenomenon. Customers talk with text and video, some because they want to share opinions, others because they are hungry for fame and others because they want to meet new friends or, simply, transcend their everyday lives.

Unlocking control with Web 2.0

Customers have unlocked 'control' from companies, with Web 2.0 facilitating user-generated content (UGC). Not surprisingly, UGC is not totally controllable. Online social networks are here to stay. They will continue to grow in line with the very human need for social contact. Customers have been mobilized by blogs, social network sites and invitations to create their own UGC, whether comments and feedback or conversations, joint research or creating advertisements, services or even products. Customers are no longer slovenly couch potatoes, and some are active co-creators who produce discussions, advertisements or even products: hence the term 'prosumer' (see 'The ladder of engagement', Chapter 1).

We are possibly on the cusp of a customer revolution bringing an end to accepting sloppy service and, also, an end to the mass dumbed-down customer. Online digital markets facilitate obscure niche markets as easily as mass markets. In the online world, the 'Long Tail' (Anderson 2006) suggests it can be as profitable to serve 100 customers spread across the world with 100 different digital products as it is to serve 100 local customers with one standardized product. This opens a gate to discrete consumer taste, which effectively moves markets away from the mass market and its tyranny of the lowest dumbed-down denominator. Instead of a handful of powerful marketers recommending, and often determining, what is in and what is out, there are now mobilized niche customers, alerting their own networks about their own niche preferences.

Death of the dumbed-down customer?

'For too long we've been suffering the tyranny of lowest-common-denominator fare, subjected to brain-dead summer blockbusters and manufactured pop. Many of our assumptions about popular taste are actually artifacts of poor supply-and-demand matching – a market response to inefficient distribution.'

Anderson (2006)

Global niches

Although spread across the world, customers with similar interests can communicate and share thoughts through images, audio, video and text anywhere in the world. This means that clusters of customers with similar tastes and interests are connecting with each other to form new global niches and segments. Global markets are here, eg Manchester United Football Club have an estimated 70 million fans around the world, and Al Jazeera's English-language TV news service has 100 million people in its audience worldwide. As media follow markets, media consumption may go global; therefore marketers must remember that brands with international ambitions must have a consistent global image – production should be international in mind, and content rights should be global. True brand masters also 'think global and act local' by paying attention to local market needs and having the nous to express this in local terms.

Creating content that users can pass on via their social networks is an increasingly important channel of communication. But, as Universal McCann (2007) suggests, 'when using these channels it is fundamental that brands and media organizations think global'. Multiple local and conflicting brand identities fragment the brand. In addition, localized brand names can often exclude brands from international sales.

Some brand names restrict international sales or global brand ambitions. See Chapter 9, page 214 for a list of names that damage the brand when used in some international markets.

The internet's new business dynamics

The internet, and broadband in particular, has changed business dynamics. It has created a level playing field for the smaller niche brands to compete with the established global players. Small brands have access to bigger, global markets and can communicate directly with customers across the world in new and more meaningful ways – ways never dreamt of 10 years ago.

Power will be prised away from those major brands that are not prepared to change. Maybe it will be the database holders that take control. Imagine consumers opening a fridge and as they take the last can of Guinness the fridge asks 'Would you like a new delivery of beer, but this time at a special price from a different brand?' Here, it is the database holder that knows who drinks what beer, when and where, as it records the last beer's bar code when the beer is taken out of the fridge. The key to accessing the customers' databases embedded in fridges, microwaves, cars, phones and PDAs is not the hardware but the intelligence (or software system) to know exactly when customers might like to replace something. The invasion of the infomediary starts here.

So marketers who ignore new trends and real customer needs and, worse still, deliver sloppy service are simply pressing a self-destruct button that damages and ultimately destroys a very valuable brand.

Before exploring the right way to nurture a brand (ie the branding process), consider exactly what a brand is and what its component parts are.

Brand components

What exactly is a brand?

A brand is far more than just a name, term, design or symbol that identifies and distinguishes a product or service from that of other competitors. A brand is still a badge of origin, a promise of performance and a point of differentiation. Today, a brand is a holistic experience that stretches beyond the physical and into the psychological. It is the sum of the real product or service experience and the perceived values, images, associations and promises made through marketing communications.

'Brand' is both a verb and a noun. It is a verb, as it is a continual process, and a set of skills is required to create and nurture brands. Branding is a core competency for serious marketers. 'Brand' is also a noun, as it is an asset on the balance sheet and something people buy. Some commentators define brands as simply the difference between a bottle of sugared, flavoured, fizzy water and a bottle of Coca-Cola.

> 'Harley-Davidson does not sell motorcycles. Starbucks do not sell coffee. Club Med does not sell vacations. And Guinness does not sell beer. Think about it.'
>
> Peters (2003)

A brand's rational and emotional appeals

A brand is a cluster of rational or functional and emotional aspects that match customers' rational and emotional needs. Strong brands are designed to trigger specific emotional responses in the minds of customers. Nike promises 'personal achievement', while Coca-Cola promises 'carefree fun'. What we buy says more about a person than he or she might want to admit. It reveals our inner, often unconscious desires and aspirations. If the brand gets it right (understands a customer's deep needs and reflects these through a range of communications) then buyers are simply buying some of their own aspirations. They are, in fact, buying a slice of their ideal self.

Brands, therefore, have both rational and emotional benefits, eg Red Bull's physical (rational) benefit is that it keeps you awake (physical stimulation), and its emotional benefit is that you feel you can do more (feel stimulated). Natural food drinks' functional benefit is 'pure fruit juice', and their emotional benefit is 'feel healthy/feel good'. Kellogg's Corn Flakes' physical benefit is 'breakfast nutrition', and the emotional benefit is 'a great start to the day'. As a brand develops, it should elicit an emotional connection from customers.

Some authors, like Kapferer (2008), see strong brands as a deeply held belief or 'an attitude knitted into consumers' hearts. This attitude goes from emotional resonance to liking, to belonging to the evoked set (or consideration set), to preference, attachment, advocacy, to fanaticism.' Some customers are really attached to their brands and simply will not buy anything else.

The emotional connection

Once upon a time brands used to be all about trust and a seal of quality. Today quality is taken for granted. Now brands fight for an emotional connection as a way of differentiation. Another platform for brands to slug it out is corporate values. Who is the brand, or the corporation behind the brand? Is it socially responsible, environmentally friendly, an animal tester, politically neutral, charitable, or good for its community? The founders of some of the world's strongest brands, like Guinness, Cadbury and Boots, had huge commitments to their employees' and communities' lives, ranging from building spacious towns, to better schools, hospitals, libraries and parks. Today's brands also need a platform of social responsibility.

> ### There's never been so much emotion in business
>
> 'What will happen is based on emotional drives. That's why you can't predict the future. If people worked on pure economic logic, I could predict the future, but I can't.'
>
> Sir John Browne, BP (in Jones, 2001)

The brand components include brand equity, brand identity, brand positioning, brand promise, brand personality, brand values, brand association and, last but not least, the customer experience. They must all integrate with each other. Here is an explanation of each component.

The brand components

Brand equity

Brand equity is the total awareness and perceived value of the brand in the mind of customers. Badly managed brands can result in *negative* brand equity. Brand equity components include the brand identity (brand name, symbols, jingles, colours, associations and any sensory features such as unique smells or tactile experiences) and reputation. Brand awareness, brand preferences and brand loyalty are also part of the brand equity. Above all, actual brand experiences contribute to brand equity.

Brand essence

Brand essence is the brand's soul and spiritual centre, which draws on its core value(s). It is the brand's mission statement (how it will help the world) that motivates customers (and employees). The brand essence is the primary functional and emotional benefits, eg Apple Computer's essence might be 'artful technology', while Amazon's might be 'unparalleled breadth of selection' and Hallmark's might be 'helping people define and express themselves'. The brand essence must have 100 per cent recall amongst the whole business team and influence every decision they make. It starts with what the brand excels at and then connects to an important cultural truth or trend, eg Apple: the world would be a better place if people had the technology to unleash their potential.

Brand experience

Brand experience is what the customers feel or experience when actually consuming a product or service. This includes all touchpoints of the brand (see below). Somehow this seems to be forgotten by many companies. The actual experience customers enjoy, or suffer, directly affects the brand image. Brand moments are all those moments of contact between the brand and the customer. This includes the website, e-mail responses, telephone responses, handling enquiries, the actual consumption of the product or service, and handling complaints and after-sales, as well as all the marketing communications contacts with the customer. These are critical brand moments.

Brand identity

Brand identity is part of brand equity. Identity is how the brand looks and is sometimes called the 'visual narrative', ie logo, colours and graphics. Brand image, on the other hand, is perception, ie how consumers see the brand based on identity plus all other communications, discussions and experiences. Identity is reality. Image is perception. Identity precedes image. Identity helps customers to remember a brand, recognize it and eventually build associations with the brand values, personality and promise promoted through all communications tools.

Brand personality

People have relationships with brands just as they do with people. That's why marketers define the brand personality carefully. Some brands have subtle, and often unconscious, relationships with customers. A brand's personality has those human personality traits. What kind of person would the brand be if it were human? Think of brands as actual people. How would the brand talk, dress and walk? What kind of clothes would it wear? What kind of car would it drive? What kind of parties would it go to? For example, the Marlboro Cowboy and the Singapore Girl have very different but well-defined personalities.

'Hello Gorgeous'

Virgin's website greets you with 'Hello Gorgeous'. This is part of the whole brand experience and is consistent with the brand values and slightly naughty brand personality.

Brand positioning

Brand positioning is how the brand is specifically perceived by customers in the marketplace vis-à-vis the competition, using only two (or sometimes a maximum of three) criteria. Brand positioning is all about perception – how the brand is to be seen, or perceived, by customers using just one or two key variables. For example, a certain drink could be positioned as a young sick person's drink or a healthy adult's drink. A positioning statement identifies the best space for a brand to be positioned in the minds of customers. As markets change (customers' attitudes and needs change) so too brands change to meet customer need. Positioning studies identify what is important to customers, where competitors are positioned (or what they are seen as by customers) and if there are any gaps for a brand to fill or take over. This is brand strategy and absolutely critical to success.

Choosing a positioning

1 Is it important to our target customers (will it drive their buying behaviour)?

2 Is it distinctive and specific?

3 Is it sustainable or can the competition copy it?

4 Can the brand deliver it?

Brand promise

Brand promise or proposition is what the brand offers the customer. For example, Perrier might be a premium-priced carbonated mineral water with unique packaging, etc. It is quite product related as opposed to consumer benefit related. Another brand of water might be the healthiest water for your body. The actual proposition flows from the positioning.

Brand role

What role does this brand play in target customer lives? The brand role is an extension of brand personality or lifestyle, or as a social facilitator. Where does it fit in the life of the customer? Is the brand a champion, a chum, a comforter, a confessor, a conscience, an enabler, an expert, a friend, a guide, a guru, etc? For example, Red Bull might be a 'portable comforter for tired people' or Ryanair possibly enables people to access Europe.

Brand values

Brand values are not necessarily seen, as they are declared internally. Imagine the brand as a person. What does your brand believe in? What does it stand for. What standards does it attain? How should it behave? Brand values are a belief system or a way of working and communicating. Mose (2003) asks:

> Which values are so inherent in your company that, if they disappeared, your company would cease to exist as it is? Thousands of companies disappear every year. So why has your company survived? Why are investors still investing in your company? Why do your customers still buy your product? Why do people come to work for your company? Why do you still work for your company? These questions can help determine your company's true core values.

Brand vision

Brand vision is what the brand should be. In Virgin's case it might be to provide a service that is 'the people's champion and which shakes up the status quo'. In Nike's case the vision is one of achievement, of personal best, of being part of a community of athletes. The brand allows people to reconnect with an Olympic ethos that sits somewhere deep inside the psyche.

> 'Do not relax until you have identified the irreducible core of a brand – what drives its connection with consumers. This will mean getting inside consumers' heads, and understanding deep-seated motivations and thought processes.
>
> Braun (2004)

Sensory branding may become more of the brand experience, as trademark regulations in almost all countries are accepting applications for registering components of the brand that incorporate all five senses. Lindstrom (2005) reported that:

> decades ago, Texas developed the Texas touch, albeit on their calculators. Texas was one of the first companies to actually trademark the specific 'clicks' – the feel of the number pad on their calculators. The interesting fact is that users of the product may not recognize Texas's logo, but they still recognize the 'touch'. Singapore Airlines currently has 9 patents including a patent on the Stephan Florida Smell – the characteristic 'Singapore Airline smell' of the hot towels served onboard. Kellogg's invested in the power of auditory stimulus, testing the crunching of cereals in a Danish sound lab to upgrade their product's 'sound quality'. We all recognize Intel's jingle even in other brands' advertisements.

Brand touchpoints are sometimes called 'brand moments' or 'customer touchpoints'. Touchpoints are anywhere the brand touches the customer, eg packaging, advertisements, websites, telephonists, sponsorship, events, etc. While customers are waiting on the phone, what brand experience do they experience? While they are receiving a bill, letter, fax or e-mail, what experience do they have? These are part of the brand experience. Marketers need to pinpoint the relevant attributes that distinguish the brand and the touchpoints that can deliver these (in order of importance). This requires input from everyone – from CEO, MD, marketing, operations and sales teams to advertising people and webmasters.

One of the ultimate touchpoints for a brand is experiential marketing – traditionally live events offline where customers get to interact with the brand in a new and immersive environment.

> 'Great marketers do not sell products.
> They evoke emotion.'
>
> Scott Farrell (2008)

The branding process

A big prize awaits brands that can develop deeper and longer-lasting brands with their customers. Marketers should treat the word 'brand' as a verb and not a noun, as branding is a continual process. Brand building and brand maintenance are, in fact, a core competency. Outstanding marketers use a development process when creating an advertising campaign, an exhibition, a website or an actual brand. They also use it when reviewing and updating a brand, since brands have to be redefined for a new era (otherwise markets can move away from old, outdated brands). The best brand stewards or brand guardians have an inbuilt review process to ensure the brand is kept fresh. They ensure the brand does not allow obsolescence to creep into it and tweak it if necessary. So, whether you are creating a brand new brand or maintaining an existing brand,

here are the four main steps in the process: brief, concept generation, concept development and roll-out/delivery. Figure 2.1 shows the process required to create and maintain strong brands.

A clear brief covers details of the target market, required brand role, personality, values, positioning, etc. Concepts or ideas are generated. One or two are selected and developed, and finally one is rolled out as the new brand.

What's missing in this process? Research is missing. Research is required before and after each stage. So now the brand development process reads:

FIGURE 2.2 The brand development process including research

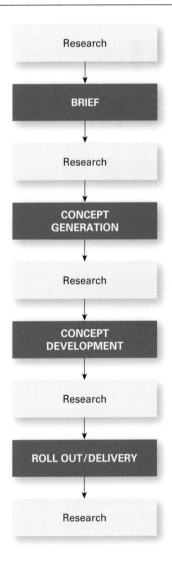

FIGURE 2.1
The brand development process

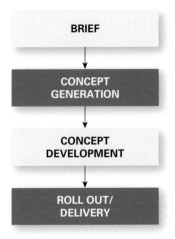

FIGURE 2.3   The complete brand development process

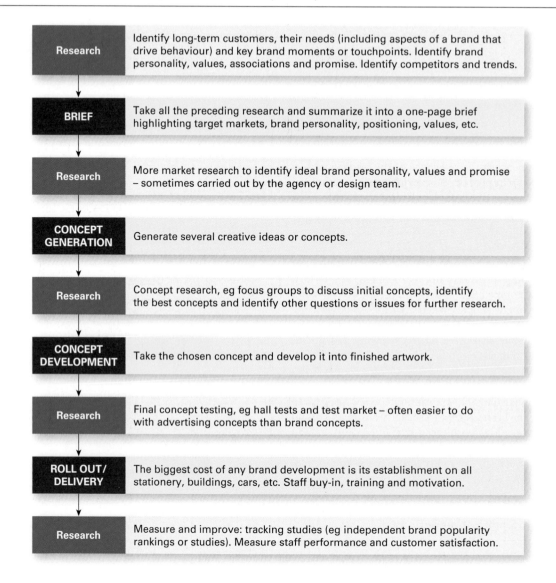

Research	Identify long-term customers, their needs (including aspects of a brand that drive behaviour) and key brand moments or touchpoints. Identify brand personality, values, associations and promise. Identify competitors and trends.
BRIEF	Take all the preceding research and summarize it into a one-page brief highlighting target markets, brand personality, positioning, values, etc.
Research	More market research to identify ideal brand personality, values and promise – sometimes carried out by the agency or design team.
CONCEPT GENERATION	Generate several creative ideas or concepts.
Research	Concept research, eg focus groups to discuss initial concepts, identify the best concepts and identify other questions or issues for further research.
CONCEPT DEVELOPMENT	Take the chosen concept and develop it into finished artwork.
Research	Final concept testing, eg hall tests and test market – often easier to do with advertising concepts than brand concepts.
ROLL OUT/ DELIVERY	The biggest cost of any brand development is its establishment on all stationery, buildings, cars, etc. Staff buy-in, training and motivation.
Research	Measure and improve: tracking studies (eg independent brand popularity rankings or studies). Measure staff performance and customer satisfaction.

Research

In order to explore the brand opportunity, research is used at the early stage of a brand's development (way before any brand names, logos and colours). Target markets are analysed, buyer behaviour drivers explored, brand personalities defined and the most cost-effective brand moments identified.

Successful brands use a platform of information to help to nurture the brand. Initial exploratory research is used to:

- identify long-term profitable customers;
- develop a deep understanding of the customer;
- identify aspects of a brand that drive behaviour;
- identify the emotions that drive brand behaviour;
- identify personality, values, associations and the promise;
- identify critical brand moments – or critical touchpoints;

- identify the most cost-effective, high-impact brand moments.

Let's consider each of these.

Identify long-term profitable customers

Do not invest branding efforts in unprofitable segments (particularly those with weak long-term potential). The profit potential of each segment needs to be measured. Also watch out for trends that may affect the relevance of the traditional segmentation approach (eg size, income, age, ethnicity, consumption patterns, loyalty, locations, lifestyles, needs and attitudes), eg the business traveller hotel segments may be changing from service-oriented business travelling to value-driven business travelling and luxury-driven business travelling. The latter may split into 'fashion seeker' segments (who see their hotels as a way of expressing who they are) and 'escape seeker' segments (who want to feel pampered and far from the pressures of business).

> Identified trends are a marketer's friend.

Develop a deep understanding of the customer

Who, what, why, where, when and how were Rudyard Kipling's six wise old friends (questions). Outstanding marketers can answer all of these questions about their customer segments. The most difficult is 'why' – why do customers buy? (See also Chapter 4.) Excellent marketers know their customers better than they know themselves. A deep understanding of the customers is required, eg a hotel might uncover that the core need underlying the desire for comfort is to 'feel as though I'm at home while I'm away'. As desires change, trends must be watched continuously to ensure the right offers are made, eg some retail sectors have discovered that speed is now far more important to customers than credit card facilities and accordingly offer cash-only transactions. An airline may have to prioritize between easier upgrades, more onboard services, faster check-in, a bigger baggage allowance and more frequent-flyer miles. Getting the proposition right is critical when building brands.

> ### Invite a brand into your life
>
> 'Marketers need a deeper understanding of what makes people invite certain brands and propositions into their lives and what makes them reject others.'
>
> Fauconnier (2006)

Identify aspects of the brand that drive behaviour

A brand's specific features may clearly distinguish the brand from competitors but not be important to customers. This is what McKinsey's refer to as the 'fool's gold of branding'. Different but non-important features are irrelevant if they do not drive customer behaviour. Without knowing which features really do affect customer behaviour, an organization can squander limited resources promoting unwanted aspects of the brand. It's a little bit like getting high satisfaction scores but wondering why customers are leaving in droves. You're probably measuring the non-important features that were important in previous years. Customer desires change, and so trend spotting and brand adjusting are required to keep brands up to date and out of the great brand graveyard in the sky.

> ### Branding requires a deep understanding of human psychology
>
> 'The new marketing approach is to build a brand not a product – to sell a lifestyle or a personality to appeal to emotions. But this requires a far greater understanding of human psychology. It is a much harder task than describing the virtues of a product.'
>
> *Economist* (2001)

Identify the emotions that drive brand behaviour

A brand is much more than a product. It is a lifestyle or a personality that appeals to the emotions as well as the rational, thinking side of the brain. Emotions are very important. Branding is about creating and maintaining emotional ties. Marketers must probe and discover their customers' emotions, since they often drive behaviour.

Le Pla, Davis and Parker (2003) identified three triggers to create an emotional tie that ultimately strengthens brand loyalty: 1) congruence with deeply rooted life themes (values); 2) helping the accomplishment of life projects; 3) resolution of current concerns. 'If all three triggers can occur through the customer's personal relationship with the brand then it is likely that the customer will see the brand as a friend or partner, or see the brand at the heart of a community of users – where the community becomes a significant part of the customer's life.'

In the US car market, the Mini created huge sales and high brand loyalty when it appealed to the emotions of drivers. The advertisements declared 'opposition to bigness' and promised to 'wage war on SUVs'. The Mini 'celebrated the joy of motoring' as opposed to 'the lobotomized, cruise control movement of most car-transport on America's highways and streets'. GM's Saturn also used emotion in car advertisements that said very little about the car but lots about the company's ideology. The car wasn't even shown in the advertisements, but the ordinary people who made it were. The ad explained GM's beliefs and values. The car became the top-selling small car two years after launch, with a community built around the brand (some 45,000 customers and families turned up at a factory to meet each other and the company at its open day, which had barbecues, bands and a factory tour).

> 'We don't know how to sell on performance. Everything we sell, we sell on image.'
> Robert Gouezeta, ex-CEO, Coca-Cola

Identify personality, values, associations and promise

Identify the kind of brand personality that reflects the ideal personality that the target market aspires to or admires. Build in the values and associations that matter to the target market. Make a very clear simple promise and stick to it – never break it.

Identify critical brand moments – or touchpoints

These are the places, often beyond the consumption of the actual product or service, where a large part of the total brand experience is really delivered. This is where the customer has a large emotional investment, eg a phone call to customer service to make a complaint. This includes anywhere that customers interact with the brand (phone, store and web, as well as ads and events, etc).

Identify the most cost-effective, high-impact brand moments

Channel creativity and resources into these high-impact areas. This is where the brand will be enhanced or destroyed. Remember, a beautifully designed logo and clever brand name mean nothing if the website doesn't work or the customer service person cannot solve the problem. Equally, a wonderful product can be destroyed if it is delivered uncaringly.

Service training or website redesign?

Which is the priority? Creating a new customer service training programme or redesigning a website? Answer: find the high-impact touchpoints and allocate resources that have the biggest effect on these high-impact touchpoints.

Equipped with answers to all of the research questions, we now know what we want and what is the priority. Having completed the research, we can now write the brief.

The brief

The starting point for any branding initiative is to ask what its objectives are: what is it trying to achieve in the customers' minds? The brief should include the brand promise, personality, values, associations and positioning (as well as the 3Ms: men/women, money and minutes – who is responsible for what, how much budget is allocated to creating this brand, and how much time there is before the launch, testing and concept development stages). Brand logos and clever names come later. A good brief should be written and agreed or signed off by all the key decision makers.

As well as defining the target market, the brief includes the brand's promise to customers. What makes it different? What needs is it fulfilling? In addition to target markets, distribution channels and regulatory guidelines, the brief should include brand vision, values, role, personality, positioning, promise or proposition, and essence.

An example of promise is Volkswagen promising the most reliable car. Volvo promise the safest. The brand's personality (the tone, manner and style of how you speak to customers, what you look like and how your staff behave) gives guidelines both for marketing communications and for staff behaviour. Virgin's personality is consistently irreverent, eg Virgin's airport luggage-size signs state 'The size of your bag has a limit – but the size of your ego can't be too large!' Brand values are included, as they influence how you work, your beliefs and your standards of behaviour. The brand's positioning must be crystal clear. This summarizes all the other questions and is key to marketing strategy. Positioning defines how your brand's distinctive benefits should be perceived by customers alongside competitive offers.

Two important aspects for any brand brief are relevance and differentiation. The proposition must make customers an offer, firstly, that fits their needs and, secondly, that the competition cannot (easily) offer. Relevance and difference increase the likelihood of success. But, remember, relevant product differentiators may change over time.

A useful *aide-mémoire* for any brief is SOS + 3Ms, which is taken from the marketing planning system called SOSTAC®. The SOS brief provides a useful framework, as it includes situation analysis (where are we now?), objectives (where are we going?) and strategy (how do we get there?); the 3Ms are men/women (the brand manager and team who decide), money (budget) and minutes (timescale). For more on SOSTAC®, see Chapter 10.

> A brand that does not stand for something stands for nothing.

Concept generation and development

The answers to questions about the brand's promise, personality, values, associations, and positioning give clear guidance to any creative ideas. A good brief saves a lot of time, as it steers creative thinking in the right direction and avoids generating time-consuming concepts that do not fulfil the brand prerequisites.

However, once the brief has been signed off, some additional research may be carried out into customers, distributors and even competitors. On the basis of a clear brief and any additional research required, brand names and brand logos can be generated and then researched, with the best one(s) being selected for refinement or development. The finished brand name and logo are then tested once more. Early-stage research should include global use, ie whether the name or the logo has any strange meaning in other key languages, and whether it is protectable. Let us look at brand name development and brand logo development.

Brand name development

Developing brand names is a specialized business in itself. A brand name should be distinctive and easy to say, spell and remember. It should also be relevant, brief (maximum four syllables) and legally protectable (ie not generic) and lend itself to advertising and promotion. Lastly, a really good name can be used almost globally.

Three different approaches to brand name development are: product function; classic names (Latin or Greek); and benefit based. Product function (eg International Business Machines (now IBM) is difficult to protect. The classic approach is more protectable, eg Nike is a Greek name, which relates to the specific cultural values of the Olympic Games and the glorification of the human body. Thirdly, benefit-based names are less directly associated with a product or service's functions and closer to a name that evokes product benefit or even a certain state of mind, eg Nectar for a 'reward points' programme.

And there are always exceptions to the rule. Richard Branson claims to have named his brand Virgin because he was a virgin when it came to business. Tech giant Cisco's name comes from the last five letters of San Francisco, reportedly chosen when the founders were inspired by a drive past the

Golden Gate Bridge en route to register the company. Aldi supermarket's founder, Albrecht, supposedly combined his name with 'Discount'.

Names need to be distinctive and protectable (to register them as trademarks). Functional or descriptive names are difficult to register, as they may be deemed to be generic words commonly used by others (and therefore owned by everyone).

Once a short list of names has been generated, a name search is carried out in the target market (and potential target markets) to check to see if anyone has registered these names already in the same business sector. After that, some simple concept testing in each target market reveals whether the brand name has any negative meanings in different languages, as Coca-Cola discovered in China (see Chapter 9). Without these checks, subsequent opportunities for global expansion are curtailed without an expensive and time-consuming rebranding exercise.

Horlicks and Birds Eye Fish Fingers – strange but true

Nomen est omen – a name is an omen. A brand name therefore is often linked to its intentions, eg Nike. IBM came from International Business Machines, and Microsoft has obvious roots in microcomputers, chips and software. However, Horlicks and Birds Eye Fish Fingers are, perhaps, an indication of the irrational nature of brands as to how their names ever became brands.

Brand logos

The crucifix, the hammer and sickle, the swastika, the red cross or a national flag immediately arouse emotions, feelings, images or interpretations of some kind. Logos are a language (sometimes international) of emotional response. Symbols, shapes and colour all have conscious and unconscious meanings. Visual symbols or devices can also be powerful as a means of increasing awareness by facilitating easy recognition. A logo can act as a focal point to summarize or encapsulate an organization, although it should not be too complex. If an identity needs too much explaining, then it isn't work-

ing. The acid test for a logo is: distinctive, easily recognizable, memorable and reducible (can work when reduced on to a business card or postage stamp). It should work in black and white as well as colour, since many corporate images appear in black and white in the press. Ideally, the logo should also be symbolic, or relevant to the business, but this is rarely the case. With the growth of the internet it is increasingly important that it works well on-screen, as well as in its more traditional applications.

Logos are an important part of the brand identity and often are described as a key component of brand equity, eg Nike's swoosh and McDonald's Golden Arches help audiences and customers to recognize the brand instantly and also help to differentiate the brand. A logo also acts as a stamp or guarantee. It should, ideally, reflect the values of the brand. Logos can protect a trademark when combined with generic words (as generic words themselves are usually not protectable on their own, but the combination of the word with the logo may be). Good logos (unique, easily recognizable, relevant and well maintained) become icons, and not only are they recognizable but even parts of them are recognizable, such as the Heinz chevron or the 'M' in Marlboro.

Don King's hair

World boxing promoter Don King's elevated hairstyle (brushed up 6 inches or more into the air) makes him stand out in a crowded post-fight boxing ring. His unique visual symbol helps to ensure that he is easily recognized and seen to be involved with the big fights.

Colour also plays an important part. Colours instantly access our emotions (think of what the colour red does to a bull). Colour also affects our physiological state and propensity to make a decision.

Logo development

The process of developing a logo is similar to the process of developing any aspect of marketing communications: brief, concept generation (and selection), concept development and finally launch or roll-out. In between each stage, research gives crucial feedback. This helps to select the best concept, which when guided by feedback (research) is developed into the final logo design. It does get one last check with more research before roll-out (launch).

One UK design consultancy developed a new logo for Saudi Arabian Airlines that looked, to the uninitiated, distinctive, unique and easily recognizable. The logo contained golden palm trees, crossed Arabian swords and a crescent moon and appeared to be suitably upmarket and regal. It contained four major errors:

1 the wrong type of palm tree – Saudi Arabia is the number two producer of dates, but the palm tree shown was not a date palm tree;

2 the wrong type of sword – the traditional Saudi sword is a fighting sword, but the sword shown in the logo looked weak, old and ceremonial;

3 the wrong moon – the crescent of the new moon used by Saudi Arabia represents a new beginning, but the proposed crescent was that of an old moon, suggesting 'the end';

4 the wrong colour – the old green colour was replaced by cream, which represents hot, barren sand in the desert when Saudi Arabia was trying to irrigate the kingdom and make it green.

This confirms the need for designers to invest in detailed research before attempting to develop any design concepts. Designers who neither budget nor plan for research (or several stages of research) vastly increase the likelihood of problems. Worse still, if problems occur after implementation of a new design, the costs immediately spin out of control, and there is a highly embarrassed management team.

Research is also carried out into logo trends. In the 1970s, corporate images hardened. The 1980s saw them becoming soft and decorative. Some cynics say that, if you wanted to make an abstract organization look purposeful in the late 1980s, you gave it a face – preferably a neoclassical one. The Woolworths group, on the other hand, changed its name, logo and total identity to Kingfisher, which was certainly distinctive, easily recognizable, memorable, and symbolic of its progressive leadership expansion and growth potential (although some argued that the bird had a life expectancy of only one year and that robins and blue tits were more popular anyway). Bovis construction company chose a humming bird, which again fitted the above criteria. Others suggest that there was a trend towards humanizing logos, since organizations are all about people.

FIGURE 2.4   The Prudential logo

More recently, there has been a trend towards purely graphic devices (in other words, away from figurative symbols). This has been driven by a number of factors. On the one hand, it is part of a general trend towards more direct communications, which has resulted in a stripping out of superfluous elements. On the other, the internet has become a more important channel of communication for many organizations. As Mark Wilson of identity specialists Bamber Forsyth says, 'The lower resolution of the internet and digital television has driven us towards simpler, highly graphic identity elements that are seen smaller, and in more places, than ever before', eg Google and Amazon.

Shanks & McEwan, a waste management business, updated its identity at the turn of the millennium, simplifying its name and adopting a straightforward graphic logo. When introducing the new identity to staff, the company said:

> We're linking the phrase 'waste solutions' to our name in order to emphasize that we are a problem-solving company. We're also using the 's' as our symbol to make the new identity more distinctive and memorable. The full stops within the logotype and after the 's' symbol are important. This is our way of saying that we're the last word in waste management.

FIGURE 2.5   The Shanks logo

shanks. waste solutions.

The logo can be literal (eg Shell), a logotype (a stylized treatment of the company name with no additional symbol, eg Kellogg's), wordmarks that integrate a graphic element into the name (eg BHS), company initials (eg IBM) or purely abstract. Whichever type of logo is chosen, it is essential to research the choice carefully, particularly in global markets where symbols, colours and words can have very different meanings.

End of logos?

'A logo today has turned out to be a warning sign of a commercial message. The trend is that it will disappear and be replaced by other non-conscious signals – everything from iPod's whiter ear plugs, to Tiffany's blue packaging, to the United Colors of Benetton photos or whatever you are imaging.

'If you look at Formula 1 today, you'll see that most of the Ferrari cars have these funny red coloured bar codes. That is the secret logo from Marlboro. There's no logo, there's no name on it.'

Martin Lindstrom, in Rothery (2009)

Roll-out/delivery

The roll-out of a brand requires far more than just press launches and lavish branding events. The rolling out of a new brand (or a revamped brand) starts internally. The whole organization needs to be mobilized. The whole organization must live and breathe the brand. This starts with the CEO acting as brand champion and cascades down through the organization by:

- living the brand;
- linking operational targets to brand ratings;
- linking rewards to customer satisfaction and brands ratings;
- putting brand values in job specifications.

Living the brand means internalizing the brand and living its values. What a business does reveals its personality and values far more than any amount of advertising. Any significant disconnection between what an organization says about itself and what it actually does will seriously undermine people's relationship with the brand.

Living the brand occurs when employees actively and enthusiastically deliver the brand promise day in, day out. It helps if the brand and brand responsibilities are written into the job description of every member of the team. This is where marketing and HR work closely together. The brand effectively becomes everybody's business.

'When you develop a brand the primary audience for it is the employees.'

Ken Morris, Siehel+Gale

Do all employees know (and memorize) what the brand promise and brand values are? Do they know what the business stands for? Are they able to tell the brand story in a compelling way to different stakeholder audiences including shareholders, employees, customers and vendors? To ensure that a brand comes to life throughout the organization, ask whether you need structural or departmental changes. It is that important. Consider every aspect of the organization from employee behaviour to premises. Inject the brand DNA into your organization structure.

Motivate and train staff

Develop operational targets to build the brand. Try linking customer satisfaction scores and brand ratings to operational targets. (You should measure criteria that are important to customers, not those you think are important.) All staff are brand ambassadors.

Brand consistency stops a brand from splintering, diluting and ebbing away. Crystal-clear brand guidelines can include templates for all marketing collateral so that brochures, websites and signage are all consistently produced anywhere in the world. The brand guidelines also include the Pantone colours,

---

Logos – an international language

'Logos, by the force of ubiquity, have become the closest thing we have to an international language, recognized and understood in many more places than English.'

Klein (2000)

size and layout of logos and straplines for a range of different uses, online and offline, as well as above the line and below the line.

At first a new logo has little or no value because it has no franchise. First it must be associated with the right kind of images, and then its recognition levels can be developed (eg Lloyds Bank's black horse). This takes time, since initial reaction to change or anything new is often quite negative. Sometimes the initial reaction is one of upset, dislike or disgust, as the new logo does not fit in with the previous set of cognitions (and thereby creates 'cognitive dissonance' and possibly tension). The value of the logo eventually starts to increase as the years roll by and it becomes better understood. However, it helps enormously if internal marketing carefully brings staff on board throughout the development and ultimately before the launch.

Whether the logo trend is towards simplicity, swooshes or sharp-edged internationally understood symbols, the corporate identity demands careful management across all the points of public contact.

Brand maintenance

Creating a brand is relatively easy. The difficult part is maintaining a brand. Great brand managers constantly develop or reinvigorate the brand so that it is constantly seen as relevant (not 'hip' nor necessarily modern, but definitely always relevant to the target market). Remember, target markets move and change. The classic Lucozade drink once upon a time was positioned as a sick child's drink. As the market demographics moved on from a disproportionately large number of children in the 1960s to a disproportionately large number of young adults in the 1980s, Lucozade repositioned itself as a healthy adult's drink. Today it has moved on again, twisting and tweaking itself to stay relevant to its key target market. Maintaining a brand requires vision, system, determination and people.

Mobilize staff and channel partners

The brand requires a system that mobilizes the entire organization. Bringing a brand to life requires a completely integrated approach beyond marketing. Operations and HR must develop a system that inspires and motivates all staff to support the brand. Ideally, job descriptions should explain the responsibilities that staff have to 'live the brand'. Operational targets can be linked to building and maintaining the brand (such as measuring relevant customer satisfaction). The brand needs to be embedded into the DNA of the business.

This, in turn, helps the company to live the brand, ensuring that all those crucial 'brand moments' (when the business interacts with the customer) actually reflect the brand. The primary audience for a brand is the employees – as they need to be mobilized to support the brand. Then come the channel partners (distributors). Brand managers need to ensure that the brand is never compromised or tarnished on its journey to the end customer.

A fatal mistake some marketers make is an over-focus on external marketing communications (developing advertising campaigns, direct mail campaigns, websites and opt-in SMS campaigns to boost cross-selling and up-selling), rather than ensuring all customer touchpoints are consistently executed.

Instigate brand policing

Brand managers are brand guardians who need to ensure the brand is consistently used in all touchpoints.

Air travel worries?

Attention to detailed design management can subconsciously influence air travellers. The same logo, typeface, primary and secondary colours and trim on all visual points of contact help to reassure the traveller, while reinforcing the airline's identity. The check-in desk logo, signs, colours and trims should be coordinated with the uniform (and badge), ticket holder, baggage tag and departure lounge carpets, right through to the plane's exterior graphics, interior carpet and even the trim on the china and linen. Without this coordinated corporate identity, cognitive dissonance can set in. There is a subconscious unease or discomfort created by the inconsistent messages. A coordinated identity reduces this often unconscious tension, which in turn creates a more satisfied passenger. The cohesive identity does not make the traveller leap off the plane and scream for joy on arrival, but it might make the subconscious difference next time around when choosing between two airline companies if one airline offers a reassuring sense of order.

Brand policing is important. If an organization's identity is not coordinated or managed precisely, confusing signals about the organization go out to different audiences around the world. A splintered identity fragments the corporate image, which in turn dilutes the corporate presence among key audiences. The potential asset (corporate brand) depreciates to the point where it becomes a liability. The organization dilutes its presence and has an uncoordinated image. This sends out disorganized messages that weaken the initial or final impression left by the organization.

A logo displayed prominently in an office or on a letterhead makes a good strong statement, but it is the consistent 'echoing' of the logo, its exact primary and secondary colours, the specific typeface and the overall design style on the 'secondary format' of products, packages, business forms and employee uniforms, that provides the all-important, if subtle, consistent reinforcement.

There is a need to think it through in detail and then to police the usage of all visual points of contact. This is where a design manual guides managers in different buildings and in different countries to specify, in a consistent manner, the exact graphic requirement for *every* point of visual contact.

a lack of consistency between the brand name, the packaging and the advertising is subconsciously recognized by the consumer and leads to a feeling of detachment, ultimately resulting in brandswitching'. So it is important to be consistent and to reinforce identity through all the appropriate points of public contact. This should include advertising and all elements of the communications mix, which includes permanent media like corporate headquarters.

The logo is just the tip of the iceberg. It is often the most visible part of an organization. A corporate identity scheme may have a logo at its heart, but it will generally include a whole array of other elements, often referred to as 'visual language'. This may include typefaces, a colour palette, the use of photography and illustrations, a layout style for using these items and even a particular style of written language, as well as briefs for interior design and exteriors of buildings (plus, today, eco-friendly building requirements).

Sweaty identity

In corporate identity terms, attention to detail needs to spread beyond just graphics. The classic *1990 US Hall of Shame* reported the following: 'To upgrade its image in 1982 AT&T told its repair people to wear dress shirts and ties, gave them attaché cases for their tools, and renamed them "system technicians". But Ma Bell didn't install air conditioning in its cars. So during the summer the technicians arrived on the job looking like they had just stepped out of a sauna. Said a union official, "It's hard to have corporate appeal if your shirt is wringing wet."'

Nash and Zull Products (1989)

The Intel, Oracle, Microsoft and IBM offices

'Intel's blue fortress in San Jose is about power and control. Oracle's shining towers on Redwood Shore are brash testimony to the showmanship of its founder, Larry Ellison. The scattered low-rise blocks at Microsoft's Redmond campus imply a laid-back informality, but the intense figures trotting along ordered paths suggest a restless insecurity. IBM's new headquarters at Armonk in New York state is so discreetly tucked into a valley that it cannot be seen until you are almost upon it. It politely curves in an S-shape around the trees and rocks that could have easily been blasted away. For a company that employs 270,000 people and earned revenues of nearly $80 billion last year, it is implausibly tiny. Inside, it is light, open-plan, discreetly high tech, and very, very calm. It is a stealth headquarters, the antithesis of the swaggering IBM buildings from before "The Fall".'

Economist (1998)

The importance of consistency applies right across the communications spectrum. In John Murphy's book *Branding* (1991), Klaus Morwind Henkel points to consumer research that 'has indicated that

A good corporate brand can help sales and boost employee relationships, financial relationships and media relationships during a crisis. Corporate branding, however, requires a lot more than just a corporate identity. The impact of a corporate identity programme goes far beyond a logo or a lick of paint. It influences almost every manifestation of an organization, its corporate headquarters, its staff and even the way they work. All of the components need to be in place. A new logo raises stakeholder expectations.

Boards, doors, logos and skunks

'A new letterhead and a new logo is no substitute for a new board of directors.'

Rodney Fitch (2003)

'Painting the lavatory door won't cure the plumbing.'

Bernstein (1984)

'If you take a lousy low-profile company and give it a major corporate revamp, you end up with a lousy high-profile company.'

Wally Olins (1989)

'Even if you paint out a skunk's stripes it will still smell extremely nasty.'

Source unknown

Corporate brands and sub-brands

An umbrella brand, such as the Virgin brand, can have various sub-brands, such as Virgin Atlantic, Virgin Cola and Virgin Trains. A corporate brand, such as GlaxoSmithKline (GSK), Unilever or Procter & Gamble (P&G), on the other hand, remains in the background and offers an endorsement, while a mainstream brand like Persil can have sub-brands such as Persil washing-up liquid and Persil powder.

Invest in the brand asset

Constant investment is also required to maintain a brand's profile to avoid getting buried in the communications clutter. Some companies take the long-term, brand investment view, eg Coke is investing $65 million in sponsoring the Olympics from 2009 to 2021.

Constant reviews of brands, and in particular large portfolios of brands, can result in a major strategic consolidation of the brand portfolio, as in the case of Unilever when it cut its portfolio of 1,600 brands down to 400. Brands are under increased challenges today.

Brands fade as tastes change, unless of course they are maintained and nurtured carefully to meet the new market conditions. Even in steady-state markets where there are no great trends pulling the market away from the brand, marketers still need to ensure that the brand is policed carefully, particularly as a brand grows globally. Rigorous use of brand guidelines is required here to ensure that exactly the same brand features appear correctly any time and anywhere.

Review the brand

Brands require constant reviews and investment of energies and money. Brands often need to be reinvented or reinvigorated to avoid being left behind by a fast-changing marketplace. A constant flow of market research ensures the brand really addresses customers' deep needs, which change over time. Otherwise brands fade as tastes change. Constant market research also reveals how the brand is positioned against existing competition and new competitors. As Olins (1989) says, 'In a complex and changing company the corporate identity [for an overall company] bears a great strain, twisting and turning to fit every new requirement. But a good corporate identity should last a generation.'

When does a brand identity become out of date? Can the business environment change and move away from the organization and its values, leaving behind the obsolete, irrelevant and even damaging corporate identity? When do the staff and other audiences get tired of it? Mergers and acquisitions sometimes necessitate a new corporate identity. Occasionally, legal reasons force a change. Sometimes overseas ambitions are restricted by the use of a home-grown logo (eg BT's old logo clashed with that of overseas companies).

Shell reviews and updates its corporate identity. The shell device has served it well, despite its being a petrol company with a 'high explosive' name.

Global markets are constantly moving and changing, so much so that some organizations fear they are being left behind by the global update. A review and redesign help an organization to keep abreast of trends and avoid being left isolated by a redundant identity.

FIGURE 2.6   The Shell logo and its redesigns

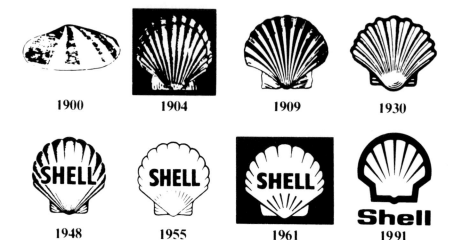

1900   1904   1909   1930

1948   1955   1961   1991

Aggressive hand-held torch of learning gets the chop

The National Union of Teachers' 25-year-old 'hand-held torch of learning' was considered to have become 'too strident, aggressive and uncaring, with none too desirable connotations of the Conservative party and the Greek fascist party'. Although it was designed in the 1960s, it had a 1930s look. It appeared that the time was right to move the logo on but keep it relevant and maintain the link with the union's heritage. The updated design shows an outstretched hand embraced by the spelt-out words of the NUT, tying the symbol together as one cohesive form, either male or female, adult or child, to avoid alienation.

FIGURE 2.7
Hand-held torch of learning

Sometimes new brand identities are developed simply because old management wants to say something new or a new CEO wants to announce he or she has arrived. This is a dangerous game, as a new brand identity or a new corporate identity raises expectations that the organization has new ways of working, new customer benefits or new customer experiences.

Lipstick on a pig

'Long before the phrase "lipstick on a pig" became an election issue, I had warned of the dangers of putting "lipstick on a bulldog" – that is, making superficial cosmetic change in organizations rather than looking at the real underlying problems. The problem with putting lipstick on a bulldog is that it is hard to wrestle the bulldog to the ground long enough to do it and then doesn't change the nature of the beast...

'George Orwell warned of the evils of lipstick-clad bulldogs that co-opt words and distort their meaning. In his book *1984*, the war department was called "The Ministry of Peace".'

Kanter (2009)

Constant watch: the customer experience

Brand maintenance also requires careful attention to the customer experience (which as we've seen is often very poor). Poor product quality and sloppy service destroy brands more quickly than any large advertising budget can build them. Poor product or service quality, complicated order forms, late delivery, incomprehensible customer service agents and error-laden websites all destroy a brand. Slow e-mail responses damage the brand. Non-responses can kill it.

Attention to the customer experience offline and online is important. Online brands still deliver offline (eg Amazon books); hence marketers monitor the offline aspects carefully also. And all brands (online and offline) have opportunities to extend the brand experience online by layering in new and exciting value-adding benefits. They add some 'sizzle'. Embellishing and extending the brand experience online can be achieved with 'sizzle', which cannot be found offline.

Nurturing brands can include lavishing wonderful brand experiences on customers, otherwise known as experiential marketing. Nurturing brands also includes engaging customers and moving them up into higher levels of brand engagement (see Chapter 1, 'The ladder of engagement').

Finally there is the experience – the quality of the experience, both online and offline, directly affects the brand and its image. Remember, sloppy websites, unanswered e-mails and comments, unpleasant receptionists and any other touchpoints can damage the brand, if not managed carefully. Many marketers now see the online opportunity to build both the brand image and the overall company value.

> In just a few seconds sloppy websites destroy brands that took years to build.

Social media now engages the customer in new ways (as discussed in Chapter 1). The brand's own website can add deeper, richer brand experiences by adding some 'sizzle' (Chaffey and Smith, 2008).

> Ask 'What experience could a website deliver that would really wow customers?'

What experience could a website deliver that would really add value for customers, be truly unique and be representative of the brand? Ultimately ask 'How can my website help my customers (or other stakeholders)?' Here are a few examples:

- A camera company can help customers to take better photographs by simulating taking photographs with different settings and allowing customers to compare and contrast the results (and can also give tips on how to maintain cameras and protect films and photos, and can invite customers to send their best photos in for a competition).
- A travel company can give you a 'virtual friend'. After you tell the company what your interests are (via an online questionnaire), the 'friend' can suggest ideas for things you would like to do in the cities you choose to explore.
- Cosmetic companies offer online games, screensavers, viral e-mails, video clips and soundtracks to help customers use the products.
- Food companies online offer printable recipes, video demonstrations and discussion forums, as well 'ask the expert' sessions.
- Chocolate companies generate ideas for desserts (using the chocolates), dinner party games and designs for table layouts.

Create customer engagement

If marketers understand customer engagement better than their competitors, then this helps them develop brand loyalty. How else can the ideal customer engage with the brand? The ideal customer, or most valuable customer, does not have to be someone who buys a lot. The ideal customer could be an influencer who may be a small irregular buyer who posts ratings and reviews. The reviews can influence another 100 people. 'Engaged customers' are probably going to become brand zealots if they are kept engaged.

Marketers can easily monitor the type, quantity and frequency of blog posts, forum discussions, reviews, profile updates, etc. This identifies opportunities and also acts as an early warning system to any possible future problems. Consider targeting brand evangelists rather than just purchasers.

A customer who doesn't care about the product or service is likely to be less committed or less emotionally attached to the firm supplying the product or service. On the other hand, a customer who is engaging is likely to be more emotionally connected to the brand. Marketers need to know about the sentiment, opinion and affinity a person has towards a brand. This is often expressed through repeat visits, purchases, product ratings, reviews, blogs and discussion forums and, ultimately, the person's likelihood to recommend a friend.

Ask 'How well are we measuring engagement amongst different online audiences?' and then close the loop by using the data to identify the advocates and deliver more relevant communications.

> Engaged customers = customer engagement = stronger brands.

Brand expansion/strategy

Brand extensions and the brand portfolio

There are few single-product companies. Many companies start up as single-product companies, but they soon develop other products as the company grows and markets fragment. A product line is a string of products grouped together for marketing or technical reasons. Guinness started as a single-product company. Since then Guinness has extended the product line to fill market needs as they emerged. It has also expanded beyond the basic product line of beers. It also offers whiskeys, soft drinks and more: different lines of product.

Add all the product lines together and you get the product mix. Finding the right product mix is a subtle balancing act. How far should a product line be extended? How many different lines should be in the product group?

Advantages

'Brand (or line) extension is attractive but dangerous' (Smith 2003).There are advantages and disadvantages lurking behind this apparently easy option.

It is one of many different ways of increasing sales by extending an existing brand name on to a new product. Some feel that this reduces the risk of launching an unknown brand. Using a recognized brand name on a new product can give the new product immediate presence in the marketplace – customers can recognize, trust and try the new product more easily. This also creates savings in advertising and other promotions, so as the original product brand matures the extended brand ensures some continuity and survival of the brand in the longer run. Generally, brand extensions work if the new product actually satisfies a real relevant need amongst customers and they like the idea. Ultimately the new product should enhance the promise of the original brand as opposed to cannibalizing it. Careful consideration must be given to what happens if the extension fails.

Brand extension is a tempting option, as it uses the same sales team with the same distribution channels and often the same customers. It can also fill or occupy any unoccupied positions in the market, which might otherwise invite unwanted competitors into the market. Finally, a full product line builds the image of the complete player, a big player, which in turn suggests reliability.

Disadvantages

But there are disadvantages lurking behind brand extensions and line extensions. A low-quality product will damage the original brand's reputation. A really good new product can also cannibalize the original product if the new product merely takes sales away from the old product. When contemplating

> ### Failed extensions
>
> 'Unfortunately, the hard truth is that many brand extensions *don't* work. Each brand has its own special positioning. The extension won't succeed if it works against that. Any time a brand is extended, its focus gets blurred in the minds of consumers. When the image is unclear, the original promise is broken. When the promise is broken, the brand loses value and me.'
>
> Jacobson and Knapp (2008)

brand extension, ask how much of the 'extra sales' actually replace existing sales of the original product. Constant brand extensions may dilute the brand's strength and its unique positioning, particularly if the extensions are not appropriate to the central brand. When easyJet extended into easy-Internetcafes it was reported to have lost £75 million (Taylor, 2004), whereas easyJet Holidays appears to be a better fit. Although Virgin is another successful company and has enjoyed a variety of brand extensions, some of its brand extensions have failed, including Virgin Vodka, Virgin Jeans, Virgin Brides, Virgin Balloons and Virgin Cosmetics.

In a sense, product deletion should be a standard activity, as companies constantly replace old products with improved ones. Some corporations like to balance the product portfolio by ensuring they have a minimum of 30 per cent of 'new products' (products developed in the last five years). Phasing out and deleting products that have had their day is a delicate task. They have to be withdrawn carefully and gracefully without damaging employee morale or upsetting small groups of customers who may still want spare parts or simply to continue consuming the product. Interestingly, one of the world's best marketing companies, Unilever, chopped its product portfolio from 1,600 to 400 in 2004.

Although criticized by some, the Boston Matrix can help to balance the product portfolio, as it helps managers identify which products generate surplus cash, which need extra marketing resources to support them and which need a lot of resources. 'Cash cows' (high market share in a low-growth market) generate the surplus cash that in turn funds other products, such as the high-growth 'star' products. Low-growth (and low-market-share) 'dogs' often absorb a disproportionate amount of management resources. This analysis is from a cash flow perspective as opposed to the customers' perspective.

Riezebos (2003) on the other hand analyses a brand portfolio from a competitor perspective. Different types of brands have different roles to play within the brand portfolio. Bastion brands are the key brands, usually the most profitable, with a large market share. Their success attracts competitors. Some companies expand their portfolios to protect their brands by introducing 'flanker brands' and 'fighter brands'. The flanker brand may be priced differently or have a different set of attributes and tends to fend off any new competitors that are considering occupying that space. Fighter brands are lower priced and compete with existing or potential competitors trying to occupy lower price points (the quality perceptions need to be shifted downwards so as not to dilute the bastion brand). Many organizations prefer to lose some premium-priced brand sales to an internal less profitable brand than to lose the sales to competitors. However, today many companies of a certain size reject brands that will not become star performers, as they prefer to direct their limited resources to major winners. The tasks of product extinction and extension require rigorous analysis of customers, competitors and overall trends. The marketer's task of being the guardian of the brand is a challenging one.

Brand summary and the challenges ahead

Twenty-first-century brands face new challenges, including hyper-competitive markets, unknown competitors (category-less and borderless), shortened product life cycles, more demanding, time-pressed and information-fatigued customers, media fragmentation and message clutter, anti-brand pressure groups, own brands and two other internal challenges – short-termism and fear of the boardroom.

The rise of the anti-brand

A direct challenge to brands are the 'ethical anti-branders', who attack premium priced branded training shoes (allegedly made in sweatshops in the Far East).

Various anti-brand feelings have been aroused by many publications, ranging from Vance Packard's 1957 classic *The Hidden Persuaders* to Eric Schlosser's *Fast Food Nation* (2002) to Robert Frank's *Luxury Fever* (2000) to *The World Is Not for Sale* (2001) by José Bové (a French farmer who is best known for vandalizing a McDonald's restaurant) and François Dufour. Brands are vulnerable to a rising tide of antipathy to branding and marketing.

The demise of major corporations like Enron has further fuelled a cynicism towards big business. However, Naomi Klein's *No Logo: Taking aim at the brand bullies* (2000) articulated a certain kind of brand frustration where global brands represent, in her words, 'a fascist state where we all salute the logo and have little opportunity for criticism because our newspapers, TV stations, internet servers, street and retail spaces are all controlled by multinational corporate interests'. The ubiquitous global brand bullies effectively reduce the colourful variety of choice and force a grey cultural homogeneity on customers instead of an array of interesting local alternatives. Even the *Economist* magazine back in 2001 pointed the finger at today's global businesses: 'So companies are switching from producing products to marketing aspirations, images and lifestyles. They are trying to become weightless, shedding physical assets by shifting production from their own factories in the first world to other people's in the third.'

This provides all the more reasons for brands and the businesses behind them to behave ethically and to demonstrate publicly their social responsibility. This includes environmental policies (and actions), supporting charitable endeavours and local communities, racial integration, not supplying or contributing to military regimes, and political donations. (See Chapter 11.)

And of course there are the brand haters who create anti-brand websites dedicated to venting their frustrations and anger about certain brands, usually resulting from alleged poor customer service, eg **www.aolsucks.com**, sometimes even without consuming the brand and simply because they don't like the brand, eg **www.ihatemanunited.com**. As Dell has demonstrated by listening to these criticisms, addressing the reasonable issues and fixing them can strengthen a brand and grow its relations and sales.

The rise of the own brand

As major retailers flex their muscles and demand that suppliers also create and deliver the retailers' own brand in almost every category, it is easy to understand why brand owners are concerned, particularly when they have to deliver a constantly high-quality own brand also. Many retailers' brands are so strong that customers are happy to give them more and more share of their wallets. Look at Tesco: what can't they sell to customers now that customers trust the brand to deliver a consistent quality at reasonable prices?

The brands do, however, have a source of continual competitive advantage, and that is continuous innovation. Although own brands are getting smarter and smarter, Saatchi & Saatchi CEO Kevin Roberts (2009) says:

> The game has changed. Own labels deliver quality. They are as strong in many categories as traditional consumer brands. Own label tend to deliver quality now. But will they deliver innovation? No. This is where real marketing comes into play. A big retailer cannot possibly develop the innovation in a category that a P&G, Unilever or a Nestlé can. So as long as those companies continue to keep their core, their focus on innovation, they will continue to develop new value in this reclaimed world.

Short-term sales versus long-term brand building

Brands are not for the short term. They are strategic assets that need to be nurtured and grown over the long term. Think of them like people. They need to grow and be nurtured. After that, relationships can last a lifetime and beyond, as some brands are handed down from generation to generation (if the brands manage to stay relevant to the needs of the next generation). There is a constant tension between sales and marketing and, for that matter, finance and marketing. Quarterly-results-driven businesses require quarterly results, which usually means seeing quarterly growth in sales and profits. Brands do not deliver quick returns, particularly new brands and repositioned brands. They take time to research and develop. They take time to build relationships. Although some brands have developed in one or two years, these are exceptional. Certainly brands emerging within a quarter is, even today, highly unlikely.

The impatience of the CFO or the board or the shareholders may jeopardize the long-term work of the brand builder. This also manifests itself in the advertising debate: whether a campaign is sales or brand building. Ad campaigns can of course do either, but rarely can do both really well. One usually takes priority. Yes, campaigns can deliver sales and grow a brand, but each objective has different priorities. Brands are for the long term and can secure higher sales, higher prices and higher profits. These are some of the factors that can bring the marketer back into the boardroom.

Brands – the bridge between marketing, finance and the boardroom

Marketers may have slipped from the potential heroes of the boardroom when back in the 1980s brands were suddenly touted as a 'surefire means of differentiation in the face of increased competitive pressures and rampant product proliferation activities. They were secret weapons of sorts: legally-protectable assets that brought unrivalled powers to the firms that developed them' (Madden, Fehle and Fournier, 2002).

A study revealed that shareholders should insist on systematic performance feedback on branding. It actually suggested systematic performance feedback on all key items in the balance sheet including branding. However, it suggested that very few companies had this optimal balance between financial performance and branding (Ohnemus, 2009). The report went on to say that 'the board of directors should systematically assess and monitor the strategic branding position of their company and how their branding investments are performing against key competitors'. Board directors acknowledge the value of brands but do not understand how brands are built and sustained and, in particular, how marketing makes this happen.

What has marketing got to do with brand building?

'To quote David Bell, Chairman of the *Financial Times*: "The value of brands as shareholder assets has been widely recognized, but the crucial role of marketing and advertising in building this brand equity and so enhancing these assets now on the balance sheet is still not fully recognized."'

Beenstock (1998)

The irony of it all is that, now that brands appear on the balance sheet, they are recognized as a financial asset of the business, yet budgets required to grow them are considered to be 'expenses rather than investments' (Ohnemus, 2009).

When Harvard's Madden, Fehle and Fournier (2002) suggested that 'the demonstration of brand

value to stockholders would prove most useful in reconceptualizing marketing from expense to investment', an opportunity knocked for marketers. But the lingering, unanswered question remains to this day, 'Do brand-building investments really pay off? Lacking conclusive evidence concerning branding and the bottom line, brand "investments" remain "expenses," and the promise of the brand remains unfulfilled.'

Marketers must learn the language of finance and apply it to marketing. Marketing language and jargon have been charged as 'inaccessible and disconnected from the financial metrics by which firms are ultimately steered' (Davis, 2001). If there is no common language, there is no communication and with that comes no understanding of marketing's crucial role in brand building.

The adversarial relationship between finance and marketing

'Most companies and CFOs will tell you that there is an adversarial relationship between finance and marketing. The CFO is viewed as the person who wants to cut the marketing budget, and marketing fails to effectively explain the return on investment for communications. The result is a wall between the two departments, and no connections between.'

CFO of Ekco Group Inc (in Banham, 1998)

In the words of the late great Peter Doyle (2000):

Marketing managers rarely see the necessity of linking marketing spending to the financial value of the business. Given today's enormous pressure on top managers to generate higher returns to shareholders, it is hardly surprising that the voice of marketing gets disregarded. The situation will never be resolved until marketing professionals learn to justify marketing strategies in relevant financial terms.

If managers can show that marketing will increase returns to shareholders, marketing will obtain a much more pre-eminent role in the boardrooms of industry. The discipline itself will also obtain more respect for its rigor and direction.

Marketers have much internal marketing work to do. But, with some work, the doors of the boardroom will be flung wide open for marketers so they can secure funds to develop great brands and, in return, deliver dividends back to shareholders.

Conclusion

Brands are being challenged. However, brands are powerful assets that generate many benefits to both an organization and its customers. Surprisingly, many brands allow themselves to self-destruct with sloppy service and inconsistent brand applications. Brand components include name, logo, colours, positioning, promise, personality, values, association and experience. Brand creation is a process that starts with a brief and goes through concept generation, concept development and roll-out. Copious research is carried out before and after each step. Brand maintenance focuses on the customer experience, extending it online and considering customer engagement as a way to move customers up the ladder of engagement towards brand zealots. Experiential marketing is also considered. Finally, brand expansion/strategy has both advantages and disadvantages. The strategic corporate brand is also explored.

> **Strong brands survive through careful management**
>
> It is no accident that these brands have been around for over 100 years: Bass, Coke, Kellogg's Corn Flakes, Guinness, Pears Soap.

Key points from Chapter 2

- Brands help customers and the organizations behind them.
- Branding and why is a strategic issue and can create competitive advantage.
- There is a disciplined approach to the brand-building process.
- Brands, like any other asset, need to be maintained and require resources.

References and further reading

Anderson, C (2006) *The Long Tail: Why the future of business is selling less of more*, Hyperion Books, New York

Atkin, D (2004) New priests for the new religion, *Marketer*, September

Aufreiter, N, Elzinga, D and Gordon, J (2003) Better brands, *McKinsey Quarterly*, **4**

Banham, Russ (1998) Making your mark: Time for finance to play a role in brand management, *CFO: The magazine for senior financial executives*, **14** (3), 1 March

Bayley, S and Mavity, R (2008) *Life's a Pitch*, Corgi Books, London

Beenstock, S (1998) Raising brands' stock in the City, *Marketing*, 26 November

Bernstein, D (1984) *Company Image and Reality: A critique of corporate communications*, Holt, Rinehart and Winston, London

Bové, J and Dufour, F (2001) *The World Is Not for Sale*, Verso Books, London

Braun, T (2004) *The Philosophy of Branding*, Kogan Page, London

Chaffey, D and Smith, P R (2008) *eMarketing eXcellence*, 3rd edn, Kogan Page, London

Clifton, R (2004) The big debate, *Marketer*, July/August

Davis, S (2001) Taking control of your brand's destiny, *Brandweek*, 15 October

Doyle, P (2000) *Value-Based Marketing*, Wiley, Chichester

Economist (1998) The rebirth of IBM – blue is the colour, 6 June

Economist (2001) Who's wearing the trousers? 6 September

Eltvedt, H and Flores, L (2005) Beyond online advertising – lessons about the power of brand websites to build and expand brands, ESOMAR Online Conference, Montreal, June

Farrell, S (2008) A million dollar branding secret, How-to Internet Marketing Network

Fauconnier, C (2006) Humanising the marketplace: A manifesto for brand growth, *Admap*, **471**, April

Fitch, R (2003) in Balmer, J and Greyser, S (2003) *Revealing the Corporation: Perspectives on identity image reputation*, Routledge, London

Fletcher, W (2010) author, lecturer and former chairman of the Royal Institution in conversation with PR Smith

Frank, R H (2000) *Luxury Fever: Money and happiness in an era of excess*, Princeton University Press, Princeton, NJ

Harris Interactive (2006) Second annual *Customer Experience Impact Report*

Hooker, S (1991) Applying psychology to market research: The theory of raised expectations, *Market Research Society Newsletter*, January

Jacobson, T and Knapp, K (2008) Brand extensions, Vistage chief executive organization online papers

Jenkins, N (1991) *The Business of Image*, Kogan Page, London

Jones, B (2001) *The Big Idea*, HarperCollins, London

Kanter, R (2009) The downsides of branding, 23 July, **http://blogs.hbr.org/kanter/2009/07/the-downsides-of-branding.html**

Kapferer, J (2008) *The New Strategic Brand Management*, 4th edn, Kogan Page, London

Klein, N (2000) *No Logo: Taking aim at the brand bullies*, Flamingo, London

Le Pla, F J, Davis, S and Parker, L (2003) *Brand Driven: The route to integrated branding through great leadership*, Kogan Page, London

Lindstrom, M (2005) *Brand Sense*, Kogan Page, London

Madden, T, Fehle, F and Fournier, S (2002) Brands matter: An empirical investigation of brand-building activities and the creation of shareholder value, Working paper, Harvard Business School, Boston, MA

Millward Brown Optimor (2010) *BrandZ Top 100 Most Valuable Global Brands*, Millward Brown Optimor, New York

Mose, M (2003) *United We Brand: How to create a cohesive brand that's seen, heard, and remembered*, Harvard Business School Publishing, Boston, MA

Murphy, J (ed) (1991) *Branding: A key marketing tool*, Macmillan, London

Nash and Zull Products (1989) *1990 US Hall of Shame*, Universal Press Syndicate, Kansas City

Neumeier, M (2007) *Zag*, New Riders, Berkeley, CA

Ohmae, K (1994) Interview with P R Smith, *Marketing CDs*, P R Smith

Ohnemus, L (2009) B2B Branding: A financial burden for shareholders?*Business Horizons*, **52** (2), pp 159–66

Olins, W (1989) *Corporate Identity: Making business strategy visible through design*, Thames & Hudson, London

Olins, W (1996) *The New Guide to Identity*, Gower, Aldershot

Olins, W (2003) *On Brand*, Thames & Hudson, London

Packard, V ([1957] 1960) *The Hidden Persuaders*, Penguin Books, Harmondsworth

Peters, T (2003) *Re-imagine*, Dorling Kindersley, London

PRTV (1993) *Corporate Image Video*, PRTV, London

Reynolds, J, Cuthbertson, C and Bell, R (2004) *Retail Strategy: The view from the bridge*, Elsevier Butterworth-Heinemann, Oxford

Riezebos, R (2003) *Brand Management: A theoretical and practical approach*, Pearson, Harlow

Roberts, K (2009) Short cuts (part 2), 6 July, **http://www.saatchikevin.com/sisomo/Speeches_Ideas/KR_Short_Cuts_part_2/**

Ronay, A (2004) Emotional brands, *Marketer*, **5**, September

Rothery, G (2009) All in the mind, *Marketing Age*, **3** (6), November

Schlosser, E (2002) *Fast Food Nation*, Penguin Books, Harmondsworth

Smilansky, S (2008) *Experiential Marketing*, Kogan Page, London

Smith, P R (2003) *Great Answers to Tough Marketing Questions*, Kogan Page, London

Taylor, D (2004) More bangers for your bucks, *Marketer*, **5**, September

Universal McCann (2007) Power to the people: Tracking the impact of social media wave, 2.0, May

Valentine, V (1988) *Signs and Symbols*, Survey, Market Research Society, London

Yeong, C L and Yu, H-y (2006) Chinese president's itinerary for U.S. visit: Gates first, Bush later, *International Herald Tribune*, 13 April

See Kenichi Ohmae in the video browser in P R Smith, *Marketing CD*, No. 6: Product decisions, talking about obsoleting strategies. The section on the product portfolio considers how to balance product lines and mixes, old and new. He also talks about how he reduces the axes of risk.

03
Customer relationship management

LEARNING OBJECTIVES

By the end of this chapter you will be able to:

- Discuss the importance of relationship marketing and how CRM creates competitive advantage
- Outline the CRM planning process
- Understand the benefits and resources required by CRM
- Identify and avoid the classic CRM errors
- Present the case of long-term brand building vs short-term sales growth

Introduction to CRM

What is CRM?

Some call it customer relationship management (CRM); others call it customer experience management (CEM); others call it customer managed relationships (CMR). Carefully managed brands help customers develop relationships with brands (see Chapter 2). There is a direct overlap between nurturing a brand and nurturing customer relationships. CRM is a set of processes, usually linked to a database, that help an organization keep in contact with customers and deal with their requests, complaints, suggestions and purchases.

Think about how personal relationships grow stronger and stronger: listening, understanding, responding and communicating; understanding what is important and what makes a difference; delivering it regularly; never breaking the promise; occasionally surprising or even delighting the other person; caring about the person; helping the person when things go wrong; always being there for the person. The same applies to customer relationships. It is not rocket science.

Even remembering someone's name makes a difference. People generally like it when their names are remembered, particularly when their preferences and needs are remembered. How nice is it when a waiter or receptionist remembers a customer's name? 'Your name is the most important sound in the world' say the classic sales training programmes. Remembering names and needs (and satisfying them) helps to build relationships. This applies to a restaurant with 50 customers or a website with millions of customers.

Remembering a customer's particular needs and providing the right response is rarely the result of guesswork. In the case of a company with a small number of customers, it requires a good memory, good interpretive skills and attention to detail. In the case of an organization with many customers on a database, it is largely dependent on accurate analysis of customers and building up valuable insights. As customers are more demanding and have more channels of communication, organizations simply have to be able to respond to them continuously – wherever, whenever and however required.

The higher the relevance, the greater the value – it's a continuum

'If you want to protect and enhance the value of your brand, your offer must be valuable.'

'Customers get what they want; your margins are protected; everyone's a winner.'

dunnhumby (2006)

Business is entering the post-'ad loyalty era', where the power of advertising is waning as other communication tools, particularly WOMWeb (word of mouth accelerated by Web 2.0 or social networking tools), generate fast high attitudinal shifts. The old loyalty model used advertising primarily to build brand awareness and, ultimately, to build a lasting bond with customers. Securing loyalty today is a never-ending process requiring outstanding CRM and ongoing customer engagement.

The power of CRM

CRM builds a protective wall around customers, in the same way as a brand does. In fact they are one and the same. Excellent CRM enhances the relationship with the brand. As the relationship strengthens, loyalty keeps a customer from the inevitable onslaught of competition. Relationships built on price simply don't last. Relationships built on relevant excellent service are more enduring.

Regardless of what it is called, managing customer relationships is critical to an organization's future. Nurturing excellent customer relationships builds this defensive wall around a business that most competitors struggle to break down. Customer relationships also boost sales and profits and add value to the brand, which boosts the balance sheet assets.

Your best defence

'Customer relationships are the only thing that cannot be replicated by a competitor.'

Hochman (2008)

Company benefits

Boost sales

Good customer relations boost sales, as they simply make it easy for customers to repeat-buy during their 'customer lifetime', as well as buy other products and services as they increase their share-of-wallet spend with the same trusted brand (look at how customers buy almost any product or service from Tesco). Good relations also help to recruit new customers, as happy customers talk to, and even recruit, new customers.

Excellent CRM systems can predict customer preferences and prompt customers with tempting offers when they are ready to buy or sometimes just before they are ready to buy.

Equally good CRM systems can identify potential defectors (customers who are about to leave), pre-empt them and trigger win-back programmes for any potential defectors who might otherwise have slipped through the net.

Strengthen the brand

Stronger relations create stronger brands. This builds brand loyalty, which effectively builds a defensive wall around the customer, protecting the customer from the inevitable onslaught of hyper-competition as it advances across this 'borderless and category-less' marketplace (see Chapter 1). Good relations also boost the brand image and consequently the brand value, which is eventually reflected on the balance sheet.

Boost profits

Marketing to both existing customers and referred customers costs a lot less than marketing to new customers. Estimates suggest it is six times more profitable selling to existing customers, hence the importance of customer retention over customer acquisition. Keeping existing customers happy boosts profits.

Create a database asset

One other advantage that CRM creates is a quality database. This is an asset and, although not shown on the balance sheet, it is a very real asset to a company. Some companies quantify the value of their databases by calculating lifetime values of different customer profiles and discounting back to today's net present value.

> **One per cent customer satisfaction = $500 million**
>
> Some years ago IBM calculated that each percentage point improvement in customer satisfaction translates into $500 million more revenue over five years.

Resources required

CRM is a strategic decision and has a long-term impact on how a business is run. However, CRM programmes cost resources, the 3Ms: men/women (commitment, including the CEO's support, an expert project director and teams of trained people to carry out the service); money (to pay for the software, outside consultants, installation, testing, training and motivation programmes); and minutes (the time required to develop a major CRM project can be several years, and even the training can take months). An excellent CRM system often requires a cultural change, which may be a challenge for many organizations.

CRM fails without senior management support cascading right down throughout the organization. CRM implementation is disruptive, expensive and time-consuming and requires extra resources, training and motivation programmes. Return on investment (ROI) can also be difficult for some companies to measure.

Overambitious CRM system suppliers sometimes recommend a 'rip and replace implementation'. Here CRM suppliers convince the client company to dump their existing systems and start again from scratch. This can then be compounded by the classic disaster scenarios, including scope creep and lack of training and motivation, where the system is delayed, late, over budget and finally resisted by staff, as they have not bought into the new approach. We will explain how to avoid these classic errors later.

Integrating customer interactions and data across a range of channels from website to mobile to telephone to sales rep to e-mail still presents major challenges, particularly when trying to integrate the legacy (old) database with the new channels of customer interaction.

Finally, maintaining a database and managing a CRM system continuously cost time, money and expertise, all of which can be in short supply. It is a continuous process and requires constant resources.

Blame storming

'Companies who do not appreciate the importance of an effective complaint handling system risk internal friction (passing on the blame). This may lead to a vicious circle, as internal friction generates poor motivation and cynicism, staff disloyalty and worse service. This is why customer loyalty and staff loyalty are closely linked.'

Merlin Stone, Neil Woodcock

CRM failure

Organizations are sitting on a customer service time bomb. Customers are more demanding, and marketers are not delivering. Yes, many products have got better (eg rustproof cars), but service and CRM are generally going backward, as witnessed by the declining customer satisfaction scores and customer defections (even when they do give a 'satisfactory' score). Customers are not happy. They are ready to swap suppliers. They are bombarded with competitive offers. They have less time but more demands. And marketers are not delivering, perhaps because marketers are not in control of the CRM, eg IT may have hijacked the process (Mahoney, 2002). Regardless of the reasons, the stats do not seem to get any better over time.

Here are the reported CRM failure rates identified by Michael Krigsman (2009):

- 2001, Gartner Group: 50 per cent;
- 2002, Butler Group: 70 per cent;
- 2002, Selling Power, CSO Forum: 69.3 per cent;
- 2005, AMR Research: 18 per cent;

- 2006, AMR Research: 31 per cent;
- 2007, AMR Research: 29 per cent;
- 2007, Economist Intelligence Unit: 56 per cent;
- 2009, Forrester Research: 47 per cent.

Although different measurement criteria from different research companies make these comparisons less accurate, there is no denying a lack of skill in managing CRM. Gartner's *Trip Report* (2009) confirms that more than 55 per cent of CRM projects deliver unacceptable results. Another report (Forrester Research, 2009) confirms that 'More than 50 per cent of CRM projects fail to fully meet expectations.'

The Gartner report (2009) continues to paint a picture of sloppy CRM:

> CRM success continues to elude most companies. 86% of survey respondents say that CRM will be important to their companies over the next three years. Despite this, more than 40% of respondents do not have a formal CRM strategy in place. Of those who do, 44% say that they have seen only 'acceptable' results from their efforts.

Working the maths here suggests that of the 60 per cent of companies that do have a formal CRM strategy only 44 per cent have seen acceptable results, ie 26 per cent of companies (60 per cent × 44 per cent) have seen acceptable results. This means 74 per cent of companies have either no CRM strategy or unacceptable results.

'80% of companies believe they deliver a superior customer experience, but only 8% of their customers agree.'

Allen, Reichheld and Hamilton (2005)

Harvard's Allen, Reichheld and Hamilton (2005) think the CRM problems have something to do with growth. They call it 'the dominance trap' and explain it as follows:

> The larger a company's market share, the greater the risk it will take its customers for granted. As the money flows in, management begins confusing customer profitability with customer loyalty,

never realizing that the most lucrative buyers may also be the angriest and most alienated. Worse, traditional market research may lead the firm to view customers as statistics. Managers can become so focused on the data that they stop hearing the real voices of their customers.

Some years earlier, another Harvard Business School professor, Susan Fournier (in an interview with Manda Mahoney, 2002), suggested that IT was hijacking CRM projects:

> Most customer relationship management technology (CRM) programs are failing. Why? CRM programs are expensive and take a long time to install. One consequence is that IT has 'hijacked' the process. In emphasizing technology decisions over marketing decisions, we've lost the opportunity to build better relationships with customers. To get back in balance, marketers have to help design CRM systems from the get-go.

Given that 74 per cent of IT projects fail (Tranfield and Braganza, 2007), there is a natural concern over IT driving CRM. Incidentally, this 74 per cent failure rate is surprisingly the same percentage as found in the survey by Standish Group and Gartner Group back in 1980 (IBM, 2004).

nightmare continues. Researchers established that companies continued to:

- *Ignore customer e-mails.* Thirty-eight per cent of major UK companies ignored incoming customer e-mails, despite the number of e-mails increasing. Retailers had the best track record, responding to 70 per cent of e-mails, but telecoms had the worst – 58 per cent of e-mails were simply ignored (Egain, 2007).
- *Fail to get to know customers.* Fifty per cent of the FTSE 1000 did not know who their customers were. Even when they had the raw data collected and safely stored, they still could not profile their own customers (MORI, 2003). Has it improved since?
- *Fail to satisfy customers.* Of all calls to Fujitsu call centres, 50–70 per cent were for value restoration (fixing a problem, eg late delivery, wrong delivery or poor product quality) rather than value creation, eg adding value with helpful advice over the phone (Mitchell, 2004). How many inbound or outbound calls today are for value creation rather than value restoration?

More CRM failures

'More than 55% of CRM projects deliver unacceptable results.'
Forrester Research (2009)

'Customer satisfaction is declining in just about every market I've looked at over the last 15 years.'
M Earls (2002)

Has it got better since these gloomy words were written?

As with websites, social media and databases, marketers have simply got to be involved in the development and management of any CRM systems. Effectively, marketers need to take control of CRM to ensure a cohesive, integrated system is embraced by all departments. A fragmented approach, with different departments running different CRM systems or, as mentioned earlier, IT hijacking CRM, loses the critical usefulness that CRM should provide to customers. They don't want to be passed from department to department. Nor do they want to fall through the cracks left by an unintegrated and poorly managed CRM system. The customer

The next section explores why CRM is failing, what goes wrong and how to avoid these classic errors. Meanwhile customers are angry. They understand how to use publicity, and now they use social networks to spread messages like wildfire.

Why CRM failure?

Organizations have steadily got worse at CRM because of the lack of a customer-driven culture (failed leadership), poor CRM project management skills (in particular scope creep, lack of training and lack of motivation programmes) and constant cost cutting.

Militant complainers – smashing your car

The chairman of a Chinese wildlife park destroyed his $60,000 SLK230 Mercedes sports car as a protest because he was unhappy about the warranty. With an astute understanding of the media, he 'intended to cause maximum embarrassment' to Mercedes-Benz by inviting hundreds of spectators and journalists to watch five workers with sticks smash the car. After that he attached ropes to the wreck and got several bulls to tow it through the city. Compensation negotiations resumed immediately but progressed too slowly, so Mr Wang (who wanted a full refund) asked a friend to also destroy his Mercedes. The friend obliged and drove his white S320 1,000 miles from Beijing to Wuhan. 'In another public event, six men armed with batons smashed the windows and doors.' Mercedes-Benz claimed that Mr Wang had 'used the wrong fuel and had subsequently refused a complimentary cleaning of the engine'.

August (2002)

Many CEOs fail because they lack an understanding about the development and implementation of customer-driven marketing. Many marketers fail because they have not mastered CRM systems, managed to integrate the culture across the organization, or helped the CEO to understand the importance of CRM.

Poor project management skills stop CRM systems from being implemented on time and within budget. CRM projects are relatively large to any organization. Failings like scope creep (constantly adding extra and late requirements into the brief), unnecessary and often poor system design, and with an over-dominant IT department also wreck potential CRM programmes. One possible reason why 74 per cent of IT projects fail is because they are called IT projects (IT is a service that supports business functions, not an end in itself). IT simply uses information technology processes to help run a business.

As with any changes introduced to an organization, they need to be supported by training and motivation programmes. Many CRM projects lack buy-in from staff who both fear and resist change.

Motivation and training programmes are required to bring people on board. This was recognized as a problem a few years ago when a BusinessEurope.com survey (2004) revealed that 25 per cent of marketing professionals record customer details incorrectly and 40 per cent of marketing professionals do not share customer contacts with colleagues. Training and motivation are critical components in any CRM programme.

Last but not least, constant cost cutting and operational failings have shifted the emphasis of many CRM programmes from value creation to value restoration. Overburdened staff may also be struggling with a work overload.

In addition, as mentioned in *eMarketing eXcellence* (Chaffey and Smith, 2008), 'Old CRM systems were effectively automated selling systems that took little or no account of what customers actually want. Danger bells should start ringing when an IT consultant offers a front end automated solution that cuts costs and streamlines operations and processes because this does not necessarily make marketing more effective.'

Wanted: strong marketing managers

'But new technologies are being implemented with the overriding aim of driving efficiencies and cost savings rather than enhancing the customer service. A strong marketing director who is respected throughout the organisation can, at worst, ensure that the customer is not adversely affected by a new IT investment, and, at best, ensure that the investment delivers tangible customer benefits.'

Wright (2007)

CRM success

The good news is that poor CRM presents a golden opportunity to create competitive advantage by developing an integrated CRM system that creates value or adds value to customers' experiences, brings them closer to the organization, listens to them, collects data and serves their needs better than ever before. This grows sales from both repeat sales (lifetime customers) and share of wallet (what else does the customer need that the company can supply?). Organizations like McKinsey forecast the after-sales market (after-sales service, consultancy and training) to be where many companies will find new growth. This emphasizes the critical importance of CRM systems that actually work.

The CRM philosophy

Building a customer-driven business requires a specific corporate culture where the organization, at all levels, recognizes the need for customer service and customer focus. A real CRM philosophy sees customers at the centre of the universe. This customer focus requires a longer-term, strategic view of the business as opposed to a short-term 'transactional marketing' approach that focuses on quarterly sales results.

The CRM philosophy is one where the organization continually seeks to learn about customer needs and preferences, in order to deliver excellent relevant services, and how to satisfy customer needs in better ways. The organization must also continually measure the right criteria. Ultimately, a CRM philosophy seeks to move customers up the ladder of loyalty from suspect to advocate.

The ladder of loyalty was devised by Considine and Raphel (1981) and is now widely used. Organizations seek to move prospects up the ladder of loyalty from suspects to devoted loyal customers who advocate an organization's product or service. There is some overlap with moving customers up the brand engagement ladder (discussed in Chapter 1), where customers engage more and more with the

brand and ultimately become advocates. In fact, some relationship marketing works so well that the seller is not seen as a vendor but as a friendly helper who knows the customers and helps them with their lives.

> ### Never sell to a stranger
>
> 'Think of the old corner shop. If the shopkeeper ordered a new type of pickle, he wouldn't expect strangers to flock in and buy it. He'd recommend it to his regular pickle buyers and to people buying cheese and pork. You wouldn't call that hard sell. You'd call it personal service, based on the shopkeeper remembering the preferences of individual customers and using this knowledge to anticipate their needs. No matter what the size and character of your marketplace, direct marketing now lets you offer that personal service to every customer.'
>
> Young (nd)

This customer-sensitive culture is based on permission-based marketing as defined by Seth Godin in 1999. Marketers gain permission to speak to customers firstly; then they develop trust and, ultimately, loyalty. The first step is to get customer's permission for future communications, whether by mail, e-mail, RSS feed, etc. Although incentives are often used when gaining permission, relevance is key. The next step is collaborative, where marketers help customers to buy and customers help marketers to sell (customer forums and testimonials). The third step is dialogue between the organization and the customers and trialogue between the organization and customers and customers amongst themselves. A triialogue can flow via blogs, discussion forums, focus groups, feedback forms or even real meetings between customers and sales reps, as well as amongst customers themselves.

When customers 'opt in' for further e-mail, they give their permission to be e-mailed. This is a first step in using their permission to develop the relationship. Do not abuse this permission by passing customers' data on or contacting them too frequently. Ensure future contact with customers always adds

FIGURE 3.1 The ladder of loyalty

value. It is a moral and legal requirement (in B2C markets) to offer the customer the option to 'opt out' every time you contact them. The number of existing customers who opt out from further contact is the 'churn rate'. Marketers watch the churn rate closely and try to understand why it varies.

All of these approaches are dependent on an overall customer philosophy that is more strategic than tactical, with customers being nurtured over the medium to long term rather than by a one-off transactional sale approach. This strategic approach requires several components to be in place, including an IT architecture and a human architecture, which depends on a customer culture (see 'CRM components required' below). These take time and require an investment of the three key resources, the 3Ms: men/women, money (budgets) and minutes (time).

Permission can be specific – ask customers exactly what they prefer

- *Content* – news, products, offers, events.
- *Frequency* – weekly, monthly, quarterly or alerts.
- *Channel* – e-mail, direct mail, phone or SMS.
- *Format* – text vs HTML.

CRM components required

There are several components required for CRM success. Without all of these components in place, the system will fail. In addition to the overall strategic attitudinal shift towards a customer culture, organizations also need:

- CRM architecture (both IT and human);
- processes:
  - profiling;
  - tailored contact strategies;
  - database management;
- credibility factors.

IT architecture

Technology has been both a curse and an important enabler to CRM/CEM. Ill-conceived websites that damaged brand values and the appalling experience of many call centres have created a need for more technology to monitor and improve the customer experience. In essence, CRM needs an integrated enterprise architecture; much of the software that will enable better CRM delivery in future does not go under the CRM banner. Software applications likely to be needed for CRM/CEM include:

- knowledge management;
- content and collaboration, eg instant messaging, community support on websites;
- business information and analysis;
- experience feedback;
- enterprise process management;
- portals and self-service;
- applications that turn call centres into interactive contact centres.

The ways of providing the technology are also growing, with hosted, outsourced and web-service solutions becoming increasingly available from service suppliers. Organizations should make the most of these.

In highly competitive markets – markets with no categories, no boundaries and no borders – differentiation is important. What difference is perceived between Visa and MasterCard, or L'Oréal and Clairol? In such a situation, how can favourable WOM be generated? Brands should be distinct from the competition. They need a 'personality' that can be promoted and brought to life at touchpoints; then they are easier to talk about. Brand promotion gives the promise; CEM is the physical delivery of that promise. This can be achieved by:

- basing brand values on what customers want;
- involving employees in developing the values;
- linking the values to the main brand promise;
- encouraging staff to align their behaviour with the values;
- rewarding employees for delivering the brand values.

Human architecture

- Benchmark current culture with staff via story techniques about customers, their work and CRM. Establish the problem areas and use the information for internal brand alignment through change programmes.

- Spread customer insight among staff and ensure they can use it in their work. Link knowledge of management processes to customer interaction processes for greater collaboration and learning. The big mistake of previous process re-engineering was not doing this. Good customer experience depends on the learning and support that staff give each other as a natural part of everyday life.

- Establish the new skills required and 'cast' staff into the new roles. Develop skills through continuous coaching in delivering the brand values.

- Redesign organizational structures to support new ways of working. Put flexible delivery teams together, pulled from 'communities of practice' (ie similar skill pools) as and when required. CRM and CEM challenge old structures because of the need for:
  - a segmented approach to customers;
  - non-siloed thinking and working;
  - new and scarce skills.

- Link key performance indicators through performance management to staff incentives; banish incentives that misdirect activity. The right incentives are vital. Do not focus just on 'what' is being delivered in terms of financial targets. Focus also on the 'how' of good performance delivery.

The CEO needs to develop a real customer culture where staff really care about customers. This is no easy task. It's a mindset. It is more an attitude than simply a set of processes. This affects the whole organization, as everyone is responsible – not just customer services, marketing or sales departments. It's everyone's job, from the delivery driver to the receptionist to accounts and finance. Everyone can use every customer experience to create a strategic advantage over the competition.

> ### 150 rules are not as good as one simple value statement
>
> 'I know an organisation whose number one value is *To conduct our business with integrity and professionalism.* The MD just keeps asking the question "Do you think that sale/meeting/task was completed in a professional way?"'
>
> Butler (2004)

Database

A database gives an organization access to its own private marketplace. The database is at the heart of CRM. A database can contain a lot of information about customers depending on how many 'fields' or variables they want to capture. It contains customer names and addresses, enquiries, purchasing patterns, preferences, areas of interest, incentives and a lot more depending on how many 'fields' are kept and what kind of analytics are used. A good database contains highly relevant and up-to-date customer data. It is a valuable repository of information on prospects and customers from all sources and channels, including websites, interactive TV, sales reps and customer service staff. Organizations with properly managed databases enjoy a competitive advantage over competitors without databases. A good database is a powerful asset.

There are two types of information kept: historical data and predictive data. Historical data ('transactional data' or 'back data') include name, address, recency and frequency of purchases, responses to offers and value of purchases. Predictive data identify which groups or subgroups are more likely to respond to a specific offer. This is done through statistical scoring: customer attributes (eg lifestyle, house type, past behaviour, etc) are given scores that help to indicate the customers' future behaviour. The database can identify best ('ideal') customers and worst customers. The worst customers have 'negative value': these are customers who are bad debtors or who buy only when special offers are available.

Database opens up new sales

Rothmans cigarettes' sales promotion built a
powerful database by offering their customers
a free pack of cigarettes when they collected 10
coupons and returned them with a completed form.
They generated 750,000 names within 18 months;
500,000 of this new customer database were
subsequently offered an FGF promotion (friend get
a friend). The database members were entered into
a free competition after sending in their own name
and the address of any friends who were over
18 years old and who smoked a competitor's brand.
There were 250,000 smokers of competitors' brands
named. Follow-up market research showed that
90 per cent were genuine. This database would
be offered a stream of tempting offers to switch
brands. The lifetime value of a smoker is £73,000
(for an average 20-a-day smoker). If only 10 per
cent convert, this generates over £2 billion sales
(if all 250,000 convert, this generates over
£18 billion worth of sales).

So the database is a powerful asset containing a lot of personal information (in the case of consumer databases) and possibly sensitive information (in the case of B2B databases). Directors are legally responsible to ensure data are backed up and stored safely and securely. Now consider the processes required to deliver excellent customer service.

Data analytics

Data analytics improves customer intelligence, which in turn improves targeted marketing, which in turn improves campaign management and, most importantly, customer relationship management. Forget how this boosts profitability for a moment, and just consider how more relevant benefits make customers happier, and happy customers generate more business and more word-of-mouth referrals. It's a virtuous circle that starts with a bunch of processes: identifying customer needs, delivering more relevant products, services and incentives in a timely and cost-efficient manner and, ultimately, boosting customer satisfaction. ROI improves. The

deep analytic tools can now also be applied to online social media as well as the more traditional scenarios. First, consider how data mining works to build better customer profiles and contact strategies while exploiting purchasing cycles with automated marketing.

Profiling

Fifty per cent of the FTSE 1000 do not know who their customers are. They cannot describe how their ideal customers are different to their negative-value customers (ones that cost the organization money). They cannot profile them. They may have their names and addresses, etc, but they cannot build useful profiles describing them. If an organization doesn't know its customer profiles (identities, needs and preferences), how can it, firstly, give them relevant offers that satisfy them better and, secondly, find other customers like them? It is like searching for a needle in a haystack if customers are not profiled.

Chaffey and Smith (2008) explain how profiling can combine explicit data (customer information collected from registrations and surveys) and implicit data (behavioural information gleaned from the back end, ie through the recorded actions of customers on a website). Valuable profiles combine both implicit and explicit data continually. This provides a real picture (or profile) of the target markets, the characteristics that define each segment and how to serve each segment. For example, certain car buyers might have different demographic profiles, show an interest in particular features (pages) of a car and request a test drive. If this group of visitors (or segment) fits the ideal customer profile then they may get a DVD and an immediate incentive to buy now, whereas another group, or segment, of visitors with a less likely profile may only get an e-newsletter once a month.

Website visitors are observed as they leave an audit trail of what they did, what they looked at and for how long. Cookies enable marketers to track which pages they access, what they are interested in (pages visited, times, duration spent there) and what they buy, which then helps to build their profile. Drill down deeper to see how well different segments respond to different offers or features in a newsletter. Profiling helps to identify who the most profitable customers are and whether they have any similar characteristics (eg whether they respond to certain mailshots, came from a certain type of site or search engine, searched using a particular key phrase, or spent a certain amount of time on particular pages).

Build profiles of both customers and enquirers and then segment them according to their different interests, enquiries, requirements or purchases. Marketers can build sophisticated consumer profiles based on previous purchasing decisions and even identify the consumer hierarchy of criteria, whether quality, speed of delivery, level of service, etc. This enables tightly targeted tailored offers that match the specific needs of each segment or profile type. Get this right and this 'virtuous cycle' delivers superior service and simultaneously creates competitive advantage that protects customers from the inevitable, new, competitive offers looming on the horizon.

The better the profiling, the better the results, because the more accurate the targeting, the less resources are wasted. Different customers have different needs. It is actually easier to satisfy them by dividing them into groups sharing similar needs (segments) and then treating each segment differently (different contact strategies for each).

Profiling is a continuous activity, which includes continually collecting customer information, mining it and using it to profile and target more successfully. For example, Grattan's ladies' fashion mail-order company decided to experiment with a new product, a grandfather clock. They guessed the likely target profile would be something like middle-aged, well-off ABs living in ACORN types J35 (villages with wealthy older commuters) and J36 (detached houses, exclusive suburbs). They then asked their computer to print out names and addresses that fitted this profile. The subsequent mailing produced 60 orders at £1,000. They then analysed those 60 orders with a view to identifying any hidden characteristic that could be added to the profile and fed into the database again to produce a different, more accurate target list. When they mailed this list they sold every one of the 1,000 limited-edition clocks.

Data mining

Data mining and segmentation can identify those customers who are potential long-term, loyal customers as opposed to other customers who are promiscuous 'bonus seekers' (short-term shoppers who grab sales promotions and then switch when another brand offers a new sales promotion). The latter are costly and increase the 'churn rate' (customers who leave). Since these long-term loyal customers are far more profitable and the promiscuous customers are loss making, every business needs to know where each of these segments comes from, ie which channels and incentives work best. Within channels, businesses need to know which offline advertising, online advertising, direct mail (online or offline) and social media (specifically which ones) are generating the right traffic or conversions and the wrong traffic or conversions.

Intelligent miner saves Safeway's top customer

Before Safeway delisted a particular cheese product, ranked 209th in sales, an intelligent miner discovered that this cheese was frequently purchased by its ideal customer profile – the top-spending 25 per cent of customers, the last clientele Safeway would want to disappoint. Under conventional analytical principles, the product would have been delisted; in actual fact, the item was quite important.

DB2 (1997)

Catch the at-risk customer defectors

Existing customers cannot and should not be ignored, as they are on average six times more profitable than new customers. It is surprising how many major brands do not have any alarm systems to highlight customers who are about to switch to a competitor. They can be easily identified or profiled by their behaviour (or lack of behaviour/spending). At-risk (of defecting) customers or even recently 'churned' customers need to be contacted (if they fit the ideal long-term customer profile).

Databases have to be stored securely. Large databases require large warehouses. Data mining drills down into these data warehouses to discover patterns and relationships previously hidden in the data. Data mining applies advanced statistical analysis and modelling techniques to data to find useful patterns and relationships. It can, for example, explore each and every transaction of millions of customers and how they relate to each other. Data mining can find correlations that are beyond human conceptual capability (see the seafood bikers and cellist DIYers in the 'Unexpected relationships' box below). A range of statistical tools is used, including regression analysis, time-series forecasting, clustering, associations, logistic regression, discriminant analysis, neural nets and decision trees. A sequence-discovery function detects frequently occurring purchasing patterns over time. This information can then be layered with demographic data (from the main database) so that a company can tailor its mailings on each household's vulnerability or propensity to buy certain items at certain times.

Unexpected relationships

Unexpected database connections revealed that 82 per cent of motorcycle owners buy frozen seafood and 62 per cent of amateur cellists buy power tools. It can be mathematically interesting to see these techniques in action. However, it is also important that a manager knows roughly what the purpose and possible benefits are of any such data-mining analysis. The ability to ask a good question or write a good data-mining brief is a relatively new skill for today's marketing manager.

Building a profile with fields of data

So what kind of data, or 'fields', should be captured? In addition to a customer's name and address, there are obviously other fields of data worth capturing for either a B2C business or a B2B business. FRAC is a useful mnemonic. It stands for: frequency (of purchase/visit), recency (of purchase/visit), amount (of money spent on purchases) and category of purchase.

Chaffey and Smith (2008) show how some CRM systems use RFM (recency, frequency, monetary value) analysis for targeting e-mails according to how a customer interacts with a website. Values could be assigned to each customer as shown in Table 3.1.

Customers can be combined in different categories and then appropriate message treatments sent to encourage purchase. There are many approaches here; for example, a theatre group uses nine categories to tailor its direct marketing for customers who have attended once, twice or more over the last year, previous year, etc. Other companies will have hundreds of segments with very tailored offerings.

There are a lot of other useful data worth collecting also, such as promotions history or responses to specific promotions, share of wallet or customer share (potential spend), timing of spend and more. In B2B, we are interested in business type (standard industrial classification (SIC) codes), size of business, holding companies and subsidiaries, competitive products bought, etc. Customers can be segmented by their activity or responsiveness levels, and then strategies to engage them can be developed. For example, Novo (2004) recommends the use of hurdle rates, which are the percentage of customers in a group (or segment) who have completed an action. Hurdle rates can then be used to compare the engagement of different groups or to set targets to increase engagement with online channels, as the examples of hurdle rates below show:

- 60 per cent of registrants have logged on to the system in the past year;

TABLE 3.1   Using RFM analysis

Recency	Frequency	Monetary value
1 Over 12 months	1 More than once every 6 months	1 Less than £10
2 Within last 12 months	2 Every 6 months	2 £10–£50
3 Within last 6 months	3 Every 3 months	3 £50–£100
4 Within last 3 months	4 Every 2 months	4 £100–£200
5 Within last 1 month	5 Monthly	5 More than £200

- 30 per cent have clicked through on e-mail in the past year;
- 20 per cent of customers have visited in the past six months;
- 5 per cent of customers have made three or more purchases in the past year.

When marketers identify their customers' purchasing cycles, they can increase sales significantly, by targeting customers with attractive offers just before they start their next search. Delaying this by a month or a week reduces the probability of purchase because, once they start searching, customers explore competitive offers. Data mining reveals the average purchasing cycle and subsequently identifies those customer segments that are about to start their buying process again. The database can then automatically trigger an e-mail or direct mail or telephone call to a customer (once certain sets of rules are applied). For example, a computer company mined its database to identify individual purchasing cycles, to identify how frequently different types of customers replaced their PCs. Once the frequency was identified, the company started sending catalogues and discount offers inside the buying frame, with a 95 per cent confidence level, ie 95 per cent of the prospects were just about to start searching for a new PC. Sales jumped up.

Data analytics treble conversion ratios

Wolters Kluwer UK provides publications such as Croner's information and consulting services that help businesses and professionals comply with constantly changing laws in key areas including tax and accountancy, health and safety, and human resources. The company has annual revenues of around €3.7 billion and employs over 19,000 people. After the company installed and employed SAS Analytics, ROI on marketing spend increased threefold; customer retention rates increased from 75 to 83 per cent; improved efficiency and targeting meant reduced marketing headcount and costs; in customer acquisition, sales conversion rates improved from 1 in 33 (3 per cent conversion) to 1 in 11 (9 per cent conversion). The overall project ROI ratio was 2.25:1.

Predictive analytics

Data mining can also be used to analyse buying behaviour to identify clues for cross-selling and up-selling. For example, a bank that monitors its customers' spending may identify a segment of customers buying products from Mothercare, which suggests the customers have young children. This can be combined with typical profile information such as age and marital status to further identify a cluster, or segment, of the bank's customers who might be likely to consider buying a bigger car (as their family is growing). The bank's subsequent offers of a car loan might receive a 30 per cent conversion rate (request more information, call the bank, register an interest or take out an actual loan).

Internet gaming company Victor Chandler uses SAS to do a behavioural analysis to predict lifetime values of new customers. For example, if a new customer comes in and bets on casinos (instead of poker tables), the company can predict whether that customer is more likely to become a long-term customer or a short-term, expensive, loss-making customer. The predictive analysis suggests which customers are worth investing in (with regular contact and regular incentives) and which are not worth investing in – those loss-making 'bonus seeker' customers, whose profile is: young male, tight betting (as opposed to betting all of their stash), declining betting frequency, infrequent betting, and middle-aged female. If visitors display these characteristics, they'll stay three weeks and leave and therefore do not warrant any relationship-building efforts (ie no regular contact or incentives). The other customers are worth investing in, and it is worth developing 'retention activity' (a regular attractive incentivized contact strategy) for them. Predictive analytics use historical data to highlight and optimize marketing messages that work better for certain social networks.

Deleting older home dwellers – a less scientific profile building In the absence of completely reliable data, a less scientific analysis is sometimes used to separate or take out names that do not fit the target profile. For example, Rediffusion cable services felt that older home dwellers did not fit their ideal prospects' profile, so they took out older-generation Christian names such as Albert, Alfred, Alice, Amelia, Arthur, Bertram, Constance,

London Fire Brigade data analytics predict fires

Database mining can even be used for non-marketing purposes, such as fire prevention. Take the London Fire Brigade. It carries out 65,000 home safety visits each year, but with over 3 million homes in London it would take over 50 years to cover everyone. More than 60 different data elements are fed into the model, including census data and population demographics, broken down into 649 geographical areas (ward level), plus type of land use, data on deprivation, Mosaic lifestyle data, historical incidents and past prevention activity. The model predicts where fires are most likely to occur. London Fire Brigade use the information to predict where there is a high risk of fire, eg in a small estate of houses or industrial buildings, so they can then send in an assessor to investigate and perhaps circulate information, set up some advisory services and ultimately reduce the number of fires.

Grace, Harold, May, Mildred, Rose, Sabena, Samuel, Victor, Violet and Winifred.

Costs

Projects range from several hundred thousand customer records to several million (or in some cases 40 million records). A data integration, data-mining campaign optimization and a full direct marketing suite from companies like SAS range from £500,000 to £5 million, with social media customer link analysis starting at around £250,000.

Processes: *general*

How does the organization manage complaints, money-back requests, queries, compliments, suggestions, and requests for additional services? How does it handle a sale, a cancellation, a complaint or a customer defection? Are there processes or systems in place? After a sale, do you send out an order acknowledgement, followed by a delivery alert, followed by a post-sales service satisfaction questionnaire or score sheet or feedback request?

What happens with this information? Who decides to act on a particular customer suggestion? Who tells the staff? Who tells the customer? How many times should a customer be contacted? If customers have outstanding issues, it is not the time to sell them something else. Should different types of customers get different types of offers? Who decides? Who implements this? Processes are important.

Does everyone know how to process an order or a complaint? What happens if someone phones with an unusual enquiry? Who deals with it? How many times are customers left hanging on the phone, being passed around from department to department?

Some companies value customer feedback. They encourage it with 0800 numbers, feedback buttons on websites, questionnaires, rating cards and even outbound telemarketing to collect customer feedback. Listening is just the beginning. It is vital to have a system, or process, that enables a listening process as well as a constructive response.

Maximize the customer's opportunity to complain

Companies can set up suggestion boxes and other feedback systems to maximize the customer's opportunity to complain, compliment, create or engage with the brand.

Feedback (even negative) is food and drink to marketers. However, only 1 in every 24 dissatisfied customers bothers to complain, according to E-Satisfy Ltd (formerly TARP). Rather than facing an unknown enemy of bitter, disappointed and dissatisfied customers, an organization, through its complaints process, can offer a chance to sort out previously unknown problems. It also gives the organization the opportunity to find the enemy within (internal problems such as quality control or demotivated staff). One company chairman takes time to listen to taped telephone complaints while driving home in his car. Many services companies actually ask their customers to fill in a form about levels of satisfaction or dissatisfaction. Solutions are relatively easy. Identifying the problem is the difficult part. Complaints are generally helpful. Welcome complaints.

Complaints help innovation

3M claims that over two-thirds of its innovation ideas come from listening to customer complaints.

The 1–10–100 rule

Federal Express's 1–10–100 rule is: For every pound your company might spend on preventing a quality problem, it will spend 10 to inspect and correct the mistake after it occurs. In the worst case, the quality failure goes unanswered or unnoticed until after your customer has taken delivery. To fix the problem at this stage, you probably pay about 100 times what you could have paid to prevent it from happening at all.

Some organizations have systems and processes that stop complaints before they happen. Compared to fixing a complaint, telemarketing (or even an e-mail) can provide a low-cost method of ensuring customer satisfaction. For example, some customers may have a question that does not merit them making a telephone call, but nevertheless they would like it answered. If left unanswered, the question can fester into a source of dissatisfaction, so regular outbound telephone contact (the company calls the customer) picks up any issues or problems before they become major ones. This is more cost-effective than fixing problems. Inbound (0800 and freephone) customer service lines can also reassure customers if they are made aware of the facility. ICL computer company has a team of telephone diagnosticians who handle fault reports from customers. Linked to a sophisticated computerized diagnostic kit, they can identify whether the fault really exists or not. Many problems arise from the user's lack of knowledge, which means many potential problems or frustrations can be sorted out over the phone. If a fault is identified, the diagnosis informs the engineer in advance so that he or she arrives with the right spare part.

Stew Leonard's US retail chain's listening process

There are monthly focus groups and a daily suggestion box. Suggestions are typed up by 10 am the next day, and store managers either act or call the customers about the complaints or suggestions. The chain averages approximately 100 comments per day – they are the pulse of the store.

By actively listening to customers (and their complaints), companies can save, rather than spend, money.

Processes: detailed contact strategies

Too much contact can wear out a relationship. As in personal relationships, you can become a bore, a nuisance or irrelevant. On the other hand, too little may close the relationship-building opportunity. The key to building the best relationship is to have the right number of contacts of the right type at the right time for specific types of customers. This is a contact strategy. It specifies which kinds of customers and enquirers get which sequence of contacts and incentives and from what method (e-mail, mail, telephone, personal call, etc). Some organizations ask their customers how they prefer to be updated about special offers, reminders and announcements (including, if e-mail, whether text or HTML is preferred). The database stores their preferred media and ensures that they are contacted in the preferred manner. So organizations vary their contact strategy depending on how customers (and prospects) react.

Some garages maintain contact with their customers via e-mail or SMS, sending them reminders when their car is due for a service. If no response is generated then this triggers a prompt for staff to make a phone call to see whether the customer still wants to receive reminders (maintaining permission).

A contact strategy defines an initial welcome strategy when the prospect is first added to the database based on the best interval and sequence of messages. The contact strategy should then be extended for later stages in the customer life cycle, with messages designed to convert customers to purchase, encourage repeat purchases, encourage customers to try new products or reactivate customers when their interest wanes. Here are three steps to a contact strategy from Chaffey and Smith (2008):

1   Develop a welcome programme where over the first three to six months targeted auto-triggered e-mails are sent to educate subscribers about the brand and its benefits and deliver targeted offers. For example, the Renault B2C welcome strategy has a container or content pod within its e-newsletter to deliver personalized information about the brand and model of car in which a prospect is interested. This is updated each month as the customer gets to know the brand better and the brand gets to know the customer better!

2   Segment list members by activity (responsiveness) and age on the list. Assess the level of e-mail list activity (ask what percentage of list members haven't clicked within the last three to six months – if they haven't, they are inactive and should be treated differently, either by reducing frequency or by using more offline media).

3   Some customers become less responsive. A specific contact strategy is required to reactivate waning customers.

Here is how Tesco, arguably the world's most sophisticated relationship marketer, develops different contact strategies relevant to different customer types and customer relationship stages, eg new website visitor, first-time customer, repeat customer, lapsed customer. Tesco monitors customer actions during the customer life cycle. Different customer actions trigger different automatic responses (ARs) by e-mail:

- *Trigger event 1*. The customer first registers on the site (but does not buy).
    - AR1: Two days after registration, an e-mail is sent offering phone assistance and a £5 discount off the first purchase to encourage a trial.
- *Trigger event 2*. The customer first purchases online.
    - AR1: An immediate order confirmation is sent.
    - AR2: Five days after purchase, an e-mail is sent with a link to an online customer satisfaction survey asking about the quality of service from the driver and picker (eg item quality and substitutions).
    - AR3: Two weeks after the first purchase, a direct mail approach offers tips on how to use the service and a £5 discount on the next purchase intended to encourage reuse of online services.
    - AR4: A generic monthly e-newsletter with online exclusive offers.
    - AR5: A bi-weekly alert with personalized offers for the customer.
    - AR6: After 2 months, a £5 discount for the next shop.
    - AR7: A quarterly mailing of coupons.
- *Trigger event 3*. The customer does not purchase for an extended period.
    - AR1: The dormancy is detected, and a reactivation e-mail is sent with a survey of how the customer is finding the service (to identify any problems) and a £5 incentive.
    - AR2: A further discount incentive is used in order to encourage continued usage after a break.

Remember, markets are conversations. Listen to what customers say or watch what they click on and use this information to tailor relevant added value with every contact you make. Then ask customers how often they want contact and what type of information or offers they would like. This increases relevancy – a key success factor.

Defectors' process

All organizations lose customers. It's called 'churn'. Some customers change job, leave the country, grow old or die, and some switch to a competitor. Organizations need a process for following up any lost customers. Essentially the organization needs to listen carefully, find out why customers have defected, clarify what can be done to win back the business, and ask for the business (sometimes with an added incentive). All of this has to be recorded on to the database for review (particularly why customers are leaving).

Patience is required, as the defecting customer may have just bought a competitor's product or service and the organization has to wait for the next purchase cycle to start again. So be patient. Keep in touch. Make it easy to come back to the organization. When defectors actually do return, the organization has to go out and win their business every day.

Marketers must know what aspect of the organization's procedures, customer care and customer experience causes customers to leave. Marketers must also know which types of customers are defecting. If it is a disproportionate number of high-value customers, then alarm bells ring.

Marketing automation

Marketing automation (MA) can improve campaign results, as it generates automatic tailored communications triggered by profiles and events (such as purchases). It is all rules based, using variables including transaction history and cost history (call centre returns, order volumes and order frequency). It delivers a single customer view and identifies which media (including social media tools) work best using propensity models (propensity or likelihood to open, propensity to buy, etc).

Marketing optimization analyses all contact history to identify what communications mix generates the best return on investment. It identifies which channels (or tactical tools) generate the best results, whether e-mail, direct mail (snail mail), call centre, search engine traffic (resulting from SEO campaigns), social media or any other sources of customer acquisition (or retention).

Personalization and tailored offers

The most important sound in the world is... your own name! It's personal. It's a compliment – an expression of respect. Marketers depend on a good database to remember customer names, needs, interests and preferences. Specialized software combined with an up-to-date and well-cleaned database allows marketers to personalize communications such as e-mails, voicemails (voice-activated e-mails), snail mails (traditional direct mail), SMS text messages (for mobiles) and, most interestingly, websites – personalized websites.

Personalization can help to build relationships. When someone remembers your name and, even more importantly, your interests, it demonstrates that the person cares about you. Similarly, an organization that remembers your name and your interests is, at least, trying to do a good job.

> ### Relationships with an unknown lady
>
> Research into senior business executives who travel with BA revealed that most of them felt they had a personal relationship with the lady who wrote the BA executive newsletter – in so far as, if they ever had a travel problem, they could ask her to sort it out for them.

There are three distinct approaches to personalization as explained by Chaffey and Smith (2008): customization, individualization and group characterization. Customization is the easiest to see in action: it allows visitors to select and set up their specific preferences. Individualization goes beyond this fixed setting and uses patterns of a visitor's own behaviour (and not any other user's – it is known that it's a particular customer because of the log-in and password choices) to deliver specific content to the visitor that follows his or her patterns of contact. In group characterization, visitors receive recommendations based on the preferences of people like them, using approaches based on collaborative filtering and case-based reasoning. Mass customization is where a different product, service or content is produced for different segments – sometimes hundreds of different segments. Personalization is different. It is truly one to one, particularly when not only the website and communications are personalized but also the product or service.

Another way of thinking about the many options for online personalization is suggested by the Gartner Group (ranging from simple to complex):

- *Addressing customers personally:*
  - Address customers or prospects by name in print communication.
  - Address customers or prospects by name in electronic communication.
- *Real-time personalization:*
  - Keyword query to change content.
  - Clickstream data to dynamically change website content.
  - Collaborative filtering to classify visitors and serve content.

- *Customer profile personalization:*
  - Geographic personalization to tailor messages in traditional media.
  - Demographic personalization to tailor messages in traditional media.
  - Geographic personalization to tailor online messages.
  - Demographic personalization to tailor online messages.
  - Give website visitors control over content from set preferences.
  - Registration data to change website content.

There are other interesting options for tailored offers and ads, including 'content interested in' (pages visited) combined with other live data such as a bank account balance. For example, when HSBC Bank International wanted to move customers into more valuable segments, it tested personalized banner ads on its own website. *New Media Age* (2007) reported that this was a challenge: since '60% of total weekly visitors to offshore.hsbc.com log on to the internet banking service, HSBC wanted to market to them effectively while they were engaged in this task, disrupting their banking experience without infuriating them'. HSBC developed some rules to serve different offers dependent on the type of content accessed and the level of balance in the customer's account. The personalized approach worked, with new banners having an 87.5 per cent higher click-through rate than non-personalized banners (6.88 per cent versus 3.67 per cent); savings accounts opened via internet banking increased by 30 per cent (based on the six months pre- and post-launch); and non-premier customers upgrading to premier accounts (requiring a balance of £60,000 or more) increased by 86 per cent (based on the four weeks pre- and post-launch of the targeted banners).

Personalization enhances relationships. Personalized web pages help to give customers a sense of ownership – not the marketer owning the customer, but the customer owning (or controlling) the site. When you make customers feel that their home page is truly theirs, then the offers you make available to them are the customers', the information they access is put together just for them, and you allow the customers to own you.

Personalization challenges

Many personalized sites require users to log in with a password, which can be frustrating when customers forget. Many visitors give up and leave the site. The use of cookies here can avoid the need for passwords and log-ins. However, privacy laws now require e-marketers to ask permission before placing a cookie on a user's PC (and also explain the use of cookies within the privacy policy). Here are some other personalization problems.

Although personalization is important, it is possible to overpersonalize. American Express once tried too hard to be too personal and upset customers. UK Online for Business reported that American Express call centres discovered that customers resented being greeted in person until the customers had actually declared who they were, even although a powerful database can recognize an incoming phone number and reveal the caller's name, address, purchases, issues, etc. The practice of immediate personalized greeting was swiftly discontinued.

Dear Rich Fat Bastard

Security becomes even more important when personalized information is collected. A credit card company once had a direct mailshot to 30,000 of its best customers (its gold card holders) intercepted by a disenchanted employee. He changed the salutation in each of the personalized letters to 'Dear Rich Fat Bastard'.

Nike's website once offered customers the opportunity to personalize their own shoes by stitching on their own personal logo. One customer filled out the online form, sent the $50 and chose 'sweatshop' as a personal logo. Nike refused. The publicity soared.

Automated personalized systems can present challenges. However, listening to feedback, ensuring security measures are in place and motivating staff to spot issues (eg Nike) are all simply best practice. Now let's consider a key component that customers expect – credibility and trust.

Credibility and trust

Develop credibility before raising visibility. If you don't do this you will waste an awful lot of money annoying customers. Many organizations spend a lot of money on advertising and generating traffic to their websites (raising visibility) before they have established their credibility. Effectively, all they have done is to take a poor low-profile company and make it a poor high-profile company. What is the point of that? Yet how often do you see this?

So how do you develop credibility and trust on a website?

Firstly, ensure that your product or service has sufficient quality to match the promises made in advertising and other communications. Use customer

TABLE 3.2   20 ways to develop credibility, boost online trust and drive repeat visits

		Yes/No
1	Privacy statement	
2	Security icons	
3	Guarantees	
4	Memberships of professional bodies	
5	Credible third-party endorsements	
6	Customer endorsements	
7	Customer lists	
8	Awards won	
9	Demonstrate expertise	
10	Real people in the About us/Contact us section	
11	Community links	
12	Ethical policies (corporate citizenship)	
13	Text-only version	
14	Full address and contact information	
15	Proof everything – typo free?	
16	Reliable systems	
Four factors that drive repeat visits:		
17	High-quality content	
18	Ease of use	
19	Quick download	
20	Updated frequently	
Score out of 20		

feedback regularly and rigorously. Then check your website works all right (usability testing).

These days, all marketing communications carry the organization's website address. Use the 20 credibility factors listed in Table 3.2 to ensure you do not damage your credibility but in fact strengthen it. Make sure you tick them all before you start to raise your web profile.

CRM creation and maintenance

Writing a CRM brief

Careful thought and considerable advice are needed in setting up a CRM system. It requires vision, strong leadership, CRM experience, integrated skills and an integrated team. When choosing a CRM system, you need to consider the current and future requirements. This involves:

- objective;
- scenarios;
- contact strategies;
- communications tools.

Objective means purpose. What are you trying to achieve with a new CRM system (customer retention, customer win-back, customer acquisition, complaint processing or customer feedback)? How can it help customers? Then how can it help you and your team? What kind of scenarios does this involve (customer feedback, suggestions, complaints, enquiries, sales – all of these can be online and offline, or on a telephone line)? Is the system designed to facilitate 'welcome cycles' (welcome letters and new member offers), up-selling (moving the customer on to higher quality levels), cross-selling (other products or services) and reactivation (of previous customers), all of which help to nurture the relationship? What kind of contact strategies might this involve? What kind of marketing tools will generate the data, eg e-mail, snail mail, outbound telemarketing, inbound telemarketing, sales teams and website dialogue?

Customer data are collected from website registration, guarantee forms, sales promotions' telemarketing, customer service teams on the phone,

and salespeople either face to face or over the phone. Often the best source of data lies dormant, thrown in the bottom of a drawer or a customer file somewhere in an organization. Every customer and his or her purchasing pattern, every enquiry and every complaint, comment or item of feedback can be stored in a database. The database can build up a detailed customer's profile, identifying issues, preferences, incentives that work and the buying cycle. This facilitates sequence selling, where interest is aroused and relevant tempting offers are made through a series of communications (contact strategy) rather than going for an immediate straight sale.

The system should accommodate and develop a dialogue or a two-way flow of information between the customer and the organization. Does it prompt three-way communication ('trialogue') by sharing engaged customers' opinions, scores, ratings and reviews with other prospects? Every time customers respond, they can be encouraged to give information about their needs and situation (eg whether they want to opt out or stay on the database).

Remember, input is one thing, but retrieval in a sensible format is another. The art lies in the retrieval of the data in an appropriate format, eg a list of 'all enquirers for product x from the south-west in the past six months', a list of a particular category of business customer (SIC code), a list of 'customers who have bought all product x but not product y', and so on.

Scale is important too. Will the database grow? How many sources of data might there be? How many scenarios might exist?

A marketing lead from an interdisciplinary team is required in creating and developing a CRM system. A strong CRM project leader is also required. The project team comprises different users of the system, analysts to understand their requirements, technical staff to create the system and a project manager with sufficient time to devote to the job. You've got to involve all departments that may use the CRM system, from customer services, sales and marketing to finance (invoicing), admin, production and quality control. And don't forget IT, but I strongly recommend that marketers must take control, not IT – IT simply supplies the service expertise. It rarely has a customer focus. Remember, the primary reason is to help customers to do business with you. This is not a technology-driven project. It has to be a customer-driven project with measurable customer criteria, such as increased sales, satisfaction, referrals, etc.

Using SOS 3Ms in a brief

Taken from SOSTAC® marketing planning (see Chapter 10), SOS + 3Ms helps briefings. SOS stands for situation (what kind of CRM do we have now and why does it need improving?), objectives (what are we trying to achieve with the new CRM system?) and strategy (how does CRM integrate with all the company's operations?):

- Situation (where are we now with CRM?).
- Objectives (what do we want to achieve?).
- Strategy (how will we get there?) This is why the brief is critical, as it should be clear about contact strategies and scenarios (including how it can now and in the future integrate with other systems, such as invoicing and debt collection).

3Ms include money (the budgets required for software licences plus training and motivation schemes to ensure staff buy into the new system), minutes (the timescales required to specify the brief, source it, test it, modify it, train the team and roll out the system), and men/women (who will champion the project, do the work and be involved in data capture, analysis and use). Every brief must have these. When should the new system be tested, staff training take place and the system eventually go live?

Beware of scope creep

Scope creep destroys projects. Finally, when you've done your research, discussed everything, written up a detailed brief, got it signed off by the key people and issued it to a supplier or several suppliers, some member of staffs thinks of something really quite helpful and asks for it to be included in the brief. This is scope creep. It delays projects, allows suppliers to be late with delivery ('you changed the brief') and allows suppliers to charge a lot more money. Although it's tempting to keep adding extra ideas, a CRM project manager has got to be strong and comprehensive in the initial exploratory discussions and ensure everyone knows that this is the last chance to discuss the brief before it goes out to tender, because once it goes out it stays out.

Systems development should follow a structured approach, going through several stages. Note though that, just as for website development, prototyping is the most effective approach, since it enables the system to be tailored through users' experience of early versions of the system. Ultimately, CRM is an attitude as much as a system. Success depends on a customer culture where all staff always ask 'How can we help the customer?'

Marketers need to improve IT skill sets. They need to get better at speaking the language of IT and develop a greater understanding of how technology can translate into improved customer knowledge and ultimately an improved customer experience. As Wright (2007) says, 'IT people use scary language, and marketers step back from it. But if marketers constantly brought conversations back to the benefits for the customer, that would help build a common language around the customer and put technology back in its place.'

CRM system creation, development, testing and roll-out

Systems development should follow a structured approach, going through several stages (see Figure 3.2).

Prior to developing a brief and system design, marketers need to improve their IT skill sets. Marketers need to understand and speak the language of IT and develop a greater understanding of how technology can be used to improve customer knowledge and ultimately an improved customer experience.

FIGURE 3.2

CRM development process

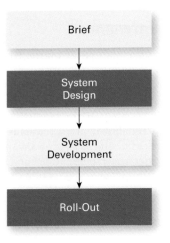

Prior to each stage there is research or testing. Prior to drawing up a brief, a lot of research goes into reviewing what each department requires and how it all integrates. After the brief is issued several supplier tenders are reviewed and researched. These may be off-the-shelf solutions, tailor-made solutions or a mixture, ie an off-the-shelf system tweaked to suit the organization's specific requirements. When a system is selected and developed it is then tested before being rolled out.

System development involves prototyping and refining the prototype. This enables the system to be tailored through users' experience of early versions of the system. However, beware of 'scope creep'. Ultimately, CRM is an attitude as much as a process or system. Success depends on a customer culture where all staff always ask CRM designers and developers and consultants 'How does this help the customer?'

Roll-out requires an investment of the 3Ms into training and motivation. Training ensures all staff are fully familiar with the system, how it works, how it can make their lives easier, how it will help the customer and how it will help the business.

Front end is fun, back end is business

Marketers are reasonably good at developing websites (front end) but we have to become experts with the database and the e-CRM systems (back end) required to build continual success.

CRM maintenance

Although it does not appear on the balance sheet, the database is an asset. Like any asset it deteriorates or depreciates over time if it is not properly maintained. In the same way that a physical asset, like a building, needs to be maintained to avoid it becoming run down and eventually become a liability (if tiles fall off the roof or a wall collapses), a database asset needs to be cleaned and maintained to stop it deteriorating and eventually becoming a liability, eg sending out direct mail to people who have died naturally upsets the relatives. Careful management of the database is required.

Managing the database

The database is at the heart of the CRM system. The database manager has many responsibilities in addition to the database design (which allows relevant customer data to be accessed rapidly and queries performed):

- Data quality – ensuring data are accurate, relevant and kept up to date.
- Data security – ensuring data cannot be compromised by attacks from inside or outside the organization.
- Data coordination or user coordination specifies exactly who has access to data retrieval and who has access to data input. Too many uncontrolled inputs may result in files being deleted or changed by too many different people. The database spins out of control.
- Data back-up and recovery – ensuring that data can be restored when there are the almost inevitable system failures or attacks.

The manager also monitors performance, particularly checking the system is coping as either the database grows or the number of interactions grows (driven by the contact strategies).

Costs and timescales

When it comes to the crunch question of 'How much does it all cost?' there are many variables to consider:

- the set-up costs of the system;
- the type of system;
- the scope of the system;
- the size of the system;
- the choice made about the database management system;
- the maintenance programme;
- where the physical database management system is geographically located.

It is a complex job but, once all these variables are taken into consideration, a task breakdown can be performed, and analysis, design, set-up, maintenance and running costs can be calculated.

What's missing is customer service staff, who are a key component, particularly when they are handling wide-ranging, non-standard requests or complaints. Here's a crucial question: how many customer service staff are required?

The other key question is: how long does it take to set up a CRM system? The variables are similar to those for cost:

- time allowed for the investigative stage;
- time allowed for design;
- time for writing programmes;
- time for data capture, reassessment and input;
- time for trials, piloting, testing and debugging.

A strong project manager

An effective CRM programme needs a strong project manager who can unite the business and technical team members. A defined database administrator is also required who will champion the system and own it to ensure appropriate data quality, security and performance. Planning using the systems development life cycle provides a framework for costing, scheduling and monitoring the project. Remember also that CRM programmes never end; they evolve.

Control issues

One of the toughest jobs is to know which data matter most – especially where there are conflicting data. Some customers will give incorrect information, consciously or unconsciously. Some staff input data incorrectly. Other staff leave data fields empty. Marketers and data managers have to come up with ways to acquire the correct and relevant information in the first place and then make it useful to the organization.

The issue of the invasion of privacy is a difficult one. Laws, ethics and codes of practice come into play. Ethics have a role, but the main arbiters of 'How much contact is too much contact?' are the customers themselves. They reveal how ready they are to be communicated with by their response (or lack of response). Permission to contact customers is only temporary. Organizations have to continually

win it by delivering relevant added-value communications continuously.

Asking for information is a delicate affair. Marketers can be too greedy. Beyond the basic information, you may need to offer incentives for more information or simply wait for the relationship to develop and permission to ask for more. But remember that customers value their privacy. All organizations' privacy policies should be clearly posted on the website and any other access points customers may have with you.

Measuring customer satisfaction

Call centre agents' performance is often measured by number of calls taken. This ignores customer satisfaction, although customer service is a stated aim of many companies. Many marketing managers view call centres as a means of gathering customer data as opposed to a highly influential brand-building 'brand moment'.

Those marketers who do measure customer care also need to tread cautiously, as it can be misleading. For example, an increasingly high customer care score (say up from 84 per cent to 92 per cent) may seem good, but it ignores two critical elements. Firstly, which service components are very important

The customer cube

One-dimensional customer surveys usually rate product quality, after-sales service, maybe price, etc with 1 extremely dissatisfied, 2 dissatisfied, 3 neutral, 4 satisfied, 5 completely satisfied. This ignores how the customer ranks the importance of each variable.

Two-dimensional customer surveys weight these satisfaction factors according to how important they are to the customer: 1 not important, 2 of minor importance, 3 fairly important, 4 very important, 5 essential. However, this ignores how customers compare the brand to those of the other competitors.

Three-dimensional customer surveys also ask customers to rate the organization versus the competition for each customer service component: 1 significantly worse, 2 somewhat worse, 3 about the same, 4 somewhat better, 5 significantly better.

to customers? The ultimate goal is to score 5 out of 5 ratings for all those customer service components given an importance rating of 5 by the customer. Secondly, how do customers rate the experience in comparison to that from competitors?

Some authors are even suspicious of three-dimensional customer satisfaction scores, as they believe conventional customer satisfaction scores 'typically only draw responses from the bored, the lonely and the seriously aggrieved' (Reichheld and Allen, 2006). The key, they suggest, is to ask customers one simple question: 'How likely is it that you would recommend us to a friend or a colleague?'

Companies like GE focus on one statistic that nets the percentage of unhappy customers (scoring 0–6) from the percentage who are very happy customers known as 'loyal promoters' (scoring 9 or 10). This net promoter score provides a crystal-clear single number that is as actionable as net profit or net worth.

Accountants cannot distinguish between good and bad profits

'Business measures success based on profits but accountants cannot distinguish between a dollar of bad, customer abusive, growth stifling profits and a dollar of good, loyalty enhancing, growth accelerating profits.'

Reichheld and Allen (2006)

CRM summary and challenges

CRM is a strategic issue requiring a long-term perspective. Winning a sale is short-term transactional marketing. Building a relationship where the customer comes back again and again is long-term

strategy. Building good customer relations requires a cultural shift in the organization to ensure that the whole organization wants to help customers. Some CRM projects take several years to research, develop, test and launch. There will always be some tension between the pressure to hit the short-term monthly and quarterly sales (and profit) targets versus the longer-term customer relations scores. Marketers need to educate boards about how CRM, in the long term, grows quarterly sales and profit results.

The shift to a relationship-building organization can start with a website or even the fundamental products and services themselves. Ask how the organization or the brand can help customers even more than it does now (see the discussion of National Semiconductor in 'The colouring department is dead', Chapter 1). Some years ago Unilever made a major strategic decision to move Persil from a product-centric portal (a lot of product information) to a customer-centric portal. The new website had two main sections: 'Time in' and 'Time out', including lifestyle and time for 'yourself', which meant relaxation, minding your skin, diet and children, time with the children, tips for a happy family, and getting creative with the children. In addition, the subsequent brand engagement strategy and contact strategy have to be worked out carefully, as discussed in the previous sections.

ROI of customer satisfaction

'In fact, when we looked at the top 100 e-retailers, we saw that increasing satisfaction by just one point drove over $112 million in additional sales.'

Atchinson (2008)

Table 3.3 is an interesting way to end the chapter – a nice simple survey to get a feel for an organization's approach to CRM.

TABLE 3.3 Customer sensitivity quotient

Are your customers getting the service they deserve? Answer the following questions 'yes' or 'no' to find out how your organization is doing.

		Yes/No
1	Do you know what percentage of customers you keep each year?	
2	Do you know what percentage of customers you lose each year?	
3	Do you know the top three reasons your customers leave?	
4	Do you know your customers' number one service expectation?	
5	In the past three months, have you personally contacted 10 former customers to find out why they left?	
6	Do you (and everyone else in your company) understand the lifetime value of a customer?	
7	Do you have written customer service quality standards (that your people helped you develop, so they own them)?	
8	Do you articulate your quality standards in understandable and measurable terms?	
9	In the past six months, have you checked to see if any of your customers' expectations have changed?	
10	Do you know how many members of your staff serve internal versus external customers?	
11	Are your customer service performance standards tied to any incentives?	
12	Is everyone in your company required to take a minimum number of hours of customer care training programmes each year?	

If you scored...	You are...
12	A CSQ legend!
10–11	A CSQ star!
7–9	Jo(e) Average
4–6	A benchwarmer
Below 4	In the penalty box

© JoAnna Brandi

Key points from Chapter 3

- Relationship marketing (and CRM) can create competitive advantage.
- CRM is all about long-term brand building vs short-term sales growth.
- There is a disciplined approach to the CRM planning process.
- CRM requires resources and a disciplined set of processes.
- Many organizations allow scope creep and lack of training and motivation to destroy their CRM.

References and further reading

Allen, J, Reichheld, F and Hamilton, B (2005) The three 'Ds' of customer experience, *Harvard Business School Working Knowledge*

Atchinson, S (2008) The ROI of customer satisfaction, Interview with Larry Freed, President and CEO of ForeSee Results, *ClickZ*, 24 July

August, A (2002) Smashing time for Chinese consumers, *Times*, 14 March

Bird, D (1989) *Commonsense Direct Marketing*, 2nd edn, Kogan Page, London

Brann, C (1984) *Cost-Effective Direct Marketing: By mail, telephone and direct response advertising*, Collectors' Books, Cirencester

BusinessEurope.com (2004) BusinessEurope News Feed, 4 February

Butler, J (2004) Developing a customer culture, *Successful Entrepreneurial Management*

Chaffey, D and Smith, P R (2008) *eMarketing eXcellence*, 3rd edn, Kogan Page, London

Considine, R and Raphel, M (1981) *The Great Brain Robbery*, The Great Brain Robbery, Pasadena, CA

DB2 (1997) IBM Developer Works

Direct Marketing Centre (1992) *The Practitioner Guide to Direct Marketing*, Direct Marketing Centre, London

dunnhumby (2006) *The dunnhumby Way*, dunnhumby, London

Earls, K (2002) *Welcome to the Creative Age*, Wiley, Chichester

Egain's State of Customer Service (2007) *New Media Age*, 31 May

Exhibition Venues Association (2000) *UK Exhibition Facts*, Vol. 12, Exhibition Venues Association, Mayfield, East Sussex

Forrester Research (2009) *Answers to Five Frequently Asked Questions about CRM Projects*, Forrester Research, Cambridge, MA

Gartner (2009) *Trip Report: Gartner customer relationship management summit 2009*, Gartner, Stamford, CT

Godin, S (1999) *Permission Marketing*, Simon and Schuster, New York

Hochman, L (2008) Guide to customer loyalty, *Marketing Age*

Howard, M (1989) Telephone marketing vs direct sales force costs, Commissioned by Datapoint (UK) Ltd, London

IBM (2004) Reported by Mike Devlin, CEO, IBM and Paul Levy, CEO, *Rational Software and the New Business Economy*, 9 March 2004, Developer Works, IBM [online] **http://www.ibm.com/developerworks/rational/library/3771.html**

Krigsman, M (2009) CRM failure rates: 2001–2009, *ZDNet*, 3 August, **http://www.zdnet.com/blog/projectfailures/crm-failure-rates-2001-2009/4967**

McCorkell, G (1997) *Direct and Database Marketing*, Kogan Page, London

Mahoney, M (2002) 'Putting the R back in CRM': It's time to reinstall the 'R' in your customer relationship, Interview with Susan Fournier, Harvard Business School Working Knowledge, 7 January, **http://hbswk.hbs.edu/archive/3000.html**

Mitchell, A (2004) Heart of the matter, *The Markets*, 3 June

MORI (2003) Managing your customer insight capability and the drivers for change – client managed, cosourced, insourced or outsourced – a survey of UK FTSE 1000 organisations, Commissioned by Detica

Moriarty, R and Moran, U (1990) Managing hybrid systems, *Harvard Business Review*, November–December

Moriarty, R and Swartz, G (1989) Automation to boost sales and marketing, *Harvard Business Review*, January–February

New Media Age (2007) Impulse buying, by Emma Rubach, *New Media Age*, 30 August, **www.nma.org.uk**

Novo, J (2004) *Drilling Down: Turning customer data into profits with a spreadsheet*, 3rd edn, published by Jim Novo

Reichheld, F and Allen, J (2006) How companies can end the cycle of customer abuse, *Financial Times*, 23 March

Royal Mail (1991) *The Royal Mail Guide to Successful Direct Mail*, Royal Mail, London

Stevens, M (1991) *The Handbook of Telemarketing*, Kogan Page, London

Tapp, A (2001) *Principles of Direct and Database Marketing*, 2nd edn, Financial Times/Prentice Hall, Englewood Cliffs, NJ

Toffler, A (1980) *The Third Wave*, Collins, London

Tranfield, D and Braganza, A (2007) *Business Leadership of Technological Change – Five key challenges facing CEOs*, Chartered Management Institute

Watson, J (1989) The direct marketing guide, *Marketing Magazine*, 9 February

Wright, H (2007) Reclaiming the customer high ground, *Marketer*, July/August

Young, M (nd) Never sell to a stranger, Ogilvy & Mather Direct

Further information

British Quality Foundation
32–34 Great Peter Street
London SW1P 2QX
Tel: +44 (0)20 7654 5000
www.quality-foundation.co.uk

British Standards Institution
389 Chiswick High Road
London W4 4AL
Tel: +44 (0)20 8996 9001
Fax: +44 (0)20 8996 7001
www.bsi-global.com

Institute of Customer Care
2 Castle Court
St Peter's Street
Colchester CO1 1EW
Tel: +44 (0)1206 571716
www.instituteofcustomerservice.com

04
Customer psychology and buyer behaviour

LEARNING OBJECTIVES

By the end of this chapter you will be able to:

- Appreciate the complexity of buying behaviour
- Understand the critical nature of a continual feed of information on customer behaviour
- Appreciate the emotional influences in decision making
- Compare and contrast various approaches to buying models
- Apply the psychology of marketing by exploring different intervening variables

Introduction to understanding customer buying behaviour

The first step in formulating a marketing communications strategy is to identify, analyse and ultimately understand the target market and its buying behaviour. This chapter considers some of the theories and models that the marketing professional can use to help to communicate with and influence the buyer at various stages before, during and after purchasing. Buying behaviour is often more complex than it appears. Individuals are generally not very predictable, but, in the aggregate, groups of customers (or percentages of markets) can be more predictable.

Whether in the industrial or consumer market, or whether they are buying products or services, buyers respond in different ways to the barrage of marketing communications that are constantly aimed at them. Theoretical frameworks borrowed from psychology, sociology, social psychology, cultural anthropology and economics are now added to by both commercial and academic market research into consumer and industrial buyer behaviour. All of this contributes to a better understanding of buyer behaviour. It is this understanding that helps to reveal what kind of marketing communications work best.

This chapter can provide only an outline of the vast amount of work written in this area. The complex burger buyer example is used to open up some of the types of question that need to be considered. The chapter then looks at types of purchases and the buying process (including some buying models) and then considers how the 'intervening variables' of perception, motivation, learning, memory, attitudes, beliefs, personality and group influence can influence the communication process and, ultimately, buying behaviour.

Three key questions

There are three key groups of questions that have to be answered before any marketing communications can be carried out:

1 Who is the buyer (target market profiles and decision-making units)?

2 Why do they buy (or not buy) a particular brand or product?

3 How, when and where do they buy?

The second question, 'Why do they buy?', is the most difficult to answer. It requires *qualitative* rather than *quantitative* data (which generally answers the other questions). Products and services are bought for a range of different reasons or benefits, some conscious, others unconscious, some rational, others emotional. Many buyers buy for a mixture of reasons. Consider a simple hamburger.

The complex burger buyer

Why buy a burger? The answer might be as simple as 'Because I was hungry – so I bought a Big Mac.' The real reason, however, may be quite different. Perhaps the buyer was in a receptive state for food because of the time of the day. In the same way that a stimulus such as a bell for Pavlov's dog (see 'Learning', page 105) can cause a dog to salivate, the highly visible yellow McDonald's logo can act as a stimulus to customers to remind them of food and arouse feelings of hunger – even salivation. Perhaps the yellow logo also acts as a cue, by triggering memories of the happy advertising images that are learned and stored in memory banks.

A teenage burger buyer may prefer McDonald's because friends hang out there and it feels nice to be in with the in-crowd (Maslow's need to be accepted or loved; see 'Motivation', page 107). Maybe the friendly image and the quick service simultaneously satisfy two basic needs – love and hunger. Many convenience purchases today are, in fact, about purchasing time, ie buying a time-saving product or service releases free time to do something else, to satisfy another need. It is likely that buyers have many different reasons with different orders of importance. Different segments can seek many different reasons with different orders of importance. But why don't they go into a Wimpy restaurant or a fish and chip shop instead of a McDonald's?

Choice is often influenced by familiarity with the brand, or sometimes the level of trust in a brand name. Familiarity can be generated by actual experience and/or increased awareness boosted by advertising. If one brand can get into the front of an individual's mind ('front-of-mind awareness') through advertising, etc, then it will stand a better chance of being chosen in a simple buying situation like this, unless of course the buyer has a preferred set of fast-food restaurants that specifically exclude a particular brand. In this case the buyer is usually prepared to search a little harder (even cross the road) before satisfying the aroused need.

The choice of another group of burger buyers can be determined simply by location – offering the right goods or services in the right place at the right time at the right prices. Assuming this is all supported by the right image (eg clean and friendly, nutritious, fast service, socially responsible), then the marketing mix has succeeded in capturing this segment of non-loyal burger buyers who have no strong preferred set of fast-food outlets.

More health-conscious buyers may prefer a nice warm cup of soup. Why? What motivates them? Health? A desire to live longer? A fear of death? A desire to be fit, stay slim, look good (esteem) or just feel healthy and feel good (self-actualization; see Figure 4.8)? Or perhaps it's cheaper than a burger? Or is it because everyone else in the office recommends the local delicatessen's soup (pressure to conform to group norms, desire to be accepted by a group – again, the need to be loved)?

There are other possibilities that lie in the dark depths of our vast information storage chambers, otherwise known as our unconscious. For example, in 1957 Vance Packard suggested that 'the deepest roots of our liking for warm, nutritious and plentiful soup may lie in the comfortable and secure unconscious prenatal sensations of being surrounded by the amniotic fluid in our mother's womb'.

Impulse buying and repeat purchasing of low-cost fast food obviously differ from the buying behaviour involved in the purchase of, say, a new audio system, a house, a holiday or a fleet of new cars for the company. It is likely that more 'information search' will occur than in the simple stimulus–response buying model (McDonald's yellow logo stimulates the senses and arouses hunger, which generates the response – buy a Big Mac). Regular low-cost purchases are known as 'routinized response behaviour' and therefore have a different buying process than a high-cost, high-risk, irregular purchase, which is known as a 'high-involvement purchase'. Some basic buying models help to explain the different types of purchases and the types of buying process involved. These will be considered later in this chapter.

Who is the customer?

So many organizations do not know who their customers are. This means they have no real idea who they are trying to target. This is high-risk marketing, something akin to trying to find a needle in a haystack. In fact there is more chance of finding the needle, because at least we can describe what a needle looks like. But in marketing if we cannot describe (or profile) who the ideal customer is then the organization is almost totally dependent on luck. The few outstanding marketing companies out there really do spend a lot of time and effort constantly researching and analysing exactly who is their target market (in great detail), the needs of the target market (why they buy) and how they buy.

It can be more difficult online. Some people behave differently online than offline. They assume different pseudonyms and personalities. Sometimes it's hard to know who's who online. As they say, 'Who knows you're a dog online?'

Different personalities below the surface

A 25-year-old New York stockbroker had an online fling with a 21-year-old blue-eyed blonde Miami beauty. They arranged to meet at JFK airport with red roses. The young New Yorker was horrified to see a 70-year-old man sitting in a wheelchair, wearing a red rose and roaring with laughter at him.

Knowing who is the customer is not as easy as it seems. As discussed in Chapter 3, 50 per cent of British companies did not know who their customers were. Despite having large databases, they did not know how to put profiles on their customers. Without this information, companies are shooting blind and just hoping for the best. This is high-risk marketing. For example, a European battery supplier noticed that its highest-margin, high-tech batteries were frequently sold out in one of its most powerful retailers. As it wanted to boost sales at this retailer, it invested in a new point-of-sale. It assumed the high-tech batteries were bought by high-tech users. It designed a prominent new display rack describing the batteries' benefits for digital services. Sales fell. Research revealed that ordinary (non-high-tech) users were buying the batteries, as they perceived the hi-tech batteries would simply last longer (a fact not emphasized in the displays). The company returned to the original displays, and sales went up by 20 per cent (Forsyth, Galante and Guild, 2006).

Decision-making units

As mentioned previously, there are often several individuals involved in any one person's decision to purchase either consumer or industrial products and services. The choice of a family car may be influenced by parents, children, aunts, uncles, neighbours, friends, the Automobile Association and so on. Each may play a different role in the buying process. Similarly, the purchase of a new factory machine may have been instigated by a safety inspector, selected by a team of engineers, supervisors, shop steward and production manager, agreed by the board, bought or ordered by the purchasing director and paid for by the financial director or company secretary.

PAGES is a simple acronym that helps to build a marketing communications decision-making unit (DMU) checklist:

Purchaser	The person who orders the goods or services
Adviser	Someone who is knowledgeable in the field
Gatekeeper	A secretary, receptionist or assistant who wants to protect his or her boss from being besieged by marketing messages
End user	Sometimes called 'the customer'
Starter	The instigator or initiator

The actual decision maker is sometimes separate from the purchaser and/or the user. The payer (cheque authorizer) may be different to the purchaser in the B2B environment.

One other, non-human, influencer that needs to be added to the DMU is the intelligent shopping bot. Some are here already. They can take many different forms. One form is the futuristic 3D floating holograms that appear beside the customer when the customer is in the buying mode, giving advice, or even haggling with the salesperson (if buying offline). Another form is the intelligent fridge

(referred to in Chapter 2), which can offer the customer a tempting online voucher to replace the last can of Guinness with an alternative brand. Another form is the mobile phone. My iPhone has various apps: one identifies the prices at all petrol stations near my location, and another scans in bar codes and compares prices locally. As mobile phones become smarter, with predictive contextual devices delivering real-time contextualized and personalized services and information, the device knows, through the aggregated filters of our location, our timeline and our social graph, what we did just before and what we are expected to want or do later on (courtesy of our online calendar, contacts database, web search history and geo-location information). Very soon, context-based technology will predict our needs and desires. It is 'aware' because it holds a complete record of our past actions and habits and of our future intentions – where we are heading and who we will meet via calendar entries, contacts, web/search history, etc (Frank, 2010).

It's only a matter of time before your mobile device knows your every want and need

'I am on a business trip to Madrid, have just finished my meetings and have three hours until my flight back to New York. My device "senses" I started moving and 'knows' my schedule, therefore it asks me if I prefer to get a taxi to the airport, or if I prefer to stay in the city since the drive to the airport takes about 15 minutes. I choose the second option, slide the "ambient media streams" all the way from "privacy please" to "hit me with everything you've got," and the device offers me all the tourist attractions around me, even a nearby coffee shop that has received exceptionally high ratings (I love coffee). I choose the coffee shop, and as I am drinking my second cup, the device alerts me that my flight has been delayed by an hour and will board through gate E32. I drink another cup of coffee and read from my device the history of Madrid until the next alert updates me that I should call a taxi – immediately providing me with an application that directly books one.'

Frank (2010)

Why do they buy?

Marketing people really do need to know the reasons why buyers buy. More often than not, customers do not even know the real reasons they buy (they like to think that they are rational decision makers). There is a range of conscious and unconscious reasons underlying why people buy what they buy. Some reasons are more important than others to a particular segment. Some reasons are rational, and some are emotional. The split between the two is called the 'emotional–rational dichotomy'. The late Robert Gouezeta, former CEO of Coca-Cola, once said, 'We sell on image. We don't know how to sell on performance. Everything we sell, we sell on image.'

Rational shoppers?

'Typically, shoppers give the correct price of only 50 per cent of what they have just put in their trolley. Consumers remain loyal to brands even when better products are available. Consumers rarely complain to suppliers when dissatisfied about a product. Is this a time-efficient way of dealing with repetitive purchases, or emotional madness?'

East et al (2008)

The rational–emotional dichotomy

This rational and emotional quagmire is not restricted to consumer purchasing but applies also to supposedly hard-nosed rational professional buying behaviour. Take small businesses selling to other businesses: they don't have the option of scale, price or bulk orders to gain an edge over the competition; they have to have a story or relationship, and need to cultivate that 'unreasonable loyalty' (Roberts, 2010b). And B2B buyers do buy into relationships built on reliability, trust and personality, as B2C buyers buy on emotion. In fact, as noted in Chapter 2, Harley-Davidson does not sell motorcycles, Starbucks do not sell coffee, Club Med does not sell vacations, and Guinness does not sell beer. Coke doesn't sell cola. Porsche buyers (many of them) don't buy a transport vehicle; they buy it because they 'simply want to prove to themselves that they

have the ability to buy such a car' (Kapferer, 2004). (See the box 'The invisible badge: motivation beyond conspicuous consumption' on page 109.)

Perhaps Professor East was conservative when, in fact, many UK customers are prepared to pay 800 per cent more for the 'the real thing' than for an own-brand cola from Asda. A 2-litre bottle of Coca-Cola may sell at £1.20 while on the same shelf an Asda own-label 2-litre cola was selling for £0.15. John Roberts (in Egan, 2007) believes that Coca-Cola's 'core concept is product engagement, how warm customers feel towards the brand, how engaged and intimate their relationship has become through the events. You'll never see a Coke ad with just one person.' And, for this intimate privilege that reflects our deep desires (the magic formula), we are prepared to pay an 800 per cent price premium.

As one of the masters of the magic marketing formula, Kevin Roberts, CEO of Saatchi & Saatchi Worldwide, acknowledges, 80 per cent of decisions are emotional. Yet 80 per cent of marketing communications (marcomms) are rational. Rational decision making equals conclusion, whereas emotional decision making equals action. Hence master marketers search for emotional benefits as well, eg the back pain medication rational approach is 'This medication solves the problem', whereas the emotional approach shows the joy of movement. That's why Roberts says: 'Let emotion rip!'

The difference between emotion and reason

'You spend three seconds. You do not think about every benefit, every attribute, every demonstration. There's an emotional connection through the packaging, through the advertising and through your memory that you make. And then you decide. Neurologist Donald Khan says the difference between emotion and reason is: "Reason leads to conclusions – emotion leads to action."

Most of the research asks: "Do you remember it? Do you get the brand benefits?", whereas the only question you need to ask in research is: "Do you want to see it again? Does this connect with you?"'

Roberts (2006a)

The bottom line is that marketing managers have constantly to ask the question: 'Why are they buying or not buying our products or services?' Customers need to be probed deeply to find the answers to questions like: 'How do you feel about the brand? Does the brand connect with you? How? How much emotional connection have you got with the brand?' The answers are not static, one-off pieces of research findings but a constant flow of information. Rational reasons need to be understood also. And remember: reasons change; people change; markets change; competition and technology change. A valid reason for buying a particular product yesterday may become obsolete tomorrow. Likewise, an apparently irrelevant feature yesterday may become a key reason for buying tomorrow.

A company executive might buy one brand of a computer rather than another simply because of a distant fear of being fired. This is further complicated by the fact that some customers buy the same product for different reasons. For example, Americans may buy iPods because they enable them to listen to their favourite music without being disturbed by others, while Japanese buy iPods to listen to their favourite music without disturbing others. Even an apparently simple product like toothpaste presents a complex web of reasons for buying. The toothpaste manufacturers respond by supplying different images of different benefits of different types of toothpaste to different segments who have different reasons (needs or motives) for brushing their teeth. The following toothpaste test explains.

The now classic Colgate 'ring of confidence' was one of the UK's best-known toothpaste advertisements. It was basically selling a tube of social confidence. This need to be accepted is relatively obvious although not always admitted initially. There are, however, deeper feelings, emotions, memories, moods, thoughts, beliefs and attitudes locked up inside the dark depths of our unconscious. Sigmund Freud suggested that the mind was like an iceberg in so far as the tip represents the conscious part of the mind while the greater submerged part is the unconscious. Even long-forgotten childhood experiences can affect buying behaviour, including that of hard-nosed US industrial buyers (see 'Mommy's never coming back', page 144). Some theories of motivation are discussed further in this chapter ('Motivation', page 107).

In the UK many organizations use in-depth research, eg Guinness carries out in-depth research to tap into drinkers' deeply ingrained feelings about the product. Individuals are asked to express their (often unconscious) feelings through clay modelling, picture completion and cartoon completion techniques. This kind of research has revealed that people associate natural goodness and quasi-mystical qualities with the brand. The section 'Motivation' (page 107) looks at in-depth feelings.

The toothpaste test

Why do you buy toothpaste? 'To keep teeth clean.' 'To stop cavities and visits to dentist.' 'To keep a full set of beautiful shining teeth.' Some people will admit that 'it is habit' or that 'my parents taught me always to clean my teeth'. All of these answers suggest different benefits that different groups or segments want from their toothpaste, and so the toothpaste suppliers oblige by positioning certain brands as those that deliver a particular benefit. But when do you brush your teeth? First thing in the morning? If people were serious about seeking the benefits they would carry a small portable brush and use it after each meal. Why do most people brush first thing in the morning? To avoid bad breath (which destroys one's confidence). Yet many people do not like admitting it. The real reason is often hidden beneath the surface reasons.

Bloatware – emotional wins over rational

Forty-five per cent of software features are never used, 19 per cent are rarely used, and 16 per cent are sometimes used, so some software suppliers launched 'liteware' with fewer functions and lower prices. It flopped. Why? Because people didn't want to be without features that other people had – so bloatware prevails.

Brain science

There is no doubt that conscious reasoning accounts for only a small part of our thinking. David Penn (2005) talks about how brain science helps to throw some light on the dark depths of emotion and consciousness:

> By reuniting psychology with philosophy and biology, it shifts the scientific focus back onto the mysteries of consciousness and emotion. Increasingly, we've come to understand that unlocking the mystery of consciousness actually depends on figuring out the unconscious functions of the brain. Not Freud's unconscious – a repository for repressed memories – but rather the many things the brain does that are not available to consciousness. Unconscious processes include most of what the brain does – we can often be aware of what we're doing when these things happen, but much of the time consciousness is informed after the fact through the cognitive unconscious. The area that's generating hottest debate is emotion, and its operation through the so-called emotional unconscious, and it's here that the fusion of biology and psychology is changing the whole way we understand human behaviour. The unconscious explains most of what we feel, think and do. Conscious reasoning accounts for only a small part of our 'thinking'.

Penn warns of the dangers of overemphasizing the importance of brand awareness when he says: 'It is clear that if we only base an assessment of effectiveness [advertising effectiveness] on conscious recall, we potentially miss out on those [customers] who are positively affected yet have no conscious recall of having seen it [an ad or a product].'

Penn highlights the four big ideas in brain science:

1 Unconscious processes (either cognitive or emotional) account for most of what we think, feel and do.

2 Conscious reasoning may account for only a small part of our 'thinking', with most taking place in the cognitive unconscious.

3 Emotion precedes our conscious feelings and works in tandem with rational thinking to help us make (better) decisions.

4 The interconnectedness of the thinking and feeling parts of the brain facilitates the interaction of rationality and emotion in decision making.

Each one of these has fundamental implications for marketing and research. Marketers must tread with caution and measure the emotional aspects – some of which are often unconscious emotional connections. Now consider the different types of buying situations in which customers have different approaches to choosing products and services.

Goethe and the magic marketing formula

'Behaviour is a mirror in which everyone displays his own image.'

Goethe, *Elective Affinities*, 1809 (quoted in Schifman and Kaunk, 1991)

Marketers sometimes say 'We are what we shop.'

Effectively, marketers have to know their customers better than the customers know themselves. This involves deep customer insights, sometimes generated by intense psychoanalysis, sometimes by employing anthropologists and sometimes by cleverly looking at customers through several lenses to get a deeper insight. Here is how Tesco varies its research techniques to generate customer insights that they then apply to their marketing immediately. Tesco is reported to have spent 20 years watching the US market before launching its Fresh & Easy chain. A team of 20 executives was dispatched to the United States to carry out in-depth research and to visit every rival. The company hired a team of anthropologists to live with consumers for two weeks and analyse what they bought and why. It also built a mock store and asked selected customers to try it. Tesco discovered that US consumers were less bothered by the selection of wines on offer, but wanted better-quality meat than UK consumers (Jones, 2008). In the UK, Tesco combined loyalty card data on what customers were buying at Tesco with survey research on what customers were not buying. This revealed that, 'in some formats, young mothers bought fewer baby products in its stores because they trusted pharmacies more. So Tesco launched Baby Club to provide expert advice and targeted coupons. Its share of baby product sales in the UK grew from 16% to 24% over 3 years' (Forsyth, Galante and Guild, 2006). The better marketers look at customers through a variety of lenses. Take Walmart in the United States: it integrates shopper research, point-of-sale data, and demographic analysis to find out who its customers are, ie what the profile of their local customers is.

Tesco varies the individual store's format to reflect the needs of its local customers (the magic marketing formula). For example, 'stores located near large concentrations of affluent male professionals, for example, offer more high end home theatre equipment, specialized financing and same day delivery while stores closer to soccer moms feature softer colours, personal shopping assistants, and kids oriented technology sections. Sales surged by 7 per cent and gross profit by 50 basis points' (Forsyth, Galante and Guild, 2006). So knowing your customers really does pay dividends.

> ### Know your customers intimately – their hopes, dreams, fears and aspirations
>
> 'The job now is to be so intimate with consumers, so empathetic with their hopes and their dreams, their aspirations and their fears that we can develop revelations which we then put into creative departments and from great revelations awesome ideas will come, eg T-Mobile UK – revelation – life is for sharing, the power of tribes, the power of communities, and the power of all this social stuff.'
>
> Roberts (2009b)
>
> See the full case study in Chapter 13.

How do they buy?

Types of buying situation

The amount of time and effort that a buyer is prepared to put into any particular purchase depends on the level of expenditure, the frequency of purchase and the perceived risk involved. Relatively larger expenditure usually warrants greater deliberation during the search and evaluation phases. In consumer markets this buying process is classified as 'extensive problem solving' (EPS) if the buyer has no previous product experience and the purchase is infrequent, expensive and/or risky. The situation is different where the buyer has some knowledge and experience of, and familiarity with, a particular product or service. This is called 'limited problem solving' (LPS). In the case of strong brand loyalty for a habitually purchased product, routinized response behaviour (RRB) can be identified by the repeat brand purchasing of convenience products like baked beans. The buyer chooses quickly and has a low involvement with the purchase. EPS requires high involvement from the buyer, which means that the buyer spends time and effort before actually deciding to buy a particular product or brand. This can be complicated by further advisers and influencers who form part of the decision-making unit. LPS requires lower levels of involvement than EPS but more than RRB.

Industrial buying is even more clearly influenced by decision-making units, particularly when the purchase is considered large, infrequent or risky. As in consumer buying, types of purchase situation also vary in industrial markets. A 'new task' buying situation means what it says – the organization has no experience of the product or service and is buying it for the first time. A 'modified rebuy' situation is where the industrial buyer has some experience of the product or service, while a 'straight rebuy' is where the buyer, or purchasing department, buys on a regular basis.

New currencies required: privacy, trust and time

In the online world, privacy, trust and time are new currencies that have a very high value in customers' minds. Customers are cautious about giving up private information. They are also busy and don't like wasting time (if you can save your customers time, they will like you even more). They expect their privacy to be protected (hence privacy statements are *de rigueur* for every website). Equally, customers resent being asked for too much information or being asked for information when they haven't yet established any relationship – so much so that many customers just lie when filling in online forms.

Trust is increasingly important, as online customers live in a dangerous environment of privacy invasion and identity theft. Surprisingly many customers trust a website more than a person. People trust well-known and well-respected brands. Why else would customers give an unknown American their credit card details, home address and money? Trust. In the UK, several major brands score higher in trust than the church and the police. Well-managed brands are trusted as long as their promise is never broken. How does it feel when a website remembers your name? And when it remembers your preferences? It seems customers are happy to have unconscious relationships with brands, robots and machines as well as people. Enlightened companies remember information for customers, not just about them. This builds trust in the relationship. Ask: what is a website that might attract a visitor to come back a second time and, ultimately, regularly revisit the site and develop a relationship? Remember, the second visit is the start of the relationship.

Models of buyer behaviour

There are many different models that attempt to model the buyer's behaviour. Figure 4.1 shows how a buyer in either an EPS or an LPS situation moves through the purchasing cycle or purchasing continuum. The basic model can be borrowed and used in industrial markets also. It highlights some of the stages through which a potential buyer passes. Sources and channels of information plus buying criteria can also be identified, which in turn provide a checklist for the marketing plan, whether online, offline or integrated.

The buying process

We can demonstrate this simple buying model by considering, say, the purchase of a new compact disc player. Somewhere, somebody or something makes the customer aware that he or she needs an in-home theatre system. This is known as problem recognition, which is followed by 'information search'. This may involve ads and editorial in magazines, visits to stores, discussion among friends, etc. Next comes evaluation. Leaflets, catalogues, ads and discussions are amassed, and a set of criteria is further refined. This may include size, shape, colour, delivery, guarantee, etc. Performance is really difficult to assess, since few of us can read sound graphs, let alone decipher a good sound in a shop full of other speakers. However, customers do check other people's opinions online before buying almost any type of product or service today. Customer comments on the official site and on other sites influence customers. Finally, a decision is made to choose a particular model. It isn't over yet. The chosen brand may be out of stock (in which case the communications mix has worked but the marketing mix has failed, since distribution has not got the product on the shelf). Another brand is eventually purchased.

This is when waves of worry, doubt or 'post-purchase dissonance' arise. This may be addressed by reassuring the buyer (with a congratulatory note, additional advertising, after-sales service and, most of all, a product or service that lives up to the promise made in the advertising). And, if the product matches the promise, then both repeat business and word-of-mouth referrals are more likely to occur over the longer run.

The simple buying model shown in Figure 4.1 serves as a useful checklist to see whether you are filling in all the communication gaps in the buying process. Interestingly, many websites now use this as a checklist to ensure that the site helps different customers to move through different stages of their

FIGURE 4.1   A simple model of the buying process for a high-involvement purchase

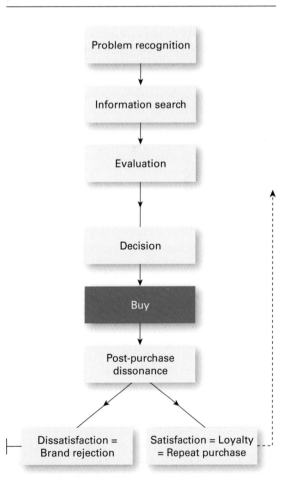

buying process. The model should not be hierarchical, since in reality there are loops, eg between information and evaluation, as the buyer learns about new criteria not previously considered.

This model is more relevant for a high-involvement purchase, whether extensive problem solving (consumer) or new task (industrial). A routinized response situation, like buying a beer, is low-involvement, and therefore it would not involve any lengthy decision-making process.

Low-involvement purchases can sometimes appear to be thoughtless (impulsive) responses (purchases) to stimuli (point-of-sale displays or well-designed packs). If attention can be grabbed, then some brands can be bought, apparently, without much considered thought processing. Basically, if you see the brand, you try it, and if you like it you rebuy it. Some advertising aims to remind customers and reinforce the benefits of the brand.

Advertising can also reassure existing customers that they have bought the right brand. This defensive advertising (defending market share) reduces any post-purchase dissonance (or worries) and also keeps the brand on the buyer's shopping list (or repertoire of brands).

In contrast with attitudes towards high-involvement purchases, attitudes towards low-involvement brands can be formed after the brand experience and not before. In the more considered, high-involvement purchases attitudes are formed after awareness but before any purchasing behaviour actually occurs. The attitude may subsequently be reinforced by, first, the real experience of buying and using the brand and, second, any subsequent advertising or word-of-mouth communications.

Ehrenberg's 1974 awareness trial reinforcement (ATR) model suggested that consumers become aware of a brand, try it (buy it) and then are exposed to reinforcement by advertising (or even the actual brand experience).

Trial can occur many months after an advertisement has created awareness. Advertising here is also seen as defensive, in so far as it reassures existing buyers that they have made the right choice, as opposed to advertising that might make them run out and buy the advertised brand immediately. Ehrenberg acknowledges that some advertising actually does prompt (or 'nudge') buyers to buy, as demonstrated with his more explicit 1997 awareness trial reinforcement plus occasional nudging (ATR + N) model. Ehrenberg's specific views differ

FIGURE 4.2   The ATR model

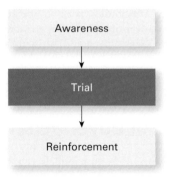

from many other approaches highlighted in this chapter, yet his research findings are used by top blue-chip companies around the world.

Many other academics believe that different buying situations (high- and low-involvement) require different thought processes and timescales. Even within the same product sector, different processes can occur. Take grocery shopping. Australian academics Rossiter and Percy (1996) have identified differences in thought processes within the grocery sector. They suggest that most grocery brands (65 per cent) need recognition at the point of purchase, since buyers tend to see the brand first and then realize they want it. Less than 10 seconds elapse between recognition and putting the product into the trolley. The other 35 per cent of groceries are chosen in advance, so brand awareness (before purchase) is important for these.

It does not stop there. There are more differences depending on whether the purchase is a relief purchase (to solve a problem such as dirty clothes) or a reward purchase (to provide gratification, like ice cream). The relief purchases require a more rational approach and the reward purchases a more emotional approach. So each market and each brand needs to be carefully analysed. Robert Shaw (1997/98) points out that 'many different measures such as brand knowledge, esteem, relevance or perceived quality may need to be monitored'. Any marketing manager, whether industrial or consumer, product or service, has constantly to watch the market, its segments and how it is fragmenting.

Marketers need to understand their customers' buying process, whether online, offline or a mixture of both. Dulux paints found that its brand share is

11 per cent higher when customers choose their paint colour at home rather than in-store. But 75 per cent of colour decisions are made in the store. It therefore tried to lock people into a Dulux purchase before they visit a shop by creating a value-added online experience whereby users can decorate a virtual room (with colour coordination suggestions) and receive free swatches delivered free to their home with directions to their nearest Dulux retailer.

Now you have it, now you don't – Oasis CD

The music band Oasis fully understand their customers' buying process and their desire to hear the songs before they are officially released. So, to satisfy the hunger for previews and reduce the number of illegal downloads from the internet, Oasis released four trial tracks seven days prior to the release of their *Heathen Chemistry* CD. The tracks were offered to readers of the *Sunday Times* as a free cover-mounted CD that was encrypted so it could only be played four times. After that, the CD was automatically wiped and the user was directed to HMV.co.uk to buy the album. In addition, HMV donated 50p (for each CD sold) to the Prince's Trust charity.

Response hierarchy models

Although the ultimate objective for most marketing managers is to build repeat purchases from profitable customers, there are many stages between creating problem recognition or need arousal and purchase (as shown in Figure 4.1). The communication models in Figure 4.3 show what are thought to be the sequence of mental stages through which buyers pass on their journey towards a purchase.

These models are sometimes called 'message models' or 'response hierarchy models', since they help to prioritize the communication objectives by determining whether a cognitive, affective or behavioural response is required, ie whether the organization wants to create awareness in the target audience's mind, or to change an attitude, or to act in some way (buy, vote, participate, etc). (See 'Attitudes' on page 110 for a more detailed explanation of the cognitive, affective and behavioural/conative elements of an attitude.) Message models are helpful but not conclusive, since 1) not all buyers go through all stages, 2) the stages do not necessarily occur in a hierarchical sequence, and 3) impulse purchases contract the process.

Although expanding repeat purchase (loyal behaviour) from profitable customers is the ultimate marketing goal, a PR campaign, advertisement or sales promotion may have a tactical objective focusing on a particular stage in the above models, eg increasing awareness, changing an attitude or generating trial. In fact, Hofacker's (2001) online information processing model shows how online messages from banner ads and websites are processed (see Appendix 4.1 for more detail).

These hierarchical communication models identify the stages through which buyers generally pass. An understanding of these stages helps to plan appropriate marketing communications. DAGMAR (defining advertising goals for measuring advertising results) was created to encourage measurable objectives for each stage of the communications continuum.

Some of the stages can sometimes occur simultaneously and/or instantaneously, as in the case of an impulse purchase. Buyers can also avoid moving in a straight line or hierarchy of stages when making a more considered purchase (extended problem solving). For example, during the evaluation stage a potential buyer may go back to the information stage to obtain more information before making a decision to buy. Each hierarchical model really requires a loop from the 'last' stage up to the first stage – to show that the sale (action) is not the end stage, but rather the beginning of an ongoing dialogue that nurtures a relationship and a report buying process.

Ideally, these models should allow for these and other loops caused by 'message decay' (or forgetting), changes in attitudes, competitive distractions, etc. The models also ignore the mind's 'intervening variables', some of which are identified in both the 'personal-variable models' of Fishbein (1975) and the 'complex models' of Howard and Sheth (1969) and Engel, Blackwell and Kollatt (1978). The complex models, do, in fact, allow for both loops and the complexities of the intervening variables (see page 102).

Three types of model, 'black-box', 'personal-variable' and 'complex', will now be considered

FIGURE 4.3   Response hierarchy models

Stage	AIDA	Lavidge & Steiner	Adoption	DAGMAR	Howard & Sheth (excerpt)	Online information processing
						Exposure ↓
				Unawareness ↓	Attention	Attention
		Awareness ↓	Awareness	Awareness		
Cognitive	Attention ↓					
		Knowledge ↓	↓			
				Comprehension	Comprehension	Comprehension and perception
	Interest ↓	Liking ↓	Interest ↓	↓	↓	↓
Affective		Preference ↓	↓			
	Desire ↓	Conviction ↓	Evaluation ↓	Conviction ↓	Attitude ↓	Yielding and acceptance ↓
			Trial ↓		Intention ↓	
Behaviour	Action	Purchase	Adoption	Action	Purchase	Retention
	E K Strong	L & S	E M Rogers	R H Colley	H & S*	Hofacker
	(1925)	(1961)	(1961)	(1961)	(1969)	(2001)

*The Howard and Sheth excerpt is taken from the full model shown on page 102

briefly. Black-box models consider external variables that act as stimuli (such as price, shops, merchandise, advertisements, promotions and the social environment, including families and friends) and responses such as sales. Personal-variable models focus on some of the internal psychological variables such as attitudes and beliefs. The complex models attempt to include both the internal and the external variables in one grand model. To some this proves impossible. As Gordon Foxall (1992) pointed out, 'No one model can capture human nature in its entirety; nor can a handful of theoretical perspectives embrace the scope of human interaction.'

Black-box models

The behaviourist school of psychology concentrates on how people respond to stimuli. It is not concerned with the complex range of internal and external factors that affect the behaviour. The complexities of the mind are left locked up in a 'black box'. The resulting stimulus–response models ignore the complexities of the mind (including the intervening variables such as perception, motivation, attitudes, etc) and focus on the input or stimulus, eg advertising, and the output, eg purchase behaviour. A classical approach to stimulus–response models is

FIGURE 4.4   Black-box model

FIGURE 4.5   An enlarged black-box model

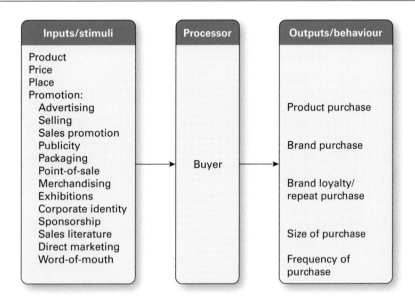

considered in 'Learning' on page 105. Figure 4.4 shows a black-box model.

As Williams (1989) says: 'Black box models treat the individual and his physiological and psychological make-up as an impenetrable black box.' Only the inputs and outputs are measured. Any internal mental processes (the intervening processes) that cannot be measured are ignored. The model in Figure 4.5 shows some examples of 'input' and 'output'.

The black-box approach considers only the inputs and outputs. Careful analysis under controlled tests (using reasonably sophisticated computer models) can reveal the optimum price, the optimum level of advertising and so on.

Personal-variable models

These models take a glimpse inside the black box of the mind. The models only involve a few personal variables such as beliefs, attitudes and intentions. These kinds of model are sometimes used within more complex models. Three types of personal-variable

models, 'linear additive', 'threshold' and 'trade-off', are briefly considered below.

Linear additive models

Linear additive models like that of Fishbein are based on the number of attributes a particular product or service has, multiplied by the score each attribute is perceived to have, multiplied by the weighting which each attribute is deemed to have. This model opens up attitudes by indicating which attributes are considered to be important to the customer and how each attribute is scored by the customer. Attitudes are not always translated into purchasing behaviour. Even intentions are not always translated into action. Nevertheless, marketing strategies can be built around changing beliefs about attributes, and altering their evaluation or scores.

Threshold models

Most purchases have cut-off points or thresholds beyond which the buyer will not venture. It may be

FIGURE 4.6   A simplified version of Howard and Sheth's model

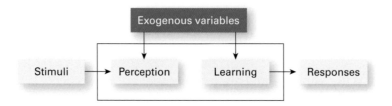

FIGURE 4.7   The complete Howard and Sheth model

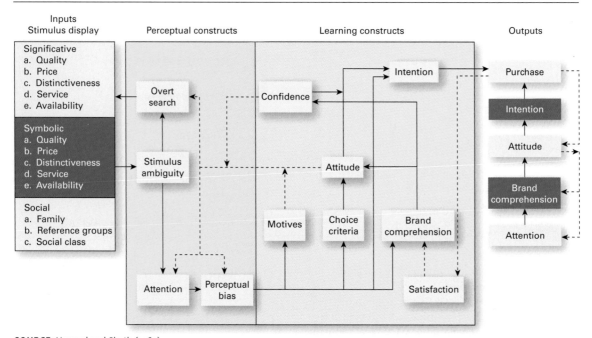

SOURCE: Howard and Sheth (1969)
© Copyright (1969) John Wiley & Sons. Reprinted by permission of John Wiley & Sons Inc

price or some particular feature that a product or service must have (or must not have in the case of some environmentally damaging ingredients) if it is to be considered at all. Here, the buyer has a selection process that screens and accepts those products or services within the threshold for either further analysis or immediate purchase. Those beyond the threshold are rejected and will not be considered any further.

Trade-off models

Buyers generally have a wide array of choices, many with different types and amounts of attributes. A trade-off occurs when the buyer accepts a product

that is lacking in one attribute but strong in another. A sort of compensatory mechanism emerges. When someone is buying a car, engine size and price can be traded off against each other, eg a bigger engine means a worse price (higher price). A number of combinations of price and engine size can be researched to find the value or 'utility' for different prices and engine sizes.

Complex models

The cognitive school attempts to open the lid and look inside the mind's black box. Here more complex buying models, like that of Howard and Sheth

(1969), try to incorporate into the hierarchical communication models the intervening variables of perception, motivation, learning, memory, attitudes, beliefs, group influence, etc – in fact, almost everything inside the mind.

Howard and Sheth

A simplified version of Howard and Sheth's complex model divides the black box into perceptual constructs and learning constructs, as shown in Figure 4.6. The exogenous variables are external to this model and include personality traits, social class, financial status, the social/organizational setting and even the importance of the purchase to the individual.

The complete complex model in Figure 4.7 includes perception, learning, attitudes and motivation. Stimulus ambiguity implies inadequate information to make a decision. Perceptual bias (see 'Perception' below) basically means that there is a certain amount of distortion in the way that an individual perceives a stimulus.

This complex model has been criticized for lacking a clear definition of the relationships between some of the variables and for a lack of distinction between the endogenous variables (within the model) and exogenous variables (external to the model). The model is, for many readers, difficult to understand and, for many practitioners, impossible to use. Nevertheless it does provide a useful insight into the possible workings of the mind.

The remainder of this chapter looks at some of the influencing variables such as perception, learning, motivation, values, attitudes and lifestyles, and considers how an understanding of them helps to make more effective marketing communications.

The intervening psychological variables

Perception

Perception means the way stimuli, such as commercial messages, advertisements, packaging, shops, uniforms, etc, are interpreted. Messages and images are not always perceived in the manner intended by the advertiser. As Chisnall (1985) says: 'Our perceptual system has a tendency to organize, modify and distort information reaching it.' Perception is selective. We see what we want to see.

Here's a simple test. Ask smokers to recall exactly what the health warning says on the side of their packet of cigarettes. Few will be able to tell you the exact words. This is because we all selectively screen out messages or stimuli that may cause discomfort, tension or 'cognitive dissonance'. Imagine that smokers allow the message (warning) to be perceived. This will cause discomfort every time a cigarette is taken, since the box will give the smokers an unpleasant message. In order to reduce this tension, the smokers have two options: 1) change behaviour (stop smoking) or 2) screen out the message and continue the behaviour (smoking).

Many stimuli are screened out by the perceptual system, which, it is estimated, is hit by between 500 and 1,500 different advertisements a day. The example in the box shows how preferences and motivations affect perception.

The infamous Brian O'Driscoll incident

The captain, and some say potential match winner, of the British and Irish Lions rugby team, Brian O'Driscoll, was spear-tackled by two players, off the ball, in the first minute of the first test match in New Zealand. O'Driscoll's shoulder was shattered and his test series over. He was lucky not to have broken his neck, as a spear tackle involves lifting and throwing a player head first to the ground. It can result in a broken neck. It is extremely dangerous and totally illegal. The Lions' manager, Sir Clive Woodward, called for a citing and disciplinary action. It never happened. Here's the interesting bit about perceptions. The author interviewed over 100 New Zealand fans, and every one of them saw no problem with the incident. Ask Lions fans, and every one will say it was an absolute disgrace. Everyone saw the same thing, but the two groups saw (perceived) something different. Perception is selective and biased by motivation.

So perceptions are biased by our underlying motivations. Take this example from Hong Kong, where in 1997 China regained control over this former

British colony. The committee responsible for celebrating the resumption of Chinese sovereignty chose the white dolphin as its symbol. A British newspaper, the *Independent*, pointed out that this was a species threatened with extinction in Chinese waters. The committee also chose to place it alongside the new symbol for the future special administrative region of Hong Kong, the Bauhinia flower, which, reported the newspaper, was a sterile hybrid that produces no seed. The newspaper perceived Hong Kong to be marching into the future under the symbols of an endangered species and sterility. The Hong Kong committee saw the friendly dolphin as appealing to everybody, especially children: 'Its leaping movement symbolizes Hong Kong's vibrancy.' They differed vastly even over the same symbol or stimulus.

Perceptions can vary even within the same region. A UK TV advertisement for Unilever's Persil washing powder showed a Dalmatian shaking off its black spots, a white horse breaking away from black horses and a skater dressed in white beating other skaters dressed in black. The advertisement was perceived by some as being racist. Despite the advertisements having been tested with Afro-Caribbean women before going on air, the Independent Television Commission (ITC) received 32 complaints.

Before perception occurs, attention has to be gained by, say, the advertiser. As Williams (1989) says, interests, needs and motives determine 'not only what will arouse attention, but also what will hold it'. For example, advertisements for a new house are ignored by the mass population. But there is a sector of the population that is actively looking for a house. This sector has a need for a new house, and it is therefore receptive to any of these advertisements. Individuals from this sector positively select information relevant to their needs. This is known as 'selective attention'.

There are also certain physical properties that increase the likelihood of a message gaining attention: intensity and size; position; sound; colour; contrast; and movement (eyes are involuntarily attracted to movement because of the body's instinctive defence mechanism). Given that an individual's attention is constantly called upon by new stimuli, repetition can enhance the likelihood of a message getting through. Novelty can also be used to jar expectations and grab attention.

Perceived differences in brands are not necessarily dependent on real product differences (in either

function or form). As Chisnall (1985) says, 'Consumers evaluate products against the background of their experiences, expectations and associations. Perception is seldom an objective, scientific assessment of the comparative values of competing brands.'

> ## Colour affects our perception
>
> 'Red is a colour that makes food smell better.'
>   Kanner (1989)

Perceptions are delicate and need to be managed carefully. Take Google: it is loved by everyone, but could easily be feared by all if it was perceived to be too powerful (as perhaps Microsoft experienced). Kennedy (2009) suggested: 'One of the main hurdles Google faces in its quest to manage the world's information, becoming a virtual library of books, movies, music, maps, tools, news, communication even our very voices, is that it also becomes a figure of suspicion. How safe is that information, are they reading our every email, do they know too much about us?' Google CEO Eric Schmidt admits these are real fears, and he says:

> Trust means there is a sacred line the company must never cross. In fact, it's greatest strength is, in truth, its Achilles heel. If it crosses that line it can never go back. Privacy and trust are sacrosanct. There's a lot of things we could do that would upset our users so there's a line you can't cross. We try very hard to stay very much on the side of the consumer (Manyika, 2008).

Even if the company stays on the right side of the line, it still has to manage customer perceptions very carefully.

An understanding of the way our perceptual system organizes information has helped some brand advertisers to exploit perceptual systems through an understanding of gestalt psychology. Gestalt means 'total figuration'. One of the four basic perceptual organizing techniques from the gestalt school is 'closure'. Individuals strive to make sense of incomplete messages by filling in the gaps or shaping the image so that it can fit comfortably into their cognitive set (or set of knowledge). Marlboro's 'MARL' advertisements and Kit-Kat's 'Kit' advertisements play on the need to fill in these gaps. This may happen so fast that viewers are not aware of what is going on inside their heads. Effectively, the mind momentarily becomes the medium, since the complete image is visible only inside the head, while the external advertisement shows the incomplete image. In a sense, a giant billboard inside the forehead is switched on by an incomplete stimulus. The natural perceptual tendency towards 'closure' completes the advertisement's image inside the audience's mind. Perception is also inextricably linked with past experiences, motivation, beliefs, attitudes and the ability to learn.

Everybody is scared

'Everybody is scared; everybody is insecure; everybody is nervous. Nobody knows what's coming next. Nobody. So people are looking for intimacy. They're looking for brands that understand them. They're looking for services that deliver for them in their new environment. I think most brands and most companies are operating in a time lag and a time warp. Consumers are way ahead of us. Their insecurities are much more to the surface... The challenge is to get more intimate with her fears, her needs, her desires. Let's face it: she needs to enjoy her life today – because there's not a lot of it coming her way. So she will still use brands. She will still find some pleasure in shopping. What we've got to do is provide that pleasure, provide that joy, that delight so that we can delight her in her new environment through being very intimate in her current situation.'

Kevin Roberts, CEO, Saatchi & Saatchi Worldwide (2009c)

Learning

Marketers obviously want customers to learn about, first, the existence of their brand or company and, second, its merits. A knowledge of the learning process is therefore useful in understanding how customers acquire, store and retrieve messages about products, brands and companies. How are attitudes about companies, products and brands developed (or learnt)? Advertising and sales promotions can

help customers learn in different ways (see 'classical conditioning' and 'operant conditioning' in 'Connectionist learning theories' below). In addition, how many times (frequency) should an advertisement be shown before it is remembered or, alternatively, before it causes irritation? Should it be repeated regularly once a week for a year (a 'drip' strategy) or concentrated into 12 times a week for four weeks only (a 'burst' strategy)? Differing levels of intelligence, memory capacity, motivations, perceptual systems, associations and rewards (reinforcement) affect the learning process.

The party

When introduced to someone at a party, do you ever forget the person's name? An inability to learn and remember names can create embarrassment. Perhaps the host should increase the frequency of the branding process by repeating the individual's name three times during the introduction? Or would this be irritating? Perhaps it would be better if the individual's name was inserted in a 'drip' strategy rather than a 'burst' strategy, ie occasionally the host would pass by, casually drop the individual's name into the conversation and move on.

Connectionist learning theories

Simple connectionist theory suggests that associations can be made between messages, or stimuli, and responses, hence the term 'stimulus–response model'. In the late 1890s the Russian physiologist Ivan Pavlov demonstrated how 'classical conditioning', or involuntary conditioning, worked on dogs. By regularly hearing the ringing of a bell before being presented with food, a dog learnt to associate (or connect) the bell with food. After a period of conditioning the dog would salivate (respond) upon hearing the bell (stimulus) without any food arriving. As Williams (1989) says, 'It is the idea of association that underlines the concept of branding in modern marketing.' Constant repetition can build associations between needs, products and brands, eg if you are thinking of beans, think Heinz: 'Beanz Meanz Heinz'. Associations can also be built by linking celebrities with the brand. For example,

Coca-Cola GB has signed the Hollywood actress Kim Basinger as part of a three-year plan to 'link Diet Coke with movies and glamour'.

Humans conditioned by music learning

'High tempo music may be appropriate in fast food restaurants because it encourages faster knife and fork activity, leading to quicker table turnover. Customers buy more expensive wines in a retail environment playing classical music rather than pop music. French wine significantly outsold German wine in a store when stereotypical French accordion music was played. Marketers frequently match the volume of music in different time zones of their store to the age band of the target market... younger shoppers spend more in a retail environment playing loud music, while shoppers aged 50 and over spend more in an environment with quiet background music.'

Oakes (2008)

'London Underground started piping "uncool" classical music in the booking hall of tube stations in December 2005 to deter youths from loitering, resulting in a 33 per cent drop in abuse against staff.'

Marketer (2010)

'Operant conditioning', on the other hand, is voluntary in so far as the participant actively searches for solutions. The Skinner box was devised by Dr Skinner in the United States during the 1930s. By placing a hungry rat in a box where food only arrived once the rat pressed a lever, Skinner observed that the rat would search, investigate and, eventually, press the lever accidentally. Food then arrived. Over a period of time the rat, when aroused by the hunger motive, learned to press the lever for food. An association or connection was made between the lever pressing and the drive to satisfy the hunger need. This approach to building associations through voluntary participation suggests that sales promotions can actively invite the buyer to participate, be rewarded, and eventually connect a particular product or service with a particular stimulated need.

Stimulus–response

Connectionist theories of learning highlight the importance of, first, timing and, second, frequency of marketing communications. The establishment of a connection or association between a stimulus and a response is fundamental to the conditioning process. Advertising jingles, pictures and even smells are some of the stimuli that can arouse emotional or behavioural responses. Some people still feel good when they hear the Coca-Cola jingle 'I'd like to teach the world to sing...'; others are aroused and excited when they hear the sound of a sports commentator's voice with crowd sound effects in the background. Ice cream van jingles arouse children. McDonald's large, highly visible yellow 'M' logo can trigger a response, particularly if an individual is involved in goal-oriented behaviour (is hungry and is ready to consider eating food). Could this yellow logo be the equivalent of Pavlov's bell? Do some humans salivate just at the sight of the logo?

Cyber-logo makes customers salivate

'Seeing your logo on the net made me hungry' (feedback from a McDonald's website visitor, demonstrating classical conditioning).

Smith, Berry and Pulford (1999)

Certainly the release of certain aromas can stimulate immediate responses. For example, as customers leave a pub and walk down the street they are often greeted by the wafting smell of frying chips, which can stimulate or arouse the need for food, and lead to an immediate purchase.

Lunn Poly created a full sensory holiday environment in its stores using a coconut aroma, fresh coffee in the Parisian-style café area, holiday music, travel images and a variety of film footage.

Reinforcement and reward enhance the learning process. In other words, good-quality products and services reward the buyer every time. This consistent level of quality reinforces the brand's positive relationship with the buyer. On the other hand, if the quality is poor, there is no reward (the response does not satisfy the need), and the response (to buy a particular brand or visit a particular shop) will not be repeated.

Positive reinforcement helps the learning process (or helps the buyer to remember the brand or shop). It is possible to 'unlearn' or forget ('message decay'), so many advertisers seek to remind customers of their products, their names and their benefits. Some advertisements seek to remind buyers what a good choice they have already made by frequently repeating messages. The connectionist approach ignores all the other complex and influential variables involved in learning and, ultimately, buying. Arguably, it oversimplifies a complex process.

Packaging design can also act as a cue to arouse momentarily the happy images conveyed in the previously seen and unconsciously stored advertising images. This is where a 'pack shot' of the product and pack in the advertisement (usually at the end) aids recall of the brand, the advertisement and its image when the consumer is shopping or just browsing along shelves full of different brands.

All brand managers would like to have their brand chosen automatically every time. Some brands achieve this through an unconsciously learned response. How? By building a presence through frequency of advertising and maximum shelf facings (amount of units displayed on shelves – see Chapter 19) and, most importantly, by supplying an appropriate level of reinforcement (an appropriate level of quality in the product or service itself). Chapter 3 emphasizes the importance of quality in the long-term repeat-buying success strategies of today and tomorrow.

Cognitive learning

Cognitive learning focuses on what happens in between the stimulus and the response. It embraces the intervening mental processes.

Insight, meaning, perception, knowledge and problem solving are all considered relevant concepts. Cognitive learning is not dependent on trial and error. It depends on an ability to think, sometimes conceptually, and to perceive relationships and 'what if' scenarios. It is not dependent on an immediate reward to reinforce the learning process; in fact, 'latent learning' occurs in the absence of reward and without any immediate action. Of course, an individual has to be suitably motivated to achieve this kind of learning. The next intervening variable – motivation – will now be considered.

China learns about Coca-Cola, Pepsi and Starbucks

Just as they helped the Europeans to learn to eat with their hands (McDonald's) and drink ice-cold beer (Budweiser), mostly through classical advertising, Coca-Cola, Pepsi and Starbucks are conditioning a massive market to learn a new way of satisfying their needs, especially young Chinese. These brands are turning a tide in tastes. Tea houses in China already are being replaced by coffee houses and Starbucks.

Motivation

Motivation is defined as the drive to satisfy a need. Some motives are socially learnt (eg wanting to get married), and others are instinctive (eg wanting to eat when hungry). Sigmund Freud suggested that an individual is motivated by conscious and unconscious forces. Many motives are unconscious but active in that they influence everyday buying behaviour. Brands carry covert messages that are fleetingly understood at a subconscious level. As the Market Research Society said in its 1996 conference paper, 'It is often this deeper meaning which is what is exchanged for money. These deep underlying feelings are often the real reason why people buy products or services.'

Freud's psychoanalytical approach broke the personality into the id (instinctive drives and urges, eg to eat food or grab food), the ego (the social learning process that allows the individual to interact with the environment, eg to ask politely for food or pay for food) and the superego, which provides a conscience or ethical/moral referee between the id and the ego. Freud suggested that all actions are the results of antecedent conditions (see how childhood experiences might affect industrial buying behaviour some 30 or 40 years later in 'Mommy's never coming back', page 144). Occasionally these unconscious stirrings manifest themselves in dreams, responses to ambiguous stimuli and slips of the tongue (Freudian slips).

Clinical psychology uses thematic apperception tests, Rorschach tests and word association tests to help it to analyse the underlying and sometimes unconscious personality traits and motivations of an individual. In-depth market researchers (qualitative researchers) use metaphors, picture completion and montages in an attempt to throw the interviewee's ego off guard and dip into the real underlying feelings that interviewees find difficult both to become aware of and to express in an articulate manner.

In the 1950s, Vance Packard was concerned about how in-depth researchers like Ernest Dichter were attempting to extract buyers' unconscious feelings, aspirations and motivations, which were then subtly reflected through advertising imagery, which in turn manipulated buyers unconsciously. Although discredited by some and criticized by others, Dichter's *Handbook of Consumer Motivations* (1964) is an extremely thought-provoking and entertaining read.

Here are some other well-known, in-depth research findings from the 1950s that supposedly reveal the deep underlying motivations that drive certain forms of behaviour, including buying behaviour:

- A woman is very serious when she bakes a cake, because unconsciously she is going through the act of birth.

- Soon after the trial period, housewives who used a new improved cake mix (no egg needed, just add water) stopped buying it. The new improved cake mix provoked a sense of guilt, as the cooking role of the housewife was reduced.

- A man buys a convertible car as a substitute mistress.

- Smoking represents an infantile pleasure of sucking.

- Men want their cigars to be odoriferous in order to prove that they (the men) are masculine.

- Shaving for some men is the daily act of cutting off this symbol of manliness (stubble). It is therefore a kind of daily castration.

This is all arguably outdated now. Humans are rational animals and are not concerned with such psychoanalytic interpretations of everyday, ordinary and, supposedly, common-sense behaviour. Consider 'A close shave?' opposite.

A close shave?

There is a simple test that has been used in lectures with different groups. A question is posed, with a request for male respondents only. The question is 'How many of you find shaving a hassle?' Usually a unanimous show of hands emerges. 'How many of you would like to be able to dispense with the aggravation of shaving?' Slightly fewer hands emerge. 'Well, here is a cream that will solve your problem. This cream closes your hair follicles so that hair will never grow there again. It is medically approved and cleared for a market launch next year. Who would like to try some right now?' All the hands are gone. The question 'Why not?' is usually answered faintly with 'Freedom to choose to have a beard later in life' and so on. Or is there something deeper here? Dichter would have said 'Yes'.

Abraham Maslow's (1954) hierarchy of needs provides a simple but useful explanation of the way an individual's needs work. Essentially he showed that one is driven or motivated initially to satisfy the lower-level needs and then, when satisfied, move up to the next level of need. This theory also implies that motivation can be cyclical, in so far as buying a house may be motivated initially by the lower-level survival needs and subsequently by the higher-level need of esteem. Figure 4.8 shows Maslow's hierarchy of needs.

Cars transport people from A to B. Sometimes the need to buy a car is a basic survival need (eg to get to work, to earn money to buy food). Sometimes it can provide a cocoon (or shelter) from the mass of bodies scrambling for the public transport system. Sometimes it can provide freedom to explore the countryside, visit friends or do what you want (self-actualize). Cars can also act as status symbols (esteem). Some cars position their benefits (power, speed, safety, environmental, etc) so that they dominate the ad and appeal to the predominant need of a particular segment.

Sometimes customers simply do not understand the new benefits delivered by innovative products and services. For example, research originally rejected

FIGURE 4.8   Maslow's hierarchy of needs

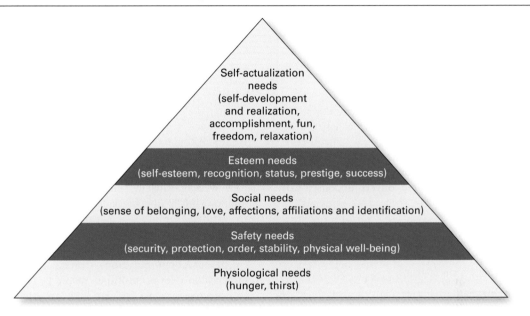

The invisible badge: motivation beyond conspicuous consumption

In 1899 Thorstein Veblen introduced 'conspicuous consumption', which suggested consumers buy products to impress other people, with his example of the man who parades down Main Street in 'stainless' linen, with a superfluous walking stick. These items told a story and provided 'evidence of leisure' – to an audience of strangers. Today's customers also wear badges (Guinness is a badge that tells everyone that the drinker is a discerning beer drinker). Even hybrid cars are said to be eco-status markers (or signals) that show 'conspicuous concern' about the environment. According to Walker (2008), conspicuous consumption

is no longer valid: 'There is a better idea – the invisible badge. What the Joneses might think is, really, beside the point. Because what you are really doing is telling that story to yourself. In other words, yes, a fancy "product" really is a badge in the sense that it's a symbolic confirmation or expression of identity (an identity that we may wish for rather than actually embody – aspirational rather than authentic). But the fact that hardly anyone sees it, let alone accepts the meaning it supposedly projects, hardly matters. In fact, if the real audience is us, the badge may as well be invisible.'

ATMs, with typical comments like 'I wouldn't feel safe withdrawing money on the street.' Interestingly, the wheel is turning full circle, as customers are once again becoming nervous about cash withdrawals on crime-ridden streets.

Different people (or groups of people) extract different benefits from the same product. Some people want to drive a Porsche because it gives

them power; others want to because they see it as a symbol of success (good for the ego and esteem); others just want the thrill of driving very fast (self-actualization, as in the case of the driver's last wish in Nevil Shute's *On the Beach*); others again may simply want a very fast, reliable car that allows them to get from A to B (around Europe) without delay (see the iPod example on page 5). Markets

What motivates Sears' best customers?

Which of the following benefits motivates customers of the US department store Sears?

- Priority repair service.
- Special zero financing.
- Free special catalogue.
- Private sale events.
- Money-saving certificates.
- Personal recognition.

Answer: Personal recognition – customers love it when staff call over the store manager to meet the VIP customer. You can see how this fits with Maslow's hierarchy of needs.

can be broken up into 'benefit segments' so that communications can be tailored to develop the ideal positioning for a particular segment. In some cases benefit segmentation demands different products for different segments, as in the case of the toothpaste market (page 94).

Attitudes

Attitudes affect buying behaviour. Attitudes are learnt, and they tend to stick; they *can* be changed, but not very quickly. As Williams (1989) says: 'If a marketer is able to identify the attitudes held by different market segments towards his product, and also to measure changes in those attitudes, he will be well placed to plan his marketing strategy.' An attitude is a predisposition towards a person, a brand, a product, a company or a place.

An interesting question is 'Which came first, the attitude or the behaviour?' Are attitudes formed prior to purchase or post-purchase? Can attitudes be formed without any experience? The answer is 'yes' to both. Attitudes are sometimes formed without direct experience and, equally, products are often bought without any prior attitude. In the latter case, however, it is likely that an attitude will form as a result of word of mouth, or an engaging advertisement.

Attitudes can be broken down into three components, which are often explained as 'think', 'feel' and 'do' or 'cognitive', 'affective' and 'conative'. The cognitive element is the awareness or knowledge of, say, a brand. The affective element is the positive or negative feeling associated with the brand. The conative element is the intention to purchase. It can be important to measure all three components, since an isolated element can be misleading. For example, Rolls-Royce scores highly on the cognitive and affective elements of the attitude, but few of those who express awareness of and liking towards a Rolls-Royce will actually buy one. Identifying the levels of each attitudinal element helps to set tighter communication objectives. For example, the creative strategy for increasing brand awareness would be different from the strategy required to change the target market's feelings (or reposition the brand). A different communications strategy (perhaps an emphasis on sales promotions) would be required if the objective was to convert high awareness and positive feelings into trial purchases.

Attitudes can be changed, but it does take time. There are several options:

1 Change the beliefs held about the product or service (or its attributes and features).
2 Change the importance ratings (or weightings) of various attributes.
3 Introduce another attribute.
4 Change the association of a particular product or service with the others.
5 Change the perception of competitors' products or services.

Groups also influence attitudes: hence the importance of opinion formers and opinion leaders. Now consider group influence in the buying process.

Group influence

Much of human behaviour, and buyer behaviour in particular, is shaped by group influence. Whether cultural, religious, political, socio-economic, lifestyle, special interest groups or just family, social groups affect an individual's behaviour patterns. Watch explicit group influence occur as thousands of people perform a Mexican wave at football matches, the Olympics, etc.

The effects of group influence are often seen in a queue or waiting area where charity collectors are attempting to collect money. Success or failure is often determined by the reaction of the first encounter, ie if the first person acknowledges the collector and makes a contribution, the next person is more likely to do so too. We have often seen a whole platform generously giving money after a successful start. Equally, we have seen almost total rejection by a whole queue once the initial contact has refused to donate. This is a bizarre or perverse form of charity giving and seems to be about peer group pressure. In a sense, a donation buys some relief from guilt or embarrassment.

Most individuals are members of some kind of group, whether formal (eg committees) or informal (eg friends), primary (where face-to-face communications can occur, eg family) or secondary (eg the Chartered Institute of Marketing). Groups develop their own norms or standards that become acceptable within a particular group. For example, normal dress among a group of yacht club members differs considerably from the norm or type of clothes worn by a group of clubbers. Yet both groups adhere to the rules (mostly unwritten) of their own group. Both groups also go through some sort of purchasing process.

Roles are played by different members within a group. An individual may also have to play different roles at different stages of the same day, eg a loving mother, tough manager, loyal employee, client entertainer, happy wife and, perhaps, sensuous lover. In the online world the same person can adopt different roles and even multiple personalities (see 'Different personalities below the surface', page 91).

Activities, interests and opinions can form useful segmentation criteria. Roles within groups help to target decision makers and influencers in the decision-making units. Roles are also identifiable from the family life cycle, which shows how an individual moves from single to newly wed to full nest 1 (youngest child under six) to full nest 2 (youngest child six or over) to full nest 3 (dependent children) to empty nest 1 (children moved out) to empty nest 2 (retirement) or solitary survivor 1 (still working) to solitary survivor 2 (retired). The income levels,

needs and spending patterns are often predictable as the income earner moves through various family life cycle roles. Spending patterns, influenced by changing roles, can be monitored and forecast before communicating any marketing messages. For example, direct mail companies often mail new mothers within a few days of the arrival of their baby.

Like everything else, roles are changing. Men aged 25–39 are experiencing a massive role change, and some find it hard to cope. 'Generation Y and X men expect to balance work and family, whereas their parents didn't' (Kimmel, 2008). Perhaps this is something women have been doing for some time. And perhaps this multitasking, multi-role life is more alien to young men, as Harold, a 39-year-old Swede, says in the Discovery Channel survey into the male species: 'Men of my age have to be successful in their jobs *and* take care of the house, kids, cook, fix the car and be a great lover' (Discovery Channel, 2008).

Many young men today even see their home as having a different role to that of their parents' home. For many, home is a 'refuge from an uncertain world' and a 'haven from the stresses of life'. In addition to being a long-term financial investment, a home can also be a hub of technology that 'connects a guy with his sense of self through a variety of media experiences'.

Absenteeism out, 'presentee-ism' in

'Men have to work harder than ever before to make themselves indispensable, to the point where we are now seeing "presentee-ism", which occurs when men feel that they have to get to work earlier and leave later to show their commitment. This is having a detrimental effect on their home lives.'
Coopere (2008)

Finally, the mix of communications tools helps move customers through the stages of a buying model from unawareness to reassurance. Each tool can affect different stages. Although there is always some vagueness at exactly where the effectiveness starts and stops, Figure 4.9 is arguably an oversimplified graphic that may help in understanding which tools do what.

FIGURE 4.9   Which communications tools do what

	Unawareness	Awareness	Acceptance	Preference	Insistence/buy now	Reassurance
Advertising		→		→		→
PR		→				
Sponsorship		→				
Direct mail		→			→	
Selling					→	
Packaging		→			→	
Point of sale		→			→	
Exhibitions		→				→
Sales promo						→
Website		→				→
Social media						→
CRM/WOM						→

Summary and conclusion

The marketing professional must understand the target market's buying behaviour before, during and after the actual purchase. Even the apparently simple act of purchasing a hamburger can reveal a host of hidden motives. In-depth research reveals some deep and unconscious reasons that demonstrate some of the complexities of buying behaviour. The time and effort spent in the buying process depend on the type of buying situation. Decision-making units affect the process. Buying models highlight some of the stages through which the buyer passes, offering a kind of checklist for marketing communications to ensure that they carry the buyer through each stage successfully. The behaviourist school differs from the cognitive school of more complex buying models. Motivation, perception, learning, values, attitudes and lifestyles all interact and influence the buying process.

Once marketing professionals are equipped with a clearer understanding of both the motives for buying and the buying process itself, a marketing communications strategy can be developed to ensure that it covers as many avenues to the mind of the buyer as resources allow.

Reasons and motives range from the rational to the bizarre. Motives are, however, only one variable among many other intervening variables that integrate and influence buying behaviour. For example, beliefs and attitudes affect motives, which in turn affect the way an individual sees or perceives things (images, ads, products, shops, etc). We learn these opinions, attitudes and beliefs partly from groups (such as friends and colleagues), partly from commercial messages carefully aimed at us through advertising, sales promotion, etc, and partly from real experiences of products or services.

All these influences interact with commercial stimuli such as advertisements. The effects are ultimately reflected in our behaviour (or lack of behaviour in some circumstances).

In consumer markets, buying behaviour is affected by the complex web of mostly internal intervening variables (motivation, perception, attitudes, learning, memory, lifestyle, personality and groups). Sex, age, income and even an individual's face or body affect their behaviour. Other external variables such as laws and regulations, the weather, opening hours, an out-of-stock situation or an emergency can all change buying behaviour.

An industrial buyer is also influenced by internal variables, including the organization's objectives, policies, procedures, structure and systems, and variables external to the organization such as the state of the economy, the level of demand and competition, the cost of money, etc.

Some argue that it is impossible, as Foxall (1992) says, to 'capture human nature in its entirety' because of the complexity of the decision-making process. This complexity is created by the web of rational and emotional factors that are generated from internal processes and guided by external influences.

Marketing communications can change a nation's behaviour. Marcomms do affect aggregate buying behaviour, as evidenced by changed behaviour patterns after the National Lottery integrated campaign, which stimulated some 65 per cent of the British adult population into shops to buy lottery tickets on a regular basis. The same changes in buyer behaviour are evident in China and across Europe, where marketers really do change customer behaviour patterns. It is no accident. It is never the result of guesswork. It is, as dunnhumby (Tesco's database agency) says, 'largely dependent on accurate analysis of customers and building up valuable insight. If you want to protect and enhance the value of your brand, your offer must be valuable. The higher the relevance, the greater the value – it's a continuum. Customers get what they want, your margins are protected. Everyone's a winner' (Humby, 2008). The magic marketing formula works.

> Perhaps Oscar Wilde was too generous when he said that 'man is a rational animal except when asked to act within the dictates of reason'.

Key points from Chapter 4

- Buying behaviour is complex.
- There are many different approaches to buying models.
- Marketers need a continual feed of information on customer behaviour.
- Emotional influences in decision making are still dominant in B2C and exist in B2B markets.
- Marketers must understand how the intervening psychological variables influence buyer behaviour.

Appendix 4.1: Hofacker's online information processing

One approach to online information processing is Charles Hofacker's five stages of on-site information processing.

1 Exposure.
2 Attention.
3 Comprehension and perception.
4 Yielding and acceptance.
5 Retention.

Each stage acts as a hurdle, since if the site design or content is too difficult to process, the customer cannot progress to the next stage. The e-marketer fails. The best website designs take into account how customers process information. Good e-marketers are aware of how the messages are processed by the customer and of corresponding steps we can take to ensure that the correct message is received.

The first stage is *exposure*. This is straightforward. If the content is not present for long enough, customers will not be able to process it. Think of splash pages, banner ads or Shockwave animations: if these change too rapidly the message will not be received.

The second stage is *attention*. The human mind has limited capacity to pick out the main messages from a screen full of single-column format text without headings or graphics. Movement, text size and colour help to gain attention for key messages. Note though that studies show that the eye is immediately drawn to content, not the headings in the navigation systems. Of course, we need to be careful about using garish colours and animations, as these can look amateurish and distract from the main message.

Comprehension and perception are the third of Hofacker's stages. They refer to how the customer interprets the combination of graphics, text and multimedia on a website. If the design uses familiar standards or metaphors, it will be most effective, since the customer will interpret them based on previous experience and memory. Once relevant information is found, visitors sometimes want to dig deeper for more information.

Changing the layout of a website will be as popular with customers as a supermarket changing its store layout every six months! Metaphors are another approach to aid comprehension of e-commerce sites; a shopping basket metaphor is used to help comprehension.

Fourthly, *yielding and acceptance* refers to whether the information you present is accepted by the customer. Different tactics need to be used to convince different types of people. Classically a US audience is more convinced by features rather than benefits, while the reverse is true for a European audience. Some customers will respond to emotive appeals, perhaps reinforced by images, while others will make a more clinical evaluation based on the text. This gives us the difficult task of combining text, graphics and copy to convince each customer segment.

Finally, *retention* – how well the customer can recall their experience. A clear, distinctive site design will be retained in the customer's mind, perhaps prompting a repeat visit when the customer thinks, 'Where did I see that information?' and then recalls the layout of the site. A clear site design will also be implanted in the customer's memory as a mental map and they will be able to draw on it when returning to the site, increasing their flow experience.

To summarize, understanding how customers process information through the stages of exposure, attention, comprehension and perception, yielding and acceptance, and retention can help us design sites that really help us get our message across and deliver memorable messages and superior customer service.

Appendix 4.2: The post-PC customer

The post-PC customer may occasionally accept payment to view some ads. The rest are screened out by both sophisticated browser software and little 'TiVo-type' boxes attached to wall-to-wall screen TVs. Neither governments nor society permit old-style intrusive advertising any more. No more intrusive evening telephone calls from script-reading intelligent agents. It is also illegal to litter anyone's doorstep or house with mailshots and inserts. Heavy fines stopped all that a long time ago. The only ads that do get inside are carried by the many millions of private media owners who rent out their cars, bikes and bodies as billboards.

The tedious task of shopping for distress purchases like petrol, electricity or memory storage is delegated completely to embedded shopping bots.

Non-embedded bots spun out of control some years ago when they first appeared in three-dimensional hovering holograms – always at your side, always double-checking the best price for hire cars, hotels, even drinks at the bar. Some are programmed to be polite, aggressive or even abusive. All are programmed to be intrusive whenever anything is being bought. Delays on buses and traffic jams regularly occurred when argumentative bots engaged in lengthy negotiations. Frustration broke out. Bots attacked bots, people attacked bots and bot owners. Eventually bots were banned from buses, planes, trains and several 'peaceful supermarkets'.

Next came the great worm wars: programming bots so they only buy your brand – for life. But, unlike humans, bots can be reprogrammed by a competitor. The advertising agent worm was born. Agent eaters soon followed. Despite being information fatigued and time compressed, the post-PC customer lives a lot longer than many bots. And certainly longer than most of the new brands that seem to come and go. The 150-year-old person has already been born.

Meanwhile, back at the ranch, microwaves insist on offering suggestions of ideal wines to go with your meal, offering instant delivery from the neighbourhood's wired-up 24-hour roving delivery van. Your fridge offers special incentives to buy Pepsi when you run out of Coke (or whichever brand owns or

Live longer

Humans may develop smaller ears (from constant use of headphones) and better body organs, replaced as a result of early-warning systems carried by miniature submarines constantly patrolling in the bloodstream. These wireless database-driven devices identify wearing parts and organs, check cloned stock availability, reserve beds and preferred surgeons and estimate time before breakdown replacement is required. Discounts for early bookings into leisure hospitals are also negotiated automatically.

hires the fridge-linked database). Children happily play chess and interact with their opponents on the giant vertical screens, called refrigerators. Voice-operated computers are considered noisy and old fashioned as discreet, upmarket, thought-operated computers operate silently, but extremely effectively.

And all the time blue-tooth type technology facilitates ubiquitous communications, which allows constant interaction between machines. Man and machine integrate into a vast database. We have more IT power in today's average luxury car than the rocket that went to the moon. Yes, Moore's law suggests the tectonic shift will continue. Yes, marketing will continue in a new guise (probably not even called marketing but just common sense).

Time-compressed, information-fatigued and disloyal, the post-PC customer seeks relationships not from brands themselves but from databases that know, understand and seemingly care about them. Witness the virtual girlfriend relationships in Japan, relationships with shops and vending machines, oh, and relationships with people, real, quaint, touchy, feely, physical people.

And all the time the technology, if truly mastered, can free up time to do the important things in life, to give the post-PC customer a genuinely higher quality of life both at work and at home with family and friends.

References and further reading

Chisnall, P (1985) *Marketing: A behavioural analysis*, McGraw-Hill, Maidenhead

Colley, R H (1961) *Defining Advertising Goals and Measuring Advertising Results*, Association of National Advertisers, New York

Coopere, G (2008) Species – a user's guide to young men, Discovery Channel, Discovery Communications Europe

Dichter, E (1964) *Handbook of Consumer Motivations: The psychology of the world of objects*, McGraw-Hill, New York

Discovery Channel (2008) Species – a user's guide to young men, Discovery Channel, Discovery Communications Europe

East, R, Wright, M and Vanhuele, M (2008) *Consumer Behaviour: Applications in Marketing*, Sage, London

Egan, J (2007) *Marketing Communications*, Case study 4.1, Thomson Learning, London

Ehrenberg, A (1974) Repetitive advertising and consumer awareness, *Journal of Advertising Research*, **14**, pp 25–34

Ehrenberg, A (1997) How can consumers buy a new brand?, *Admap*, March, pp 20–27

Engel, J F, Blackwell, R D and Kollatt, D T (1978) *Consumer Behaviour*, 3rd edn, Dryden Press, Hinsdale, IL

Engel, J F, Kinnear, T C and Warshaw, M R (1994) *Promotional Strategy: Managing the marketing communications process*, 7th edn, Irwin Shaw, Homewood, IL

Fishbein, M (1975) Attitude, attitude change and behaviour: A theoretical overview, in P Levine (ed), *Attitude Research Bridges the Atlantic*, American Marketing Association, Chicago

Forsyth, J, Galante, N and Guild, T (2006) Capitalizing on customer insights, *McKinsey Quarterly*, **3**

Foxall, G (1992) *Consumer Psychology in Behavioural Perspective*, Routledge, London

Frank, O (2010) Goodbye, smartphone; hello, predictive context device, *Advertising Age*, 25 June

Hofacker, C (2001) *Internet Marketing*, 3rd edn, Wiley, New York

Howard, J A and Sheth, J N (1969) *The Theory of Buyer Behavior*, Wiley, New York

Humby, C (2008) *Brand is Dead, Long Live the Customer*, Dunnhumby

Jones, H (2008) How to tackle foreign markets, *Marketer*, 8 September

Kanner, B (1989) Colour scheme, *New York Magazine*, 3 April

Kapferer, J (2004) *The New Strategic Brand Management*, Kogan Page, London

Kennedy, J (2009) A wave of optimism, Interview with Eric Schmidt, *Marketing Age*, November

Kimmel, M (2008) Species – a user's guide to young men, Discovery Channel, Discovery Communications Europe

Kotler, P (1998) *Practice of Marketing*, Prentice Hall, Englewood Cliffs, NJ

Lavidge, R and Steiner, G (1961) A model for predictive measurements of advertising effectiveness, *Journal of Marketing*, October, p 61

McGovern, G (2010) The rise of the anti brand – Ryanair, **http://tinyurl.com/ydwk943**

Manyika, J (2008) Google's view on the future of business: an interview with CEO Eric Schmidt, *The McKinsey Quarterly*, September

Marketer (2010) Facts and stats, Marketer, March

Market Research Society (MRS) (1996) Research is good for you – the contribution of research to Guinness advertising, Conference papers, MRS, London

Maslow, A (1954) *Motivation and Personality*, Harper & Row, New York

Oakes, S (2008) Mood maker – music to set your till ringing, *Marketer*, September

Packard, V (1957) *The Hidden Persuaders*, Penguin Books, Harmondsworth

Penn, D (2005) Brain science, that's interesting, but what do I do about it?, Market Research Society Conference

Peters, T (2003) *Re-imagine*, Dorling Kindersley, London

Roberts, K (2006a) Except from a Saatchi & Saatchi presentation, Madrid, 8 June, **http://www.saatchikevin.com/sisomo/Speeches_Ideas/Emotion_not_Reason/**

Roberts, K (2006b) Saatchi & Saatchi presentation, Madrid, 8 June, **http://www.saatchikevin.com/sisomo/Speeches_Ideas/KR_Short_Cuts_part_5/**

Roberts, K (2009a) Short cuts (part 1), 6 July, **http://www.saatchikevin.com/sisomo/Speeches_Ideas/KR_Short_Cuts_part_1/**

Roberts, K. (2009b) Short cuts (part 5), 6 July, **http://www.saatchikevin.com/sisomo/Speeches_Ideas/KR_Short_Cuts_part_5/**

Roberts, K (2009c) Annual City Lecture to the Worshipful Company of Marketors, 6 November

Roberts, K (2010a) Creativity, 21 January, KRconnecttoblogspot.com

Roberts, K (2010b) Spreading the love, *Marketer*, February

Rogers, E M (1961) *Diffusion of Innovations*, 1st edn, Free Press, New York

Rossiter, J and Percy, L (1996) *Advertising Communications and Promotion Management*, 2nd edn, McGraw Hill, New York

Schifman, L G and Kaunk, L L (1991) *Consumer Behaviour*, 4th edn, Prentice Hall International, London

Shaw, R (1997/98) Appreciating assets, *Marketing Business*, December/January

Smith, P R (1996) Video interview with Kenichi Ohmae

Smith, P R (2001) *Online eMarketing Course: eCustomers*, Multimedia Marketing.com, London

Smith, P R (2010) Video interview with Kevin Roberts, CEO, Saatchi & Saatchi Worldwide

Smith, P, Berry, C and Pulford, A (1999) *Strategic Marketing Communications*, Kogan Page, London

Strong, E K (1925) *The Psychology of Selling*, McGraw-Hill, New York

Veblen, T (1899) *The Theory of the Leisure Class*

Walker, R (2008) The invisible badge: Moving past conspicuous consumption, ChangeThis.com, 47.01

Williams, K C (1989) *Behavioural Aspects of Marketing*, Heinemann, Oxford

Williams, T G (1982) *Consumer Behavior*, West Publishing, St Paul, MN

Further information

Market Research Society (MRS)
15 Northburgh Street
London EC1V 0JR
Tel: +44 (0)20 7490 4911
www.mrs.org.uk

Ofcom
Riverside House
2a Southwark Bridge Road
London SE1 9HA
Tel: +44 (0)300 123 3000
Fax: +44 (0)20 7981 3333
www.ofcom.org.uk

Semiotic Solutions
1 Manor Cottages
Kenninghall Road
Garboldisham
Norfolk IP22 2SJ
Tel: +44 (0) 1953 681012
www.semioticsolutions.com

05
Customer communications theory

LEARNING OBJECTIVES

By the end of this chapter you will be able to:

- Understand that communication involves a two-way flow of information
- Appreciate the subtle variables involved in communications
- Apply communication theories to practical marketing situations
- Exploit contemporary models to ensure successful innovations
- Explain why new models are required to meet the changing communications landscape
- Understand why new skills are required to match new communications models

Introduction to communications theory

A dictionary definition of 'communications' is as follows: 'communication n. 1. a transmitting 2. a) giving or exchange of information, etc by talk, writing b) the information so given 3. a means of communicating 4. the science of transmitting information'.

What is interesting is the exchange of information. Communication is not a one-way flow of information. Talking at or to someone does not imply successful communication. This only occurs when the receiver actually receives the message that the sender intended to send. Message rejection, misinterpretation and misunderstanding are the opposite of effective communication.

Millions die from ineffective communications

'There is evidence that a mistake in translating a message sent by the Japanese government near the end of World War II may have triggered the bombing of Hiroshima, and thus ushered in atomic warfare. The word "mokusatsu" used by Japan in response to the US surrender ultimatum was translated by Domei as "ignore", instead of its correct meaning, "withhold comment until a decision has been made".'

Cutlip, Center and Broom (2004)

This is an extreme and tragic example of communications gone wrong. Communication errors in marketing generally do not cost lives but can, if allowed to continue unchecked, cost market share, company survival and jobs. On the other hand, good marketing communications help an organization to thrive by getting its messages across in a focused and cost-effective way.

Good marketing communications is not as simple as it may appear. Even David Ogilvy, the advertising guru, was once reported to have used the word 'obsolete' in an advertisement only to discover that (at the time) 43 per cent of US women had no idea what it meant. The delicacy and difficulty of creating effective communications to target

audiences can be explained by Douglas Smallbone's analogy of radio communication.

Perfect transmitting conditions might exist if there were no noise (extraneous factors that distract or distort the message, such as other advertisements, poor reception, a flashing light, a door bell or an ambulance). Without noise, perfect transmitting conditions would exist. In reality, there is almost always noise, so perfect transmitting conditions do not exist. Cinemas may be the exception, where a captive audience is in an attentive state and receptive to, say, a well-produced X-rated advertisement. But even when the target audience is seemingly tuned in (watching, listening to or looking at a particular organization's package, promotion, advertisement, etc) it may not be on the same wavelength because of the hidden internal psychological processes that may be reshaping or distorting the message to suit the audience's own method of interpretation.

The human receiver is in fact equipped with five distinct means of receiving messages or information or marketing communications – the five senses of hearing, sight, touch, taste and smell. Marketing communications tools can address many senses simultaneously (eg packaging).

The human radio

'Given good transmitting conditions and receiver and transmitter tuned to the same wavelength, perfect reception can be effected.'

Smallbone (1969)

Non-verbal and non-symbolic communications

Although verbal and visual communications gain a lot of conscious attention, there are non-verbal and non-symbolic ways of communicating, such as space, time and kinetics. Crowded areas, or lack of space, send messages to the brain that, in turn, can stimulate a different set of thoughts and a different behavioural response. The opposite is also true: a spacious office or living room conveys different images. In Western cultures the use of time creates images, eg a busy but organized person gives an impression of authority. 'Thanks for your time' immediately conveys a respect for and an appreciation of a seemingly important person's time. A busy diary can project an image of importance. 'I can squeeze you in on Friday at...' implies seniority in the relationship. In the UK, the term 'window' is now used for free time or space in a busy diary. Some advertisements sell products and services primarily on time-saving and convenience benefits. In fact, banks are really time machines that allow an individual to move forward in time by buying, say, a house that would not normally be affordable for 30 years. Finally, kinetics communicate. Gestures and movements send messages. Even the simple, swift clicking of a briefcase, entering or leaving a room or closing or not closing a door can communicate (in China sitting opposite the door means you are paying for the meal). Most of all, body language and facial gestures are powerful communicators. An understanding of body language allows an individual to learn more about what another person is really feeling. A smile, for example, communicates immediately, effectively and directly. (More smiling, please.)

Symbolic and semiotic communications

The field of semiotics (or semiology) opens up a rich discussion of how symbols and signs are used in communications, particularly advertising. Audiences often unconsciously perceive images stimulated by certain symbols.

Engel, Warshaw and Kinnear (1994) demonstrated how Lever's fabric softener Snuggle used a cuddly teddy bear in its advertising. It has been suggested by some psychologists that 'the bear is an ancient symbol of aggression, but when you create a teddy bear, you provide a softer, nurturant side to that aggression. As a symbol of tamed aggression, the teddy bear is the perfect image for a fabric softener that tames the rough of clothing.'

Engel, Warshaw and Kinnear (1994) comment: 'The key point here is that if marketing communicators are not aware of the subtle meanings of symbols, then they are liable to communicate the wrong message.'

Carol Moog's advice to Pierre Cardin on its men's fragrance advertisement, which was designed to show men who are 'aggressive and in control' splashing on fragrance, was accepted but rejected! Moog saw 'cologne gushing out of a phallic-shaped bottle' creating a conflict of images, since it 'symbolized male ejaculation and lack of control'. Pierre Cardin acknowledged that she was probably right, but decided to keep the shot, as it was 'a beautiful product shot plus it encourages men to use our fragrance liberally'.

Source credibility

The success or failure of an advertisement, or any message, is partially determined by whether it is a credible message in the first place. This, in turn, is influenced by the credibility of the source of the message, the deliverer of the message and the chosen media vehicle.

The perceived credibility of the message source is influenced by trustworthiness and expertise. These are key factors that organizations must constantly prove so that they have a platform of credibility ('Develop credibility before raising visibility': see Chapter 3). Endorsements from customers and venerable bodies, published papers, conference speeches, awards won, memberships and of course the perceived quality of the brand itself all help to establish trustworthiness and expertise, ie source credibility. In addition to the credibility of the brand, the message credibility is also influenced by the individual delivering the message, such as the presenter in an advertisement. For example, some brands in the UK stopped using supermodel Kate Moss when her public behaviour was deemed to be 'unsuitable'. On the other hand, a highly credible presenter adds credibility to a brand.

The media vehicle affects the credibility, eg a message that 'using a PC damages your fertility' would have less credibility if it came from the *Sun* newspaper than it would have if it came from the *FT*, or even more credibility if it came from a learned medical journal rather than a newspaper survey. The media vehicle's perceived expertise, prestige and editorial tone (style, eg upmarket or mass-market, and other content, eg sex and violence) all affect the credibility of a message.

Kelman (1961) suggested that the message source has three variables: 1) perceived source expertise and neutrality (or objectivity); 2) perceived source attractiveness (if it is deemed attractive, the recipients may be more likely to develop a similar opinion or position); and 3) perceived power to reward or punish message receivers (eg a teacher or perhaps an owner of a social media group). In summary, a great message delivered from a source with low 'source credibility' will not be as effective as the same message coming from a source with high 'source credibility'.

unleash an epidemic of demand for products and services' (Marsden, 2004).

Connectors, opinion leaders, style leaders, innovators, early adopters, influential individuals and opinion formers: call them what you want, they spread messages.

Message likeability

This is about how much an individual likes an advertisement. It is determined by how interesting, meaningful, relevant and enjoyable an advertisement is deemed to be. When researching advertisements, and in particular, how much customers like an advertisement, 'likeability is deemed to have four elements: entertainment, relevance, clarity and pleasantness.'

Connectors know a lot of people

'They are the kind of people who know everyone. All of us know someone like this. But I don't think we spend a lot of time thinking about the importance of these people. I'm not even sure that most of us really believe that the kind of person who knows everyone really knows everyone. But they do.'

Gladwell (2000)

Opinion formers, opinion leaders and connectors

Opinion formers and opinion leaders include journalists, judges, consultants, lecturers, religious leaders and group leaders. Today they also include bloggers, Facebook fan page owners, Facebook group owners, LinkedIn group owners and many more online group leaders. Officially, opinion formers are formally paid to give their opinions (eg journalists), while opinion leaders are not paid for their opinions (eg many bloggers). Identifying influencers is important, and high-profile bloggers can be easily identified, as can group leaders, whether on Facebook or LinkedIn. Indeed LinkedIn now has a feature that identifies the top influencers in a group and not just the group owners.

Malcolm Gladwell's fascinating *The Tipping Point* (2000) explores how to create an epidemic of demand for a product or service or idea. He calls opinion leaders 'socially contagious connectors' and suggests that, instead of pandering to the mass-market herd, marketers should focus on satisfying the connectors' needs. Connectors are estimated to be 10 per cent of a target audience (Keller and Berry, 2002).

It is worth identifying and partnering with the 'infectious few' so that organizations can focus on the 'consumers that count, who have the power to

Marketers recognize that in each market there are smaller target markets of opinion leaders who influence other members in the marketplace. Major brands can maintain their credibility by talking (advertising) specifically to these leaders, as well as talking to the mass through other media channels (sometimes with messages tailored for the two groups). Whether marketers are advertising hi-fis, fashion, tennis rackets or social issues, multi-step communications can be employed.

In the world of fashion, the leaders are called **'style leaders'**. Even cult fashion products can be mass-marketed by carefully splitting the messages between style leaders and the mass. While the leaders want to set themselves apart from the rest, the mass market consciously and/or unconsciously looks to the leaders for suggestions about what to buy. The difficulty lies with success – as the mass market buys more, the leaders lose interest unless they are reinforced with brand values that preserve the brand's credibility among the cognoscenti. This is important because, if the leaders move away today, the mass sales will eventually start falling away next year or the year after. So, in addition to the mass advertising, some brands use small-audience, targeted, opinion-leader media to send the 'right' messages to reinforce the leaders' relationship with the brand.

Hi-fi trendsetters need a different kind of advertising than just colour supplements with glossy brand images. These innovators and early adopters read additional magazines and look for more detailed technical information in music magazines or specialist hi-fi magazines, buyers' guides, etc. Less knowledgeable buyers often refer to a friend who is a bit of a music buff (innovator or adopter) for an opinion on a brand of hi-fi before deciding to buy.

Just getting the product into the hands of the opinion leaders can help a brand competing in a large market. US marketing guru Philip Kotler (2000) suggests that special offers to opinion formers can work wonders: 'A new tennis racquet may be offered initially to members of the high-school tennis teams at a special low price. The company would hope that these star high-school tennis players (or influential individuals) would "talk up" their new racquet to other high schoolers.'

An understanding of multi-phase communication processes can contribute something to the development of social issue campaigns, such as that concerning AIDS. The initial stages of the campaign were temporarily restricted by inaccurate editorial coverage. Some tabloid journalists were feeding conflicting messages to the same mass that the advertising was addressing. The factual advertising was switched into the press so that opinion formers (journalists) could not write any more conflicting and inaccurate reports.

The power of influential individuals and influential organizations can also be seen in industrial markets. An entire industry may follow a well-respected and highly successful company that makes an early decision to buy. Expert sales teams focus on these kinds of companies initially. Marketers in consumer markets can also focus on the people who are the first to buy new ideas. Better information today can provide a focused approach through database marketing (see page 69), while the imagery used can reflect the lifestyles, attitudes and aspirations of these innovators and early adopters of fresh ideas.

Who are these early adopters of new products and services? Are they different from the other potential customers in the same market? How do they 'adopt' new products or services? Is there a particular type of process through which they pass?

Communications models

No simple diagram can reflect all the nuances and complexities of the communication process. This section considers some basic theories and models.

A single-step communications model

There are three fundamental elements in communication: the sender (or source), the message and the receiver, as shown in Figure 5.1.

This basic model assumes that the sender is active, the receiver is inactive or passive and the message is comprehended properly. In reality this is rarely the case. Chapter 4 demonstrates how we see what we want to see and not necessarily what is sent. An understanding of the target receiver or audience helps to identify what is important to the audience and how symbols, signs and language are interpreted. The message is 'dressed up' or 'coded' in an appropriate way, sent through a media channel and, if it gets through all the other noise, finally 'decoded' by the receiver. Guinness advertisements basically ask their target audience to drink Guinness, but they are very carefully coded. For example, 'It's not easy being a dolphin' were the only words uttered in one of their television advertisements. The audience decodes the message (correctly or incorrectly) and ultimately rejects, accepts, stores or decides whether to include Guinness in its 'considered set of brands' or not. Correct decoding does not always work, eg an anti-drink ad campaign backfired by inadvertently glamorizing the habit (see the box 'Decoding drunken messages' below). Amidst the careful coding and decoding there is noise, the extraneous factors that distract or distort the coded messages; Figure 5.2 demonstrates this.

The sender monitors feedback (eg whether the receivers change their behaviour, facial expression, beliefs or attitudes) so that the message (and/or the channel in which it is sent) can be modified or changed. With so many other advertisements out there it is easy to understand why so little communication actually gets through and works on the target market.

FIGURE 5.1

A simple communications model

FIGURE 5.2   The communication process (based on Schramm's 1955 model)

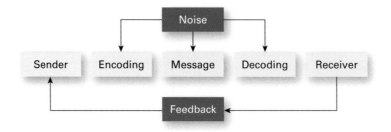

Decoding drunken messages

'Drinks manufacturer Diageo's "The Choice Is Yours" campaign implied that being very drunk with friends carries a penalty of social disapproval. However for many young people the opposite is often the case. University of Bath research team found adverts which show drunken incidents – such as being thrown out of a nightclub, or passing out in a doorway – are often seen by young people as being typical of a "fun" night out, rather than as a cautionary tale. Lead researcher Professor Christine Griffin said: "Extreme inebriation is often seen as a source of personal esteem and social affirmation amongst young people."'

BBC News Channel (2007)

Despite the attractions of one-to-one marketing, mass communications such as television advertising are still considered attractive because they can reach a large audience quickly and cheaply (when comparing the cost per thousand individuals contacted – see page 170). In fact, although TV channels are fragmenting, TV viewing is increasing year on year in most of Europe and the United States (see Chapter 7). Having said that, much of this kind of mass advertising is often ignored or distorted by an individual's information processing system. However, there is usually, within the mass audience, a percentage who are either actively looking for the particular product type or who are in a receptive state for this type of message (see the financial services example in the box 'Floating targets' on page 232).

Mass communication is therefore of interest to many marketing communicators. It is not the single-step process it was considered to be in the early mass communications model shown in Figure 5.3.

This kind of inaccurate model of mass communication suggests that the sender has the potential to influence an unthinking and non-interacting crowd. Audiences (receivers) are active in that they process information selectively and often in a distorted manner ('We see what we want to see'). Receivers (the audience) talk to each other. Opinion formers and opinion leaders also influence the communications process. Today's communications models are more sophisticated.

A two-step linear communications model

Katz and Lazarsfeld's two-step hypothesis (1955) helped to reduce fears of mass indoctrination by the

FIGURE 5.3
One-step communications model

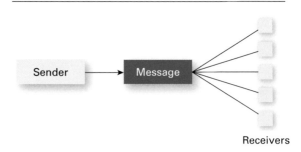

Receivers

all-powerful media. It assumed that mass messages filtered through opinion leaders to the mass audience. Figure 5.4 shows how messages are filtered through opinion leaders, as well as going directly to some members of the target audience.

When **opinion formers (OF)** are added in, the communications model becomes a little bit more interesting. Opinion formers can be separated from opinion leaders, as shown in Figure 5.5. Opinion formers are formal experts whose opinion has influence, eg journalists, analysts, critics, judges or members of a governing body. People seek their opinions, and they provide advice. Opinion leaders, on the other hand, are harder to identify – they are

not formal experts and do not necessarily provide advice, but other buyers are influenced by them. Other customers look toward them. Opinion leaders often enjoy higher social status (than their immediate peer group), are more gregarious and have more confidence to try new products and services. Endorsements from both opinion formers and opinion leaders are valuable.

The opinion formers are often quoted in promotional literature and advertisements, while the style leaders are often seen with the brand through clever editorial exposure engineered by public relations professionals. This can be generated by collecting third-party endorsements, creating events around

FIGURE 5.4   Two-step communications with opinion leaders

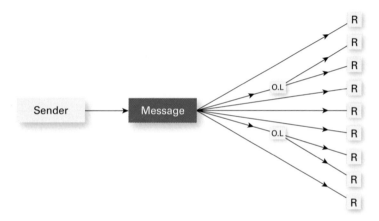

FIGURE 5.5   Two-step communications model with opinion leaders and opinion formers

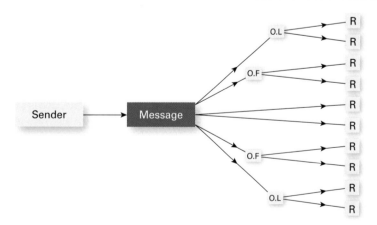

FIGURE 5.6   Multi-step communications model (a)

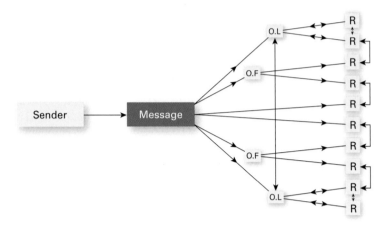

celibrities and 'placing' products alongside cele-brities (eg branded mineral water on the top table at press conferences or actual product placement in films). In **B2B markets**, blue-chip customers are opinion leaders and are much sought after, as their presence on a customer list influences other custom-ers. Both opinion formers and opinion leaders can contribute towards credibility. 'Credibility before visibility' means that a solid platform of credibility should be developed before raising visibility with any high-profile activities.

Multi-step linear communications models

Communication is in fact a multifaceted, multi-step and multi-directional process. Opinion leaders talk to each other. Opinion leaders talk to their listen-ers. Listeners talk to each other (increasingly with discussion groups and internet groups) and subse-quently feed back to opinion leaders, as shown in Figure 5.6. Some listeners or readers receive the message directly.

Noise, channels and feedback can be added to the multi-step model to make it more realistic, as shown in Figure 5.7.

The process of communicating with groups is fascinating. Group roles (leaders, opinion formers/leaders and followers), group norms and group attitudes are considered in 'Group influence' (page 110). In fact, all the intervening psychological variables can be added into the communications

models to show how perception, selection, motiva-tion, learning, attitudes and group roles all affect the communication process. The intervening vari-ables and some more complex models of buyer be-haviour are considered in more detail in Chapter 4.

James Bond – opinion leader

Product placement does not always have to be expensive. In 1997 European Telecom touted their new piece of mobile technology (a car fax) to all the major product placement agencies that act on behalf of the film company giants. They had no budget for any deals or link-ups with any film, but they had a visually interesting piece of technology. To their surprise and delight, the placement agency handling the James Bond film *Tomorrow Never Dies* requested two working prototypes, which were duly delivered and demonstrated at Pinewood Studios. The product was shown as Moneypenny receives a fax from the clearly branded prototype, and hands it to Bond, who is sitting alongside M in the back of the Daimler. An additional car fax is also clearly seen alongside Bond in the back of the car. Now the PR team can really milk the opportunity. After all, 'a portable fax that is approved by James Bond surely has more cachet than one that isn't'.

(Lucas, 1997).

FIGURE 5.7   Multi-step communications model (b)

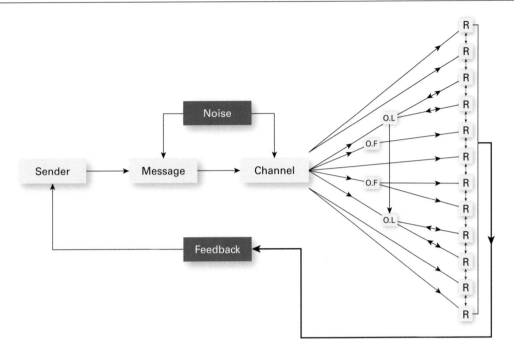

Winning over opinion leaders can be key to any marketing communications campaign, whether B2B or B2C. Take B2B: IBM linked up with the Marketing Society, as its 3,500 members represented key movers and shakers in the business world. Consider B2C: KangaROOS trainers targeted opinion-leading celebrities such as Cat Deeley, Edith Bowman and children's TV show presenters by giving them free shoes. P&G, Unilever and Microsoft trial products with hundreds of thousands (see page 131).

Multi-step non-linear communications models

Let's take this a stage further and consider today's new web communications models, which revolve around the brand instead of simply being sent to the masses by the brand owner. Markets are conversations. The ladder of engagement in Chapter 1 is an example of this. Word of mouth works much more quickly online than offline. With the internet came the easier facilitation of customer communities, where customers can talk, **first, to each other (C2C)** and,

secondly, back to the company (C2B). The flow of communications eventually becomes like a web of communications between customers and opinion leaders – all built around the brand. See Figure 5.8.

The company facilitates these conversations. In doing so, it keeps close to customers, as it can look and listen to what's being said. It can also communicate easily with the customers and ultimately develop strong relations with them. Newsgroups and discussion rooms hosted by the brand discuss the brand, its applications, problems, issues, ideas, improvements and a broader array of topics linked with some of the brand values. In a sense, a web of conversations is spinning around the brand. Customers talk to each other. For example, more than half of eBay's customers come from referrals (Reichfield and Schafter, 2000).

The marketing team also monitors the blogosphere (including Twitter) and user group sites it does not host; some of the truths may be painful but extremely useful. C2C communications can be negative. Remember the Pentium chip problem? It spread like wildfire as the worry spread online. C2C communications can also be fuelled by some customer groups who set up fake sites and hate sites that

FIGURE 5.8
Simple web communications model

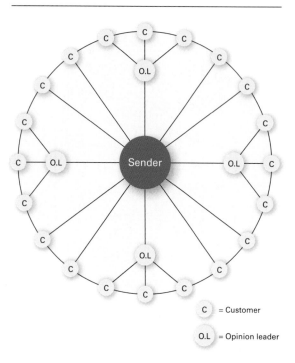

FIGURE 5.9
Advanced web communications model

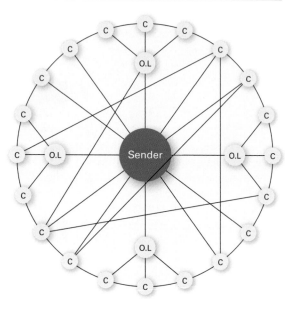

are devoted to spreading negative messages about brands. One type of C2C that is positive – and in fact generates a lot of business – is referrals, where happy customers become advocates and recommend other customers. Another positive form of C2C and P2P is viral, where customers pass the message on. This is accelerated word of mouth. Clever, creative messages with interesting ideas, amazing ideas, special offers, announcements and invitations are good for viral marketing, where messages are passed between customers and from opinion leaders to customers and from opinion leaders to opinion leaders and, of course, from the brand also. See Figure 5.9.

Affiliate marketing also spreads awareness of a brand among a community of relevant customers, who in turn talk to each other and can spread ordinary or clever viral messages among their own communities. Implicit in all of these communications models is permission-based marketing. In this time-compressed, information-cluttered world, customers resent unsolicited spam. Marketers must win permission to send future messages. If the customer agrees, a message is finally sent.

Individuals do talk to each other (at least 500 million on the internet and billions on the phone), particularly when sharing personal product experiences. In fact, dissatisfied customers tell up to another 11 people about their bad experience, whereas satisfied customers tell only three or four. As marketing guru Philip Kotler says, 'Bad news travels faster than good news'. Although this is not in the realm of mass communications, it does demonstrate how everything an organization does communicates something to someone somewhere. Chapters 2 and 3 looks at this whole process in a lot more detail. Suffice to say, at this stage, that many advertisers use teaser, surreal and puzzle advertising (by sending incomplete or obscure messages) to arouse involvement and discussion among target audiences.

Classic and contemporary communications models

Adoption model

Several different hierarchical message models are considered in Chapter 4. The adoption model (Rogers,

Rumours spread in Egyptian university town Al-Mansura that after chewing certain brands of gum female students experienced uncontrollable passion for their male peers. *Time* magazine reported that 'in a society where girls are expected to remain virgins until marriage the news has generated considerable anxiety. Suspicion of who might be spiking the gum with aphrodisiacs fell on the usual suspect, Israel, frequently accused of supplying the Egyptian black market with pornography. However, laboratory analysis showed that some gum samples actually lowered the libido.' Scientific fact may not be relevant. For once a rumour gets going, 'the suggestibility factor can be so strong that it can greatly affect one's mind and actions without there being a scientific explanation', says sociologist Madiha El Safty.

Time magazine (1996)

FIGURE 5.10   The adoption model

Guinness – an individual's adoption process

Although it is not a new product, Guinness has adapted the adoption process. They researched the adoption process for a pint of Guinness because high increases in consumption among young session drinkers resulting from the previous Guinness campaign were not sustained. This prompted the questions: How does one adopt a pint of Guinness? How many pints, sessions or weeks does it take before becoming a regular, fully converted, loyal Guinness drinker? The answers to these questions were carefully collected before the commencement of the campaign.

1962) is such a model. As shown in Figure 5.10, it attempts to map the mental process through which individuals pass on their journey towards purchasing, and ultimately adopting (or regularly purchasing), a new product or service. This somewhat simplistic hierarchical model is nevertheless useful for identifying, first, communication objectives and, second, the appropriate communications tools.

For example, television advertising may create awareness, while a well-trained salesperson, expertly designed brochure or product comparison website (or iPhone app) may help individuals in the evaluation stage. In reality, the process is not simply hierarchical. Some individuals move directly from awareness to trial, while others loop backwards from the later stages by never actually getting around to trying the new idea, subsequently forgetting it and then having to go through being made aware of it again.

The diffusion of innovations

Rogers was also interested in how a new idea spreads or diffuses through a social system or market. He defined diffusion as 'the spread of a new idea from its source of invention or creation to its

ultimate users or adopters'. Several groups who moved towards adoption – at different rates – were identified. The first group to try a new product were called 'innovators'. They represent approximately 2.5 per cent of all of the buyers who will eventually adopt the new product. Their profile was very different from those who were last to try a new idea (the 'laggards'). Opinion leader characteristics were part of the innovators. The key to successful marketing of innovations is to identify, isolate and target resources at the innovators rather than everyone (84 per cent will not buy the product until they see the innovators and early adopters with it first). The 'early adopters' are the second group to adopt a new idea (they represent 13.5 per cent of the total market), followed by the 'early majority' (34 per cent), the 'late majority' (34 per cent) and the 'laggards' (16 per cent). (See Figure 5.11.)

Each group has a different profile, encompassing income, attitudes, social integration, etc in a B2C market. Innovators are venturesome and socially mobile, and they like to try things that are new. The early adopters tend to be opinion leaders who carefully adopt new ideas early. In the retail sector, Nielsen identified early adopters as multiple card holders (among other things), who are very different from single card holders in that they are significantly more promiscuous in their card usage. The early majority adopt earlier than the majority of the market, and they are even more careful, almost deliberate, in their buying process. The late majority adopt only after they have seen the majority of people try it. They tend to be sceptical. The laggards are self-explanatory – tradition bound and the last to adopt.

Crossing the diffusion chasms

Geoffrey Moore (1999) adopted the diffusion of innovations and applied it to the B2B sector and, in particular, technology innovation. Although he gave different names to the segments, the principle was the same: focus and find the innovators and early adopters first. When they have been penetrated and are happily using the product or service, the next segments can be approached. The key point is that there are gaps between the segments – vast gaps so big that they are like chasms into which many companies fall and never climb back out. (See Figure 5.12.) The gap between early adopters and the early majority is massive. Whereas the former seek innovative products, like exploring how they work and accept some teething problems, the latter group (the early majority) will accept only a tried-and-tested fully functional solution with zero risk. They will also seek a different package. In the e-learning market, whilst early adopters like IBM were happy to buy CDs and make them integrate with their training programmes, the early-majority customers like BT needed a different solution: CDs, workbooks, textbooks, workshops and accredited training programmes. This was a completely different solution (to the same problem), albeit a much more lucrative sale. So many other e-learning companies did not understand the difference between the two types of customers and the subtle but deep chasm between them. Many threw millions of dollars at the e-learning market and it all fell into the chasm. Casualties followed.

FIGURE 5.11

The diffusion of innovations (Rogers, 1962)

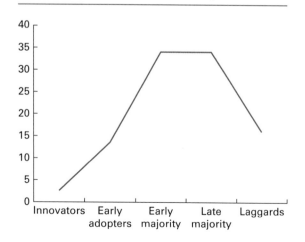

FIGURE 5.12   Diffusion of innovations: the chasm between the segments (Moore, 1999)

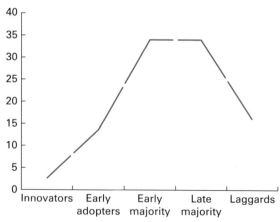

The same principle applies: identifying and targeting the innovators and then moving on sequentially through the other segments. In addition, however, marketers must recognize that the different segments are different, ie they have different needs. Offering exactly the same solution to the total marketplace will fail. Matching the proposition (and the actual solution delivered) to the needs of each segment will generate success. It is the magic marketing formula once again (identify needs, reflect and deliver).

Accelerating diffusion – the tipping point

Malcolm Gladwell's *The Tipping Point* (2000) applies to both B2B and B2C. It explores that moment when ideas, products, trends and social behaviour cross a certain threshold and spread like wildfire. In his book, Gladwell suggests three key initiatives that release the viral potential of new ideas, products or services:

1 *The law of the few.* A relatively small group of adventurous influencers are powerful. Marketers need to identify these gregarious and socially active 'connectors' and then develop relationships with this small group of 'socially infectious early-adopters' or connectors (Gladwell, 2000).

2 *The stickiness factor.* The product, service, idea or message has to be intrinsically infectious. Marketers need to systematically 'tweak and test' or refine and improve against diffusion criteria. 'By tinkering with the presentation of information we can significantly increase stickiness' (Gladwell, 2000).

3 *The power of context.* Ideas and innovations spread quickly when they fit the context or are relevant to the group or its environment. You can exploit the bonds of memory and peer pressure in groups of 150 or less. 'In order to create one contagious movement, you often have to create many small movements first' (Gladwell, 2000). That's why many small, tightly targeted movements are better than one large movement.

Many organizations, including giants like P&G, Unilever, Diageo and Microsoft, started their tipping point initiatives several years ago. P&G set up its 'connector panel' in 2002 in the United States with 200,000 infectious teen connectors used to research and seed new products. Prior to that, Microsoft recruited 450,000 early adopters to trial Windows 95 in 1995 ('ensuring that one in every 189 PC users had a pre-release copy'), enabling Microsoft to 'capture critical pre-launch feedback for the mass market launch whilst giving the consumers that count a unique preview of their product that would generate word of mouth' (Marsden, 2004).

Future communications models

The end of the traditional marcomms funnel model?

Marketers aim to reach customers at the moments that most influence their purchasing decisions. **The old 'funnel' communications model started with creating awareness** (the wide end of the funnel with many brands) and then familiarity, followed by consideration followed by purchasing a single brand (followed by repeat purchasing of the same brand, ie loyalty, where only one brand is chosen). The number of brands is reduced as customers move through the funnel and finally end up with a single brand.

McKinsey's David Court *et al* (2009) suggest the funnel is out of date: 'Today, the funnel concept fails to capture all the touch points and key buying factors resulting from the explosion of product choices and digital channels, coupled with the emergence of an increasingly discerning, well-informed consumer.'

> ### The old funnel is dead – change your model
>
> 'Consumers are moving outside the purchasing funnel – changing the way they research and buy your products. If your marketing hasn't changed in response, it should.'
>
> Court *et al* (2009)

A more sophisticated model is required to help marketers plan their marketing communications. The old linear funnel model misses many of the new touchpoints, which can occur late in the buying process, eg a customer is looking at buying brand X, but just before clicking the 'buy' button checks for customer comments and ratings both on the same site and on other sites, effectively going back to the 'evaluation' stage of other buying models despite being apparently at the 'decision' stage.

Marketers need to be where these points of influence occur, whether at the offline point-of-sale or merchandising point or the online point-of-sale, or in the offline and online word-of-mouth discussion. For the latter, marketers monitor discussions about their brand (and their competitors' brands), whether on Twitter, forums or blogs, and automatically post their messages (some 'canned' or pre-prepared) into the conversation, with links to videos, demonstrations, testimonials or the brand itself. This can be done manually or as part of automated marketing (scanning, identifying and rules-based selection of responses).

Late deciders wait until inside the store

'Consumers want to look at a product in action and are highly influenced by the visual dimension: up to 40 percent of them change their minds because of something they see, learn, or do at this point – say, packaging, placement, or interactions with salespeople.'

Court *et al* (2009)

Marketers need to increase relevancy, ie more tightly targeted ads (the magic marketing formula: identify needs, reflect them and deliver the product or service). Today, marketers can create dozens or hundreds of variations of an advertisement to reflect the context of the past browsing behaviour of customers (and also match what an organization wants to promote according to stock levels or trials of new product variations). 'Many airlines manage and relentlessly optimize thousands of combinations of offers, prices, creative content, and formats to ensure that potential travelers see the most

relevant opportunities' (Court *et al*, 2009). Marketers now have the tools to do this.

Integrated marketing communications are more important than ever. CMOs now have a broader role, which realigns marketing communications with the new realities of customer decision making. Firstly, they have to manage the usual marcomms, product development, market research and now data management. Interestingly, McKinsey recognizes the importance of marketing: 'It's hard but necessary to unify these activities, and the CMO is the natural candidate to do so' (Court *et al*, 2009).

Make way for the semantic web – new models required

The **semantic web** is the next phase of the web's development. Essentially, it enables any piece of data to communicate with other data. It will integrate web-based connectivity into any pieces of data (not just web pages) 'so that it can communicate with other information' (Richards, 2008). It will give access to structured collections of information as well as sets of inference rules that can be used to conduct automated reasoning, eg if the phone rings and music is playing in a the same room, as soon as the phone is answered the phone automatically sends a message to all of the music audio devices to instantaneously lower the music volume while the phone conversation is taking place. The iPod already does this when taking a call: it automatically lowers the music volume. Customers will probably enjoy much more sophisticated applications than anything on the 'traditional' web. This semantic web may change communications models, as clever technology will serve up extremely relevant messages that will help satisfy needs even before they emerge into the customers' conscious stream of thoughts.

Berners-Lee (the inventor of the World Wide Web), Hendler and Lassila explained in 2001 that:

> The Semantic Web is not a separate Web but an extension of the current one, in which information is given well-defined meaning, better enabling computers and people to work in cooperation. The first steps in weaving the Semantic Web into the structure of the existing Web are already under way. In the near future, these developments will usher in significant new functionality as machines become much better able to process

and 'understand' the data that they merely display at present.

Seven years later Tim Berners-Lee (2008) believes that the semantic web could wipe out Facebook and Myspace.

The semantic web wipes out Facebook and Myspace

'Facebook and Myspace will eventually be superseded by networks that connect all manner of things – not just people. Using the semantic web, you can build applications that are much more powerful than anything on the regular web. Imagine if two completely separate things – your bank statements and your calendar – spoke the same language and could share information with one another. You could drag one on top of the other and a whole bunch of dots would appear showing you when you spent your money. If you still weren't sure of where you were when you made a particular transaction, you could then drag your photo album on top of the calendar, and be reminded that you used your credit card at the same time you were taking pictures of your kids at a theme park.'

Berners-Lee (2008)

John Markoff of the *New York Times* coined the phrase 'Web 3.0' when he referred to the next generation of internet-based services in 2006. Merlin Stone (2009) suggests that these new services constitute 'the intelligent Web', using semantic web, microformats, natural language search, data mining, machine learning, recommendation agents, and artificial intelligence technologies. These technologies emphasize machine-facilitated understanding of information to provide a more productive and intuitive user experience. Stone feels that the main characteristics of Web 3.0 seem to be an open, intelligent, seamless, interoperable, access-anywhere-by-any-channel, distributed system where software is a service. Perhaps customers' lives are about to get a little easier, with the semantic web communicating and helping to satisfy their needs. New communications models are required.

Information-smart marketers or just traditional marcomms marketers?

'Marketing is increasingly split between people who are information smart and those who are involved in more traditional marcomms functions... knowing where your competitors are moving in terms of the market place will have a far greater impact than doing a focus group or logo... New marketers are going to have to be much more IT savvy.'

Regis McKenna, in Rothery (2008)

Instead of watching ads, building brand relationships over time and eventually buying a particular product or service, customers can now speak into their phone and ask it to get a certain product or service. It duly obliges, as Google Voice searches carefully and delivers useful suggestions for purchase. A high Google ranking, for some, acts as an endorsement of quality (or at least relevance). Another phone app compares prices (by just swiping the phone screen over the bar code or just keying in the brand name). An ability to work with this rapidly changing marketing environment is now essential for marketers. New skills are required.

New marketing communications skills required

Scott Brinker (2009) suggests marketers need five new skills:

1 *Analytical pattern skills.* Mastering the flow of data from social media feedback, web analytics, transaction histories, behavioural profiles and industry aggregates.

2 *Agile project management.* As tactical campaigns fragment into more granular, relevant, niche-like propositions, each one targeted at dozens, hundreds or even thousands of different contexts, fast-moving, multiple project management skills are required.

3 *Experimental curiosity and rigour.* As marketers seek constant improvement on

their marketing ROI, marketers manage a constant flow of tests, testing new alternatives, exploring new creative executions and monitoring changes in response rates to identify immediate opportunities and threats.

4 *Systems thinking.* Marketing is a set of processes. This means connecting all the parts. Who gets customer comments, summaries and key issues arising from social media conversations? Which decisions does it influence? Who else needs this information (eg salespeople, PR people, the board of directors) and what decisions can it affect?

5 *Mashable software fluency.* Those marketers who understand the mashable web – a world of mash-ups, widgets and application programming interfaces (APIs) – will have competitive advantage. For example, it is possible to connect and integrate a website's

content management system with site search, RSS feeds, e-mail alerts and e-newsletters, all serving very relevant content. Rose (2006) defines mashable in terms of a 'Web page or application that uses and combines data, presentation or functionality from two or more sources to create new services'.

Many of the previously discussed models offer some insight into the communication process but, almost invariably, they distort or oversimplify the process of communication. Chapter 4 draws on some of the communication models discussed here and looks at buying models, the buying process and the intervening psychological variables. How do we buy? Why do we buy? What influences our choices? Are there unconscious motives playing havoc with our day-to-day shopping behaviour? Chapter 6 attempts to look inside the customer's mind and answer some of these questions.

Key points from Chapter 5

- Communication involves a two-way flow of information.

- Communication theories can be applied to practical marketing situations.

- New models are required to meet the changing communications landscape.

References and further reading

BBC News Channel (2007) Warning on anti-drinking adverts, 10 December

Berners-Lee, T (2008) Google could be superseded, says web inventor, *Times Online*, 12 March

Berners-Lee, T, Hendler, J and Lassila, O (2001) The semantic web, *Scientific American*, May

Brinker, S (2009) 5 new skills for the future of marketing, *Chief Marketing Technologist* (blog), 23 February

Carroll, G (2010) CoJargon watch: Delinkification, *Renaissance Chambara* (blog), 5 June

Court, D *et al* (2009) The consumer decision journey, *McKinsey Quarterly*, June

Cutlip, S, Center, A and Broom, G (2004) *Effective Public Relations*, international edn, Prentice Hall International, Englewood Cliffs, NJ

Ehrenberg, A (1988) *Repeat Buying*, 2nd edn, Charles Griffin, London

Engel, J, Warshaw, M and Kinnear, T (1994) *Promotional Strategy: Managing the marketing communications process*, 8th edn, McGraw-Hill Education, Homewood, IL

Floch, J-M (2001) *Semiotics, Marketing and Communication*, Palgrave, Basingstoke

Gladwell, M (2000) *The Tipping Point*, Little, Brown, New York

Godin, S (1999) *Permission Marketing*, Simon & Schuster, Hemel Hempstead

Guirdham, M (1999) *Communicating across Cultures*, Palgrave, Basingstoke

Katz, E and Lazarsfeld, P (1955) *Personal Influence: The part played by people in the flow of mass communications*, Free Press, New York

Keller, E and Berry, J (2002) *The Influentials: One American in ten tells the other nine how to vote, where to eat, and what to buy*, Simon & Schuster, New York

Kelman, H (1961) Process of opinion change, *Public Opinion Quarterly*, **25**, Spring

Kotler, P (2000) *Marketing Management: Analysis, planning, implementation and control*, international edn, 11th edn, Prentice Hall, Englewood Cliffs, NJ

Lucas, Jeff (1997) License to sell, *Marketing Director International*, October

Markoff, J (2006) Entrepreneurs see a web guided by common sense, *New York Times*, 12 November

Marsden, P (2004) Tipping point marketing, *Brand Strategy*, 1 April

Moore, G (1999) *Crossing the Chasm*, 2nd edn, Capstone, Oxford

Reichfield, F and Schafter, P (2000) Eloyalty: Your secret weapon on the web, *Harvard Business Review*, July–August

Richards, J (2008) Google could be superseded, says web inventor, *Times Online*, 12 March

Rogers, E (1962) *Diffusions of Innovations*, Free Press, New York

Rose, B (2006) Marketing mashup tools, *iMedia Connection* (blog), 27 June

Rothery, G (2008) The real deal, Interview with R McKenna, *Marketing Age*, February

Schramm, W (1955) *The Process and Effects of Mass Communications*, University of Illinois Press, Urbana

Smallbone, D (1969) *The Practice of Marketing*, Staples Press, London

Smith, P R (2001) *Online eMarketing Course: eCustomers*, Multimedia Marketing.com, London

Smith, P R and Chaffey, D (2001) *eMarketing eXcellence*, Butterworth-Heinemann, Oxford

Stone, M (2009) Staying customer-focused and trusted: Web 2.0 and Customer 2.0 in financial services, *Journal of Database Marketing and Customer Strategy Management*, **16**, June

Time magazine (1996) Chewing gum hysteria, 22 July

Tuck, M (1976) *How Do We Choose? A study in consumer behaviour*, Methuen, London

Further information

Greg Rowland Semiotics
172 Court Lane
London SE21 7ED
Tel: +44 (0)20 8693 1413
www.semiotic.co.uk

Nielsen Company BV
Ceylonpoort 5–25
2037 AA Haarlem
The Netherlands
Tel: +31 2354 63000
http://en-us.nielsen.com

Ofcom
Riverside House
2a Southwark Bridge Road
London SE1 9HA
Tel: +44 (0)300 123 3000
Fax: +44 (0)20 7981 3333
www.ofcom.org.uk

06
Marketing communications research

LEARNING OBJECTIVES

By the end of this chapter you will be able to:

- Understand how market research reduces risk and improves decision making
- List and explain the different types of research tools available
- Apply the marketing research process
- Appreciate the advantages and disadvantages between online and offline research
- Identify and avoid the potential problems

Introduction to market research

Relevant information reduces risk, increases power and creates competitive advantage if used correctly. Today's marketers have to be ruthless with their information needs and know exactly what it is they need to know, prioritize that, collect it, digest it and then make better decisions equipped with this information. One of the ultimate users of market research is Simon Cowell and the TV phenomenon *The X Factor*. He researches various products (singers) by testing them with customers (audiences at home and at the theatre). The customers provide free market research, revealing which product they prefer. The customers also pay for this privilege (as they vote by phone). He then refines the product concepts (trains them and adds some production effects) and repeats the market research exercise (all the time making money from the research). The final product testing is done with a chosen song, which has already been recorded by each finalist. This final layer of market research almost guarantees the success of the new product (a pop star). The finalists present their version of the song. The market research respondents (audience) complete the 'survey' via a text message (whilst paying for this privilege and simultaneously being highly engaged with the *X Factor* brand). The most popular product is identified (most votes). The product (star) is launched and usually becomes a chart-topping product.

Relevant information reduces risk

As more and more relevant information became available, the risk was eventually reduced to zero and a certainty emerged. The young woman could pick the ace as soon as she knew what the other three cards were. Market research (information) also reduces risk. So why not use research to reduce all risks? There are three reasons: it costs men/women, money and minutes – the three key resources (the 3Ms). First, knowing exactly what information is required and how to gather it (whether commissioning a research agency or handling the research in-house) is a relatively rare management skill; second, research costs money; and third, it takes time to define and write a brief, carry out

The card trick

An Oxford Street card trick man places four cards face down on a portable table. As the crowd gathers, he shouts, '£10 to anyone who picks the ace.' Embarrassment, scepticism and even mistrust run through the crowd. No one responds to the offer of a simple £1 bet to win £10. As the card man leans forward to show the crowd a crisp £10 note, a grinning young man leans behind the card man and sneaks a look at the outside card. It's a jack of diamonds. Word quickly spreads through the crowd that the outside card is not the ace. Prompted by the fund (and the improving odds) someone shouts, 'That's not a real tenner.' The card man responds by stepping into the crowd to allow a closer inspection of the £10 note. A second stranger boldly leans across and briefly turns the other outside card over. It's a two of hearts. The card man returns. 'Come on now. Who wants to win £10?' A well-spoken young woman replies, 'If you show me one of the two middle cards, I will place a £2 bet against your £10.' The card man accepts. What has happened here?

the fieldwork, analyse the data, write and read a report and, ultimately, act upon the information. The fieldwork (asking the questions and collecting the answers) can also give competitors an early warning of intended activities. In a sense, it can give them time to respond.

Relevant information increases power

In both military and marketing strategies, information creates power. If an organization knows what its customers really want, and its competitors do not, then it has a powerful advantage. If the organization knows what a competitor's next move is before it makes it, then the organization is in a stronger position to react or even pre-empt the move. In negotiations, if one party knows more about the other party, then the information holder carries a hidden advantage. The classic salesperson versus buyer situation emphasizes how sales and profits can be increased as a direct result of information:

the salesperson desperately wants an order and is prepared to cut prices to get the business. The buyer desperately needs to buy the salesperson's product because all the buying company's existing stocks were destroyed the night before in a fire in one of its factories and the salesperson's company is the only company that can supply the goods immediately. If the buyer knows how desperate the salesperson is, then a low price will be negotiated by the buyer. On the other hand, the salesperson seizes control over the negotiations (power) if he or she has been informed about the buyer's desperate situation. In addition, the salesperson takes total control if the buyer does not know how desperate the salesperson is for the order. In this situation the salesperson will make the sale, probably at a higher price. Information is power.

Notice how senior managers always seem to ask questions that are potentially embarrassing (because sometimes you don't know the answers). When they ask the question, you might think, 'I wish I'd thought of that.' Questions are indicators of ability and seniority, or potential seniority. The ability to ask the right question is a precious skill that usually takes time and practice to develop. **The ability to ask the right question is the precursor to providing the right answer.** This is becoming increasingly important as too much information becomes available and the potential for information overload and information fatigue grows.

Information advantage: world chess championship

To avoid giving his competitor too much information, Bobby Fischer wore a green visor to stop Spassky, the challenger, from looking into his eyes during an alternative world chess championship.

Relevant information improves decision making

The best marketing managers always ask whether they have enough information to make a good decision. They define what information they need to make their decision making easier. They get this information, digest it and then, and only then, do they make a decision. This is an informed decision. The alternative is guesswork, which relies on luck, which is usually an unnecessary, high-risk activity. On the other hand, proprietary relevant information (or knowledge) effectively creates competitive advantage, eg if an organization has unearthed some deep customer insights that no one else has. Research is an aid to decision making and not a decision in itself.

Information overload

By the end of today, another 4,000 books and another 7 million new web pages will have been published around the world. Billions of e-mails are sloshing around and increasing in number. Do you find it increasingly difficult to find the ones you really need to read?

> Never before in history has the human being had such an ability to create information. Never before have we been faced with so much information. It's not faster computers. It's not bigger hard drives. It's information literacy we need. We need to create less information of a higher quality. We need to be able to manage information much, much better, getting rid of the junk and out-of-date stuff. We need skills that help us search better, and to be able to judge better and faster the quality of the stuff we find.
>
> (McGovern, 2000)

It has been said that information is the principal source of competitive advantage. University of California at Berkeley professors Varian and Lyman (2000) note that our ability to create information has far outpaced our ability to search, organize and publish it: 'Information management – at the individual, organizational, and even societal level – may turn out to be one of the key challenges we face.' Marketing managers must learn to manage information pollution; otherwise they will make ill-informed decisions and may well end up suffering from 'information fatigue syndrome'. Reuters reported that information overload combined with analysis paralysis and poor quality of life reveals that 'one in four people admit to suffering ill health as a result of the amount of information they now handle' Reuters (2009). Out of 1,300 managers, two-thirds said that their social life was affected by having too much information to process at work.

In the UK's top 200 companies, staff spend 30 minutes every working day looking for lost information:

- 60 per cent of staff waste 15 minutes looking for info on their PCs;

- 15 per cent waste 30 minutes each day;

- 7 per cent waste 60 minutes each day.

'In a 1,000-person company there are 33 people permanently looking for information' (Lynch and Manchester, 1999). This was written in 1999; how much worse is it now? Knowledge workers spend 25 per cent of their time looking for information, according to the brain trust firms such as IDC and Delphi Group. Enterprise search: the Holy Grail of KM?

(Moole, 2004)

Information junkies

Other reports reveal that a growing proportion of internet users find themselves addicted to information on the internet. Over 50 per cent of managers were accumulating information they didn't have the capacity to assimilate; rather they were overwhelmed by it. Over half the respondents pronounced themselves information junkies who got 'cravings' for new information, especially from the internet.

Not often considered, however, is one simple way of dealing with stress. Laugh, as it cures stress by pumping adrenalin and endorphins into the bloodstream. It reduces muscular tension, improves breathing and regulates the heartbeat (Nurden, 1997). This is much required in today's hyper-competitive marketplace.

Information prioritization

There is an unlimited amount of information available to all marketing managers. There is more information available and obtainable than any manager can absorb, let alone pay for, in any one period. So the key is to define what the problem is and outline the kind of information that might help. An experienced market researcher (whether in-house or from an agency) can guide the marketing manager towards defining specifically what kind of information is needed. Since the research budget is usually limited, the manager may then have to prioritize which kinds of information are more important than others. Ask for ambiguous information and a lot of ambiguous answers will be delivered.

A certain amount of discipline is needed to focus on relevant issues and not become sidetracked by indulging in 'interesting' bits of information. When briefing a market researcher as to the kind of information that is required, it is often tempting to add extra, 'interesting' questions. Before adding extra information requests, check that the following questions are answered satisfactorily:

- What will I do with this information?
- How will it affect my strategy or tactics?
- What action or withdrawal may result from this information?
- How much is the information worth?
- How much will it cost?
- Can I afford it?
- When do I need it?
- Have I checked all secondary sources? (See Table 6.1 below.)

Do not forget common sense. For example, the highly successful ice cream manufacturer Ben & Jerry's observed an increase in complaints from buyers of Cherry Garcia ice cream. Many customers were upset because they felt that the product had too few cherries. What would you do? What extra information would you collect? This is what they did – they asked the following questions. First, was it only a regional problem? They checked by matching shipment records with complaints. Second, did the problem arise from the manufacturing process – was the quality not up to scratch? But the ingredients turned out to be normal. After questioning almost every aspect, they finally found the source of the problem. The photograph on the ice cream carton was not of ice cream but of frozen yogurt, which appeared laden with cherries in comparison with the paler pink ice cream. They simply changed the image on the carton and the complaints melted away.

Types of research

There are basically two types of research sources: primary and secondary. Primary data are gathered specifically for and commissioned by an organization for a particular purpose (eg a research survey to find out about attitudes towards a company's brand). Secondary data, on the other hand, already exist and have been gathered by someone else for some other reason (eg government statistics, newspaper features or published reports). Desk research can be carried out in a library or office, since it requires researching secondary sources. It is worth doing some desk research before embarking on the more expensive primary research.

There are essentially two types of research: quantitative and qualitative. Quantitative research uses surveys based on a representative sample of the population or target group. Qualitative research involves an in-depth, unstructured exploration with either small groups of individuals (group discussions or focus groups) or individuals on a one-to-one basis (depth interviews).

Research can provide the marketing professional with information on just about anything from markets to distributors, to customers, to competition, to new products, new packs, new promotions, new advertisements, new prices and so on. Different types of research can reveal information about customers, where they are located, what they buy, read and watch on TV, how they spend their holiday time, which competitors they prefer and so on.

Ideas on new or modified products, packs, brand names or advertisements can be discussed initially in focus groups (six to eight people), which generate information explaining how people feel about a concept. This kind of concept testing can be used to reduce a number of ideas to only one or two for further testing, or can be used to give feedback to the creative people so that they can refine a particular concept. These qualitative interviews open up and identify areas that may need further investigation on a larger scale (a quantitative survey) to find out how important certain aspects are among a statistically valid sample (minimum 400 in the sample). In the case of a new advertising concept, or a new pack or brand name concept, the refined concept can then be shown in a hall test (where respondents are invited into a hall to make comments). The packs and brand name concepts can

be shown as mock-up artwork, and the advertisements might be shown as either a storyboard or an animatic (video cartoon). A new product (concept) can be tested by using in-home trials or hall tests. Some data sources, such as the Target Group Index (see 'The Target Group Index' below), are often used in the early research stages of consumer campaigns to identify buying behaviour, socio-economic groups, lifestyles, locations and appropriate media channels.

After all this, a new pack or brand name (or product) can be test-marketed. This reduces the risk by holding back from national or international roll-out until the advertising campaign (or pack or name or product) can be tested within a representative test area. Owing to the high cost of test marketing, and the increasing difficulty in the UK of truly isolating the test market area (especially in terms of distribution, where the national retail chains do not want to limit stocks to certain parts of the country), companies often prefer to conduct a simulated market test instead of carrying out a test marketing exercise. The main research companies in the field are Burke (BASES test), Nielsen (QUARTZ model) and Research International (MICROTEST). These models use information from the concept test or product test, simulate an expected level of distribution penetration (percentage of stores that will stock the product), assume a certain level of advertising spend required to generate certain levels of awareness, and then assume competitive activity, prices and other factors to predict the likely sales of a new product with an accuracy of +/–20 per cent.

Since television advertisements are so expensive, many companies prefer to do all the careful checking and testing through focus groups and hall tests instead of testing the advertisement in a specific test region. They can, and do, however, test the weight of advertising in different regions and measure the incremental sales to help them to find the most cost-effective levels (frequency and timing) of advertising expenditure.

If a product is launched nationally or regionally, its launch can be monitored in several ways. Its usage (user profiles, frequency of purchase, etc) can then be monitored through consumer panels. Retail audits provide information about distribution penetration and how the product is moving off which shop shelves. It is also likely that tracking studies will monitor the immediate reactions and effects of the launch advertising. Pre- and post-quantitative surveys can monitor the levels of branded awareness before and after a new campaign breaks, and can then be used again to measure the effect of the advertising and the product's development in the marketplace.

Summary of types

Table 6.1 summarizes some of the many different types of research information that are readily available. The cost figures give only a very rough indication of the budget requirements. They have been included to give some idea of the costs involved.

Anything can be researched and tested, including sales promotion ideas (concepts), mailshots and even press releases and journalists' attitudes to particular companies and brands. A new and exciting area of research is that of websites, which can be tested before, during and after development. Media research and planning are discussed in Chapter 7.

Qualitative research

An in-depth interview with an individual provides a lot of qualitative information. There is usually a series of individuals interviewed on a one-to-one basis. This type of research attempts to reveal what customers sometimes don't even know about themselves by delving deep into their unconscious motivations. In-depth interviews can reveal deep customer insights.

How young men retain their youth (unconsciously)

Amongst the most popular destinations from the stresses of life are the worlds of the computer game: 'One way that men retain their youthfulness is by spending large amounts of time playing video games.'

Kimmel (2008)

TABLE 6.1   Types of research or information available

Information on	Type of research or information	Sources	Approximate costs
Markets	Market reports (analysing market size, structure, market shares and trends, prices, key players, etc)	Mintel Jordans Keynotes	£750–£2,500
		Syndicated	£1,000–£15,000
		FT and trade magazines	£1
Distributors	Retail audit (analysing a brand's penetration into various retailer store categories, average stocks bought, held and sold per period, retail prices)	Nielsen	£15,000–£50,000*
Customers' attitudes and awareness	Surveys – recommended minimum of 200 interviews; preferably a minimum of 500 interviews	Quantitative market research agencies	£10,000–£60,000 £10–£100 per person interviewed**
		Omnibus surveys	£750 per question
Customers' motivations and perceptions	In-depth research, sometimes using projective techniques, children's groups, supergroups	Qualitative market research agencies	£650 per individual, £1,950 per group of eight
Customers' future lifestyles	Social forecasting, futurology, etc	Future forecasting	£1,500–£5,000 annual subscription

TABLE 6.1   *Continued*

Information on	Type of research or information	Sources	Approximate costs
Customers' buying behaviour and trends over time	Who's buying what, when and from where; how buyers respond over time to various marketing activities, eg special offers, new ads and competitor activities	Consumer panels, eg AGB's Super	£15,000–£40,000
Customers' penetration	Penetration of production into percentage of homes and frequency of usage	Omnibus survey	£500 per yes/no question; £1,500 per multiple answer/ranking
Competition	As for markets, distribution and customers, if the budgets are available. The sales force and marketing departments' 'ear to the market' can also provide much competitive information	As for markets, distribution and customers	As for markets, distribution and customers
Simulated test market	Total mix test of product, brand name, price, positioning	Nielsen Research International; RSGB	£25,000–£100,000
Test market	Running a new product or variation of its mix in a test area	Sales analysis	–
Product	New product concepts can be researched ('concept research')	Focus groups	£1,950 per group of eight
Packs	New pack design concepts can be discussed	Focus groups Hall tests	£1,950 per group of eight £5,000+
Advertisements	New advertisement concepts can be researched before going to expensive production. Pre- and post-advertising research measures levels of awareness before and after a campaign (tracking studies)	Focus groups Hall tests Quantitative survey Online tests	£1,950 per group of eight £1,000+ £20–£40 per person £1,500–£3,000
Exhibitions	Stand design, memorability, number of passers-by, number who stopped and looked, number who visited, percentage of total exhibition visitors	Exhibition surveys	

* Prices can vary enormously, eg a single brand retail price check might be carried out for as little as £750, while a full-blown retail audit for multiple products can run into hundreds of thousands of pounds.

** depending on location and methodology plus set-up plus analysis costs.

As Gordon (1991) says, 'Consumers are often unaware as to why they do or don't use/buy/choose a particular brand. Asking for this kind of information in a direct way is like shouting at a foreigner in the belief that he will then understand English more easily.' So in-depth researchers employ a range of techniques designed to throw the ego off guard and reveal real answers.

Work and family aren't the only important things in life

'As time pressures increase on young men, so does their value of "me time". There's more of an "I deserve it" attitude towards leisure activities. What's more, leisure can enrich and reconnect a young guy with his sense of self.'

Discovery Channel (2008)

In-depth researchers employ a variety of techniques (including psycho-drawings, word associations, metaphors, collages, picture completion, clay modelling and role playing) that throw the ego off guard and allow the subconscious feelings to be expressed. Chapter 4 considers the underlying motivations and complex information processes through which buyers pass on their journey towards a purchase.

Mommy's never coming back

In-depth research for a US manufacturer of security doors revealed deeply ingrained unconscious fears of being trapped inside, or abandoned, when doors are closed. The report suggested that a young child's first experience of a door is when its mother puts it to bed and closes the door behind her as she leaves. The child fears that it may never see its mother again. Many years later, the adult's unconscious mind can react to the sight of a closed door with an 'underlying feeling of discomfort and anxiety'. The Simpson Timber Company was reported as having gained a significant increase in its market share when they changed their advertisements to show partly open security doors rather than their traditional images of securely closed doors.

Knave (1991)

Focus groups

Group discussions can be a more cost-effective way of collecting information that is perhaps less in-depth but nevertheless useful in understanding why and how people (in the target market) feel about certain brands, advertisements or just new ideas (concepts).

A variety of creative stimuli materials are used within these groups, including cartoons, pictures, words and brand maps. One of the most common types is the collage or mood board, which is made up from scrap art taken from a wide variety of magazines and newspapers. It is used to explore a variety of themes, such as user lifestyles, occasion usage and abstract concepts such as freshness or vitality. Two examples of collage boards are featured here and have been developed by The Collage Shop for use in focus groups. Figure 6.1 is a simple mood board showing different eating experiences or occasions. Figure 6.2 is more complex, exploring concept pack themes for a shower gel.

Some companies, like MTV, use online discussions and discussion groups as online focus groups – 'a yearlong focus group'. But all of this is wasted if the right questions are not asked (see the box below).

If the Russian president were a tree

During the final stages of the 1996 Russian election campaign, focus group operators were asking respondents, 'If Yeltsin were a tree what kind of tree would he be?' in a standard approach to throw the respondents' egos off guard and extract real answers. US consultants came in and cancelled these questions, since they urgently 'needed to know whether voters would move to Yeltsin if he adopted a particular policy', and not whether he was a tree or not.

Knave (1996)

Concept research

Concept testing helps every element of the communications mix. Whether it is an advertisement, new sales promotion, new piece of packaging, new

FIGURE 6.1   Eating experiences and occasions

SOURCE: Collage provided by The Collage Shop

direct mail leaflet or even a product or service, the concept should be researched and discussed at least among colleagues and customers and, ideally, among unattached, unbiased focus groups that are representative of the target audience or customer.

Advertising concept testing measures responses to advertisements before they are fully produced. Storyboards, and key frames (see Chapter 13, the Hovis campaign concept) or animatics are made up and shown to focus groups. This kind of group discussion is used to identify the best idea from a range of different concepts, to iron out any glaring problems with a chosen concept or simply to help to refine the concept itself.

Qualitative research is also used to define parameters or types of questions that should be asked in future quantitative research. For example, focus group or qualitative research into newspapers may have revealed that some readers feel mentally un-

comfortable if they don't read all of their newspaper before throwing it out. This is obviously a problem if part of the paper's advertising proposition is 'the newspaper you can digest on the way to work'. So quantitative research will seek to substantiate the variables or issues revealed during the initial qualitative stage. The quantitative stage may be carried out by surveying several hundred or a thousand respondents. The interviewer's questionnaire might ask, 'Which papers on this list do you find a quick and easy read [or long, difficult, etc]?'

Quantitative research

Whereas qualitative research asks individuals and small groups of customers difficult questions like 'Why do you buy [or like] something?', **quantitative research asks larger panels or surveys numerical**

FIGURE 6.2   Concepts for shower gel packs

SOURCE: Collage provided by The Collage Shop

questions like 'Who?', 'What?', 'How?', 'Where?' and 'When?' – who buys this (what percentage of different types of buyers buy it or saw the ad), where do they buy, when do they buy it, etc.

The Target Group Index

The Target Group Index (TGI) collects and compiles information on consumer brands and the profiles of heavy, medium and light users, and non-users, in a vast range of product categories and subcategories. This is all cross-referenced to types of papers read, TV programmes viewed, and lifestyle or attitude statements. It can even classify 'light users' according to whether they buy a brand exclusively ('solus users'), whether they prefer it to another brand also used ('most often users') or whether they are more casual in their use ('minor users'), again cross-referenced to demographic data, lifestyles and

media used. Advertisers use the TGI to find out who the users of a particular brand are and what they read, watch and listen to. The same information is available on competitors and their brands.

Elsewhere the index also gives lifestyle data, eg 'heavy drinkers of low-alcohol lager'. This gives an insight into what motivates them. The excerpt in Figure 6.3 shows that they are keen pub-goers and have a propensity to try new drinks. They are highly image conscious, aiming to keep abreast of new fashions. They appear to be fairly 'flash with the cash' and admit to being no good at saving money. In spite of, or maybe because of, this, they show a strong tendency to seek the advice of a financial consultant. They see their holidays as a way of achieving total relaxation, not wishing to do anything but eat, drink and lie in the sun.

Just about anything can be cross-referenced with any other variable. For example, the index can

FIGURE 6.3   An example of lifestyle data from the TGI

```
Base: NEW 18+
Pop: 20699
Private Eye Target: HEAVY DRINKERS OF LOW ALCOHOL BEER AND LAGER
Pop: 1155(000)    X of Base: 5.57
```

		INDEX	UNWTD RESP	PRJ (000)	VERT (%)	HORZ (%)
1	D8 DRINK LAGER RATHER THAN BEER THESE DAYS	176	183	366	31.68	9.83
2	PA9 I LIKE TO KEEP UP WITH LATEST FASHION	165	53	121	10.47	9.20
3	T7 HOLIDAY-ONLY WANT TO EAT, DRINK, SUNBATHE	165	75	158	13.67	9.18
4	PA15 MEN'S FASHION MORE EXCITING NOWADAYS	161	105	238	20.60	8.96
5	F7 I TEND TO SPEND MONEY WITHOUT THINKING	160	65	141	12.20	8.96
6	SP3 CO'S/PRESTIGE SPONSOR ART/SPORT	157	88	190	16.45	8.76
7	DH6 HEALTH FOODS ONLY BOUGHT BY FANATICS	155	78	179	15.49	8.65
8	D9 I LIKE TO TRY NEW DRINKS	155	70	143	12.38	8.65
9	D12 I REALLY ENJOY A NIGHT OUT AT THE PUB	146	164	345	29.87	8.12
10	P4 I WOULD LIKE TO BUY A HOME COMPUTER	142	58	148	12.81	7.92
11	F4 I AM NO GOOD AT SAVING MONEY	138	87	190	16.45	7.72
12	F15 USUALLY CONSULT FINANCIAL ADVISOR	138	62	114	9.87	7.68
13	PA2 IT'S IMPORTANT TO LOOK WELL DRESSED	137	104	247	21.38	7.65
14	T11 TRY TO TAKE ONE+ HOLIDAY ABROAD A YEAR	135	60	116	10.04	7.55
15	PA13 I REALLY ENJOY SHOPPING FOR CLOTHES	134	70	130	11.25	7.50

identify Heinz beans users and what kind of cars they drive. Another package, called 'trender', can be used to track product, brand, attitudinal, demographic or media trends. The index can also link into various online geodemographic packages.

Geodemographics

Geodemographics mixes geographical population data together with basic demographic data. It uses neighbourhood types to predict the kind of people who live within them and thus their behaviour as consumers. If a brand is found to appeal to certain geodemographic groups, their locations can be mapped and the subsequent communications can be targeted at the geographical areas that offer the greatest potential.

ACORN (a classification of residential neighbourhoods) uses postcodes to identify different types of houses and generally gives useful indica-

tions about buying behaviour. Other UK online demographic analyses can be cross-referenced, eg PINPOINT, which uses 60 different neighbourhood classifications. MOSAIC has 58 neighbourhood categories linked with financial information. SUPER PROFILES uses 150 neighbourhood types.

Test marketing

Test marketing refers to new packs, new brands and new products that are marketed only in a limited test region or geographical area, eg the Yorkshire TV area. A full marketing drive (distribution and advertising, etc) is released in the test area only. This gives the company a chance to spot any last-minute problems that previous research has not identified. If the test market proves to be positive, then the marketing campaign can be extended nationally.

As mentioned, everything can be tested. A new advertising campaign, a new sales promotion or

FIGURE 6.4   Awareness questionnaire

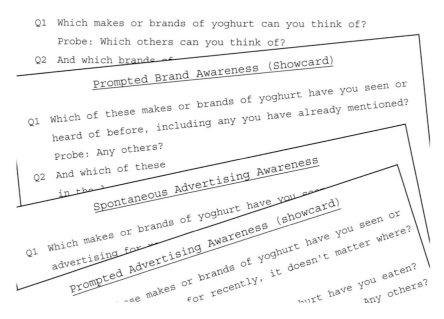

Spontaneous Brand Awareness

Q1 Which makes or brands of yoghurt can you think of?
    Probe: Which others can you think of?
Q2 And which brands of

Prompted Brand Awareness (Showcard)

Q1 Which of these makes or brands of yoghurt have you seen or
    heard of before, including any you have already mentioned?
    Probe: Any others?
Q2 And which of these
    in the

Spontaneous Advertising Awareness

Q1 Which makes or brands of yoghurt have you
    advertising for

Prompted Advertising Awareness (showcard)

...se makes or brands of yoghurt have you seen or
for recently, it doesn't matter where?
...urt have you eaten?
any others?

even a direct mail campaign can be tested among a few thousand names on a mailing list (in direct mail, some companies test right down to whether different-coloured signatures affect direct mail response levels). Some organizations do not, however, test-market because of the associated problems of security, timing, costs and seasonality.

Some tests are considered to create security problems since they can alert the competition with an early warning about, say, an intended new brand. Testing also costs time and money, which may not be available as launch deadlines loom closer. The limited time period of a test often restricts the accuracy of the measured results, since additional time may be required to monitor whether repeat purchases continue beyond the 'trial period'. That is, do customers keep buying, or still remember a particular advertisement, after the impact of the initial launch has died down? Seasonal products and services are further complicated, since they may need to be tested 12 months in advance. Testing, of course, costs money, which needs to be budgeted for at the beginning of the planning period. Both freak results and results manipulated by competitors

can also invalidate certain tests. If this kind of inaccurate information is used to decide whether to launch or not, or to find out how much advertising spend is required nationally, etc, then the results could be disastrous. As mentioned in Chapter 5, Microsoft has 450,000 early adopters who trial its software, and P&G has 200,000 on its 'connector panel' who research (test) and seed new products.

Tracking studies

Advertising tracking involves pre- and post-advertising research that aims to measure levels of awareness and brand recognition before and after an advertising campaign. It can also be used to measure the series of mental stages through which a customer moves: unawareness, awareness, comprehension, conviction and action. These are the stages identified in **DAGMAR** (defining advertising goals for measuring advertising results). It is worth remembering that some elements of the communications mix, such as sales promotions, packaging and point-of-sale, can be more effective than advertising when pushing the customer through the final stage of 'action' or buying.

An analysis of the sales figures can identify an advertising campaign's effect on overall sales. Home audit panel data like SuperPanel can reveal information on what is happening within the total sales figures, such as who is switching brands, who are the heavy users, etc. Quantitative techniques involving street surveys, in-home interviews or telephone surveys (obviously not used if prompting respondents with visual prompt material, eg storyboard, press or poster ad) can measure the other DAGMAR stages listed above.

The percentage of respondents with spontaneous awareness (which brands of beer can you remember seeing an advertisement for this week?) is always lower than those with prompted awareness (since the interviewer prompts the respondent by showing a list of brand names or a storyboard of the ad). See *Marketing Magazine*'s weekly brand awareness results for an example of who is leading the awareness tables. Incidentally, telephone surveys cannot currently be used for measuring prompted awareness of a TV campaign (they can be used to research a radio campaign) since prompt materials such as storyboards, press advertisements or lists of brands can only be shown to a misrepresentative sample (homes with videophones). Verbal prompts can be made, but this is obviously not the ideal situation. This situation may change as more homes begin to use videophones (ie as penetration increases and 'the diffusion of innovations' occurs).

Although awareness is of interest, 'salience' is, as Gordon (1991) points out, 'a far more valuable tool for understanding what a brand means than brand awareness'.

Retail audits

Retail audits monitor share of shelf space, prices and turnover of particular brands (including competitors') in a large and representative sample of retailers. It is worth noting that Boots, Sainsbury's and Marks & Spencer do not allow auditors to come into their stores. This means that the audit results have to be weighted and adjusted. Where auditors are allowed access, they check shelves, facings, prices and stock levels. Most FMCG companies buy these audits, since they provide a picture of what is happening at the retail level. Bar codes

and laser scanning can provide much of this information online directly to the user. Sales out of shops do not necessarily reflect actual customer usage. Home audits (see below) can provide customer purchase information.

Home audits

Instead of, or in addition to, retail store research, home audits research the customer directly. The retail audit data can be backed up with customer usage data. Representative families (sample size: 8,500) are recruited and asked to log all their purchases using a bar code recorder. The device asks for the name of the store and the price paid per brand, etc. Non-bar-coded items are recorded on paper. Analysis of this wealth of data over time shows consumers' repertoire of brands, the effects of sales promotions on purchases, frequency of purchase, etc. This is automatically cross-referenced with the household's demographic data already held. Diaries and dedicated dustbins used to be used to collect this type of information. Today the automated online bar code system is preferred.

Social media audits

Look before you leap. It is essential to carry out an audit before jumping into the blogosphere. As always, the brand and the organization need to check that it is credible and ready to become more transparent, as social media can probe into many previously protected areas of the business. **A social media audit explores how an organization (and/or its brands and high-profile staff) and its competitors are seen in relevant online communities:** what is being discussed, what is required, whether the organization has existing assets (contents, eg speeches) and how ready the organization is (includes training, systems and processes and generating content and participating in discussions). The audit also looks at current presence, whether blog, Twitter, Flickr or YouTube, and the levels of engagement and traffic or followers. The audit explores the organization's social media goals (eg a direct channel with customers, to gather research, to improve customer service, to reach out to new audiences or markets, to add value to existing customers, etc), as well as its resources and restrictions (policy issues about content or trade secrets, any legal or political constraints or any internal issues about sensitive information).

Opinion-forming panels

Chapter 5 highlighted companies that use opinion-forming panels, including Microsoft (450,000 early adopters), Procter & Gamble (nearly 200,000 recruited respondents in its 'connector panel').

'Connector panels' are used to research and seed new products. *Note:* In the UK market, research cannot be blended with selling (it's called 'sugging' – selling under the guise of research). Not only are these testers giving very valuable feedback, but they are also taking ownership of the product and the brand as they become more and more engaged.

Neuroscience

Neuromarketing and biometrics have received a lot of publicity as marketing research tools. Whether it is about mapping eye movement or measuring heart rate, sweat response or any neurological activity, many marketers are sceptical, yet companies like Google, Microsoft and Mercedes-Benz use neuromarketing to improve their marketing communications (Rothery, 2009).

Specialist companies such as Mindlab, Innerscope, Eyetracker, NeuroFocus and Neurosense all use slightly different approaches, and each one is more likely to be associated with hospitals or university laboratories rather than 'normal' marketing approaches.

Think 'secondary' first

All communications plans should be based on sound research. Expensive primary data should be used only when all possible secondary data sources have been checked. Why pay £25,000 for a market research report analysing your industry when it may be possible to subscribe for less to a syndicated survey carried out specifically for a group of companies in an industry sector (eg air travel or car manufacturers)? Alternatively, some markets are researched regularly by market report companies such as Mintel, Keynotes and Jordans. These reports can be purchased by anyone for a few hundred pounds. Academic institutes often publish reports on various markets or aspects of the marketing process within a particular industry. Sometimes these are available at not much more than the cost of duplication and dispatch. A newspaper like the *Financial Times* may have done its own analysis or survey, which costs less than £2. Other research reports are available free of charge, as the commissioning companies see published surveys as a useful marketing tool to generate free media coverage. It also gives them something to talk to clients and prospective clients about. On the other hand, some free survey results may be biased in favour of the organization that commissioned the research in the first place, particularly if they have a vested interest in revealing certain positive results or trends. In addition, some surveys can be hijacked or manipulated.

The market research process

Define what you need to know

Before going through the steps of the market research process, it is worth emphasizing the importance of defining exactly what information you need and which decisions it will affect. Otherwise you get information creep, delays and confusion. Rushing into research will probably deliver sloppy market research or well-structured research findings but miss some key information.

Same secondary source – completely different 'factual' reports about David Beckham

'Gaultier-saronged, posh-spiced, cool Britannia, look-at-me, what-a-lad, loadsamoney, sex and shopping, fame-schooled, day-time-TV, over-quaffed twerp'.

> *Daily Telegraph*, June 1998, after Beckham was sent off in the World Cup

'Elegantly-dressed, charmingly-espoused, golden-jubilees, self-effacing, paternally perfect, deservedly-rich, superbly tasteful, uniquely tele-visual, gloriously-maned hero'.

> *Daily Telegraph*, June 2002, after Beckham captained England in the World Cup

Even the Telegraph recognized the vagaries of newspaper reporting, as it reprinted both paragraphs side by side in June 2002.

Bank misses key information

A major bank tracked performance by product group (eg credit cards, mortgages) and by channel (branches, phones, online, e-mail). It went on and compared sales, costs, profits, attrition rates, cross-sell penetration, and customer satisfaction across products and channels. It missed some crucial information, which made the research worthless. What did it miss? 'It didn't link performance in individual customer segments – such as investors, retirees, home owners, renters and students with aggregate financial results objectives and results. Management therefore couldn't pinpoint how strategies to improve customer acquisition, increase penetration, and lower attrition across the bank's key segments were related to the bank's sales and profit goals.'

> Collins, Dahlstrom and Singer (2006)

It is important to identify specific segments and what information is required from each segment.

A one-size-fits-all survey will not yield the quality of market research findings that a carefully refined and tailored survey will. Although 'most companies lack the roles, processes, and integrated customer metrics needed to create unique customer experiences for select segments or to respond quickly to shifts in a segment's value' (Collins, Dahlstrom and Singer, 2006), the few that do really must ensure their research is tailored to different segments. (See the box 'Flawed research – males and females all the same', page 156.)

This applies to any kind of research online or offline. There has been an increase in the amount of research carried out online. It is worth considering the advantages and disadvantages of online vs offline research.

Online vs offline research

Qualitative research such as in-depth interviews and focus group discussions gives insights into the real reasons why customers buy or don't buy, or what they think about new ad or pack design. A lot of this can be done online. In addition, accessing real-time discussions and layering them with shared uploads such as photos and videos adds a richness to research. These insights shape marketing strategies, product development and ad campaigns. Marketers can now carry out a lot of qualitative research online. With more anecdotal information accessible than ever before, how does a marketer choose between online and offline research?

The *Guardian*'s Robert Gray (2010) believes the digital revolution has been both a blessing and a burden for market research: 'A wave of new research techniques has emerged in recent years, bringing immense opportunities for heightened understanding, but also making it harder than ever for those commissioning research to decide on the right method.' So should online research be part of the research mix?

Online advantages

1 Access – it is easier (and cheaper) to get respondents online than to drag them out of the office.

2 Researchers can observe consumers in their own community (without taking them somewhere else).

3 Researchers can observe passively as people interact with each other very naturally online.

4 It is quicker – online dialogue and feedback are immediate and in some cases within minutes of something happening, as opposed to face-to-face surveys, which might take days, weeks or months, which gives people time to think, forget or get confused.

5 It allows for more longitudinal studies – instead of an intense one-hour dialogue, online can encourage conversation over months or years, which can yield very different insights to traditional face-to-face.

6 There is a wider spread of respondents, as online focus groups can recruit from across geographical and social boundaries.

7 Respondents can upload videos and share photos and online diaries and use these as stimuli.

8 It is cheaper than offline equivalents.

Online disadvantages

1 Too much information generated by too many social media conversations means marketers potentially face 'an overload of untargeted data that is costly to analyse and requires specific expertise and resource' (Gray, 2010).

2 There is less control. As the discussions reside within their own online communities, the role of a focus group moderator has become more passive and observational, with less control over the direction of the discussion. This can open up new, previously unknown aspects, but can also make it harder to get feedback on specific questions.

Facebook research platform

Restaurant chain Nando's asked its Facebook fans for their thoughts on a possible new product. Overnight, more than 500 fans clicked their 'like' button, and there were 657 comments for marketing to analyse.

TABLE 6.2   The market research process

Step		Actions
1	Problem definition	Decide clearly what information is needed and why it is needed. Is it qualitative and/or quantitative? What will be done with it?
2	Research plan	Agency briefing. Data sources: secondary/primary. Research techniques: observation, survey, experiment, focus group. Sample: size and type. Degree of confidence. Fieldwork: face-to-face, phone or post. Questionnaire design. Cost and timing.
3	Fieldwork	Actual interviews/data collection and supervision.
4	Data analysis	Coding, editing, weighting, summing, consistency/check questions, extracting trends and correlations, if any.
5	Report presentation	The interpretation of the figures, summary, and sometimes conclusions.
6	Action taken/not taken	If the information is not used, then perhaps it wasn't worth collecting in the first place.

Websites and research

Websites can help identify customer needs:

- Identify what customers are interested in (the most popular web pages).
- See what customers really want by looking at key phrases used to arrive at the site and within the site (seeing what phrases are keyed into the onsite search engines).
- Employ polling for brand names, straplines, packaging design concepts or any concepts.
- Use questionnaires sparingly, as they can cause people to leave a site, particularly if the questionnaire is on the home page.

Every click potentially captures data, building a better profile about visitors and their interest. Chat rooms offer a wonderful opportunity to listen, free of charge, to customers discussing your product or service. And more sophisticated data-mining software can drill down into data mines and build profiles that help companies to understand their customers better.

The market research process

The key to using information efficiently lies in the ability to define exactly what information is required. This is a valuable management skill. Defining the problem or defining the research objectives is the first step in the market research process (see Table 6.2).

Briefs, proposals and agency selection

Research brief

Depending on the type of research, the brief can include SOS from SOSTAC® plus 3Ms (see pages 229–37):

- Summary.
- Situation analysis (including target and marketing mix).
- Objectives of the research (problem definition – what information is required and what decisions should be made as a result of the research finding?).
- Strategy (why the information is required and how the research findings may affect the communications strategies).
- Men/women (who will liaise with the agency?).
- Money (how much is the research budget?).
- Minutes (timing – when is the information needed?).

Note that some clients prefer not to divulge too much strategic or tactical information for security reasons. On the other hand, the more the research agency knows, the more useful the contribution to the success of the project will be.

Research proposal

If an external research agency has been briefed, its research proposal should incorporate a research plan (step 2 in Table 6.2). You will also want to look at the agency's credentials.

Subcontract research but not understanding

'There are certain research functions, marketing research functions, that are sometimes provided by outside firms that are specialists in doing nothing but research. But the core aspect of marketing, which is understanding our customer and having a close bond with the customer, that should never be turned over to anybody else.'

Kanter (1996, 2000)

Agency selection

If the organization is not handling the research in-house, a market research agency will be chosen. Some of the usual agency selection procedures

will apply (see 'Agency selection process overview', page 189).

A shortlist of agencies can be developed from personal recommendations from colleagues and advertising agencies, and from the organization's own observation of research agencies and their advertisements or editorial coverage. Agency size, specialism or expertise, reputation, location and whether the agency works for any competitors can be used as shortlisting criteria. The agencies that 'pitch' or make a presentation will then be judged by the quality of their research proposal, security of data, cost, and spin-offs (like free training). Even small details can make an impression – for example, the number of bound reports that will be delivered when the research findings are eventually presented, or e-mailing presentations and providing client access to extranets, so that clients can monitor project progress. The personal chemistry or relationship between the client and the agency presenter is often the key variable that swings the choice of agency one way or another. It is also important to find out who will be handling the project and, if it is a junior member of staff, the degree of supervision that will be offered. The Interviewer Quality Control Scheme (IQCS) follows rigid procedures to supervise and check the quality of the information.

Some agencies demonstrate great care about the security of the data they hold. Computer hackers pose a problem to any computer stored

My girlfriend

'About 10 years ago my girlfriend used to work for a well-known market research agency in London. On Fridays, I would go in and collect her before going to the pub. Whenever I was late I would dash through the main front door, past the security guard and go up in the lift. Occasionally I jumped out at the wrong floor and found myself wandering through empty offices full of live, unattended, expensive (and competitor-sensitive) research projects. Such a situation would not be allowed to happen today, and the particular agency has since changed its security procedures.'

Anonymous

data. Product test samples need to be controlled carefully and securely. All samples, mock-ups and concept boards need to be returned by the interviewers, and logged as returned once they are received by the research agency. Samples, mock-ups and concept boards can then be kept under lock and key.

Research problems and challenges

There are many challenges associated with getting good market research. These include: researching new ideas, sloppy briefs, sloppy interviews and much more.

Researching new ideas

How can answers to questions about anything that is new, unseen or previously untried be valid? The first commercially produced electric car, the Sinclair C5, had the benefit of some product research, but how can research ask people about something they cannot experience? Driving a C5 in a hall is very different from driving one along a coast road or a busy, wet and windy dual carriageway with a 40-foot truck trying to overtake. Here lies one of the difficulties with researching a new idea: how can the reality of some markets and product usage be

simulated? Another problem lies with the difficulty in taking the novelty factor out. When presented with something new, buyers may be prepared to give it a try, but can the marketing people sustain the marketing effort after the excitement of the initial launch?

The same applies to advertising. Most advertisements try to be new, different and refreshing. So how can research help produce something that is radically different to people's existing levels of expectancy? One of the UK's most successful advertising campaigns, 'Heineken refreshes the parts other beers cannot reach', had the normal focus groups and concept research carried out. It 'researched poorly', ie the results said, 'This is rubbish. We don't understand this type of ad. Don't do it.' Sir Frank Lowe (chairman of the advertising agency Lowe Group) tells the story of how he had to tell the client (Heineken) about the negative concept research findings on their radically different advertising concept. 'He [the client] took a very brave decision and placed the research report document in the bin. He said, "We had best leave that alone and get on with the ad!"' Expensive and carefully prepared market research findings are sometimes ignored.

Expensive research also gets it wrong if it fails to ask the right question. Even world-class companies can ask the wrong question and make huge mistakes. Take Coca-Cola – although it researched the taste of the new Coke, its 1985 flop occurred because it failed to research how consumers felt about dropping the old Coke. Here is Philip Kotler (2000):

> Blind comparisons which took no account of the total product... name, history, packaging, cultural heritage, image – a rich mix of the tangible and the intangible. To many people Coke stands beside baseball, hotdogs and apple pie as an American institution. It represents the fabric of America. The company failed to measure these deep emotional ties, but Coke's symbolic meaning was more important to many consumers than its taste. More complete concept testing would have detected these strong emotions.

Real innovations are difficult to research because both customers and experts struggle to visualize their benefits. Henry Ford once said: 'If I'd listened to my customers, I would have invented a faster horse.' This is echoed by Clayton Christensen (2003)

Flawed research: Coke flop

'Sometimes research gets it wrong because it fails to understand that people can only buy a complete brand. People don't buy products; they don't buy packages; they don't buy brand names. They most certainly don't buy advertising. They buy the sum total of all those things. At one point the Coca-Cola company thought they could improve Coke and invented a new Coke. They had thousands of consumers in the US blind-test new Coke vs old Coke without telling them what it was. New Coke won. So the Coca-Cola Company launched new Coke. It failed miserably. When the company researched new Coke versus old Coke they missed the understanding that the brand Coca-Cola was far more than just a product. It's the sum total of all elements of the brand.'

Bradt (1996, 2000)

in *The Innovator's Dilemma*: 'Listening too much to customer input is a recipe for a disaster.' Listening to experts in the field can also be a recipe for disaster, as demonstrated by the, now classic, quotations regarding innovations from so-called industry experts (see Chapter 1, page 26).

Dangers to guard against

Here are some of the areas where problems can occur in market research:

1 ambiguous definition of the problem;
2 ambiguous questions;
3 misinterpretation of the written question by the interviewer;
4 misinterpretation of the question by the interviewee;
5 misinterpretation of the answer by the interviewer;
6 interviewer bias (street interviewers may select only attractive-looking respondents and exclude anyone else from the sample);
7 interviewee inaccuracies (trying to be rational, pleasant, offensive, disruptive, knowledgeable when ignorant, etc);

8 interviewer fraud (falsely filling in questionnaires);
9 non-response (a refusal to answer questions);
10 wrong sample frame, type or size;
11 incorrect analysis;
12 freak clustering or result (an inherent danger of sampling);
13 timing (researching seasonal products out of season).

Marketing intelligence and information system

Every organization should have a marketing intelligence and information system (MIIS) that lists secondary data sources. The system can be a useful starting point. An MIIS should be built and constantly refined as new sources become available and old ones become redundant.

Internal figures, such as sales, percentage of sales expenditures (of say advertising), response levels,

Flawed research – males and females all the same

Recent testing on both sexes [of rats] has revealed variations in pain thresholds and quite different responses between male and female rats to the same medicines… [This implies that the] body of drugs research has been built on a false premise, "one size fits all".

Women today influence 80% of consumer decisions.

1 Women's sensory perception levels are higher on all five counts… more sensitive to sales environments.

2 Women use the internet and shop online differently.

3 Women talk more about their experiences – word of mouth and referral rates are higher.

4 Women buy differently at every stage of the buying cycle.

Dunkley (2008)

cost per order or enquiry, etc, can and should be compared with external industry averages or competitor activities. Not all the information is readily available immediately, but competitors' sales figures (of grocery products and some other large markets) are available from companies such as Nielsen Retail Audits. Information on levels of advertising is available from Nielsen Media Research.

In an ideal marketing department, competitors' products, leaflets and advertisements should be filed, monitored and counted (so as to estimate the competitors' advertising spend), but busy marketing departments sometimes find this too time-consuming. Certain monitoring companies offer to collect competitors' press clippings and published advertisements. They will also estimate a competitor's advertising spend, if this is not available from MIIS. Again, this costs money and therefore it may be deemed to be outside the budget, particularly if it was never included in the annual marketing budget in the first place. Estimating a competitor's advertising spend can also be done by collecting all the competitor's press ads and calculating the spend from rate card costs less bulk discounts.

A marketing log filing previous marketing activities, advertisements, mailshots, editorial clippings, etc should be tagged with 'cost, objective and result'.

Comparing internal sales figures with external figures (eg total market size) gives you market share figures, which can also be used to calculate your competitors' market share and, more importantly, whether it is growing. Figures in isolation are relatively useless. Figures have to be pushed backwards and across. Backwards gives you the trend over, say, the past five-year period, and across gives you a comparison across your market (including your competitors).

The sales force can, if trained, provide the most up-to-date and relevant information from the MIIS. They are closest to the marketplace and in touch with what is happening. They need to be encouraged to collect relevant information.

Staff members throughout an organization can be trained or briefed as to what type of information is considered important. Different members of the team can identify their choice of newspapers and/or trade journals. They can then scan them for anything relevant. Alternatively, a press clipping agency (eg Romeike & Curtice) can be hired to do this

The intelligent rep

In the United States one particular chain of stores that sold Christmas crackers held buying days when their buyers would see visiting sales representatives. Appointments were not accepted and, once they had registered with the receptionist for the appropriate buyer, reps proceeded to queue in a waiting room on a first-come, first-served basis. The room had rows of desks with telephones, where the reps sat down quietly filling in order forms, drafting letters, completing call sheets and making phone calls. Although it was only 7.30 am, a dozen registered reps were already busily working away. By 8.05 am the room was packed. The large chap beside me was on the phone at 8.00 am reporting some hot information he had come across during another breakfast appointment earlier that day. He told his boss how the competition had offered the other buyer a new buyer-incentive scheme which would commence next month, followed by a new consumer-incentive programme scheduled four months down the road. They had now four months to react or pre-empt the competition!

Today's reps should be asking buyers what words and phrases they use to search for the sales reps' products and services. The answers need to be regularly and systematically sent back to the marketing team to be added to the key phrase inventory for SEO and pay per click (PPC) PR Smith (nd) purposes.

work. An online database like Textline accepts keywords, companies, products, people or issues. Once you have keyed in what period of time (3, 6, 12 months, etc), what area (UK, Europe, United States, etc) and what types of journals or magazines, the screen will register how many references there are and ask you if you would like to read or print the headlines, read or print all the abstracts, or refine the definition or choice of keyword if too many references are recorded.

Some of this information can then be used in a SWOT analysis (strengths, weaknesses, opportunities and threats). This is particularly useful in monitoring uncontrollable external opportunities and threats (OT) variables such as political, economic, social and technical (PEST) factors. PEST developments can be difficult to forecast, but the portents cannot be ignored (see Chapter 11). Many forecasting companies specialize in certain aspects such as social forecasting, and they will also carry out econometric forecasting, which correlates the likely sales effect resulting from a change in pricing or advertising expenditures (price elasticity or advertising elasticity).

In conclusion

Research is valuable but, as can be seen, it does require experienced advice and strict control if the data are to be usefully applied. 'Dodgy data is worse than no data!' Having said that, good data can make the difference between winning and losing. Asking good questions is a great skill. It is important to know what you need to know, as demonstrated by the following poem:

> There is something I don't know
> that I am supposed to know.
> I don't know what it is I don't know,
> and yet am supposed to know,
> and I feel I look stupid
> if I seem both not to know it
> and not know what it is I don't know.
> Therefore I pretend to know it.

> This is nerve racking
> since I don't know what I must pretend to know.
> Therefore I pretend to know everything.

> I feel you know what I am supposed to know
> but you can't tell me what it is
> because you don't know that I don't know
> what it is.

> You may know what I don't know, but not
> that I don't know it,
> and I can't tell you. So you will have to tell
> me everything.

Source: A poem about information from R D Laing's *Knots*. Reproduced by kind permission of Tavistock Publications.

Key points from Chapter 6

- Budgets allowing, research can reveal anything required.
- Consider carefully exactly what information is required, because there is too much information out there.
- Always check secondary sources before commissioning expensive primary research.
- Consider online as well as offline research.
- Set up a marketing intelligence and information system.

References and further reading

Birn, R (ed) (2003) *The Handbook of Market Research Techniques*, Kogan Page, London

Bradt, G (1996, 2000) *Online Marketing Course 5: Marketing research*, Multimedia Marketing.com, London

Cerha, J (1970) Inventing products to fit the future market, Paper given at ESOMAR, Neu-Isenburg, November

Christensen, C. (2003) *The Innovator's Dilemma*, Harper Business Essentials, New York

Collins, S, Dahlstrom, P and Singer, M (2006) Managing your business as if customer segments matter, *McKinsey Quarterly*, August

Crimp, M (2000) *The Marketing Research Process*, 5th edn, FT Prentice Hall, Englewood Cliffs, NJ

Crouch, S, Housden, M and Wright, L T (2003) *Marketing Research for Managers*, Butterworth-Heinemann, Oxford

Discovery Channel (2008) Species – a user's guide to young men, Discovery Communications Europe

Douglas, T (1984) *The Complete Guide to Advertising*, Papermac, London

Dunkley, C (2008) Gender psychology – differentiate to accumulate, *Marketer*, October

Gordon, W (1991) Accessing the brand through research, in *Understanding Brands*, ed D Cowley, Kogan Page, London, pp 31–56

Gordon, W (1999) *Goodthinking*, Admap, Oxford

Gray, R (2010) How to do 'qual' research, *Marketer*, June

Holder, S (1999) Talking to the right consumer, *Design Week*, May

Holder, S and Young, D (1995a) A journey beyond imagination, Paper given at ESOMAR, Berlin, February

Holder, S and Young, D (1995b) Managing change: Moving towards a leaner future, Paper given at Business Industry Group, May

Holder, S and Young, D (1997) Researching the future in the present, Paper given at ESOMAR, Edinburgh, September

Holder, S and Young, D (2000) Getting to the future first, Paper given at AEMRI, Paris, June

Kanter, R (1996, 2000) *Online Marketing Research Course 5: Marketing research*, Multimedia Marketing.com, London

Kimmel, M (2008) Species – a user's guide to young men, Discovery Channel, Discovery Communications Europe

Knave, M (1991) Unlocking deepseated reactions makes ads more sympathetic, in *Marketing Breakthroughs*, ed Bruce Whitehall, December 1991, p 9

Knave, M (1996) Rescuing Boris, *Time* magazine, 15 July

Kotler, P (2000) *Marketing Management: Analysis, planning, implementation and control*, millennium edn, Prentice Hall International, London

Lynch, M with Manchester, P (1999) How to uncover knowledge and make it available, *Financial Times*, 10 November

McGovern, G (2000) Information overload – the sequel, *New Thinking*, 23 October

McNally, F (2002) Wolfe Tones' rebel ballad beats off Bollywood classic to be top choice, *Irish Times*, 21 December

Marketing guide 6: Market research (1989) *Marketing Magazine*, Haymarket Publishing, 13 April

Market Research Society (1986) Research is good for you: The contribution of research to Guinness advertising, Conference papers, MRS, London

Marsden, P (2004) Tipping point marketing, *Brand Strategy*, 1 April

Moore, A (2004) Enterprise search: the Holy Grail of KM?, *KM World*, 1 January

Murray, R (1997) Clone zone, *Creative Review*, November

Nurden, R (1997) Managers pay price for office pressures, *European*, 27 November

Reuters (2009) Information overload, 15 August

Rothery, G (2009) All in the mind, Interview with M Lindstrom, *Marketing Age*, 3 (6), November

Smith, PR (nd) Personal anecdote from the 1980s when the author was marketing Christmas crackers in the USA

Varian, H and Lyman, P (2000) *How Much Information?*, UC Berkeley School of Information Management of Systems

Wurman, R (1996) Information anxiety, system overload, *Time*, 9 December

Further information

British Market Research Association (BMRA) (formerly known as Association of British Market Research Companies – ABMRC)
Devonshire House
60 Goswell Road
London EC1M 7AD
Tel: +44 (0)20 7566 3636
www.businessmagnet.co.uk

European Society for Opinion and Market Research (ESOMAR)
Eurocenter 2
11th floor
Barbara Strozzilaan 384
1083 HN Amsterdam
The Netherlands
Tel: +31 20 589 7800
Fax: +31 20 589 7885
www.esomar.org

Market Research Society
15 Northburgh Street
London EC1V 0JR
Tel: +44 (0)20 7490 4911
www.mrs.org.uk

Millward Brown (London)
24–28 Bloomsbury Way
London WC1A 2PX
Tel: +44 (0)20 7126 5000 (Dale Beaton)
Fax: +44 (0)20 7126 5001
www.millwardbrown.com

Nielsen Media Research (formerly known as Media
Monitoring Services)
Atrium Court
The Ring
Bracknell
Berkshire RG12 1BZ
Tel: +44 (0)1865 742742
Fax: +44 (0)1865 732461
www.nielsenmedia.co.uk

07
Media buying and planning

LEARNING OBJECTIVES

By the end of this chapter you will be able to:

- Appreciate the importance of media planning and buying
- Discuss media choice
- Understand the advantages and disadvantages of various media
- Embrace media language
- Evaluate media options according to consistent criteria

Introduction – the challenge of the media mix

The media mix is where the big money is traditionally spent. A £10 million TV ad campaign may spend £1 million on producing the TV ad, but it spends £9 million on media, ie nine times more on the media. It follows, in this case, that nine times more time and effort should be spent on choosing the right media mix. And the mix has got a lot bigger.

Some marketing managers and agency media people consider that media include communications tools such as sponsorship, direct mail and point-of-sale, as well as the mainstream media such as TV, cinema, radio and the press. Buildings, they would say, are permanent media, which, planning permission allowing, can be used to carry a message. For the purposes of this chapter, 'media' means the more traditional advertising media (press, TV, cinema, radio and posters), as well as new media such as web radio, interactive television, mobile messaging and websites. Although good media planners also consider media outside the traditional advertising realm, this chapter focuses on the mainstream advertising media, while other communications tools are addressed separately in their respective chapters in Part Two.

Deciding to include advertising in the communications mix is a relatively easy decision compared to deciding which media and which media vehicles (eg the specific magazine title) to use. Should the press, TV, radio, cinema and/or posters be used, online and offline? If so, how much of each? Should they be mixed together (the media mix)? If press advertising is chosen, which publications should be used – national dailies, Sunday newspapers, evening newspapers, daily or weekly regional papers, or magazines? How many times should the audience see or hear the ad (optimum frequency)? When should it happen? On which page? Even a great advertisement will not work if 1) it is in the wrong place, 2) it is placed at the wrong time or 3) it is in the right place at the right time but not seen enough times (insufficient frequency).

Today it gets even more complicated, as changing media consumption patterns show more and more online media consumption, yet TV viewing in most markets is also at an all-time high. What about when TV audiences watch their programmes on their mobiles, iPads and plain old PCs? Media mashing means audiences are multitasking (watching TV and being on the internet). The media planners' and buyers' job has become even more complicated, with a plethora of channels, social media sites, apps and more. All of these are considered later in this chapter.

Since most of the advertising budget gets spent on the media, careful attention to detailed media planning and razor-sharp negotiating skills is important. Expert media planners and buyers get the best out of advertising by finding the right spaces or places for an ad campaign at the lowest cost. Media planning is both a science and an art. Traditionally it has been based on number-crunching media analysis and the application of complex computer models. Today media planners are also interested in the qualitative side, which tells them how audiences actually use (and feel about) different media. First, consider the changing media consumption patterns.

Changing media consumption

Media consumption is continually changing. Newspapers and radio are down. Online and TV are up, when measuring where audiences go to gather their news, although both newspapers and radio are consumed via the internet. This research is from the United States, as many European media consumption patterns follow the US trend.

TV viewing is at an all-time high in many countries around the world (Nielsen Wire, 2009). Media meshing or multitasking (watching TV and using the internet simultaneously) is growing (EIAA, 2010). For advertisers, combining TV and online increases positive brand perception and significantly increases the likelihood of purchase (IAB and Thinkbox, 2008).

Internet usage is growing. In some countries internet usage is bigger than TV consumption, eg Canada (IPSOS Reid, 2010). In some demographic segments, eg Millennials (born between 1981 and 2001), internet usage is three times greater than TV usage (Markiewicz, Sherman and Jaworski, 2008).

And YouTube just keeps on growing. In fact, more video has been uploaded to YouTube in the last two months than if ABC, NBC and CNN had been airing new content continuously since 1948 (which was when ABC started broadcasting) (XPLANE, 2009).

FIGURE 7.1   Media source by generation

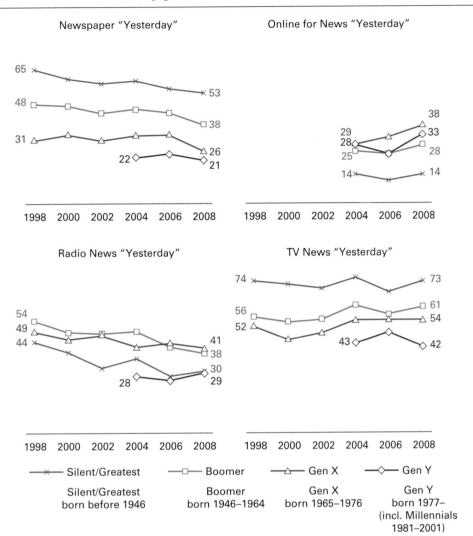

TV being at an all-time high may be because of multiple sets, more channels to watch or TiVo technology, and perhaps the recession means some audience members have more time to watch TV. The average American watches 38 hours per week, up from 36 hours per week the previous year (Nielsen Wire, 2009). And, surprisingly, TV viewing amongst children is almost five times greater than watching DVDs and almost 20 times greater than using games consoles (Nielsen Wire, 2009).

Invisible kids

Time spent by the average child watching television: 1,491 minutes per week or almost 25 hours per week.
Nielsen Wire (2009)

Parents' time spent in meaningful conversation with their children: 3.5 minutes per week.
TV Free America (2010)

FIGURE 7.2 Hours spent per week using media

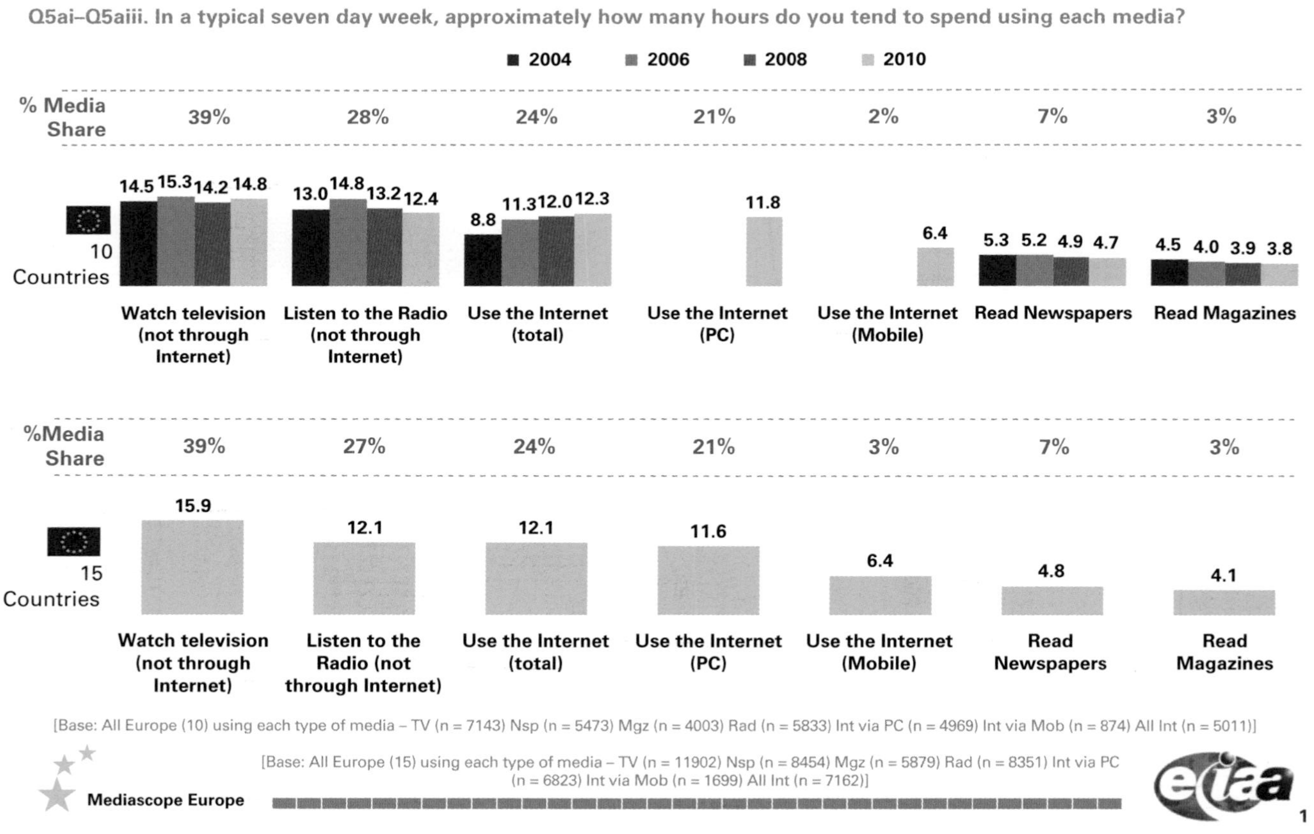

Q5ai–Q5aiii. In a typical seven day week, approximately how many hours do you tend to spend using each media?

■ 2004 ■ 2006 ■ 2008 ■ 2010

10 Countries

% Media Share	39%	28%	24%	21%	2%	7%	3%

Watch television (not through Internet)	Listen to the Radio (not through Internet)	Use the Internet (total)	Use the Internet (PC)	Use the Internet (Mobile)	Read Newspapers	Read Magazines
14.5 15.3 14.2 14.8	13.0 14.8 13.2 12.4	8.8 11.3 12.0 12.3	11.8	6.4	5.3 5.2 4.9 4.7	4.5 4.0 3.9 3.8

15 Countries

%Media Share	39%	27%	24%	21%	3%	7%	3%

Watch television (not through Internet)	Listen to the Radio (not through Internet)	Use the Internet (total)	Use the Internet (PC)	Use the Internet (Mobile)	Read Newspapers	Read Magazines
15.9	12.1	12.1	11.6	6.4	4.8	4.1

[Base: All Europe (10) using each type of media – TV (n = 7143) Nsp (n = 5473) Mgz (n = 4003) Rad (n = 5833) Int via PC (n = 4969) Int via Mob (n = 874) All Int (n = 5011)]

[Base: All Europe (15) using each type of media – TV (n = 11902) Nsp (n = 8454) Mgz (n = 5879) Rad (n = 8351) Int via PC (n = 6823) Int via Mob (n = 1699) All Int (n = 7162)]

Mediascope Europe

Research into what media people use to get news revealed that printed newspaper consumption is, not surprisingly, falling across all demographic groups. Radio is falling also, except for Generation Y (born after 1977). Whilst TV is still generally growing across most age groups in the United States, there is one exception, and that is Generation Y. Online news is growing right across all segments, including 'the Silents' – those born before 1946 (Pew Research, 2009).

For European media consumption statistics, the European Interactive Advertising Association (EIAA) (2010) reveal similar patterns. Over a five-year period to January 2010, TV is up, radio is down (excluding internet access to radio), newspapers are down and internet usage is up.

Both TV and online have an identifiable effect on purchase and response, eg TV is stronger at:

- telling people about a new brand they haven't heard of before (74 per cent);
- sparking interest in a brand (74 per cent);
- giving new information about a brand people are already aware of (72 per cent);
- persuading people to try a brand or product (59 per cent).

Online advertising also has these effects, but performs relatively better at:

- helping people decide which brands are relevant (50 per cent);
- causing a re-evaluation of a brand (41 per cent);
- giving enough information to make a purchase decision (41 per cent).

IAB and Thinkbox (2008)

In 2008 the internet was still being used primarily for research/finding information (75 per cent) and communication (66 per cent), while TV was mainly used for entertainment (80 per cent) and relaxation (73 per cent) (IAB and Thinkbox, 2008). However, this has been changing, as more and more internet usage is for entertainment (including iPlayers, streaming radio and even newspapers online). As faster and more reliable broadband rolls out, the popularity of watching selected TV programmes will grow.

With hundreds of channels, television has moved from broadcasting to narrowcasting, from broad or mass audiences to smaller and more distinct target audiences. The new, wider choice means that audiences are fragmenting into many smaller interest groups fed by sports channels, kitchen channels, children's channels, educational channels, religious channels, music channels, etc. Different channels attract different audience profiles or different psychographic and demographic segments. This gives marketers access to more distinct and tighter target audiences.

However, audiences will continue to migrate online away from the traditional TV viewing model as TV is watched on other devices (eg mobiles, iPads and car TVs). Demand for measurable ROI will keep taking marketing budgets away from TV and direct channels and on to the internet. The marketers' dilemma of whether to use ads for brand building or making sales may be beginning to blur as 'engagement' becomes the burning issue. How can advertisements or any marketing communications engage customers so that they are aware of the brand, embrace it and engage with it to ensure stronger brand relationships and, ultimately, better lifetime sales? And before the debate broadens to the new challenges and opportunities presented by social media, marketers have a new arsenal of advertising tools, including:

- transactional banners (see below);
- contextual ads (serving ads relevant to whatever a visitor is searching for);
- geolocation ads (serving ads relevant to your location);
- mobile ads (new mobile ad models emerging);
- gaming ads (ads placed in games);
- one-second ads (Miller Beer in the United States);
- long-form ads (see Chapter 1, p 20, on the 27-minute ad);
- intelligent media units (banner-sized panels with useful widgets and streams);
- PPC vs PPA (pay-per-click ads vs pay-per-customer acquisition);
- apps (see page 166);
- virals (a natural extension of many TV ads).

Transactional ads let users purchase items by interacting with the banner instead of having to click through to another page or website, helping impulse buyers buy immediately. (See Chapter 13.)

Free coffee if you watch my ad

Apex Japanese vending machine company developed a dispenser that gives free coffee in return for watching a 30-second video advertisement while it prepares and pours the coffee.

Marketer (2008)

Is old advertising media out?

There is a shift in vision and philosophy amongst advertisers. Media owners now have to think differently. Consider Facebook: although it primarily earns revenues from selling engagement ads that drive people to brand pages, 'marketers and agencies want it to focus less on selling media and more on helping them solve problems and create big ideas' (Learmonth, 2010). Big marketers like Unilever, with its $7.4 billion advertising budget, have been visiting the Googles, Facebooks and Hulus (and lesser-known up-and-coming start-ups) of Silicon Valley for years, to understand 'new' concepts like social media, search-contextual advertising and geolocation advertising.

It has been suggested that Silicon Valley companies could be incentivized less on ad sales and

---

The internet creates bigger interactive relationships and not just ads

'But marketers have realized the internet isn't just a place for ads but a means to create bigger interactive relationships with consumers. For savvy digital players such as Unilever, the digital tour (of major social media owners) wasn't about CPMs or page views; rather, it's about learning how to interact with consumers who spend more and more of their time online, and to discover new social tools to participate in what's going on there.'

Learmonth (2010)

---

more on creating bigger and better programmes. The days of just selling ad space are over. Marketers need media owners to think creatively about using the media for reaching out and building stronger relations, as well as selling more products.

Is mixed media – mobile and apps with TV – in?

Apps (or mobile phone applications) can put brands back on screens that are currently 'stealing attention from TV viewership'. Mobile could bring back some of those lost ad revenues to those TV networks if they bundle mobile and TV into new advertising packages for brand owners. Although apps are not yet a prerequisite for a successful TV series, they do 'create context for its shows and let the network interact with viewers while simultaneously laying the foundation for additional revenue streams' (Patel, 2010).

Here is how Fox TV network's app for *Glee* (the musical comedy series) works. It costs £0.59 to download, and within a few weeks it had several hundred thousand users. These customers are engaging beyond the show, as they get extra information about the show, or they sing karaoke to songs performed in the show and then share their work of art by posting their recordings to social networks. Of the first 200,000 subscribers, some 60,000 have been published. Thirty per cent high-level engagement like this is powerful (see 'The ladder of engagement', Chapter 1). Users can also buy additional songs. On average, the app is used once or twice per week at 8- to 10-minute sessions, mostly when the show is off-air. Is this an ad or a product extension or both?

The app helps to restore a sense of being in an audience or in a group, particularly if the app allows the audience to share their thoughts, feelings and, in this case, songs with each other. Apps that integrate with social media help get a brand quickly discussed.

Social TV and its supporting apps extend a brand's reach, enhance the customer experience, deepen the engagement and the brand relationship and simultaneously earn a new revenue stream from subscriptions. Such 'walled garden' experiences mean more 'marketing utopia' (see Chapter 1) – it's a great time to be a marketer.

Additional revenue streams may follow if additional brand advertising is added to the app. The

Glee app developers are actively talking to brands about sponsorship opportunities, such as providing free songs to users.

Apple TV beats cable TV?

'Widget or APP-based TV is just rolling out, and will be built into the majority of flat-screen TVs sold during the holiday season. Early adopters in the US are pulling their cable and dish now and downloading the shows they want to watch on their computers and Apple TV. When that occurs, networks will directly distribute their content to a large portion of their customers, who will pick and choose all programming they watch, when they want to watch it – sort of like it has evolved to now with DVRs and on-demand, but with much greater control by the viewer, who will buy or subscribe to the programmes they watch without having to buy bundled purchase packages. When any part of the old TV spectrum is released to transmit the internet, speeds will accelerate to the point instant real-time on-demand viewing will take place with minimal need for downloading.'

Rodney Mason, CMO, Moosylvania Marketing (2010)

Are apps the 'new media'?

An app is simply a piece of software for an iPhone or iPad that can do anything from keeping up with the sports news, to following a favourite team or player, playing a game, reading free books, analysing a golf swing, taking better photographs, learning to speak French, finding the lowest prices, managing the household bills, Skyping the family, Twittering with friends, making rude noises, stopping snoring, consuming a mobile version of a media brand or consuming a new experience for any brand.

'Some companies are using the App Store as a form of advertising. Developers can create gadgets or widgets that can push their client names onto millions of devices worldwide' (Kennedy, 2009). BBC, Time and Sky News are all available on iTunes, because they know that having their brand name (and services) on a screen that customers carry with them everywhere extends their reach and builds brand loyalty. If a brand can find something of value and something of relevance to its target market then users can continue engaging with the brand long after the ad campaign is over.

Building social media like Twitter and Facebook into an app is potentially very powerful. Other 'walled garden' experiences, such as the Xbox, are developing social media aspects to their games so that players can keep in touch with their friends and compare scores, etc, as they lean over the 'wall' into the social media networks. Others are also using apps as an added-value extension of the brand experience. Few brands as yet appear to be using apps as revenue generators (fees for downloads or additional brand advertisements).

Here are some early apps highlighted by Kennedy (2009):

- *Zippo*. The US lighter manufacturer created an app that replicates an image of a typical Zippo flame. Five million people downloaded it, many of whom don't even smoke. It is now popular at gigs.

- *Kraft Foods iFood Assistant* is a sticky iPhone app with 50 per cent of downloaders continuing to engage with it three months after first downloading it. This builds ongoing brand loyalty.

- *Public transport app*. The Avego app gives updates on public transport and is used in 60 countries. The app gives personalized information for bus passengers, tailored maps and online payment 'on the go'. Silicon Valley's *San Jose Mercury News* referred to it as 'one of the most innovative companies'.

- *House-buying app*. *Irish Times*-owned MyHome.ie partners with Phoneware to show home buyers listings, floor plans, photos and agent contacts, all linked to Google Maps to see what schools, parks and motorways are nearby. Filters allow searchers to explore it by price, number of bedrooms and property type.

- *Affiliate charity contribution app*. Vodafone is mixing affiliate marketing with a clever app. If a local club signs up a Vodafone user, the club receives a percentage of the contract. The app lets the club representative see how much Vodafone is giving back to local clubs.

Print

Technology today allows low-cost entry into the world of publishing. This has reduced the publishing industry's traditional high-investment barrier to entry. In effect, this means that we are seeing new magazines, journals and newsletters appearing alongside multi-edition, tailor-made magazines such as the *US Farmers' Journal* (which produces over 1,000 different editions of each month's publication targeted at over 1,000 different types of farmer). The result? More accurately targeted media that allow advertisers and PR people to target their messages more effectively.

The internet

The internet offers a whole gamut of communications opportunities, including two-way communications, ie listening as well as talking, and collecting as well as sending information. Banner advertising (eg placing an approved advertisement on other websites) is just one form of advertising available on the internet.

Is ambient media the new media?

Beyond TV, radio, cinema, posters, the press and the internet, there are many other advertising media, ranging from scented posters, mirrored posters and graffitied posters, to floor posters, from heated bus stops, painted train platforms, tunnel entrances, taxis, buses, trains and planes, to banners in space visible from earth, to aerial balloons, to the bottoms of beer glasses, to lottery balls, to screen savers, to the back of stamps (and around the front edge of stamps in the United States), to cutting fields into patterns (crop circles), to free bookmarks at the checkouts of bookstores.

The misery of choice

David Ogilvy once described the increasing array of choice as 'the misery of choice'. It applies to media planners and buyers today also.

Which medium?

Should the press and/or radio be used? How should a client or an agency choose which medium to use? Which TV stations and/or publications should be used? Which vehicles within a particular medium (eg the *Guardian* or *The Times*)? The press includes national dailies, Sunday newspapers, evening newspapers, daily and weekly regional papers, and magazines. Television, radio, cinema and posters are considered. The key points are as follows:

- Audience size (reach or penetration). Some media cannot carry national brands because they cannot offer national coverage. Media such as the regional press are generally considered to be local media, since they talk to the community. Television can get to large audiences quickly.

- Audience type (eg 15- to 24-year-olds don't watch much TV but do go to the cinema; on the other hand, not many over 45-year-olds watch the music station MTV).

- Budget (production cost, media cost and cost per thousand – CPT).

- Message objective:
  - Response required: is action required after the ad (eg filling in a coupon or phoning an 0800 number)?
  - Creative scope: are colour, sound and movement needed (eg TV's movement can show impulsive purchases)?
  - Demonstration: product usage is often best shown on TV, but all media can show product benefits.
  - Technical detail: TV is not good; the press is better.
  - Urgency: TV, radio and national papers can be topical and announce urgent commercial news.
  - Compatibility, 'rub-off' or image effect of media and vehicle on the product itself. For example, would Harrods advertise in the *Sun*? TV puts a product or company alongside the major players and therefore enhances the image, since many viewers think they must be good if they're on national TV.
  - TV adds credibility: 'as seen on TV'.

- Ease of booking:
  - Lead times for space: magazines, TV and cinema have long lead times or notice of booking.
  - Lead times for production: some press can be knocked out overnight, whereas a cinema production takes months.
- Restrictions. Some products, eg cigarettes, are totally excluded from all advertising, and certain media restrict the promotion of some products, eg alcohol in children's programmes.
- Competitive activity. Advertisers watch, copy and sometimes avoid the places where their competitors advertise.

Media selection

Audience size

TV allows commercial messages to 'reach' large numbers of people on a national or regional level. TV used to be known as a mass medium, but, as the number of stations increases, more niche channels are emerging on cable, satellite and mainstream terrestrial TV, which means that TV is becoming less of a mass medium. Radio attracts smaller regional audiences, although it can offer national coverage. Cinema attracts small audiences and can offer slow national coverage among younger audiences, but can be great for 15- to 35-year-olds. The national and regional press deliver what they say – national and regional audiences respectively. Because posters can prove difficult to coordinate on a national scale, there are poster-buying specialists. Direct mail can address large national and international audiences, but because of its high cost per thousand the target audiences are likely to be tightly defined and targeted. Finally, TV's audience size is seasonally influenced, with the audience increasing in winter and reducing in summer.

Audience type

Generally, 15- to 24-year-olds are busy doing other things and don't have time to watch TV, whereas cinema can attract this target group. Radio is popular with housewives and commuters. The national daily newspapers tend to target specific socio-economic groups and political sympathizers, while magazines reach targeted groups defined by their lifestyles, income levels, ages and sex. Posters can target commuters who travel by car, bus and train.

Audience state of mind

Audience state of mind or receptivity to messages varies across the media spectrum. TV audiences can be relaxed and passive, sometimes viewing in a trance-like manner (the 'couch-potato syndrome'). TV and its ads can become a form of visual wallpaper, sometimes used as company and sometimes to 'warm up' a room. Radio can also be used in the background, but listeners do tend to work with the radio, as they create visual images from verbal messages. The cinema delivers a captive audience that is happy to be involved in the suspension of disbelief and will not leave the room to make a cup of tea. In fact, many viewers thoroughly enjoy the special cinema ads. The national press is deliberately read, as information is sought. Some research reveals unconscious feelings of guilt (waste and/or inadequacy of knowledge) if a newspaper is left unfinished. Magazines are absorbed in a more relaxed mood.

Cost of production

The cost of producing a TV ad can range from £5,000 to £5 million, depending on the length, complexity and actors involved, whereas radio has a lower cost of production ranging from £500 to £20,000. Stationary pictures with a voice-over promoting the local Indian restaurant can cost just a few hundred pounds, while a more lavish 90-second full-production cinema advertisement could cost up to £1 million or more. Radio and the press sometimes provide free help with basic productions. Posters can be produced for as little as £125 for a 6-sheet (1.83 × 1.2 metre) poster or £11,000 for a backlit 96-sheet (12 × 3 metre) poster campaign for two weeks. Direct mail can be as cheap as the cost of a letter, but if a four-colour brochure is specially designed and produced then the costs can be anywhere from several hundred to several thousand pounds for design and artwork alone.

Minimum cost of space

Advertising space is rarely bought in single units. A single ad is unlikely to achieve as much as a campaign or a series of ads would. Ads are generally scheduled and bought over a period of time rather than as one-offs. The cost of space is relatively high on TV compared to radio; a single off-peak 30-second spot on a regional radio station could be as little as £20, compared to £500 for TV. A national 30-second spot in the middle of *Coronation Street* could cost up to £100,000. A one-off, full-page, four-colour ad in the *Sun* or the *Financial Times* costs £45,386 and £50,151 respectively. Smaller space can be bought, right down to the square column centimetre (approximately £205 and £190 for the *Sun* and *Financial Times* respectively).

Cost per thousand

Within a particular medium, say the press, there is a wide range of media vehicles available, from *Amateur Gardening* to *The Economist*. The CPT varies vastly across different media vehicles (eg from approximately £5 in the *Sun* to £70 in the *FT*) and across different countries (eg 70 cents in Bulgaria to $19 in Norway for 30-second peak-time viewing). Although CPT varies greatly, the actual selection of a particular medium (say, the press versus television) and a specific media vehicle (say, *Amateur Gardening* versus *The Economist*) is influenced by the quality of the media as well as the relative cost.

Message

TV has sight, sound, colour and movement, which makes it an ideal medium for product demonstrations and impulse purchases, but the time constraint and viewing mode make detailed messages almost impossible. It is time constrained (whereas a press ad is not). Ads are viewed serially, whereas press ads compete with other ads and editorial, often on the same page. Remote control channel zapping has made TV more vulnerable as an advertising medium. TV, radio and cinema are highly transitory, in that the viewer cannot refer back to an ad once it has been shown (unless it is taped). On the other hand, the audience can refer back to press ads, posters and direct mail. TV's fleeting messages leave no room for detail but can grab attention, create awareness and arouse interest. More and more ads across the media spectrum, including TV, are tying in with direct response mechanisms (0800 numbers, web addresses or coupons to fill in) so that more detailed information can subsequently be delivered to the audience.

Ease of media buying

Some popular TV programmes (and magazines) require long lead times for booking space. Advertisements are still pre-emptable (they can be outbid and kicked off a particular spot on the day they were booked to be broadcast). Big agencies generally do not get pre-empted. Different rates or prices can be bid; the top rate guarantees the spot, but agencies and clients want to avoid paying these extremely high rates, so they make bids at prices lower down the scales (giving various amounts of notice about pre-emption). Clearcast pre-approves most British television advertising. Clearcast is now owned by seven UK commercial broadcasters. Clearcast replaced the Broadcast Advertising Clearance Centre (BACC) in 2008. This takes time. Cinema can have longer lead booking times but shorter clearance time from the Cinema Advertising Association. Radio is the most flexible of all, with same-day clearance and short lead booking times. The national dailies tend to have flexible positions and size and short lead times, while magazines have longer lead times. Certain positions cannot be booked in the short term, eg one-year lead time. TV and radio can offer a higher frequency, since an advertisement could theoretically go out every half-hour all day. The lack of national network coverage makes the regional press a tough task for media planners and buyers involved in national campaigns.

Which media and which vehicle?

Does the impact of a double-page spread (DPS) justify the cost? Would the reach be increased by placing two single-page advertisements in two different magazines instead? Should TV be supplemented by radio, by posters or by both? Is a personal media network worth creating so that the target audience is hit with a brand's message first thing in the morning on the radio, on posters in the neighbourhood area, in the appropriate paper on the way to work, on TV that evening, in the cinema that night and finally on the radio in the car coming home from the cinema?

Media buyers' computers churn out cost-ranking analyses that list the publications in order of their cost per thousand, with the lowest at the top. CPT offers a quantitative criterion, but does it reveal heavy-user information? Perhaps a high CPT conceals within it a large chunk of the heavy users, which may make the advertisement more effective? Qualitative criteria (audience size and how they use the media, targetability, message type, ease of booking, restrictions and competitive activity) all affect the choice. In the end, experience, judgement and a little bit of creative flair influence the decision to buy space.

How much space, how often and when?

Having selected the media type, and specific vehicles within each media type, the next question is how much space and/or airtime should be booked. In what season, month, week, day or hour should the advertisement appear? How many times should the ad be seen? How many times is too many times? Can the audience become irritated? Frequency? This last question becomes more difficult when a campaign uses several different advertisements, particularly when each new ad builds on the last one. The creative side of the campaign can sell itself to the client, but the media schedule often requires much more detailed justification. Once the media schedule has been agreed, it can be passed on to the media buyer to start booking the space (within booking deadlines).

Media schedule

The media strategy is then refined into the tactical details specifying exactly what space should be booked where. Figure 7.3 shows the proposed media schedule for an Orange campaign.

Media buying

It pays to plan carefully. Plan first; then buy. A skilled media buyer can save enormous sums by playing one media owner off against another. After all, there are many different routes (or media vehicles) to the minds of the target audience.

There are series discounts (10 inserts or ads for the price of 9), and volume discounts if you spend over a certain amount. Many agencies pool their media buying together to gain the maximum discounts. Negotiating and discounting vary from country to country. Countries such as Austria and

Denmark allow very little negotiation with media owners. Media buyers and media planners or schedulers need to work closely together. A global new-media planning resource was launched in early 2001. World Online Rate and Data (WORD) will provide media planners with a database that can be used to plan domestic and global online campaigns. It is available both in print and online (**www.wordonline.net**).

Media research

Media research basically tells the media buyer and scheduler which publications are read by what type of people, how many and what type of people are likely to watch a particular television programme, who listens to what on the radio, which kinds of films attract what kind of audience, which poster sites are passed by most people, etc. Media buyers can then decide if the particular media vehicle's audience profile matches their target market, and if the audience size proves to be cost-effective in terms of cost per thousand, coverage, frequency, opportunities to see (OTSs), TV rating points (TVRs) (see pages 177–79), etc.

How many people watch *Neighbours* or the *ITV News*? How many listen to Capital Radio's breakfast radio show? How many people read the *Sun*? Advertisers are even more interested in what type of people are in the audience and whether they are heavy, medium or light users of the product type or even the specific brand. Although the *Sun* is considered to be a working man's paper, 31 per cent of its readership are ABC1s. So some strange anomalies do exist, and media buyers must tread cautiously. Information concerning socio-economic groups, product usage types and lifestyle data all help to build a profile, which the advertiser can then use to target the most relevant audience.

An initial search into the British Rate and Data (BRAD) directory reveals a limited amount of information regarding circulation and audience type (socio-economic groups). This can be cross-referenced (or cross-tabulated) with the Target Group Index (see page 146) to reveal, for example, types of audience according to lifestyles and typical product purchases, in addition to the usual demographic information.

The qualitative data explain how the media are used by target audiences – the role the media play in people's lives. Some advertising agencies use focus

TABLE 7.1 Summary of media characteristics

	TV	Radio	Cinema	Daily and Sunday press	Evening and regional press	Magazines	Posters	Direct mail	Internet
AUDIENCE									
Audience size	Some wastage, large and national, new niche opportunities	National coverage now available	National coverage	Large and mostly national	Small, some networks	Mostly national (and international)	National coverage can be difficult	Large national and international	Rapidly growing national and international audience
Audience type	Few 15- to 24-year-olds, high 55+	Many housewives, commuters	Young, upmarket	Socio-economic	Geographic segments	Lifestyle/demographic	Commuters, car drivers, etc	Any target available	Targeted by site type – any target available
Audience state of mind	Moving towards active viewers with interactive potential	Often active audience – background/audio wallpaper	Captive audience, willing suspension of disbelief	Deliberately read	Deliberately read	Relaxed and involved with magazine			Active, inquisitive
COST									
Cost of production	High	Low	High	Low–medium	Low	Low–medium	Medium	Low	10–30% of the cost of media
Minimum cost of space	High (for peak time national exposure)	Low	High	Medium	Low	Low–medium	Low–medium	High but can experiment in small quantities	Generally no minimum Large portals require £1,000 minimum spend

Average cost per thousand	Low (£7.80)	Very low (less than £2.50)	£55	Low–medium (£8)	Medium (£30)	Medium (£12–£70)	High (£500)	Banners = £15, pop-ups = £30, other rich = £35+
Extra advantages	Adds credibility to product or company, rapid, high coverage, interactive capability	Transportable medium	High impact and captive audience	Quick coverage build	Location specific	Quality and low wastage		Generates fully accountable direct response and dialogue with audience
MESSAGE								
Variable/sense	Sight, sound, colour, movement, time constraint	Sound and time constraint	Big impact, enhanced sight and sound	Now mostly colour with some black and white	Black and white with some colour	4-colour	4-colour, big impact	4-colour and 3-D possibility; Infinite colour, 3-D, sound, interactive
Serial ad sequence	Viewed serially, no competition from other ads or editorial but zapping prevalent	Serially, less zapping	Serially and no zapping	Must compete with other ads and editorial on same page	Slow coverage build with monthly mags			Non-linear medium, can jump back and forward

TABLE 7.1 *Continued*

	TV	Radio	Cinema	Daily and Sunday press	Evening and regional press	Magazines	Posters	Direct mail	Internet
Transitory	Highly transitory since you cannot refer back to ad once shown (unless taped, or with interactive ads that can be bookmarked)		Can keep clippings or refer back if desired			Can refer back, walk	Can refer back/keep back or drive past	Can refer until coupon campaign ends	
Demonstration	Idea for usage and impulse purchases	Difficult	Yes	Benefits or results can be shown but not product usage		Only short image benefit	Yes	Yes	
Detail/technical	Viewer cannot absorb detail	Urgency and topical	Visual and audio	Yes	Yes	Yes	No	Yes	Yes
Urgency/topicality	Difficult to adapt ads to daily events, high level of recall	Unique immediacy, urgency and topicality	No	Yes	Yes	Magazine image spills on to ad		Cut image?	Yes
EASE OF MEDIA BUYING	Complicated	Inflexible	Flexible	Flexible	Flexible	Flexible	Inflexible	Flexible	Timing flexible, rates negotiable
Lead times	Long	Short/ medium	Short	Short	Short	Medium Long	Long	Short Medium	3–10 days, depending on richness of media

Clearance	Script (1 week), finished film (1 week), Clearcast	Same day clearance, Clearcast	One week clearance, CAA						Generally required for editorially driven content and where advertiser is potential competitor
Audience research*	BARB and TGI	RAJAR and TGI	CAVIAR, TGI and EDI	NRS, QRS, TGI and BMRC	JICREG and TGI	NRS (and ABC), QRS and TGI	Postar and TGI	TGI	ABCE, Nielsen Net Ratings
High-frequency facility	Yes	Yes	No	Yes	Daily and weekly	Weekly/monthly	Yes	Yes	Yes
National coverage	Expert's job but network exists and international cable/satellite	National network through NNR	Yes	Yes	No national network but all major conurbations covered	Yes	Yes	Yes	Nearly half all adult UK population covered London/South-East of England bias

Code of advertising practice (clearance is not compulsory)

*Audience research: see 'Further information', page 180

SOURCE: Media Planning Group

FIGURE 7.3   Proposed media schedule for an Orange campaign

MEDIA PLANNING
Press Schedule

Page 179: Media Schedule

| Client: | Orange | | | Period: | 3rd July - 6th August 2000 | | Date: | 23rd August 2000 |
| Campaign: | Best Network | | | Status: | Booked / v10 | | Format: | Page / tabloid page |

Media (all 4clr)	Size	No. Ins.	Cost per Insertion	Total Gross Cost	Total Client Cost	July 10th	17th	24th
		Page / tabloid page equivalent.				All dailies on Wed / Fri option unless otherwise specified.		
The Guardian	38x6	4				3 x Tabloid Page (Thu/Fri)	Tabloid Page	
The Times	37x6	5				3 x Tabloid Page (Thu/Fri)	Tabloid Page	Tabloid Page
Telegraph	38x6	3				Tabloid Page (Wed) 1/2 price	Tabloid Page	Tabloid Page
The Independent	38x6	2				Tabloid Page (Thu/Fri)		Tabloid Page
Financial Times	38x6	2				Tabloid Page (Thu/Fri)	Tabloid Page	
The Sun	page	3				Page (Thu/Fri)	Page	Page
Daily Mirror	page	3				Page (Thu/Fri)	Page	Page (Tues)
Daily Mail	page	3				Page (Thu)	Page (Mon - Fri)	Page (Mon - Fri)
Sunday Times	37x6	2					Tabloid Page	Tabloid Page
Sunday Telegraph	38x6	4				3 x Tabloid Page	Tabloid Page	
Independent on Sunday	38x6	4				3 x Tabloid Page	Tabloid Page	
Observer	38x6	2				Tabloid Page	Tabloid Page	
Sunday Business	38x6	2				Tabloid Page	Tabloid Page	
News of the World	page	2				Page	Page	
Sunday Mirror	page	2				Page	Page	
Sunday People	page	1				Page		
Mail on Sunday	page	4				3 x Page	Page	
Regional Titles								
Metro	page	2				Page (Thu/Fri)		Page
Evening Standard	page	3				Brand Page (Mon - Fri)	Page (Mon - Fri)	Page (Mon - Fri)
Belfast Telegraph	38x6	2				Tabloid Page (Thu/Fri)	Tabloid Page	
Irish News / Newsletter	page	2				Page (Thu/Fri)		Page
The Glasgow Herald	38x6	2				Tabloid Page (Thu/Fri)		Tabloid Page
Daily Record	page	2				Page (Thu/Fri)	Page	
Scotsman	38x6	2				Tabloid Page (Thu/Fri)	Tabloid Page	
Scotland on Sunday	38x6	1				Tabloid Page		
Sunday World	page	1				Page		
Sunday Mail	page	1				Page		
O Magazine	page	1					Page	

Total Cost to Client	£	
Total Budget	£	
Difference	£	

	Cov and Freq	Scotland Cov and Freq	N. Ireland Cov and Freq
ABC1 Adults	82% @ 4.1	92% @ 3.8	84% @ 4.0
All Orange	81% @ 4.1	96% @ 3.8	83% @ 4.0
Non-Orange	82% @ 4.3	93% @ 4.3	84% @ 4.1
AB Businessmen	90% @ 5.2	93% @ 5.1	91% @ 5.0
Decision Makers	93% @ 5.6	97% @ 7.3	94% @ 6.0

N.B. Performance figures are for national press and magazines.

groups to research the obscure media used by a particular group of opinion leaders or to investigate how an audience uses the media.

Media research bureaux

TV audiences are measured by the Broadcast Audience Research Bureau (BARB), which monitors a sample of 4,500 homes through its people meter. The meter records what stations are turned on, and the hand-held remote control unit inputs data about who is watching the TV.

Radio audiences are measured by Radio Joint Audience Research (RAJAR). In 1992 RAJAR replaced the Joint Industry Council for Radio Audience Research (JICRAR).

Cinema uses Cinema and Video Industry Audience Research (CAVIAR) to measure cinema and video audience size and profiles. Admissions are also measured by Gallup/EDI.

Newspaper and magazine readership is measured by National Readership Survey (NRS), which carries out 35,000 in-home interviews each year. The Audit Bureau of Circulation (ABC) audits the sales or circulation of over 2,000 different publications, including the nationals. ABC also audits and verifies website traffic.

Freesheets or local newspapers use the Verified Free Distribution (VFD) system.

Posters use Poster Audience Research (Postar) and the Poster Audit Bureau (PAB).

British Rate and Data (BRAD) is the media buyer's reference book, because it lists all the circulation or audience figures, as well as the costs (rate card costs). It also gives detailed information on deadlines, mechanical data and commissions on 2,706 newspapers, 3,130 consumer publications, 5,208 business publications, 1,838 new media, radio and TV networks, and much more. The monthly book, which contains over 1,200 pages, costs £600 for a single copy or £970 for an annual subscription. The information is also available online for the same price, or as part of planning version BRADnet for £2,120.

Media jargon and vocabulary

Cover and reach

'Coverage' is the percentage of the target audience reached by the advertising. If, for example, *ITV News* reaches 5 million viewers, 16 per cent of whom are ABC1 male, then an ad placed during the break will reach 0.8 million ABC1 males (16 per cent of 5 million viewers). If ABC1 men are the target audience and there are, in fact, 10.6 million ABC1 men in the UK, then although the advertisement reaches 0.8 million ABC1 men the coverage is only 8 per cent (0.8 million as a percentage of the total target market of 10.6 million).

Frequency

This is the number of times an ad is shown or placed in a particular period of time. How many times should an ad be shown and seen? Between four and six times? The optimum frequency is often really unknown. Should it be concentrated over a short period (a 'burst strategy') or spread steadily over a longer period (a 'drip strategy')? For example, an advertising frequency of 60 can be built up by either 1) having the same advertisement shown before, during and after *ITV News* every weekday for four weeks, or 2) having one advertisement every six days throughout the year.

Opportunities to see (OTSs)

OTSs are the number of exposures or opportunities that a particular audience has to see a particular advertisement. In the previous example there would have been 5 million OTSs for adults and 0.8 million for ABC1 men. If the ad went out every night for five nights during the *ITV News* break, the total number of ABC1 men OTSs would be 5 × 0.8 million = 4 million OTSs.

Cost per thousand (CPT)

CPT calculates the average cost of reaching 1,000 of the population. If it costs, say, £100,000 to place a 30-second spot (advertisement) on national TV with a peak-time audience of, say, 10 million, then the cost per thousand or the cost of reaching each or any group of 1,000 people within the audience is £100,000 divided by 10,000 (10 million = 10,000 groups of 1,000 people). The cost per thousand here is £10. CPT allows cross-comparisons across different media types and media vehicles (although quality of media must also be analysed). For example, if a full-page advertisement in the *Sun* reaches, say, 9.5 million (bought by 3.5 million but read by 9.5 million) and costs, say, £45,000, then the CPT is £45,000 divided by 9,500 (9.5 million = 9,500 lots of 1,000 people), which gives a cost of £4.74 per thousand. CPM (cost per mille/thousand) is the same as CPT and is commonly used in the United States.

Ideally, cost per enquiry or order generated gives a truer picture, but this can only be measured after the advertisement has run (and if the advertisement was designed to achieve these kinds of responses rather than, say, increase awareness or change attitudes). Experience and knowledge provide useful insights into media scheduling and buying. CPT varies according to the actual selection of a particular medium (say, the press versus television) and a specific media vehicle (say, *Amateur Gardening* versus *The Economist*). The quality of the media affects

CPT, as does the quality of the audience, ie advertising to high-income earners will cost more per thousand than reaching a larger, middle-income audience.

TV rating points (TVRs)

TV rating points are referred to as gross rating points (GRPs) in the United States and overseas. GRPs can be used across different media, whereas TVRs refer to TV in the UK. One TV rating point is 1 per cent of the target audience. The percentage of the target audience viewing a spot ('reach') multiplied by the average number of opportunities to see gives the TVR. Television companies will sell packages of guaranteed TVRs. For example, a target of 240 TVRs means that 60 per cent of the target audience will have, on average, 4 OTSs. It could also mean that 40 per cent have seen it six times. Reference to the media schedule quickly identifies the frequency. Four hundred TVRs (80 per cent seeing the message five times) is considered an average-sized one-month campaign. Eight hundred TVRs in one month is a big campaign. It has been suggested that some confectionery and record companies run a lightweight campaign and buy 100 TVRs so that they can tell the retail trade that they are running a television advertising campaign (the 'pull' helps the 'push').

Impacts

Impacts refer more to TV than the press. Impacts measure the total number of people who saw the ad multiplied by the number of times they saw it. In the *ITV News* case it would be 0.8 million × 5 = 4 million impacts (for ABC1 men). To make more sense of impacts, divide them by the universe (number of people within the target market) to get TVRs (television rating). Impacts are more useful when converted to TVRs.

Drip

Drip means spreading relatively small amounts of advertising over the whole campaign period. A 'steady drip' of advertising creates presence over a longer period of time.

Burst

Burst is the opposite to drip. Here the ads are concentrated into a shorter period of time. Effectively this creates a bigger impact but only for a shorter period of time.

Continuous patterns

Continuous patterns of advertising are a regular and uniform presentation of the message to the target audience. A rising pattern is where the ads are increased up to a particular event. A fading pattern is where the ads are slowly reduced after the event (or after a product launch).

Flighting patterns

Flighting patterns are where the advertiser spreads the ads over a longer period of time. It can mean boosting advertising at certain times to match seasonal demand, match a competitor's ad campaign, support a particular sales promotion, respond to adverse publicity or simply seize a one-off market opportunity.

Pulsing

Pulsing supposedly combines both continuous patterns and flighting patterns, ie to incur high levels of ad spend when required but also to maintain some advertising in between times so that the target audience does not forget the brand. This 'safe option' is an expensive option. Pulsing is also known as the 'long tail approach'. In conjunction with econometric modelling it can actually prove better value.

Pulsing can save money

A radio ad campaign in the Irish Republic found that the campaign caused an uplift in awareness for three weeks after it was broadcast. As a result the agency recommended to the client to move from a bi-weekly burst to a three-weekly burst. This retained the impact of the campaign, saved a lot of money and allowed the campaign to run longer in a 'long tail' format. *NB*: This is not the same as the niche market long tail concept.

Position

Position refers to the place where the ad is shown. Back pages, inside cover pages, right-hand pages,

TV pages and so on have greater readership and more impact than other pages (eg the third right-hand page has a bigger impact than the first left-hand page). Similarly, some positions on a page are more effective than others. Media buyers are aware of this and so are the media owners, since their rate cards (prices) reflect the value of, and demand for, certain positions. Boddingtons beer media strategy was built around position, ie it concentrated its advertisements on the back page of glossy magazines to the extent that it 'owned' the back pages for a period of time.

Environment

The environment or context in which an ad is exposed affects the message itself. The types of features or editorial, and other advertisements, that run alongside an advertisement affect the likely effectiveness of that advertisement. An advertiser can lose credibility if the programme is a parody of the product being advertised, for example the film *Airplane* with an airline ad in the break.

Summary

Media consumption patterns are changing, as are media. Great care is required in developing the right media mix and vehicle mix, as well as timing and pulsing, since this is arguably marketing's single biggest spend. Small savings here can free larger budgets for elsewhere (eg social media campaigns).

Key points from Chapter 7

- Media choice is growing continually.
- Media planning and buying have more of an impact on the bottom line than producing an ad.
- Different media have different advantages and disadvantages – careful planning is required.
- Evaluate media options according to consistent criteria.

References and further reading

Account Planning Group (1987) *How to Plan Advertising*, ed D Cowley, Cassell, London

Davies, M (1992) *The Effective Use of Advertising Media*, 4th edn, Business Books, London

Douglas, T (1984) *The Complete Guide to Advertising*, Papermac, London

EIAA (European Interactive Advertising Association) (2010) *Multi-Screeners Report 2010*

Engel, J, Warshaw, M and Kinnear, T (1991) *Promotional Strategy: Managing the marketing communications process*, Irwin, Homewood, Ill

IAB and Thinkbox (2008) Combine TV and online to boost brand perception, *Brand Republic*, 10 June

IPSOS Canadian Interactive Reid report (2010) *2010 Fact Guide*

Kennedy, J (2009) App-fab, *Marketing Age*, November

Kohler, E (2007) Hyperlocal is more about ads than news, *Technology Evangelist*, 9 August

Learmonth, M (2010) Top marketers to Silicon Valley: Help us get ahead of consumer. Through visits to tech hub, big advertisers getting more than sales pitches, *Ad Age*, 17 May

Marketer (2008) Watching the coffee channel, May

Markiewicz, P, Sherman, N and Jaworski, D (2008) *Millennials and the Digital Entertainment Age: A sourcebook for consumer marketers*, Digital Media Wire, West Hollywood, CA

Mason, R (2010) Moosylvania Marketing, *Advertising Age*, 4 November

Media International, Reed Publishing Services, London

Media Week, EMAP Business Publications, London

Nielsen Wire (2009) TV viewing among kids at an eight-year high, 26 October

Patel, K (2010) Will growing crop of TV apps engage viewers, advertisers?, *Ad Age*, 17 May

Pew Research (2009) Newspapers face a challenging calculus, 26 February

TV free America (2010) Invisible Children blog 2010, TV's ugly stats

XPLANE (2009) Did you know? YouTube video, Fall

Further information

Audit Bureau of Circulation (ABC)
Saxon House
211 High Street
Berkhamsted
Herts HP4 1AD
Tel: +44 (0)1442 870800
www.abc.org.uk

British Audience Research Bureau (BARB)
18 Dering Street
London W1R 9AF
Tel: +44 (0)20 7591 9610
www.barb.co.uk

British Rate and Data (BRAD)
Brad Insight
Greater London House
Hampstead Road
London NW1 7EJ
Tel: +44 (0)20 7728 4315
www.brad.co.uk

Cinema and Video Industry Audience Research (CAVIAR)
Digital Cinema Media
12 Golden Square
London W1F 9JE
Tel: +44 (0)20 7534 6363
Fax: +44 (0)20 7534 6464
www.carltonscreen.com

Joint Industry for Regional Press Research (JICREG)
c/o The Newspaper Society
8th Floor
St Andrew's House
St Andrew Street
London EC4A 3AY
Tel: +44 (0)20 7632 7400
www.jicreg.co.uk

National Readership Survey Ltd (NRS)
40 Parker Street
London WC2B 5PQ
Tel: +44 (0)20 7242 8111
Fax: +44 (0)20 7242 8303
www.nrs.co.uk

Postar Ltd
Summit House
27 Sale Place
London W2 1YR
Tel: +44 (0)20 7479 9700
www.postar.co.uk

Radio Joint Audience Research (RAJAR)
2nd Floor
5 Golden Square
London W1F 9BS
Tel: +44 (0)20 7292 9040
Fax: +44 (0)20 7292 9041
www.rajar.co.uk

Verified Free Distribution (VFD) – contact the Audit Bureau of Circulation (ABC)
Saxon House
211 High Street
Berkhamsted
Herts HP4 1AD
Tel: +44 (0)1442 870800
www.abc.org.uk

08
Marketing communications agencies

LEARNING OBJECTIVES

By the end of this chapter you will be able to:

- Understand the range of different types of agencies
- Draw the structure of a large agency and modify it with new marketing tools
- Discuss different methods of remunerating agencies
- Set up a selection process
- Nurture relationships between agency and client

Agency types

Introduction

This chapter covers agencies, types of agencies, their structure, fees and working relationships, from shortlisting to briefing, selecting, hiring and firing.

There are many types of agencies, including advertising, sales promotion, direct mail, PR, corporate identity design, web design and more. Some call themselves agencies and others, consultancies. Regardless of title, the barriers created by the separate disciplines are falling. Corporate identity design consultants' services are spreading into advertising campaigns (to launch the new identities); sales promotion consultants are tempted into direct mail, as this communications tool requires a constant flow of incentives, premiums and sales promotions; advertising agencies are dropping the word 'advertising' and PR consultants are dropping 'PR', as these terms restrict them from developing and delivering the integrated marketing communications services their clients require. The overall approach by, and structures of, advertising agencies is changing. Most agencies have moved their total focus beyond the one-way 'tell' medium of traditional broadcasting, with its limited levels of interactive responsiveness. These agencies are now integrating more closely with the 'responsive disciplines', such as direct mail, sales promotions and social media. Moving from 'tell campaigns' to 'listening campaigns' requires a constant customer dialogue nurtured and integrated across many media.

Some agencies see new structures as an exciting challenge for the agency world. 'At the very least, the shaking up of structures and processes that pre-date the new technology by about 100 years can't fail to have a liberating effect that should be greatly to the benefit of clients', says **Sir Martin Sorrell (1996), Chairman, WPP Group. Other agencies feel that the required changes in agency structure require not just new structures but new language.** 'Impact' is being replaced by 'dialogue' (and even 'trialogue'), 'poster advertising' by 'street dialogue'. Perhaps 'direct mail and radio' should change to 'kitchen dialogue'. 'Engagement' has become the new mantra, replacing 'response'. The process of change among agencies is being driven partly by unsettled clients, visionary agency directors, the media explosion and new types of competition emerging.

> ### Agency opportunity
>
> 'Many brands today are dying. Not the natural death of absence but the slow, painful death of sales and margin erosion. The managers of these brands are not complacent – in fact, they are constantly tweaking the advertising, pricing and cost of their brands. At the heart of the problem is a more fundamental issue: can the original promise of the brand be recreated and a new spark lit with today's consumers? We believe it can. Most brands can be reinvented through brand renaissance.'
>
> Excerpt from a Boston Consulting Group brochure

Although advertising agencies are under siege from aggressive management consultants, young, hungry integrated agencies, expert SEO and viral marketing specialists, social media consultants and disgruntled marketing clients, the advertising agency's structure is still used here, as it offers a broad base upon which other agencies and consultancies often develop their structures.

One of the best-known ad agencies in the world, Saatchi & Saatchi, dropped the word 'Advertising' from its title. It is now just plain Saatchi & Saatchi, the Lovemarks company. It describes itself as a 'full service, integrated communications network'. It even commissioned a short video called 'The last ad agency on earth' (see YouTube) to confirm that the old agency concept was no longer its concept.

DIY, full-service or specialist

As 'ad agencies' are by far the biggest type of agency, TV consumption is still going up and offline budgets are still far greater than online budgets (across the board), 'advertising agencies' will be used here (despite their restructuring into new forms of agency). The larger ad agencies offer a full service, including creative, research and planning, media planning and buying, and production and now social media planning. Some full-service agencies also have departments specializing in forecasting, market intelligence and business planning, together with support services for the advertising campaign, including point-of-sale design, sales literature, sales

TABLE 8.1   The pros and cons of different working relationships

Aspect	Full services (under one roof)	Specialist services	In-house
Management and control	Easier, since it is all under one roof	More work (coordinating)	Total control, but more work involved
Security	Limited risk – sensitive information is shared with agency	More risk – more people have access to information	Minimal risk – no outsiders
Speed/response	Reasonably good	Possible problems if à la carte = more coordination	Fast, since all decision makers are available
Cost	Expensive, high overheads, but lower media costs with agency buying power	Cheaper, fewer overheads	Cheaper, but less media buying power
Fresh views	Yes	Yes	No
Expertise	Yes (jack of all trades, master of none?)	Yes (fill in gaps in client's skills)	No (lack of specialized knowledge)
Stress	Less pressure/workload	Delegate some workload	More stress – more work

conferences and other below-the-line activities such as sales promotion, PR and direct mail. The agency, like any other business, also has other departments that are of little interest to the client, such as accounting and finance, personnel, administration, etc. (See Table 8.1.)

Advertisers can choose to use only their own in-house staff to run a campaign. Do-it-yourself or in-house advertising also varies, as some advertisers prefer to contract out some of their requirements to specialist services such as a specialist media scheduling and buying agency known as a 'media independent'. Similarly, the creative work can be put out to a 'hot shop' or 'creative shop'. Saatchi & Saatchi started as a creative shop. Alternatively, the advertiser can go à la carte by picking and choosing separate agencies with specialist services for different parts of the process, eg using four different agencies for the research, creative, production and media planning/buying stages. There are other types of specialist agencies that focus on a particular industry sector.

A recent discrete development in the à la carte option is the agreement of a large, well-known, full-service advertising agency to subcontract the large agency's creative services to a small communications consultancy on an ad hoc basis. This may last only as long as the agency has spare capacity or is searching for extra revenue. Some clients demand that their full-service agencies work alongside the client's separate choice of media independents. Some full-service agencies get only a portion of the full job. A recession can force some clients to cut back their own in-house advertising department and operate a less costly and more flexible ad hoc project arrangement with various agencies.

Agency structure

Different types and sizes of agencies have different structures. The structure of a large advertising agency is shown in Figure 8.1, which illustrates the many different departments, people and skills that have to work together to create an advertisement. Companies that have their own in-house advertising departments, and smaller, external agencies, will subcontract (or hire) any of the departments they do not have. Many of the bigger agencies also hire, or subcontract, directors, producers, camera people, photographers, film companies, print and production facilities. Any other agent, agency, consultant or consultancy – whether public relations, direct mail, sales promotion or corporate identity – also relies on the ability to bring together many different skill sets and departments, as shown in Figure 8.1. Although pure ad agencies are growing into integrated agencies offering an additional suite of social media services, TV advertising is not going away and still takes a disproportionately large chunk of any brand's budget. Therefore the original ad agency structure is still worth exploring.

Agencies are evolving from 'pushing advertising campaigns to nurturing communities of consumers and matchmaking them with brands' (Farey-Jones, 2008). There is a new breed of agencies with greater data analytics and planning skills emerging. It is possible that, instead of pitching for a brand's business, agencies may offer a new service – selling access to groups of consumers' groups with similar interests that they have nurtured (eg a Facebook group or a LinkedIn group). Successful agencies will probably connect themselves with clearly defined communities of consumers and 'cultivate insights into their behaviour' (Farey-Jones, 2008). These communities can be online and offline, eg an agency funding a community hall. So many new skills and new departments need to be added to Figure 8.1, eg social community creators, developers and nurturers.

FIGURE 8.1   Structure of a large advertising agency

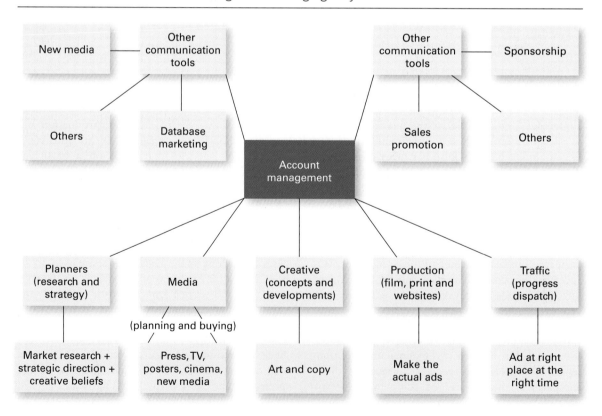

The account executive

Sometimes also called an account representative, the account executive is dedicated to a particular client. The account executive wears two hats – the client's when talking to the agency and the agency's when talking to the client. Responsibilities include: attendance at all client meetings, writing up 'contact reports' and general liaising between the many different members of the agency's team and the client. Many agencies write up contact reports (after each meeting), because they confirm and clarify all key points discussed, conclusions reached and any actions to be taken. This cuts out the opportunity for any misinterpretation further down the road when the client says 'I never said that' or 'I never asked for that.' When agreed by the client, vital documents, such as a summary of the agency's interpretation of the client's brief, or concept proposals, are sometimes required to be signed by the client as 'approved'. This keeps communication clear, reduces ambiguities and, if a row does break out over a particular strategic direction or over the details of copy (the words in the advertisement), the agency can pull out a signed 'approved by' copy. This is particularly helpful when a manager leaves a client company, because it confirms the stage-by-stage approval of the development of a campaign.

to absorb, summarize and translate large market research reports into simple lay terms for inclusion in the creative brief that they, in conjunction with the account manager, give to the creative team. Second, the information has to be interpreted at a strategic and tactical level for discussion with the account executive, account manager, account director and often the client. Planners provide an objective voice, unhindered both by the account executive, who sometimes wants to 'sell' an advertising concept to the client simply because the creative director wants to get on with it, and by clients, who sometimes want to get on with it by quickly running some advertisements to satisfy the sales force, who are anxiously waiting for news on the new campaign.

> ### Joint planning required
>
> 'Decisions about where to run ads and the nature of those ads need to be planned by the same person. I urged marketing departments to call for a joint planning approach in order to achieve a better return on investment for their advertising.'
>
> Stengel (2006)

> ### Account execs – new community managers?
>
> Account people will evolve into 'community managers', who will help the community sell itself to certain brands. 'The agency would know which brand would be best to let in, which brands should be kept out, and what information can be shared and with whom it can be shared.'
>
> Kemp and Kim (2008)

Planners are experts in making sense of market research data and condensing the information into creative briefs. Marketing clients may also want more analysis and insights from customer communities and groups. Research into top marketers from Coca-Cola, Procter & Gamble and HSBC as well as agency bosses from WPP Group, Publicis Groupe and Omnicom revealed that clients will value the importance of passing on information on selected brands which will, in turn, 'boost agency demand for specialists in data analytics and insight' (Kemp and Kim, 2008).

Planning department

Planners are more than glorified researchers. They have to know the right kind of questions to ask in the research, commission the research and interpret the results at two different levels. First, they have

Creative department

It is unfair to stereotype creative people as coming in late, lying around and dreaming up the big ideas and concepts that drive all advertising campaigns. They can work long hours under extreme pressure to deliver unique, creative ideas that grab attention, build brands and win customers. They constantly search for the big idea that has to fit the single-minded strategy presented in the creative brief that is developed by the planning department. Creative people usually work in pairs, covering words and pictures, ie a copywriter (or wordsmith) and an art director.

Creative people – an appreciation

'Somebody finally has to get out an ad, often after hours. Somebody has to stare at a blank piece of paper. Probably nothing was ever more bleak. This is probably the very height of lonesomeness. He is one person and he is alone – all by himself – alone. Out of the recesses of his mind must come words which interest, words which persuade, words which inspire, words which sell. Magic words.'

Leo Burnett, Founder, Leo Burnett Company

Creatives will work more on content required for generating ongoing dialogues with individuals and less on one-way campaigns to a mass audience. Outsourcing will include user-generated content (see Chapter 1), harnessing champions and brand advocates as user-generated content becomes more important.

Creatives' role will change

Creatives will still be important, but will work less on one-way campaigns to a mass audience than on 'ongoing dialogues' with individuals.

Kemp and Kim (2008)

Media department

The media department basically plans and buys the space where the advertisements are eventually placed (press, posters, TV, radio, cinema, etc). Media planners or schedulers are sometimes separate from media buyers, who negotiate and ultimately buy the space from the media owners. Both media planners and media buyers can be further separated into those who specialize in TV, press or new media, etc. The emergence of cable and satellite TV, low-cost print technology and thousands of new websites increases the range of media available to media buyers. As markets fragment and media explode into many more magazines, TV stations and websites, large audiences become more difficult to buy. Despite this, the media explosion presents new opportunities for schedulers and buyers, as these new media vehicles have access to more tightly defined target markets. **The media department now analyses the appropriateness and cost-effectiveness of much more media than ever before.** This is quite a responsibility, as the bulk of the advertising spend is in media and not production (eg a £20 million campaign might have a £19 million media budget and a £1 million production budget). On top of this, media departments can deliver highly creative media strategies that find new ways of delivering advertisements to target audiences. See Chapter 13 for examples.

You think you are overworked – try the media department

The explosion of blogs and other social media has opened new media channels which reach various target groups. If this is where significant numbers of the target audience spend time (consuming this media experience), then surely media buyers and planners now have an awful lot more work to do.

Production department

The production department actually makes the advertisement. Many agencies subcontract various parts of the production, eg hiring a studio, camera crew or photographer, director, editing suites, etc. This can involve long pre-production meetings finalizing all the minute details, flying around the world to shoot some film, and the less glamorous, lonely post-production – working around the clock in a dark and dingy editing suite.

> **Creating games, funny virals and some ads**
>
> Production departments (and outsourced production companies) will be full of clever people, some of whom can create great 60-second movies (and longer-form ads – see Chapter 13), as well as online games and of course contagious virals.

Traffic department

Dispatch, or traffic, is responsible for getting the right artwork or film to the right magazine or TV network at the right time. This becomes complicated where posters, cinema, radio and magazine inserts are included in the media strategy. Multiply this by several different campaigns for a range of different clients, and the need for a traffic manager becomes self-evident. Add in games and virals, and life is going to get busier.

The account management team

In a large agency this can involve an account director, account manager, account executive, planner, creative director, copywriter, art director, TV producer, media director, TV media scheduler, TV airtime buyer, press planner and press buyer.

The three key components

The three key components of the agency are:

1 planning and strategy;
2 creative;
3 media.

Agency remuneration

Agencies have three basic methods of calculating their remuneration: commission, fees and pay-by-results (PBR).

Commission

Although this has changed drastically, historically media owners have given recognized agencies a 15 per cent discount off the rate card price. Thus, in the case of a £10 million TV advertising campaign, the agency gets invoiced by the TV station at rate card £10 million less 15 per cent, ie £8.5 million. The client then gets invoiced by the agency at the full rate card price, ie £10 million (this can be checked with British Rate and Data (BRAD) or the media owner's published rate card). The 15 per cent commission really represents a 17.65 per cent mark-up, ie the £1.5 million commission is the mark-up which the agency adds on to its media cost of £8.5 million:

Agency invoiced by TV station less 15 per cent	£8.5 million
Agency invoices client at full rate card	£10.0 million
Agency mark-up	£1.5 million
Agency mark-up	17.65 per cent

The agency will also apply its agreed mark-up to other services that it subcontracts, such as market research and so on. Thus a piece of research that costs the agency £10,000 would be charged to the client (+17.65 per cent) at £11,765. One of the problems with the commission system is that it can tempt agencies to get clients to spend, spend, spend. Incidentally, the commission system does not necessarily cover all production costs, so production costs are often separately invoiced directly to the client by the agency. Over the past 10 years the number of clients using this method has declined significantly, in favour of a combination of the payment methods outlined below. In fact the 15 per cent commission has been slashed in half by some media owners. Back in 2006, Yahoo announced that it would pay 10 per cent commission to agencies that spend £80,000+ per month on search marketing, 5 per cent to those spending £20,000+ and nothing to agencies that spend less than that.

Commission rebating

Specialist media-buying companies – with much lower overheads – can work with commissions as low as 2 or 3 per cent. Some clients insist that the full-service agency only takes a smaller commission, say 10 per cent, with the balancing 5 per cent going back to the client. Commission rebating occurs when an agency passes on some of its commission to the client. There is no actual refund or rebate. The agencies simply invoice the client at rate card costs less the level of rebate, in this case 5 per cent. Commission rebating opens the door to agencies competing on price instead of on quality of service, as they have done traditionally. Most industries dislike price wars, and advertising is no exception. In 1984, Allen, Brady & Marsh (ABM) resigned its £3.5 million B&Q account after a request for rebates. It also took a large advertisement in the advertising trade press explaining that the 15 per cent commission left most agencies with 2 per cent profits after tax and any reduction would affect the quality of advertising. It fought against the tide of change, and refused to become involved in commission rebating. ABM was a fantastic agency generating some classic advertising campaigns, but, sadly, it no longer exists.

Many clients today are moving towards fees instead of solely commission-based remuneration.

Fees

Smaller clients with smaller media spends do not generate sufficient commission, so a fee will generally be agreed. Larger clients are also moving towards fees – an annual, quarterly or monthly retainer or, alternatively, a project fee. No commission means no media bias, since the agency is then free to recommend, say, direct mail, without losing any of its income (which would have been generated through commissions).

Many agencies receive a fee along with some level of commission, and/or some level of pay-by-results. The agency's remuneration essentially depends on how much work is involved and how much the client is likely to spend (on media). The trend, particularly with larger clients, appears to be moving towards a fee basis or a mixture of fees, commissions and results.

Pay-by-results can be mutually beneficial. It is sometimes disliked because of the lack of control that the agency may have over its own destiny.

Pay-by-results (PBR)

Not so long ago, major agencies would dabble in some PBR, while the newer agencies, hungry for

business, were prepared to put their heads on the block and offer most of their services on a pay-by-results basis. Today PBR has become the norm rather than the exception, with the majority of British advertisers remunerating their creative advertising agencies according to the results they achieved. Media agencies had an even bigger majority, with 60 per cent being paid subject to PBR factors (ISBA, 2010). Media owners like Google offer another form of PBR: CPC (cost per click) and CPA (cost per action). If no one clicks on the sponsored phrase or no one buys (if that is the goal) then Google do not get paid a penny.

The problem with PBR is that some results are beyond the agency's influence, eg poor product quality control, late delivery or inadequate distribution, a price change, a strike at the factory or competitor activities such as doubling advertising and cutting prices. So if sales form the main criterion for payment then the agencies are vulnerable by the very nature of their dependency on so many uncontrollable variables.

If, on the other hand, the payment is linked to results directly influenced by advertising, say level of awareness or a shift in image or positioning, then the agency has more control over its own destiny. Results, of course, have to be measured through market research. **One area where PBR is relatively easy to manage is direct mail campaigns that deliver a certain number of enquiries, orders or customers.** Similarly, an SEO campaign can be linked to number of visitors generated by SEO. Another area where results are easily measured and are directly related to the agency's input is media buying. If an agency achieves media buying at a price that is better than average, then the saving can be shared between client and agency. For example, if the average advertising cost per thousand to reach, say, housewives with children is £3.50, and if the agency gets this for 10 per cent less, then the saving might be split 8 per cent to the client and 2 per cent to the agency. (Note: quality of the media is also taken into account.) Some agencies, like BBH, prefer a fixed bid with shared risk system. For example, if an advertisement is produced under budget, the production company keeps a percentage and the client receives a percentage. If the advertisement is 10 per cent over budget, the client pays; anything over 10 per cent and the production company pays.

PBR extends beyond advertising into other disciplines as far away as design. This can apply to new product design (as a royalty) or even packaging design, when the packaging design consultancy bases its fee (or a portion of its fees) on the client's increase in sales occurring after the launch of the newly designed pack. Although PBR appears attractive to the client, it can generate extra administrative work, as exact results have to be measured, royalties and contributions calculated, invoices requested and cheques raised for each agreed accounting period.

The method of agency reimbursement is fundamental to the client–agency relationship (both working and contractual). An agency's range of reimbursement packages can influence the client's selection process.

Agency relationships – selection and retention

The coordination of any campaign's development, launch and measurements requires time and management skills. Powerful personalities in agencies need to be managed. The ability to ask the right question is a valuable management skill. **The fatigue factor in negotiations or discussions can also cause rash decisions to be made.** Marketing people tend to be energetic, enthusiastic, action-oriented achievers. Sometimes steely patience needs to be exercised. Perhaps a decision has to be delayed until further research can answer some emerging questions. Painstaking attention to detail may sometimes seem irksome to the advertising agency, but it is often the mark of a true professional. On the other hand, a key resource, time, may be running out. More research reduces the risk but costs time and money. Can deadlines be moved? Is there money left for more research? Is there time before the competition launches its new offer? A decision made in haste is rarely the best one.

Agency selection process overview

Defining exactly what is required is the first stage of agency selection. This is because an appropriate choice is partly determined by a specific requirement. Some furniture retail chains may consider the strength of the media department the key criterion when choosing an agency, particularly if the store

primarily wants maximum media coverage for its relatively straightforward black-and-white product information advertisements. Another client may be looking for a radically fresh approach and have a bias towards agencies with abundant creative talent. Either way, a clear brief should be prepared to identify exactly what – in marketing and advertising terms – the new advertising campaign is trying to achieve (see Chapter 2, 'The brief').

The agency selection procedure is as follows:

1 Define requirements.
2 Develop a pool list of attractive agencies.
3 Credentials pitch (by the agencies).
4 Issue brief to shortlisted agencies.
5 Full agency presentation or pitch.
6 Analysis of pitch.
7 Select winner.
8 Agree contract details.
9 Announce winner.

Some clients prefer to get on with it by issuing a full brief to the shortlist of, say, six agencies without going through the agency credentials presentation. Other clients prefer to restrict the valuable research findings and strategic thinking to as few agencies as possible, because the unsuccessful agencies are free to work for the competition at any time in the future.

Pool list

Most advertising managers and marketing managers observe various campaigns by watching advertising and noting any particularly attractive campaigns. Agencies working for the competition need to be excluded or treated with extreme caution. Some desk research, both online and offline, can reveal the agencies behind the brands by reference to organizations such as Nielsen Media Research or Adforum.com, which allow advertisers to look for agencies using sensible criteria. Advertisers can create shortlists, preview creative work and explore an agency's profile, online and free of charge. Many marketing managers have a fair idea of who is doing what advertising in their sector by constantly reading the trade press. Other managers simply increase their advertising dosage by spending a few weeks watching more advertising than normal. Some clients sift through the agency portfolio videos, which can be bought from Campaign Portfolio or Marketing Week Portfolio for a few hundred pounds (the agencies pay a lot more to acquire this advertising space in the first place). In these videos, agency after agency present themselves in a sometimes surprisingly tedious fashion. Some clients prefer to do their own screening and request an agency reel (video) or an agency information pack directly from a particular agency so that they can view the agency's best work. Try some online sources (eg **www.adforum.com** and **www.mindadvertising. com**) initially, where you can get some agency info, preview some of their creative work (peruse some ads) and sometimes see some interesting updates and communications articles and news alerts. Remember, selecting agencies is hard work and requires rigorous attention to detail. Bad selections are very expensive.

Another way of building a pool list is through the professional associations. Upon receipt of information about a potential client's basic requirements, professional bodies or trade associations such as the **Institute of Practitioners in Advertising (IPA), the Incorporated Society of British Advertisers (ISBA) and the Advertising Association (AA)** all offer to provide lists of agencies that they feel are suitable to handle a specific type and size of business. Similar services are offered by the relevant professional institutes of other service sectors such as public relations, sales promotion, design, direct mail, etc (see 'Further information' at the end of each chapter). This service is normally free, and the associations are extremely helpful to the uninitiated.

There are also agency assessors, such as the Advertising Agency Register, and intermediaries whose business is agency selection. They can handle the development of the pool list, pitch list, pitch analysis, agency selection and even performance assessment of the agency when it starts working for the client.

Probably fewer than 10 per cent of agency hires in the UK are through intermediaries (Bashford, 2008). The assessor services are popular with international clients that need help in all aspects of their quest for the right agency. Similar services are available for PR, direct mail, sales promotion and corporate identity. Intermediaries can help agencies find new business by producing daily reports identifying potential new opportunities, eg when a new marketing or PR director is appointed, which could suggest the need for extra services. Some agencies interview any new senior decision makers, to explore their communications plans and then relay this information back to their clients. Retainer fees can vary, from single-user fees starting at £950 per annum to £60,000 per annum, which then provides an entire outsourced new business function from identifying opportunities to acting on them.

Credentials pitch

Some clients, before issuing a full brief, prefer to ask the pool of agencies to present their credentials. This includes examples of current and previous work, team members' profiles, and company history, structure and facilities. It is worth visiting the agency, and sometimes at short notice, as this gives the client a feel for the potential agency, and its atmosphere, organization, professionalism, etc. From this a final shortlist is selected and issued with a detailed brief.

Long shortlist

Some years ago, Westminster City Council invited 10 agencies to pitch for its communications work. A long shortlist creates an unnecessary amount of unpaid work for everyone concerned.

Briefing, pitching and selecting take time and skills. Apart from creating a lot of work, a large pitch list sometimes leaves sensitive marketing information with many different people. Some cynics see it as an opportunity to get free strategic and tactical ideas from the best brains in each agency.

Issuing the brief

Briefs vary in size, structure and level of detail. Some clients may summarize on to a single A4 sheet of paper; others issue a much more detailed briefing document (one Guinness brief was 100 pages). Essentially, the brief should incorporate at least the situation, objectives and strategy (SOS) and the 3Ms (men/women, money and minutes), part of the SOSTAC® planning system explained in Chapter 10.

The brief tends to be brief, while a marketing communications plan has much more detail. Since the brief usually goes out to several agencies pitching for the business (only one of which will get the business), a difficult dilemma emerges. How much confidential and strategic information should be revealed in the brief, given that the majority of the recipients will not work for you and may one day work for your competition? Food for thought. At the bare minimum, the brief will usually include the following:

1 *Situation* – where you are now, including the market, channels, segments, target markets, trends, competition, market share, position, current and previous campaigns, strengths and weaknesses, unique selling propositions (USPs), features and benefits of the brand and the organization.

2 *Objectives* – where you want to go: marketing objectives and communications objectives (see page 233 for examples) plus specifically defining exactly what is the problem (or opportunity). Include the required positioning and tone of voice. Ensure also that effectiveness criteria and evaluation methodology are clearly specified.

3 *Strategy* – how you are going to get there (including how the marketing strategy fits in with the overall corporate strategy). This may also include a campaign strategy if this is already worked out.

4 *Control* – how you will know when you've arrived. Both the agency and the client should agree on what success and failure will look like. What are the key criteria, and how will they be measured?

5 *3Ms:*
   – Men/women: who makes the final decision, members of the team, who reports to whom, contacts for additional questions.
   – Money: key question for the agency – what is the budget?
   – Minutes: timescale and deadlines for pitch, agency selection and eventual campaign launch.

Control is sometimes included, as it outlines how the campaign will be measured, which in turn motivates the team to get it right. A smaller client may prefer to replace the advertising and/or marketing objectives with a statement of the problem and subsequently ask the agency to present a complete promotional plan. It is likely that the agency's first question will be: 'How much do you have to spend?' As mentioned, there are obvious dangers of releasing strategic information to several agencies, the majority of whom will never work for you (since there is usually only one winner or single agency selected). The corollary is that too little information reduces the quality (and possibly strategic direction) of the proposals. For that reason, it can be helpful to show examples of the kinds of ads that are preferred: this can help creatives to get a feel for what you want. So start collecting ads, sales promotions, web pages, packaging, etc now.

It is important to get the brief correct and concise. If there are specific requirements, spell them out, eg 'It must be clearly legible from 8 feet away' or the 'The brand name must stand out from the crowd', etc. You must work hard at stating your positioning and of course benefits, USPs, etc. Remember, a casual brief will probably generate casual concepts followed by frustrations and accusations. Get the relationship off to a good start with a clear, concise, yet comprehensive, brief.

Pre-pitch agency efforts

The shortlisted agencies are invited to make a full presentation or sales pitch. This usually involves several members of the agency staff and is viewed by several members of the client company. The cost of a major pitch varies from £10,000 to £50,000 (up to six agency people involved for six weeks, £36,000, plus £10,000 for materials plus £4,000 research). Preparation for a pitch is usually an intensive affair and can include researching the client's market, media, company structure and individual personalities (prior knowledge of who will attend the pitch and hopefully some background information on their personalities and interests), strategic planning, brainstorming, concept development (advertising ideas), slide shows, videos, rehearsals and even meditation. Without doubt, new business pitches increase the adrenalin flow inside agencies.

US-owned McCann Erickson is reported to draft in a professional teacher of meditation and

TABLE 8.2   Pre-pitch agency initiatives

Client	Agency	Stunt
Kiss FM Radio	BBDO	Delivered a framed poster to the Kiss MD bearing the legend 'We'll put your name on everyone's lips'*
Kiss FM Radio	Saatchi	Covered Kiss HQ with pink balloons on Valentine's Day
Guardian	Publicis	Booked a 96-sheet (40' × 10' poster) site opposite the newspaper's offices during the week of the pitch and ran flattering ads that changed each day*
Financial services company	Publicis	Sent a safe containing the agency's credentials
Toyota	Saatchi	Three Toyota cars suspended above Charlotte Street, hanging out of the agency's offices*

* Won the account

relaxation techniques before every pitch. JWT practises its pressure presentation techniques with bizarre scenarios like asking its teams to imagine that they discover one of their art directors pushing cocaine and that, as they prepare to fire him, they discover his wife is dying of cancer and in need of private medical treatment.

Real empathy, sound strategy, exciting creative work and reasonable costs are often considered to be the key factors during a pitch, but some agencies take initiatives before the actual pitch, as Table 8.2 shows.

Pre-pitch feelings – a client's view?

Other potential or prospective clients would deny any such self-imposed pressure. They may see the pitch as an exciting and stimulating process full of fresh ideas and strategic thinking presented by clever, articulate (and sometimes entertaining) people. Client egos are massaged, and generally the prospect is treated as a revered guest. Other prospective clients see pitches as a more tedious affair, since they have to repeat their brief in detail several times over and then sit through the inevitable credentials bit before they get to the heart of the matter – the agency proposals.

Will they love me?

'Our research has shown that, generally speaking, clients are not happy about changing agencies. Such events are usually a signal that they are unable to sustain a productive relationship with other people, which is something that none of us is pleased to accept, however difficult the other people might be… the prospect [potential client] is under pressure from his boss to get it right quickly… so when he steps from the bustle and stress of his own trade into the palm-fringed oasis of Berkeley Square or Charlotte Street or Covent Garden it is possible that he has two questions in his mind: "Will they love me?" and "Can they save my neck?"'

Brian Johnson, New Business Director, JWT

Most selling situations, including pitches, are about the removal of uncertainty. So understanding the problem, and identifying clear solutions with enthusiasm and conviction, is a winning formula.

The pitch

After weeks of intensive preparation of exciting creative ideas, ingenious media plans and pitch rehearsals, copies of the proposal or pitch document are laser-printed, bound and made ready for client distribution after the main presentation. The pitch itself is where an advertising agency has the opportunity to advertise or sell itself. Given that most campaigns try to be different, grab attention and make an impression, it is understandable that some agencies should regard a pitch as a creative opportunity also. There are many stories of daring pitch techniques, some of which work and some of which do not. Here are a few.

Legendary 1980s agency ABM created the classic British Rail pitch, which purposely created client tension when the top executives from British Rail were kept waiting in a smoke-filled reception area while the receptionist ignored them throughout her gossip-filled telephone conversation. Eventually a space was cleared among the empty cans and orange peels, and the executives were invited to wait, as the agency people were 'busy'. After some minutes the British Rail executives had had enough. As they got up to leave, the agency chairman, Peter Marsh, clad in full BR uniform (complete with cap, whistle and flag), burst in and said, 'You don't like it. Why should your passengers?' He then invited them to listen to how he and his colleagues were going to solve their problems.

Don White, formerly of Benton & Bowles, is reported to have dressed up as a Butlins redcoat for a Butlins pitch. The client took one look, said 'Anyone dressed like that isn't suitable for my business' and left. David Abbott of Abbott Mead Vickers is reported to have greeted Metropolitan Police Commissioner Sir Robert Mark with a high-pitched nasal 'Hello, hello, hello' as he arrived to hear the agency pitch. Not amused, Sir Robert left the building and was never heard of again.

Agencies pitching for the Weetabix breakfast cereal account were invited to make their pitches in a hotel. As ABM was the last agency to pitch on the final morning, it decided to redecorate the function room in the ABM colours. This required an overnight painting and carpeting exercise. A stage was built, and a special chair was delivered to the function room for Mr Robinson, the arthritic and ageing Weetabix chairman. As the Weetabix panel seated themselves the next morning, the lights dimmed until they were all immersed in an enthralling darkness. A spotlight burst a stream of light on to the stage, where Peter Marsh knelt as he opened his pitch with: 'As one of Britain's few remaining wholly owned independent advertising agencies, it gives me great pleasure to present to you, Mr Robinson, as chairman of one of Britain's few wholly owned cereal manufacturers...' ABM won the account.

One final ABM classic pitch was for Honda. ABM hired the 60-piece Scots Guards bagpipe band to play the Honda jingle 'Believe in freedom, believe in Honda', while marching up and down London's Norwich Street (where ABM was making its pitch). Again, ABM picked up the account. Another agency, AMV, had Hollywood hero Bob Hoskins at its pitch for BT (which it won).

Strict adherence to the time and type of presentation (specified by the client) is essential. When Burkitt Weinreich Bryant was pitching for Littlewoods, it was asked to make a 'short and sweet' final pitch, since the then 92-year-old chairman, the late Sir John Moores, would be in attendance. The trade press reported that 'after over 30 minutes managing director Hugh Burkitt was asked to finish as it became obvious that Sir John's interest and attention was waning'. A row broke out as Hugh Burkitt persisted and a senior Littlewoods executive tried to stop the pitch.

In 1992, when British Airways moved from Saatchi & Saatchi to Maurice and Charles Saatchi's new outfit, M&C Saatchi, all the agencies involved threw everything at this prestigious £30 million account. In an attempt to dramatize BA's global reach, Saatchi & Saatchi did the pitch in different rooms for different stages. Each room had been completely redecorated in the styles, natural habitat and climate of particular parts of the world – tropical rainforests, etc. When Bartle Bogle Hegarty (BBH) got its chance, it reassured BA about BBH's ability to create extremely satisfied clients by providing ready-made testimonials after the presentation – a wall went back and BA were surrounded by the key decision makers of every one of BBH's clients, who then had lunch with them. When M&C Saatchi got its chance, Maurice Saatchi stood up and talked about the importance of music to the BA brand, explaining that they had commissioned their own composer to create a unique blend of popular classical music that BA could own. A growing murmur of approval was heard. He went on to say that they would like the client to meet the composer, at which point in walked Andrew Lloyd Webber.

Dropping your guard

During an intense, high-profile, multimillion-pound pitch, the client called for a 10-minute break. Unfortunately for the agency (which will remain unnamed), a senior agency member had forgotten to remove his scribbled notes, which the client accidentally read. 'Watch out for the — in the glasses', it said at one point.

Not surprisingly, the agency lost the pitch. Some time later, the same agency was pitching for another piece of the business and, as the agency opened its pitch, all of the client team simultaneously donned pairs of glasses! The agency coped and went on to win this separate piece of business.

Pitches, like presentations for major campaigns, are now an ongoing process where effort is concentrated on developing a relationship (relationship marketing) with the client before the final presentation. This can sometimes involve client exposure to the strategy and even the advertisements before D-Day. One UK agency, Howell Henry Chaldecott Lury, has tried to appropriate this process on its own with what it calls 'tissue groups', ie a series of build-up meetings with the client. In the United States the most notable exponent, Chiat Day, has been doing this for a long time. Without doubt there is a cultural shift to ongoing pitches rather than a big finale.

An online pitch

The British Interactive Media Association accepted pitches only via Facebook and Twitter. 'We read about BIMA's agency trawl in *PR Week*, so one of our consultants became a follower of the BIMA Chair, Paul Walsh. Within minutes he came back to us with a brief and we started on the pitch', said Jennifer Janson from Six Degrees, the agency that eventually won the pitch.

Williams (2008)

Analysing the agency

As Nigel Bogle, CEO of Bartle Bogle Hegarty, says: 'The key questions today are less about an agency's ability to execute brilliantly and more about visionary strategic thinking, razor-sharp positioning, pinpoint targeting and ingenious media solutions.'

The order of importance of the following questions can vary, depending on what the prospective client really wants. Some clients may consider the agency's location and car parking facilities relevant, whereas other clients would discount this as trivial and irrelevant to good advertising. Here are the 20 most vital questions to help choose the right agency:

1 Does the agency really have a feel for my product and market? Does it really understand my brand's situation and potential?

2 Has it got strong research and planning capability?

3 Does it know the best media to use? Will its media-buying skills make my budget go a long way?

4 Has it got creative flair? Does it win awards? Does it suggest new ideas?

5 Is it full-service, or does everything get subcontracted out? Can it handle a pack redesign, public relations, sales promotion and direct mail if called upon?

6 How much integration experience with above-, through- and below-the-line as well as online does it have?

7 Is it international? Can its headquarters force it to resign the account should it decide to seek business in the same industry overseas? Alternatively, can it take on a lot of our coordination work through its own international management network?

8 What will it charge? And on what basis? How much time will it spend on the account?

9 How does it allocate resources in the planning, testing and evaluation process?

10 Does it display cost-consciousness?

11 How will it measure its effectiveness?

12 Are we a small fish in a big pond? Is it too small or too big for us? Do we have contact

with the principal partners? Will it fire us if a competitor offers it a bigger account (should we insist on a five-year contract)?

13 Who will work on the account? Are we likely to get on together (chemistry)? Will the pitch team be involved? How stable will our account team be? Are the people who worked on the case histories still with the agency? (This is a crucial question.)

14 Does it have a good track record? Do clients stick with it and place repeat business with the agency? If not, why not?

15 How is my investment going to be returned? (This should feature prominently in the agency's pitch.)

16 How much experience does the agency have in marketing integration (particularly with the internet)?

17 What is the agency process (not just a bunch of arrows in a fancy PowerPoint slide)? Ask how it intends to allocate resources (time and people) to particular aspects of the campaign, including planning, concept development, testing and evaluation, etc. This helps in making interesting comparisons with other agencies. If an agency is unclear about this, then perhaps it is running an inefficient business (which might cost you money).

18 Ask how much time it will devote to your account.

19 Also, what are the agency retention rates?

20 Check its references. References of past clients can also be requested.

Choosing an agency – an assessment form

The assessment form shown in Figure 8.2 can be weighted and scored as appropriate for each client's needs. A rating scale of 1–6 can be used. Agencies should be assessed using the same criteria. Few agencies perform so outstandingly that they remove all doubt in the client's mind as to which agency it should choose. The criteria should be agreed in advance by the team involved in the selection process. The assessment form in Figure 8.2 shows one approach that attempts to formalize the selection

by using consistent criteria. Each company obviously tailors its own approach.

And some agencies add a little extra hook, sometimes proprietary applications, widgets or iApps, eg a South Africa multimedia agency won the UK Tourism account when it presented a digital workflow system that enabled regional offices to remotely customize English-language campaigns to their specific needs. Called Dynamic Positioning Mode, it was a new system of profiling consumers and generating consumer relationships using digital marketing tools.

The pitch is never over

After making a good pitch, a well-known agency kindly offered a chauffeur-driven car to take the clients to the next agency on the pitch list. During the journey the client team analysed the previous pitch and commented that the media strategy appeared 'off-brief'. The next day the agency found a way of representing the media strategy – and it won the business. The limo driver was an account man at the agency. Ethical or not, it's reality.

After the pitch – the agency awaits the decision

Post-pitch tension is agonizing. Awaiting the outcome of a pitch is a tense and worrying time. When the phone eventually rings and it turns out to be the prospect, everyone holds their breath. Rejection means total failure. All the brilliant ideas, the careful research, the buzz of excitement, the long hours – all down the drain. Selection means total success. The post-pitch wait makes the mind wander. Were there any clues as to what the client thought of the pitch? Len Weinreich, advertising guru, gives a nervous insight in 'Scratching an indecent living' (see Figure 8.3 on page 197) and an almost unbearable wait in 'No news is bad news' (see Figure 8.4 on page 198).

Agency rejection

A rejected agency's managing director has the difficult job of picking up the shattered team and building up the agency morale again. The rejected

FIGURE 8.2 Choosing an agency – an assessment form

AGENCY	Understand our product and company?	Commitment to our project?	Research, planning & strategic thinking	Media planning and buying	Creative	Size, in-house resources, full service	International	Location	Fee/cost	Will we get on?	Opinion of existing clients
1											
2											
3											
4											
5											

FIGURE 8.3

Scratching an indecent living

My ferrety acquaintance, Crispin Neat, intrepid slogan detective, telephoned recently. "Hello, Lenny," he burbled. "I thought you might like to know that I'm branching out. Diversifying."

"Excellent news, Crispin," I replied, feigning enthusiasm. "What other services will you offer the hard-pressed advertiser?"

"Scratch pad deciphering."

"What's that?"

"Simple, Lenny, old chum. You gather and despatch the scratch pads after a crucial meeting and we'll decipher the scribbles and the doodles. We'll interpret the curious, dubious squiggles that clients leave behind."

"Crispin, that is the most ridiculous scam I've ever encountered."

He paused to draw breath on the other end of the 'phone. "Lenny, Lenny," he admonished. "If cynicism is your only reaction to my new sca . . . I mean, venture, then I have to tell you that you've been ignoring one of the most invaluable sources of high-grade intelligence in the business."

"Talk me through it." I was compelled to listen.

"Well, look at it this way. You've got this captive audience. You're either presenting for the account, or pleading to retain the business. Either way, it's hypertension ad biz max stressworld for all participants and the anxious clients need to combust mega-kilojoules of excess nervous energy."

"Hence the doodling?"

"Correct. But (and here's the brilliance of the idea) it's their *sub-*

Len Weinreich

conscious that's doing the doodling. So, whatever materialises on the pad is an action diagram of the client's thought processes. See?"

"I see. But how do you decipher their darkest thoughts if they're only scribbly doodles? And anyway," I added, "some clients actually tear their encrypted messages off the pad and tuck them into pockets. What's your action then?"

"The rub, Lenny. The old brass rubbing lark. We massage the undersheet delicately with a 9B pencil and a palimpsest of the jotting appears, by magic. From then on, interpretation is everything."

"OK. I How do you interpret?"

"You mean you've missed my new book: *Corporate Doodling: The Direct Line To Your Clients' Intentions.* It reveals all."

"I missed the book. Supply the topline, please."

"Well, many symbols are clear. Sketches of knives, revolvers, bludgeons, barbed wire and strategic nukes mean that he or she

might be firing the agency."

"Crispin, what about clients who can't draw? Can you explain *their* scratch pads?"

"All in my book, old chap, £9.50 at leading booksellers. Since you ask, anything resembling a maze represents confusion on their part. Blurred shading or scratchy hatching means they think you're a shifty bunch of crooks."

"Crispin, in my experience, they generally scribble down a few low key phrases from the presentation or make a few critical comments for subsequent reference."

"Of course, Lenny, of course. But each one can be a telling pointer. In order to cope with that eventuality, we've cobbled together a computer program called SNOOP which correlates their scratch notes with the agency slides and overheads in order to present you with an Attention Rating Admiration Factor and Purchase Property Index on a scale of one to ten."

"What happens if they've only scribbled a 'phone number or an enigmatic address in SW10?"

Crispin was wounded. "Haven't you read *any* of my books?"

"Er . . . which of your *oeuvre* have I missed now, Crispin?"

"*Corporate Blackmail for Profit and Pleasure* one of my all-time chart-toppers and money spinners. A right little cash cow."

"Thanks, Crispin. Don't call us . . ." *Clickbrrrrrr*

Len Weinreich is a vice-chairman of Burkitt Weinreich Bryant Clients and Company

Reproduced by kind permission of Haymarket Marketing Publications Ltd and Len Weinreich
SOURCE: *Marketing*

FIGURE 8.4

When no news is bad news

"Why don't they ring? It's been four, no, three, days since they were in for the presentation. Didn't they say they'd make their minds up the next day? God. No news is bad news. Or is it good news? I can never quite remember.

"Anyway, I don't think we won it. I mean, we would have heard, wouldn't we? That guy, the one down the end of the table with the woolly khaki tie, he never liked us. He asked the worst questions. Like that one about putting all their press money in TV. That was a stinker, maliciously inserted to distract me. Quite arrested my flow, log-jammed my drift. No sense of unfolding drama, silly sod.

"The woman liked us though. I had a feeling she'd marked us down because we had too few women in the presentation team. But I could tell she warmed to me. Smiled a lot when I projected in her direction. God! Why haven't they rung yet? It's not as if we really need their lousy business, after all it's only an account. Ad agencies are like re-volving doors: one account leaves and another one follows, I mean, enters. Have you seen this year's free-fall figures? The income from their billing would make good the loss of those bastards from . . .

"We won't get it. They hated the

Len Weinreich

creative work. Detested it. They sneered at the ads. You would've thought they'd never seen a real commercial before. On the other hand, they'd asked us to be radical. Their brief advised ignoring all re-straints. Still, I think it might have been wiser to check the script with the ITVA before the presentation. The naked couple and the golden retriever might be a little rich for today's audience.

"We spent a month assembling this presentation and now, a week, okay, maybe three days later, not a dicky bird. Not a peep. Not even a whimper. Not even one of those mysterious calls to the media de-partment dishing them undercover dirt. Nothing.

"Perhaps we should have bribed them. Maybe we should have taped a few large denomination notes to the inside covers of their docu-ments. Perhaps I really should have nobbled the top man when he dashed out for a pee.

"Quite frankly, I think they loathed the work. And my suit. And our media director. It didn't help that our creative (ho, ho) di-rector completely cocked up the or-der of the storyboards. Or that our dizzy planner addressed their com-pany by the wrong name, twice. This instant they obviously are ap-pointing someone else because they have no wit, taste, imagination, discernment or balls.

"I'm not so sure we'd be happy handling their business. They'd be terrible clients. Endless trips to their remote offices to niggle over a charity ad mechanical.

"Stuff their lousy business. Prob-ably seriously unprofitable. In fact, I shouldn't be surprised if they went belly up. I've heard some interest-ing City whispers concerning the bizarre hotel bedroom habits of their chairman. Apparently . . . ***, is that the phone?"

Len Weinreich is a vice chairman of Burkitt Weinreich Bryant Clients and Company

Reproduced by kind permission of Haymarket Marketing Publications Ltd and Len Weinreich
SOURCE: *Marketing*

agencies usually ask the prospect for some feedback for future reference. Here are some answers that re-jected agencies have recorded upon asking why they had failed:

- 'I just didn't like you.'

- 'I'm afraid you are not European.'

- 'You're too small.'

- 'They [the other agency] have more experience of this sector.'

- 'You have too much experience in this sector. We're looking for a fresh approach.'

- 'If it wasn't for the other agency you would have come first.'

- 'The final decision was evenly split and you lost 8–7.'

- 'Although we preferred your creative work, the other agency does have a place to park in London on Saturdays – and it's terribly handy for the shops.'

As managing directors are never told that their pitches are terrible and come last, having always been narrowly beaten into second place, there is a plea from the advertising industry to clients that they should tell it like it really is!

After the pitch – the agency still waits

Occasionally the prospect client actually helps the agency by giving an answer that identifies where they saw a real weakness. The agency can then eradicate the weakness before the next pitch. Similarly, a successful agency will be interested to find out why it was chosen, so that it can capitalize on its strengths.

Skip the pitch – marketing clients meet media owners directly

'Yahoo and Google established agency-relations teams to build relationships and teach agencies the peculiarities of online display and search. Since then, Google focused its agency relations on building its display business and promoting YouTube; Yahoo on moving offline dollars to digital. AOL's agency-relations team was rebuilt by ex-Google execs now running the company. Microsoft launched its agency-relations team in May of last year.'

Learmonth (2010b)

In 2010 Unilever had an intense week-long series of media meetings including Google, Yahoo, Facebook, Fox Interactive, Amazon, Microsoft, Vevo, LinkedIn, Formspring, Millennial Media, several venture capital firms and, of course, Huddler.

Firing the agency

Campaign magazine survey identified the following reasons for sacking an agency (in order of clients' importance):

1. receiving no fresh input;
2. account conflict at the agency;
3. a new marketing director arriving;
4. a change of client's policy;
5. other accounts leaving the agency.

A derivative of number 2, conflict of interests, arises with mergers and acquisitions. After acquiring Gillette for $57 billion, P&G sacked Gillette's agency, Mindshare (part of the WPP Group). Gillette explained that it was removing its $800 million global media planning and buying business. Mindshare already works for Unilever, P&G's arch rival (*WARC*, 2005c).

An example of number 3 above is when BA appointed its new CEO Willie Walsh. After 23 years, M&C Saatchi lost its prized BA account worth £60 million (and estimated to be between 6 and 7 per cent of Saatchi's turnover). Prior to that, Saatchi's had only one pitch, 10 years previously, when it retained the business by the skin of its teeth after Bartle Bogle Hegarty prematurely broke out the champagne (*WARC*, 2005a).

In the international arena, business relationships (including agency relationships) are even more delicate, as WPP discovered when it was fired by China's largest advertising conglomerate (Citic and its Beijing Guoan Advertising arm). Citic's vice-chairman, Yan Gang, claimed that WPP's CEO, Sir Martin Sorrell, had treated him 'very rudely'

What's straining the agency–marketer relationship today?

'Too many agencies are wondering, "Am I going to have a job six months from now? What does my client really think?" When the agency doesn't know where it stands or if the client believes in it, it becomes dysfunctional. That's the biggest thing that's missing. If the client's not happy, get on with it. Tell them what's wrong and what they need to do. Marketers also shouldn't be afraid to challenge their agencies. The best teams ask outrageous questions of their agencies. And agencies love that. And when you answer those, you get great work.'

Stengel (2010)

during an April meeting in London to discuss management problems at the joint venture (*WARC*, 2006).

Although over a decade old, *Campaign* magazine's '13 ways to be a loser' article identifies many recurring reasons why agencies still get fired:

1 **Control of brand's advertising switches to rival of client:** Gold Greenlees Trott lost Fosters when Elders IXL and its Courage division took over control of marketing Fosters from Watneys, a GGT client.

2 **Agency produces irrelevant or inappropriate advertising:** Lowe Howard-Spink lost some of its prized Mobil account after its 'breakthrough' Dan Dare campaign failed. Insufficient planning was cited as a reason behind the fiasco.

3 **Client is unsettled over too many changes at agency:** Foote Cone and Belding lost £22 million worth of business – including Heinz and Cadbury – because of management upheaval.

4 **Client unhappy over excess negative publicity surrounding its agency:** IBM is uncomfortable over the widely reported lawsuits involving its agency and breakaway Lord Einstein O'Neill and Partners. Could result in IBM choosing neither and picking a new shop.

5 **Takeover of agency infuriates client:** Goodyear, Philips, Pilsbury said goodbye to JWT after it was taken over by WPP. Most cite 'disruption' as a reason for leaving.

6 **Client rationalizes its agency roster:** Toyota chose its dealer agency Brunnings over its main agency Lintas London after a creative shoot-out. British Telecom reviewed its entire account and picked three main agencies – BBH, Abbott Mead and JWT.

7 **Total breakdown in agency–client relationship:** GGT resigns the *Daily Express* after repeated clashes and an inability to work with title's marketing staff.

8 **Agency fails to come to terms with account:** BMP got the sack by Comet, its first major retail client. Former vice-chairman Paul Leeves said BMP won the business 'one year too soon'.

9 **Lack of solution creatively:** Abbot Mead couldn't crack the *Daily Telegraph*. Later the agency admitted to producing tasteless series of press ads which aroused the ire of women, among others.

10 **New client arrives:** Allen Brady & Marsh's long-standing Milk account was reviewed after new NDC chief Richard Pears joined.

11 **Agency can't master the client's politics:** JWT lost British Rail. Agency was allied to the central advertising body while the chairman, Bob Reid, was committed to devolution. Network SouthEast chief Chris Green was not keen on JWT after it produced two poor ads, one in which it was in legal hot water with the *Monty Python* people.

12 **Agency merges with another, producing conflict and massive disruption:** Difficulties surrounding the merger of Reeves Robertshaw Needham and Doyle Dane Bernbach resulted in massive client fall-out.

13 **Client is subject of a merger or takeover:** Fast becoming a major reason for account moves.

Reproduced by kind permission of Haymarket Marketing Publications Limited and Laurie Ludwick

Are agency managers egotistical?

McCann chiefs are said to have reacted with disbelief and anger at Ben Langdon's suggestion that the London agency be rechristened McCann Langdon, followed by the names of the agency's other principals. It appears that his suggestion helped to convince McCann's worldwide chairman and chief executive, John Dooner, that it was time for Langdon to step down. Bosses of the Interpublic-owned network are jealous guardians of one of the most famous brands in US advertising and opposed to anything that might dilute it.

Firing the client

Agencies sometimes resign accounts, particularly if a larger competing account is offered to them. Occasionally, they are obliged to resign if an agency takeover or merger brings in some competing accounts and thereby creates a conflict of interest. New demands by a client sometimes become so difficult that the account becomes unprofitable or, as in the case of ABM, a reduced commission is considered unsatisfactory.

Arrogance and egos

Some years ago, a continually critical senior marketing manager commented at the end of yet another long, unsatisfactory meeting, 'If this were my company [which it wasn't; he was an employee], I would fire the agency.' The long-suffering creative director responded, 'If this were my agency, which it is, I would fire the client, which I am.'

He left the room, with the marketing manager knowing he now had to face colleagues and break the news that there was no campaign ready to roll out, no agency, and an agonizing new pitch process required.

How to ensure good agency relationships

1 Agree a system of remuneration – fees, commissions, mark-ups, time, expenses and method of billing – in writing. Remember, it is better to argue over a quote than an invoice.

2 Trust the agency team (share research and information with them, and involve them).

3 Make them become part of the marketing team. Use their expertise.

4 Ask relevant questions. Listen carefully to the answers. Do not be intimidated by strong agency characters. All propositions should be justifiable. The final decision is the client's.

5 Explain to the agency who makes what decisions, ie who has authority for which decisions.

6 Sign or approve in writing each stage from brief to concepts – finished artwork, running proofs and so on.

7 Keep briefs short and unambiguous.

8 Regular reviews help to plug any gaps in performance, whether creative, strategic or personal.

9 Write an occasional thank-you note to the team.

10 A stable relationship builds a real team, since the agency gets to know the client, the team, the company and the market inside out. In addition, the client does not have to worry about unfriendly, discarded agencies that have previously had access to sensitive information.

How to upset the client and get sent to jail – overcharge them

Thomas Early (former senior partner and finance director) and Shona Seifert (former president) at Ogilvy & Mather (O&M) New York were both reported by *WARC* to have been found guilty in 2005 of fraudulently overbilling the White House Office of National Drug Control Policy in 1999 and 2000. The guilty pair were allegedly responding to the anger of O&M North America's co-president Bill Gray at the loss of anticipated income. Gray was not among the accused. Early got a 14-month prison sentence and $10,000 fine. Seifert got an 18-months prison sentence and $125,000 fine (she was also ordered to write a code of advertising industry ethics). O&M extricated itself (but not its employees) from the affair with a $1.8 million settlement in 2002.

WARC (2005b)

Key points from Chapter 8

- Clear communications between client and agency are important if the right messages are going to be successfully communicated to target audiences.

- Agencies, consultancies and consultants can become more than just suppliers of marketing services; they can become strategic partners of the client.

- Careful selection is crucial to ensure the development of a mutually beneficial long-term relationship.

References and further reading

Bashford, S (2008) The rise of the intermediary, *PR Week*, 4 July

Burnett, L (nd) Quote bank, WARC (World Advertising Research Centre)

Cowley, D (ed) (1989) *How to Plan Advertising*, Thomson Learning, London

Farey-Jones, D (2008) Consumer relationships key to future agency success, *Brand Republic*, 8 February

IPA (2003) *The Client Brief: A best practice guide to briefing communications agencies*, Joint industry guidelines for young marketing professionals in working effectively with agencies, IPA, ISBA, MCCA, PRCA, London

ISBA (2010) in conjunction with the Advertising Research Consortium, *Paying for Advertising 5*, ISBA, London

Kemp, M and Kim, P (2008) The connected agency, Forrester report

Learmonth, M (2010a) Do you know the ABCs of DSPs? Agency-relations teams pitch in, *Ad Age*, 26 April

Learmonth, M (2010b) Top marketers to Silicon Valley: Help us get ahead of consumer, *Ad Age*, 17 May

Rijkens, R (1993) *European Advertising Strategies*, Thomson Learning, London

Sorrell, M (1996) Beans and pearls, D&AD president's lecture

Stengel, J (2006) Top P&G marketer urges agencies to integrate planning, *WARC*, 7 February

Stengel, J (2010) How to save the troubled agency–marketer relationship, *Ad Age*, 26 April

WARC (2005a) British Airways ditches Saatchi Brothers after 23 years, 10 November

WARC (2005b) O&M's Early jailed for ONDCP fraud, 14 July

WARC (2005c) WPP's 'Chinese walls' fail to reassure P&G, 6 October

WARC (2006) Chinese ad giant drops WPP pact in favor of Omnicom, Data sourced from AdAge.com, Additional content by *WARC* staff, 16 June 2006

Weinreich, L (2000) *Seven Steps to Brand Heaven*, Kogan Page, London

Williams, H (2008) Six Degrees lands BIMA retained brief, *PR Week*, 29 August

Admap, NTC Publications, Henley-on-Thames

Advertising Age, Crain Publications, Detroit, MI

Campaign, Haymarket Marketing Publications Ltd, London

Marketing, Haymarket Marketing Publications Ltd, London

Marketing Business, Chartered Institute of Marketing and Maxwell Publications, London

Marketing Week, Centaur Communications, London

Media Week, EMAP Business Publications, London

Further information

AdForum MayDream SA
18–20 rue Jacques Dulud
92521 Neuilly-sur-Seine CEDEX
France
Tel: +33 (0)1 41 43 71 93
Fax: +33 (0)1 46 37 33 82
www.adforum.com

Advertising Agency Registrar Services
AAR Group
26 Market Place
London W1W 8AN
Tel +44 (0)20 7612 1200
www.aargroup.co.uk

Advertising Association
7th Floor North
Artillery House
11–19 Artillery Row
London SW1P 1RT
Tel: +44 (0)20 7340 1100
www.adassoc.org.uk

Agency Assessments International
100 Pall Mall
London SW1Y 5NQ
Tel: +44 (0)20 7321 3828
www.agencyassessments.com

British Rate and Data (BRAD)
Brad Insight
Greater London House
Hampstead Road
London NW1 7EJ
Tel: +44 (0)20 7728 4315
www.brad.co.uk

Incorporated Society of British Advertisers (ISBA)
Langham House
1b Portland Place
London W1B 1PN
Tel: +44 (0)20 7291 9020
Fax: +44 (0)20 7291 9030
www.isba.org.uk

Institute of Practitioners in Advertising (IPA)
44 Belgrave Square
London SW1X 8QS
Tel: +44 (0)20 7235 7020
Fax: +44 (0)20 7245 9904
www.ipa.co.uk

09
International marketing communications

LEARNING OBJECTIVES

By the end of this chapter you will be able to:

- Understand the globalization of markets and the international opportunities arising
- List and explore the international challenges arising in international markets
- Avoid the classic errors in international markets
- Discuss the strategic global options available to marketers interested in growing on a global scale

The globalization of markets

This chapter examines opportunities and the difficulties, strategic options and actual implications for implementation of international marketing communications, in particular global communications.

The global opportunity – is it really happening?

Look around you. Yogurt, pizza, spaghetti, rice, kebabs, Indian cuisine, Chinese meals, Mexican food and American burgers are popular and also easily available in many countries around the world. Not too long ago they were considered sophisticated luxuries. The Rolling Stones and Shakespeare also have a universal appeal. There are more people learning English in China than speak it in the United States. Back in 1985 approximately 1 billion people from different time zones across the world watched the Live Aid charity concert simultaneously. In 2002 over 2 billion people watched football's World Cup final. The London to Brussels train is quicker than that from London to Newcastle. Perhaps clichés like 'The world is getting smaller' are nothing more than oversimplified generalizations cast upon a culturally complex world?

> '70% of search worldwide is not in English.'
> Oban Multilingual Translation Services

Some say that human beings have more things that bind them together than separate them; others argue that market differences are greater than market similarities. There are, in fact, what Young & Rubicam creative agency calls 'cross-cultural consumer characteristics'. These identify the common ground. The person living in a smart apartment block in London's Knightsbridge probably has more in common with his or her counterpart living in a smart apartment block off New York's Central Park than with someone living in a drab south London suburb. There are indeed some common denominators and some common sets of needs and aspirations that can be identified, particularly in similarities of lifestyle.

Global markets are here. For example, Manchester United Football Club has an estimated 70 million fans around the world, and Al Jazeera's English-language TV news service has a 100 million audience worldwide. As media follow markets, media consumption may go global; therefore marketers must remember that brands with international ambitions must have a consistent global image – production should be international in mind, and content rights should be global. Creating content that users can pass on via their networks is an increasingly important channel of communication. But, as the Universal McCann (2007) report suggests, 'when using these channels it is fundamental that brands and media organizations think global. Multiple local and conflicting brand identities will not work.'

We are global – the internet says so. Although spread across the world, customers with similar interests can communicate and share thoughts through images, audio, video and text anywhere in the world:

> This means that clusters of customers with similar tastes and interests are connecting with each other to form new global niches and segments. The Internet and broadband, in particular, has changed business dynamics. It has created a level playing field for the smaller niche brands to compete with the established global players. Small brands have access to bigger, global, markets and can communicate directly with customers across the world in new and more meaningful ways – ways never dreamt of 10 years ago.
>
> Chaffey and Smith (2008)

Respecting global complexity

The total global concept suggests that the big global marketing players can accelerate the globalization process by transcending cultural boundaries and bringing their messages, goods, services and traditions to the markets they choose. There are some cultural norms that suggest that the total global concept will not happen everywhere, at least not in the next few generations. Lailan Young (1987) reported that the Barusho bride in the Himalayas has a tough time on her wedding night, as she has to share the bridal bed with her mother-in-law until the marriage is consummated.

Post-natal male exhaustion

In the southern Indian state of Kerala, Puyala women return to the fields to tend the crops after the birth of their babies, while the husband goes to bed. The rest of the family ministers to his needs until he recovers. In the Andaman Islands especially anxious husbands will stay in bed for anything up to six months.

Young (1987)

Understanding other cultures – the oppressed male

The Kagba women of North Colombia practise not only free love but free rape, and few men are safe.

Young (1987)

If this is deemed to be strange, consider how other cultures might view the seemingly bizarre behaviour patterns of the tea-drinking, nose-blowing, ballroom-dancing and kissing population of Europe.

Nose blowing

'Where most North Americans are repulsed by an Indonesian who blows his nose on to the street, the Indonesian is repulsed by the North American who blows his nose in a handkerchief and then carries it around for the rest of the day in his pocket.'

Ferraro (2001)

The lost kingdom of the Minaros was 'discovered' in a mountain hideaway 16,000 feet up in the Himalayas by a French explorer in 1984. The Amazon-like women totally dominate their men, marrying several at a time and keeping them in line by brute force. The former Kwakiutl of Vancouver Island demonstrate what is almost a parody of industrial civilization: the chief motive of this tribe was rivalry, which was not concerned with the usual concerns of providing for a family or owning goods, but rather aimed to outdo and shame neighbours and rivals by means of conspicuous consumption. At their potlatch ceremonies the people competed with each other in burning and destroying their valuable possessions and money. This is in contrast to the Dobu of north-west Melanesia. This culture is re-ported to encourage malignant hatred and animosity. Treacherous conduct unmitigated by any concept of mercy or kindness and directed against neighbours and friends is expected. The Zuni (a branch of the Pueblos of New Mexico) are a people whose life is centred on religious ceremonial, being prosperous but without interest in economic advancement. They admire most those men who are friendly, make no trouble and have no aspirations, detesting, on the other hand, those who wish to become leaders. Hence tribal leaders have to be compelled by threats to accept their position and are regarded with con-tempt and resentment once they have achieved it. Even cultures that are relatively better known have their own intricacies over something as simple as a handshake, eye contact and the use of colours. For example, brown and grey are disapproved of in Nicaragua; and white, purple and black are the colours of death for Japan, Latin America and Britain respectively.

The reader may be surprised to know of a tribe where it is not uncommon for the men of the tribe to behave in a promiscuous manner with other men's wives and daughters in public. It is so popular it is even broadcast on their television networks. The country: the UK. The practice: ballroom dancing. Here is a description of this behaviour:

It is common in such dancing for the front of the bodies to be in constant contact – and they do this in public. In spite of the close physical touching involved in this type of dancing (a form of bodily contact not unlike that assumed in sexual intercourse), our society has defined it as almost totally asexual. Although ballroom dancing can involve high levels of intimacy, it is equally possible that there is no sexual content whatsoever. Many adult men in the United States have danced in this fashion with their mothers, their sisters, the wives of the ministers at church socials without anyone raising an eyebrow. Yet many non-American cultures view this type of dancing as the height of promiscuity and bad taste. It is interesting to note that many of those non-Americans for whom our dancing is a source of embarrassment are the very people we consider to be promiscuous, sex-crazed savages because their women do not cover their breasts.

Ferraro (2001)

Cannibalistic disease: kissing

'A whole lot of people think kissing is not at all natural. It is not something that everybody does, or would like to do. On the contrary, it is a deplorable habit, unnatural, unhygienic, bordering on the nasty and even definitely repulsive. When we come to look into the matter, we shall find that there is a geographical distribution of kissing; and if some enterprising ethnologist were to prepare a "map of kissing" it would show a surprisingly large amount of blank space. Most of the so-called primitive races of mankind such as the New Zealanders (Maoris), the Australian Aborigines, the Pauans, Tahitians, and other South Sea islanders, and the Esquimaux of the frozen north, were ignorant of kissing until they were taught the technique by the white men… The Chinese have been wont to consider kissing as vulgar and all too suggestive of cannibalism… the Japanese have no word for it in their vocabulary.'

Pike (1966)

The international marketer embraces other cultures, researching and respecting the local culture as being right and proper and perhaps adopts Geertz's (1983) insight:

> the world… does not divide into the pious and the superstitious… there are sculptures in jungles and paintings in deserts… political order is possible without centralized power and principled justice without codified rules; the norms of reason were not fixed in Greece, the evolution of morality not consummated in England… We have, with no little success, sought to keep the world off balance, pulling out rugs, upsetting tea tables, setting off fire crackers. It has been the office of others to reassure; ours to unsettle.

Touching a global nerve

Despite the complexities of cultural idiosyncrasies, there are many common needs that manifest themselves into common wants and purchasing patterns, particularly where there are similar levels of economic wealth. It follows that, if a manufacturer or service supplier targets roughly the same socio-demographic groups in different countries and touches a common nerve within these target markets, then the same product or service can be packaged and promoted in a uniform manner. The pricing and distribution may vary, but the branding, packaging and even advertising can be the same. The manufacturers of world brands can therefore position their products in a similar manner in the minds of millions across many different cultures. This is the result of careful analysis and planning by expert marketing professionals rather than a trial-and-error approach to market extension.

The next challenge lies in moving the rest of the communications mix in a uniform manner so that not just advertising and packaging but also sales promotions, direct mail, sponsorship, etc, reap the benefits of a global approach. This globalization issue has revealed itself through the increased use of the internet. Even local firms going on to the net attract customers from all over the world. A web presence can deliver a global presence. However, this does present challenges, as Pepsi discovered, with its European blue can being seen by its US customers, who much prefer the traditional red can. Similarly, Tia Maria, although it is consumed around the world, has different age segments in different countries, eg in the UK Tia Maria is about girl power, targeted at 18- to 24-year-olds, while in the Netherlands it's drunk neat by pensioners. Now this 'common nerve' presents a positioning challenge. Despite these difficulties, Coke and computers have proved that large, lucrative global markets do exist.

Forces driving globalization

It is not just a product-orientated corporate push for growth but more of a market-orientated reaction to the emergence of common global lifestyles and needs. These are emerging as cheap travel, combined with higher disposable incomes, allows travellers to leap across borders, visit other cultures and return home with a little bit of that culture's soul in their own. Television itself has brought into the sitting rooms of Europe's homes pictures and images of the United States' *Sopranos*, Australia's *Neighbours*, Africa's famines and atrocities, and Tiananmen Square's students. It has also brought stunning scenes from the depths of the oceans, the balmy beaches of the Caribbean, the rugged beauty of the bush and the once rich and fertile Amazon rainforest. This global awareness is exploited by the corporate push for growth, which has forced many suppliers from saturated local markets to venture into overseas markets. Improved production, distribution and marketing techniques have accelerated the movement of products and services from all around the world into local markets. Professional buyers now scour the world in pursuit of new suppliers. The internet gives immediate access to a world of new sources. Political barriers are falling in China and the eastern bloc and, of course, Europe's own internal political barriers are being dismantled also. The doors of the world's markets are opening. The key, it seems, is to identify core benefits that are common to different cultures, along with any relevant cultural idiosyncrasies.

The elite global players

The significant benefits derived from a global brand and a global communications strategy are currently reserved for a relatively small number of players. This elite brand of players recognize the right conditions and apply thorough research and planning to exploit the brand's assets on a global scale. Although Rein Rijkens (1993) has identified a 'trend towards greater internationalization and centralization', it should be remembered that a single communications strategy (incorporating everything from branding to the complete range of communications tools) rarely works for all the players operating in international markets. The desire to harness the global opportunity is natural, because international markets offer huge rewards. They also present intricate problems. Careful cultural homework needs to be included in the detailed research and planning that go below the surface.

Below-the-surface similarities

Similar buying behaviour and buying patterns do not necessarily mean a uniform market with uniform needs, uniform communications channels, uniform

decision-making processes, uniform decision-making units, or even uniform reasons for buying. Take the case of buying premium-priced water. In a Khartoum slum an impoverished family pays 20 times the price paid by families with water main connections, while half a world away a middle-class family buys bottles of mineral water. This demonstrates 'unreal similarities'. The buyers appear to behave similarly by purchasing expensive water. They are, however, very different; in fact, they are from totally dissimilar groups with different aspirations, motivations, lifestyles and attitudes, not to mention disposable income. On the surface there is a market for private water in both countries, but the distribution channels, communications channels, advertising messages and levels of disposable income are poles apart.

An analysis that goes below the surface (or below the sales results) will reveal a range of different motives, aspirations, lifestyles and attitudes to the same product. Surface information can create a false sense of simplicity. International markets can also suggest surface solutions that ignore the cultural complexities and intricacies of distant markets. As Sir John Harvey-Jones once warned (1988):

> Operating in this milieu requires much greater sensitivity to national differences than we are accustomed to having. The mere fact that one stays in the same sort of hotel almost anywhere in the world, that one arrives in the same sort of car, that it is now possible to call by telephone or telex directly from almost anywhere in the world, all gives a superficial feeling of sameness which is desperately misleading and must never be taken for granted.

South Korea – 'Would you like plastic with your credit?'

A completely different mindset applies to customers in other countries. In South Korea, the Visa credit card company will ask you on a new Visa card approval on the phone 'Do you want plastic with the credit?', as the credit card functionality will automatically be enabled on your cell phone and the old-fashioned plastic card for your wallet is a free optional extra, only really needed if you travel outside South Korea.

Ahonen and Moore (2007)

Globalization, intertwined with cultural idiosyncrasies, is emerging in many markets around the world. The marketing maxim 'Think global, act local' remains valid. Although the late great Professor Theodore Levitt's 'globalization of markets' is still criticized by some academics, it is happening and it does offer huge rewards for those who seize the opportunity.

Below-the-surface external differences

There are, of course, many differences below the surface also. In practice, the European Union is splintered by different levels of economic development (north and south), culture, attitudes and lifestyles, languages, retail trends, direct mail trends, sources of information, time taken to make a decision, and so on. Different marketing mixes and communication mixes are required for different European countries. For example, in the Netherlands, dentists derive 40 per cent of their turnover from the sale of products such as toothbrushes. In Germany, supermarkets are expected to sell only cheap, utilitarian brushes, while the pharmacies handle the premium brands. In Italy, a premium brush has to carry a fashionable, exclusive label. This makes any above-the-line campaigns difficult. The communications mix was built around direct mail to dentists supported by point-of-sale and product literature, packaging design and sales presenters.

Below-the-surface internal differences

The marketer's challenge goes beyond communicating with new international customers and into working with international partners whose idiosyncrasies and languages pose many problems.

To some, overcoming local customers' idiosyncrasies may seem relatively easy compared to overcoming local partners' working practices. Whether the local partners are suppliers, distributors, sales agents, advertising agents, strategic partners or prospects, it is essential for success to understand and work with very different approaches to business. Take nomenclature for a moment. The French normally refer to advertising as *publicité*, which can cause some confusion, while the Yugoslavian word for advertising is *propaganda*. Other cultures have

difficulty translating 'marketing', 'marketing communications' and 'advertising', as they have not yet created such words.

> ### Southern Europeans work to live and northern Europeans live to work
>
> 'Somewhere in the world there are people who think the Germans are messy and unpunctual. (The chances are they are in Switzerland.) There are countries where Greece is regarded as a model of efficiency. There are countries in which French bosses would seem absurdly egalitarian and others where Italian company life would seem oppressively regulated.'
>
> Mole (1998)

International difficulties

International markets are riddled with hidden cultural differences that make global advertising an intriguing challenge even for the most capable international marketing expert. Here are some of the intricacies that contribute towards the difficulty of global marketing:

- language;
- literacy;
- colour;
- gestures;
- culture;
- original national identity;
- media availability;
- media overlap;
- lack of media data;
- lack of media credibility;
- varying media characteristics;
- different media usage;
- different media standards;
- different cost structures;
- legal restrictions;
- competition;
- non-global names.

Language

Language obviously requires careful translating, whether it is straplines, product descriptions or instructions. There are exceptions to the rule (where the language reflects beneficial cultural aspects of the product, eg Audi's *Vorsprung durch Technik* strapline). And some brand names simply don't work when used in foreign languages and thus restrict the brand's international growth potential or dilute the brand's presence through the need to have two brand names.

Language barriers can be expensive

Even the same language can have different meaning in different markets, eg a 'boot' refers to the rear of a car (in the UK) as well as a shoe. In the United States, the rear section of a car is called a 'trunk'. This is relatively minor, but how about exactly the same word having radically different business meanings? Take a trillion. In the United States and France a trillion is 1 followed by 12 zeros:

1,000,000,000,000

New English Dictionary (1932)

In the UK and Germany, a trillion is 1 followed by 18 zeros:

1,000,000,000,000,000,000

Collins Pocket Dictionary (1992)

Be careful also with a billion, as it has different meanings – in the United States and France a billion is 1 followed by 9 zeros, and in the UK and Germany it is 1 followed by 12 zeros. In the United States and France, it is a thousand million: 1,000,000,000; in the UK and Germany, it is a million million: 1,000,000,000,000.

Literacy

In many developing countries literacy is low (Dudley, 1989). This limits the amount of explanation in advertising. Even with high literacy, the reading of translated **Western-style advertisements still causes** problems, eg before-and-after toothpaste advertisements if they are not adjusted for Arabic readers, who read from right to left. In other low-literacy countries, pictures may be used to explain the contents. When Gerber first sold baby food in Africa it put a picture of a Caucasian baby on the label and didn't realize that, in Africa, companies routinely put pictures on the label to show what's inside, as there is a high rate of illiteracy.

Colour

Colour has a direct access to our emotions. Watch how red is commonly used in advertising in the West. Colour, however, does not have uniform meaning across the world. Asians associate red with prosperity and good luck. Consider a financial services website: if Asians see *no* red, they will leave; if Westerners see red, they might leave. Never wrap a gift in red in Finland, as it is associated with Russian aggression during the Second World War. Blue in Iran means immorality. **White in Japan means death** (hence McDonald's white-faced Ronald McDonald has problems). Black means death, unlucky or morbid in some countries. Websites designed with black backgrounds may be seen as 'hip' in the West, but can suffer lack of traffic from China and Hong Kong.

Gestures

When greeting or bidding farewell, physical contact beyond a handshake in South America, southern Europe and many Arab countries is a sign of warmth and friendship, but in Asia it can be considered an invasion of privacy. After a meal in Egypt it is considered rude not to leave something on your plate, while in Norway and Malaysia leaving anything on your plate would be considered rude. Basic body gestures are not global. In some parts of India, Sri Lanka and Bulgaria, shaking the head from left to right means 'yes'. Touching the lower eyelid may be just an itch, but it also suggests to a South American woman that a man is making a pass, or to a Saudi man that he is stupid. Scratching an earlobe has five different meanings in five Mediterranean countries: 'You're a sponger' (Spain), 'You'd better watch it' (Greece), 'You're a sneaky little…' (Malta), 'Get lost, you pansy!' (Italy), while a Portuguese will feel really pleased. The A-OK gesture (thumb and index finger in a circle with the rest of the fingers open) means money to a Japanese, zero in France, 'OK' in the United States, a rude gesture in Brazil and 'I'll kill you' in Tunisia. Even the thumbs-up sign is deemed to be a devastatingly obscene gesture to a Sardinian woman and insulting in Iran. Thrusting your palms towards someone's face may be meant to be endearing, but to a Greek there is no greater insult, since this gesture is called a *moutza* and comes from the Byzantine custom of smearing filth from the gutter in the face of condemned criminals.

Culture

Culture creates a quagmire of marketing problems: religion, sex, eating, greeting, habits, lifestyles, the role of women – the list is endless. Ferraro (2001) points out nine critical dimensions that contrast the United States with the rest of the world's cultures. She says that US culture places a high value on 1) individualism, 2) a precise reckoning of time, 3) a future orientation, 4) work and achievement, 5) control over the natural environment, 6) youthfulness, 7) informality, 8) competition and 9) relative equality of the sexes.

As always, the web complicates matters. For example, Scandinavians are reluctant to use credit cards, the currency of the internet; the French dislike revealing personal information; the Germans prefer to pay with a cheque, after delivery of the goods. In meetings, the Dutch and the Germans want to get straight to the point in business dealings, whereas in countries like Spain, Brazil and Hong Kong some general chat is the most important part. In France, family is private and not part of business discussions. In Hong Kong, expressing an interest in family, general health, and observations of the country help to nurture good relations.

Even protocol for follow-ups to a meeting vary from country to country, as some countries place more importance on the written word than the spoken word, and vice versa. As Julian (2009) points out: 'In Spain for instance, it's important to follow-up an email with a phone call, but in Germany you must do the opposite and put your phone conversations into writing.' As for humour, use it sparingly, if at all. **In Germany, humour is generally considered inappropriate in business.** It is essential to take advice from expert export advisory services such as UK Trade & Investment in the UK.

Christmas in other cultures

Taking advantage of the Christmas opportunity requires an understanding of each international market. For example, in Brazil and Spain the celebration continues until 6 January (when festivities end). In Russia the celebrations start on 7 January. In India Christmas Day is called *Bada Din* (Big Day) in Hindi, and it is a national holiday that allows people from all religions to celebrate with their Christian friends. In China the main celebration occurs at the end of January (the Chinese New Year or the Spring Festival). In other countries Christmas does not happen (in fact the word is illegal in some countries).

Original national identity

National identity can be an asset or a liability. For example, Dudley (1989) reported that Marathon Oil makes a point of stressing its US association in Italy, where US high technology is beneficial, but in Germany Marathon avoids the issue of its US parentage because of the German concern over US control in the German energy industry.

Media availability

Television is sometimes unavailable, since 1) developing countries do not have a high penetration of televisions in domestic households, 2) some countries do not have commercial TV stations, and 3) others do but they restrict the amount of advertising time. Unilever and BAT make their own medium available in East Africa by running their own mobile cinemas.

TV helps

The further away from a TV screen, however, the more difficult many experts say it becomes to create and to deliver a pan-European message.
Mead (1993)

Media overlap

Television, radio and the internet from one market can spill over into other markets, eg half the Canadian population has access to US television. The Republic of Ireland receives the UK's BBC and ITV channels. In mainland Europe local TV is received by neighbouring countries.

Lack of media data

Great Britain and Ireland have well-structured and categorized media analysis data (audited data). Without reliable media data the optimum cost and effectiveness of the overall campaign are unlikely to be achieved. Properly structured media markets are easier to work in.

Lack of media credibility

Unregulated or poorly regulated media in some countries may flout the principles of legality, decency, honesty and truth, which in turn may make these media untrustworthy or create audience scepticism about the particular source of information.

Varying media characteristics

Coverage, cost and reproduction qualities can and do vary from country to country. Some countries are technically more advanced than others, eg they may have massive penetration of high-speed broadband, while other countries do not even have many cinemas.

Different media usage

Kahler and Kramer (1977) suggest that the British tend to see TV as a visual medium, while TV to the Americans is a visual accompaniment to words.

Different media standards

A lack of uniformity of standards means that different types of both film and artwork may be required for different markets, eg the United States and the UK have different standard page sizes that may require different artwork, which increases cost.

Different cost structures

Different countries have different forms of negotiation and bartering. The Americans and the Japanese are poles apart. In less developed countries cash may not be available, but barter, or counter-trading, can offer an acceptable alternative.

Legal restrictions

Whether voluntary codes or actual law, there is as yet no harmonized set of laws or regulations. For example, Lands' End's website in Germany cannot mention its unconditional refund policy, because German retailers successfully sued in court. (They normally do not allow returns after 14 days.) This presents the advertiser with different problems in different countries. In Sweden, misdemeanours by advertisers may be charged under the criminal law, with severe penalties.

Competition

Different markets have different key players using different strengths. For example, Ford's position of 'safety engineering' worked in many countries, but not in Sweden, where, of course, Volvo occupied the position. Competition may react in different ways in different markets.

Language, literacy and logic

Combine these three in the international arena and a new challenge emerges – writing instructions. It is a skill in one language, and attempting to translate instructions is a complex skill. This is an extract from the instructions for assembling a 'knapsack':

1 Lead for hind leg in an opened position.

2 Lead the frame of the sack support up.

3 Insert the blushing for blocking in the proper split, push it deeply and wheel in an anti-time sense till it stops.

International mistakes

Here is a selection of global misses or international mistakes made by brands attempting to sell into international markets. It includes wrong brand names, wrong advertising slogans or, worse still, a fundamentally unsuitable product for a particular international market.

Some marketers carefully choose names that work for their local domestic market but never consider that one day the successful brand could sell into several markets. This insular perspective more than likely restricts any future growth opportunities into international markets and almost certainly restricts the brand from developing into a global brand.

Wrong names

Here are a few examples:

- Sic (French soft drink);
- Pschitt (French soft drink);
- Lillet (French aperitif wine);
- Creap (Japanese coffee creamer);
- Irish Mist (in Germany 'mist' means manure);
- Bum (Spanish potato crisp);
- Bonka (Spanish coffee);
- Trim Pecker Trouser (Japanese germ bread);
- Gorilla Balls (American protein supplement);
- My Dung (restaurant);
- Cul toothpaste (*cul* means anus in France);
- Scratch (German non-abrasive bath cleaner);
- Super-Piss (Finnish car lock anti-freeze);
- Spunk (jelly-baby sweet from Iceland);
- the Big John product range was translated as Gros Jos (slang for 'big breasts') for French-speaking Canada.

Even sophisticated marketers get it wrong. General Motors discovered that Nova meant 'it won't go' (*no va*) in South America. Ford launched the Pinto in Brazil and soon realized that it was slang for 'tiny male genitals'. Coca-Cola's phonetic translation in China meant 'Bite the wax tadpole'. After launching into English-speaking markets, Japan's second-largest

tourist agency was surprised to receive a steady influx of enquiries for sex tours. The Kinki Nippon Tourist Company soon changed its name.

These translation problems are not insurmountable. For example, Curtis shampoo changed its name from 'Everynight' to 'Everyday' for the Swedish market, since the Swedes wash their hair in the mornings. Mars changed its well-known 'Marathon Bar' to 'Snickers' to fit in with the worldwide brand name communications strategy.

Wrong strapline

The New York Tourist Board found 'I love New York' difficult to translate into Norwegian, since there are only two Norwegian verbs that come close: one translation is 'I enjoy New York', which lacks something, and the other is 'I have a sexual relationship with New York'. Scandinavian vacuum cleaner manufacturer Electrolux used this in a US campaign: 'Nothing sucks like an Electrolux'. When Parker Pens marketed its ballpoint pen in Mexico, its advertisements were supposed to read: 'It won't leak in your pocket and embarrass you'. Unfortunately, *embarazar* does not mean embarrass. It means impregnate, so the slogan had an entirely inappropriate meaning. The Mitsubishi Pajero had problems, since *pajero* in some parts of the Spanish-speaking world means a liar, in others a plumber and in others something much worse. Other expressions that have been imprecisely translated include US cigarettes with low asphalt (tar), computer underwear (softwear) and wet sheep (hydraulic rams). Attention to detail is required when translating, as even the smallest error, such as missing out an accent on a letter, can drastically change the meaning. For example, in the United States, a bilingual banner celebrated '100 ano of municipal history'. In Mexican Spanish, *año* is year but *ano* is anus.

I saw the potato

During the Pope's visit to Miami it was reported that some T-shirts were printed supposedly saying 'I saw the Pope'. However, the translation was 'I saw the potato', because *Papa* with a capital P means Pope, whereas *papa* with a small P means potato.

Wrong product

In the attempt to get the packaging, advertising and branding right, global marketers can sometimes forget the fundamental product and whether it is suitable for the market in the first place, leading to campaign failure. Here are some examples of international product failures arising from the basic product itself: Christmas puddings in Saudi Arabia (where the word 'Christmas' is illegal and 50,000 of the Anglo-Saxon population go on leave during Christmas anyway); and toothpaste to combat betel nut stains (stained teeth imply wealth in some cultures, as does being overweight in others). General Foods' packaged cake mixes found the Japanese market too small for them (3 per cent of homes had ovens). Coca-Cola had to withdraw its 2-litre bottle from Spain, because few Spaniards owned refrigerators with large enough compartments. Tennent's Caledonian, a successful Scottish lager, flopped initially in the UK because it came in 24-packs rather than six-packs. Philips had to change the size of its coffee makers to fit into the smaller Japanese kitchens and its shavers to fit smaller Japanese hands.

The global web

Like it or not, once you're on the World Wide Web you're global. This presents great opportunities but also new challenges. Web positioning on a global scale is not easy. Apart from language, literacy, colour, gestures and culture, marketers now have to try to think how global audiences search for information – what words, what search engines, etc. Even if you do translate correctly, you probably have to redesign your web pages, as many other languages require more words and more space to deliver the same message.

Even the major global players can get it totally wrong. Microsoft was reported (Brown, 2004) to have released its colour-coded world map with time zones showing the disputed Jammu and Kashmir region as not being in India. Under Indian law, this is an offence. Result: the Windows 95 operating system was banned, with hundreds of millions of dollars in lost sales. Office 97 was subsequently launched without colour coding.

Microsoft employees were arrested in Turkey when Kurdistan was shown as a separate entity, so Kurdistan was subsequently removed from all maps. 'Of course we offended the Kurds by doing this but we had offended the Turks more and they were a much more important market for our products. It was a hard commercial decision, not political' (Tom Edwards, Microsoft's senior geopolitical strategist quoted in Brown, 2004).

Another mistake that caused catastrophic offence was a game called Kakuto Chojin, a fighting-styled computer game with a rhythmic chant from the Koran. Despite being alerted by a Muslim staff member as to this insult to Islam, Microsoft still launched the game in the United States on the assumption that it would not be noticed. After a formal protest by the Saudi Arabian government, Microsoft withdrew the product worldwide. The list goes on. China, Korea, Spain and Uruguay have all been upset by various Microsoft products. In Korea its software showed the Korean flag in reverse and prompted government objections. In Spain, *hembra* means woman, but in Nicaragua and some other Central American countries it means bitch. In China, when Microsoft referred to Taiwan as a country, the police moved in and questioned staff. In Uruguay, a proud republic, Microsoft's Outlook referred to 30 April as 'the Queen's birthday', which offended the government.

Strategic global options

More and more businesses have to compete in the global arena. For many companies there is nowhere left to hide. Those that do not move into the global market will probably find that the global market will come to them, as new international competitors target their once-safe local market. There is a need

---

Microsoft pays dear for insults through ignorance

'Insensitive computer programmers with little knowledge of geography have cost the giant Microsoft company hundreds of millions of dollars in lost business and led hapless company employees to be arrested by offended governments.'

Brown (2004)

to be proactive rather than reactive. Those that ignore this small part of the globalization process may not be around in 50 years.

A defensive strategy (eg consolidating the existing customer base, staying native, and blocking competition from entering with, for example, a series of flexible distributor promotions) may safeguard the company, at least in the short term. Offensive strategies are required if a company is seeking entry into new markets, eg increasing promotional spend in key national markets, supported by a flexible operations system. Strategic alliances and joint ventures offer a lower-cost, lower-risk (and possibly lower-margin) method of entry into these new, large and increasingly competitive markets. Global competition has even prompted global co-operation in the marketing communications industries. Advertising and PR independent networks are popping up alongside the global agencies that have expanded to meet their clients' global requirements.

Global marketing strategy

Keegan and Schlegelmilch (2001) identified five marketing (product/communication) strategies for multinational marketing. These were determined by the state of the various international markets, analysed by 1) whether the need (or product function) was the same as in other markets, 2) whether the conditions of product use were the same as in other markets, and 3) whether the customer had the ability to buy the product:

1 *Same product/same communications.* This applies to markets where the need and use are similar to those of the home market, eg Coca-Cola, with its centrally produced advertisements that incorporate local differences in language.

2 *Same product/different communications.* This applies to markets where the need or function is different but the conditions of product use are the same, eg bicycles in Europe and bicycles in Africa (recreation and transport, respectively).

3 *Different product/same communications.* This applies to markets with the same product function or need but with different conditions of product use, eg different petrol formulae but the same advertising image (eg Esso's tiger).

4 *Different product/different communications.* This applies to markets with different needs and different product use, eg greeting cards and clothes are held to be 'culture bound', but it should be noted that some clothing companies (like Levi's) use the same, centrally produced, wordless advertisements internationally.

5 *New product (invention)/new communications.* This applies, for example, in the case of a hand-powered washing machine.

It is highly unlikely that the complete communications mix can be standardized by centrally controlling and producing everything from advertising to sales promotions to point-of-sale to PR to direct mail, etc, because of, first, the differences in regulations and laws, which vary from country to country, and, second, the array of differences highlighted above. There are of course exceptions to the rule. IBM's Aptiva ran a 'win tickets to the 1996 Olympics' campaign across 12 European countries, while a new point-of-sale campaign rolled out to 15 European countries. Mars also developed a pack specifically for the Euro 96 football championships, featuring a green colour base with white netting effect, which appeared in shops in the UK, France and Germany.

Not a totally pan-European approach

All promotional ideas for Snickers' sponsorship of Euro 96 were shared with each European office, and the individual brand managers then assessed the viability for their marketplace. Language barriers will often dictate the feasibility of an individual promotion. For example, the 'Snickers – tackles your hunger in a BIG way' strapline was not utilized in any country other than the UK, owing to language interpretation difficulties.

Gordon Storey, Mars external relations manager

Global advertising strategy

The question of whether at least the advertising can be standardized (same communication) is a source of great discussion. Kahler and Kramer (1977) suggest that successful standardization is dependent on the similarity of the motivations for purchase and the similarity of use conditions. For culture-free products such as industrial goods and some consumer durables, the purchase motivations are similar enough to permit high degrees of standardization. Culture-bound products, in contrast, require adaptation. Customs, habits and tastes vary for these products, and customer reaction depends on receiving information consonant with these factors. It has been argued that 'buying proposals' (the benefits proposed in the advertisement) have a good chance of being accepted across large geographical areas, whereas the 'creative presentation' (creative treatment) does not.

Essentially, if the international market had a similar set of needs and interests (to the established market), then a successful adaptation of the advertising message was more likely (as in the case of pattern advertisements – see 'Central strategy and local production (pattern advertisements)' below). Simon Majaro (1993) observed that the gap between the time a product reaches its decline stage in the most advanced market and the introduction stage in the slowest market is narrowing. If this trend continues, the point will be reached where the pattern of the life cycle in a domestic market will become identical with the pattern in the foreign markets. This will of course have a tremendous impact on the communications strategy of firms operating internationally. It would mean that in time it would become possible for the communications objectives of such firms to become more and more homogeneous, thus allowing for a larger measure of standardization. In other words, if the trend continues, it should become possible for the same campaign, subject to the manipulation necessitated by linguistic and cultural variations, to be undertaken in all markets. This is indeed the kind of standardization that Coca-Cola has achieved in world markets. This strategy stems in the main from the fact that the product life cycle profit of Coca-Cola is pretty homogeneous throughout the world. Rijkens (1993) confirmed the trend towards 'greater internationalization and centralization', where basic creative ideas are centrally produced for international use. Kahler and Kramer (1977) felt that transferability of advertising was dependent on the possibility of a more homogeneous consumer, who might, for example, evolve out of the ever-integrating European community. If the European consumer

showed a willingness to accept the products of countries within the community, and if that consumer was motivated similarly to consumers in other countries, a common promotional approach would be practical; but if national identities prevailed, separate campaigns would be more likely to succeed.

Four global advertising strategies

The four basic strategies available for global marketing communications are:

1 central strategy and production;
2 decentralized strategy and production;
3 central strategy and local production (pattern advertisements);
4 central strategy with both central and local production.

Central strategy and production

Advertisements are controlled and produced by the head office (or its agency). This includes message modification, such as translations and tailor-made editions for various markets. Examples of centrally controlled and centrally produced advertisements include Coca-Cola's emotion-packed 'General Assembly' advertisement showing the world's children singing happily and harmoniously together, which was similar to their 1971 'I'd like to teach the world to sing' (McCann) in that it was packed with emotion and carried a universal theme. The 21 language editions of this advertisement opened with 'I am the future of the world, the future of my nation' and ended with the tag line 'a message of hope from the people who make Coca-Cola'. Each country then edited in its own end shot of the appropriate child's face. Incidentally, the German edition was dubbed slightly out of synchronization, since Germans associate quality films with dubbed (slightly out of sync) US and British films. Scottie's nappies save production costs by omitting any dialogue and just using a different voice-over for each country. Levi's does not bother with voice-overs, dubbings or translations, as there is no dialogue – just music by Steve Miller. Its unified logo and brand image does away with the need for different pack shots (close-ups of the pack/label) for each country, so its commercials, produced by the London agency BBH, are used throughout Europe.

Decentralized strategy and production

Advertisements are controlled and produced by each local subsidiary and its agency specifically for the local market. This approach generates lots of different advertisements by the same company. Each division or subsidiary works with its own local agency to produce tailor-made advertisements for the local market. As well as being an expensive approach, it can destroy uniformity and a consistent global presence, but it does allow more creativity to suit the specific needs of the local market. Different positionings in different markets do require different campaigns, sponsorship and retail strategies. For example, if Rolex epitomizes 'achievement' in New York and 'trendiness' in Tokyo, it must implement two of everything: two product lines (one stately, one flashy), two ad campaigns, two sponsorship series and two retail strategies (Doctoroff, 2005).

Central strategy and local production (pattern advertisements)

The pattern provides uniformity in direction but not in detail, which allows the advertisements to be locally produced but within the central strategic guidelines. This is where head office guides the strategic direction of the advertisements but allows local production. These advertisements work to a formula, or pattern. In the Blue Band margarine advertisements, whether in Scandinavia or Africa, the appropriate happy mother could be seen spreading margarine on bread with her happy family sitting around eating it. Impulse fragrance used a 'boy chases girl' formula across Europe, but still allowed for cultural idiosyncrasies like eye contact, sex appeal and law-abiding citizens to be tailored into each country's different production. Renault's pan-European strategy was to 'endow the car with its own personality'. In France the car was shown with eyes. In Germany the car talked back. In the UK the end line was 'What's yours called?'

Central strategy with both central and local production

Centrally produced non-verbal commercials are used to build a unified identity, while local productions supplement this platform. This is demonstrated by the Levi's example given below. Although 'standardized' generally refers to production, it can also include centrally controlled media strategies, planning and buying. The centralized or standardized global campaign problems are discussed below. As Rijkens (1993) says:

> As far as advertising is concerned, the company will continue its policy of central production of non-verbal commercials and cinema films, to be shown throughout Europe and intended to establish a uniform identity for Levi Strauss as a business and for its products. Advertising produced locally by the Levi Strauss subsidiaries will respond to local circumstances and to the local competitive scene.

This formula, also applied by other companies marketing a uniform product and using one advertising strategy on an international scale, has proved successful and may well be further developed once the single market really comes about.

Advantages of central strategy and central production

1 *Consistent image.* A consistent image (and positioning) is presented around the world, allowing consumer awareness and familiarity to prosper.

2 *Consolidated global position.* It leaves the brand in a stronger position to protect itself from any attack.

3 *Exploits transnational opportunities.* It reduces message confusion arising when advertising in one country spills over to another (eg boundary-bouncing satellite TV) or when migrants and tourists physically travel to another geographical area (geographical segment).

4 *Saves costs.* Economies are enjoyed by not having several different creative teams (and production teams if central production) working on the brand around the world

(saves reinventing the wheel). There is the possibility of centrally produced (or at least centrally designed) point-of-sale material also. Levi's has found that it saves £1.5 million by shooting a single TV ad to span six European countries (at £300,000 production cost per each one-minute TV ad).

5 *Releases management time.* It may also reduce the size of the marketing department, which might otherwise be tied up briefing creative teams, approving creative concepts, supervising productions, etc. It may even save time invested with packaging designers, sales promotion agencies, etc, if pack designs and promotions are run from a central office.

6 *Facilitates transfer of skills.* It does this within the company and around the world, since in theory it is the same job anywhere around the world. It also stimulates cross-fertilization of company ideas if staff are moving around internationally.

7 *Easier to manage.* It is easier to manage centrally, since there is in total a smaller number of decisions and projects to manage:

   – One creative decision facilitates harmonization of creative treatments, particularly in areas of media overlap.

   – Media policies – manage the media overlap between countries to maximize effectiveness and recommend preferred media choice in specific territories.

   – Budgets – determine local budgets for each product in each market so that the method of allocating resources is balanced.

   – Agree an activity programme and a specific reporting system to facilitate easier management.

Disadvantages of central strategy and central production

1 *Stifles creativity.* It stops local creative contributions from both company staff and the local advertising agency (whether part of an international group or an independent agency). The account may be considered by the local agency staff to be dull and boring, and the supposed 'best brains' (from the creative department) may avoid being involved with it.

2 *Frustrated local management.* Although the local office may be accountable for its performance, it does not have control over its own destiny, since advertisements are centrally produced or directed. This may lead to a sense of frustration.

3 *Minimal effort from the local agency* (if using an international agency with its network of overseas branches). The high global advertising spend may put the brand high on the agency's head office list, but the local agencies may find it is uneconomic to spend too much time and top brains on it.

4 *Lost opportunities.* The opportunity to react quickly to changes in the local market is lost.

5 *Different product life cycles.* Different markets may be at different stages of their life cycle, which may make the standardized approach unsuitable. It may, however, still be possible to standardize each stage of the brand's development, eg Boots launch of Nurofen in the UK and northern Europe.

6 *Wrong idea.* Some central advertising concepts may simply not work as well as a locally created original idea. Sales therefore perform below their potential.

7 *Difficult translation.* Some ideas just do not lend themselves to translation, eg Pepsi's 'Come alive' was translated in some countries as 'Come from the dead' or 'Come out of the grave'.

8 *False savings.* Local language adaptation or modification costs may negate the cost savings generated by the centrally controlled creative work.

9 *Market complexities.* The many other local market differences (eg variations in consumer protection regulations and media availability) may make a standardized message extremely difficult.

10 *Inexperienced staff.* A lack of suitably qualified expert staff who can manage the coordination of transnational standardized campaigns may make the whole centrally controlled advertising concept too risky.

Rudyard Kipling's advice to McDonald's

'Asia is not going to be civilized under the methods of the west. There is too much Asia and she is too old.'

Rudyard Kipling (1891)

McDonald's India now offers tailored products for the Indian market – mutton, chicken, fish and vegetable products, not beef, pork or their by-products. The Big Mac is called the Maharaja Mac.

Agencies in the international arena

There are several different types of agency from which an international advertiser can choose:

- international agencies (multinationals);
- independent networks, associations or confederations of agencies;
- local independent agencies;
- house agencies.

In addition to deciding whether to centralize control over advertising (and effectively standardize it), the international marketing manager must decide whether to put all international advertising in the hands of one international agency or hand it out to local independent agencies. Many local independent agencies have grouped themselves into networks or associations, which means that they have a ready-made network of contacts with the other network member agencies in the various international regions. A fourth and less common option is for the client to set up its own house agency specifically to handle its own worldwide advertising. Two options will now be considered: whether to choose a single international agency or several independent local agencies.

Choosing an international agency or independent local agency

This question is linked to whether the communications should be controlled centrally or left to run autonomously. Should the marketing team at headquarters work with just one large multinational advertising agency or should it allow a range of independent agencies to use its unique skills on a local basis? A coordinated message can be developed in either situation. For example, centrally produced advertisements (with local modifications, translations, etc) and pattern advertisements (formula advertising) can work under either system. Although a centrally produced advertisement is more likely to be handled by a large international agency, there are exceptions where local independent agencies with local media buying and production skills (if pattern advertisements are required) may be preferred. It is possible to choose to work with a range of independent local agencies while adhering to centralized policies. These policies can help the client to manage the whole advertising process by giving specific guidance on creative directions, media strategies, budgets and activity programmes. As Majaro (1993) says, 'Obviously where the product profile justifies communications standardization, it may be advisable to use the services of an international agency with offices in all markets.' Majaro continues: 'Hoping to attain the same results by using a host of local agencies with no international expertise is a formula for waste in worldwide marketing.'

Advantages of using an international agency

Compared to local agencies, the international advertising agency claims the following advantages:

- Full service – because of the international agency's size, it can offer a full range of services, including research, planning and translation, under one roof.

- Quality – some clients feel reassured by the quality feeling of a large international agency (as opposed to taking a chance with a smaller local agency). Quality and standards should, in theory, be universal.

- Broad base of experience – training and transferring personnel is common among the international agencies.

- Presence in major advertising centres – the agency branches are located at the centre of most major cities or marketing territories.

- Cost saving – less duplication in areas of communication, creative and production departments.

- Easier to manage – a single central contact point combined with the points listed in 'Advantages of central strategy and central production' on page 218.

Disadvantages of using an international agency

It is arguably easier for a single international agency to standardize the message. The disadvantages of standardization (see page 219) therefore apply where central control moves in. In addition, the overseas subsidiary may lack enthusiasm if the account was won elsewhere. It is as if, by necessity, various branches of the international agency are brought in. The lack of excitement may be compounded, particularly where all the creative work has been handled by head office. In a sense, the branch's job is relegated to media scheduling and planning.

The key to successful central communications

'If Shakespeare and the Rolling Stones can do it, so can advertising.'

Maurice Saatchi

Rather than engaging in high-risk new product development many corporations prefer to consider the lower-risk new market development approach. Harmonization of brand strategy across different markets has been on the agenda for years. Making it actually happen is another thing altogether. Take advertising: although more and more advertising is used in more than one country, only some of it works successfully.

Understanding the disadvantages in addition to the advantages is the first step towards implementing centralized communications. Identifying the barriers reveals the levels of resistance among distant marketing managers. It follows that internal marketing skills are also required. Before international communications are standardized (centralized), management thinking must first be harmonized internationally. Diminishing local autonomy without diminishing local responsibility requires skilful management handling. Indeed, maintaining management motivation requires people skills, particularly when their responsibilities for advertising budgets are being slashed.

Many local managers will perceive the central advertising campaign to be dull and disappointing because it is based on the lowest global common denominator – those common cross-cultural characteristics that somehow find commonality across borders that can result in dull ideas.

Inspiring managers to continue to excel under a blanket of apparently bland advertising is a challenging job. It becomes more challenging the longer internal communications are delayed.

Global cross-fertilization

Reckitt Benckiser (RB) may have low corporate brand recognition, but its 17 'powerbrands' include the well-known Dettol, Clearasil, Nurofen, Vanish and Strepsil. 'RB has grown faster than its competitors – P&G, Unilever and Colgate – in the last few years, despite the recession. The most distinctive aspects of the company are its people and culture: it has spent 10 years building up a culture of global mobility amongst its employees. For example, an Indian runs its Chinese business, while a Frenchman heads up its Russian organization. This means that many of its products – 35% to 40% in the last three years – are the result of global cross-fertilization.'

Becht (2010)

International marketing communications require even more attention to detail than domestic marketing communications. But, even closer to home, care is required to ensure the correct translation processes are in place. A process is required to ensure copy is sent off for translating, translated, double-checked and then uploaded into the correct section of the foreign language site. This is particularly needed when using free machine translations

Swansea Council translation process gone wrong

A sign that read 'No entry for heavy goods vehicles. Residential site only' was sent, by e-mail, for translation into Welsh. As the translator was not in the office, an auto-response e-mail was returned to the sender saying: 'Nid wyf un y swyddfa ar hyn o bryd. Anfonwch unrhyw wiath i'w gyfieithu', which means 'I am not in the office at the moment. Please send any work to be translated.' Since the original message had two sentences, it was assumed the Welsh message was the translation, and the sign was duly printed and erected.

like Google Translate. For example, the word 'home' is automatically translated into *maison*, the French for 'a home to live in' (as opposed to 'home page'). In Italy, machine translation for the word 'hi-fi' generates a machine translation of *ciao-fi*. *Ciao* means hi or hello.

In conclusion

International markets present many challenges and many rewards. There are many similarities amongst customers around the world, but there are also many differences lurking below the surface. Even more attention to detail is required in international markets, as the opportunities for errors increase. Systems, processes and teams have to be harnessed to make it all work successfully.

Key points from Chapter 9

- The globalization of markets is ongoing.
- There are, however, cultural idiosyncrasies that need to be accommodated.
- There are many other challenges that arise in international markets beyond just culture,

including language, media, laws (or lack of them) and much more.

- The classic errors are made even by the big established brands. They can be avoided by checking and researching.

References and further reading

Ahonen, T and Moore, A (2007) *Communities Dominate Brands*, Future Text, London

Anholt, S (2001) *Another One Bites the Grass*, Wiley, Chichester

Becht, B (2010) How I did it: Building a company without borders, *Harvard Business Review: The Magazine*, April

Brown, P (2004) Microsoft pays dear for insults through ignorance, *Guardian*, 19 August

Chaffey, D and Smith, P R (2008) *eMarketing eXcellence*, Butterworth-Heinemann, Oxford

Doctoroff, T (2005) *Billions: Selling to the New Chinese Consumer*, Palgrave Macmillan, New York

Dudley, J (1989) *Strategies for the Single Market*, Kogan Page, London

Ferraro, G P (2001) *The Cultural Dimension of International Business*, 4th edn, Prentice Hall, Englewood Cliffs, NJ

Geertz, C (1983) *The Interpretation of Cultures: Selected essays*, Hutchinson, London

Harvey-Jones, J (1988) *Making It Happen: Reflections on leadership*, Collins, London

Inskip, I (1997) Marketing international brands in Asia needs fresh thinking, *Marketing Business*, May

Julian (2009) The 'lucky seven' tips when collecting payments from overseas companies, *Octempo: RM Blog*, 18 December

Kahler, R and Kramer, R (1977) *International Marketing*, South-Western Publishing, Cincinnati, OH

Kashani, K (1989) Pathways and pitfalls of global marketing, *Marketing Business*, June

Keegan, W J and Schlegelmilch, B B (2001) *Global Marketing Management: A European perspective*, Financial Times/Prentice Hall, Englewood Cliffs, NJ

Kotler, P (2002) *Marketing Management: Analysis, planning, implementation and control*, 11th edn, Prentice Hall, Englewood Cliffs, NJ

Majaro, S (1993) *International Marketing*, 2nd edn, Allen & Unwin, London

Mazur, L (1997) Successfully managing cultural differences, *Marketing Business*, September

Mead, G (1993) A universal message, *Financial Times*, 2 May

Mole, J (1998) *Mind Your Manners*, Nicholas Brealey Publishing, London

Morris, D (1988) Watch your body language, *Observer*, 23 October

Pike, K (1966) *Language in Relation to a Unified Theory of the Structure of Human Behavior*, Mouton, The Hague

Rijkens, R (1993) *European Advertising Strategies*, Cassell, London

Universal McCann (2007) Power to the people: Tracking the impact of social media wave, 2.0, May

Usunier, J C (2000) *Marketing across Cultures*, Financial Times/Prentice Hall, Englewood Cliffs, NJ

Winick, C (1961) Anthropology's contribution to marketing, *Journal of Marketing*, 25

Young, L (1987) *Love around the World*, 2nd edn, Hodder & Stoughton, London

10
The marketing communications plan

LEARNING OBJECTIVES

By the end of this chapter you will be able to:

- Write an outline marketing communications plan
- Understand the importance of gathering intelligence and research for the situation analysis before writing the rest of the plan
- Explore strategy, knowing that it is an area of weakness for most organizations
- Establish control systems

Outline marketing communications plan: the SOSTAC® planning system

There are many different approaches to building a marketing plan or, more specifically, a marketing communications plan. There is no single common approach, but there are essential elements that every plan must have. **SOSTAC® (P R Smith, 1998) is a simple aide-mémoire that helps managers to recall the key components of a marketing communications plan.** SOSTAC® can in fact be applied to any kind of plan – a corporate plan, marketing plan, marketing communications plan, social media plan, direct mail plan or even personal plan.

S – Situation analysis (where are we now?).

O – Objectives (where do we want to go?).

S – Strategy (how do we get there?).

T – Tactics (the details of the strategy).

A – Action (or implementation – putting the plans to work).

C – Control (measurement, monitoring, reviewing and modifying).

SOSTAC®'s simple structure is applicable at different levels and in different situations. In each chapter in Part Two, SOSTAC® is applied at a lower level for each of the communications tools, an advertising plan, a direct mail plan, etc. SOSTAC® can also be used to check other plans to see if they are comprehensive and cover the key items that every plan needs. You don't have to use the same terminology, or even the same sequence, but SOSTAC® should help the development of a logical structure combined with the key elements of a plan.

SOSTAC® has been adopted as a planning system by literally thousands of managers worldwide, including:

- Sam Howe, Director of CATV Marketing, Southwestern Bell: 'SOSTAC® is a great approach for anyone going ahead and building a marketing plan.'
- David Solomon, Marketing Director, TVX: 'It appears that we are following the principles of SOSTAC®.'

- John Leftwick, Marketing Director, Microsoft UK: 'We use SOSTAC® within our own marketing planning.'
- Peter Liney, BA Marketing Manager: 'I think SOSTAC® is very good in terms of identifying, if you like, major component parts of what you're doing in marketing.'

Philip Kotler acknowledged the simplicity and usefulness of this approach to planning when he said: 'SOSTAC® is a system for going through the steps and building a marketing plan' (Kotler, 2001; Smith, 2004).

SOSTAC® provides an outline or a structure upon which a comprehensive plan can be built. A real plan requires much more detail, and the first component, the situation analysis, is often considered so important that it can take up half of the total plan. Objectives and strategies should be written in a concise manner, while the tactics and action plans can require a lot of detailed planning. Control, feedback and monitoring mechanisms should be built into the plan so that managers know if the plan is succeeding or failing early on rather than at the end of the year, when it is too late to change. So SOSTAC® and the 3Ms (the three key resources) provide a simple approach for building a marketing plan (and marketing communications plans in particular).

The 3Ms

Every plan must include the three key resources, the 3Ms:

1 men/women (the human resources);

2 money (budgets);

3 minutes (time).

Men/women are the human resources: who is required to do what? It means professional men and women skilled and capable of handling specific activities. Some can be drawn from within the organization; others have to be brought in from an agency or consultancy or recruited as full-time members of staff. Many organizations may not have this calibre of person or, if they do, these people may be kept so busy that they cannot do any additional tasks. Is it worth asking over-busy people to give half their attention to a project or asking under-qualified and underutilized people to have a go? Perhaps the marketing communications task is too important to be casual? There is no doubt about the importance and limited supply of the human resource.

Minutes, the third M, is the most limited resource – time. Is there enough time to do the job, to carry out the research, to develop a new pack, to prepare properly for a good mailshot, etc? Timescales are fundamental. Without them any plan becomes uncontrollable, because there are no time-related milestones. Timescales for objectives, and deadlines for each activity (eg proposals, concept development, concept testing, regional testing, national roll-out, European launch), are required. How much lead time do you need if you want to launch a new toy at Christmas? When should the product be ready? In February, if it is going to make the New York Toy Show, when major US retailers place their orders. How long would a new pack take to create? Six to nine months. So, even if you allow four months to develop a mailshot and simultaneously four months for a TV advertisement, you still need a total of 18 months for the pack and exhibitions. Managers have to manage teams of people who have different attitudes to deadlines. Time is a precious commodity and deserves careful attention. Some consider it now to be the currency of competitive advantage.

Whooshing deadlines

'I love deadlines. I like the whooshing sound they make as they fly by.'

The late Douglas Adams

Money means budgets, and senior management will tend to scan budgets first and foremost. There are many different ways of setting marketing communications budgets, and there is not a generally agreed methodology but rather a whole range of approaches that can be described as either scientific or heuristic.

Managers tasked with setting a budget ask themselves a series of 'What if?' questions about what would happen if a particular strategy and series of tactics are pursued. A combination of judgement, experience and rational evaluation is applied to develop an appropriate budgeting method for organizations.

Budget setting

Outlined below are the most common forms of budgeting:

1 Objective and task – identifying the overall objectives and then breaking these down into specific tasks and calculating the budget accordingly. For example, to sell x million cans of Coke would require x per cent levels of awareness, which would require x number of impressions, which would require x amount of advertising, which would cost £x. This is sometimes called the 'ideal' or 'task' approach.

2 Modelling involves the use of a variety of econometric and simulation techniques to determine how various budget levels may affect performance (eg sales). An example of this is Unilever's AMTES area market-testing model.

3 Profit optimization tries to find the optimum marketing spend that would generate the most profit. It is based on ensuring that the marginal revenue derived from each marketing communications activity exceeds the marginal cost.

4 Percentage of sales is a crude but quick way of calculating a budget. For example, taking 5 per cent of £1 million forecasted sales means the marketing budget is £50,000. In B2B markets, the percentage ranges from 0.5 to 2 per cent, and in B2C markets it ranges from 5 to 20 per cent.

5 Competitive parity analyses competitors' marketing communications spends. Basically, it suggests that if an organization wants to match a competitor it should spend the same amount as that competitor.

6 Affordability is usually driven by accountants, who draw up business plans, work out profitability and then allocate some budget to marketing based on what is left over or affordable. This is the opposite of the objective and task method. It is based upon what is affordable after talking all costs and an amount of profit away from sales.

7 Payback period is the time taken for an integrated campaign to pay back the costs (or budget) of the marketing communications.

8 Arbitration requires a senior member of staff to arbitrate between different views of the marketing team and the rest of the business.

Some academics categorize these different budgeting approaches as scientific and heuristic. Scientific planning approaches include: objective and task; modelling; payback period; and profit optimization. Heuristic planning approaches include: percentage of sales; competitive parity; affordability; and arbitration.

Marketers inevitably have to justify to the financial director the actual return on investment (ROI) of the marketing communications investment. ROI calculates the profit (created from the extra sales generated from the integrated marketing communications campaigns) as a percentage of the investment. This can be done for the whole mix or, more easily, for a specific marketing communications tool such as an advertising campaign or even a tool such as exhibitions (see 'costs' on page 408). The usefulness of ROI is debated in the section 'Control' below.

In reality several budgeting approaches are used. Although a manager might use the ideal task approach, the review panel (of senior management) will immediately convert it into a percentage figure, compare it with the competition's spend and ask 'Can we really afford it?' and 'Does it deliver the required level of profits?' It is not unusual to find the initial budget request cut back by senior management as other divisions and departments compete internally for limited funds for the following year's marketing. Few companies have sophisticated optimum profit models that attempt to identify the optimum spend.

Allocating budget between online and offline marketing

The answer lies in where customers are spending their time consuming media, interacting with colleagues and engaging with particular types of brands. This determines where the budget should be allocated, eg if a particular audience spends 50 per cent of its time on online then 50 per cent of that target market's budget should go online.

However, Forrester Research (2009) forecasts that by 2014 only approximately 21 per cent of total marketing budgets will be allocated to interactive marketing (search marketing, display advertising, e-mail marketing, social media and mobile marketing). It is likely that search and mobile will take a larger portion of the budget.

Allocating budget between customer retention and customer acquisition

Another interesting question is how to split the budget between customer retention and customer acquisition. If selling to existing customers is supposed to be on average six times more profitable than selling to new customers, there is a school of thought that suggests that marketers should spend at least equal resources on 1) keeping customers happy (eg CRM) and 2) acquiring new customers. Businesses like Amazon reportedly pay £50 to acquire a customer, and Virgin pays up to £150 (a free laptop), while Reichfield (2006) estimated the Dell average customer to be worth $210 (five-year net present value), with a detractor (someone speaking negatively about Dell) costing $57 and a promoter generating $328. In the world of online marketing it is increasingly easy to calculate the cost of customer acquisition. See the section 'Control' at the end of the chapter.

Allocating budgets to social media

A burning question emerging across all markets is 'How much resource should we allocate to social media?' It really depends on the strategy and how active an organization wants to be. At a minimum, any marketer needs to have someone listening to conversations, participating in discussions and ultimately driving the discussions. Beth Kanter (2008) suggests 55–75 hours per week for a non-profit-making organization:

- Listen to Google alerts, Technorati, Twitter, and RSS readers. The key skill is pattern analysis. (5 hours per week)

- Participate. Join the conversation direct or via other bloggers. (10 hours per week)

- Generate buzz. Buzz tools include FriendFeed, Twitter, StumbleUpon and Digg. (10–15 hours per week)

- Share your story – blog, podcast, Flickr, YouTube and social networks. (10–15 hours per week)

- Community building and social networking. Nurture a community – Ning and LinkedIn. (20 hours per week)

So SOSTAC® + 3Ms works for any type of product or service in both consumer and business-to-business markets, as demonstrated in the short case studies used in this book. Although the case studies provide only an outline plan, they show how easily SOSTAC® can be applied to either planning the overall marketing communications or just planning a campaign for a single communications tool such as direct mail. In reality, the plan would cover a lot more detail. Consider now each SOSTAC® component in more detail.

Situation analysis

The situation analysis needs to be comprehensive. Over 2,000 years ago Sun Tzu wrote *The Art of War* (Wing, 1989), which has become a classic read, particularly for some enlightened marketing managers. Here is an excerpt:

> Those who triumph,
> Compute at their headquarters
> A great number of factors
> Prior to a challenge.
>
> Those who are defeated,
> Compute at their headquarters
> A small number of factors
> Prior to a challenge.
>
> Much computation brings triumph.
> Little computation brings defeat.
> How much more so with no computation at all.
>
> By observing only this,
> I can see triumph or defeat.

The analysis should include a review of the performance (sales, market share and profitability) during the most recent period. Comparisons with previous years reveal any trends, and comparisons against competitors reveal relative performance. The analysis should include a summary review of the overall marketing performance, the marketplace, the competition, and strengths and weaknesses. The marketing communications plan does not require a full **SWOT analysis**, which is usually found in the full marketing plan. The situation analysis in the marketing communications plan must keep the focus on communications aspects such as performance (identifying which elements of the communications mix work best), target markets and positioning. It should certainly include an explanation of the product or service's positioning – how the product is perceived in the minds of the target market. Lucozade was positioned as a sick child's drink until the marketing people saw a bigger opportunity and repositioned it as a healthy adult's drink. Perceptual maps plot where different brands and product types are positioned on certain criteria, as shown in Figure 10.1.

The situation analysis can include a **PEST** analysis specifically relevant to communications, eg political (what new laws or regulations affect communications); how economic fluctuations might affect media and messages; social trends and changes in attitudes and media usage; and technology's fast-changing impact on communications.

A vital part of any analysis is the market and its structure. How is it segmented? What are the most suitable segments that can become target markets? Are the target markets big enough? Are they profitable enough? Are they vulnerable to competition? Do the existing distribution and communications channels serve them properly? Are customers satisfied in each target market? Do they intend to repurchase? Who is involved in the decision-making unit (DMU)? Do the key opinion leaders and opinion formers support the brand?

Segmentation and target marketing

Segmentation and target marketing are so important that they appear almost everywhere in a marketing plan: in the situation analysis in detail, in the objectives briefly and in the strategy (as a fundamental component); they are also referred to in all tactical campaigns and events.

Target marketing involves the division of a large market into smaller market segments. Each segment has its own distinct needs and/or its patterns of response to varying marketing mixes. The most attractive segments are targeted according to the organization's resources. Attractive target markets are those that will generally be more profitable, eg segments located closer to the organization, or loyal customer groups, or heavy users of a particular

FIGURE 10.1   A perceptual map showing Lucozade's classic repositioning from a sick child's drink (when the UK had a disproportionately large child population) to a 'healthy adult's drink (when the UK demographic shifted to a disproportionately large young adult population)

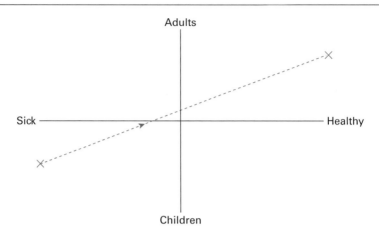

product or service. Targeting reduces wastage of resources (eg money spent on mass advertising) and, ultimately, it increases sales, since better-prospect customers are contacted. Segmentation and target marketing are absolutely fundamental approaches to marketing. Some communication channels are more wasteful than others, eg TV, but the **Target Group Index** (**TGI**) (see Chapter 6) helps to identify what kind of brands people buy, the papers they read, the programmes they watch, etc. As mass markets fragment and splinter into mini-markets or segments, and technology provides more tailored communications, there is less requirement for mass marketing and mass communications. The ability to segment a market accurately is a key skill that marketers need to spend time on again and again, revisiting their marketplace and thinking about how it can be broken into segments.

Segment criteria

Ideally, segments should satisfy the following criteria:

- *Measurable*. Is it quantifiable? Can buyers who fall into this category or segment be identified?
- *Substantial*. How many buyers fall into this segment? Is there a sufficient number of buyers in the segment to warrant special attention and targeting?

- *Accessible*. Can this group be contacted? Can they be isolated or separated from other non-targeted markets? Are there specific media and distribution channels that provide access to them?
- *Relevant*. The benefits of the product or service being offered must be relevant to the target. There is no point picking measurable, accessible and substantial segments if they have no interest in what is being offered in the first place. Know your own customers. Knowing the ideal customer's profile is fundamental to success. Some database companies actually carry out 'profiling' or an analysis of an organization's own customers into groups with distinctive profiles. This helps in targeting the appropriate message through the appropriate medium.

£50 Rembrandt

A Rembrandt probably would not sell (even for £50) in the wrong target market, whereas in the right target market it would fetch several million pounds.

Some segments are obvious. Cat food is bought by cat owners, petrol is bought by motorists, and heavy-duty cranes are bought by both large construction companies and leasing companies. Other segments are less obvious. Expensive cars are bought by high-income groups, while cheaper cars are bought by both high-income groups (as a second or third car) and low-income groups. Who are the heavy users, eg who are the 9 per cent of the UK adult population who drink 65 per cent of the lager consumed? Who are the buyers? Gift boxes of chocolates are bought for women by men. Who are the deciders? Cola drinkers may tend to be young, but who does the buying, who makes the decision, who influences and who pays? This is where segmentation focuses on the decision-making unit.

Decision-making units

The DMU is made up of influencers, advisers, deciders, users, buyers and payers. It applies to all types of markets (industrial, consumer, products and services). A baby's pram may be used by mother and child, bought by the mother and father, influenced by the grandmother, and decided on by the whole family. Similarly, the purchase of a new photocopier may have been instigated by a secretary who keeps complaining to the boss about the old machine breaking down. The end user may be several secretaries; the decider may be the financial director; the buyer may be the organization's professional buyer or the managing director. In some organizations the DMU may be a committee. In other organizations there is a central decision maker, or there may be a decentralized approach with each branch or region making its own decisions. The acronym SPADE (starter, payer, adviser, decider, end user) helps to identify some of the different members of the decision-making unit.

The DMU can consist of several people or committees, or it can sometimes be just one person. There is one other influential member of a business-to-business or industrial DMU, and that is the 'gatekeeper', who acts as a screen and sorts out unsolicited sales pitches from more important incoming communications. The gatekeeper is often a secretary or personal assistant, who may decide whether to interrupt a manager with a phone call or allow a direct mailshot to land on the manager's desk.

Global segments

Segments do not always have to be localized or defined on a geographic basis. Values, attitudes and lifestyles (VALs) can be used to identify cross-cultural common characteristics. For example, the advertising agency Euro RSCG identified the four main European psychographic segments as follows:

1   modern materialists: 117 million (acquire goods and services);

2   new radicals: 50 million (concerned with change and reform);

3   get what you deserve: 110 million (more conservative and resistant to change);

4   bygones: 83 million (oldest, most moralistic group, threatened by consumerism).

Global idiosyncrasies complicate the supposedly simple global segments. Chapter 9 looks at the international arena in more detail.

Global convergence

'So tastes are converging and to discover that all you have to do is talk to my teenage son. I have taken him with me on trips all over the world and I keep introducing him to a local boy who he can spend the day with to learn something about the life in those countries. And in every country he's visited, whether it is Jakarta, Indonesia; São Paulo, Brazil; Manila in the Philippines or a small town in The Netherlands, he has spent the day exactly the same way. They have gone to a local shopping mall, played video games and eaten a McDonald's hamburger.'

Kanter (2001)

B2C (consumer) segments

Segmenting markets into groups of buyers and targeting those groups that are more likely to be the best customers are absolutely vital if marketing communications are to be both effective and efficient. Markets can be broken into segments using many different criteria. Here are some typical consumer criteria:

- demographics:
  - age;
  - job type (socio-economic groupings);
- geodemographics: geographical location, type of neighbourhood and demographic data;
- psychographics;
- lifestyle: see Chapter 6, 'The Target Group Index';
- attitudes, beliefs and intentions (as above);
- benefits sought: see Chapter 4, 'The toothpaste test'.

Floating targets

Many markets have a floating percentage who move in and out of the market. Take insurance. Like most financial services, it is considered to be so dull and off-putting that most people rather not think about it. So, if customers reluctantly review, say, their insurance suppliers every 4 years, then you have only got 25 per cent of the market active each year. Divide this by 12 months and you have only got approximately 2 per cent of the market active in any particular month. That's why there is no point advertising specific product benefits when the 'active' market is so small. Instead, many brands just want to maintain awareness levels, so that they are at least considered when the customer becomes ready to buy.

B2B (industrial) segments

In industrial markets and business-to-business markets, segmentation criteria are different but nonetheless vital. Here are some commonly used segmentation criteria for industrial markets:

- type of company (Standard Industrial Code – SIC);
- size of company;
- structure of company (autocratic vs centralized);
- location or geographical area;
- heavy or light users;
- existing suppliers;
- benefits sought;
- title or position of key decision makers.

Most airlines target at least two different segments on each plane: the business traveller and the leisure traveller. These segments can be further segmented, eg the business traveller may be divided into club class, executive class and so on. These can be further divided into different benefit segments, eg those who want a fast check-in, those who want frequent flights, those who want top-class in-flight service, those who want a reasonable price, and those who want 'seamless travel' (connections for the next flight, cars and hotels all booked for them). Most travellers want all of these benefits, but usually consider some more important than others, so much so that they choose one airline over another because of a particular key benefit. If this type of flier proves to be significant in number, then it is a valid segment. The organization then decides if it has the resources and sustainable advantages suitable to target this segment.

To continue the airline example, Transavia Airlines segmented various companies that might have had some connection with the Netherlands (and therefore might have had a need for its services) into five different target groups of business fliers and travel agents. As shown in Figure 10.2, a different communications strategy was developed for each segment. A gift/food hamper and a boxed presentation were delivered personally by the sales manager to those accounts (customers) that warranted this kind of attention (resources). Lighter users had a smaller mailing. Top travel agents got a boxed mailing, while other travel agents just got a mailing.

Segmentation requires careful analysis

In reality, all the target customers rarely fall neatly into one single segment, eg 67 per cent of the *Sun*'s customers might be C2DEs and 33 per cent ABC1s. As mentioned, not all buyers of small cars are in lower- to middle-income groups. Many small cars are bought by mid- to higher-income groups as a second or third car in the family. There is, however, usually a core target made up of heavy users or easily convertible prospects, eg Lyons Tetley's Quickbrew tea is targeted at women aged 35+ (core C1C2D). Some markets have several people involved in the decision making (DMUs). For example, the advertising campaign promoting Shell's free miniature

FIGURE 10.2   Business traveller segments and communications mixes

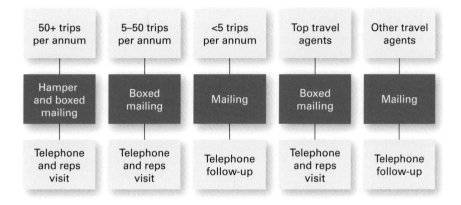

classic sports car collection was aimed at ABC1 fathers aged between 25 and 64 with children aged three to nine; within this they also had to ensure high coverage of high-mileage drivers (heavy users). Other markets have customers who drift into the marketplace and then out again, as in the case of financial services.

However, sophisticated technology can help the marketer today by adding new segmentation variables on top of the traditional variables. For example, it will be possible to segment buyers by their brand purchases and their stockholding (in the fridge) as well as the usual age, income and geographic criteria. Infomediaries (owners of information), such as manufacturers of fridge-freezers with inbuilt online capacity to reorder automatically when products are taken out of the fridge, hold valuable data about customers' stock levels. If consumers agree to share this information with other third parties, this opens up interesting segmentation opportunities. For example, Pepsi might like to make a special offer to a ripe segment like Coca-Cola consumers who are out of stock. It's worth considering how this might apply in the B2B sector, eg office stationery or software supplied by an intermediary.

Objectives

After analysing the situation through secondary and primary sources (see Chapter 6), a clear picture of 'where we are now' emerges. The next step is to define as specifically as possible 'Where do we want

to go?' Ideally objectives should be quantified in terms of success or failure criteria. Timescales should also be set. Clearly defined objectives make the management task of control much easier. Drawing up objectives for the first time is a difficult task. In future years, the previous year's objectives and corresponding results will help to make the planning job a little easier, as everyone has a better idea of what is realistic and what is not. Establishing clear objectives is necessary to give a focus to the organization or division. Clear objectives also give direction to subsequent creative efforts. Some marketing managers and agencies break objectives into many different types; other marketers use just one set of objectives (and sometimes without quantification or numbers attached). As a discipline it is useful to break up objectives so that performance can be measured more accurately. Objectives should be SMART:

S – specific
M – measurable
A – actionable
R – realistic
T – time specific

Two types of objectives are examined here: marketing objectives and communications objectives.

Marketing objectives

Typical marketing objectives refer to sales, market share, distribution penetration, launching a number of new products, and so on. For example, marketing objectives might be:

- to increase unit sales of product/brand X by 10 per cent over the next 12 months;
- to increase market share by 5 per cent over the next 12 months;
- to generate 500 new enquiries each month;
- to increase distribution penetration from 25 per cent to 50 per cent within 12 months;
- to establish a network of distributors covering Germany, France, The Netherlands and Italy during the first six months, followed by Switzerland, Austria, Belgium and Luxembourg in the second six months.

It is worth noting that not all marketing objectives are growth oriented. In Denmark, electricity boards no longer pride themselves on how much electricity they sell but on how little. Product withdrawals are another example where objectives are not attached to year-on-year growth. In very competitive mature markets, with new entrants appearing on the market, maintaining market share and consolidating sales might be more appropriate than expecting big growth. Given that marketing is shifting towards retention of profitable customers and deselection of unprofitable customers (see page 63), the emphasis in some companies has moved from growth in turnover or sales to growth in profit or ROI.

Communications objectives

These typically refer to how the communications should affect the mind of the target audience, eg generate awareness, attitudes, interest or trial. Again, these tend to be most useful when quantified. DAGMAR (defining advertising goals for measuring advertising responses) and AIDA (attention, interest, desire, action) provide yardsticks for communications objectives by trying to separate the various mental stages a buyer goes through before buying. (The response hierarchy models are discussed in Chapter 4.)

The mental stages suggested by DAGMAR and AIDA are as follows:

DAGMAR	AIDA
Unawareness	–
Awareness	Attention
Comprehension	Interest
Conviction	Desire
Action	Action

Here are some examples of communications objectives:

- to increase awareness from 35 per cent to 50 per cent within eight weeks of the campaign launch among 25- to 45-year-old ABC1 women;
- to position the service as the friendliest on the market within a 12-month period among 70 per cent of heavy chocolate users;
- to reposition Guinness from an old, unfashionable, older man's drink to a fashionable younger person's drink over two years among all 25- to 45-year-old male drinkers;
- to maintain brand X as the preferred brand (or number one brand) of photocopiers among at least 50 per cent of current UK buyers in companies with 1,000-plus employees;
- to include Bulgarian wines in the repertoire of possible wine purchases among 20 per cent of ABC1 wine buyers within 12 months;
- to support the launch of a new shop by generating 50 per cent awareness in the immediate community one week before the launch;
- to announce a sale and create 70 per cent awareness one day before the sale starts;
- to reposition the *European* as an upmarket business paper (from a general mid-market newspaper) (see Figure 10.3).

The *European* newspaper positioned itself in new market space, where the management saw a gap in the market. But was there a market in the gap? No other paper was offering a high-quality, European business newspaper. Was there a real need for a weekly European newspaper at that time? The *European* has now ceased publication.

FIGURE 10.3   Repositioning the *European* newspaper from a medium-quality newspaper to an upmarket European business newspaper

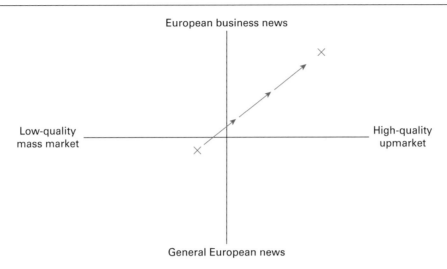

Objectives can cover a variety of goals. It is useful to separate marketing objectives from marketing communications objectives. Detailed, specific objectives ensure that the subsequent choice of strategy is clearly focused.

Strategy

Strategy summarizes 'how we get there' – how the objectives will be achieved. Strategy drives tactics in the same direction. Strategy summarizes tactics. Communications strategy helps to harmonize and integrate all of the tactical communications tools. Communications strategy can include selection of target markets, positioning, selection of communications tools, sequence of communications tools (are different tools used at different stages?), and more.

> ### Most of us are afraid of strategy...
>
> '...because we don't feel confident outlining one unless we're sure it's going to work.'
>
> Godin (2009)

Marketing communications strategies are hard to find. Often the strategy is retrospective in so far as the tactics are planned and then a strategy is created to make sense of the tactics. This is far from ideal. One aide-mémoire for the components of marketing communications strategy is STOP & SIT:

Segmentation (how is the market broken up?)

Target markets (what target markets are chosen plus who is the 'ideal customer'?)

Objectives (strategy must fulfil objectives)

Positioning (of the product or service, which also drives the overall proposition)

and

Stages (is there a sequence or series of stages?)

Integration (does it all integrate smoothly, perhaps through a database?)

Tools (TV, opt-in e-mail, PPC or social media, etc? Or, if you are considering using a social media strategy, you should state clearly whether you build your own network or use someone else's)

Ideally the communications strategy should succinctly answer all of these questions. Objectives, by the way, don't have to be regurgitated, but do keep an eye on them, as any strategy that ignores objectives is a waste of time. Razor-sharp strategies are required now more than ever before. A lot of people work very long hours, and they are very loyal and committed people, but if the strategy is wrong all that hard tactical work is wasted.

> 'There's no point rowing harder if you're rowing in the wrong direction.'
>
> Ohmae (2000)

Positioning is strategic. Careful analysis is required to find a positioning that is actually needed by customers, that is not delivered by the competition and ideally that the organization can genuinely deliver better than competitors. Some brands may be strategically positioned to fill different gaps in the marketplace. Getting it wrong can destroy a business, and getting it right can save a business.

> ### Radical repositioning strategy: Reebok reposition from fashion to action
>
> Adidas repositioned Reebok from 'fashion' to 'action'. It's previous positioning as street-cred fashion with endorsements by rappers like Jay-Z and 50 Cent is being changed to 'sports performance'.
>
> *WARC* (2006)

Developing good marketing communications strategies requires careful consideration. Although occasionally frustrating, it is worthwhile because:

> developing marketing communications strategies delivers many benefits. It is important to remember this because developing and agreeing strategic decisions costs time, money and energy. Many marketers have an inner urge to get on with the job, get creative, develop wonderful advertising campaigns, wacky sales promotions, delightful new sales literature, sensational exhibition stands and more. Other marketers are under pressure to get out and talk to customers, bring in some

sales, generate revenues and justify their existence. So seemingly self-indulgent navel gazing such as strategic contemplation may not always appear worthwhile – in the immediate term. But, beyond the immediate term, a good strategy will reap many benefits.

> Smith, Berry and Pulford (1999)

Here are five examples of marketing communications strategy taken from Smith, Berry and Pulford's *Strategic Marketing Communications* (1999), each demonstrating a very different approach:

- *Tupperware marketing communications strategy.* 'A multimillion-dollar direct-response campaign… the company maintained its personal selling approach but modified its party format to accommodate the increasing limitations for working women… installed a toll-free number to link customers to a local dealer… catalogues were originally available only for dealers, hosts and hostesses, they were made accessible to everyone and reached 30 million people' (adapted from Engel, Warshaw and Kinnear, 1994).

- *IBM insurance marketing communications strategy.* Position the business as a solution provider that fully understands client needs and is easily able to provide complete and successful solutions. All communications reinforce the company's unique capability, which combines marketing and IT in an integrated manner. The key target group is 'European insurers with medium to large customer bases (usually over 1 million)'. All communications are below the line, editorially driven, and drawn from sound research into leading-edge solutions. The published papers are used across a series of public conferences, own conferences and training awareness days, along with a constant media relations campaign.

- *ETC human resource company's marketing communications strategy.* A client relationship strategy focusing on a few key sectors (industry, health, local government and financial services) instead of the previous machine-gun (broad advertising) approach. Direct mailings and seminar events aimed at key opinion formers developed through targeted mailings create a tightly focused database for future presentations and high-value mailings.

- *Daewoo marketing communications strategy.* Position Daewoo as the most customer-focused car company in the UK. Car buyers are happy with the cars but unhappy with the dealers. Daewoo must own customer service. This differentiates Daewoo.

  - Stage 1: Build corporate credibility through TV and motoring press.

  - Stage 2: Develop Daewoo dialogue, collecting information about likes and dislikes about car ownership.

  - Stage 3: Launch brand.

  This necessitates integration throughout the marketing communications and operational implementation. Advertising will build brand awareness and direct people into Daewoo's telemarketing database. The complete mix includes retail design, interactive point-of-sale, sales promotion, direct marketing, database construction and management, PR and advertising.

- *Telewest communications strategy.* Create/educate the market (get consumers to a point where they are predisposed to consider cable from Telewest Communications); build the brand (by teaching customers to value most what Telewest does best); stimulate acquisition (through three big sales promotion ideas); build and manage relationships (through good service and constant database dialogue).

There is no one single approach to building marketing communications strategies. In fact many companies do not put them together at all. A good communications strategy helps to keep all the subsequent tactical communications tools integrated and moving in the same direction, delivering bigger impacts and reducing costs. A simple way to practise writing marketing communications strategies is to generate several alternative strategies, so that strategic options can be considered. Try generating a bad strategic option so that you can begin to see, first, that there is always more than one strategy available to choose from and, second, that some strategies are better than others.

Few social media strategies

MarketingSherpa's US study (December 2008) found that the vast majority of those surveyed rated social media marketing effective at influencing brand reputation, increasing awareness and improving search rankings and site traffic. Although many organizations have a corporate blog or Facebook page, few have strategies in place and even fewer have written social media policies. In fact, only 33 per cent of larger firms had a written policy to manage brand communications, and a mere 13 per cent of smaller businesses had a written policy.

eMarketer.com (2009)

Tactics

Tactics are the details of strategy. In marketing, communications tactics are the communications tools such as advertising, PR, direct mail, etc. The tactics in the marketing communications plan list what happens when and for how much. They are often best expressed as a Gantt chart, as shown in Figure 10.4.

Action

The action stage reveals the details of tactics. Detailed project plans are required in order to implement the tactics. Detailed action plans bring the tactics to life. Actions implement the tactics. This is the not-so-glossy side of marketing, which requires attention to detail, good project planning skills, time management, prioritizing, people management skills, and an ability to handle pressure and to get things done. In reality the action/implementation of the marketing communications tactics requires an ability to get other people (staff, agencies, printers, etc) to deliver on time and within budget. It also requires an ability to plan for contingencies, because things do go wrong (eg advertisements fall down).

FIGURE 10.4   Tactical timings of different communication tools

	Jan	Feb	Mar	Apr	May	Jun	Jul	Aug	£
Advertising – TV – Press – PPC									
Social media – Blog – YouTube – Facebook									
Website – SEO – Inbound links									
Sales promotion – Sample drop – Competition – Collection									
Direct marketing – Mailshot – Telesales									
Publicity (and public relations)									
Sponsorship									
Exhibitions									
Packaging									
Point-of-sale and merchandising									
Internet									
Word of mouth – Viral marketing – CRM NGN									

This is just a shortlist of some of the tactical tools employed by an organization.

Any kind of project planning can be used here, whether critical path or just a Gantt chart. A detailed project plan is required for each tactical communications tool. For example, the production of a mailshot can be as shown in Figure 10.5.

This is just for one mailing. More detailed planning is required if there is a series of mailings. The response handling also needs to be planned carefully. With hybrid and automated marketing systems (see Chapter 17), the responses can be routed to an inbound telesales team, who filter respondents, rank them in terms of urgency, size and location, and pass the enquiry to a relevant salesperson or dispatch further information and update the database for future activities. All of this requires careful planning to ensure sufficient resources are available to make the strategies and tactics actually happen.

FIGURE 10.5   An action plan for one communication tool – a mailshot

	Wk 1	Wk 2	Wk 3	Wk 4	Wk 5	Wk 6	Wk 7	Wk 8	Wk 9	Wk 10	Wk 11	Wk 12
Creative brief	X											
List brief		X										
List proposal			X									
Visual concepts			X									
Visuals approved				X								
List order				X								
Final copy/design					X							
Artwork brief					X							
Print quotes					X							
Set artwork proofs						X						
Receive lists						X						
Data preparation						X						
Finished artwork							X					
Printer brief							X					
Printer proofs								X				
Merge purge lists								X				
Print									X			
Computer bureau output files									X			
Live laser proofs									X			
Mail house brief									X			
Print delivery										X		
Laser print letter										X		
Mail house delivery											X	
Mail house sort/enclose											X	
Mail												X

Control

Plans should include control systems – how performance will be monitored, measured and controlled. Managers need to know at an early stage (rather than when it's too late) how a campaign is running and whether it is an advertising campaign or a mailshot. If it is not working, it should be stopped. **Control systems need to be in place to help monitor any campaigns or activities** (see Figure 10.6). This is where clear objectives can once again help, since the objectives can usually be broken down into more detailed objectives covering shorter periods of time. Once marketers are armed with clearly defined, precise objectives, money can be spent on measuring performance against the objectives (whether defined as sales, enquiries, awareness, enquiries, sales, or return on investment, etc).

Marketers can now measure and compare all activities: inbound (social media campaigns) and outbound marketing (ad campaigns), online and offline. If a campaign is focused on boosting brand awareness or repositioning a brand in the mind of the target audience, this can be measured separately through surveys. If the campaign is focused on engagement and/or sales, this can be easily measured by identifying if visitors, enquirers or customers are emerging from each communications tool – assuming the campaign is focused on generating engagement at some level, eg interaction on a website or Facebook page (posting a comment or voting), registering for a newsletter, taking a trial or making a purchase. The web analytics reveal where visitors are coming from, and telesales, reception and sales staff should also always log where new enquiries are coming from (how visitors heard about the business and what key phrases they used to find the website).

Cost per order, cost per enquiry and cost per visitor can be easily calculated. Other variables need to be closely monitored, including:

- cost per order and cost per customer acquisition;
- net promoter score, satisfaction score and recommendation score;
- reputation/social conversation scores (social media monitoring);
- return on investment.

Note that the figures in Figure 10.7 are not real. Over time, professional marketers learn what are realistic conversion ratios of enquirers or website visitors to customers. For example, in Figure 10.7, 1 per cent of visitors generated by search engine optimization (SEO) convert to customers, while only half of 1 per cent of visitors from a viral marketing campaign convert to customers. The figure would probably be higher for visitors generated from PPC campaigns.

FIGURE 10.6   Control systems

Quantified objectives State each quantified objective and its time period	Means of measuring Sales analysis; number of responses; surveys	Frequency of measurement Daily; weekly; monthly; quarterly; annually?	Accountability Who does it?	Cost How much does it cost to measure?	Action? Who needs to be alerted if significant variances are found?

FIGURE 10.7 Cost per order/cost per customer acquisition

	Volume of people/ size of audience	Total cost	CPT/CPM (cost per thousand people reached)	Percentage CTR (click-through rate/visit website/ enquiry)	Unique visitors	Cost per visitor/ lead	Conversion rate of visitors to customers	Number of orders/ customers	Cost per order
SEO	n/a	£20,000	n/a	n/a	20,000	£1.00	1%	200	£100
Viral A	20,000,000	£30,000	£1.50	10%	2,000,000	£0.15	0.5 of 1%	10,000	£3
Blog	n/a	£20,000	n/a	n/a	10,000				
Banner ad	100,000	£1,000	£10	1%	1,000				
PPC ad	n/a	n/a	n/a	n/a	n/a				
Opt-in e-mail	10,000	£2,000	£200	2%					
Online sponsorship	50,000	£5,000	£1,000	1%					
E-zine/e-newsletter	1,000	£10,000	£10,000	5%					
Press ad	1,000,000	£5,000	£5.00	1/100th of 1%					
Direct mail List A	10,000	£5,000	£500	2%					
Telemarketing – outbound	5,000	£20,000	£4,000	10%					
Exhibition B	6,000	£18,000	£3,000	n/a					

Consider SEO. In Figure 10.7, it generates 20,000 visitors and costs £20,000. This gives a cost per visitor of £1 (£20,000 divided by 20,000 visitors). If the site converts 1 per cent of these visitors into customers, then the SEO generates 200 new customers (1 per cent of 20,000 visitors). The cost per order (CPO) generated by SEO is £100 (£20,000 divided by 200 orders).

If a viral marketing piece costs £30,000 (to create and seed) and it generates 20 million players of which 10 per cent click through to the website, this generates 2 million visitors. Say only half of 1 per cent convert, because many of them are from international markets not relevant to this service. This generates 10,000 customer 'uniques' (unique visitors). Feel free to fill in the rest of the figures yourself.

The table in Figure 10.7 can be extended. You can create your own, more accurate, analysis by adding another column for percentage of visitors that convert to enquirers (and a percentage of them eventually convert to customers, and a percentage of them convert to repeat customers, at which point the costs decline significantly and large profit margins emerge). A longer list of tactical communications tools can be added, including different exhibition events, different e-mail campaigns, different virals, etc, so that the marketer can see what works best and ultimately do more of what works and stop what doesn't.

The lifetime value of potential repeat sales of a customer can give a truer picture of the real value of a customer. Remember, lifetime value can include 'share of wallet': other products or services that a customer might be prepared to buy from the same organization.

You also need a rigorous structured approach to measuring relative satisfaction (compared to competitors) for each stage of the online experience – product search, evaluation, enquiring, purchases, post-purchase communications, after-sales support, etc. You need this more than once a year.

Net promoter score, satisfaction score and recommendation score

It is important to monitor satisfaction scores (though remember that the satisfaction criteria can change and leave an old system irrelevant if not updated). Some blue-chip marketing directors like to keep a simple system monitoring just what percentage of customers would recommend the organization. Other marketers take advocacy and 'detractors' (customers who feel negatively about the organization or brand) and develop reporting systems that combine both variables to highlight a net promoter score (Reichheld, 2006).

Reputation/social conversation scores (social media monitoring)

Marketers need to keep abreast of what is being said about their brands, their organizations and their staff (as well as the competition) in the vast array of conversations in social media platforms around the world. Marketers need to know about the quantity and intensity of commentary about brand or product. In addition to the free services of Google Alert, there are other social monitoring

Social media control myth

'One of the most common fears I focus on defeating among executives and brand managers is that in new media brands lose control by publishing content and engaging in social networks. The general sentiment is that by sharing information and creating presences within public communities that they, by the nature of democratized participation, invite negative responses in addition to potentially positive and neutral interaction. By not fully embracing the social Web, many believe that they retain a semblance of control. The idea is that if brands abstain from providing a forum for hosting potentially disparaging commentary, it will prevent it from earning an audience – in this case, an audience that can impact the business and the reputation of the brand. However, retaining control, following the socialization of the Web, is nothing more than pure legend. While many companies retain control during the stages of defining and shaping messages, control is relinquished at the point of distribution. Once messages are published, they are at the mercy of consumers, peers, and influencers online and offline.'

Solis (2010)

tools, including Google Blog Search, Icerocket, Twitter Search, Yahoo Pipes, BlogPulse, BoardReader and BoardTracker. There are also some more comprehensive licence fee systems with their own scoring systems, which include Radian6, Market Sentinel and Precise Media.

So I continue to ask: if a conversation takes place online and you're not there to hear it, did it actually happen?

Return on investment

As mentioned in Chapter 1, marketers must learn to speak the language of the boardroom. This includes ROI on marketing expenditure. Can marketers demonstrate rigorous professional discipline and track what communications campaigns deliver a better ROI than others? Can marketers convince the board that the return from investment in marketing is better than the return generated by investing the money elsewhere (eg in a high-interest deposit account)? It is possible to calculate the cost per order, profit per order and cumulative profit from a campaign. Ambler (2006) explored four measurement mechanisms – return on investment (ROI), or return on marketing investment (ROMI), or return on marketing expenditure (ROME), discounted cash flow (DCF), return on customer, and net advocates (Reichheld, 2006) – and concluded that no single metric does it all. In fact, a combination of metrics is required.

Control includes various areas of market research and testing, so measurement systems need to be built into the plan.

Planning is really an iterative process. A manager puts together a plan and a budget. Senior management agree it or reduce it by way of budgets. The

> ### ROI is not the only measure
>
> 'Despite all evidence to the contrary, the belief that a single number can be used to assess marketing performance is persistent. Some say that top management can only handle a single number, or silver metric, so we must choose the least bad one. Others believe that ROI is so standard as not to be worth challenging. Others again claim modernity for customer concepts such as customer equity, customer lifetime value and Peppers and Rogers' new 'Return on Customer'. Yes, they are new and, yes, they have value, but these measures are not the silver metrics their promoters claim them to be.'
>
> Ambler (2006)

manager revises the plan in the light of the resources available. The plan is then rolled out, results watched carefully and action taken to change the plan if necessary (ie if it is not working). If something is not right, it is better to find out why, make corrections and move on – hence the importance of control mechanisms. They provide a manager with useful feedback as to whether the plan is working or not. Everything a manager does is a learning process since, assuming the desire for constant improvement, a manager is monitoring what works best and what doesn't. Each year, as experience is gained, improvements can be made through this longer-term iterative process. Procter & Gamble asks its managers to build on their 'learnings' (what they have learnt from the marketplace). They constantly learn from the marketplace and then incorporate those 'learnings' in their next marketing plan.

Key points from Chapter 10

- SOSTAC® provides a very effective structure for any plan.
- Market research and intelligence create a winning platform. It is essential to gather key information before making any decisions about strategy or tactics.
- STOP and SIT are the key components for writing a strategy. Write several options before choosing the best one.
- Build control systems into the plan.

References and further reading

Ambler, T (2006) Use a dashboard when driving your marketing, *Market Leader*, **33**, Summer

Doyle, P (2001) *Marketing Management Strategy*, 3rd edn, FT Prentice Hall, Hemel Hempstead

Doyle, P, Saunders, J and Wright, L (1987) A comparative study of US and Japanese marketing strategies in the British market, Warwick University report

eMarketer.com (2009) Social media best practices, 29 July

Engel, J, Warshaw, M and Kinnear, T (1994) *Promotional Strategy: Managing the marketing communications process*, Irwin, Boston, MA

Forrester Research (2009) *US Interactive Marketing Forecast, 2009 to 2014*, Forrester Research, Cambridge, MA

Godin, S (2009) When tactics drown out strategy, *Seth Godin's Blog*, 7 August

Kanter, B (2008) How much time does it take to do social media?, *Beth's Blog*, 1 October

Kanter, R M (2000) *Marketing CD 2: Segmentation, positioning and the marketing mix*, **www.prsmith.org**

Kanter, R M (2001) *On-line Marketing Course 2: Segmentation, positioning and the marketing mix*, 2nd edn, **www.prsmith.org**

Kotler, P (2001) In conversation with Paul Smith

Kotler, P et al (2000) *Marketing CD 3: Marketing planning*, **www.prsmith.org**

Ohmae, K (2000) *Marketing CD 2: Segmentation, positioning and the marketing mix*, **www.prsmith.org**

Reichheld, F (2006) *The Ultimate Question: Driving good profits and true growth*, Harvard Business School Publishing, Boston, MA

Smith, P R (1998) *Marketing Communication: an integrated approach*, 2nd edition, Kogan Page, London

Smith, P R (2003) *Marketing Planning Toolkit*, **www.prsmith.org**

Smith, P R (2004) *SOSTAC Marketing Plans* (CD)

Smith, P, Berry, C and Pulford, A (1999) *Strategic Marketing Communications*, Kogan Page, London

Solis, B (2010) The myth of control in new media, *Brian Solis*, 25 January

WARC (2006) Adidas to reposition Reebok from fashion to action, 26 January

Wing, R L (1989) *The Art of Strategy* (translation of Sun Tzu, *The Art of War*), Aquarian Press, Wellingborough

Further information

Euro RSCG
Havas Media
Privacy Office
Dr Fleming 17
08017 Barcelona
Spain
Tel: +44 (0)20 7257 6077
www.eurorscg.co.uk

International Organization for Standardization (ISO)
1 ch de la Voie-Creuse
Case postale 56
CH-1211 Geneva 20
Switzerland
Tel: +41 22 749 01 11
Fax: +41 22 733 34 30
www.iso.org

National Readership Survey Ltd (NRS)
40 Parker Street
London WC2B 5PQ
Tel: +44 (0)20 7242 8111
Fax: +44 (0)20 7242 8303
www.nrs.co.uk

Target Group Index (TGI)
Ealing Gateway
26–30 Uxbridge Road
Ealing
London W5 2AU
Tel: +44 (0)20 8433 4000
www.kantarmedia-tgigb.com

11
The changing communications environment

LEARNING OBJECTIVES

By the end of this chapter you will be able to:

● Embrace the constant nature of change in markets and ergo marketing communications and recognize the opportunity offered to marketers

● Be aware of the importance of checking the laws and regulations relevant to marcomms

● Consider building risk assessment into marketing plans, particularly including economic risks

● Accept the need to understand social change and integrate this change into marcomms to reflect changing social norms, values and roles

● Dispel any fears of technology and embrace technological changes as aids to marketing

Introduction

We are children of change. Right now business is going through 'the biggest change since the industrial revolution' (see Chapter 1), and with this comes radical change for marketing communications. This chapter looks at how marketing communications are affected by the rapidly changing business environment and its many uncontrollable factors.

Markets are pulled and pushed in different directions by forces that are outside an organization's immediate control. New laws, changing regulations, fluctuating economic cycles, demographic shifts, new social values, attitudes and cultural norms, fast-changing technology, and aggressive, borderless and category-less competitors are some of the key factors that constantly move markets away from the status quo. As a result, yesterday's marketing communications strategy can soon become obsolete.

This means that the marketing intelligence and information system (MIIS) should constantly feed back information on patterns, trends or sudden changes in any of these uncontrollable forces. This requires, in turn, a constant alertness and preparedness to change products, services, advertisements, images, communications and even an organization's attitudes or culture.

The 'SW' part of a SWOT (strengths, weaknesses, opportunities and threats) analysis monitors the external opportunities and threats that emerge in the business environment. The PEST acronym provides a useful starting point to scan the business environment for any of these change factors that directly or indirectly affect a business and how it communicates:

Political (including legal and regulatory)

Economic (global economic shifts and cycles of recession and boom)

Social (new values, attitudes, lifestyles, ethics and demographics)

Technological (the internet, databases, digital TV and much more)

Competition could also be added as a key factor operating in an organization's environment. For the purposes of this chapter, the focus will be on the PEST factors. Any of these change factors could ultimately push a business into extinction if the changes are constantly ignored. There is a tendency to resist change, perhaps because of the insecurities it heaps upon an individual. Some organizations wait until the last moment before changing. Others see an advantage in being proactive rather than reactive. We will now consider how these PEST factors affect the organization's marketing activities, and its communications in particular.

New borderless, category-less competitors changing the marketplace

It is a rapidly changing market: Microsoft is following Google and Yahoo into the telco market. The BBC works with Google's video-sharing service and with YouTube. Meanwhile the UK telco company BT now offers TV. And on it goes – this is the borderless, category-less merry-go-round continually changing the structure of markets.

Politics (regulations and laws)

UK business legislation provides laws that essentially support the principles of being honest and truthful. There is also a host of self-regulatory professional codes that draw on the same set of basic business principles, ie that marketing professionals should conduct their business in a legal, decent, honest and truthful manner.

Before looking at the laws, it is worth mentioning that short-term, dishonest deals that slip through any regulatory systems generate only short-term gains and do not tend to generate long-term sales, since repeat business does not come back. The 'everlasting customer' or the 'lifetime customer' concept is a long-term winning strategy, since the marketing perspective focuses on selling 10 cars, 10 fridges, thousands of cans of food or beer, or 50 years of office cleaning to one customer over a long period of time instead of grabbing a one-off, short-term sale. It costs five times as much to sell to a new customer as it does to sell to an existing customer. Fooling a customer is myopic. You can only cheat a customer once. Flouting the law or regulations restricts a business to a short-term vision. Incidentally, Japanese management guru Kenichi Ohmae claims that the most fundamental difference between Eastern and Western business strategies is the time horizon. Japanese companies build long-term strategies, while Western companies plan short-term profits.

EU directives are subsequently adopted into local laws by each country independently. **In the UK a statute is a law, also called an Act, that has to be voted in by Parliament. Acts are the primary legislation. Regulations are refinements of an Act**, and they are brought into force by the Secretary of State (minister). Regulations form part of the law in the UK.

UK television advertising alone has approximately 150 statutes and regulations that affect it.

The Unfair Commercial Practices Directive 2005 harmonizes unfair trading laws across the European Union and prohibits businesses from treating consumers unfairly. The directive was implemented through the Consumer Protection from Unfair Trading Regulations 2008 (CPRs).

Unusual trademark applications

Trademark applications include the sound of a dog barking (Dulux paint), the musical jingle for Mister Softee's ice cream, car tyres that smell of roses (a Japanese company), Microsoft's catchphrase 'Where do you want to go today?' and 'Ooh aah Cantona' (Eric Cantona).

- The Trade Descriptions Act 1968 effectively stopped false claims and will be amended or replaced by the CPRs.

- The Sale of Goods Act 1979 demands that goods sold match their description.

- The Trade Marks Act 1994 adapted UK trademark law to fit with European legislation. This means that a wider range of products and service attributes can now be registered as trademarks.

- The Control of Misleading Advertisements Regulations 1988 provide legislation in respect of advertisements.

- The Data Protection and Privacy Regulations 1999 emerged from the Data Protection Act 1998.

- The Communications Act 2003 was driven by the Electronic Commerce (EC Directive) Regulations 2002.

- The Enterprise Act 2002 ensures fair competition.

- The Consumer Protection (Distance Selling) Regulations 2000, sometimes referred to as the Distance Selling Regulations, protect consumers by insisting marketers supply, in writing, full details of the goods or services offered, delivery arrangements and payment, suppliers' details and the consumers' cancellation right before they buy (known as 'prior information'). This information must also be provided in writing. Consumers can cancel the order during the cooling-off period of seven working days. These regulations apply when selling via the internet, TV, mail order, phone or fax.

- The EU Directive on Privacy and Electronic Communications Regulations (PECR) came into force in 2003.

- The Consumer Protection from Unfair Trading Regulations 2008 seek to tackle unfair sales and marketing.

- The Business Protection from Misleading Marketing Regulations 2008 combined with CPR also provide protection for businesses.

- The Digital Economy Act came into force in 2010, regulates digital media and offers new protection against copyright infringement.

The overall guiding principles are the same in law as in voluntary regulations: simply be legal, decent, honest and truthful. If all else fails, the Office of Fair Trading (OFT) provides a safety net, and complaints about marketing communications (advertising, shop-window displays, etc) can be referred to the OFT for scrutiny.

International Financial Reporting Standards cost $54 billion

International Financial Reporting Standards require companies to value their intangible assets (eg brands) on their balance sheets, subject to annual review for impairment, which means that the difference between the price paid and the current value of an acquired brand must be calculated. Any resulting write-downs can have a significant impact, as AOL Time Warner discovered in 2002. It had to write off $54 billion for the value lost when AOL acquired Time Warner at the end of the dotcom boom in 2000.

London Olympics 2012 vs ambush marketers

The London Olympic Games and Paralympic Games Act 2006 and the Olympic Symbol etc (Protection) Act 1995 protects sponsors' rights by attempting to prevent ambush marketing and to protect exclusivity of official sponsors, which effectively means that only official sponsors, suppliers and licensees are allowed to use the Olympic marks, while the law prohibits non-official advertisers from the unauthorized use of:

- logos: the Olympic marks, such as the London 2012 logo, the Olympic rings or any other logo that can be confusingly similar to the Olympic marks;

- images: such as the Olympic torch, Olympic flames, athletic images and the colour combinations of the Olympic rings;

- mottoes: the Olympic and Paralympic mottoes;

- words: 'Olympic', 'Olympiad', 'Olympian', 'Olympix' and similar words;

- word combinations and phrases that falsely suggest an association between a business, its goods or services and the Games;

- sounds, designs, images and marks: advertising, marketing material, sales promotions, goods with words (spoken or written), sounds, designs, images and marks associated with the Games.

There are, as mentioned, many other laws and regulations, both national and international, that affect a business and its marketing communications. For example, the EU Telecommunications **Data Protection Directive (enforced by the Data Protection Registrar)** makes it illegal for companies to fax homes or businesses that have opted out. (See Fax Preference Service details on page 261.) Some of the legislation may not appear to affect the marketing communications directly, eg product liability laws, but caution, coupled with expert advice, is required, particularly in the international arena. Product liability puts an increasing onus of responsibility on manufacturers, distributors and retailers to make sure that the products they market are safe and sound. It also affects marketing communications (and it even affects the instructions on a pack, as shown in the box below). The 'borderless world' knows few barriers when it comes to liability. Bloggers and twitterers take note (libel cases and breach of trade secrets cases will emerge).

Sparkling wine shooting

The 20-year-old case of a US consumer suing a UK paint company (for alleged injurious effects of a lead-based paint) strikes fear into the heart of many potential exporters. According to Pohl (1991), a growing awareness that a manufacturer carries a heavy and detailed obligation to warn potential users about any dangers that might lurk in the use of its products has prompted some sparkling wine manufacturers to print disclaimers on the packaging warning against possible risks involved in uncorking their products.

Breach of privacy regulations costs money and brand image

A television company in the US has been fined £3 million for flouting the Do Not Call laws. Five telemarketers allegedly called on behalf of Direct TV, contacting consumers registered on the Do Not Call database. One of the firms did not put the required live salesperson on the line within two seconds of the consumer answering the phone (Precision Marketing, 2006).

Nationwide was fined £980,000 when an employee's laptop containing confidential customer information was stolen from the employee's house in August 2006. The FSA's action is based solely on Nationwide's breach of the FSA's Principles for Businesses, Principle 3: Management and control: 'A firm must take reasonable care to organise and control its affairs responsibly and effectively, with adequate risk management systems' (Anning, 2007).

An individual recipient of an unsolicited e-mail, Gordon Dick, sued online IT product vendor Transcom in respect of a single e-mail, which it said it sent out once a year to customers and those who had contacted Transcom about its services. Dick denied ever being in either category and threatened to sue Transcom unless it 'treated for peace and made him an offer'. He won over £1,000 (Anning, 2007).

Adult site Nortycams sent salacious unsolicited e-mails to UK recipients who had not opted in to receive them. The ISP, Microsoft, claimed its image as a service provider was being damaged, and Nortycams settled for a combined damages and costs figure of £45,000 (Anning, 2007).

Data security disasters

Memory sticks, discs, laptops, and files lost or stolen from homes or cars or left behind on a train included information about the following:

- 10,000 prolific offenders – profiles and other information;
- 84,000 prisoners – profiles and other information;
- 30,000 people with six or more convictions in the last year;
- 100,000 personal details about members of the armed forces;
- 600,000 people interested in, or who had applied to join, the Royal Navy, Royal Marines and RAF;
- 25,000,000 child benefit claimants;
- Gulf War invasion plans stored on a computer stolen from an RAF officer's car in 1990.

BBC News Online (2008a, 2008b)

Self-regulation: codes of practice

Various professional bodies draw up their own codes of practice to which their members must adhere. Failure to do so may result in expulsion and sometimes negative publicity, along with a form of blacklisting. In the case of advertising or a sales promotion, a breach of a code can also result in the withdrawal of an advertisement or sales promotion, etc. This can be expensive, as the development of any campaign costs money. The risks are arguably higher in television, where a 60-second advertisement can easily

cost a million pounds. Most advertisers want to stand out from the crowd. To do this they sometimes have to be daring, bold and controversial. The advertiser's dilemma here is whether 1) to be so controversial that the advertisement teeters on the brink of being pulled off the air or 2) to play safe with a less controversial creative treatment.

Although marketing communications must adhere to the laws of the land (ie one cannot misrepresent or blatantly mislead), the voluntary codes are both cheaper and quicker to apply should any complaints or claims be made. The codes also offer useful guidance to the marketer, so that most problems are ironed out before an advertisement goes out on air or is published in the press. Essentially, advertisements should:

- be legal, decent, honest and truthful;
- show responsibility to the customer and society;
- follow the basic business principles of fair competition.

Professional bodies need to be vigilant in order to maintain the credibility of their profession. This is particularly true in advertising, where the consumer's scepticism and resistance to advertising are heightened or lowered according to the credibility of the advertising industry. This credibility is founded upon the industry's reputation and determination to maintain standards of legality, decency, honesty and truthfulness.

Regardless of legislation and regulations, common sense and good ethics dictate that marketing professionals should adhere to permission-based marketing. This means that all e-mail campaigns and all telemarketing campaigns should be built around 'opt-in' lists or databases. These are lists or databases of customers or prospects who have readily given their permission for further contact by 'opting in'. These lists are of a much higher quality in terms of response than are 'opt-out' lists, where the customer or prospect has to consciously make the effort to tick a box to ensure there will be no further contact. 'Opt-in', by contrast, ensures that customers or prospects consciously make an effort (eg tick a box) to request further communications from the marketer. There is increasing resistance to intrusive online marketing (including SMS messaging). Arguably, this resistance is also spreading to offline marketing, including direct mail. Therefore it follows that best practice should be permission-based marketing.

In addition, marketers need to tread carefully when using new technologies. There is the well-publicized fine handed to a Leeds company, Moby Monkey, for an SMS promotion. This came about as the result of a mass SMS broadcast to hundreds of thousands of randomly generated numbers – it was inevitable that many of these included mobile phones owned or used by children (Murphy, 2003). Then, in late 2002, the Australian high court made history (in Gutnick *v* Dow Jones) by declaring that anyone publishing information on the internet could face legal proceedings anywhere in the world (Keegan, 2002). So, although caution is required, common sense and good ethics should prevail and act as useful guidelines for marketers.

Press and print advertisements and the ASA/CAP

Press and print mean all non-broadcast media, ie the press, posters, leaflets, direct mail, video cassette commercials, teletext and cinema advertising. **In the UK, the Committee of Advertising Practice (CAP) is the custodian of the British code of advertising practice.** It provides a rulebook for all advertising except radio, TV and cable (which is covered by the ITC). The code offers guidelines as to what is acceptable and what is not.

If any member of the public objects to a published advertisement he or she can contact the Advertising Standards Authority (ASA) and complain in writing. The ASA is the customer side of the CAP; the CAP deals with the trade or the advertisers directly. Complaints are analysed to determine whether they are worth further investigation. If the complaint is deemed to be reasonable, and the association consequently upholds the complaint, then the advertiser is asked to withdraw the advertisement immediately. The ASA is not a legal body and therefore has non-statutory powers. Some advertisers may choose to ignore a request to withdraw an advertisement. The ASA will then issue a media warning to all CAP member organizations (including media owners). This effectively blacklists the advertisement. The result is that the advertiser will find very few media owners prepared to sell it any advertising space. The media may implement their terms and conditions of business, which require adherence to the codes. Agencies that persistently breach the codes jeopardize their membership of professional and trade organizations. This means trading privileges and financial incentives

may be forfeited, and potential new clients may exclude agencies that are not members of recognized professional bodies. If all else fails, the association can invoke the final legal backstop of the Control of Misleading Advertisements Regulations 1988. Although rarely needed, these empower the Director General of Fair Trading to obtain an injunction against the advertiser.

It is worth checking with the CAP before printing a mailshot or publishing an advertisement. However, many campaigns are published without prior CAP approval and run the relevant risk.

It has been suggested that some of the more controversial short campaigns seek to gain free editorial coverage by being banned. There are, of course, risks associated with this kind of exposure.

Television advertisements and Ofcom

TV advertisements, on the other hand, must gain approval before broadcasting. **Ofcom came into being in 2003, having been created by the Telecommunications Act 2003,** and for the first time a single entity regulated what traditionally had been seen as disparate forms of media.

Ofcom combines the role of five bodies into one powerful organization. The Independent Television Commission (ITC), the Radio Authority (RA), the Radio Communications Agency (RCA), Oftel and the Broadcast Standards Commission all now come under the control of Ofcom, operating from its headquarters in London.

Initial scripts are approved by Clearcast, and a clearance certificate is issued. However, this does not guarantee that the finished production will also be acceptable, as the film's treatment is sometimes difficult to envisage from a script or storyboard, and so it is also screened for final approval by Clearcast before broadcasting. Even after an advertisement is cleared for broadcasting, it can still be pulled off the air if the ITC requests it. Its attention can be aroused by complaints from the public. If, after it has examined the material and considered the complaint, it feels that the complaint should be upheld, it can then pull the advertisement off the air.

In addition to advertising, other marketing services have their own regulations and codes. For example, the Code of Sales Promotion Practice is also published by the CAP and basically provides guidelines for sales promotion activities. The Institute of Practitioners in Advertising (IPA), Chartered Institute of Public Relations (CIPR), Public Relations Consultants Association (PRCA), Institute of Sales Promotion (ISP) and other professional bodies all have codes of practice to which their members must adhere. Any breach of the code can result in a member being warned or ultimately struck off the institute or association member list. This may have some short-term negative publicity plus, in the medium to longer term, exclusion of that member from pitch lists. Some clients refer to the appropriate institution or association when choosing a new agent or consultant.

Direct marketing

Since 1992 the ASA/CAP has had the responsibility of regulating the direct marketing industry. Essentially this is to ensure that consumers receive as much or as little direct mail as they want. The CAP's rules require direct marketing campaigns to:

1 give consumers a choice before transferring their names to other companies;

2 remove names from lists on request;

3 correct personal details immediately upon notification.

The direct marketing industry is currently under scrutiny from the EU. The European Advertising Standards Alliance (EASA) consists of the organizations in Europe that already operate self-regulatory codes of advertising practice. It hopes to coordinate the disparate activities and act as the focal point for pan-European consultation. Whether voluntary codes of practice will be preferred to centralized legislation remains to be seen.

This will affect all direct marketing activities, including telemarketing. At present there is little EU harmony in either regulations or legislation, eg cold calling is banned in Germany. It is also banned in some US states. Equally, sales promotions, incentives, premiums and free gifts are generally unacceptable in Germany and also cause problems in France. The EASA may provide a platform for promoting self-regulation and harmony across Europe.

Macro-political effects on business and communications

We now move from national and international regulations and legislation, which affect marketing communications, to international political negotiations, which affect the world economy. It should be remembered that the larger international trading companies need to monitor the results of worldwide political agreements. Plans are prepared to meet a range of scenarios built around possible results from, say, the current major economic disputes. *Fortune* magazine describes two scenarios used by an oil company.

Scenario 1, sustainable world and global mercantilism, assumes that all the major international economic disputes are solved, there is European unity, the United States and Japan agree trading terms (and avoid a trade war), free trade prevails across the globe, and stable growth is maintained. As a consequence, environmental issues receive more attention. The implications for Shell are new emission restrictions and a reconfiguration of the energy industry in which less oil and more natural gas are used.

Scenario 2, global mercantilism, this assumes a gloomier world where regional conflicts basically destabilize the world, trade wars and recessions rage, trading blocs form, and consensus on environmental issues is never achieved. This scenario implies less regulation, a piecemeal approach to environmental issues and much more oil consumption.

Worldwide political agreements not only affect product portfolios (the range and types of products or services), but they also affect the social agenda, which determines what are considered to be the most important social issues in the minds of customers. This, in turn, affects the organization's social responsibility policies and subsequent communications programmes. The social factors examined in 'Social change' below also indicate how the agenda can change over relatively short periods of time. First, we will consider how the national economy affects organizations and their marketing communications.

Economics

Economic changes affect markets and, in turn, a marketer's choice of marketing messages. Economies move in cycles, but few can forecast exact economic trends across different regions. Some market economies are more risky than others, particularly at certain periods or stages in their cycles. Marketers must be in tune with economic trends. **Since 2005, UK company reports must, by law, include a description of the principal risks and uncertainties facing the company** (as well as a description of the resources available to the company and a statement of the business's objectives and the strategies of the company). Businesses now need marketers to analyse the risks of various markets and the risk of particular strategies. **In the United States, the Sarbanes–Oxley corporate governance legislation requires a risk management approach to business.** Interestingly, the 2004 Enterprise Risk Management Integrated Framework mentions the word 'customer' 71 times and the word 'marketing' 11 times. Marketers are well positioned to analyse risk and integrate at board level.

Shift to the East

'The dominance of the US and the dominance of Europe – particularly Western Europe – is eclipsed. What we're witnessing is a sharp shift in wealth in a relatively short period of time from West to East.'

Martin Sorrell, WPP,
at the 2006 World Economic Forum, Davos

Economic effects on markets and communications

Industrial and consumer markets are directly and indirectly affected by the state of the economy. The global shift in economic power from West to East is affecting many markets. Exchange rates, interest rates, unemployment, levels of disposable income, etc all affect how much money is around, how much will be spent and, in a sense, the size of many markets or industries.

During a recession almost everyone cuts back on spending. Consumers spend less. Companies spend less. Many organizations cut back on all types of spending, including marketing (although there are exceptions, such as Procter & Gamble, which, according to Bill MacNamara (1991), ex-Asda divisional marketing director, 'automatically raise their marketing expenditure in a recession'). A classic fall in derived demand emerges: as primary consumer demand falls, the secondary demand (for the commercial products and services required to make and market the consumer products) also falls. This reduces growth in the marketing service industries like advertising and design. It becomes a buyer's market as prices

tumble and better deals are demanded by clients. Several agencies and clients go into liquidation. There is therefore an increased need to check the financial stability of any agency, partner, supplier or customer.

Meanwhile, advertisers have to address the difficulty of encouraging people to buy during a serious recession. See how advertisers fight the enemy of recession by using its own images. During a recession many buyers search for better deals, which include price cuts, extended terms and value-for-money sales promotions. These promotions do not necessarily increase brand loyalty. The scars of an economic recession may be permanently expressed in terms of buying patterns, attitudes, values and, ultimately, the advertising imagery, which reflect the changing norms, roles and values of a culture.

Recession-induced psychological change

Even a phenomenally strong economic recovery may not bring back the consumer spending patterns of the 1980s. Values, attitudes and lifestyles may combine to create lower levels of consumption, new buying processes and an overall pattern of trading down (away from premium-price brands). The worldwide recession brought job cuts and quality-of-life worries out of the headlines and into millions of homes. Some feel that consumer markets have changed because of a recession-induced psychological change that moved people away from the self-indulgence and excess of the 'me, mine, more' mentality of the pre-millennium to the 'learning to live with limitations' of the post-millennium.

This could affect buying behaviour and the supporting advertising messages, for example a move away from images of personal achievement to images about personal relationships, or even a move away from advertising that is built around the user imagery (from where 'the user is the hero' to where 'the product is hero'). This suggests that advertising will have to provide more hard information as consumers buy more carefully, seeking out the best deal, and display a price consciousness that rejects premium-price brands for better-value products that provide relevant benefits and excellent performance. Marketing messages change to match the mood created by the state of the economy. Equally, marketers must monitor the overall business environment for high-impact events such as a recession or banking crisis, to be ready to react and, ultimately, to reflect the changing set of needs that people acquire as their circumstances change.

Companies that ignore Black Swan events will go under

'Black Swan events are almost impossible to predict. Instead of perpetuating the illusion that we can anticipate the future, risk management should try to reduce the impact of the threats we don't understand. We don't live in the world for which conventional risk-management textbooks prepare us. No forecasting model predicted the impact of the current economic crisis, and its consequences continue to take establishment economists and business academics by surprise. Moreover, as we all know, the crisis has been compounded by the banks' so-called risk-management models, which increased their exposure to risk instead of limiting it and rendered the global economic system more fragile than ever.

'Low-probability, high-impact events that are almost impossible to forecast – we call them Black Swan events – are increasingly dominating the environment. Because of the internet and globalization, the world has become a complex system, made up of a tangled web of relationships and other interdependent factors. Complexity not only increases the incidence of Black Swan events but also makes forecasting even ordinary events impossible. All we can predict is that companies that ignore Black Swan events will go under.

'Instead of trying to anticipate low-probability, high-impact events, we should reduce our vulnerability to them. Risk management, we believe, should be about lessening the impact of what we don't understand – not a futile attempt to develop sophisticated techniques and stories that perpetuate our illusions of being able to understand and predict the social and economic environment.'

Taleb, Goldstein, and Spitznagel (2009)

Social change

Norms, values and roles change. Today, fathers change nappies, cook dinners and shop in supermarkets. Many women earn more than their male partners. Roles are becoming less clearly defined. It is no longer abnormal to have two working parents. Children are growing old younger, and many adults feel fatigue beyond their years as they suffer 'information fatigue syndrome' (too much information), which weakens the effectiveness of marketing communications, as audiences simply cannot digest all the information being thrown at them. Meanwhile roles continue to change.

'Metrosexuals'– straight urban men who enjoy such things as shopping and using beauty products – are emerging. However, young men find a lot of pressure out there and are not sure what their role is (see Chapter 4 for more). Global research from Millward Brown reveals that children are growing old younger. This is substantiated by the following statement: 'Corporate brands are starting to replace character brands. Kids are starting to grow up at an earlier age and so move away from characters and into brands sooner. Their pocket money is spent on items such as mobile phones and branded merchandise' (Levy, 2003). Young people also prefer to text rather than to talk when using their mobiles. They also see grammatically correct sentences in ads, on television or the internet, as outdated (Lindstrom, 2003). Tweens (8- to 14-year-olds) around the world revealed they had common fears, including terrorism and family breakdown. Their view of the world around them is changing. Marketers must reflect these changes in their messages.

Changing world – no longer black or white

Who would have thought the world's favourite golfer would be a black man and the world's favourite rapper would be a white man? Tiger Woods and Eminem are still top of their respective charts.

Adults are growing old faster than kids! This means the world's population is ageing. This has significant social and economic implications, as Harvard's Farrell, Ghai and Shavers (2005) observed:

> The world's population is aging, and as it gets even grayer, bank balances will stop growing and living standards, which have improved steadily since the industrial revolution, could stagnate. The reason is that the populations of Japan, the United States, and Western Europe, where the vast majority of the world's wealth is created and held, are aging rapidly. During the next two decades, the median age in Italy will rise to 51, from 42, and in Japan to 50, from 43. Since people save less after they retire and younger generations in their prime earning years are less frugal than their elders were, savings rates are set to fall dramatically.

And older people's needs are changing too. They may flex their muscles with grey power votes or just demand younger lifestyles; for example, senior citizens considering retirement lifestyles and homes want Pilates, Chinese chicken salad and wireless-ready housing. Meatloaf, bingo and chair exercises are not required. 'In the past it was about healthcare and the nursing staff, but this group is saying I am not ready for that. I want Pilates, a lap pool, gourmet dinner and I want to lead my own life with flexible choices' (Dwight, 2007).

Adults are changing too. An Accenture research report carried out in 2001 found that people were fed up with marketing communications. Eighty per cent of a target audience could be reached with one 30-second off-peak TV spot in the early 1980s. At the beginning of the 21st century, reaching that same audience required 200–300 primetime spots. 'It's getting worse every day... unsolicited interruptions are unwanted – in *all* media... People are fed up. They're overloaded with information. Their time and attention is being wasted... people no longer respond the way they used to' (Brøndmo, 2003). Impatience and intolerance of irrelevant information continue to grow today as customers juggle multiple tasks in their busy lives. This is partially why Google is so successful. It fits a need: to find information quickly. Google is 'in the business of revolutionizing the nature of knowledge; search has become integral in the way we think and act' (Andrew Keen, in Smith, 2008).

Attitudes towards issues change. Once environmentalists were considered to be hippies, communists,

> **OK, Google, now figure out my life, please**
>
> 'We cannot even answer the most basic questions about you because we don't know enough about you. The goal is to enable Google users to be able to ask questions like "What shall I do tomorrow?" and "What job should I take?" This is the most important aspect of Google's expansion.'
>
> Smith (2008)

anarchists or outcasts because of their lack of conformity with other people's beliefs, values and attitudes. Today, most political parties and major corporations recognize the importance of environmental groups.

Ethics

Social consciousness among buyers is important. However, the degree of importance can change over time. Perhaps it is linked to economic cycles; for example, during economic downturns does ethics fall down the ladder of importance? However, many customers want to know more about products and their producers. Do the products or producers damage the environment? What do the producers do in the community? Do they donate political funds? Do the organizations disclose information, and so on?

Many buyers are becoming aware that the supermarket is the economic ballot box of the future. And investors also are becoming increasingly interested in the corporate citizenship of organizations that they might consider funding.

Banks are becoming weary of lending funds to higher-risk, environmentally poor companies. Insurance premiums will also reflect the higher risk of non-green companies. The corporate responsibility record is now a criterion in joint ventures. For example, who wants to invest time and money in an organization that has a poor environmental record? To put it another way, who wants to inherit a green time bomb?

Some estimates suggest that a 'green screen', or false green claims by corporations, will last only a short period, since probing pressure groups, investigative journalists, scrutinizing financial analysts and information-hungry customers will eventually reveal a much bigger problem than that which was originally hidden. This implies that the marketing people have a vested interest in ensuring that an organization operates in a socially responsible manner. Corporate attitudes towards altruism and ethics are changing, as are personal religious beliefs.

Finally, one extraneous factor that affects the business environment is the environment itself. If the world continues to heat up, northern European attitudes, emotions and feelings about different stimuli (particularly colour) may change. This would affect almost all forms of marketing communications, and possibly even radio.

Demographics

The statistical analysis (or division) of a population or audience by age, sex and social status helps marketers to segment and target markets. This can be combined with location or geography (hence the term 'geodemographics') and contextual or behavioural information (see Chapter 13). In addition, there are demographic cycles, trends and movements that can help an organization to learn about its market many years in advance. Some years ago, forecasts (Gwyer, 1992) revealed that by 2030 the UK population would start to shrink and deaths would exceed births. The period total fertility rate (PTFR) is now at 1.8 children per family, which is below the replacement level of 2.1. By 2030 the over-80s market will expand to 3.4 million (3.5 times more than in 1961). Demographic shifts affect markets and consequently marketing communications.

For example, the demographic shift during the 1980s pulled the market away from Guinness, as a disproportionately large number of younger drinkers (20-year-olds) emerged after the 1960s baby boom. Guinness was positioned as an older, unfashionable drink. To chase the moving market, Guinness and the now extinct but then brilliant advertising agency Allen, Brady and Marsh repositioned the product as a younger and more fashionable drink. The 1990s saw the demographic bulge move on to create a disproportionately large number of 30-year-olds. Guinness chased this swell by using a maturing blond-haired man to help to position the drink appropriately. During the early 2010s Guinness might decide to reposition itself as a 50-year-olds' drink. The beer market will shrink, since

volume customers are the younger session-drinkers who seem intent on pouring a lot of alcohol down their necks on Friday and Saturday nights. In-home drinking of wine and beer is another social trend, which marketers reflect in their special offers for cases of beers. Perhaps the ozone layer will completely crumble and the weather will warm up, followed by increased liquid consumption, including beers. Or will there be another baby boom (as fewer women use the pill because of cancer scares), creating a vast 18- to 25-year-old market by the early 2030s? Or then again perhaps an even bigger health trend will curtail all regular drinking behaviour. Or will the EU ban all alcohol advertising and 'promotion'? Maybe real estate companies will force pubs to increase their prices and thereby push drinkers back into their homes to consume canned draught beers. Or perhaps the decline of Western civilization will follow the decline of the Roman and Greek empires with over-indulgence and decadent lifestyles, including heavy drinking, and thereby create a short- or medium-term boost in the beer market before a major slump.

What are the implications of an ageing UK population? Bigger typefaces and print to help older eyes read commercial messages? Many products and services repositioned as the more mature person's choice? There will still be youth markets, but they may not be as attractive, since they will shrink in size and competition may become quite ferocious. Then again, AIDS may yet wipe out a whole middle generation, leaving behind a polarized society of very old and very young.

The falling marriage rate, the increasing divorce rate and the increasing number of births outside marriage contribute towards the sad term 'disintegrating family'. In addition, the number of single-person households is expected to increase. The traditional happy-family advertising formula is becoming obsolete, and marketing campaigns have been reflecting this for years. Oxo ads have shown the husband cooking the family lunch while the wife is out at play. Persil ads also reflect the changing demographics and roles, eg one ad shows a friendly grandchild who helps his grandmother to wash up with a top brand of washing-up liquid. The traditional 'housewife' (woman) shopper is no longer the sole key decision maker. Just take a look around a local supermarket on a Saturday morning, where you will see male shoppers buying Fairy Liquid, Ariel and Palmolive soap.

Decision-making units (DMUs) are changing (see Chapter 10, 'Segmentation and target marketing'). Over 60 per cent of mothers in the UK work either part time or full time, compared with 10 per cent in the 1930s and 20 per cent in the 1950s. Incidentally, it has been suggested that guilt-ridden working mothers may ease their discomfort by buying the 'best' brands for their families instead of buying the store's less expensive own brand. A Gallup poll suggested that 90 per cent of working mothers suffer some psychological discomfort in combining the roles of mother and worker.

The effects of the changing structure of DMUs apply to a broad sweep of products and services and not just FMCGs. Insurance, health care and double glazing target both partners instead of the head of the household or the main income earner. Many telesales phone calls fix an appointment to visit only when *both* partners or spouses are available for a sales presentation.

In 1990 futurologist Alvin Toffler forecasted that technology could facilitate vast demographic shifts as populations migrate from the cities to work in their own electronic cottages (complete with phone, fax and computer). Although there has been some movement, the vast demographic shift has not yet occurred. Technology, meanwhile, has relentlessly marched on into new realms of marketing.

Hanging out at the oxygen bar

Here is an IBM future vision from many years ago: oxygen bars offering 'nutraceuticals' (staple foods packed with vitamins and minerals) and gas for the jet-set hyperactive executives and fun lovers. Memory drugs, male birth control pills and remote-control surgery might all affect markets, their structure, the communications channels and communications tools.

Technology

Technology keeps changing the face of marketing communications. Web 2.0 (social media) has had a huge impact on marketing (see Chapter 1), and Web 3.0 (the semantic web) is emerging. Social change and technology change are driving new business models and new marketing models. It is a wonderful time for marketing, as these new opportunities allow marketing-driven business models to satisfy customers in new ways, deepen brand loyalty, spread messages and improve overall business operations. This takes marketers into new territories and into the boardroom.

Think of customer care announcements, automatic bank dispensing tills, robot-operated compact disc stores, and outbound and inbound telesales voice machines. Home computer shopping in the United States allows customers to move their home computer's mouse to scan aisles, pick up products, examine them in three dimensions and put them into an electronic basket. Payment is by credit card, and delivery comes the next day.

Point-of-sale technology, ranging from robots to light-sensitive supermarket displays, reacts when triggered by a passing customer. Shopping cart video screens promote 'today's special offer' as the customer passes various sensors, which trigger new relevant ads.

Pepsi can page groups of its customers with brand bleepers already supplied. In fact, bleepers and other items with computer chips can be triggered by simply moving within a certain range of a pack or product. Today, location-based marketing means that mobile phones can alert customers to special offers as they enter the vicinity of the retail outlet. **The Massachusetts Institute of Technology (MIT) has used 'hot badges' that flash when two like-minded people come within range of each other at a party.**

Packaging technology has, for many years now, provided self-heating tins and special Coca-Cola cans for use in US spaceships. And spaceships themselves are available for advertising purposes. Technology permeates every aspect of marketing and marketing communications.

Print technology allows magazines to run liquid-filled ads, heat-sensitive ads, double-image ads (which create the effect of movement), 3D ads, scratch-and-sniff ads, perfumed ads and, of course, singing and speaking press ads and mailshots.

There is also projection technology – perhaps we will soon see brand logos projected on to the moon.

Push technology means that specific relevant messages can be pushed out and delivered on a one-to-one basis through the internet.

The internet also provides virtual meeting places, virtual discussion groups, virtual greetings cards,

Moore's law

Every 18 months, processing power doubles, while costs hold constant.

'Gordon Moore, founder of Intel, observed that each new generation of computer chips (semiconductors) doubled in power every 18 months. This has been valid for 30 years and is predicted to continue for the next 30 years... has held since the 1960s, and recent developments in so called "molecular electronics" – arranging molecules in electronic circuits – suggest improvements are likely to continue for another 30 years.'

Krugman (2000)

This means that in just over 30 years computer chips will be 1 million times more powerful than today. *Note:* Today's modern luxury car has more computer power than the first human spaceflight craft that landed on the moon.

Digital body language

'Marketers who continue to pursue their mission with a disconnected set of communication tools and non integrated data set of communication tools and non integrated data sets cannot gain the multi-perspective visibility into their prospects that is required to understand and leverage their digital body language.'

Woods (2009)

virtual gifts and virtual exhibitions. Invisible computers will be in everything that uses electricity, and 3D environments and avatars will increase – both in virtual worlds (see Figure 11.2) and in traditional web environments. Virtual reality and augmented reality draw from a mash-up of data, allowing even richer and more relevant customer experiences.

Bar codes and information-collecting technology have increased in diversity and accuracy, so companies like Tesco can continually increase the relevancy of their tailored offers to customers.

Behind technology's physical manifestations, more subtle technology advances are occurring. Witness

Fast-forward to the semantic web

'Now, fast forward a few years. You're still happily employed as a software consultant, and today you're taking a working lunch with one of your biggest clients. Her company has an emergency project at its San Francisco branch for which they need you to consult for two weeks, and she asks you to get to San Francisco as soon as possible to begin work. You take out your hand held computer, activate its Semantic Web agent, and instruct it to book a non-stop flight to San Francisco that leaves before 10 AM the next day. You want an aisle seat if it's available. Once your agent finds an acceptable flight with an available aisle seat, it books it using your American Express card and assigns the charges to your client's account in your accounting application. It also warns you that you'll be missing a dentist appointment back home during your trip and adds a note to your calendar reminding you to reschedule. Next, you specify that you want a car service to the client's site, so your agent scans the availability of limos with "very good" or higher service ratings and books an appointment to have you picked up 30 minutes after your flight lands. Your agent also books you at your favourite hotel in San Francisco, automatically securing the lowest rate using your rewards card number. Finally, the agent updates your calendar and your manager's calendar with your trip information and prints out your confirmation documents back at your office.

'With just a few clicks your Semantic Web agent found and booked your flight, hotel, and car service, then updated your accounting system and calendars automatically. It even compared your itinerary to your calendar and detected the scheduling conflict with your dentist appointment. To do all this, the agent had to find, interpret, combine, and act on information from multiple sources. This example, of course, is a long-term vision for applying the Semantic Web. It's one that may or may not come to fruition, and only the future will tell. However, the vision itself is important for understanding the potential of Semantic Web technologies.'

Altova (2010)

FIGURE 11.1   Years taken to achieve 25 per cent market penetration, showing the ever-accelerating speed with which new ideas are adopted

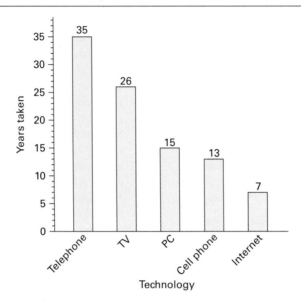

marriages between technologies such as geographic information systems, analytical modelling market analysis and data mining. (See the box below, and Chapter 12, 'Digital body language reports' and 'Digital body language and joined-up marketing'.)

Google Alert and Google News can even do a lot of a manager's reading by scanning journals, newspapers and trade magazines for relevant material and printing out headlines, summary abstracts or complete articles. Robots make our lives easier.

The semantic web will make life even easier. Software will talk to software, documents and a lot more. Tim Berners-Lee, the British inventor of the World Wide Web, defines the semantic web as 'a web of data that can be processed directly and indirectly by machines'. Data can be processed independently of application, platform or domain; in fact, data become part of the web.

The increasing pace of change

There is no doubt that change will continue to affect organizations. Those who ignore significant trends do so at their peril. However, marketers must develop their ability to recognize and separate significant trends from insignificant fads.

Today's must-have may be forgotten tomorrow

'I can confidently predict that every month for the next 100 years there will be a new "Must Have" application, portal or community that one of your employees will discover, and then try to convince you that your company will implode if you don't immediately join, link, or retweet. In five years, all but three of these ideas will probably be forgotten.'

Byron, Kievman and Schrum (2010)

Summary

An open mind helps in exploiting trends and emerging opportunities more quickly than a closed mind. Change is constant. It churns up new opportunities and threats in all markets. The only certainty is that all markets constantly pull away from the status quo, fuelled by an ever-increasing array of variables easily categorized under the PEST factors. It is every marketer's responsibility to observe, analyse and anticipate future developments in the marketplace and, in particular, in the changing communications environment.

Key points from Chapter 11

- The constant nature of change in markets presents a constant flow of opportunities and threats.
- The laws and regulations change also. Ignoring them can be a costly affair.
- Building risk assessment into marketing plans (particularly including economic risks) makes sense.
- Mapping social change is critical as marketers aim to reflect customers' social feelings, values, roles and norms.

FIGURE 11.2   Virtual worlds can, and do, co-exist alongside the real world

References and further reading

Adams, R, Carruthers, J and Hamil, S (1992) *Shopping for a Better World*, Kogan Page, London

Altova (2010) What is the Semantic Web?, Altova Library, **www.altova.com**

Anning, P (2007) FSA helps ICO with £980K data fine as Halifax could be next, Osborne Clarke

BBC News Online (2008a) Company loses data on criminals, 21 August

BBC News Online (2008b) Previous cases of missing data, 25 May

Brinker, S (2008) Marketing in the Semantic Web, *Chief Marketing Technologist*, 2 March

Brøndmo, H (2003) Save the customer attention ecosystem, *ClickZ*, 14 July

Byron, D, Kievman, N and Schrum, R (2010) Why executives hate social media: An executive's guide to social media, *Deming Hill*

Central Statistical Office, *Social Trends* (annual) (gives demographic breakdowns and forecasts)

Cetron, M and Davies, O (1992) The Futurist (World Future Society), summarized in *Crystal Globe: The haves and the have-nots of the new world order*, St Martin's Press, New York

Chartered Institute of Management (CIM) (2010) *Fact File: Marketing and the law*, CIM, Maidenhead

Doyle, P (1992) What are excellent companies? *Journal of Marketing Management*, 8, pp 101–16

Dwight, M (2007) Lifestyle stories, *Services, PE.com*, March

Economist (2003) Real men get waxed, 3 July

Enterprise Risk Management Integrated Framework (2004) COSO (Committee Of Sponsoring Organisations of the Treadway Commission)

Farrell, D, Ghai, S and Shavers, T (2005) The demographic deficit – how aging will reduce global wealth, *McKinsey Quarterly*, web exclusive, March

Grey International Advertising (1992) *The Post-Recession Marketplace: Life in the slow lane*, Grey International Advertising, New York

Gwyer, M (1992) Britain bracing for the age bomb, *Independent on Sunday*, 29 March

Keegan, V (2002) The web needs its own police, *Guardian*, 19 December

Knowlton, C (1991) Shell gets rich by beating risk, *Fortune*, 26 August, pp 51–53

Krugman, P (2000) Unleash after 100 years of trial and error, *Fortune*, 6 March

Levy, A (2003) Unlock the equity in your brand, *Marketing*, 24 April

Lindstrom, M (2003) *Brandchild*, Kogan Page, London

MacNamara, W (1991) A new discipline, *Marketing Week*, 6 December, pp 34–37

Murphy, D (2003) Stopping careless texting to children, *Marketing*, 3 April

Ohmae, K (1983) *The Mind of the Strategist*, PenguinBusiness Library, London

Ohmae, K (1999) *The Borderless World*, rev edn, Collins, London

Ohmae, K (2002) *Triad Power: The coming shape of global competition*, 2nd edn, Free Press, New York

Pohl, M (1991) UK unaware of legal pitfalls in US, *Marketing Week*, 13 September

Precision Marketing (2006) Privacy: Do Not Call means business, 6 January

Rijkens, R (1992) *European Advertising Strategies*, Cassell, London

Smith, D (2008) Google, 10 years in: Big, friendly giant or a greedy Goliath?, *Observer*, 17 August

Taleb, N, Goldstein, D and Spitznagel, M (2009) The six mistakes executives make in risk management, *Harvard Business Review*, guest edn, *The Magazine*, October

Toffler, A (1990) *The Third Wave*, Bantam edn, Bantum Books

Woods, S (2009) *Digital Body Language*, New Year Publishing, Danville, CA

Further information

Advertising Standards Authority
Mid City Place
71 High Holborn
London WC1V 6QT
Tel: +44 (0)20 7492 2222
www.asa.org.uk

CIPR
Public Relations Centre
52–53 Russell Square
London WC1B 4HP
Tel: +44 (0)20 7631 6900
www.cipr.co.uk

Department for Business, Innovation
and Skills (BIS)
Victoria Street
London SW1H 0ET
Tel: +44 (0)20 7215 5000
www.bis.gov.uk

European Association of
Communication Agencies (EACA)
EACA Secretariat
152 Boulevard Brand Whitlock
B-1200 Brussels
Belgium
Tel: 00 32 2 740 07 10
Fax: 00 32 2 740 07 17
www.eaca.be

European Marketing Confederation (EMC)
Pl Chasseurs Ardennais 20
1030 Brussels
Belgium
Tel. +32 2 742 17 80
Fax +32 2 742 17 85
www.emc.be

Fax Preference Service (FPS)
DMA House
70 Margaret Street
London W1W 8SS
Tel: +44 (0)20 7291 3300
Fax: +44 (0)20 7323 4426
www.dma.org.uk

Institute of Practitioners in Advertising (IPA)
44 Belgrave Square
London SW1X 8QS
Tel: +44 (0)20 7235 7020
Fax: +44 (0)20 7245 9904
www.ipa.co.uk

Institute of Promotional Marketing
Arena House
66–68 Pentonville Road
London N1 9HS
Tel: +44 (0)20 7837 5340
www.theipm.org.uk

Institute of Public Relations
The Old Trading House
15 Northburgh Street
London EC1V 0PR
Tel: +44 (0)20 7253 5151
www.ipr.org.uk

ITV Consumer Limited (ITV plc)
ITV Network Centre
200 Gray's Inn Road
London WC1X 8HF
Tel: +44 (0)20 7156 6000
www.itv.com

Ofcom
Riverside House
2a Southwark Bridge Road
London SE1 9HA
Tel: +44 (0)300 123 3000
Fax: +44 (0)20 7981 3333
www.ofcom.org.uk

Public Relations Consultants Association (PRCA)
Willow House
Willow Place
London SW1P 1JH
Tel: +44 (0)20 7233 6026
Fax: +44 (0)20 7828 4797
www.prca.org.uk

PART TWO
Communications Tools

12
Selling, sales management and key account management

LEARNING OBJECTIVES

By the end of this chapter you will be able to:

- Understand the purposes of different types of sales teams
- Map out the key stages and skills required of key account management
- Begin to manage the sales force
- Identify different ways of extending your sales force

Introduction

The word 'sales' is conspicuous by its absence in job titles on business cards. 'New business development', 'Account manager', 'Key account manager', 'Relationship manager' and 'Marketing executive' are often preferred, yet selling's impact on most markets at some stage is vital. The 'selling' stigma is surprising, given the size and importance of selling. A study called *Balancing the Selling Equation* (Abberton Associates, 1997) indicates that there are approximately 470,000 professional salespeople in the UK alone. The London Business School's Associate Professor of Marketing, P J S Law, cites selling as a vital ingredient: 'I cannot think of a product or service which has not, at some stage on its journey from producer to customer, been the subject of face-to-face negotiations between buyer and seller.' The sales force budget allocation varies according to industry type, but generally, in B2B markets, more budget is spent on selling than on advertising or PR.

B2B markets depend on personal selling more than others. Winning an order for, say, a heavy industrial machine cannot be done by advertising, direct mail or telesales (telephone selling). This kind of selling requires a top-level sales professional. Consumer goods, on the other hand, rarely use personal selling to the end user or consumer because of the high cost per visit (ranging from £27 to £500, depending on the seniority of the salesperson, the frequency and length of the visit, etc). Nevertheless, consumer products need salespeople to sell or 'push' the product in the retail chains (and wholesalers).

There was an era when selling was all about short-term tactics, quick sales, in–out and on to the next unsuspecting prospect. This is short-term transactional marketing, which in the long run reduces sales and profits. It is probably best summarized by the well-known Heaven and Hell story.

Today, selling has moved away from the short-term, quick-sale scenario. Combative salespeople are being transformed into 'customer servants'. Selling today is more about 'partnering' and relationship building: 'You don't sell to people; you partner with them.' This is particularly true with key account management (KAM), which requires a more strategic approach to selling. Today selling is about building durable relationships that are dependent on satisfying the customer constantly.

A dead prospect

A man dies and arrives at the Pearly Gates, where St Peter tells him he cannot enter until Hell has been given an equal opportunity. Although the man knows he wants to go to Heaven, St Peter insists that he checks out Hell first. To his amazement, the man discovers that Hell is a party town, with free-flowing drink, good music, lots of friendly supermodel lookalikes everywhere, perfect weather, immaculate golf courses, football pitches, internet connections and white sandy beaches. Best of all, everyone is friendly and concerned that the man feels comfortable in his new surroundings. St Peter appears and asks the man for a decision, upon which the man says, 'Hell's for me!' When he returns the next day, all he sees is bodies, scorched, burning and screaming. 'But this isn't the same place', he shouts at St Peter in the distance. 'Oh, yes, it is', St Peter replies. 'Yesterday you were a prospect. Today you are a customer.'

IBM today is following a growing trend towards paying the sales force salaries partly on customer satisfaction. Many companies are now measuring success not just by units sold but also by the far more rigorous yardstick of customer satisfaction. Selling has moved beyond the marketing and sales departments as companies realize that in today's heated competitive markets the whole company must sell.

The changing salesperson

'I sold systems that people didn't want, didn't need and couldn't afford.'

Bill Gardner, IBM veteran with 23 years' service, now retired

'Forty-five per cent of the variable component of my pay cheque depends on how Jon Gorney at National City Corporation rates me.'

Don Parker, IBM salesperson

Functions of selling

The purpose of selling is not just to sell. Master salespeople gather intelligence and build relationships (which can, in turn, create competitive advantage). Research suggests that as little as 10 per cent of a salesperson's time is in fact spent actually 'selling'. In addition to prospecting, appointment setting, letter writing, travelling, training and administration, many salespeople are also responsible for some customer care, post-sales service, entertaining, intelligence gathering, forecasting, understanding customers, developing customized solutions, team selling, etc. Some managers say that 'Customers seek longer-term relationships with fewer suppliers than formerly, and in return for security of business ask their suppliers to do more for them.' Forecasts suggest that there will be a concentration of key accounts (large customers) and they will need suppliers who work with them as strategic partners instead of adversaries (see 'Consultative selling' and 'Key account management (KAM)' below). Team selling may become more popular as research and development, production, distribution, sales, marketing and even legal and financial people work with the customer.

The best salespeople are expert listeners. They ask intelligent questions and listen carefully. The best salespeople are masters at capturing data. Since the sales force is in the front line of the market, it provides a fast and accurate feedback mechanism. Competitor activity, customer needs, and new opportunities and threats can and should be picked up by the sales force and fed back, without delay, to the sales manager or marketing manager. Reasons why an old customer is lost or a new customer is won should also be fed back immediately.

Consultative selling

Looking at customers as partners with whom a company wishes to develop a long-term, repeat-business relationship requires a shift in the business paradigm from 'selling *to* them' to 'working *with* them'.

B2B selling is no longer just converting features into benefits. Selling is more to do with problem solving and strategy fulfilment (for the customer). 'What is your requirement and how can we fulfil it?' is not enough. Salespeople have to understand customers' business strategies and then see how

they can help. GE asked its largest customers what they expected from the GE sales team. Customers revealed: 'The number one thing we expect is excellent knowledge of our company, our industry and the environment in which we do business.'

Offering expert advice and consultancy demands an attitude shift where the customer is seen as a partner rather than just a sales target. The short-term 'win–lose' scenario (the seller gains at the customer's expense) is replaced by the longer-term strategic partnership 'win–win' scenario. This builds customer retention through enhanced customer satisfaction, which in turn creates a sustainable marketing advantage. These new partnerships may involve joint development programmes that might not bear fruit for five or more years. This may seem inefficient in the short term but highly effective in the medium to long term. This is a strategic shift towards KAM.

> ### 25 per cent lose money and 50 per cent only break even
>
> Half of all collaborative sellers enjoy only modest benefits from their efforts, and a quarter actually lose money in those relationships, according to a recent McKinsey survey of more than 200 sales executives at Fortune 1000 companies.
>
> Hancock, John and Wojcik (2005)

Key account management (KAM)

Key account management means managing the most important customer relationships. It is strategically important and requires highly skilled senior salespeople or senior management. In addition to salespeople being able to sell on a personal level, KAM requires many other time-consuming skills, including:

- Solutions selling and collaborative selling, which generate tailored products or services, including ensuring customer retention, growing lifetime value and share of wallet. It is all about value creation for the client or partner. The initial sale (demonstration, pitch, handling objections, building trust,

> ### Master salespeople
>
> Master salespeople are masters at gathering information. They are equipped with 'must know', 'useful to know' and 'nice to know' questions before every meeting.

presenting proposals, closing the sale and after-sales service) is just the beginning. Intense collaboration is a complex, time-consuming joint effort. KAM must help the client to identify unique sources of value. Collaborative selling is a high level of customer engagement and generates collaborative co-creation offline (see Chapter 1 for the online version).

- Project management skills (to ensure tailored products and services are delivered on time and within budget).
- Relationship building at many complex levels right across the decision-making unit (this requires the ability to analyse clients' internal structures, systems and overall organization and continually widen relevant contacts).
- Research and intelligence gathering (and sharing information).

- Negotiating skills (to nurture the long-term relationship and deal with a large decision-making unit).
- Legal skills (an understanding of legal issues and contracts).

10 Steps to KAM

McDonald and Woodburn (2007) identified 10 steps towards developing KAM within an organization:

1 Select the right accounts.
2 Categorize them for their sales and profit potential.
3 Analyse their needs.
4 Develop strategic plans for (and with) each of them.
5 Get buy-in from all functions about their role in delivering the agreed value proposition (to the key account).
6 Get the right organization to serve the selected key accounts' needs.
7 Get the right people and skill sets in the key account team.
8 Implement the plans on an annual basis.
9 Measure success, particularly in respect of whether they create shareholder value added.
10 Reward individuals and teams for their success.

TABLE 12.1   Stages of KAM

Stage	Activity
Pre-KAM	Identify potential accounts (select the best clients – who's the perfect client?). Understand how they make decisions; key criteria; key players.
Early KAM	Tentative agreements and probing; identifying how the organization can help the client.
Mid-KAM	Account review and senior management involvement.
Partnership KAM	Joint problem solving and sharing sensitive information.
Synergistic KAM	Synergy of shared values and one-entity perspective.
Uncoupling KAM	A positive move recognizing that there is no further value in the relationship.

An alternative approach to seeing how KAM evolves through the following stages was developed by Millman and Wilson (1995). This overlaps with the above but also goes beyond it by including the 'uncoupling' stage when the partnership ends.

Digital body language reports

Digital body language analysis can deliver a weekly alert to each global account manager and summarize all visitors' activity from an existing key account (or a major new prospect), whether a brief visit or a deeper investigation of a particular new product. This helps salespeople gain deeper insights into, first, what is of interest to their prospects and, second, what buying stage they are moving towards. Alternatively, reports can analyse prospect interest levels by both region and product, allowing marketers to identify areas in need of additional focus and resources. These reports can save a lot of time and effort and build stronger rapport between the sales and marketing teams, as sales teams really appreciate these valuable insights. Marketers can also instantaneously see which campaigns are generating better visits and conversions. This helps to improve resource allocations to optimize ROI. See the next section for a brief perspective on digital body language, or Chapter 21 for more detail.

Integrating the sales force with the communications mix

An organization's own sales force, or a distributor's or agent's sales force, has to be kept abreast of any new advertising, sales promotions or social media campaigns. Its product knowledge has to be kept up to scratch. Some advertisements are wasted when they succeed in pulling customers into stores only for the customers to find out that the sales staff behind the counter are not familiar with either the advertisement or the particular offer being made. Equally, salespeople may spend considerable time ensuring that wholesaler and retailer point-of-sale materials are professionally coordinated with a national advertising campaign. The amount and type of personal selling required change as a product or service moves through its life cycle (see **'Types of salespeople'** below). Using a sales force to create awareness is expensive (and slow). The

salesperson has more impact in the final stages of attention, interest, desire and action (AIDA), eg a salesperson in a retail store. Equally, salespeople can ask buyers what phrases they use when searching for the salesperson's products or services. This key phrase inventory should be fed back regularly to the marketing team who are optimizing the websites and any social media. Another level of integration is between the web analytics and the sales team (see the next section).

Digital body language and joined-up marketing

Buyers increasingly source and purchase products and services online. The opportunities for a salesperson to get to meet the prospect are reducing. Once upon a time a salesperson could gauge prospects' reactions and, ultimately, their readiness to purchase by listening carefully to their questions and comments and watching their body language. Today, marketers can, instead, watch prospects', or website visitors', digital body language (Woods, 2009) to determine how close the prospects are to buying and how they can help the prospects to make a purchase. If, for example, a prospect has returned several times to the site and downloaded three white papers, and some colleagues from the same company have visited the site, this might indicate the visitor is at an **advanced 'information collection'** stage in the buying process. This could prompt an on-screen message, a virtual assistant, an e-mail or a phone call offering help. Chapter 21 looks at digital body language in more detail.

> ### Most prospects are ignored
>
> 'The tragedy is that most prospects fall through the cracks in the floor boards. 80% of B2B leads are not followed up. Of the 20% that do get followed up, sales reps reject 70% too quickly (even though the majority of these prospects eventually buy within 24 months and often from a competitor). Effectively, only 6% of a business's hard earned leads get followed up.'
>
> Woods (2009)

Managing the sales force

Types of salespeople

Some sales reps are excellent at winning new business ('order getters') and find the servicing of regular accounts to be dreadfully tedious compared to the exciting buzz of new business. Other reps are meticulous professionals who service an account ('order takers') with such professionalism, pride and affection that they create barriers for competition by building a **'wall of warmth'** around their customers. In reality, most reps have to do a bit of both jobs. Shiv Mathur (1981) wrote an intriguing paper about 'transaction shifts', which suggested that different types of marketing managers (and salespeople) were required as a product passes through its life cycle, since the product requires different levels of service support at various stages.

In an increasingly impersonal world of faceless faxes and voicemail, face-to-face communications or personal selling can provide a reassuring, personal touch. In addition, the salesperson can respond immediately to a buyer's changing needs and moods. The salesperson can also provide instant feedback from the customer or marketplace (see Chapter 6, 'The intelligent rep'). On the other hand, a sales force can be expensive in terms of cost per thousand contacts, and sometimes it can prove to be uneconomical on a cost-per-order basis. This largely depends on the size and profitability of the order, the distance travelled to get it, the number of meetings required, etc.

The primary responsibilities of the sales force manager include recruitment, training, motivating, controlling and collecting feedback.

I perform better as a salesperson now

'I used to have a territory where I was a free agent... today the computer recommends which calls I should make... my sales aids remind me what to ask and say... my manager knows where I am and I spend half my time on training courses... but I do sell 30 per cent more per annum.'

A domestic appliance executive

Recruiting

Determining the right size and structure of the sales force is vital. What is the optimum call frequency? Who should service the account? As an organization changes or grows, so too the sales force and its responsibilities must change. Sales force attrition is a fact of life. Some salespeople move to new companies; some are promoted; others retire or are fired. This means that recruitment is a continual process that demands skills, cash and time. Recruiting the right salesperson is a resources-consuming management activity. The New York Sales and Marketing Association (2002) revealed that 71 per cent of customers buy from a salesperson simply because they like and trust the salesperson. Two out of three customers change suppliers because of a salesperson's lack of interest, attention or communication. Recruit the wrong people and sales can actually be reduced instead of increased. Keeping the right sales team together is largely determined by levels of training, motivation, control and feedback.

Making noises like farm animals – sales training

Imagine a group of people walking around a room, making farm animal noises and trying to form a circle with their eyes closed. This is part of a rigorous selection process of a field marketing team whose job is to help major marketing player Unilever to launch new varieties of an established snack product. Top marketing companies recognize that the more time they invest in selection and training, the better the result. Preparation is rigorous, including dealing with hecklers. As mystery shoppers check on the team, nothing is left to chance.

Training

Training is an ongoing affair, not a one-off activity. It is a continuous process. Like thinking, it requires practice. Tony Buzan's classic books (1988, 1989, 2003) emphasize that thinking is a skill that needs development and exercise. Basically, the sales force has to acquire and maintain three pieces of know-ledge and one set of skills – selling skills. The three pieces of knowledge that the professional salesperson must have are:

1 product knowledge (marketing mix, features and benefits, and unique selling propositions – USPs);

2 market knowledge (customers and competitors);

3 company knowledge (history, structure, etc).

The 7P approach to selling skills

There are several different stages involved in selling. The 7P sequential approach identifies areas for skill improvement. The seven stages are:

1 prospecting (looking for potential customers);

2 preparation (objective setting, continual customer research, etc);

3 presentation (demonstration, discussion);

4 possible problems (handling objections);

5 'Please give me the order' (closing the sale or getting the order);

6 pen to paper (recording accurately all relevant details);

7 post-sales service (developing the relationship).

Increasingly today, more and more sales come from past customers and through growing the share of wallet of existing customers. Both employees and past employees can help to prospect for new business. For example, **McKinsey Consultants harnesses a network of its ex-employees – recognizing that the alumni can help to generate new business. Similarly, PwC discovered that 60 per cent of new business came from ex-employees or via ex-employee contacts.**

Each stage requires a certain amount of training and practice. Training should also include non-selling activities (information-gathering techniques, time-management skills, personal expense control, etc). Preparation is continual and includes an initial analysis of the customer's business, issues and objectives, clarifying exactly what the customer wants to achieve as well as identifying its compelling

reason to act. In fact, most major sales in large B2B situations involve a huge needs analysis. This involves analysing the customer's situation and includes needs, benefits, barriers and ways forward. The decision-making unit is analysed in great detail to ensure that all key decision influencers are addressed at the appropriate stage in the selling process. The customer's financial position, access to funds and decision-making units are also carefully studied. Eventually a risk analysis will be completed, identifying potential problems, their sources and their likely impacts.

Using problems (objections) to close that special sale

'Julie says: "I don't like the way you dress, I don't think you make enough money, and you drive like a maniac." '

'Frank hears: "I don't like the way you dress [*buying signal*], I don't think you make enough money [*buying signal*], and you drive like a maniac [*buying signal*]." '

'Frank's response: "If I let you pick my suits, if I double my income, and if I promise never to exceed the posted speed limits, will you marry me then?" '

Frank Pacetta, Xerox sales manager

Motivating

Maintaining the sales force's motivation is a vital part of sales management.

It can be as easy as publishing the monthly sales figures against targets for each sales rep and circulating the figures among the sales team. This can lead to competition among members, which may inhibit them from sharing ideas, contacts, leads and even closing techniques. On the other hand, it can keep everyone focused on targets, with peer pressure as a source of motivation. It is the sales manager's job to build a team feeling and get everyone working together, sharing ideas rather than hiding them from each other.

'Psychic income' is often a stronger motivator than financial income, yet it does not need to cost the company any more money than the traditional financial incentive. **Psychic income offers rewards aimed at the higher levels of need, such as being valued, recognized, rewarded and challenged** (see Chapter 4, 'Motivation', Maslow's hierarchy of needs).

This is how it works. A bonus cheque for £1,000 tends to get spent on dull and boring things like reducing the overdraft or paying the mortgage. On the other hand, the same £1,000 spent on a holiday for two or a spectacular piece of Waterford glass acts as a constant reminder of a job well done. Even a clap on the back, a thank-you note, a presentation ceremony or a photograph in the newsletter (or in the annual report) can arouse feelings that satisfy the higher levels of Maslow's hierarchy of needs. This contrasts with the £1,000 used to satisfy the dull, boring and soon forgotten lower levels of need. The reward itself is soon forgotten here, whereas the psychic income reward tends to linger longer and therefore offer better motivational potential.

Psychic income – two holes of golf with Jack Nicklaus

The Maritz Corporation specializes in psychic income packages. They even give out pyramid-shaped paperweights that list Maslow's needs. They tailor their awards so that individuals are offered an appropriate range of stimulating options. Some of their choices have offered trips to the moon, ballooning across the wine fields of Burgundy or two holes of golf with Jack Nicklaus. As you approach the 18th green there is an 80-piece orchestra perched on scaffolding, playing the tune of your choice.

The annual sales conference should be a motivator and act as a forum for sharing ideas ('how I made a sale' contest), identifying and solving problems, improving techniques, and recognizing and rewarding achievements. The conference should also provide a pleasant environment that reinforces feelings of being glad to work with the company.

Controlling

Controlling the sales force involves analysing sales:

- by product;
- by market or region;
- by salesperson.

Sales can also be analysed by profitability or the 'contribution' each order makes towards the overall profitability of the organization. This encourages the salesperson to sell higher-margin products or services rather than succumbing to the temptation of 1) giving discounts and 2) pushing easier, low-margin items.

The bottom line tends to be turnover or sales, number of new accounts (customers) won and old accounts lost, and the quality of those accounts (size and creditworthiness). Further analysis reveals number of orders (and average order size), calls-to-orders ratios, etc. Even miles driven give some indication as to whether reps are chasing their tails or leaving room for improvement. Good planning helps control.

Good sales forecasting provides targets and yardsticks for measurement. Sales forecasts can be drawn up by sales reps for each customer for each month and eventually put together to form an overall sales rep forecast. This can be modified to allow for low forecasts that reduce target sales figures, thereby reducing pressure on the reps and making it easier for them to attain their daily, weekly, monthly, quarterly and annual targets. There are also more sophisticated forecasting models that take into account a host of factors, including prices, competitors, state of the economy, etc.

Typical quantitative standards are as follows:

- sales volume as a percentage of sales potential;
- selling expense as a percentage of sales generated;
- number of customers as a percentage of the total number of potential customers in the territory;
- call frequency ratio, or total calls made divided by total number of customers and prospects who are called (or visited) by the salesperson.

The extinguisher

There is always room for creativity in marketing, and particularly in selling. Whether it is a new form of presentation, a new way of prospecting or a new way of showing determination to win the business, the list is endless. The extinguisher's creative approach below is not to be recommended. This story is recalled from a marketing magazine of many years ago.

Having recognized the weary tread of a door-to-door salesman coming up the stairs, the giggling office staff scrambled behind doors and under desks to avoid the approaching salesman's eye contact. I only realized that a salesman was looming when I noticed the sniggering bodies scattered behind the furniture. Too late. I turned around to see a shabby little man with a greasy raincoat and coffee-stained briefcase move towards me. Before I knew it he had opened his briefcase and poured a jar of petrol over himself. Out of his inside pocket he drew a lighter and set fire to himself. Then, while standing in the classic salesperson pose (right arm holding out a spray can and left arm pointing to the label), he said 'And this, ladies and gentlemen, is the FlameZapper miniature fire extinguisher.' As he proceeded to spray himself, he continued, 'You can carry it anywhere.' He left several cans lighter and several pounds heavier.

Time – the scarce resource

The average salesperson spends less than 10 per cent of his or her time actually engaged in face-to-face selling (Abberton Associates, 1997). The rest of the time is spent filling in report forms, travelling, setting up appointments, attending internal meetings, etc. Is this the optimum use of a key resource? Definitely not, so some companies use other communication tools (eg direct response advertisement or a mailshot) to generate enquiries and then categorize or qualify the quality of the enquiry or lead into 'hot, medium or cold' prospects. An online form or an offline telesales team can then further qualify the lead by determining how urgent, immediate or serious the enquiry is (see Chapter 17 for further examples). They can even set up appointments in a way that minimizes the travel between appointments. 'The extinguisher' (in the box above) is an extreme example, where the salesman seizes the relatively rare face-to-face opportunity and makes a sale every time (although he may also soon be locked up!).

Servicing existing customers with a mixture of telephone calls and personal visits, instead of visits only, allows sales reps to become more efficient by reducing the frequency of their visits but maintaining the frequency of contact or service by phone. There is obviously a fine line between the less personal telephone call and the more personal visit. Some buyers may prefer to avoid the interruption of a sales visit and appreciate a courtesy call ('just checking to see if everything is all right or if there is anything you need'). This minimizes time wastage (for both parties) while maintaining the customer service facility. Getting the balance between calls and visits is vital, since the competition is also out there, every day, knocking on the same doors. Optimum call frequencies need to be carefully planned.

Extending the sales force

Types of sales force

The three key resources, the 3Ms (men/women, money and minutes), are limited. Selling soaks up all three resources. There are various combinations of types of sales force. An organization's field sales force can be supported by an in-house telesales team who do the prospecting and appointment setting, thereby freeing the field salespeople to do what they are best at – selling. Resources can also be invested in agents, distributors, wholesalers, retailers and their reps so that they become an extension of the sales force. Alternatively, a temporary sales team can be contracted in to screen prospects and make appointments (telesales teams) or to go out and sell or give free samples away (see 'Field marketing' below). There is no single correct sales force mix, eg within the commercial tyre market one company achieves 200 calls per executive per annum, while its largest competitor achieves over 1,600. The former company has focused on large accounts and uses agents to service the independent trade. The latter sells direct to customers of all sizes. Both companies are highly profitable, and both have highly efficient sales organizations.

The correct approach is, of course, to monitor constantly the effectiveness of each sales force mix (customer satisfaction, sales, market share and profitability) and the efficiency (number of calls, cost per call, conversion rates of enquirers to customers, etc). There is always room for improvement.

Own sales force

Although a sales force creates a large overhead, it does allow direct control over recruiting, training and motivating. The section 'Managing the sales force' (page 270) explores the processes involved in getting the best out of this key resource. First consider alternative extensions of the sales force, both online and offline, including field marketing, multi-level marketing, affiliate marketing and distributors' sales assistants.

Field marketing

It is possible to hire flexible sales forces for ad hoc tactical activities or regular repeat activities. Reduced cost, flexibility and direct measurability make a contract sales force or field marketing team attractive compared to a full-time, in-house field sales team. Cost can be further reduced by using a syndicated or shared team as opposed to a dedicated team devoted to one particular product only. There are, of course, risks, particularly if the salespeople have a tendency for hard selling, misrepresentation or even rudeness. Careful scrutiny and supervision can usually identify these potential problems before they develop into a full-blown crisis. Field marketing tends to be used by FMCG or impulse goods manufacturers, but can be used by a wider range of organizations.

Typical field marketing activities include:

1 selling into independent retail outlets, eg field sales teams sold Christmas charity cards to almost 18,000 outlets during January, February and March;

2 merchandising and display – arranging stocks and literature in retail stores and other outlets, eg 25,000 newsagents and doctors' surgeries had the Department of Social Security's Family Credit information point-of-sale material placed in them within 14 days;

3 sampling and promotions – providing teams (eg the Pepsi Challenge) in shopping precincts and superstores and at national events and exhibitions;

4 market research into shelf facings, stocking levels and positions in store (including number of shelf facings or number of units that can be seen);

5 monitoring customer care and service – with mystery shoppers who are employed to observe service and report back details of the specific levels of in-store service and customer care.

Field marketing's main advantages are widening the reach without acquiring the overhead of a full-time sales team. The disadvantages, in addition to the fees, are that training, motivation and constant monitoring and feedback are required to get the best out of the field sales team.

Telemarketing

In addition to direct selling, telemarketing (telephone marketing) is used for appointment setting, lead generation, list building or cleaning, market research, customer care and even shareholder communications. An outbound campaign requires telemarketing professionals to make the calls, as opposed to an inbound campaign, which receives calls generated from 0800, freephone, local phone, standard phone or premium-rate phone (which act as 'self-liquidating', ie generating revenues that pay for other costs) numbers listed in direct response advertisements, mailshots or websites. Telemarketing is a flexible tool. Depending on the previous day's results, a telesales campaign can change on a daily basis, with the telesales script being rewritten overnight and tested the following day.

Telemarketing can be part of a contact strategy that includes mailshots (letters, brochures and vouchers), **e-mails, visits and calls**. Equally, telemarketing can qualify prospects to determine which particular contact strategy is best, eg prospects with less immediate needs might be mailed a brochure, while telemarketing contacts the more immediate buyers with a view to setting up an appointment. Another stage will emerge when the not-so-urgent prospects who received the brochure start to mature into the buying mode. The database can prompt some telesales action, and so on. Detailed objectives for the campaign, such as total number of calls, number of calls per person per hour, conversion rates, minimum amount of information to be collected, etc, must be agreed.

Once again, sales and marketing need to work closely together, eg the telemarketing manager needs to know when the mailings go out or when the sales team are available for appointments. Script development draws on the features, benefits and USPs. It will also include open-question, presentation, objection-handling and closing techniques. The telemarketing team can then be briefed and trained. Lists, scripts, incentives, prices and timing can all be tested. The results will be carefully monitored and used to develop the optimum combination for the full roll-out of the telemarketing campaign. These results should be analysed to continually build on previous success.

Telemarketing is an expensive way to boost awareness on a cost-per-thousand (CPT) basis, but it is flexible and quick and can be cost-effective if targeting the right customer profile. It can also save costs by maintaining customer relationships with telecalls bolstered by fewer actual visits from a sales rep.

Multi-level marketing

Multi-level marketing is a system of selling goods directly to customers through a network of self-employed salespeople. The manufacturer recruits distributors, who in turn recruit (or sponsor) more distributors, who in turn recruit more distributors, and so on. Each distributor is on a particular level of discounts (depending on the size of stock purchased). Distributors effectively earn income on their own direct sales to the distributors they have recruited. Distributors also earn a percentage of the earnings of all of the other distributors connected through their chain or line of distributors.

Multi-level marketing is sometimes called network selling, retail networking or pyramid selling.

Several companies have proved that network selling can be a legal and successful method of marketing. Pyramid selling has a bad image because it was exploited unscrupulously, with new distributors being promised fortunes in return for large investments in stock that never sold. In addition, these selling systems tend to exploit personal contacts and networks, which can cause individuals to view all their friends and family (or anyone with whom they come into contact) as sales prospects. This mercenary perspective is sometimes enveloped in a kind of corporate evangelism, which gives this sales and distribution method a poor image, despite the several legitimate and successful systems that thrive in the United States.

The Trading Schemes Regulations 1997 allow a maximum initial fee of £200 (within the first seven days) to be charged for enrolment as a distributor. Goods are then purchased at a discounted wholesale price, which allows newly enrolled distributors to add their own margin of profit when selling the goods to an end user. Goods are returnable (and 90 per cent of the cost recoupable). Any training fees must be clearly stated in the written contract, and training must not be compulsory.

The advantage of multi-level marketing is acquiring a vast distribution network with no direct overhead, although margins are reduced as commissions are paid. Disadvantages include that some countries do not accept multi-level marketing and ban any form of 'pyramid selling'.

Affiliate marketing

Although it does not employ salespeople per se, affiliate marketing extends the reach of a brand's sales potential through a form of multi-level marketing online. **Affiliates generate sales on a commission-only basis.** Affiliate partners usually have access to specific communities or target markets. The affiliates basically refer visitors to the brand's website, and every time the referred visitors buy the brand the affiliate gets paid a commission. The affiliates use banner ads (usually supplied by the brand), e-mail and PPC ad campaigns.

The relatively risk-free concept is straightforward:

- Affiliate networks generate traffic to the client's website via banner ads, PPC and e-mail.

- Affiliate networks track this traffic closely (via tracking codes) and supply reports.
- Commission is paid against whatever the agreed goals are: traffic, leads or enquiries, or actual sales, eg if sales conversions are the goal and no sales are generated then no commission is paid.
- The only investment a marketer needs is 1) the copy about the company or product to attract affiliates and 2) the banner adverts for affiliates to use on their sites.

The original form of affiliate marketing was selling through clubs, associations and networks, whether online or offline. Members within networks, clubs or associations tend to trust relevant offers from within the group. For example, an insurance company might ask a football club to encourage its members to buy its credit card. Each time a football fan buys a card, the club gets a commission and the member gets a discount or a gift instead (eg a club baseball cap that costs £2 could have much greater value, as a club baseball cap is so relevant). The insurance company can do the same online, except on a potentially much bigger scale and with multiple clubs, associations and communities online. As well as boosting sales, this also increases brand awareness. In fact, affiliate marketing can get a brand's ad carried by hundreds if not thousands of websites, eg Marriott Hotels use **Commission Junction** to reach into over 700 highly relevant websites with a range of banner ads and special offers.

Amazon has an estimated 400,000 affiliates or 'associates' who offer Amazon books to their networks, eg a horse-riding website can have a book about horse riding promoted on the website in an Amazon banner that takes the buyer directly to Amazon. Everyone wins. The customer is offered very relevant books only. The website owner adds value to its website by adding highly relevant books and subsequently earning a revenue or commission on each book sold. There is no risk to the website owner, as no stockholding investment is required, and no resources are required for logistical operations (dispatch, post and packaging, and invoicing), as this is all handled by Amazon.

Advantages and disadvantages

Essentially affiliate marketing extends a brand's reach across hundreds and sometimes thousands of websites (and search engines), generating extra sales on a commission basis (30 per cent approximately). However, the affiliate may be competing for the same traffic that the brand's own website wants (or it may reach way beyond the brand's own reach). Heavy use of PPC ad words (including the brand name) by affiliates can push up bid prices for the brand itself. Some brands have strict guidelines about the use (even restrict the use) of their brand name by affiliate PPC campaigns. Brands need to check out the quality of the affiliate's website and how it portrays the brand to ensure no damage to the brand. There are two types of affiliate programmes: in-house affiliate programmes and affiliate network programmes. Ask how the brand is being portrayed and whether the brand is effectively competing with affiliates to attract the same visitor.

In-house affiliate programmes

Some brands like to have their own affiliate networks. Amazon has over 400,000 partners who place highly relevant Amazon banner ads on their own sites, delivering visitors who buy and simultaneously earning a steady stream of revenue for themselves. Many major brands list their affiliate programmes on their websites under 'Affiliate programme', 'Associate programme', 'Referral programme' or 'Partner programme', which gives a full explanation of how it works, including log-in, tracking, banners available and frequency of commission payments. **Commissions range from 5 per cent to 30 per cent.**

Affiliate network programme

A network is a collection of companies that have affiliate programmes but are managed by one company, eg Commission Junction, Affiliate Future, Trade Doubler or UK Affiliates. A lot of companies want affiliate programmes but they don't want to manage them (commissions, payments and queries), which can be costly in terms of time, money and systems. An affiliate network company like Commission Junction recruits relevant new publishers (websites), checks the quality of each new affiliate, activates existing publishers, and motivates them to boost performance and ultimately grow sales. Some affiliate networks have a set-up fee (up to £2,000) and a monthly management fee, and all have a commission override,

FIGURE 12.1   In-house affiliate programme

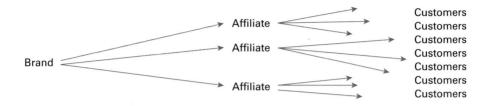

FIGURE 12.2   Affiliate network programme

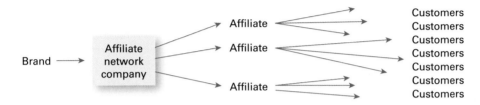

on top of the commission paid to the affiliate (say 20 per cent of the affiliate commission). For example, if an item sells for £100 with an affiliate commission of 30 per cent, £30 goes to the affiliate and £6 goes to the network (20 per cent of the £30 commission), so the brand pays a total of £36 from the £100 sale.

There are three parties involved: the merchant (eg a brand owner), a publisher (affiliate, eg a website owner) and the affiliate network (eg Commission Junction). Consider the retailer Argos ('the merchant') using Commission Junction ('the affiliate network') to reach different target markets via different publishers, eg it could target cheap furniture into its network of student sites (publishers) and camping equipment into its network of festival sites (publishers) from Commission Junction's 16,000 affiliate publishers that are in Commission Junction's network.

Distributors' sales assistants

In both B2B and B2C markets, most brands sell to distributors, who in turn sell to wholesalers and/or end users (ultimate customers). Winning the battle for the distributor's 'mindshare' (or share of mind) can be an important part of sales force management. **Mindshare means the amount of attention and effort that a distributor's sales force gives to a particular manufacturer's product.** A distributor often carries many different product lines supplied by several competing suppliers. The mindshare concept aims to develop the distributor's sales force into an extension of the supplier's sales force.

All suppliers would obviously like to have the distributor's sales force recommend, select or push their particular brand to the end user. Mindshare can be won by creating and maintaining a partnership approach that develops a mutually beneficial business relationship. This means the manufacturer must supply:

- a reasonable quality of product (and price and delivery);
- creative and frequent sales promotions (eg a distributor sales rep club where the top distributor's reps are presented with awards, in front of the distributor's own management, once they attain a certain level of sales; there might be a silver, gold and platinum club for 50-, 100- and 200-unit salespeople, respectively);
- product training;
- joint visits (the manufacturer and distributor visit the end user together);
- cooperative advertising (where the manufacturer shares the cost of the distributor's advertising when it promotes both the parties);
- merchandising and display services.

Mindshare requires a longer-term approach to selling, since the sales reps' efforts do not necessarily result in an immediate order. But mindshare will contribute to longer-term sales. It is therefore management's responsibility to develop a suitable time horizon and a mindshare strategy that works.

A US marketing consultancy, the Richmark Group, claims that a mindshare strategy has been found to be more powerful than strategies based on product differentiation and other more traditional market strategies. Manufacturers who successfully implement this strategy can build a market position that it is almost impossible for competitors to duplicate. Mindshare can make a competitor's marketing communications totally ineffective. Imagine the manufacturer makes electrical cable Z100, the distributor is an electrical wholesaler and the end user is the electrical contractor who will buy and install the cable under the floorboards of a new house. An end user (electrical contractor) customer asks a distributor's sales rep (electrical wholesaler's rep) for a competing brand, say brand A1000. The distributor's rep recommends and offers the Z100 cable instead. The end user seeks advice in selecting a specific brand. The distributor's rep recommends the manufacturer's brand Z100. The distributor's rep effectively becomes part of the Z100 brand 'unofficial' sales force.

The advantage of mindshare is spreading the sales force wider without acquiring the fixed overhead of the additional resource. The disadvantages are, once again, that training, motivation and constant monitoring are required. Note that organizations must pay heed to the new Bribery Act 2011.

Advantages and disadvantages

Here are some of the advantages and disadvantages to consider when deciding whether to increase or reduce the communications tool.

Advantages

Salespeople are great (when trained and motivated) at getting key messages across to buyers. Messages can also be changed (though it requires some training) in a relatively short lead time. If the product or service requires a personalized presentation then investing in salespeople rather than just advertising makes sense. B2B markets invest more in sales teams than advertising. Sales people are also great at collecting intelligence and market research, as well as building relationships and, of course, getting sales.

Disadvantages

A sales force cannot spread a message as quickly and as widely as advertising, sponsorship, PR or perhaps a piece of viral marketing. Sales teams require investment in training, motivation and monitoring. It is important to spend time carefully recruiting salespeople, as they are the organization's brand ambassadors. On a CPT basis, sales teams do not compete with advertising, sponsorship or PR, but on a cost-per-order basis they may very well do better than other promotional tools.

Summary

The sales force is a key marketing resource that can determine the success or otherwise of any organization. Sales teams and marketing people need to work together more closely to share intelligence and leads in a systematic process. Managing the sales resource requires clear management skills. There are many different options to extend the sales force: through its own sales team or using field marketing, multi-level marketing, affiliate marketing or mindshare through distributors' sales teams.

Key points from Chapter 12

- There are different types of sales teams, including in-house, telemarketing, multi-level marketing, affiliate marketing and distributors' sales assistants.

- KAM requires a variety of management skills, including consultative selling.

- Managing a sales forces requires recruitment, training, motivation and monitoring.

References and further reading

Abberton Associates (1997) *Balancing the Selling Equation*, CPM Field Marketing, Thame

Buzan, T (1988) *Make the Most of Your Mind*, Pan Books, London

Buzan, T (1989) *Use Your Head*, rev edn, Pan Books, London

Buzan, T (2003) *How to Mindmap*, Thorson Publications, London

Constable, J and McCormack, R (1987) *The Making of British Managers*, CBI/BIM, London

Denny, R (2000) *Selling to Win*, Kogan Page, London

Francis, K (1998) What is KAM?, *Winning Business*, January–March

Hancock, M, John, R and Wojcik, P (2005) Better B2B selling, *McKinsey Quarterly*, 16 June

Jobber, D and Lancaster, G (2000) *Selling and Sales Management*, Financial Times/Prentice Hall, Harlow

Mathur, S (1981) Strategic industrial marketing: Transaction shifts and competitive response, City University Working Paper 33, City University, London

McDonald, M and Woodburn, D (2007) *Key Account Management, the Definitive Guide*, 2nd edn, Butterworth Heinemann, Oxford

Millman, T and Wilson, K (1995) From key account selling to key account management, *Journal of Marketing Practice: Applied marketing science*, 1 (1), pp 9–21

New York Sales and Marketing Association (2002) Tips and advice in selling, *Sense and Sensibility*, 22 April

Woods, S (2009) *Digital Body Language*, New Year Publishing, Danville, CA

Further information

Institute of Sales and Marketing Management
Harrier Court
Lower Woodside
Bedfordshire LU1 4DQ
Tel: +44 (0)1582 840001
Fax: +44 (0)1582 849142
www.ismm.co.uk

13
Advertising online and offline

LEARNING OBJECTIVES

By the end of this chapter you will be able to:

- Understand the evolutionary nature of advertising
- Explore cutting-edge new advertising tools
- Appreciate the potential for integrations with social media and other marketing communications tools
- Know how to plan the stages of an ad campaign

Introduction

Advertising is changing all the time, and in the last five years it has seen some massive changes that challenge the nature of advertising itself. It is morphing into dialogues, social media, user-generated content and a myriad of wonderful new ways of communicating with customers. These include contextual advertising, behavioural advertising, location-based advertising, user-generated ads, long-form and short-form ads, apps, social TV, postmodern ads and of course good old contentious ads. This chapter explores these and uses two cases to demonstrate how a basic TV ad campaign and a social-media-driven TV ad campaign are developed.

The end of advertising?

Many current critics believe advertising is on its way out, eg Regis McKenna (1991) announced that we are 'witnessing the oblivion of advertising'. More recently, some other marketers have said that location-based services remove the need for advertising. **The fortunes of advertising have grown alongside the growth of the mass media.** Now that this growth has stopped, questions are being asked. The mass media have fragmented (200 TV stations, millions of websites and an explosion of new magazines and radio stations). Martin Sorrell (1996) of WPP said: 'Massive audiences become more and more difficult to buy.' It is therefore suggested that the current lavish advertising productions, which depend on mass audiences to make them cost-effective, will decline as well.

Eric Schmidt (2009), CEO of Google, said the former and Johnson the latter (in the *Idler*, 1759). So some feel advertising is a maturing industry. Although advertising does have a unique ability to simplify and condense a complicated selling message into an emotionally charged 30-second piece of film, media proliferation has meant that the traditional 30-second TV advertisement is no longer the answer to everything. But brilliant advertising, particularly if it integrates with social media, still has a role to play. Customers will consume them if they cut through the clutter and are relevant.

More TV and radio stations, newspapers and cinemas still need advertisements to fill them. But the days of media owners just selling ad space are over. 'Marketers need media owners to think creatively about using the media for reaching out and also building stronger relations, as well as selling more product X.' Learmonth (2010) refers to this in more detail (see Chapter 7). There is a shift in vision and philosophy amongst 'advertisers'. Interruption marketing (ads shouting at customers) has less of a role today. Marketing campaigns are no longer just about cost per thousand (CPT) and page views and more about learning how to interact with customers and participate in their activities as they spend more time online. Customers want to be engaged with relevant added-value content. They want to find relevant information only when they want it and share it with whomever they desire. Despite the hype, advertising is not going away. It's just reinventing itself to meet the needs of social media demands. Contextual advertising, behavioural targeting and location-based advertising are clear examples of advertising reinventing itself.

Media owners and advertisers are thinking more creatively and, in some cases, thinking way 'outside

'Advertising [is] one of the most fundamental ways to sort out information. And that's the gift of advertising: to connect with people in a human way, to make the kind of emotional connections that are at the core of storytelling.'

'Advertisements are now so numerous that they are very negligently perused.'

Which of these statements is the more recent? One is by Google's CEO, and the other by Samuel Johnson 250 years earlier.

Half of my advertising is wasted

The days are over when clients politely smiled as Lord Leverhulme's legacy echoed: 'I know half my advertising is wasted. I just don't know which half.' Today, better-disciplined clients demand more measurement, more integration and more dialogue from all of their communications.

the box'. They understand customers' needs for interaction and involvement and are developing strategies to maximize them. This is demonstrated in the integrating social media, new variants of advertising (see below) and radical rethinking by companies like Coca-Cola, which is shaking up its view of marketing by not relying on traditional advertising and, instead, investing serious money into ideas that bring entertainment value to brands. It is developing content and partnerships with media companies, as it sees its brands such as Coca-Cola as 'portals' offering a 'network' or means of distribution in their own right. This concept has been dubbed **'brand entertainment'**, and companies such as Coca-Cola, Nike, Orange and Mercedes-Benz are busy integrating brands into such varied areas as sport, entertainment, music, travel and gaming.

New advertising

Customers still want relevant advertising to inform them, entertain them and challenge them just as it always has. After all, advertising does inform, persuade and remind. It can still, very quickly, help to build brands, raise awareness and nurture brand relationships, and all in a relatively controlled environment (compared to the vagaries and uncontrollable nature of editorial exposure generated by PR, sponsorship and social media campaigns – see Chapter 14, 'Lack of control'). So, although it will not be the same as before, there is a future for integrated advertising. This means that managers will still have to be able to manage the development of an advertising campaign, which will be explored after considering the new forms of advertising:

- contextual advertising and behavioural advertising;
- location-based advertising;
- user-generated ads;
- long-form ads;
- short-form ads;
- sponsored TV;
- apps – the new ads;
- integrated mobile, apps, TV and social TV;
- postmodern ads;
- creative ads.

Contextual advertising and behavioural advertising

Marketers are now free from the limitation of segmenting and targeting customers with 'monochrome' classifications such as 18- to 25-year-old ABC1s. In addition to age and sex, location, workplace and college, today marketers can target customers according to their actual behaviour, interests and passions (by keywords used). As each targeting criterion is selected, Facebook displays the approximate number of users that fit the profile.

Other online organizations, such as newspapers, can now serve very specific ads to readers online determined by the words on the pages they read, the number of pages they read and how often they read these pages. Ads can be selected according to a customer's changing status or status updates on Facebook. For example, a man who announces to his network of friends that he is getting married or updates his status with 'I'm getting married' or 'I've just got engaged' will find that he is subsequently served ads about wedding photographers, suit hire, limousines, romantic honeymoon holidays and maybe even wild stag venues. This is contextual advertising.

It is also called **behavioural targeting**. For example, if a 23-year-old male living in a major city is online comparing car prices, Microsoft can serve (or target) him with an ad for a Mini Cooper, while a 40-year-old suburban businessman with children might be served an ad for a people carrier.

It gets more interesting. Ads can be made even more relevant according to the geographic location of the customer. This is location-based advertising (LBA).

Location-based advertising

For some time now, it has been possible for ads tailored to geographic areas to be served online by Google, Facebook and other platforms. This is called **geo-targeting**, which basically serves ads tailored to where website users are geographically located (recognized by either the locations of their internet service providers or the registration details, which include their home or office address). **Location-based advertising**, on the other hand, uses location tracking technology in mobiles to target customers with specific ads relevant to their actual location as they travel around. There are many types of LBA ads, such as a text message display ad. Push-based ads are sent by a media company once the customer 1) has opted in to receive relevant ads (often opting in while signing up for a mobile phone service) and 2) is in a particular location. Cinema goers may be offered free soft drinks, trailers to download or two for the price of one as they walk past a cinema. The LBA push approach serves ads to a customer when the customer is in a specific location. An 18- to 25-year-old male who likes Guinness may be offered a free pint in specific pubs within a certain area.

Seth Goldstein, co-founder of SocialMedia.com, in an interview with Kohler (2007), said: 'People talk about location-based advertising, but location removes the need for advertising. If you know where the consumer is, and that she is physically touching your brand, then you do not need to rely upon traditional mass-media channels to reach her.' A restaurant, pub or night club may incentivize customers to share a special offer whilst sharing their location with friends to attract their friends into the venue. Other customers might value knowing that a friend is having a coffee around the corner – as long as they are happy for all their network to see what they are doing and with whom.

Sharing of location information with your network may become as common as sharing your status update with your network.

A simplified variation of LBA can also be released with other vehicles. For example, if a local newspaper collects postcodes as part of its registration process and has, say, 10,000 readers in a certain postcode area, it could serve local restaurant ads and special offers to just those 10,000 customers who live near those particular restaurants. The paper can still cover national and international and local news whilst delivering very relevant local ads. As Kohler (2007) says, 'It's not about hyper local news, it's about hyper local ads.'

Interestingly, many banner ads are now '**transactional** banners' or, alternatively, branded applications (apps), which means customers can buy directly from the banner without being taken away from their preferred platform to a website. Customers on Facebook can order a pizza delivery while on Facebook.

Targeting specific customer types can be much tighter. It can also be more flexible, as it can be on **cost per click** (CPC) or impressions or cost per thousand (that can see the ad).

Coca-Cola's Twitter ad campaign

Coca-Cola had 86 million 'impressions' or views of the ads in 24 hours, and an engagement rate of 6 per cent, compared with the approximately 0.02 per cent of people who click on a regular online advertisement.

Bradshaw (2010)

McDonald's location-based functionality

'McDonald's is building a location-based functionality with Facebook that will allow users to 'check in' at restaurants and share menu items with friends. That campaign is expected to be rolled out sometime after the consumer launch, when Facebook integrates brands into the system.

'The social impact of including a physical location in a virtual sharing app is immense; so is the marketing application as brands are then able to turn their physical locations into media channels connected to real people across Facebook's social graph.'

Kohler (2007)

The creative age is here

There is no doubt that more creative thinking is required to cut through the clutter, engage customers and nurture communities. Chapter 1 discusses the need for creativity. More user-generated ads will emerge (as mentioned in Chapter 1), and more apps, games, virtual worlds, massively multiplayer online role-playing games (MMORPG), intelligent media units, long-form ads and short-form (one-second) ads, as well as postmodern ads and plain old contentious advertising. Let's explore these.

User-generated ads

The ladder of engagement in Chapter 1 explained how UGC added a dimension to customer engagement. Chevrolet's Tahoe opened up the concept by

> ## Google's perfect ad
>
> 'I've always argued that the correct ad in YouTube is itself a YouTube story. Once you start watching, it's so good you can't stop – don't have a 30 second limit in principle – and the best ads may be an ad about a refrigerator that is so compelling you will drop everything in your life and drive at full speed to get to the refrigerator store. That's the job of advertising companies: to come up with that narrative that will get you to really want that refrigerator.
>
> That's what they compete over; our job is to host them.'
>
> Eric Schmidt, in Kennedy (2009b)

placing the winning user-generated TV ad during the Superbowl. It is increasingly popular, arguably because it employs the magic formula (identify needs, reflect them and deliver them). Users (customers, prospects and sometimes even non-prospects) are invited to create an ad, whether TV or press. The PR machine works hard behind the scenes helping to spread the word of mouth as the final selections are narrowed down to a winner. Social media communities ideally buy into it and spread the word even further. Naturally, there are some disadvantages, as negative ads can be created and posted for public viewing. It can be moderated, but as with most aspects of social media it is best to be transparent. Another interesting development of UGC ads is UGC films or UGC long-form ads.

Long-form ads

Long form ads can help a brand stand out from the clutter and do not necessarily cost more than a traditional 30-second or 60-second ad, as, firstly, they can be repurposed and, secondly, there is less need to buy media space. Nike created a three-minute ad about the art of dropping beats using sneakers. Waitrose's mini-cooking show with celebrity chefs giving cooking tips used the whole three-and-a-half-minute ad break. Absolut Vodka created a 15-minute documentary commercial featuring Jay-Z called NY-Z; Kraft Foods Greek chocolate brand Lacta created a 27-minute user-generated branded

movie initially for online consumption but eventually seen on local TV (free), as it generated so much buzz. An extension of long-form ads is sponsored TV programmes (when major soap powder brands sponsored TV dramas, the 'soap opera' was born).

> ## Lady Gaga's nine-minute ad and product placement
>
> Lady Gaga's nine-minute video included product placement for Virgin Mobiles, Wonder Bread (unpaid) and Miracle Whip (paid). It has had '28 million views on YouTube, been watched on MTV.com nearly 500,000 times and shared on Facebook and tweeted directly from the pop star's site some 150,000 times'.
>
> 'Featured throughout "Telephone" are shots of a Virgin Mobile cellphone, a nod given to the mobile sponsor of Gaga's Monster Ball tour, as well as a Polaroid camera and photo booth as part of Gaga's new role as the camera company's creative director. Several characters are also seen listening to music on Heartbeats by Gaga headphones from Interscope Music and surfing the internet on the "Beats" laptop from Hewlett Packard, all of which were unpaid extensions of Gaga's marketing partnerships.
>
> 'Online, music-video site Vevo bought a slot on the YouTube home page that referred users to the "Telephone" page on Vevo.com, which crashed the morning of the clip's premiere. The video broke all Vevo single-day traffic records and had already generated close to 4 million views on YouTube in less than 24 hours.'
>
> Hampp and Bryson York (2010)

Short-form ads

Somebody had to do it sooner or later, and Miller beer did it – a one-second TV spot during the Superbowl 2009 (the American football final). The ad cost a fraction of the $3 million normally charged for 30-second spots during the Superbowl. The ad, played by actor Windell Middlebrooks, gave one second of inspiration and reminded viewers that 'High Life is common sense in a bottle'.

Sponsored TV

As already mentioned, a natural extension of long-form TV ads is sponsored TV programmes, including soap operas, sport and entertainment. Interestingly, BBC (a non-commercial broadcaster) now only considers commissioning new TV programmes that satisfy their 'Find, Play, Search' criteria. This includes finding the programmes or user-generated content related to it across several social media platforms, sharing them with friends, drilling down to new depths of knowledge, and encouraging user-generated creativity in everything from apps and widgets to more traditional user-generated content. New-styled sponsored TV programmes, like 'Bud House' (see the box below), draw on social media and UGC.

Budweiser experiment with World Cup sponsored reality TV and social media

Budweiser created a World Cup online reality TV show and social media integrated web series with 32 fans from 32 countries living, eating, breathing and watching World Cup matches together. Fans were grouped together in rooms based on the actual World Cup groups of countries. Fans were sent home as their teams were eliminated. The last-standing fan presented the Man of the Match trophy to the final team's most valuable player after the last game of the World Cup. New episodes were uploaded to the Bud United channel on YouTube several times a day. Viewers kept in touch and shared content with their favourite 'Bud House' fans via Facebook and Twitter. Viewers also influenced events in the house via the 'You Decide' polling tube on Bud United's YouTube channel.

Apps – the new ads

'Apps' are useful software applications that provide, or allow users to do, just about anything from a mobile phone, eg calculator, petrol prices locator, music identifier (point the phone at a radio and it lists the name of the track, the album and the band), sports news, weather forecasts, golf swing analysis, stock market feeds, managing bills, learning

a language, and 'On this day' (famous people's birthdays). Kraft Foods iFood app offers help and reinforces the brand value. One of the most popular is Zippo's app, which displays a flickering flame (popular at concerts). Skype, Twitter and Facebook all have apps that allow customers to use their services even more frequently. Some brands commission their own relevant apps; other apps are created by developers and sold to organizations that find them useful for their customers and, ideally, relevant to their brands. Few brands are actually using their apps as revenue generators (see the *Glee* exception below). Apps or widgets (used on websites), by extending brand usage, add value to customer experiences, brand awareness and brand affinity.

Apps or widgets can effectively put a brand name on to millions of devices worldwide. Each time they are used they boost awareness, eg 50 per cent of those who downloaded the Kraft Foods app continue to engage with it three months after first downloading it (Kennedy, 2009a). Apps are putting brands back on screens (mobile phones) that were previously stealing attention from TV viewership.

Screen wars hyper-competition

As mobiles steal audiences from TV, Apple TV also challenges cable TV (Chapter 1), and now the United States' CNN TV sees Facebook as its major threat, as its US president, Jonathan Klein, suggests: 'although rival Fox is currently winning the ratings war in the US, their real threat comes from Facebook'.

Whatmough (2010)

Integrating mobile, apps, TV and social TV

Apps extend the user experience beyond the TV with a much wider array of engagement activities and, although the TV programme may be over, prolong the sense of being in an audience or group, thereby adding value, extending the customer experience, deepening engagement and boosting satisfaction levels, awareness levels and, ideally, recommendation levels (see Chapter 10, 'Net promoter score, satisfaction score and recommendation score').

Fox TV network's app for *Glee* (the musical comedy series) is a good example. It costs £0.59 to download and within a few weeks it had several hundred thousand users. Customers use the app once or twice per week for 8- to 10-minute sessions, usually when the show is off-air. The app combines karaoke and social singing. Sing to the app, and the pitch indicator tells customers if they are on the note or if they're sharp or flat. The app corrects the pitch and optionally adds harmony. Saved recordings can be uploaded and used to create a band of like-minded 'gleeks' who follow customers' tracks and share them via Facebook, Twitter or Myspace feeds. The 'Broadcast' button allows users to add their performance to *Glee*'s global sing-along, which also allows other users to add their own voices on to another user's – effectively extending the virtual glee club. *Glee* has several other apps such as 'Unofficial Glee Trivia' and 'Unofficial Glee Facts', both selling on iTunes for £0.59.

Postmodern ads

A new style of advertising, postmodern advertising, may at first seem a little abstract, and certainly

> ### Social singing: singers wanted – no talent required
>
> ' "The thrill begins once you start singing into this app. You cannot sound bad. Period." – David Pogue, *NY Times*. Sing your favourite songs with friends, strangers or the cast. *Glee* will enhance your pitch and harmonize your voice while you sing. Share your top songs with friends to get Gleeks and earn more free songs, like just added "Bohemian Rhapsody"!'
> The official App Store

unconventional, as neither the user nor the product is the hero. Old-fashioned ad people find it difficult to understand how an ad that doesn't appear to address a brand's values or have any apparent link to the brand can work. Perhaps this is best explained by Cadbury's drum-playing gorilla ad. This postmodern ad has no apparent link to the brand, as drums, music, gorillas and animals are not part of the brand equity. However, there is a link between

FIGURE 13.1   Cadbury's drum-playing gorilla

the brand and the ad – it is fun and enjoyment. It is 'feeling good', which is how people feel when they eat chocolate. What engages people better than a gorilla sitting behind a set of drums waiting as a really well-known piece of rock music builds up to the climax, where the drums come blasting in and the gorilla thumps perfect drums? The ad didn't tell people to feel good; it simply made them feel good. Results: 2 million hits on YouTube; 100 Facebook groups; bloggers who tried to identify why they liked the ad so much and whether the gorilla was Phil Collins (the singer) in a gorilla suit; and a 9 per cent sales increase year on year. In addition, all five variants were back in growth for the first time since the beginning of 2005.

Creative ads

Marketers need even more creativity. Some websites can be information heavy, and therefore a quick creative ad can be a quick pleasurable experience. As Saatchi CEO Kevin Roberts's (2010) blog says, 'Marketers bring optimism and joy amidst doom and gloom. Marketers need to bring optimism

> ### Postmodern ad brief
>
> 'People feel uplifted when they eat it [Cadbury's chocolate]. One of the things I believe passionately is that the advertising should be as enjoyable as the product. The brief was not to tell people to feel good, it was to make them feel good and the "gorilla execution" is an expression of that.'
>
> Phil Rumbol, former Marketing Director, Cadbury, in Jones (2008)

and joy to people. We've 60m unemployed in the world. This is the Age Of The Idea... Invest in unreasonable power of creativity. If we've got a great idea, people will tell it. Humour, love, emotion and music.' So marketers have to be relevant and increasingly creative, challenging and sometimes contentious to break through the clutter. The Paddy Power ad in Figure 13.2 certainly cuts through the clutter.

FIGURE 13.2   This six-week outdoor campaign broke through the clutter but received consumer complaints via the Advertising Standards Authority towards the end of the campaign; the ads were subsequently withdrawn slightly earlier than expected

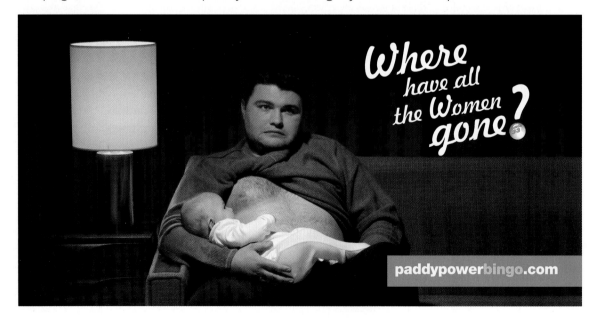

Managing an advertising campaign

This chapter focuses on how an advertising campaign is planned and managed. SOSTAC® + 3Ms (discussed in detail in Chapter 10) is a flexible system that can be adapted to any plan, whether a full marketing plan, an advertising plan or an integrated social media plan. A general approach to each stage will be considered, and then it will be applied to two case studies: 1) T-Mobile's integrated social media and TV ad campaign and 2) a drug education TV ad campaign. First, consider what each SOSTAC® stage contains:

- Where are you now? (Situation – S)
- Where do you want to go? (Objectives – O)
- How will you get there? (Strategy – S)

The advertising campaign planning process incorporates an analysis of the current situation (research) and a clear definition of the overall communications objectives, as well as the specific advertising objectives. Only then can the advertising strategy be devised. The strategy summarizes broadly what to say (message), how to say it (execution, tone or creative strategy), who to say it to (target audience), where to say it (media choice or media strategy), when to say it (timing) and, sometimes, how much it will cost (budget). Strategy can also guide the integration or links between advertising and all of the other communications tools.

The situation

There is a lot of research to be done before any exciting creative work can be started. What are the current sales trend, market share trend and overall market trend? Are there any regions or segments that buy more than others? How big are the competition's sales (per region and per distribution channel)? What is the profile of the customer and of the non-customers who might be converted? Who is the target market now and in the future? Who are the heavy users? When do they buy? Where do they buy?

How is the brand positioned in the minds of various target markets? Why do people use or not use the brand? This can be the most difficult question to answer, because real reasons are often deeply hidden beneath apparently rational buying behaviour. What are the current features and benefits of your product or service? A feature is translated into a benefit by using three words: 'which means that'. For example, 'This car has a crush loading of over 5 tons, which means that it can roll over without the roof caving in.' Many advertising campaigns can demonstrate benefits without having to use words (in fact, wordless advertisements like Levi's may become more popular as satellite television grows – see Chapter 9), but it is the application of this three-word formula that helps to identify real benefits that can then be demonstrated. Spending time 'interrogating the product' is a good investment.

Product interrogation

In addition to the previous question, further questions, or product interrogation, can sometimes reveal hidden benefits, which advertising can subsequently highlight. Is there anything unique about the product (a unique selling proposition – USP)? Product (or service) interrogation explores and examines every angle, including product characteristics, user characteristics, ways of using, benefits of using, disadvantages of non-usage, competitor comparisons, product heritage, customer cases, newsworthiness and more. How does it compare against the competition's features and benefits both in people's imaginations and in reality?

The cunning K Shoes lady

Some years ago shoe manufacturer K Shoes and its agency BBH discovered a hidden USP. This was that the quality of the leather in the shoes was such that the shoes did not creak or squeak. This subsequently opened up the opportunity of dramatizing the benefits of squeak-free shoes. One of the TV advertisements showed a lady wearing K Shoes quietly entering an apartment in which her lover was dining with another woman. The K Shoes lady proceeded to dump a bowlful of slimy noodles on the head of the two-timing man. The K Shoes lady turned silently and walked confidently out of the apartment.

BBH

How does the product or service compare with competitors' products or services in the minds of customers (how is it positioned)? Or have they even heard of it? (What percentage are spontaneously aware of your product or service? Is it top of the mind or front of mind, ie do customers include it in the first three brands they think of when considering your product type?) What is important to the target customers? Or perhaps there is a high level of awareness but a low level of preference, possibly because of a poor product or poor image. What do customers consider to be the most important factors (key buying criteria) when making a choice? What is their ideal product?

Social media potential

Most campaigns today will be mindful of what arouses discussions and chatter in social media when it comes to ad campaigns. Topicality and trends will be monitored from a discussions perspective to see what is hot and generating a lot of buzz. Are there aspects of certain types of campaigns that lend themselves more to social media and user-generated content? Some social media tools can be used to identify hot topics, phrases and even words (eg Google Zeitgeist and Google Trends).

Trend identification

What new values, trends, attitudes, lifestyles or business styles are emerging that may affect the organization's product or service? Individualism, self-exploration, materialism, environmentalism, ageism, sexism, interaction: once the advertisers identify a relevant trend, they can then reflect it through advertising imagery.

Review of past advertisements

An analysis of competitor advertising campaigns can trigger ideas and, more importantly, provide some insights into competitor strategies, thereby helping the strategic thoughts of the advertising for the brand in question. Even the brand's past campaigns can give some guidance as to how they reflect the state of the market, what the objectives are, and what works and what does not.

Answers to all of the questions raised in the situation analysis and review are required before setting advertising or communications objectives. In a sense, researching the current situation reveals the objectives

---

Consumer research and trend identification

Another major exercise was embarked upon to understand the consumer environment that the new advertising executions would have to operate in.

The central thesis was quite simply that in the early and mid-1980s consumers felt most comfortable following the crowd and feeling a collective sense of involvement. In this context advertising that showed session drinking in the pub (men making wisecracks) was quite appropriate. Brands in the main lager arena prospered. The role these brands occupied was to lubricate the session drinking of the male-dominated pub. In the late 1980s this climate changed, and the process of change continues. Now consumers wish to stand out from the crowd and express their individuality much more. They do this by demonstrating their discernment in the clothes they wear and the brands they choose.

The implications for the advertising were fundamental: a more sophisticated audience, a change in the pub environment, less session-drinking orientation and a different attitude to premium brands. Indeed, it presented a significant opportunity for draught Guinness, which was already moving in the more fashionable image arena, to catch the crest of this wave and exploit it fully. In order for it to do so, this social change needed to be confirmed and understood in some detail.

Ogilvy & Mather

---

for the campaign. Good research makes objective setting easier.

Research, however, costs time and money (and people), so it needs to be budgeted for or, ideally, built into a continual system of information gathering (see Chapter 6, 'Marketing intelligence and information system') to help both objective setting and subsequent measurement of the campaign's effectiveness.

Objectives

After you have analysed the situation through primary and secondary research sources (see Chapter 6), a clear picture of where you are emerges. The next step is to define exactly where you want to be. 'If you don't know where you're going, any road will take you there.' Ideally, objectives should be quantified in terms of success or failure and timescale. This makes control easier, since actual results can be measured against quantified objectives. The previous year's objectives, and corresponding results, help to make the planning job a little easier, as experience provides a better idea of what are realistic objectives for the future.

Objectives should be **SMART**:

Specific

Measurable

Actionable

Realistic

Time specific

A clear strategy (how to get there) is not possible without clearly defined objectives (where you want to go). Without a clear strategy, a loose set of tactics, lacking cohesion (and sometimes pulling in different directions), is likely to emerge.

Establishing clear objectives is necessary to give a focus to the organization. Clear objectives also give direction to the subsequent creative efforts. Some marketing managers and agencies break objectives into many different types. We focus on just two types here: 1) marketing objectives; and 2) communications objectives.

Marketing objectives

Typical marketing objectives refer to sales, market share, distribution penetration, launching a number of new products, and so on. See Chapter 10, 'Objectives'.

Communications objectives

You will find examples of these in Chapter 10, 'Communications objectives'. As mentioned in Chapter 10, communications objectives typically refer to how the communication should affect the mind of the target audience, eg generate awareness, attitudes, interest or trial. The defining advertising goals for measuring advertising results (DAGMAR) and awareness, interest, desire and action (AIDA) hierarchical models reveal some of the mental stages many buyers have to move through before buying. Again, these objectives (eg 'to increase awareness') are more useful when quantified ('to increase awareness from 35 per cent to 45 per cent within a six-week period').

Another way of looking at communications objectives in a competitive market for, say, the purchase of a car is that shown in Figure 13.3. A particular campaign's objective may be to move a significant number of prospects from one set to the next. Some advertisements go further by seeking to reinforce or reassure existing buyers.

FIGURE 13.3   A way of looking at communications objectives in a competitive market for the purchase of a car

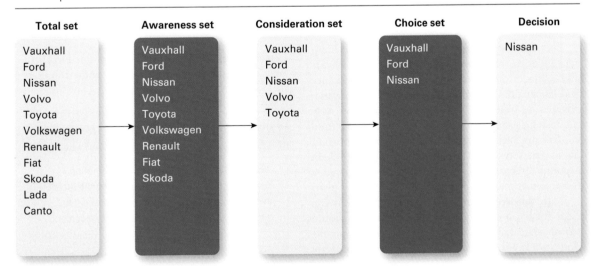

Strategy

Once the situation has been fully researched and clear objectives identified, the campaign or advertising strategy can be developed. It will include positioning, objectives, target audience, key benefits, secondary benefits and often a statement of what kind of media will be used. The strategy will not get bogged down in detailed tactics or any specific creative messages. It should offer strategic direction to the client and agency team. Some clients will work with the agencies to develop this key statement. Other agencies do all the work and present the campaign strategy to the client for approval.

The campaign strategy forms the foundation for the more detailed planning and development of the actual message (or the advertisement itself) and the selection of the media. Figure 13.4 illustrates how the initial situation, objectives and strategy (SOS) form the basis for the subsequent development of the message and media plan.

Message development (tactics)

Creative briefs

With the review complete, objectives set and strategy agreed, the creative team can finally be called in and briefed. The creative brief is a key document. Each agency has its own style (see top advertising agency BMP DDB's style in Figure 13.5). It is here where all the volumes of research findings and weeks of discussions have to be concentrated into a single-page creative brief that translates the details and research jargon into relatively simple lay terms that explain exactly what the advertisement should do.

This is the brief that the planner or account manager gives to the creative team. It succinctly covers all the key information, such as: the target audience and its perceptions, motivations and buying criteria; advertising objectives, proposition, tone and how the audience should feel after the advertisement; and constraints and choice of media. It is an important document and should be signed (or approved) by an account director before being passed to the creative team. Sometimes the client wants to approve it also.

Both the agency and the client need to have a clear focus on exactly what the advertising should say or what it should achieve. Many creative people don't want too much detail ('Just tell me exactly what you want!'). They will then set about delivering a creative idea or concept. Figure 13.5 shows the summary creative brief that BMP DDB used for the award-winning Hovis campaign.

Concepts

Ideas or concepts are roughly designed into 'roughs' or 'scamps', which can be developed into a storyboard (Figure 13.6). The idea can then be further developed into better-quality visuals known as key frames (see Figure 13.7). These, in turn, can be shot on video to create an animatic (moving cartoon of the advertisement complete with music, voice-over and sound effects). Any of these visual presentations of the advertising concept (concept board, storyboard, key frames and animatics) are discussed and/or researched before the idea is allowed to go on to the expensive production stages and eventually to the even more expensive media stage (buying space and actually advertising). If the concept 'researches well', ie gets good feedback from the focus groups, it can be taken forward for further refinement and eventual production. Even with poor research findings (ie the focus groups do not like the concept), some clients and agencies sometimes pursue an idea regardless. For example, Heineken's long-running 'refreshes the parts other beers cannot reach' campaign did not research well but was, nevertheless, produced. It eventually went on to become a successful campaign.

Advertising agency BMP DDB's rough concept idea for the Hovis campaign (Figure 13.6) was developed from the initial creative brief (shown in Figure 13.5).

Client approval

Concepts have to be justified or explained to clients. Agencies support their concepts with a message

---

Emotional decisions

'Let emotion rip. 80% decisions are emotional. Yet 80% marcomms are rational. Rational decision making equals a conclusion. Emotional pitch: back pain solution delivers the joy of movement.'

Roberts (2010)

FIGURE 13.4   The remaining stages of the campaign planning and execution

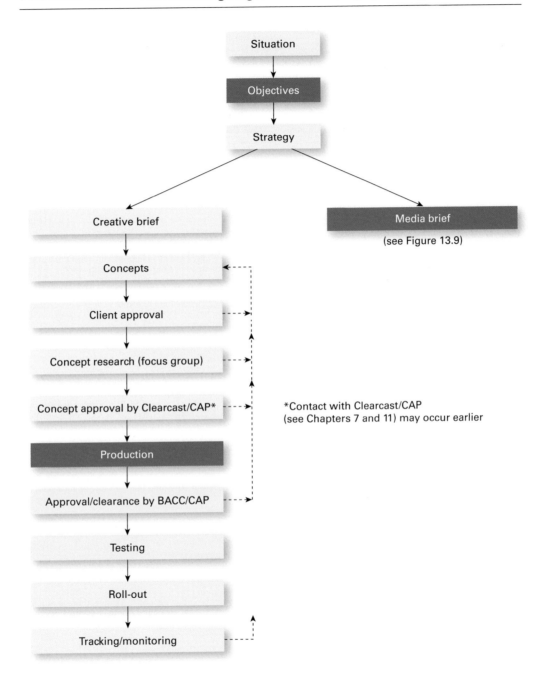

rationale, which basically explains why the concept is brilliant and guaranteed to achieve outstanding results!

The concept is developed into key frames, which are then presented along with the message rationale to the client. The key frames can also be shown during focus group research. Figure 13.7 shows a Hovis key frame.

FIGURE 13.5   BMP DDB Needham's creative brief for Hovis

F R I E F B R I E F   C R E A T I V E   B M P   D D B   P M B

CLIENT	British Bakeries	INTERIM REVIEW	
PRODUCT	Hovis	FINAL REVIEW	
JOB NO.		PRESENTATION	

What is the advertising required to do?

To convince Mums that their family will love Hovis

MEDIA BUDGET _____   PRODUCTION BUDGET _____

REQUIREMENTS (Please select by formatting requirements in bold)

One off ads	Ad in existing campaign	**New Campaign**		
TV	Cinema	Press	Radio	Poster
Size/Timelength:				

Any possible links between media channel and message?

What is the single most important thing we want to say?

Hovis is the one good thing you can do for your family everyday

Why should people believe this?

People believe that Hovis is full of goodness – more so than other brands of bread. Its name even means 'strength of man' and, even though we are talking white bread, its brown bread credentials help give it a healthy feel.
Hovis has always been associated, via its advertising, with things being done properly in an idealised world. Hovis today still does things properly (they still make their bread in essentially the same way) but the reality of the world in which it is operating has changed & these idyllic images are becoming increasingly irrelevant to today's bread buyers.

What tone of voice should we use?

Down to earth, honest, of the people.
Hovis might take bread seriously, but it shouldn't take itself too seriously

What are the mandatory requirements?

Campaign must be able to work across the Hovis product range.

Who are we talking to?

Almost everyone eats bread & Hovis is a mass market brand, so our idea must have broad appeal.

Primarily, however, our audience is Mums with kids (0–10). They get through a loaf a day on sandwiches for packed lunches, toast when the kids come home from school etc. Kids prefer white bread. Mums have all heard of Hovis & it is one of the first brands of bread that they think of. However, recently it has become more distant – a bread for other people. Kingsmill has taken over as the best bread for families.

As a group, Mums share a common trait, they all believe that looking after the family is roller coaster of positive and negatives and that looking after the family is harder today than ever before. Anything they can rely on for a spot of 'goodness' is appreciated.

Our secondary audience are the kids themselves – whatever our idea, it must have playground currency. If Mum can see that the kids like the ads it will go a long way in giving her the confidence to start buying Hovis

What do we want them to think or feel having seen the advertising?

If I buy Hovis for my family, then, whatever else might happen, at least I know I've given them a damn good start. And my kids will enjoy eating Hovis.

What is the cleverest bit of thinking on this brief?

This is really about owning a category generic. Despite not having any tangible reasons to believe, there is much in people's emotional associations & beliefs in the Hovis brand to allow Hovis to credibly own this territory.

Issued by
_____

Date
_____

Signatures:

Client	BAD	Olivia Johnson	DOC
_____	_____	_____	_____

FIGURE 13.6
Hovis 'roughs' of new characters

FIGURE 13.7
Hovis key frame

Action

Production

The production of an advertisement requires time and careful attention to detail. It may involve overseas locations, casting, contracts, rehearsals, special effects, weeks or months of sophisticated computer graphics, studio shoots, editing and more.

Control

Clearance

The finished advertisements should be checked before publication. **In the case of press advertising it is optional** (see full explanation of CAP in Chapter 11). For TV it is compulsory (see Clearcast in Chapter 7).

Testing

With the production stage completed, some clients or agencies test the finished advertisement in a hall test (see Chapter 6). Others will test the advertisements in a geographical region (eg the Anglia TV or Ulster TV region) before rolling them out nationally or internationally. Other clients put their advertisements out without testing because of time constraints. The 'first to market' with a new product or idea can

often steal the initiative. Although both strong and weak theories have some validity, some marketing professionals simply ask three questions about success criteria to determine if an advertising campaign will work or not:

1 Do I want to see it again?
2 Do I want to pass it on?
3 Do I want to add something to it?

Roll-out

After rigorous testing the finished ad (eg Figure 13.8) can be released, or rolled out, across its whole market.

Tracking

The advertising campaign can and should be monitored, or tracked, to see how it is working, eg what level of awareness it is generating or whether it is affecting attitudes or even sales. This allows any problems to be corrected sooner rather than later.

While the advertising messages are being developed, the media planners are busy devising media strategies and plans to ensure that the advertisements get the optimum exposure.

The stages of media planning

More money is spent on media than on the production of the advertisement itself. It is here that large savings can be made. Media planning is becoming increasingly scientific as press and TV proliferate. Although media buying, some argue, is an art in itself, some media planners understand the qualitative side of the media as well as the quantitative side and can therefore use media in a creative manner. The media awards in *Media Week* give an insight into the creative use of media.

Expert media planning and buying can also save vast sums of money, which can be either redeployed to buy more advertising space or saved and used elsewhere in the communications mix. There is, of course, the temptation to keep the saving and add it on to the bottom-line profits (by taking it away from the bottom-line expenses). Figure 13.9 shows the process of media planning.

FIGURE 13.8   Finished Hovis commercial

CONVERSATION

Harry: Pooh.
Alfie: Bra.

Harry: Bogies.
Alfie: Er ...

FVO: When the witty conversation
        starts to drag ...

FVO: give them a break with peanut butter
        and banana in fresh White Hovis.

Harry: Mmm.

Alfie: Mmm.
FVO: Things'll soon start to pick up again.

Alfie: Belly button.
Harry: Pants.

MVO: White Hovis.
        Get something good inside.

FIGURE 13.9   The media planning process

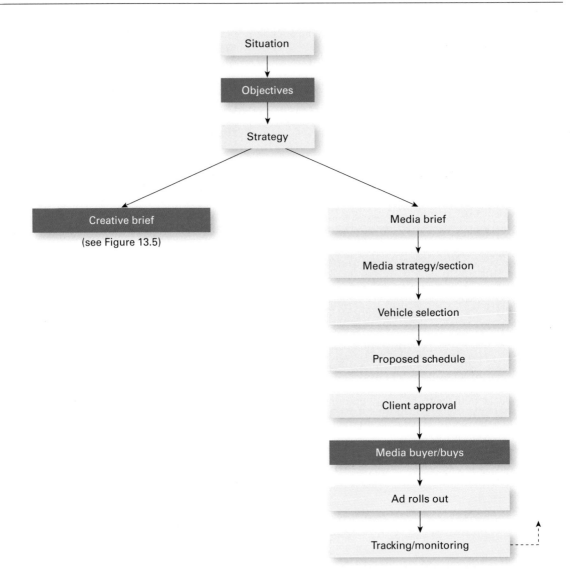

Media selection

Media people should not be briefed to book space after the advertisement has been created. They need to be involved early on, as their creative media input can influence the finished creative message. Carat Research shows that placing advertisements in unexpected positions can boost the likelihood of seeing them. From ads appearing upside down, to perfume ads in finance pages, to a McDonald's ad in *Vogue* magazine, to buying all the back pages of specific colour supplements for a year (Boddingtons), to buying an entire newspaper for one day (Microsoft and *The Times*), to an entire 3½-minute commercial break (Waitrose's mini-cooking show), the media planners have plenty of creative scope. And they have plenty of new media to play with, from video vans (with large computer screens and mobile billboards) to floor posters, to laser-beamed buildings (see Chapter 7, 'Are ambient media the new media?'), to long-form ads, to user-generated ads and right through to social media.

Message development is crucial. Eric Meyer some years ago reported that up to 30 per cent of US ads actually damage the brand. Today, perhaps some marketers get distracted by the exciting allure of highly ambient opportunities and technology interactivities rather than first checking the quality, relevance and context of the message. For example, is putting your logo on a rubbish bin appropriate for a brand like Rolex? Even if the message says something like 'Bin your old watch and buy a Rolex', it is simply not appropriate.

Here are some additional examples of how media selection can work creatively and effectively. Häagen-Dazs ice cream used the weekend press to allow the advertisements to be savoured and enjoyed at leisure, while 'the intimacy of the experience could be hinted at better through the personal communication of the press'. Part of Guinness's media strategy was to use black-and-white 'fractionals' (ads within a small space) in newspapers, which, as the *Media Week* awards explain, meant that they 'effectively dominated the mono newspaper world with fresh and extensive copy rotations, so that no reader would see any one execution more than once over a period of seven months'. Chapter 7 looks at media research, planning and scheduling.

Media schedules

In addition to the creative use of the media, careful analysis can identify the optimum media schedules. A media plan is then developed and presented to the client. This plan shows the types of places where the advertisement could be used. The space is then negotiated and bought. (See Chapter 7.)

Does advertising really work – the strong and weak theories of advertising

The strong theory of advertising suggests that basically advertising works. It suggests that advertising helps to move customers through a series of hierarchical stages towards purchase (see Chapter 4). The ultimate proof of strength is where advertising can persuade customers to buy something they have never bought before. This is challenged today, as it assumes that customers are passive and unable to process information properly. Andrew Ehrenberg (1974) challenged this and proposed the weak theory of advertising, which suggested that customers are driven by habit and that advertising reinforces rather than drives initial sales. Advertising could, he suggested, increase the frequency of purchases, as it could stimulate habitual buyers into more frequent choice of the advertised brands against a repertoire of considered brands. **He developed the awareness–trial–reinforcement (ATR) model** (see Chapter 4). He maintained that advertising could increase or maintain awareness and improve the customer's knowledge, but only for those brands that customers were already buying (or at least had some prior knowledge of). Some academics went further and suggested that advertising could not convert customers who had reasonably strong beliefs that contradicted the messages in the advertisements. The truth is that no one is 100 per cent sure of exactly how every aspect of advertising works. The same applies for every aspect of marketing. The winners will be those who have inquisitive minds and a willingness to continually learn how marketing communications work.

> ### Coca-Cola continually learning
>
> '"When it's something new, it's hard for publishers to know what the value is," she said. "We didn't know how it would work out but we wanted to learn in that space. It could have completely flopped. They [Twitter] also wanted to learn with us."
> Carol Kruse, Vice-President for Global Interactive Marketing at Coca-Cola, which is an official sponsor of the football tournament, in Bradshaw (2010)

Now consider two interesting ad campaigns, one for a mobile phone campaign and one for a drugs education campaign.

CASE STUDY 13.1   T-Mobile

T-Mobile: life's for sharing

This is an intriguing example of an organic and trusting relationship between client and agency. It demonstrates how integrated organic campaigns work well, reacting to, nurturing and developing each stage of a campaign according to consumer reactions. Each stage (or chapter) was a progression from the last, building on the excitement and interest in the brand, increasingly handing more control of the campaign to fans of the brand for them to contribute to and play with. So this case just uses SOS from SOSTAC for the initial phase and then explores SOSTAC fully with phase 3 of the campaign.

Situation analysis

The oversupplied UK telecoms market is one of the toughest in Europe. Over the last 10 years, the 'big four' (O2, Orange, Vodafone and T-Mobile) have been fighting a brutal price war, flooding the market with margin-eroding offers.

Against this backdrop, T-Mobile was lagging in fourth spot, with a decidedly static market share. Desperately, it chased customers with bold price promises and great value offers. But this only made matters worse: it attracted price-sensitive deal chasers who cared little for long-term relationships. By late 2008, T-Mobile had the lowest market share and the highest customer churn rate of the big four.

The agency, Saatchi & Saatchi, had to go back to basics and explore. It found that, while people might take mobile brands for granted, mobile phones were changing human behaviour, encouraging a new era of connection and openness. In countless ways, mobile phones enable people to share. The tapping of keypads has become an incessant cultural chatter: the silent language of people sharing their lives through calls, texts, photos, snippets of film and Facebook updates.

Mobile telephony was changing how people related to one another. Younger generations were collectively living their lives in the present tense, regardless of time or geography. Spontaneous gatherings and get-togethers were becoming the norm. Mobile telephony meant sharing was no longer closed (between friends and family) but increasingly open (between strangers and community). The boundary between the personal and collective was dissolving – we were moving from a 'me' to a 'we' society. Generosity was emerging as the new spirit of the age, a welcome reprieve from the previous 15 years of selfish capitalism.

This insight gave rise to a radical approach to brand communications. Rather than traditional advertising, the focus was real events dramatic enough to create a reaction from the general public, TV journalists, press journalists, bloggers, radio call-ins, copycats and online tributes. The events would get the nation sharing, becoming a physical manifestation of T-Mobile's beliefs and capabilities. The brand might create the events, but in the end the events would create the brand.

Objectives

The main objective was to establish an emotional brand promise for T-Mobile. T-Mobile needed to differentiate itself: give the brand new purpose and direction so it attracted higher-value customers who wanted to have a long-term relationship with the brand, guaranteeing sustainable future growth. This meant giving the brand a point of view that would reconnect it to popular culture.

Strategy

The stategy was to go beyond traditional telephony insights and acknowledge the role of T-Mobile in people's real lives. It was an active move away from talking about deals and individual conversations to give T-Mobile a brand identity through acknowledging its role in society and collective communications.

'Life's for Sharing' became a perfect articulation of this new way of living, and it also gave T-Mobile a powerful reason for being. But, because people were fed up with platitudes from corporates, it wasn't good enough to just tell people about T-Mobile's new philosophy; T-Mobile had to show it and prove that it genuinely believed in it.

The organic strategy allowed the agency to follow the flow and develop the campaign into a sequence of three TV advertisements fully integrated with social media.

Each chapter of Life's for Sharing (Dance, which saw 350 dancers break into a choreographed routine in Liverpool Street Station; Sing-along, where 13,500 joined the mass

FIGURE 13.10   T-Mobile Life's for Sharing – Dance

karoake in Trafalgar Square; and Josh's Band) was a progression from the last, building on the excitement and interest in the brand, increasingly handing more control of the campaign to fans of the brand for them to contribute to and play with. Now consider just the third phase, Josh's Band. Although the situation contained the same challenges, here are the other SOSTAC® stages for this, the third phase of the T-Mobile campaign.

Phase 3: situation – Josh's Band

As listed above in the general introduction to this case study.

Phase 3: objectives – Josh's Band

For each chapter in the Life's for Sharing campaign, there were specific short-term targets. The brief for the campaign that became Josh's Band was received in July, with the main proposition being 'free texts for life'. This offer had to be at the heart of the campaign but had to fully support the Life's for Sharing positioning.

The specific objectives for the Josh campaign were:

1 to grow the pay-as-you-go (PAYG) contributing base, driving 375,000 connections to the unlimited text and internet proposition;

2 to optimize brand creative (building on the T-Mobile brand and not just focusing on the direct response) and media principles to maximize response and drive down overall cost per acquisition (CPA) to under £200;

3 to maintain actual brand consideration at 28 per cent (people who consider buying T-Mobile when they are buying a mobile phone contract), with share of consideration remaining stable at 15 per cent, until the end of the year (share of potential mobile phone contract buyers who would think of T-Mobile over the competition).

Phase 3: strategy – Josh's Band

Josh's Band became the ultimate expression of Life's for Sharing, because it was entirely created by the great

FIGURE 13.11   T-Mobile Life's for Sharing – Sing-along

British public. Josh's Band started in September 2009 when, for a T-Mobile vox pop, amateur musician Josh Ward said that he would use the T-Mobile offer of free texts for life to start a superband. And from there the campaign unfolded in a rather unorthodox way, as Saatchi & Saatchi and T-Mobile challenged him to do just that. No one knew if the superband would materialize – it was a case of watch and see.

A documentary film crew followed Josh from purchasing his sim card to travelling around the UK gathering musicians for his band. Each beat of the story was told through commercial spots and webisodes. Josh's Myspace and Twitter pages were swamped with interest. At the start of 2010 Josh and his new band wrote the song *Come with Me*, which was then recorded around Britain by the band of 1,107 musicians. The whole campaign culminated in a three-minute TV spot in January to promote the release of the band's single by Universal Records. Each one of the band members featured on the ad.

Phase 3: tactics – Josh's Band

Facebook, Twitter and YouTube provided a continuous communication stream that helped to build the band. Filming was continous over the period, but larger band meetings were shot with a larger crew to assist with logistics. PR and news releases were sent out around major band get-togethers. Josh was encouraged to do his own PR ahead of events, getting radio stations to come down and cover the activity.

Phase 3: action – Josh's Band

The production process was an organic one. The directors spent a number of days each week with Josh documenting his activities as he tried to bring the superband to life. Day-to-day events were recorded using a small team, and Josh also had a handheld camera that he used to document his own interpretation of the experience. These edits were put on to Myspace to help engage potential participants in the story.

FIGURE 13.12   T-Mobile Life's for Sharing – Josh's Band

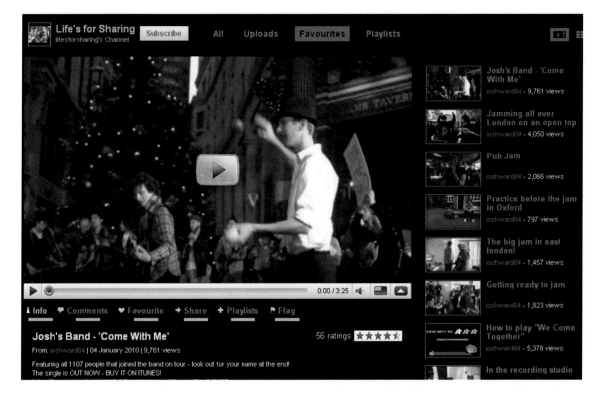

The shoots with the band involved a much larger production team. The events were still Josh's, but more control was needed over how these sessions were recorded. Both filming and photography took place on the same shoot, so this needed to be coordinated, along with release forms for members of the public who turned up to take part. TV edits were then created using this footage, which was reviewed, developed and finalized generally within a week, sometimes less, sometimes more.

Social media sites were central to how this campaign played out. Josh used texts and social media sites such as Twitter and Myspace to keep people up to date on his progress and to generate more interest in the band.

He plotted all the musicians he met on a Google map, which then became a database for British musicians. He promoted the band by organizing a number of special gigs around the country, including a jam on an open-topped bus tour around London. He plotted the route on his Myspace page so that people could see where to jump on and off.

After this, Josh and three members of the band decided to write a song with guidance from a top music producer. This was then posted on to the Myspace site for everyone

to learn, and quickly people started to send in videos of themselves playing the song. But Josh wanted to get them all together to play and organized a national tour, again using only texts and social media. Josh was given some help in identifying where his tour should go, based on the location of the members, but he was in control of getting people to join the band and turn up on the day. In the end, 1,107 people joined the tour, all of whom were recorded playing the song to make the single that was then released by Universal Records.

Phase 3: control/results monitored – Josh's Band

In order to work in such an unorthodox way the agency and the client had to in some parts relinquish control to allow the idea to develop organically; in others parts control was vital. For example, the campaign to drive recruitment for Josh's Band was run with Josh's own Myspace and Twitter accounts. They were unaffiliated with T-Mobile, and therefore content went up as it was created by Josh in his quest to get more members. There was no pre-approval process for content or posts, but content was reviewed at the end of the week and any issues identified.

Filming followed a similarly organic process. However, there was a degree of control needed during shoots where the band came together and played as a group. Anyone joining in had to sign release forms to appear in advertising, and also it was necessary to collect the required footage and shots to create the assets for the campaign.

The music was developed by Josh's Band, but it was vital that this track was catchy and simple enough to be easily replicated by new band members.

Results

There was no pre-testing of the Josh concept. The success of the campaign was measured against original objectives: sales, maintaining brand measures, and also in terms of whether Josh achieved his goal!

Josh's Band led to a staggering like-for-like 61 per cent increase in sales with PAYG customers (September to November). And T-Mobile had a record-breaking Christmas, in terms both of sales and of footfall. All brand attribution levels were up on the previous quarter.

Over the campaign Josh built up 1,529 followers on Twitter, had 1,114,995 views on Myspace, acquired around 1,000 Facebook fans, and sold thousands of records.

This followed the success of Dance and Sing-along. After Dance, T-Mobile enjoyed record footfall and impressive

year-on-year increases in sales. And although Sing-along was more focused on sim-only and PAYG, the campaign led to an increase in opt-ins. What's more, the Life's for Sharing YouTube channel had almost 30 million views for uploaded content and was the second most popular sponsored channel in the UK (**http://www.youtube.com/user/lifesforsharing**).

Men/women

Over 50 people were involved in developing the Josh's Band campaign. This includes the T-Mobile marketing team, Saatchi & Saatchi (the advertising agency), MediaCom (the media agency), TMW (direct response), Elvis (retail), Brands2Life (PR) and the production company Pulse.

Money

This is undisclosed.

Minutes

Brief: July.
Production: August to December.
Release: September.
Duration from brief to roll-out: four weeks until the first part of the campaign (vox pops) and eight weeks until the main campaign (Josh's story).

CASE STUDY 13.2   HEA drug education

How advertising turned the tide

Here is a case of how advertising fought a battle against huge odds to turn the tide of drug use in the United Kingdom. It is the story of a brave client building a strong campaign with an innovative advertising agency.

Situation

Britain during the 1990s faced an explosion of drug use among young people. In only five years the proportion of 14- and 15-year-olds in contact with drugs had doubled. Fifty-six per cent of 16- to 25-year-olds had tried drugs, nearly half of them (47 per cent) starting before they turned 15. In 1995, the government awarded the responsibility of educating the

public about illegal drugs to the Health Education Authority (HEA). The HEA chose Duckworth Finn Grubb Waters to help it develop a three-year campaign to turn the tide.

Objectives

The client's brief was to reduce the demand for drugs among young people. This was a complicated task, because it involved two important factors: first, a large number of new users starting to take drugs; and, second, only a small number of users stopping.

Given more time, the best solution would have been to tackle the adoption of drug use. Over the long term this would

FIGURE 13.13

A twofold problem

FIGURE 13.14

Tackling the problem on three fronts

have reduced the number of new users, while the older users would gradually have stopped. However, both the need for clear results within three years and the large numbers of young people already using drugs at the time meant that both problems needed to be tackled simultaneously.

Three key objectives regarding drug use were agreed:

1   to stop people starting;

2   to get current users to give up;

3   to ensure that the inevitable number of people who did continue to use drugs harmed themselves as little as possible.

Strategy

Research revealed that young people were not being pressured into taking drugs. Instead, they actively chose to take them, weighing up the pros and cons. The real problem was that, within the enclosed world of youth culture, the pros outweighed the cons by an enormous and unrealistic margin. Millions of young people were ignorant of the health risks associated with recreational drugs.

The challenge therefore was to let young people have the information and conclude for themselves that drug taking was not a good idea. They already knew, and had dismissed, the fact that drugs were illegal and their parents would disapprove. Research provided the key insight into how to persuade these young people away from drugs, which was concern for their health. The strategy was clear: give them the facts, not the fear, and their own judgement should do the rest.

Tactics

In an ideal world, the campaign would have featured every drug available. Budget constraints meant that educating the target market sufficiently for each drug would have been difficult. Selection criteria were therefore developed. Each drug featured must be one that:

- young people were likely to come across (ie be offered);

- they were likely to use or consider using;

- carried health risks about which they knew very little.

Therefore the campaigns focused on ecstasy, speed and LSD, and briefly featured magic mushrooms and mixing drugs.

Trying to persuade such a cynical audience was difficult enough, but if the government had been suspected as the source the task would have been impossible. Gone were the 'Just say no' and the 'Drugs are bad' campaigns of the past. The audience were seen as capable of making their own decisions, and were to be treated as equals.

In order to maximize the effectiveness of the campaign, the advertising also promoted the National Drugs Helpline, so as to open up a dialogue and to educate further, on a one-to-one basis.

Action: infiltrating youth culture

In order to maximize the budget of £6.8 million over three years, the agency worked closely with its media partner, New PHD. The 11- to 15-year-olds were tackled using teen magazines, while the 16- to 25-year-olds were reached through style press and dance radio. Crucially, each burst of activity combined radio and press activity to create universal coverage.

The creative work adopted an open, honest tone that allowed people to make up their own minds. The campaign information admitted that, in this untested market, doctors did not yet have all the facts. Bravely, the client (the government) agreed with the agency, allowing the creative work to acknowledge the positive effects of drugs. It was crucial in giving credibility to the campaign to admit that drugs could be fun.

The press ads featured young people in drug-taking situations, with a biological textbook 'cutaway' to reveal medical facts. The ads carried detailed information in an easily digestible form. On radio, scripted ads illustrated health risks, and

FIGURE 13.15   Media schedule

	1995	1996														1997														1998		
	N	D	J	F	M	A	M	J	J	A	S	O	N	D	J	F	M	A	M	J	J	A	S	O	N	D	J	F	M		

		Burst 1	Burst 2	Burst 3		Burst 4	
Teen mags and style press	NDH	E, Speed, LSD	E, LSD, MM	E, Speed Mixing		E, Speed, LSD	Total press and radio spend £6.8 million
Local and national radio	NDH	E, Speed, LSD	E, LSD, MM	E, Speed Mixing		E, Speed, LSD	Total PR spend £0.5 million
PR							Total spend (incl. production) £7.3 million

vox pops revealed people talking about their drug experiences to a credible young man who delivered facts about drugs. These ads contributed to and mimicked the way people learn from their peers.

Control

The success of the campaign can be demonstrated both from direct response and advertising awareness and from claimed drug use.

The advertising helped generate over a million calls to the National Drugs Helpline over the term of the campaign. Awareness levels nationally reached 62 per cent for radio executions and 55 per cent for presswork. In a selected test region, awareness reached a staggering 90 per cent.

Three years after the launch of the campaign, drug use was on the decline:

- More people claimed to have stopped using drugs within 12 months of the campaign starting (from 1995 to 1996 the figure rose from 14 to 28 per cent).

- Fewer people considered using drugs: the proportion of 11- to 25-year-olds who claimed they would definitely or possibly consider using drugs in the future went down by 14 per cent.

In addition to fulfilling the campaign's objectives, post-campaign analysis revealed that:

- With an annual £2.3 million ad spend, £28 million was diverted from the black market into the legal economy.

- The campaign saved British industry some £11 million per year in lost working days.

- The campaign added value to the field of drug education, saving organizations an estimated £3 million in potential development costs of materials.

Men/women

The HEA drug education campaign demonstrated tight collaboration between several agencies, from the advertising agency and the youth PR company, to the below-the-line agency and an innovative media agency, and of course the client. Each used different levels of human resourcing in order to effectively plan and deliver the campaign. The advertising agency used a core team managing partners, an account planner and director, and an account manager, in order not only to manage the internal process but also to effectively coordinate the work of the other agencies and ensure that time was efficiently used. Once decisions were taken, a wider team of supporting departments began work, from the print and radio departments, to media planning and buying, as well as the PR 'selling in' of stories.

Money

The HEA drug education budget was £6.8 million over three years, to change a market that accounted for 8 per cent of world trade. In the UK this market was made up of £13 billion of drugs circulating every year. Duckworth Finn Grubb

FIGURE 13.16   Campaign press ad with 'cutaway'

Waters was able to prove that over £28 million was diverted from the black market into the legal economy as a result of the campaign. British industry saved £11 million per year in lost working days.

Minutes

The HEA appointed Duckworth Finn Grubb Waters in July 1995. Much of the planning and creative work was developed during the pitch process, although there was still much to do when it was appointed to the business. The launch of the Drugs Helpline occurred in November 1995, just three months after the agency was appointed – an unusually fast turnaround time. However, for the three years of the campaign, there was continuous planning and evaluation for each burst, and constant tracking and refinement in order to reach the maximum effectiveness.

Advantages and disadvantages

Here are some of the advantages and disadvantages to consider when deciding whether to increase or reduce this communications tool.

Advantages

Advertising is great at getting messages out to large audiences quickly. Today ads can also be targeted at niche markets, as there are media vehicles (magazines and TV programmes) that target niche audiences. And of course PPC ads can now be tailored to audiences with particular interests. Location-based advertising takes this a stage further. Advertising is good for building awareness (and growing brands) but not so good at closing sales. On a CPT basis it can be quite effective. And the message can be controlled (as it cannot be in PR or social media).

Disadvantages

Message credibility is less than that of PR or social media, as it is seen as 'advertising trying to sell something', though credibility can be enhanced by source credibility. Some media advertising, such as TV ads, has a long lead time if changes are required. Such advertising also requires relatively large budgets for creating the ads. (Note that PPC ads can be small and flexible, and ads can be changed within minutes.) Advertising is less engaging than social media or an interactive website, although some ads now seek to change this, as they integrate with social media. It can be difficult to cut through the communications clutter, as ads generally cannot be personalized.

Key points from Chapter 13

- Media planning can be creative.
- Creative ads are designed to break through the clutter, but by default may be deemed contentious.
- Research can be used at all stages of the development of a campaign.
- Advertising needs to be integrated with social media and other marcomms tools.

References and further reading

Aaker, D and Myers, J (1987) *Advertising Management*, 3rd edn, Prentice Hall International, Englewood Cliffs, NJ

Belch, G and Belch, M (2001) *Advertising and Promotion: An integrated marketing communications perspective*, 6th edn, McGraw-Hill, London

Bradshaw, P (2010) Coke sees 'phenomenal' result from Twitter ads, *FT.com*, 25 June

Brannan, T (1998) *A Practical Guide to Integrated Marketing Communications*, Kogan Page, London

Broadbent, S (1994) *The Advertising Budget*, Admap Publications, London

Cowley, D (ed) (1989) *How to Plan Advertising*, Cassell in association with The Account Planning Group, London

Douglas, T (1987) *The Complete Guide to Advertising*, Pan Macmillan, London

Dwek, R (1997) Who's got the net by the eyeballs?, *Revolution*, October

Ehrenberg, A (1974) Repetitive advertising and the consumer, *Journal of Advertising Research*, **14** (2), pp 25–34

Fanning, J (1997) Is the end of advertising really all that nigh?, *Irish Marketing Review*, Marketing Institute, Ireland

Hampp, A and Bryson York, E (2010) Singer's manager dishes on all those product-placement deals (and lack thereof) in the nine-minute video, *Ad Age*, 13 March

Hart, A and O'Connor, J (1990) *The Practice of Advertising*, 3rd edn, Heinemann, London

Howell Henry Chaldecott Lury and Partners (HHCL) (1997) *Marketing at a Point of Change*, HHCL, London

http://www.adcritic.com (latest TV ads)

http://www.adforum.com

Jones, H (2008) Gorilla tactics, *Marketer*, May

Kennedy, J (2009a) App-fab, *Marketing Age*, November

Kennedy, J (2009b) A wave of optimism, Interview with Eric Schmidt, *Marketing Age*, **3** (6), November/December

Kohler, E (2007) Hyperlocal is more about ads than news, *Technology Evangelist*, 9 August

Learmonth, M (2010) 'Top marketers to Silicon Valley: Help us get ahead of consumer. Through visits to tech hub, big advertisers getting more than sales pitches, *Ad Age*, 17 May

Learmonth, M and Bryson York, E (2010) Facebook poised to take geo-networking mainstream, *Ad Age*, 10 May

McKenna, R (1991) Marketing is everything, *Harvard Business Review*, January–February

O'Neill, M (2010) Budweiser celebrates the World Cup with Bud House reality series, *Social Times*, 14 June

Parekh, R (2010) Why long-form ads are the wave of the future, *Advertising Age*, 3 May

Patel, K (2010) Will growing crop of TV apps engage viewers, advertisers?, *Ad Age*, 17 May

Percy, L, Rossiter, J R and Elliott, R (2002) *Strategic Advertising Management*, Oxford University Press, Oxford

Roberts, K (2010) Creativity, *KRconnecttoblogspot.com*, 21 January

Schmidt, E (2009) A wave of optimism, *Marketing Age*, **3** (6), November/December

Smith, P R, Berry, C and Pulford, A (2000) *Strategic Marketing Communications*, 2nd edn, Kogan Page, London

Sorrell, M (1996) Beans and pearls, D&AD president's lecture

Weinreich, L (2001) *11 Steps to Brand Heaven*, Kogan Page, London

Whatmough, D (2010) Facebook threat, *PR Week*, 19 March

Further information

Advertising Standards Authority (ASA)
2 Torrington Place
London WC1E 7HW
Tel: +44 (0)20 7580 5555
www.asa.org.uk

Broadcasting Standards Commission (formerly known as Broadcasting Complaints Commission)
7 The Sanctuary
London SW1P 3JS
Tel: +44 (0)20 7808 1000
www.bsc.org.uk

Committee of Advertising Practice (CAP)
2 Torrington Place
London WC1E 7HW
www.cap.org.uk

Incorporated Society of British Advertisers (ISBA)
44 Hertford Street
London W1J 7AE
Tel: +44 (0)20 7499 7502
www.isba.org.uk

Independent Television Commission (ITC)
33 Foley Street
London W1W 7TL
Tel: +44 (0)20 7255 3000
www.itc.org.uk

Institute of Practitioners in Advertising (IPA)
44 Belgrave Square
London SW1X 8QS
Tel: +44 (0)20 7235 7020
www.ipa.co.uk

14
Publicity and public relations – online and offline

LEARNING OBJECTIVES

By the end of this chapter you will be able to:

- Understand how PR is changing and its expanding range of PR tools
- Appreciate the potential for integration with social media and other marketing communications tools
- Plan an outline PR campaign knowing the advantages and disadvantages of PR tools

Introduction

Positive publicity nurtures good relationships with the media (media relations). This is only one of the responsibilities of public relations, as it deals with a range of different 'publics' or stakeholders. Public relations integrates with public affairs, corporate affairs, community affairs, community relations, corporate relations and corporate communications. The first part of this chapter explores what exactly PR is and where it fits with marketing; then it examines various PR tools and finally the advantages and disadvantages of PR over other marcomms tools. The golden rule 'Develop credibility before raising visibility' underpins this chapter.

What is PR?

Public relations is regularly, and sometimes worryingly, referred to as 'PR', which is often confused with 'press releases' or 'press relations'. These are, in fact, only a part of real public relations. **A simple definition of public relations is: 'the development of and maintenance of good relationships with different publics'.** The publics are the range of different groups on which an organization is dependent. These include employees, investors, suppliers, customers, distributors, legislators, regulators, governments, pressure groups, the community, the media and even the competition. Most of these groups have different (sometimes conflicting) interests in any particular organization. The UK's Institute of Public Relations (IPR) uses the following public relations definition: 'the planned and sustained effort to establish and maintain goodwill and mutual understanding between an organization and its publics'. In 1978 in Mexico, the World Assembly of PR Associations agreed what is now known as the 'Mexican statement': 'PR practice is the art and science of analysing trends, predicting their consequences, counselling organization leaders and implementing planned programmes of action that will serve both the organization's and the public interest.'

Public relations and marketing

While marketing traditionally focuses on markets or just three of the publics, ie customers, distributors (the 'trade') and the competition, public relations is concerned with many more publics. Add in the emergence of globalism (eg websites can be viewed around the world), increased media interest in business, new investor criteria (eg ethical policies), more effective pressure groups, information-hungry customers and the constant search for cost-effective communications tools, and you can soon see why PR has grown in importance. In fact, PR proved its increasing potency with the emergence of major global brands like Google, Facebook and LinkedIn without any significant advertising. The new understanding of the power of PR was clearly demonstrated when business analysts including the *Financial Times* suggested that both management and unions, before embarking on a dispute, must, first, learn to ask: 'How will this play in the media?'

> ### The classic virtual world movie *The Matrix* was powered by PR
>
> ' "As of Monday, April 28, there's 95 per cent awareness of this movie," boasted its producer, Joel Silver, to *Entertainment Weekly* weeks before its premiere. In a country where two-thirds of the population cannot name any of the nine Democratic candidates for president, according to a CBS/*New York Times* poll, that's some achievement.'
>
> Rich (2003)

Some organizations insist on public relations, advertising, direct mail people, and sales promotion people sitting in together on various project meetings so that they cross-fertilize ideas and create synergy through integrating the marketing communications at an early stage.

Who reports to whom? Is PR part of marketing or marketing part of PR? Product publicity is part of the marketing communications mix and therefore should be under the control of the marketing director or manager. Corporate PR, on the other hand, often reports to the board or CEO directly.

Product PR and corporate PR

The previous definitions give an indication of the diverse nature and far-reaching effects of public relations. We need to separate product PR (product or brand publicity) and corporate PR (corporate image enhancement). Product PR (sometimes called 'marketing PR') promotes a product or a brand and is the responsibility of the marketing manager, while corporate PR promotes a company and is the responsibility of the corporate communications director. A manager responsible for product PR would ultimately report to the marketing manager, whereas a manager responsible for corporate PR would probably report to a board director or the board itself. Both types of PR do, however, integrate with each other. Jon White, in *How to Understand and Manage Public Relations* (1991), suggested that:

> public relations is a complement and a corrective to the marketing approach… it creates an environment in which it is easier to market… public relations can raise questions which the marketing approach, with its focus on the market, products, distribution channels and customers, and its orientation towards growth and consumption, cannot. Public relations concerns are with relations of one group to another, and with the interplay of conflicting and competing interests in social relationships.

Publicity objectives can vary from promoting a product (product PR) to promoting a company (corporate PR) among employees, customers, investors, the community, local government, etc. The simplest way of expressing the difference is to 'discriminate between brand or product image and corporate or company image' (Hart, 1992). Marketing will tend to be sales or market share orientated, while public relations can, but not always, be sales or market share orientated; eg a PR objective may be to recruit the best employees, to win permission to build a new factory or to influence government. Nevertheless, today's PR people, like any marketing professionals, have to be fully versed in blogs, microblogs (Twitter), wikis, online networks, RSS feeds, social bookmarking, tags and podcasts, as well as optimized news release (social media press release, newsroom with social media functionality, social and professional networking sites such as LinkedIn, **Myspace** and Facebook, communities, forums, Yahoo groups, Google groups, Ning, virtual worlds such as Second Life, crowd-sourced news aggregators like Reddit and Digg, and e-zine articles). Today's PR is often measured less by press coverage (press clippings) and more by web traffic, registrations and sales.

The influence of public relations stretches far beyond product marketing and into corporate strategy, particularly where long-term decisions affecting choice of markets, products, factory locations, production processes, etc are concerned. External groups are becoming more demanding, and organizations are beginning to have to demonstrate their social responsibility on a global basis. Ethics and social responsibility have traditionally been the bastion of public relations. Today all managers need to develop their awareness and understanding of at least the PR implications of both boardroom and marketing decisions, strategies, policies and actions (or the lack of these).

PR is more than communications

Publicity and visibility should not be raised before a solid platform of credibility has been developed through decent, safe products, friendly customer service, caring ethics and socially responsible policies. The PR mix (see Figure 14.1) gives an indication of the diverse nature and far-reaching effects of public relations. It is more than just communications; it is part of the broader business disciplines such as corporate planning, finance, personnel, production and marketing. It cannot work effectively unless it is integrated into these areas and unless it also links with product quality, customer care and design management (corporate identity). These are the credibility elements that build a platform for subsequent publicity, which, as can be seen from Figure 14.1, is just one of the many visibility tools.

Survey after survey reveal that the public feel that industry and commerce don't pay enough attention to their **corporate social responsibilities (CSR)**. People feel that a company that supports the community is a good one to work for. People believe that companies have responsibilities to their employees and communities that go beyond making profits. Today ethical issues are highlighted by new pressure group techniques.

Although Klein's book *No Logo* (2000) was criticized, she did highlight issues and the need for constant corporate social responsibility. Amnesty International, which defends the human rights of individuals, departed from its normal focus on prisoners persecuted for either their religious or their political beliefs and, as Klein reported, 'is also beginning to

FIGURE 14.1 The PR mix

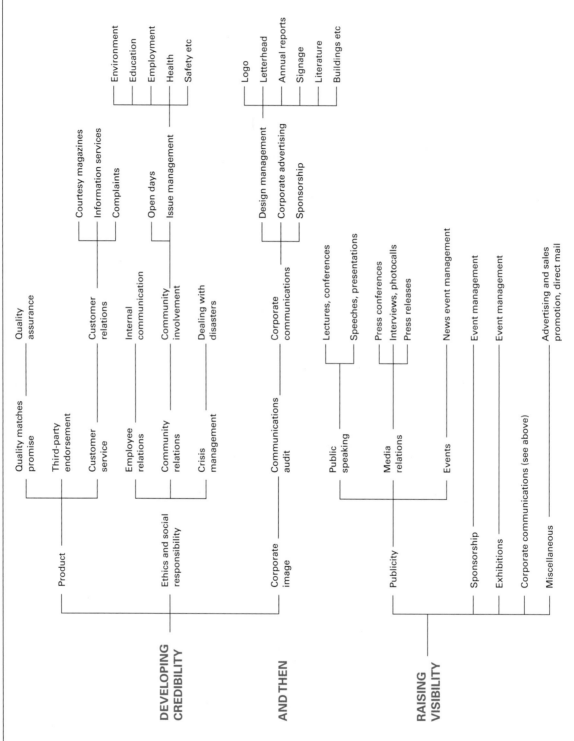

SOURCE: Adapted from the video notes of the award-winning PR video *Actions Speak Louder than Words*, with kind permission from PRTV (London) Ltd

Nike

'According to Campaign for Labor Rights, the largest ever anti-Nike event so far took place on October 18, 1997: eighty five cities in thirteen countries participated. Not all the protests have attracted large crowds, but since the movement is so decentralized, the sheer number of individual anti-Nike events has left the company's public relations department scrambling to get its spin onto dozens of local newscasts. Though you never know it from its branding ubiquity, even Nike can't be everywhere at once.'

Klein (2000)

Shell

'There was an explosion of protest and activity targeting Shell oil after the shocking hanging of Nigerian author and anti-Shell activist Ken Saro-Wiwa: 'But the most significant landmark in the growth of anti-corporate activism also came in 1995, when the world lost Ken Saro-Wiwa. The revered Nigerian writer and environmental leader was imprisoned by his country's oppressive regime for spearheading the Ogoni people's campaign against the devastating human and ecological effects of Royal Dutch/Shell's oil drilling in the Niger Delta. Human rights groups rallied their governments to interfere, and some economic sanctions were imposed, but they had little effect. In November 1995, Saro-Wiwa and eight other Ogoni activists were executed by a military government who had enriched themselves with Shell's oil money and through their own people's repression.'

Klein (2000)

treat multinational corporations as major players in the denial of human rights worldwide'.

Corporate responsibility is not just an overseas responsibility but starts in the corporations' own back gardens. A few years ago, the *Chicago Tribune* reported that Sears Roebuck had hundreds of elderly protesters picketing its store as a result of a decision to reduce pensioners' life insurance benefits. Any amount of press releases, or even advertising, announcing Sears' caring ethics would have a negative effect until this basic credibility problem was sorted out.

Even companies with a great tradition of social responsibility and, ergo, high credibility, like Cadbury Schweppes, sometimes score PR own goals when mixing marketing and social responsibility without carefully thinking through the implications. Some years ago it offered nearly £9 million worth of sports equipment to UK schools if schoolchildren bought lots of chocolate (millions of bars of chocolate had to be bought to get all the equipment). The media quickly picked up on the negative spin associated with the prospect of a teenager 'needing to consume thousands of calories before being able to play with a new basketball'. Using cause-related marketing to boost sales and corporate image is popular but needs, first, to be thought through carefully and, second, to be screened to ensure that there is a clear and positive strategic fit between the brand and the cause.

Good business is not just about achieving financial targets; it is also about behaving with a sense of responsibility. Over 50 per cent of the value of the Fortune 500 and the FTSE 100 comes from intangible assets, eg management, leadership, vision, innovation, customer loyalty, product and service quality, intellectual property, brand equity and reputation (Larkin, 2003). In September 2001 the US stock market was worth an estimated $24 trillion; by summer 2002 it had collapsed to $11 trillion. The events of 9/11 and economic uncertainty had a significant impact, but so too did the collapse of Enron and a wave of other scandals that raised fundamental questions over corporate governance. The vast majority (84 per cent) of Americans think that the people who run their companies are trying to do what is best for themselves rather than the company (Accenture, 2004). Years later, after another major economic crisis and an environmental crisis (BP), organizations now, more than ever before, need to engage in, and provide evidence of, solid ethical policies. One way is by joining a per cent club by promising to donate 1 per cent (or half of 1 per cent) of profits to the local community. There are even 2 per cent and 5 per cent clubs. Another way is by ensuring regular ethical and/or environmental audits and, of course, taking appropriate action.

Imagine your funeral

'I went on this training course (at Procter & Gamble) where you had to imagine what the minister might say about you at your funeral. When I realized that mine would say I was the leading expert on housewives' toilet cleaning products, I realized it was time for a change.'

Hamish Taylor, Managing Director, Eurostar

It is not just about making good business sense. Marketing, PR and corporate communications professionals are in the exciting position of being able to help improve their local communities, support valid causes, improve the environment, and much more. The bottom line is that it makes long-term business sense to be ethical, as it creates a platform of credibility that enriches all subsequent communications. As Bob Leaf, Burson Marsteller, succinctly says in the award-winning PR film *Actions Speak Louder than Words*, 'Ethics is good for business' (PRTV, 1991).

Cancel the Christmas party

'As CEO of Electronic Data Systems, Mort Meyerson made an unpopular decision and cancelled the Christmas party when he realized it was going to cost $360,000. Instead, he insisted, "We'll take the $360,000 and buy food and clothes and toys, and we'll get our employees to take those things personally and deliver them to the inner city, to people who don't have anything." The result was, initially, outrage that the party was cancelled, then depression, then recognition that the company was doing something different and then elation for those who actually took part in the project. This project "made them more human... made them better employees... better family members... it did a whole bunch of things". When Meyerson was CEO, he used to give 10 per cent of his time to community and philanthropic projects.'

Colvin (2003)

The PR mix

Figure 14.1 also shows how the 'visibility' or publicity-generating activities such as news releases, news conferences, publicity stunts, conferences, events, exhibitions, sponsorship and sales promotions can all integrate. Before we look at publicity in more detail, it is worth mentioning again that the key to long-term success is to develop credibility before raising visibility. Credibility is created by a proper product and/or quality of service. This means that the product must match the promise made by the marketing communications, ie do not sell a Rolls-Royce and deliver a Ford Ka. False expectations only lead to disappointment, frustration and extremely high post-purchase dissonance. This kills off any long-term repeat business. Good customer service makes doing business a pleasurable experience for all parties. Having the right sort of people or institutions associated by their using or endorsing a product improves credibility. So too ethics, social responsibility and corporate image all contribute towards building a credible image.

There is no point waving a flag or raising an organization's visibility if it does not have a solid platform of credibility supporting it. The days when the two aspects were held separately are gone. Spending

Harry Potter's anti-marketing magic builds the PR hype

'Review copies were withheld from interviews, no author interviews were allowed, and foreign translations were deferred for fear of injudicious leaks... printers and distributors were required to sign strict legally enforceable confidential agreements. Subtle hints that there weren't enough copies of the book to go around... fake TV footage of heavily armed security vans delivering Potter books to online book stores... Twenty advance copies were "accidentally" sold by an unnamed Wal-Mart in deepest West Virginia and one of the "lucky children" was miraculously tracked down by the world's press and splashed across every front page worth its salt... Another copy "accidentally" found its way to the news desk of the Scottish *Daily Record*.'

Brown (2001)

thousands or millions of pounds on raising a profile is not just wasteful but actually damaging if a lack of credibility is exposed. So today, more than ever before, it is worth investing men/women, money and minutes in getting the credibility right before raising visibility. And credibility must also be evident on websites and blogs, as journalists use these as their first port of call for gathering information.

New and old PR tools

Media relations and publicity

Take a look at the local and national newspapers, trade journals, radio programmes and television. Spot the commercial news items or features that have made news. Although they appear to be written by an editor or journalist, many of the news items and features have been written by skilled PR professionals. Like advertising, editorial publicity can achieve many similar communication goals, such as increasing awareness, repositioning a brand, generating enquiries and boosting sales. Busy editors do not have time to scout around for all the items they use. They depend on a constant feed of professionally presented news items and news releases from organizations. Despite this, sackfuls of press releases get thrown into editors' bins continually. Many of them are badly written and inaccurately targeted (sometimes even addressed to people who have long left the newspaper).

Publicity can be generated through written press releases and feature articles for the press, video news releases for television programmes, syndicated radio recordings for radio programmes and digital press packs for all and sundry. Publicity is also generated by press conferences, press receptions, media events (what the media less reverently call 'stunts') and public speaking at conferences, lectures, seminars, dinners, chat shows, etc.

News releases

News by definition is new – a new idea, a new process, a new product, a new service or even a new use of an old product. News should 'defy expectations' and provide a new way to understand the world we live in, so it has to be newsworthy. A news release should make it easy for a journalist (and a search engine) to make news. All the key information should be in the first paragraph for the journalist, and key phrases, if relevant, should be used in the title or headline and also in the opening paragraph (to optimize it for search engines). The press releases can then be distributed to the news wires, top-ranking free publicity websites, news aggregators, relevant social news sites such as Digg, and relevant online and traditional media outlets. Press release services like Pressbox, PRWeb, Free Press Release and ClickPress can do it all in one go.

Ensure the organization's web URL is included and any other links to relevant sections of a website, as not only does this help readers but it also acts as inbound links, which boost search engine rankings.

As the proliferation of online news aggregators (eg Google News) increases, the debate continues as to whether PR staff are writing news releases for people or machines – a human editor or a robot. The reality is both. A select few organizations bother to write different news releases for human editors and online aggregators.

The debate rattles on with Ryan Singel's (2006) comments:

> Standing up for the human intellect, upstart Digg is betting that its formidable legion of users can find better and more interesting news faster than any algorithm Google – or a number of upstart

This boring headline is written for Google

Journalists over the years have assumed they were writing their headlines and articles for two audiences – fickle readers and nitpicking editors. Today, there is a third important arbiter of their work: the software programs that scour the web, analysing and ranking online news articles on behalf of internet search engines like Google, Yahoo and MSN. The search engine 'bots' that crawl the web are increasingly influential, delivering 30 per cent or more of the traffic on some newspaper, magazine or television news websites. And traffic means readers and advertisers, at a time when the mainstream media are desperately trying to make a living on the web.

companies – can code. On the machine side, the purest algorithmic news finder is Google News, which made waves in the media world when it debuted. With Google News, it's code, and not a team of editors, that decides which stories make it onto the front page.

Online newsroom

If building an online newsroom or media facility on a website, make it easy to make news by considering what journalists need when writing up a story:

- news releases and press releases (easily searchable and sortable by date, by topic and by department);
- photos (linked to each news release, plus an archive or library of high-, medium- and low-resolution images);
- video (can be linked to a new release if it is a launch event, a press conference, a speech, an interview, a product demonstration, vox pops or endorsements);
- media kits to support news (all of the above in one downloadable file);
- general corporate information (corporate background, corporate financials, corporate statistics and executive team information);
- research and study data, white papers, links and related resources (including blogs, which journalists use increasingly);
- awards and recognition;
- upcoming events;
- contact information.

Note that all media assets, including videos, photos, news releases, white papers, etc, should be easily searchable, sortable and shareable. An effective online newsroom invites visitors to go deeper into the site for additional background information on the organization, its corporate social responsibility, its people and its media assets, so that journalists get to know the organization and form a healthy relationship.

Press conferences and interviews

Press conferences are an efficient way to release information to a large number of journalists, newspapers, blogs and radio and TV stations. They should include pre-prepared press packs and, ideally, rehearsed Q&As (the likely questions and sensible answers), although there is not always time to prepare Q&As.

Key staff need to be trained for press interviews. Avoid jargon, tell the truth and be topical, relevant and unusual if possible. A story that stirs up some trouble can be attractive to an editor. However, some caution is required to ensure the facts are 100 per cent correct, as journalists will investigate rigorously and any inaccuracies will subsequently cause damage. Finally, the human angle (human story) always appeals at an emotional level. Paint a picture with words; as Scott Chisholm (2010) says, 'Imagine is the most powerful word you can use in an interview.'

Video news releases

A video news release (VNR) is conceptually the same as a written press release, except that it is produced

Embeddable digital press kit

Buena Vista International's film *Starship Troopers* had an innovative 'digital press kit' available to support its launch. The kit comprised a ready-made mini-site packed with material related to the film. It was designed in such a way that it could be incorporated into other media sites. This made a convenient package for media partners, distributorships, agents and promoters to link the mini-site to their own website.

Virtual press conference in Second Life

For those international bloggers and journalists who could not physically attend the launch of Northern Ireland's creative digital hub in Belfast's Science Park, a virtual press conference was held, the next day, with some 50 bloggers attending. The Minister for Enterprise's avatar and P R Smith's avatar presented the hub and took questions for an hour afterwards. This resulted in a buzz of discussions on key international blogs, raised awareness, a new network of bloggers and a surge of valuable inbound links.

Influencers influence sales

When billionaire Donald Trump plugged GM's new Pontiac Solstice on his hit TV show *The Apprentice*, it generated online orders for 1,000 of the $19,995 sports car in just 41 minutes after the show.

WARC (2005)

on broadcast-quality digital video. A key factor is that it must be newsworthy or highly relevant as a feature item. VNRs also save broadcasters from having to send their own busy camera crews out to cover a story. The VNR consists of two sections: a 90-second 'A' roll, which carries a commentary designed to show the editor and/or journalist how the story could run on air, and a three- to five-minute 'B' roll, which is a selection of loosely cut shots ('rushes') designed to be re-edited by the broadcasters into their own style, ie the broadcasters use their own commentary, graphics and captions so that as far as the viewers are concerned the story has been originated by the broadcaster. As with a press release, **a VNR is paid for by the organization that is looking for some positive publicity. The TV stations receive VNRs free of charge.** Again, as with press releases, there is no guarantee that the material will be used, since a bigger story can break at any time. Equally, a VNR can be used negatively, since, unlike advertising, there is no control over the final message. And these videos can also eventually be used on social media sites, websites and blogs as well as form part of the press resources.

Syndicated radio interviews and down-the-line interviews

A syndicated radio interview is, on average, a three-minute recorded interview about a person, event, company, product or service. The audio file and script are distributed (or syndicated) to radio stations. The same principles as apply to VNRs apply here, ie it should be newsworthy and not a blatant plug. For just a few thousand pounds, a syndication supplier's basic package usually includes:

- preliminary discussion;
- interviewer – selecting, booking and briefing;

- structuring the interview;
- studio session (one hour);
- recording (three minutes);
- editing the master tape;
- two spare copies for the client;
- cue sheet preparation (written introduction to the taped interview);
- selecting 30 relevant radio stations (only one per area where stations overlap);
- monitoring – three to four weeks after dispatch a written report is produced, giving details of which stations broadcast the information, which is sometimes followed up with a more detailed report.

A 40 per cent take-up of a professionally produced, newsworthy, accurately targeted syndicated radio interview is considered to be an 'average success rate'. There is usually a range of optional extras (eg localized cue sheets or overseas distribution).

Syndicated producers usually offer an alternative service – 'down-the-line interviews'. This is where the interviewee is brought into the studio, linked up live to local radio stations one at a time, and interviewed on a one-to-one basis. On average the interviewee does about 10 separate interviews per day. Some interviewees have been known to do up to 15 separate interviews in one day. This is exhausting, and sometimes the later interviews are not as good, as interviewees cannot remember if they have said something before or not.

Photography

A picture paints a thousand words. A cleverly crafted photograph can catch a photo editor's eye. Some of the same criteria as for a news release apply – is it newsworthy, is it different, does it tell a story, does it catch the reader's eye and does it add value to the publication? If the photo has someone famous in it, then it is even more valuable. Ideally photos can be stored in three file sizes: high, medium and small resolution. They can be stored securely for press, or distributors only. Social photo sites like Flickr.com can store the images, embed them on the company's or individual's blog and embed them as part of an electronic press kit. Again tagging makes the images searchable and sortable. Here is a list of some great publicity photos that generated vast audiences:

- *Jarvis Cocker's blue beard for Oxfam* was part of a series taken by Rankin to promote Oxfam's 'blue faces' campaign, which was to raise awareness of the effects of climate change on poor people around the world, and was carried out across the UK festival season.

- *Dom Pedro and the 15 Second Film Festival.* Dom Pedro is the iconic character used by the 15 Second Film Festival to promote the concept of 15 Second Movies. Each movie has a beginning, a middle and an end, and Dom Pedro is the front man, deal maker and do-er who catches the picture editor's attention. www.15SecondFilmFestival.com.

- *No 10 Downing Street.* Plan UK created this image to put pressure on the prime minister to help 72 million extra children into primary school across the world. This was part of an ongoing advocacy/PR campaign to ensure the government delivered on promises to fulfil the Millennium Development Goals (MDG) at the MDG summit in New York in September 2009.

- *Projection on parliament.* Don't forget planes! – Friends of the Earth took its

FIGURE 14.2   Jarvis Cocker's blue beard

PHOTO: Rankin/Oxfam

FIGURE 14.3   (Dom) Pedro El Magico silent investor of the 15SecondFilmFestival.com

FIGURE 14.4   The 10 Downing Street image for the MDG summit

PHOTO: Plan UK/Mark Read

FIGURE 14.5   The 'Don't forget planes!' campaign

PHOTO: Friends of the Earth

FIGURE 14.6   Andrew George supporting Friends of the Earth's rainforest-free lunches

PHOTO: Warren Allot

FIGURE 14.7   Admiral Lord Nelson supporting the London bid

PHOTO: On Edition

successful campaign for aviation emissions to be included in the Climate Change Act to Parliament and mobilized huge public and political support for action on climate change, engaging a mainstream public audience, as well as environmental activists and politicians.

- *MPs support Friends of the Earth's rainforest-free lunches for planet-friendly farming.* Andrew George finds out that there's no such thing as a rainforest-free lunch if you're eating meat or dairy. He's one of 160 MPs who backed Friends of the Earth's call for government action to reduce the environmental impact of livestock farming.

- *Admiral Lord Nelson.* The stunning skyline around Nelson demonstrated the total commitment of the whole of London, its authorities and its people as part of the campaign for the London 2012 Olympics bid.

Publicity stunts

Publicity stunts are at much higher risk of error and 'egg on the face' than issuing a news release with a photograph, since the media are invited to wait and watch. Didier Pasquette promoted Vanguard while walking high above the River Thames on a tight-rope, meeting Jade Kindar-Martin heading in the opposite direction. The two had to climb over each other midstream in the first ever double tightrope crossing of the Thames – a stunt that was publicized worldwide.

Other stunts include:

- *The Archaos fish diet.* A classic 'What the –?' photo, this is a brilliant example of life mimicking art. Photographer Gavin Evans was sent to shoot a fish-throwing act. Stuck for a workable angle, Gavin stuffed a fish in the performer's mouth. Archaos subsequently made the stunt the grand finale to its routine.

- *Razorlight at the Science Museum.* Razorlight played a one-off gig at London's Science Museum to back Friends of the Earth's call for aviation emissions to be included in the forthcoming Climate Change Act.

Legendary publicity stunts

'The most celebrated was by a New Yorker called Jim Moran, who once contrived a bar-room brawl between a fairly well-known band leader and a bystander. When the judge asked what they were fighting about, the band leader told him it was over the recipe for Pimms Cup. Pimms had hired Mr Moran because they were having trouble establishing the brand name in the United States. The "brawl" received so much publicity that he solved the problem with a single blow.'

Independent on Sunday, 1 April 1990

FIGURE 14.8   The Archaos fish diet

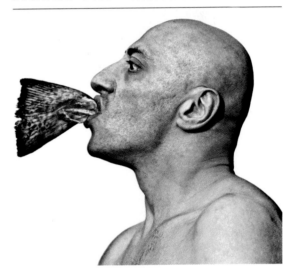

PHOTO: Gavin Evans

- *Fuel poverty stunt outside the Royal Courts of Justice.* Friends of the Earth and Help the Aged took the government to court in October 2008 over its failure to tackle fuel poverty.

- *Mortascreen* has a consumer database of over 7 million deceased individuals, with 50,000 UK deaths being added each month. Brands use the Mortascreen database to remove deceased people from their mailing lists, firstly, so families are not upset in

FIGURE 14.9   Razorlight at the Science Museum

PHOTO: Ben Queenborough

FIGURE 14.10   Fuel poverty stunt at the Royal Courts of Justice: 'Heat our homes, not the planet'

PHOTO: Amelia Collins/Friends of the Earth

FIGURE 14.11 Mortascreen's coffin with unwanted mailings

PHOTO: Eulogy

FIGURE 14.12   Mortascreen's publicity stunt delivered an immediate return on investment

PHOTO: Eulogy

bereavement with unwanted mail and, secondly, to improve the effectiveness of the brands' marketing campaigns. The PR agency Eulogy set up a photo opportunity using a traditional horse-drawn funeral procession, complete with four mourners, walking across Westminster Bridge and Parliament Square and finally coming to rest behind the London Eye. The funeral cortège contained a coffin filled with the amount of direct mail Londoners receive in one day addressed to deceased loved ones. This publicity stunt achieved 90 pieces of coverage across key national, broadcast, trade and online media (within an hour it was on YouTube and probably even more quickly on Twitter), delivering 35,000,000 Opportunities To See (OTS), with a

Publicity Value Equivalent (PVE) of £578,000. On a small budget of £8,500, this generated an ROI of £68:£1 or 6,800 per cent. It also generated £60,000 worth of licence sales, which gave a sales-to-fee ratio of 7:1.

Viral marketing

Viral marketing devices tend to be videos, games or widgets, but they can also be a photograph, a graphic or just a piece of text, as long as it is enlightening (informative), entertaining (shocking or funny), engaging (people must play or interact with it) or simply so good that you just have to pass it on to a friend or colleague. That is the acid test: is it worth looking at again, and is it deemed valuable if it is passed on? Anything that enhances the value of the sender (or person who passes it on) has viral potential. Common virals tend to be video clips, TV ads, cartoons, a funny picture, a poem, a song, a political or social message, or a news item. It has to be so amazing that it makes people want to pass it on. The best ones simply make compulsive viewing.

However, great creative material ('the viral agent') is simply not enough. It needs to be seeded, branded and measured. Seeding means identifying websites, blogs and influential people and sending them the e-mail, or posting the viral on their Facebook wall to start the virus spreading. Some agencies offer seeding services, where they have databases of people who like virals and tend to pass them on. Other marketers tend to build their own lists of their champions or brand advocates who like to be the first to see a new idea and therefore get credibility amongst their networks when they pass on useful virals. There are also websites that host virals for their audiences who like to view them, eg **www.viralmonitor.com** and **www.viralbank.com**. Branding means clear branding and a URL ideally, not just at the beginning and end where they can be cut out before being passed on. Although they cannot be controlled, virals should be measured as to what traffic they generate and what conversions come from this, as on an ROI basis.

TV channel E4's 'Stack Da Police' viral (**http://kerbgames.com/Play/?contentId=658**) mixed real video, animation, sound and gaming technology to create a viral that promoted its new TV programme. It generated 3.8 million uniques and a 14 per cent click-through, which is about 0.5 million click-throughs. The cost per click (CPC) was 6p (approximately £30,000 divided by 500,000). Kerb viral agency created and seeded it for £30,000.

The Snack Dash viral case study

The Snack Dash viral game

This is another more detailed viral case regarding the serious issue of obesity and healthy eating: **http://kerbgames.com/Play/?contentId=536**.

The situation The client, Digital Public, proposed a viral game to the School Food Trust to promote its healthy eating message, raise awareness of the School Food Trust and drive traffic to its site. The target market is a cynical age group, and the task of creating a game with such a nannying message without alienating the target market is a minefield.

Objectives The brief was to build a game that conveyed the message of healthy eating to a target market of children aged seven and over in the UK, drive traffic to the site and also for the game to sit on the site as a flagship piece of game content for the site's newly established game section.

Strategy To create more than just a game with a logo on it, or with information regarding healthy eating embedded in it, the strategy required the creation of a game with pure game play and humour that would appeal to children but that would actually illustrate the benefits of healthy eating within the game play.

Tactics The tactics were to design and build a game that requires the player to guide the main character from start to finish in the shortest possible time, whilst collecting as many points as possible along the way. In order to fulfil the brief, one of the game's key features is the inclusion of healthy and unhealthy food. Collecting healthy foods (such as apples, water and carrots) increases the player's score and protects the player from danger. Conversely, the consumption of unhealthy food (such as crisps, sweets and fizzy drinks) causes the character considerable instant weight gain. The player can still move but is unable to move quickly enough to negotiate features like the loop-the-loop or to jump over the baddies. A little bit of exercise is required to lose the excess pounds (toggling the A and S keys will make the character perform a number of press-ups in order to lose that puppy fat). However, this all takes up precious time. The only way to get a good score and speed is by avoiding the fatty foods altogether.

Action

Week 1: design.
Week 2: develop.
Week 4: test.
Week 5: seed.

Control

Results: As expected from an engaging viral, it got huge worldwide traffic, 70 million uniques, with 3 per cent coming from the UK, which equals 2 million UK uniques, without any media spend. In the first two weeks alone, the game achieved over 3 million visits, with no budget spent on media buying. It subsequently spread like a true viral. The game has been independently tracked by Meme-Counter and Viralchart. 'Out of over 400 campaigns this is the fastest moving viral that we have ever tracked' (Viralchart.com). MemeCounter recorded over 340,000 visitors in one day, which beat the previous record by over 80,000 (MemeCounter. com). The cost per thousand was £8.33, and the reach was 3 million, with a cost of £25,000. This may seem expensive, but it was a highly engaged audience. The cost per click was less than 1p (£25,000 divided by 3 million).

Men/women: Created and seeded by Kerb Viral Agency.

Money: £25,000.

Minutes: Eight weeks to create, seed and spread to 70 million users.

Blogs, Facebook and Twitter

Blogs can be for individuals or they can be corporate blogs with several authors. In either case, a content strategy needs to be worked out, to ensure the postings are relevant and of value to the target audience. A content strategy also helps reduce the workload, as it identifies content that can be tweaked for the blog, eg a speech, a white paper or a book.

Remember that, although blogs tend to be informal, they do count as legal published documents in cases of libel, disclosure of trade secrets, breach of copyright, etc, so a certain amount of caution is required. In the case of a corporate blog with several contributors, this means that an overall editor is required, along with a workflow management process for approval of postings and responding to comments.

Resources are required to moderate and respond to various comments made by the audience. As with Twitter, blogs will probably require an increasing amount of time from the marketing department or PR department. This is where resources need to be integrated.

Blogs do help to nurture relationships with target audiences. Blogs and Facebook can also extend the brand experience into another dimension. In the case of **www.greatmomentsofsportsmanship.com**, readers of the book can see videos relating to the stories, participate in discussions about certain topics of interest, send in their stories for future editions of the book and future postings on the blog, hear radio interviews of the author, and much more.

The brand experience can further be enhanced by embedding applications or widgets in blogs, Facebook pages and most social media platforms. In fact, the embedded video player in the sportsmanship site is a very basic widget that adds enormous value to the blog, which adds value to the book. See Chapter 13 for more about widgets and apps.

The other visibility tools, such as advertising, sponsorship, exhibitions, sales promotions and direct mail, are all dealt with as separate chapters elsewhere in this book. Positive editorial is usually the result of carefully managed media relations. Organizations and/or individuals must take time to understand what the journalist or editor wants, the news angle, the relevance of the piece, the appropriate time to deliver it to a news organization, the correct format or layout of the press release, and so on. One point to bear in mind is that PR campaigns, and particularly media relations campaigns seeking editorial exposure, do not have to be short-term, one-off news events.

Advantages and disadvantages of PR

As mentioned, editorial coverage can achieve many objectives similar to those of advertising, but there are three important points that differentiate editorial coverage from advertising:

1 There is no media cost.

2 The message has higher credibility.

3 There is no control over the message.

No media cost

There is no media cost since, with editorial coverage, unlike advertising, the space is not bought. There are, however, other costs, since news releases have to be written, carefully targeted and distributed to the right editor at the right time in the right format. This can be done by an in-house press officer or public relations department, or it can be handled by an external public relations agent or consultancy. There are news release distribution companies that specialize in getting releases physically or electronically to news editors' desks at the right time. The 'TSB sponsorship of Roy of the Rovers' press release and montage of press clippings show the kind of free publicity that a well-written, carefully targeted and properly timed news release can generate (see Case study 15.1). This kind of editorial coverage creates valuable positive publicity. **The editorial coverage has higher credibility than advertising copy.** No space was bought, and therefore no media costs were incurred. However, whether it is in-house PR people or an external consultancy, it does cost someone's time and expertise:

- to select the right target media (appropriate press and editors) at the right time;
- to write the news releases;
- to distribute the news releases;
- to handle any press enquiries. (There are, of course, other minor costs, some of which are hidden: photographs, stationery, stamps, phone calls, and wear and tear of the word processor, laser printer and so on.)

Editorial coverage is used increasingly to stretch the above-the-line advertising campaigns. Good press officers push the knock-on PR potential of advertising. Bruno Magli shoes enjoyed an uncontrolled estimated $100 million worth of free exposure during American football star O J Simpson's trial. The calculation is simple: add up the column inches of coverage, times by the amount of broadcast coverage and find the equivalent cost for the same amount of advertising space. There are more sophisticated methods of evaluation, which include: positive and negative comments; the position on the page; whether a picture is shown; the number of times a brand name is used, etc. Forte Hotels' constant quantitative report on editorial coverage is outlined in the box 'Scoring your PR performance' below.

Higher credibility

Editorial coverage has higher credibility than advertising because it is perceived as being written by an editor or journalist and not by an advertiser trying to sell something. There is arguably less resistance to the message. Some estimates suggest that a message carried in a piece of editorial has three times more credibility than a similar message carried in an advertisement. Despite the attraction of the message credibility factor, editorial coverage is risky because there is no control over the message. An editor can take a news release and criticize the sender for sending it. Advertisers, on the other hand, can control the message, since they buy the space and publish exactly what they want to say (within the law and advertising regulations). Despite this, editorial clippings and their associated levels of credibility are often compiled and used as endorsements in direct mailshots, sales literature, advertisements and exhibition stands. You can even see them above theatres promoting a show, where extracted comments from the press are highlighted in bright lights outside the front door. The third-party editorial coverage adds credibility to the claim that this is a good show. Equally, a reviewer can severely criticize a show and therefore damage the credibility (and viability) of that show.

Lack of control

The uncontrollable element of media relations is demonstrated by the montage of press clippings (editorial coverage) generated by P R Smith's 'nuclear missile' news release (Figure 14.13). This shows how the same news release gets totally different editorial coverage from two different editors. On the one hand, the *Wall Street Journal* gives it brief but positive front-page exposure, while *Personnel Today* treats the same news release with a lot of cynicism and, arguably, negative editorial coverage, despite a lot more detail about the promotion. It can be argued, in the case of P R Smith's award-winning PR video, that 'any publicity is good publicity', but this is certainly not the case with Ratners, IBM and McDonald's. These examples

FIGURE 14.13   PRTV News Release: The same news release can generate totally different types of editorial coverage, from positive coverage on the front page of the *Wall Street Journal* to negative coverage in a training magazine

demonstrate the dangers of uncontrolled publicity (see the next section). Even carefully controlled media events such as annual general meetings can go wrong (see the box below). Every media event has an element of risk attached to it, since if things do go wrong the press are waiting – with cameras perched and pens ready.

Fat cat pig

The production of a pig at the British Gas annual general meeting helped give the bandwagon against 'fat cats' (overpaid directors) a memorable push.
Andrew Bolger, *Financial Times*

Uncontrollable publicity – any publicity is good publicity?

The adage 'any publicity is good publicity' is not always true. Although the PR training video's negative editorial coverage (mentioned in the previous section) is, arguably, useful publicity, this is not always the case. Retail jewellery giant Ratners discovered this when it fell foul of the power of negative publicity. Its chairman, Gerald Ratner, told the press that his jewellery was 'crap'. This gained national coverage, but it also kept customers away from his shops and lowered morale among his employees. He relinquished his joint position of chairman and managing director, and the Ratners shops have since disappeared. On the other hand, unexpected editorial coverage can sometimes help, as shoemakers Bruno Magli observed when their sales jumped 50 per cent because of references to their shoes during the trial of O J Simpson. Uncontrolled editorial exposure, and particularly negative publicity, can somersault out of control, as IBM discovered during the 1996 Olympics when one of its official Olympic computers started churning out incorrect information. 'The press reported the story ad nauseam, even blaming IBM for things it had nothing to do with. In the aftermath of the tragic bombing in Centennial Park, for example, the *Philadelphia Inquirer* erroneously reported that an IBM system may have contributed to security lapses' (*Fortune* magazine, 9 September 1996). How a company handles the spotlight is a test for its

company values. When 21 customers were shot dead in California in 1984, McDonald's knocked the restaurant down within days and eventually donated the land to a local community college. Continued publicity and association with such a tragedy are certainly not 'good publicity'. More recently, BP's negative publicity threatens the very survival of this highly profitable global success story. The negative coverage has been exacerbated by extremely poor crisis management (see 'Crisis management' below for more).

Reducing the lack of control

Red faces can be avoided by checking to see if any events clash with a particular news release or event (such as launching a new hamburger bar on a national vegetarian day). There are directories available that list events and categorize them by type, region, date, etc. There are other directories that list editors' names, addresses and numbers (again categorized by type of magazine or programme). Editorial risk can be further reduced with the help of companies (such as Echo Research) that compile lists of journalists who have written articles on a particular organization or on its products, or on any particular issue, together with a favourable or unfavourable rating for each article. A further analysis compares the incidence of solicited and unsolicited press coverage, which can be cross-referenced with the ratings to identify any apparent bias in specific journalists' relationships with organizations. When a journalist calls the press office, the staff can punch in a few keywords into a desk terminal, and effectively see the profile of the caller on the screen almost instantaneously, even before the preliminary greetings are completed. So the pressurized PR manager is briefed automatically.

Despite the best preparation and briefing, things still go wrong. In advertising, the organization gets a chance to approve the final copy (or wording), but with editorial coverage deadlines are too tight even for the friendliest of editors to allow the PR manager sight of the copy and layout before it is published: hence a bad day for Mr Pimlott (below).

Controlled integration of publicity

Publicity should be integrated with other elements of the marketing communications mix. Chapter 1 explained how many major advertising campaigns

A bad day for Mr Edward Pimlott

Mr Pimlott's letter to the *Grantham Journal* led to this apology: 'In a letter printed in our July 25 issue, Mr Pimlott apparently described himself as a pillock of the community. This was our error. Mr Pimlott described himself as a pillar of the community.'

Independent, 28 August 1997

are now supported by press launches and followed up with a press and publicity campaign to maintain the visibility generated by the public relations people. The TSB sponsorship campaign (Case study 15.1) integrated with the media relations (editorial) campaign. An integrated packaging, PR and sales promotion campaign maintains the brand's share without any traditional above-the-line support. In other cases, blown-up press cuttings can be used (once permission is gained from the copyright owners) at trade fairs and exhibitions. Third-party endorsements can be used in advertising, news releases, sales literature, packaging design, sales promotion and so on. A single photographic shoot can produce a range of material suitable for advertising, packaging, exhibitions, direct mail, press packs, etc. Strategically, the marketing communications tools should all work together (eg consistent positioning) rather than pull in different directions. Ideally, each activity should be planned for maximum integration.

Unforeseen opportunities and threats invariably emerge that make it difficult to plan for everything. For example, editorial is difficult to forecast. (Even if an editor promises to use a news release, it often gets 'spiked' or replaced by some other news item at the last moment; at other times the news release gets used later than expected.) Successful positive publicity can trigger all sorts of ideas for mailings, promotions and further press coverage. Crises and negative publicity are equally difficult to forecast and plan, although top companies invest in crisis management programmes before crises occur. This allows them to respond in the most effective manner. A well-handled crisis can actually leave an organization in a stronger position, eg Johnson & Johnson's excellent handling of the 1982 Tylenol

poisoning crisis (when seven people died of poisoning from cyanide that had been inserted in their headache tablets) in Chicago.

Crisis management

Accidents happen, sometimes on a massive scale. Crisis management is standard procedure when a nightmare occurs. Top companies have crisis management procedures in place in case of a crisis – whether of their own or someone else's making. Key speakers are agreed, with key messages about the company, and specific messages for a series of different disaster scenarios. These are reviewed immediately if a crisis occurs. Media training includes a questions-and-answers document (tackling all the most frequently asked questions, including the tricky ones). Key to it all is simply to be human and decent. Show concern. Visit the site or the customers. Answer the questions. Pay for any damage (after the legal people have approved it). Communicate to all stakeholders. Avoid threatening legal action if possible. Legal options can be part of the solution, but rarely all of it. Note that legal action takes time (and money), and time is a very scarce resource during a crisis. Company spokespeople must tread with caution. As Alex Wollfall (2010) points out, 'After the global breaking crisis and the politicians' expenses scandal, public distrust of politicians, company spokespeople and big brands is at an all-time high.'

Footballer takes on the press

'John Terry was granted a super-injunction to stop newspapers reporting details of his alleged affairs. But when the judge overturned the ruling a week later, the scorned media went in for the kill.'

Luckett (2010)

There is a process, which usually includes the following steps. Firstly, survey the scale of it. Is it just a handful of moaners or something more significant, and have they good reason to moan? Secondly, don't deny it. Acknowledge the issue if it is an issue. Be open and honest and give useful information where possible. When the toy company Mattel faced a number of product recalls, the **CEO tackled the issue head on with a video message that was posted on Mattel's corporate website, spread virally across the internet and appeared on some TV news bulletins.** Compare this to TV images of queues of concerned customers trying to withdraw their savings from a crippled Northern Rock for several days, while no one really knew what was happening and rumours spread uncontrollably. Thirdly, be genuinely concerned. It seems ridiculous to spell this out, but a lack of sincerity will be sniffed out by an angry press corps very quickly. Witness the BP CEO's now infamous comment 'I want my life back', which displayed a concern for his own personal circumstances at a time when others' livelihoods were being destroyed by a massive environmental disaster. Fourthly, be open with employees. Inform them as much as the press. Fifthly, fix it so it is better than it was before the crisis. Make sure processes are reviewed so that the accident can never happen again. Finally, repair or compensate for any damage done or replace any faulty products.

Yacht holiday while Atlantic burns

'BP's Gulf of Mexico crisis is a case study in how poor communications skills will only magnify a corporate crisis. Avoid any photographs transmitting the wrong message. Of course everyone needs some time off but to be snapped enjoying yourself on your yacht in blue seas – when just across the Atlantic a BP field continues to spew oil into the ocean – is tantamount to reputational suicide. It was just the latest mistake by Hayward, who, despite correctly apologising on 30 May, stupidly added: "I would like my life back", demonstrating a lack of judgement... His performance in front of a Senate committee was evidence of this. While one sympathises with the pressure he was under, and the fears of his legal advisers, he came across as overly defensive and unemotional, playing into the hands of aggressive US journalists.'

Rogers (2010)

It may be difficult to avoid financial losses, but crisis management can, if handled properly, strengthen relationships with all stakeholders. In this way it not only repairs damage but is an investment in the future. It is worth remembering that good corporate social responsibility gives a platform of credibility, particularly during a time of crisis.

Control – measuring media relations

Free publicity, news coverage or editorial can be monitored, measured and analysed. The old approach was just 'column inches' and TV minutes of press coverage. Today news releases are also measured by impressions, shares, reads, traffic and engagement. News clippings can be compiled in-house, by an agency or by a specialist news clipping company that monitors, cuts out, pastes up and delivers the clippings daily, weekly or however regularly the client wants. Google Alert can also highlight any references to a brand or organization online.

Similar media monitoring services are available for television, radio and the internet (scanning newsgroups, online editions and search engines), such as **www.ewatch.com**. The size of file, number of references, and quantity of space or time devoted to a chosen product, organization or issue are, again, a simple method of measurement. More detailed analyses give a breakdown of: front-page mentions; exclusive mentions; size of mention or cutting; number of beneficial credits; neutral credits; adverse credits; and opportunities to enquire (includes reach of article, circulation, and whether a contact address and/or phone number, enquiry card, coupon, etc was included). Various formulae attempt to calculate the quality of the coverage rather than the quantity. These can include photographs or diagrams, position on the page, etc.

Online measurement includes the following:

- 'Reads' measures how many times a news release has been read every day.

- 'Impressions' measures how often a news release headline was displayed to how many people visiting PR websites and RSS feeds.

- 'Activities' reveals who read the release, who skimmed the headline and how many 'shares'. Social media sharing is important, and the number of times a release was shared on Facebook, LinkedIn or Twitter can be measured.

- Keywords that were used to find the news release.
- Search engines that were used to find the release can be reported on also.

All of these are hard facts, which could provide a simple format for pay-by-performance.

These factually based reports will make it easier for more PR consultancies to accept pay-by-results from their clients. The PR industry has not fully embraced pay-by-results (probably because of the large number of uncontrollable variables that affect the results).

Paul Miller, Strategic Planning Director at Porter Novelli Europe, has observed that 'the PR business is not the most sophisticated or advanced about setting good objectives. But this is now being recognized as a weakness, and what we like about performance-related fees is that they make clients really focus on what they want, so they are not wishy-washy.' In 2002 Hill & Knowlton, a leading PR agency, launched the pre-school animation series *Engie Benjy* using the TV stars Ant and Dec, and 30 per cent of its fee was contingent upon the programme achieving audience reach targets.

These forms of analysis measure what gets into the press; they do not measure what gets into the minds of the target audience, ie whether the editorial has changed or reinforced the target audience's attitudes and intentions, voting patterns, shared values, sales levels, etc. This has to be measured separately by

---

Scoring your PR performance

'When we have a story about a new hotel or product we identify five key messages we want to put across – it's never more than five – and we're lucky if we get two across in print. We then identify the key target audiences and the most appropriate publications to reach them. This establishes a matrix which ensures the maximum efficiency for our efforts. All stories are then monitored on a scale of one to five, according to how favourable they are and how many of the key messages are included.' This enables Power to give Rocco Forte and other executive directors a quantified report on just how well they are communicating.

Richard Power, Director of Corporate Communications, Forte Hotels

---

researching attitudes and behaviour patterns. Sales can be measured, but it can be difficult to isolate PR from other communications activities when attempting to gauge the effect of any aspect of public relations. Perhaps this is the reason for the apparent resistance to payment-by-results. But, despite the difficulties of isolating and measuring PR's results, performance-related fees do encourage clients to set very clearly defined, measurable objectives.

In summary, PR punches above its weight. It can be a very cost-effective communications tool that nurtures and strengthens relationships with key stakeholders.

CASE STUDY 14.1   Virgin Mobile's new tariff

Situation

Tariff announcements are essential for mobile phone providers, as they are one of the key factors affecting consumer purchase. It's a cluttered marketplace where a formulaic approach to PR is typically used. The campaign used innovative techniques in digital media to promote Virgin Mobile's new, very cheap, 30p tariff, engaged a hard-to-reach audience and delivered coverage that surpassed all client expectations for a new tariff announcement.

Objectives

- Engage Virgin Mobile customers, potential customers and key online influencers with the data tariff story – Virgin Mobile offers unlimited mobile internet for 30p a day.

FIGURE 14.14 The Virgin Mobile campaign

Virgin Mobile onlinefire

'30 peas' – the launch of the new a 30p per day mobile internet data tariff

Objective: With no organic online chatter, onlinefire was appointed to get people talking about Virgin Mobile's new plan – the most inexpensive mobile internet plan available.

Description: To get people talking, we produced a stop-motion animated film of literally '30 Peas' celebrating, under the theme "It's amazing what 30 peas can do"

To get the video into the hands of the target audience, we planned and staged the Voscars (Virgin Mobile Oscars) to premiere the 30 Peas Clip. We invited 30 of the most influential UK bloggers to the Voscars to share their favourite viral videos and creatively packaged 30 Peas and UK bloggers' favourite viral video into a feature story sold in to target media.

Results:

Increased monthly new customer acquisition by **5.5%** (37% over target)

Over **80% of sites linked** to the tariff's homepage

Secured **99 pieces of coverage** in 3 weeks, including a feature in Metro online and print

Best use of Digital
CorpComms Awards

- Find a creative way to get people talking about a dry news story.
- Increase inbound links to the tariff's homepage at **www.virginmobilepeople.com/30p.**
- Secure at least 60 pieces of coverage between online national news and blogs in three weeks.
- Increase average monthly new customer acquisition by 4 per cent.

Strategy

To build an online PR and social media campaign using innovative digital techniques to engage Virgin Mobile's customers, prospects and influencers. The campaign had to be developed with the essence of the brand in mind, so elements of youth, fun, funkiness, vibrancy and edginess were critical in positioning Virgin Mobile as the 'challenger' brand within its competitor set.

Tactics

The '30 peas' campaign was the first ever online PR and social media campaign for the launch of a new mobile phone tariff.

The creative concept was to use '30 peas' in different, digitally enhanced ways to illustrate the new 30p tariff in a fun and quirky way.

A stop motion animation film of 30 frozen peas dancing through black holes, climbing mountains and playing Pong fully encapsulated the fun of the Virgin Mobile experience, with the subtle messaging 'If you can get all of the internet for 30p a day, just imagine what 30 *peas* could do.'

The *30 Peas* film premiered at London's first interactive blogger event for the launch of a viral video called the Voscars (Virgin Mobile Oscars).

Action

The premiere of *30 Peas* took place at the Curzon Theatre in Mayfair, where a group of 30 of London's most influential bloggers were invited to showcase their favourite viral videos. Bloggers across all categories, including tech, coolhunting, mobile, social media, marketing, transport, London, food and news, took part, bringing an eclectic and vibrant energy to the event.

At the end of the screenings, the bloggers voted on their favourite videos. The winning video was packaged as a story and sold in at a 'Virgin Mobile's 30p per day Mobile Internet Tariff' premiere.

The Voscars also saw the opportunity for Virgin Mobile to engage directly with online consumers. Members of the Virgin Mobile communications team were on hand to chat about the campaign, the data tariff and Virgin Mobile's plans for the future.

What was not covered in national news was covered by the bloggers in attendance at the event. Each of the 30 bloggers wrote his or her own post about Virgin Mobile, the Voscars, *30 Peas* and the mobile data tariff plan, often linking to or embedding the *30 Peas* clip.

Additional online outreach was conducted to bloggers who were not able to make the event, as well as to non-London-based bloggers on mobile, creative, entertainment, coolhunting and technology blogs.

Control

Results

- Monthly new customer acquisition increased 5.5 per cent (over 37 per cent over target).
- There were 99 pieces of coverage, including a feature in *Metro* online and print.
- Over 80 per cent of sites linked to virginmobilepeople.com/30p.
- There was OTS of over 20 million across non-mobile blogs and websites.
- There were 10,000 video views in 10 days.
- In total, 75 per cent of placements linked to or embedded the *30 Peas* video.
- Over 95 per cent of placements mentioned Virgin Mobile.
- For every £1 spent, 952 people were reached.
- Outcome: over 80 per cent of sites linked that wrote about the plan and/or the campaign created inbound links to Virgin's site.

Men/women (human resources required for the campaign)

Account executive, managers and senior managers.

Money (budgets) – including retainer, media commission and pay-by-results

This amounted to £21,000 for all PR activity, including agency fees and third-party costs.

Minutes (timescale) – from brief to launch to campaign completion

FIGURE 14.15   Virgin Mobile campaign timescale

Week commencing	24 November	1 December	8 December	15 December	22 December
Brief delivered					
Campaign planning					
Video production					
Event planning					
Blogger engagement					
Event confirmation					
Video approval					
Event			11 December		
Top virals story developed					
Top virals story sell-in					
Campaign evaluation					

CASE STUDY 14.2   Meet the Stars in a Muzu.TV intimate environment

Muzu.TV offers free music video streaming and live events to a growing audience. It uses its own studio in its offices for live streaming events, which in turn generate more exclusive content for the site, eg Jedward did a live event in the studio. Muzu.TV does a live performance and invites 10 winners from say a national daily newspaper and 10 winners from a radio partner station to a very intimate event where the guests get flown over to meet the stars, watch the performance and get photographs, autographs, merchandise, and content for their websites, Facebook pages and Twitter feeds.

Objective

The objective was to extend the Muzu.TV experience, boost the UK audience to reach another 10 million music lovers, and boost traffic, sign-ups and embeds. The music lovers take the embed code of the video player, which

contains multiple playlists, embed it on their Facebook page and post it to their wall, where it auto-updates all their other friends.

Strategy

Muzu.TV changed its online strategy away from solely driving traffic to the main website and instead to delivering its services on many platforms and forming communities by embedding the player and simulcasting live performances and archive video jukebox, as well as live chat so friends can chat during concerts.

Tactics

Muzu.TV now get 1 million monthly uniques from the UK alone visiting the Muzu.TV site and spending 7–10 minutes there. In addition, across the syndicated publisher network (media companies, official artists' sites, official artists' social networks, radio stations, music magazines and festival websites), it gets another 2 million to 3 million uniques on a monthly basis. Muzu.TV can add pre-roll video ads or skins wrapped around the player.

A UK national daily newspaper, eg the *Sun*, might have a 6 million readership, a radio partner might have another 1 million audience, and an Irish equivalent newspaper and radio audience might boost the potential reach to, say, 8 million. If, say, only 30 per cent like music and, of those music lovers, only 10 per cent like Jedward, then approximately 3 per cent of 8 million fall into the hot target market, ie 240,000. If they alert their own social media networks (say each has 50 friends), then the potential reach via social media is 12 million.

Action

Muzu.TV's entertainment manager coordinates the logistics and events management with precision.

Control

This successful format is now rolled out to all urban crossover acts that come to Ireland, so major bands now are lined up for a private performance (and intimate fan event). Major acts have their own Facebook fan following of up to 2 million.

Advantages and disadvantages summary

Here are some of the advantages and disadvantages to consider when deciding whether to increase or reduce this communications tool.

Advantages

PR has higher credibility than advertising, as it is deemed to be a journalist's opinion or at least vetted by a third-party news source. Equipped with a good platform of corporate social responsibility, PR can work wonders. It also has much lower costs (on a CPT basis) than advertising. PR is good at generating awareness, building preference and overall brand building. It often delivers more 'bangs for your buck'.

Disadvantages

PR has no control of the message once editors receive it. They can rewrite it any way they want, whereas advertising controls its message. Editors, journalists and bloggers often dig deep under the surface to expose any inconsistencies. Also the message can spread beyond target areas. PR cannot close sales.

Key points from Chapter 14

- PR and marketing are not subsets of each other, although they do integrate.
- Editorial coverage has lower costs, higher message credibility and higher risks because of lack of control over the message.
- Social media are a natural fit for PR.
- Integrated PR contributes to marketing communications synergy.

References and further reading

Accenture (2004) *The Business of Trust*, White Paper referencing the World Economic Forum 2004

Bernays, E (1923) *Crystallizing Public Opinion*, Boni & Liveright, New York

Bernays, E (1969) *The Engineering of Consent*, 2nd edn, University of Oklahoma Press, Norman

Bland, M (1987) *Be Your Own PR Man*, Kogan Page, London

Brown, S (2001) Marketing for Muggles, *Journal of Marketing Management*, **17** (5), 5 July

Chisholm, S (2010) Getting your message across, *PR Week*, 16 April

Churchill, D (1992) The power behind the image, *PR Week*, 15 October

Colvin, G (2003) Value driven – think about this as you don your tuxedo, *Fortuna*, 18 December

Cutlip, S, Center, H and Broom, M (1999) *Effective Public Relations*, 8th edn, Prentice Hall International, Englewood Cliffs, NJ

Hart, N (1992) Is there a new role for PR in marketing?, *Public Relations*, **11**, 1 September

Haywood, R (1990) *All about PR*, 2nd edn, McGraw-Hill, London

Jefkins, F (1998) *Public Relations*, 5th edn, FT Management, London

Klein, N (2000) *No Logo*, Flamingo, London

Kosky, H (2008) Howard Kosky on PR and digital broadcasting, *Independent*, 16 June

Larkin, J (2003) Reputation under fire, *Profile*, **35**, April, IPR, UK

Lohr, S (2006) This boring headline is written for Google, *New York Times*, 9 April

Luckett, T (2010) Crisis communications, *PR Week*, 26 February

Murphy, D (1992) Don't forget the hype, *Creative Review*, October, p 16

PRTV (1991) *Actions Speak Louder than Words*, PR training video by P R Smith, Chartered Institute of Public Relations, London

Rich, F R (2003) There's no exit from the Matrix, *New York Times*, 25 May

Rogers, D (2010) Poor comms skills just magnify a crisis, *PR Week*, 25 June

Ross, D (1990) *Surviving the Media Jungle*, Mercury Books, London

Singel, R (2006) Man vs machine in newsreader war, *Wired Magazine*, 14 March

White, J (1991) *How to Understand and Manage Public Relations*, Business Books, London

Wollfall, A (2010) Crisis communications, *PR Week*, 26 February

World Advertising Research Centre (WARC) (2005), excerpt from a subscription-based article archive

Further information

CIPR Public Relations Centre
52–53 Russell Square
London WC1B 4HP
Tel: +44 (0)20 7631 6900
www.cipr.co.uk

Communications Advertising and Marketing Education Foundation Limited (CAM Foundation)
Moor Hall
Cookham
Maidenhead
Berkshire SL6 9QH
Tel: +44 (0)1628 427120
Fax: +44 (0)1628 427158
www.camfoundation.com

Public Relations Consultants Association
Willow House
Willow Place
London SW1P 1JH
Tel: +44 (0)20 7233 6026
Fax : +44 (0)20 7828 4797
www.prca.org.uk

15
Sponsorship – online and offline

LEARNING OBJECTIVES

By the end of this chapter you will be able to:

- Consider the unlimited range of sponsorship opportunities online and offline
- Assist in managing a sponsorship programme
- Discuss the advantages and disadvantages, including what can go wrong
- Monitor a sponsorship programme

Introduction

So is sponsorship worth investing in? Can it work as a short-term tactical tool? Probably 'yes' to the former and almost certainly 'no' to the latter. Certainly major brands see that some sponsorship opportunities are extremely worthwhile (as they repeatedly invest in them in the long term). Witness Coca-Cola investing again in the FIFA World Cup. In 2005, Coca-Cola committed $500 million to extend its sponsorship of the football world's governing body, FIFA, until 2022. This gives Coke exclusive rights as non-alcoholic beverage supplier to all major competitions, including the World Cup tournament, and sales rights for TV and stadium advertising. It also extended its Olympic Games sponsorship for 12 years to 2020. The Coke deal covers the 2010 Winter Olympics in Vancouver, the 2012 Summer Games in London, and the games of 2014, 2016, 2018 and 2020 (*WARC*, 2005). Note that even the signing of a sponsorship contract provides a PR opportunity – Coke took it and signed the contract on the Great Wall of China. Although this is based on anecdotal evidence, it is from one of the world's best marketing machines, which considers that its sponsorship management ('know-how') gives it a distinct competitive advantage.

Today expert sponsors leverage the sponsorship opportunity to maximize the return on their investment. It is much more than just 'badging an event (or a celebrity)', eg if a mobile phone company sponsors a summer music festival, it will seek to be allowed to collect and distribute backstage gossip, generate exclusive video content, interviews and jam sessions, and share this with its audiences, with its own customers getting extra benefits. These may include VIP access, parties and intimate performances from artists. Some phone companies loan phones so people can share their partially branded photos and videos with their social media networks.

So what should be sponsored? How does one choose what to sponsor and what to reject? Maybe arts are good for computers and sports are bad for banks? If sports sponsorship is so good for Gillette, why does it bother to advertise at all? Or perhaps its advertising doesn't work, which means any meagre improvement would be deemed to be a success? **Do sponsorship funds come out of the above-the-line budget, ie does it always mean reducing the advertising budgets, or can they come out of some corporate fund?** How much should be spent? How much is too much? When does it become less value for money? How is it measured? Finally, what exactly does sponsorship mean? These are some of the questions this chapter answers.

What is sponsorship?

Sponsorship is more than patronage, altruism or benefaction. **It can indeed help others while simultaneously achieving specifically defined communications objectives.** Some sponsors see sponsorship as a form of enlightened self-interest, where a worthy activity is supported with cash and/or consideration in return for satisfying specific marketing or corporate objectives. As sponsorship matures, its diverse range of programmes, objectives, advantages and disadvantages requires a relatively sophisticated level of management understanding.

The target audience must be researched in detail, crystal-clear qualitative and quantitative objectives must be set, and appropriate types of sponsorship vehicles must be agreed, considered and selected. A programme of integrated communications has to be planned with precision, and sufficient budgets have to be allocated to allow for 'leveraging', stretching or maximizing the overall sponsorship impact.

New and old sponsorship tools

All sectors of society can be targeted and reached through sponsorship. Just about anyone or anything can be sponsored. You can even sponsor 'the possibility of an event', eg Granada TV once sponsored Manchester's bid to host the 2000 Olympics. The range of sponsorship opportunities is limited only by one's imagination. **The obvious areas are sport, the arts, education, community and broadcast.**

Whether the events are large or small (eg blind golf and blind cricket), sport offers an effective route into the minds of various target markets. Even within a particular sport there is a range of different sponsorship opportunities. Take football, for example. It is possible to sponsor a title, eg the Carling Cup or the Barclaycard Premiership, or a stadium, eg the Reebok Stadium. Perhaps a more interesting example is where Maxwell House coffee's Taste of Chicago sponsorship maximized the off-site potential by buying all 37,000 tickets to a game and then giving them away free in return for two empty Maxwell House jars. It is also possible to sponsor: a club, eg Emirates and Arsenal, Doritos and Wolverhampton Wanderers (incidentally, since

the 1980s, five of Japan's baseball teams have been owned by railway companies, four by beverage companies, two by newspapers and one by an automobile company); a match day (eg York City gave 12 stand tickets, free buffet, free bar, free ads in the programme, hoardings in the car park and the opportunity to present the Man of the Match award and join players in the bar after the game – all for approximately £1,000); a kick-off (in the United States, Anheuser Busch sponsors NFL kick-offs, and they are referred to as 'Bud kick-offs'); a ball, eg Crystal Palace FC match ball sponsorship costs £250; a fair play award, often tied in with another sponsorship package; a sin bin (the Northern Ireland police force wittily sponsored the 'sin bin' at the Belfast Giants hockey team – essentially made up of neutral Canadians); a player (players receive individual sponsorship and in return they open stores, meet employees and acknowledge the sponsor in the programme); a pass, a tackle, a goal, a save or a miss – the Pizza Hut and American Express examples in the boxes below show US baseball creating such exciting opportunities. Score updates, gossip about players and even free betting can be sponsored. It is even possible to sponsor a fictitious team (see Case study 15.1).

Sponsoring a catch – fan catches 33,000 pizzas

Pittsburgh Pirates fan Ted Bianucci was picked at random out of a crowd at Three Rivers Stadium to take the field to try to catch three pop-ups (balls shot out of a gun used to help catchers practise defence). Sponsors Pizza Hut promised every spectator in the park a free soft drink at Pizza Hut (by showing the ticket stub), a jug of soft drink or a small pizza if the fan caught one, two or three respectively of the pop-ups. No one had ever previously caught all three. Bianucci, to the cheers of 33,789 people, caught all three balls – and $150,000 worth of pizza generates a lot of good feeling and probably extra business as 33,000 customers enter Pizza Hut's premises.

Effectively anything can be sponsored, including golf on the moon. A golf equipment manufacturer asked Russian cosmonaut Mikhail Tyurin, who was based on the International Space Station, to take a golf club and ball outside to tee off into space for what was likely to be the longest golf shot ever (IOL, 2006). It is the marketer's job to spot the opportunity and determine if it is really just a publicity stunt sponsorship or if it is a medium- to longer-term sponsorship programme.

Sponsoring a miss

American Express and Best West International Hotels jointly sponsored a programme that donated $300 to children's baseball league every time top baseball pitcher Nolan Ryan bowled or pitched an opposition player out. If Ryan pitched a 'no-hitter' (bowled the whole team out for nought), then a whopping $1.25 million would be donated by the sponsors to the league. AmEx and Best West also donated three cents every time an AmEx card was used to pay for a Best West hotel. In addition, $2 was contributed for every newly approved AmEx card member application that came from a 'take-one' box at each Best West hotel.

Arts sponsorship can be even more diverse – from sponsoring the opening of Disneyland Paris, to a film premiere, to a particularly obscure type of play to gain access to an otherwise difficult target market. Education is a sensitive area, and sponsorship can come in cash or in kind, eg a computer company donating computers to schools. **Community sponsorship** is becoming increasingly important as businesses recognize the importance of their community and their corporate responsibility. The corporate citizen is alive and well within the 'per cent club'. (In the UK, corporate members of the per cent club promise to spend one-half of 1 per cent of their profits on community programmes. In the United States, there are also 2 per cent and 5 per cent clubs.) In the UK, it is possible to sponsor the police, the fire brigade and the coastguard. Off-licence chain Thresher has sponsored a van for Avon and Somerset police force, while Newcastle Breweries has sponsored a mobile police station.

Other (unusual) types of sponsorship

Here are some other forms of sponsorship, which give an indication of the variety and potential available. An organization can sponsor an expedition (Mercury has sponsored a walk to the North Pole). British Aerospace, Memorex and Interflora signed as sponsors for a voyage into space (the package was subsequently cancelled). An organization can also sponsor a species (Systematics Association, a scientific group involved in classifying organisms, named seven wasps after the directors of Salomon Brothers when they waived a $300,000 debt arrangement). The 'Ugly Bartender' contest sponsored by the Multiple Sclerosis Society is its second-biggest revenue generator. Some years ago, cows wearing Vladivar Vodka jackets in a field near the London-to-Brighton railway line were sponsored during the Brighton festival. Akai sponsored bullfights at £10,000 a fight. BP sponsored Eugène Ionesco's play *Journeys among the Dead*. Sponsoring a war? It is possible to sponsor sections of the US Army (eg the Medical Corps). On the other hand, sponsoring peace initiatives is also possible. For example, during the height of the Cold War the *Irish Times* sponsored an official televised arms debate between Soviet and US diplomats. It is even possible to sponsor an Amnesty International tour.

Sponsoring bad sex

It is possible to sponsor bad sex – Hamlet Cigars sponsored *Literary Review's* Annual Bad Sex Grand Booby Prize. The award is given to the writer whose novel contains the worst description of the sex act.

Broadcast sponsorship offers possibilities ranging from sponsoring other people's advertisements (Midland Bank's £50,000 and Cancer Research), to the weather, specific programmes and themed weeks on cable television.

Online events in virtual worlds or online communities events (webcasts, discussions, video walls, etc) can be sponsored. Effectively any event anywhere, online or offline, presents sponsorship opportunities that can be leveraged in many ways.

Not the Salvation Army

'This is not the Salvation Army; this is business. Our programme is focused and we are able to quantify what has happened. When I am criticized for paying the wages of dancers while staff are losing their jobs I say that, by supporting dancers, I am supporting more jobs at Digital.'

Geoff Shingles, Chairman, Digital

Managing a sponsorship programme

The SOSTAC® + 3Ms acronym (see Chapter 10) can be used to develop and manage a sponsorship programme.

SOSTAC® + 3Ms involves:

1 defining target audiences;
2 defining sponsorship objectives;
3 analysing and summarizing the current sponsorship situation (including competitive review, previous sponsorship experiences, sponsorship strategies, etc);
4 clarifying the strategy (how the sponsorship programme contributes towards the overall corporate or brand mission, marketing objectives and communication objectives);
5 developing the tactical details of how it all fits together;
6 building in measurement or evaluation to see whether the programme is worth repeating;
7 identifying the resources required to leverage a programme to give the maximum return.

Situation – the target audiences

There are two different audiences. The first is the one immediately involved with the programme; the second is the one that can be reached through advertising and media coverage. Although there are many spin-off objectives that offer benefits to different target groups, the primary objective should be linked clearly with the primary audience. This involves some research into the lifestyles, attitudes, behaviour patterns, leisure activities, issues and demographics relevant to the primary target group. Previous research should have identified the current situation, ie how the sponsor is positioned in the target audience's mind. This will reveal the kinds of specific communications objectives that need to be set.

Objectives

After defining the target audiences, objectives must be fully clarified to focus both the spin-off activities (eg sales promotions linked with the core sponsorship programme) and the marketing support activities (eg advertising and publicity announcements around the sponsorship programme). A sponsorship programme can satisfy many objectives simultaneously. The range of objectives is varied:

1 *Increase awareness* – eg Canon sponsored the Football League to create a presence, become a familiar household name and generally raise awareness of a previously relatively unknown company in the UK marketplace. Its sponsorship gave it a foothold in the UK market.

2 *Build an image* – this can help to reposition or strengthen a brand or corporate image through association with particular types of sponsorship activities, eg a caring image through community programmes. The sponsorship must support the brand values.

3 *Improve or maintain relations* – with customers, the trade, employees and even investors through hospitality and entertainment at a sponsored event. Rumbelows department store sponsored English soccer's League Cup. Part of the agreement allowed the sponsor to appoint its own employee of the year to meet the teams and present the cup to the winning captain. Community relations can also be enhanced by supporting appropriate local activities.

4 *Increase sales and open closed markets* – Coca-Cola was banned in Arab markets

because it had built an Israeli bottling plant. Sponsorship of the 1989 Arab Youth Football Competition in Riyadh helped to open the door again.

5 *Increase sales (sampling and direct sales)* – action-orientated sampling opportunities abound in a captive market where the buyer is in a relaxed frame of mind, eg buying and drinking Victoria Beer at a touch-rugby competition sponsored by Victoria Beer. Some market research can also be carried out. Sponsorship can create a dialogue, whereas a lot of advertising is a monologue (although there are some campaigns that engage the customer in more than just a monologue).

6 *Attract distributors or agents* – ECON is sponsoring a radio station's weather forecasts to build awareness and attract enquiries from agents in other markets.

7 *Create promotional material* – some events offer wonderful photo opportunities with scenes, sights and stars. One climbing equipment company sponsors climbs primarily to secure stunning photographs with branded climbing gear featuring prominently.

8 *Circumventing advertising bans* – sponsorship, particularly of televised events, allows sponsors a way around mainstream above-the-line advertising bans, eg tobacco companies sponsoring sports events such as snooker. Incidentally, the famous Steve Davis vs Dennis Taylor snooker final kept one-third of the British population glued to their TV sets until 3 am.

9 *Miscellaneous* – ranging from, for example, the generation of new product ideas (new product educational competitions) to graduate recruitment.

Sponsorship strategy

The strategy statement briefly explains which types of sponsorship programmes are preferred, why a particular sponsorship programme is selected, how it will be exploited and integrated, and at what cost. To maximize the effect, sponsorship must be integrated with other elements of the communications mix, eg advertising, sales promotion, direct mail and public relations. It should also be explained internally and sometimes used internally as part of psychic income (see Chapter 12) as a means of improving employee relations.

A sponsorship policy helps the programme selection process by defining sponsorship parameters such as the preferred types of sponsorship that fit with the overall mission statement and the marketing and communication objectives. Questions to ask include the following. Is there any relevance between sponsor and subject, eg a chess competition and a computer company share values of intelligence. Is there a consistent message or objective behind all the organization's chosen sponsorship programmes? Does the association add value to the company or product? Does the sponsorship support the brand values? Is the association internationally acceptable? Think global; act local (sponsoring bullfighting is globally unacceptable, although Pepsi has sponsored it). Are there certain types or areas of sponsorship that are preferred? It is often felt that it is better to concentrate in certain areas. What is the ideal time in terms of seasonality and length of commitment, eg a three-year minimum? When should a sponsorship programme be dropped, changed or simply reviewed? Are both solus and shared or joint sponsorship programmes acceptable? Can staff involvement be incorporated? Does the sponsorship lend itself to leverage by offering potential for spin-off promotions and publicity? Does it lend itself to sales promotions? Can customers become even more engaged? Is it unique? Is it protectable from ambush marketing (see page 350)? What is the competition doing? Are 'me-too' sponsorship packages (the competition follows with a similar

---

Tiger Woods and a watch

Does the sponsorship support the brand values? The watch company Tag Heuer sponsors Tiger Woods for £1.5 million and he doesn't even have to wear one of its watches while on the golf course. Both brands, one might argue, are very similar. The trick is to balance the person and the product. Arguably, there is a good balance between Tiger Woods's and Tag Heuer's brand values: timing, focus and commitment.

sponsorship programme) preferred to unique (and uncopiable) sponsorship programmes? What kind of budget is required? What is defined as value for money?

Tactical plans

Squeeze as many benefits as possible into the programme. Sponsorship does not involve just adding the organization's name to an event, team or situation and waiting to see if awareness takes off overnight. A well-planned sponsorship programme involves attracting media coverage, corporate entertainment, new client recruitment, miscellaneous spin-off promotions and staff motivation schemes. (See Chapter 10, 'Tactics', to help develop a whole communications plan around the sponsorship package or to help integrate the sponsorship programme into the rest of the marketing communications activities.)

The launch is the easy bit. The real work starts then, as years one, two and three need constant attention to detail. A series of checklists and detailed plans (including contingency plans) have to be developed.

Action

The agreement

Agreements need to be carefully checked, as sometimes, in the frenetic search for funding, those sponsored may promise the world to potential sponsors. The potential sponsor needs to exercise some caution. Here are some points worth considering:

1 Have the contract checked by an expert. In particular, check the exit clause and exit arrangements, since it may be harder to get out of sponsorship than to get into it. For example, it is easy to start supporting a local theatre, but when the sponsor wants to switch into a different type of sponsorship the eventual withdrawal of funds may prompt the local paper to print a headline that reads 'Company X Pulls Plug on Theatre' or 'Company X Leaves Theatre in the Dark'. Consider exit strategies also.

2 Can those sponsored deliver on their promises? Can they provide proof?

Have they done it before? Have they any references? Are they financially secure?

3 Is it fair and reasonable to all parties? Sometimes razor-sharp negotiators agree a deal that is too good for the sponsors, which eventually creates problems. A good example is Nike's sponsorship deal with the Brazil football team (see the box 'Sponsor being too clever' below).

4 Are there other opportunities for brand exposure via the sponsored person or organization's other marketing activities (see the box below)?

> ### Nike piggyback on Tiger Woods's Buick
>
> 'Nike's association with Mr. Woods has worked wonders for the company. After signing him in 1996, Nike redid the deal in 2000 for a reported $105 million. That may sound like a lot of money, but not only has Mr. Woods single-handedly built Nike Golf, his apparel deal means that even when he appears in ads for his other partners, he wears Nike clothing. The swoosh is clearly visible in ads for Buick and American Express.'
>
> Thomaselli (2006)

Pilot scheme

Pilot testing is where 'action' overlaps with 'control'. In an ideal marketing world, all risks are reduced by testing and researching everything. Extra research costs resources, primarily time and money. Sometimes the nature of a sponsorship programme does not lend itself to testing, eg sponsoring the English Football League, but customers can be asked what they would think of it (before signing on the dotted line). Alternatively, a local league can be sponsored to allow management to move up the learning curve. Telstra was reported to have jointly sponsored the 2003 Rugby World Cup so that it could learn about how sponsorship worked. The cautious or delayed approach arising from testing can also cause opportunities to be lost, since the competition may snap up the best sponsorship programmes. It may however identify some opportunities and avoid some nasty problems.

Roll-out

This is the exciting side that everyone sees without fully realizing the amount of work that goes on beforehand. Nevertheless, it is deceptively hard work since, even though the sponsors are enjoying entertaining their clients, it is still work. In smaller sponsorship programmes sponsors have constantly to think on their feet while entertaining, as minute problems inevitably crop up from time to time. In larger sponsorship programmes the constant alertness, attention to detail and readiness to react can be shared between members of staff (or a consultancy). Staff will be interested in high-profile sponsorship programmes. Keep staff informed about how the programme is working and whether it is on target and generating results. Where possible, include programme prizes as staff incentives. Marks & Spencer sponsors projects that attract staff involvement.

Control – monitor, measure and evaluate

This is where the clearly defined sponsorship objectives make life easy, since results can be compared with predetermined targets. Once the result has been measured, further analysis as to why a programme was particularly successful or unsuccessful will help future sponsorship programmes. The first three objectives listed above, awareness, image and relations, would normally require some formal market research activity such as a survey. **There is, in addition, an interim method of evaluating sponsorship** – by the amount of media coverage or name mentions. There are many monitoring companies that provide such services.

35 days' continuous monitoring

When npower sponsored cricket, media monitoring services revealed it received:

- 350 hours of TV coverage (Channel 4 and Sky);
- 12,500 banner sightings;
- 625 references in the national press.

Cost: £18 million over three years.
Result: Spontaneous awareness up to 45 per cent.

Although cricket is on TV for long periods, its audience is often quite small. Sponsorship research company AGB divides broadcast time by audience size to give cricket a ranking of 67, less than half that of ice skating. There are other, sometimes simpler, approaches to measuring the effectiveness of sponsorship. For example, Volvo calculated that its $3 million tennis sponsorship generated 1.4 billion impressions (number of mentions or sightings times audience size), worth about $18 million in advertising. It is worth noting that this measures only the amount of media coverage or output. It does not measure the ultimate objectives of, say, increasing awareness, changing attitudes or improving relations with different groups. This is where money may have to be spent on commissioning a piece of research that looks inside, instead of outside, the minds of the target audience.

The other objectives can be relatively easily measured if a system of measurement is set up in the first place, eg everyone is briefed to log or identify the source of any enquiries from customers, agents or distributors. Then again, a common-sense approach may help to identify results, eg new distributors or increased sales, without changing any of the other elements of either the marketing or the communications mix (and assuming the competition has not had a strike or a factory fire).

Waffles or lager?

In 1979 Belgium was 'better known for its waffles than its lager'. When TV ads were beyond budget, sponsorship of the Queen's tennis tournament beckoned. TV exposure and tennis's 'aspirational and achievement' image matched Stella's objectives. Stella rose to number 1 in Britain's premium lager sector. Sales increased by 400 per cent.

Observer, 1 April 1988

Canon got good value for its money when it sponsored the Football League for a limited period only. As Frank Jefkins (1991) observed, 'Hardly an office in Britain is without a Canon machine. It only took £3 million and three years – peanuts in that sort of business when you think what the sales are valued at.'

sponsors' logo. Payment can be in cash or in kind. A sponsor's services or facilities are likely to have a much greater value than cost, eg a newspaper sponsoring a boxing match can offer the fight promoter free advertising space in return for exclusive sponsorship rights. The cost may be minimal if the newspaper is not selling all its advertising space, while the value to the promoter is, of course, much greater.

There are also various government sponsorship grant programmes that contribute significantly towards the cost. (Check for any government subsidies, eg Arts & Business has different subsidy programmes.)

The 3Ms (men/women, money and minutes) need to be budgeted for and built into plans. Who is responsible for what, eg the supporting advertising, the spin-off sales promotions, the hospitality tent, the invitations, the publicity, etc? Is it all handled by an agency or controlled and administered by the in-house team? Time can be the greatest constraint to leveraging a sponsorship programme fully, since there may be lots of great ideas for exploiting the opportunities to the full but each one takes time to plan and ultimately put into action. Some estimates suggest a minimum of nine months is needed to develop a proper sponsorship strategy and programme plan.

Sponsor being too clever

'There was a legislative inquiry into Nike's sponsorship deal with Brazilian football team. [Nike had negotiated a $400 million, 10-year kit sponsorship deal with the Brazilian Football Federation.] A sense that Nike had too much control over the country's affairs was magnified by original provisions in the contract allowing the company to promote 50 Nike branded Brazil friendly matches involving eight first team players...
With World Cup qualifiers and other friendlies to organize, it became clear that the original number of Nike friendlies was too large. In November 1999 Brazil found itself double booked to play two matches. This led to a second-string Brazil team playing in Australia, while most of the country's top stars featured in a game against Spain. Consequently last April Nike reduced the contractual number of games it would promote to two a year. Also under the initial contract – since changed – legal disputes with the CFB were to be settled outside of Brazil. "The CFB transferred part of its autonomy as a public entity to Nike," said Aldo Rebelo (head of the 25 member committee of Brazil's Lower House of Congress investigating Nike's sponsorship deal).'

Colitt and Garrahan (2001)

Budgets

Budget allocation may in fact determine programme choice rather than the other way around. The formulae for determining the sponsorship budget vary, but a rough rule of thumb suggests that the basic sponsorship fee should be at least doubled to get maximum leverage from the programme (Coca-Cola allows 16 times the sponsor fee to generate maximum leverage).

This then leaves a budget for supporting marketing activities such as advertising and publicity, and maybe even some direct marketing. It also allocates some money for other spin-off activities. For example, sponsors of the Olympics will tend to milk the sponsorship to the maximum by running sales promotions offering Olympic prizes and donations in addition to simply carrying the 'official Olympic

Advantages and disadvantages of sponsorship

Advantages of sponsorship

Sponsorship can be cost-effective (compared to advertising) in terms of reaching a particular audience. It does allow access to very specific types of audience that otherwise might be difficult to reach. Sponsorship can achieve many different objectives (see 'Objectives', page 345), including: increased awareness; image enhancement; improved relationships with many different publics; increased sales, sampling and database building; creating a platform for new promotional material; beating advertising bans, etc. It also offers creative opportunities, including the engagement of an audience in a relaxed atmosphere of goodwill. Hospitality events open doors and create a dialogue that conventional media simply cannot match. As Alan Mitchell (1997) says, 'sponsorship reaches the parts conventional advertising cannot'. Sponsorship lends itself to integrated communications and the cost-effectiveness of integrated activities. Finally, the effects of a sponsorship programme are measurable.

Even the uncontrollable nature of sponsorship is measurable. Consider the now classic case of the 1996 Olympic sponsors (which paid $40 million each). They were pleased to have the rights to the Winter Olympic games in Lillehammer thrown in free of charge. The US figure skater Nancy Kerrigan was violently attacked six weeks before the games began. The attack was masterminded by the ex-husband of her chief rival, Tonya Harding. However, interest in Kerrigan's recovery created an avalanche of media coverage before, during and after the event. The extra, unplanned coverage was carefully measured and valued by the sponsors.

Disadvantages of sponsorship

Some say that sponsorship is insidious and that it undermines artistic integrity. In areas such as health and education, some feel that the issues involved are too important to be left to the whim of a corporation. Although sponsorship can deliver extremely cost-effective benefits, it can be misunderstood as an excessive indulgence by employees if they are kept in the dark about it and if there are redundancies occurring at the same time. In both cases sponsorship, particularly high-profile sponsorship, needs to be presented to the employees as a cost-effective business tool that can help the business to survive and thrive in the future. Sponsorship of a competitive activity, such as a football club, can alienate the company or product from the opposition fans, eg a national audience if the teams are involved in an international competition, or an even larger audience if the team or player behaves badly. TSB got around this potential problem with an innovative sponsorship programme, which is explained in Case study 15.1.

Global media coverage may not be a good thing if what is being sponsored in one country is unacceptable in another country, eg bullfighting, camel

---

> ### Attention to detail: sponsor inside the shirt
>
> As sponsor of Middlesbrough, Cellnet emblazoned its name on the inside of top goal scorer Ravanelli's jersey, since his trademark after scoring is to lift his shirt inside out over his head.

---

wrestling, dwarf throwing, etc. If the medium is the message (ie the choice of sponsorship reflects the values of the sponsor), the message can become tarnished through its association with a socially unacceptable event. Some sponsorship deals can alienate a whole nation, particularly if the sponsor is perceived to have negotiated too good a deal for itself (See the box 'Sponsors being too clever' above). The uncontrollability of so many variables from weather to fans to strikes to riots makes sponsorship more risky than advertising. Even pop concerts are risky, as Naomi Klein (2000) points out: 'Celine Dion's concert tour was picketed by human rights activists in Boston, Philadelphia and Washington, DC. Although she was unaware of it, her tour sponsor – Ericsson cellular – was among Burma's most intransigent foreign investors, refusing to cease its dealings with the junta despite the campaign for an international boycott.' Finally, ambush marketing allows non-sponsoring competitors to soak up some benefits without paying full sponsorship fees.

Ambush marketing

Ambush marketers attack official event sponsors by running competing promotions, events and advertisements close to the official sponsors' activities. This way they create an aura of being official sponsors without paying the official sponsor fees. An example is the classic 1984 ambush by Kodak when it sponsored the ABC TV coverage despite Fuji being the official Olympics sponsor. In 1988 Kodak was the official Olympics sponsor while Fuji sponsored the US swimming team. Nike managed to 'ruin the 1996 Olympics for the official sponsors by ruthless advertising and by exploiting its star names' (Boshoff, 1997). The International Olympic Committee stepped in next time round by ordering that all poster sites in Athens be bought up and fairly distributed. For the 1998 World Cup, Adidas paid £20 million to be an official sponsor and, among other things, built a football village under the Eiffel Tower, while Nike responded with a site on the outskirts of Paris. Adidas signed up Paul Gascoigne, Paul Ince and David Beckham, as well as sponsoring the kit of nine teams, including Germany, France and Spain, while Nike sponsored six squads, including the favourites, Brazil (which cost £250 million over 10 years). The *Daily Telegraph* reported that 'rumours have it that Nike is willing to spend £20 million to hijack its arch-rivals Adidas during the competition in France'. Adidas planned a series of 'counter-stunts' and intended to 'ambush their ambush by having our own stunts and tricks'. Both companies supposedly had £20 million to spend on the five months up to and including the competition (on top of Adidas's sponsorship fee).

There is nothing really new in this, as ambush marketing has been around almost as long as sponsorship itself. Measurement of the 1991 Rugby World Cup broadcast sponsorship demonstrated its ability to influence consumers and override the main event sponsors. Spontaneous brand awareness of Sony rose among Rugby World Cup watchers by 8 points to 61 per cent (between September and November). Despite the recession, the company went on to record sales in December. Although Sony was not a sponsor of the event itself, it did sponsor the ITV coverage. ITV report that invariably the first name mentioned as sponsor of the rugby World Cup and overwhelmingly seen as the main sponsor was Sony.

However, overzealous policing can backfire. Pepsi was one of the official sponsors at the 2003 Cricket World Cup in South Africa. The drinks company had to distance itself from the embarrassment of the publicity surrounding the ejection of a fan caught drinking a can of Coca-Cola. Previously, Coca-Cola had been the official sponsor of the Football World Cup in Japan, where organizers had stopped fans from taking Pepsi into the stadium. This kind of action is not necessarily protecting sponsors from mainstream ambush marketing but is an indication of the attention to detail and the

lengths that event organizers will go to in order to protect the interests of sponsors. It can, however, backfire in publicity terms.

Shani and Sandler's (1989) study of ambush marketing revealed that it works. For example, Wendy's got what it wanted for about $20 million or so less than McDonald's spend. McDonald's didn't leverage its sponsorship well at all, advertising its super-value meals and Double Big Macs instead of its Olympic sponsorship.

For some 20 years now, the Olympics Committee has had clear anti-ambush guidelines, including the registering of all trademarks and emblems, coordination with city authorities to control the skies above venues, and ensuring that sponsors have first option for any broadcasting and advertising rights for the event in each country where the Olympics is shown on TV. In 2010 a beer company tried ambush marketing tactics inside the stadium by introducing a group of women wearing similar shirts. The women were ejected. The laws and regulations have become more stringent (the UK has specific Olympic legislation in place to stop ambush marketing).

Unpredictable sponsorship results from an ambushed knee

'When US skater Tonya Harding's associates hammered her main competitor Nancy Kerrigan's knee, they performed a dastardly deed – which happened to boost the fortunes of Kerrigan's sponsors, Campbell Soups, for the first time in a decade. Campbell was also a sponsor of the US Figure Skating Association. After the incident Campbell placed ads everywhere, and when Kerrigan recovered and came back to win silver Campbell's sales skyrocketed. Which just goes to show that no amount of planning could have produced the publicity it received from the wounded-knee incident and the sales bump that accompanied it. Campbell was even mistakenly perceived by the general public as a full-fledged Olympic sponsor in 1994, even though it wasn't.'

Schlossberg (1996)

CASE STUDY 15.1   TSB's Roy of the Rovers

This case study demonstrates how careful audience and media research identified a previously untapped sponsorship opportunity that was integrated with PR to gain access to a traditionally difficult target market.

Situation

TSB research identified sport, particularly athletics and soccer, as a key active interest of its young customers. Success in sport demands discipline and control. Young people, research demonstrates, demand control of their money. TSB's youth products offer a mechanism to help control spending (eg an instantly updated account that prevents young customers from the nightmare of an unwanted and unauthorized overdraft). The overall marketing strategy for the youth market was therefore founded on sport and financial control, and linked TSB as the bank for, and in touch with, young people. In an Olympic year the bank became a £5.2 million sponsor of major British athletics meetings.

Account opening incentives, supported by TV and press coverage, focused on money off anything from Nike trainers to Head tennis rackets at Olympus Stores. The media relations campaign focused on money control issues like 'buying a banger', 'getting a holiday job' or 'setting up a home of your own'.

The athletics opportunity had been seized, but the soccer opportunity presented a somewhat more difficult challenge. The glamour of football is sometimes tainted by uncontrollable risks such as injuries, foul play, sendings-off, disciplinary committees, boardroom coups, protesting fans, rotten results, on- and off-the-pitch violence and, of course, the weather. What marketing directors, with top brands in their custody, want their logo in full colour in a national paper if it is on the shirt of a player just sent off for a vicious and cynical foul, or if it is being worn by a mass of rioting fans?

Having said all that, football does attract audiences – intense, loyal, largely young, male, with leisure time and money to spend and save. Boys aged 7 to 12 are all targets for the bank's FirstSave account. Banks want to recruit young customers, since such customers normally stay with the same bank for life and because at least 50 per cent of these accounts are opened before the age of 16. Whether this is lethargy or loyalty is unclear, but it does reinforce lifetime value.

The dilemma

TSB faced the soccer dilemma at the launch of the Premier League's first season. The bank, a big institution, was ready to act quickly, and it set aside a budget to take advantage of any creative media opportunities.

Objective

To reinforce the link between TSB and one of its youth markets.

Strategy

The strategy was sponsorship of Melchester Rovers, supported by a media relations campaign. Melchester Rovers are the 'perfect' soccer team, which pull in 125,000 schoolboy spectators week in, week out regardless of the weather. Its captain is not only best mates with ex-England captain Gary Lineker, but even more saintly. There are no riots, no drink-driving, no smashed-up hotel bars and no spurned love children. The results can even be found out months ahead, and they usually win. The star player of this model team, Roy of the Rovers, and his squad are, of course, mythical. Roy has been Britain's best-loved footballer since his debut, in 1954, on the pages of the boys' comic *Tiger* (since 1976 he has had a comic named after him).

Tactics

In the comic, TSB logos feature on Melchester's red and yellow strip and on perimeter boards around the ground. Storylines around banking and young people are written into the comic. Competitions give away Olympus kit. There are covermounts (sales promotions attached to the comic itself).

Action

The media relations campaign involved a clear strategy:

- The race to sign up a legendary team was leaked to and covered by national TV and newspapers on a quiet Monday in the dog days of August.

- Roy and his agent, Dave Hunt (in reality his editor), were 'snatched' leaving secret talks at the Tower Hotel.

- The leak served two purposes: it put the comic back on the map, with the aim of widening the audience for TSB's sponsorship, and it ensured a packed turnout for the press conference and launch.

- The press conference to announce the sponsorship was held at the Tower Hotel and was hosted by sports broadcaster Danny Baker.

Control

The sponsorship programme launch gained media coverage on national and local TV, and in the national and regional press. New account openings jumped ahead of target.

Men/women

PR consultancy the Quentin Bell Organization (QBO) worked closely and intensively with the TSB marketing team.

Money

The sponsorship fee was £20,000, with an additional £12,000 media relations budget.

Minutes

TSB and QBO moved at breakneck speed and achieved concept to launch within three weeks.

> ### No war during the World Cup
>
> 'There will never be another war while the World Cup is being played because there would be no media coverage.'
>
> Jeff Bliss, World Cup USA Licensing Executive

Advantages and disadvantages summary

Here is a summary of some of the advantages and disadvantages to consider when deciding whether to increase or reduce this communications tool.

Advantages

Sponsorship can establish awareness and help to build a brand and its presence in a market. It can also generate goodwill and affection if managed correctly. Sponsorship programmes can be used for employee motivation schemes. Sponsorship is more effective than advertising on a CPT basis and can also engage customers if the sponsorship is leveraged into other environments such as websites, games and user-generated content. Sponsorship can be used to spread awareness over global markets (eg the World Cup) or local niches (eg a local art theatre).

Disadvantages

Sponsorship cannot close sales; it only creates awareness. It can carry only a very limited message (for the masses), usually just a brand name, although some brands leverage the sponsorship into many diverse aspects, which allows more detailed brand value messages. The message cannot be controlled, eg a football hooligan wearing a club shirt with a sponsor's brand can be on the front page of a newspaper attacking a police officer. Guerrilla marketing can also damage the sponsor's impact. It is not so easy to change a message or to exit a sponsorship programme quickly (unless carefully planned). As with PR, there is a lack of control, as strikes, riots, weather and media all affect the impact of sponsorship.

Key points from Chapter 15

- Almost anything can be sponsored.
- Almost any target audience can be reached through sponsorship.
- Choose sponsorship programmes carefully, and separate the initial excitement from the numerical analysis.
- Sponsorship can provide a cost-effective marketing communications tool, satisfying a range of different objectives.
- Maximize leverage by integrating sponsorship with other communications tools.
- Sponsorship does not have total control over the message. Have contingency plans in case things go wrong.

- Think global, but act local (today's satellite communications may highlight a sponsorship programme that is acceptable overseas but unacceptable at home and vice versa).
- Budgets should be secured to leverage the programme and maximize impact through other communications tools.
- Keep employees informed. Sometimes getting them involved increases the leverage.
- Run a small pilot scheme, if possible, to iron out any teething problems.
- Beware of ambush marketing.

References and further reading

Atkinson, S (2007) Why just a logo is now a no-no, *BBC News*, 21 June

Boshoff, A (1997) World Cup's battle of the boots, *Daily Telegraph*, 4 December

Colitt, R and Garrahan, M (2001) Nike finds Brazil deal a bad fit, *Financial Times*, 12 January, p 19

Giles, C (1991) *Business Sponsorship*, Butterworth-Heinemann, Oxford

Head, V (1981) *Sponsorship: The newest marketing skill*, Woodhead-Faulkner, Cambridge

IOL (2006) The year of golf in space, *IOL.com*, 7 December

Jefkins, F (1991) *Modern Marketing Communications*, Blackie & Son, London

Klein, N (2000) *No Logo*, Flamingo, London

Mitchell, A (1997) Sponsorship works, *Marketing Business*, September

Schlossberg, H (1996) *Sports Marketing*, Blackwell, Oxford

Shani, D and Sandler, D (1989) Olympic sponsorship versus ambush marketing, *Journal of Advertising Research*, August/September

Shank, M (2002) *Sports Marketing: A strategic perspective*, 2nd edn, Prentice Hall, Englewood Cliffs, NJ

Thomaselli, R (2006) Dream endorser: Tiger Woods as a giant of marketing ROI, *Ad Age*, 24 September

Turner, S (1987) *Practical Sponsorship*, Kogan Page, London

WARC (2005) Coke pours $500 million into soccer sponsorship, 24 November

Further information

Arts & Business
Nutmeg House
60 Gainsford Street
Butler's Wharf
London SE1 2NY
Tel: +44 (0)20 7378 8143
Fax: +44 (0)20 7407 7527
www.artsandbusiness.org.uk

Business in the Community
137 Shepherdess Walk
London N1 7RQ
Tel: +44 (0)20 7566 8650
www.bitc.org.uk

European Sponsorship Association (ESA) Office
Suite 1
Claremont House
22–24 Claremont Road
Surbiton
Surrey KT6 4QU
Tel: +44 (0)20 8390 3311
Fax: +44 (0)20 8390 0055
www.sponsorship.org

European Sponsorship Consultants Association
(ESCA)
34 Pensford Avenue
Kew
Richmond
Surrey TW9 4HP
Tel: +44 (0)20 8395 9895
www.esca.com

Institute of Sports Sponsorship
4th Floor
Warwick House
25–27 Buckingham Palace Road
London SW1W 0PP
Tel: +44 (0)20 7233 7747
www.sportsmatch.co.uk,
www.sportssponsorship.co.uk

Ofcom
Riverside House
2a Southwark Bridge Road
London SE1 9HA
Tel: +44 (0)300 123 3000
Fax: +44 (0)20 7981 3333
www.ofcom.org.uk

Sponsorship News
The Meeting Room
Unit 301b
The Aberdeen Centre
22–24 Highbury Grove
London N5 2EA
Tel: +44 (0)20 7485 2111
Fax: +44 (0)20 7485 2555
www.sponsorshipnews.com/content/en/
sponsorship-news.aspx

16
Sales promotions – online and offline

LEARNING OBJECTIVES

By the end of this chapter you will be able to:

- Discuss the difference between strategic sales promotions and tactical sales promotions
- Separate brand-enhancing sales promotions from brand-diluting sales promotions
- Begin to integrate sales promotions with other elements of the communications mix
- Work in a team developing sales promotions and understand the campaign management process
- Avoid the typical costly trial and error
- See that there is room for enhanced creativity, as social media has opened up a vast range of collaborative opportunities

Introduction

Sales promotion is big business. **In fact, it is bigger than advertising in the UK.** Its growth has been fuelled by several factors, including:

- the movement towards relationship marketing (and rewarding loyal customers);
- the growth of direct mail (and incentives);
- the emergence of promotion-literate customers who expect promotions with certain product types;
- during recessions, price-conscious customers searching for value-for-money promotions;
- powerful retailers favouring suppliers whose products sell quickly (because of heavy advertising, exciting promotions or both);
- high television advertising costs forcing marketing managers to look for more cost-effective, below-the-line tools such as sales promotions.

Isolating and calculating the exact industry figures is difficult since, first, forfeited revenues from price promotions (discounts) are included in the size of sales promotions expenditure and, second, some companies categorize promotions as part of PR, ie some companies pay for a sales promotion such as free information booklets out of their sales promotion budget, while others see it as part of public relations. Whichever way it is looked at, sales promotion is a below-the-line activity that can be used externally with end users (customers) and intermediaries (trade distributors) and also internally with an organization's own sales force. **Sales promotions, premiums, incentives and motivation schemes are used for both products and services in consumer, business-to-business and industrial markets.** There are three main categories:

1 customer promotions (premiums, gifts, prizes and competitions, eg on the back of breakfast cereal boxes);

2 trade promotions (special terms, point-of-sale materials, free pens, diaries, competition prizes, etc);

3 sales force promotions (incentive and motivation schemes; see Chapter 12, 'Motivating' for an explanation of how these become a form of psychic income).

Advantages and disadvantages

Whether they take the form of competitions, price reductions, free gifts, coupons, samples, special demonstrations, displays or point-of-sale, consumer sales promotions tend to affect the later stages of the communications and buying process (see Chapter 4, 'Models of buyer behaviour'), ie they trigger action such as a purchase or increased usage of a particular brand, whereas advertising tends to affect the earlier stages, such as awareness, interest and desire (there are exceptions, particularly where direct response advertising is concerned). However, sales promotions are an expensive way of generating awareness and need to be supported by advertising PR and social media. **Sales promotions are action orientated, particularly as they often tempt the buyer to buy, or at least try, a product or service.** These kinds of promotions often provide the final nudge that moves a customer towards buying a particular product or service.

Free Ladas boost sales by 36 per cent

After several seasons of declining gates, Russian football club Zenit used a simple sales promotion to boost attendances up to 26,000. Entry costs 1.5 roubles and tickets for the Ladas lottery cost 1 rouble. Ladas cost 8,000 roubles (equivalent to three years' salary for the average industrial worker). The biggest roar of the evening comes not as the two teams run out on to the pitch but when the three cream-coloured Ladas are driven on to the running track. The opportunity of winning a Lada just pulls in the crowd.

In terms of learning about brands and learning to use them frequently, many sales promotions, and the involvement they create (by filling in forms, collecting coupons, posting application forms, trying a free sample, etc), are considered by some to be a form of operant conditioning as demonstrated by Skinner's rats (see Chapter 4). Advertising, on the other hand, is thought by some to help buyers to learn and remember brands and their benefits by repeating the message and building associations between brands, logos, images and benefits, a form of classical conditioning as demonstrated by Pavlov's dog (see Chapter 4). Well-thought-out sales promotions that embrace the brand values and deliver real customer benefits can be enormously successful. For example, Tesco's Computers for Schools sales promotion has been running for several years, and in that time two-thirds of UK schools have actively participated, with millions of consumers. Promotions must establish a clear and desirable proposition for the target audience. Then ask: does the promotion support the brand's longer-term strategy (support the brand values)? Promotions should strengthen the brand image.

Some promotions fail for two reasons: 1) they have no link to the brand values and long-term branding; 2) they have had no attention paid to detail, so problems emerge, such as fulfilment (eg pubs find SMS promotions offering money-off vouchers to be labour-intensive, since staff have to be trained). See 'Disaster promotions' below for major disasters by, surprisingly, major brands.

Some promotions, on the other hand, enhance or add value to the image of the product or service. They can strengthen the brand. These types of promotions build 'consumer franchise'. This means that the gift is in some way related to the brand, its image or its properties (eg Johnnie Walker's gentleman with top hat and tails). Franchise-building promotions contrast with price and discount offers that dilute brand values and do not enhance brand loyalty, despite boosting short-term sales. The now classic Miss Pears competition reinforces the brand image of gentle, natural soap. This is consumer franchise building. **Consumer franchise-building (CFB) promotions tend to have longer-term implications and are therefore more strategically driven,** while non-CFB promotions can be driven by shorter-term tactical goals.

Freebies not required (always)

'It is a popular misconception that loyalty schemes have to give things away; special service or treatment can work too.'

J Bird (1997)

There is much room for more creative flair in sales promotions (see 'Creative sales promotions' below).

Effective sales promotions can creatively build the brand franchise while achieving many other objectives, such as increasing sales, cementing loyalty, building databases, generating publicity and more.

Disaster promotions

Despite the phenomenal size of the sales promotions industry and the data available for analysis, there are a frightening number of sales promotions that are relatively ineffective, and some are actually damaging in terms of branding, sales and cash flow. Take price promotions such as discount vouchers, two for the price of one, a free extra 10 per cent: they can help to boost sales in the short term, but what do they do to the brand in the long term? Discount the price and you discount the brand down to a point where it loses its brand values and competes solely on price (which is not a protectable competitive advantage). So many sales promotions damage the core values, the image and the positioning of the brand. Other promotions attract only promiscuous consumers who switch back to another brand as soon as the promotion is over.

Some promotions create a temporary boost in sales followed by an immediate drop, as customers who initially bought more and stocked up then stop buying until they have used up their extra stock (as shown in Figure 16.1). Other promotions actually damage the brand image and even the holding company's corporate image, sales, profits and cash flow (eg Hoover's £48 million fiasco; see below).

As with most marketing communications tools, things can go wrong with sales promotions and

FIGURE 16.1 Some promotions boost sales temporarily as customers stock up but don't come back for twice as long

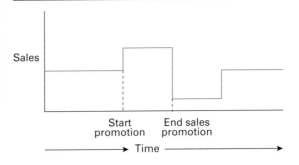

destroy many excellent ideas that have apparently been meticulously planned. Sample packs may burst and destroy other goods, or premiums may be pilfered. There can be problems of misredemption (non-buyers acquire other buyers' coupons), malre-demption (large-scale fraudulent coupon redemption), over-redemption (with millions claiming their prizes), or door-drop samples that the dog or child gets to before the adult. The possibilities of a mini-marketing disaster seem endless. In addition, the *Competitors' Companion*, a monthly subscription magazine, publishes news and views on which competitions are running, what prizes they offer, exactly where to get entry forms, which qualifiers are required (eg a label) and the closing dates. According to the magazine, 'You receive advice on the answers to their questions plus a regular list of winning slogans and tie breakers... that way, you can read what's catching the judge's eye today and make them work for you tomorrow.' Here are a few cases of promotions that went wrong, even for the biggest and the best of marketing companies:

- *Typhoo Tea's Cash Pot promotion*. In 1984 Cadbury Typhoo was reported to have had to make cash payouts of more than £1 million. According to *Marketing Week* Cadbury Typhoo's insurers were reported to have issued a High Court writ against the company seeking a 'declaration that some claims made by Cash Pot competitors are outside the rules of the competition'. Nevertheless, the expensive promotion apparently increased its market share to its 'highest level since its relaunch in 1982', but at what cost?

- *Coca-Cola's MagiCan*. In 1990 Coca-Cola's US promotion was supported by a massive $100 million push. The MagiCan looked, weighed and felt (even when shaken) like a regular can. When the tab was pulled, the winning cans had a mechanism inside that pushed real rolled-up dollar notes through the hole in the top of the can. Cash prizes ranged from $5 to $200. The winning cans had some extra liquid to ensure the cans weighed and felt the same. Inevitably there were a few duds. Most of them just didn't work, but in a few cases the seal that held the 'liquid that gives the can the feel of the real thing' had broken. Although it was not

harmful, one small boy (who was not aware of the promotion) drank the liquid and public health officials were called in. Massive media attention followed; 750,000 cans were held back while each one was shaken to determine whether the seal was broken or not. An immediate TV and press campaign was put into action to explain the promotion and to warn customers not to drink the liquid if the seal was broken (*Marketing*, 31 May 1990).

- *Pepsi's special bottle top* was offered by its Philippine subsidiary with a 1 million pesos (£26,000) prize to anyone finding a bottle top with the number 349. Pepsi paid out £8 million before it realized that thousands of winning bottle tops were appearing everywhere. When payment stopped there were public demonstrations; then Pepsi plants were attacked with grenades, and Pepsi lorries were burnt (three people were killed). Pepsi executives hired bodyguards before fleeing the country.

- *Heinz recipe book* was a printed recipe book promotional offer on its Pickering Fruit Pie Fillings. Heinz forgot to print a reply address, so no one could participate in the promotion.

- *KFC plastic figures* seemed like a good idea (giving a free plastic figure in some of its meals as a promotion). Although they tested the plastic for proximity to hot food, they did not test it for children sucking off the plastic and poking their eyes with the remaining wire. Personal injury claims followed.

- *Macy's department store talent promotion* was designed to find an Annie for a new production of the Broadway show *Annie*. The lucky 12-year-old winner later made even bigger news when she sued Macy's after she was 'dumped' from the production.

- *Hoover free flights to New York* were offered to anyone purchasing any Hoover over £100. Wrong comparisons with response rates from dissimilar 'two flights for the price of one' promotions prompted wildly inaccurate forecast response rates. (The company forecast 5,000 responses and received 600,000!) The fixed-fee limit of £500,000 was agreed with the relatively small travel agent. When the agency went bust, Hoover was exposed to a massive response (insurance is essential). Meanwhile the trade increased prices of the cheaper Hoover models to over £100 so that effectively any Hoover purchase qualified for free flights (Hoover should have restricted the offer to certain models). The promotion cost £48 million, careers and corporate image.

- *Kraft Foods' 'Win a free camper van' promotion* had a computer error that generated hundreds of winners. As the prize-winners' claims kept coming in, Kraft realized there was a problem. Some disappointed customers vowed never to buy the firm's food products again. Others sought legal action.

- *Vidal Sassoon shampoo samples.* According to *Marketing Breakthroughs* (1991), half a million special free sample minipacks of Vidal Sassoon shampoo were distributed in 1991 throughout Poland. When news of the promotion spread, around 2,000 mailboxes (mostly at apartment blocks) were pillaged. The sample packs then started appearing in street markets and soon sold out. The extra costs incurred by the damaged mailboxes added a new dimension to the sales promotion review process.

- *Alamo Car Hire's free car hire* flopped in Germany. Alamo normally offers one free day's car hire with every 30-day hire. This was fine until it discovered that it is illegal in Germany to give anything free after just one transaction. The international arena further complicates the life of the sales promotion professional, as regulations vary enormously.

- *Coca-Cola and McDonald's* got into trouble with Coca-Cola's special-edition round bottle, which was a potential 2006 World Cup collector's item – available from McDonald's outlets in the host country Germany as well as Austria, Hungary and Poland during the tournament. This fell foul of Germany's strict waste recycling regulations. Although it was stamped with the word *Mehrwegflasche*, indicating it was returnable, McDonald's did not charge the customary deposit meant to ensure the bottle was returned for recycling. The environmental lobby threatened legal action if McDonald's continued to advertise or sell the bottles.

The moral of the story? Check all possible disaster scenarios. Get advice from third parties. Test the promotion. Take out promotional insurance: professional indemnity insurance covers an agency's duty of care to its clients; product recall insurance protects against the cost of a recall of products or promotional gifts; over-redemption insurance protects against an unexpectedly high response. Whether the client pays or the agency pays is an issue that needs to be clearly agreed long before any sales promotion campaign rolls out.

There is, arguably, a worse scenario. No one responds to the sales promotion. Large stocks of premiums are left in the warehouse, and teams of order fulfilment staff (who dispatch the prizes) sit around with nothing to do.

New sales promotions

Creative sales promotions

There is always room for creative innovation. Whether it's a trip to the moon or a party in an underground nuclear shelter, the only limitation to potential sales promotion creation is one's imagination. If it is stunningly successful, it is likely that the competition will follow, unless the innovative promotion relates uniquely to the brand in a creative way. This is demonstrated by the *Sunday Sport* tabloid newspaper.

Is your mother-in-law an alien?

The *Sunday Sport* offered a free test kit that helped readers to determine whether their mothers-in-law were, in fact, aliens. The paper sold out within hours.

This 'alien mother-in-law' type of promotion is arguably just a stunt designed to generate publicity that may, at least temporarily, increase levels of awareness, boost circulation and also reinforce readers' loyalty by rewarding them with a gift that appeals to their mentality. Because the gift is relevant to both the target reader's sense of humour and the newspaper's image, it adds to the paper's branding. In a way it adds to the brand franchise or builds consumer franchise.

One sales promotion that might have impressed mothers-in-law was for Cadbury. When it launched its white chocolate, Snowflake, agency Triangle achieved significant consumer trial by negotiating a covermount of a free bar on *OK!* magazine. When it discovered that the same issue was featuring Anthea Turner's wedding, it persuaded *OK!* to give free bars to all the celebrity guests. The additional brand exposure enabled Cadbury to hit the media headlines, gain an estimated £1 million worth of editorial coverage, and ensure a spectacular launch success as a result.

Creativity and originality can work well together, as when NatWest Bank's sales promotions and direct marketing were combined as a 'direct promotion' (most mailshots use an incentive). NatWest moved away from the traditional clock/radio/calculator/travel-bag type of incentive used by the banks from time to time. Instead it offered the choice of 1 of 10 limited-edition prints that were specially commissioned from five artists. It mailed to 65,000 names (who were thought to have over £25,000 to invest) and received a 12.3 per cent response (instead of the targeted 5 per cent response level). Another highly creative and popular promotion was Guinness's inflatable armchair, which formed part of its campaign as sponsor of the Rugby World Cup. An application for the armchair was even received from Buckingham Palace!

Another highly effective yet high-risk sales promotion was created to support the Maxwell House relaunch. To provide a unique brand-related promotional campaign, agency Triangle persuaded TV personality Noel Edmonds to telephone people at random while floating across the country in the hot-air balloon featured in its advertising. Half a million pounds was given away, including a top prize of £100,000, and the brand recorded its highest market share ever during the promotional period. Highly creative sales promotions may involve an element of risk. Insurance (indemnity insurance, redemption insurance, etc) is advised with all sales promotions, but particularly recommended with highly creative and high-risk promotions. Incidentally, creative thinkers will spot the creative PR opportunities that can be exploited when creative sales promotions are developed. These can spread through social media networks, and the press are usually interested.

Social-media-driven sales promotions are explored in the case studies with three promotions where users generate poetry and music (rap), digital art and a musical soundtrack (for a film).

One other dimension that creative thinkers can explore is the huge synergies and creative potential released by marketing marriages, or joint promotions. Before all of this, consider virtual gifts as sales promotion tools in the online world and, in particular, the social media world.

Build a rocket to the moon

Google co-founders Brin and Page even have their eyes on space: they have offered a $20 million prize to anyone who can make a privately financed spacecraft able to land on the moon.

D Smith (2008)

Virtual gifts

Although marketers are puzzled by why consumers pay real money for non-existent goods (virtual goods), there is an element of conspicuous consumption involved. Marketers understand how this influences both offline and online buyer behaviour, particularly if it either is a collectable item or has status symbol attachment, or both. **The virtual American Greetings case (Case study 21.2) demonstrates how the difference between the virtual world and the real world is blurring all the time.** The film *The Matrix* explained this in a more dramatic manner. This is all brought back down to earth in the box opposite by Michael Zeisser with a useful analysis of virtual gifts.

So why do consumers want online objects that don't actually exist?

'While the notion of virtual goods – nonphysical objects used in online communities and games – still puzzles many executives, it's quite apparent that consumers love them. People acquire or compete for virtual items obsessively on Foursquare, Zynga, and many other sites. It is estimated that virtual goods have become a very real $5 billion industry worldwide.

'So why do consumers pay real money for online objects that don't actually exist? Their motives reinforce our notion that users seek online importance: they purchase virtual goods primarily for self-expression (such as virtual houses or virtual gifts) and for recognition (such as virtual badges for becoming, say, the 'mayor' of a bar on Foursquare). These behaviours are too widespread and intense to be fads, and marketers need to recognize them as meaningful. Brands should actively experiment with ways to use virtual goods as catalysts of word-of-mouth media.

'In the context of a social network, it is not a stretch to conceive of virtual gifts as important objects, especially as their availability can be strictly limited. Just think about the fervor consumers accord collectibles of all kinds, from baseball cards to dolls to coins. If virtual items prove similarly desirable, they are likely to be a big deal for consumers and marketers, as well as a great tool to create useful word-of-mouth media.

'We've also found that basic laws of consumer behaviour still apply: consumers love a bargain, and companies should take full advantage of social networks as powerful notification tools. Users can be alerted to sales or to the expiration of a promotion, but companies must be mindful that these feeds and tweets are designed as catalysts to generate virtual word-of-mouth media. They are not social-media junk mail, but legitimate content objects – actual pieces of media that we want the initial recipients to distribute to their friends.

'One final recommendation: no gimmicks. Forget dancing monkeys, artificial contests, or stupid tricks; they add no value and waste people's time. A commitment to being useful in social-media activities means a commitment to creating only high-quality interactions.'

Zeisser (2010)

Joint promotions

Joint promotions and cross-promotions have been going on for more than a quarter of a century. These marketing marriages offer economical routes to target the same customers with relevant offers. Cathy Bond (1991) gives this example: Coca-Cola led its army of soft drinks brands into a joint promotion with Cadbury in spring 1991. It was only a matter of time before arch-rival Pepsi popped up with another mega-brand deal, in this case with Kellogg's. When Deep Pan Pizza created a joint promotion with Lego, giving children free branded toys, sales of children's meals doubled. The choice of toys was changed every quarter to encourage re-peat visits, and the cost was built into the price of the meal. Caution must be exercised when choosing a partner. Equal-standing brands, budgets and branding details need to be clarified, with nothing left to chance. Stuart Hardy, Managing Director of WLK (which married Mothercare and Lever's Persil in a joint promotion), says, 'In any true relationship each side is going to have 50 per cent of the say. A lot of marketing people want 100 per cent of the say and only 50 per cent of the costs.' Although there are lots of opportunities, relatively few joint promotions seem to get off the ground. 'For every one joint promotion that gets off the ground, 10 never make it', says Roger Hyslop (1989). As with any partnership, the devil is in the detail. It must be agreed and specified who actually does what and gets what, including databases, space allocation, preferences, etc.

Social-media-driven sales promotions

Social media has become an essential element of any sales promotion campaign, as word spreads fast across social media platforms. Social media is 'social', and that means people like to be sociable, by keeping in contact, sharing relevant (useful or fun) information. In fact, people's image or status is increased if they have sourced 'free stuff' or special offers, particularly if the offers are limited offers. **Spreading useful information about sales promotions adds value to the connection,** and people are deemed more worthwhile the more good stuff they have to share, so sales promotions naturally lend themselves to social media. See 'Virtual gifts' above and the three case studies below, which demonstrate how user-generated promotions for poetry and music (rap), digital art and a soundtrack for a movie can make attractive sales promotions, which in this case are mostly driven purely by social media.

Integrated promotions

Sales promotions integrate with other marketing communications tools, particularly packaging ('on-pack' promotions), point-of-sale, merchandising, sponsorship, PR, advertising, selling and, of course, social media. Traditionally, advertising-supported promotions do better than ones that are not supported. There are, however, many occasions when media support cannot be afforded or where point-of-sale materials flagging the offer are considered to be more cost-effective than above-the-line support. In fact, this chapter shows three sales promotions that work entirely through social media channels

Coke auctions

Coke's innovative Coke Auction campaign combined sales promotions and packaging with the unique online facility of online auctions, offline radio and TV advertisements, and online e-mail viral marketing. Online auctions harness some of the internet's unique functions. With innovation at the helm, Coke has somehow converted the normally discarded ring pulls into online currency called unsurprisingly 'Coke credits'. These credits are then used to bid for items from sports tickets to becoming stars in Coke ads (having their faces on the Coke signs) in major advertising venues.

Smith and Chaffey (2001)

and platforms. But even a great sales promotion fails if no one knows about it. Some support, whether advertising, point-of-sale, PR or social media, is therefore required. Creative promotional ideas command press coverage, so some budget should always be left for PR requirements (stocks of photos, transparencies, websites and social media platforms with downloadable images and news items, etc).

Managing a sales promotion

Planning the campaign

The SOSTAC® + 3Ms checklist can be used to build a sales promotion plan. The situation analysis requires research into past, present and possible future campaigns, combined with a clear analysis of the target market.

Situation (research)

Research is required at most stages of the development of the sales promotion. An initial review of previous promotions (including competitors' promotions) can be followed by further research into the target market.

In addition to the usual demographic and psychographic information, further analysis may reveal what Philip Kotler (2000) identifies as three types of new triers who are attracted to (and respond to) sales promotion offers: 1) users of a competing brand in the same category, 2) users in other categories, and 3) frequent brand switchers. 'Deal-prone customers', the brand switchers, tend not to be loyal and are likely to switch away to the next low-price or free-gift offer that comes their way. **In the UK, Peter Holloway (1989a), former Managing Director of MS Surveys, calls this last group 'promiscuous nomads', who can be easily bought and lost the next day** – but at what cost? The group at the other end of the target market loyalty spectrum are called 'the immovables', who are locked into brand loyalty. 'No amount of promotional effort will move them, so there is no point wasting money on them', says Holloway. The real target group within the target market are called the 'loyal susceptibles'. Holloway says that 'they are there to be won (or lost if they are your brand customers) and once their loyalty is broken, their new-found loyalties can be well worth having'.

Crossing the bridge

'Crossing the bridge from your own island of subjective presumptions to the land of the real-life target consumer can be as revealing, remove as many uncertainties and avoid as many clangers as having a full medical check-up, or consulting a map before you go somewhere new. The first step towards making promotions, etc, work better for you is knowing who you really ought to be talking to.'

Holloway (1989a)

Knowing exactly who these people are and why they are more susceptible is the key to the sales promotions tapping into their susceptibilities, which in turn will increase market share beyond a short-term temporary boost.

After the real target market has been analysed, the eventual sales promotion concept should be researched in focus groups or at least with sample customers. When the idea or promotional tool is agreed, it is still worth testing it in a limited area or customer group to reveal any hidden problems or even opportunities before launching it nationally or internationally.

Sales promotion objectives

As the name suggests, a promotion is a limited-period offer. It is therefore not surprising to find that sales promotions tend to have shorter-term tactical objectives (although, as previously explained, this need not be the case).

Some typical sales promotion goals might be:

1 Increase sales (although it may be only a temporary increase, because customers can simply stock up with the goods or temporarily switch brands while the promotion is running) by:
   – rewarding loyal customers;
   – locking customers into loyalty programmes (where they have to keep buying the product or service over a period of time in order to collect the right number of coupons, vouchers, or items in a collection);
   – increasing the repurchase rates of occasional users;
   – generating trials among new customers (by triggering an impulse purchase);
   – demonstrating new features or modifications or introducing a new product or service;
   – developing new uses;
   – image development (awareness or repositioning);
   – deseasonalizing seasonal sales (eg skiing holidays in the summer).
2 Develop new sales leads.
3 Satisfy retailers with a complete package – gain trade acceptance.
4 Move excess stock.
5 Block a competitor (by offering incentives to customers to stock up).
6 Match a competitor (eg petrol tokens).
7 Build a database (some promotions also act as database builders: see how the Rothmans offer of a free pack collected 750,000 customer names, in Chapter 3, 'Database opens up new sales' box).
8 Generate publicity.

Matching types of promotions with specific objectives

Some sales promotion tools are more appropriate than others in achieving certain objectives (Table 16.1).

Some efforts have been made to rank the effectiveness of specific tools ('mechanics') against various objectives. Cummins (2003) identified how certain sales promotion techniques match up with various objectives (Table 16.2).

Strategy

All promotions should be part of a bigger and longer-term strategy. Longer-term sales promotion strategies are about building and reinforcing brand image, strengthening user loyalty, and even inviting

TABLE 16.1   Matching promotions with objectives

Objective	Promotional tool
Consumer	
Trial	Sampling; couponing; free draw; price-off; self-liquidator (send in some money, which pays the costs of the promotion); premiums; in-pack; on-pack; near-pack; reusable container; personality promotion
Retrial	Coupon for next purchase; price-off
Increase usage	Collections; games; competitions; extra-quantity or bonus packs; price-off multiple purchase
Develop new uses	Companion brand promotions; publications; workshops
Image development	Publications; sponsorship; charity
Trade	
Increase distribution, shelf facings or displays	Discount; extended credit; point-of-sale materials; tie-in with advertising
In-store promotion	Discount; extended credit; point-of-sale materials; tie-in with advertising; consumer offer; promotion allowance
Increase sales	Sales competitions and rebates (mostly independent stores and wholesalers)
Cement good relations	Gifts, holidays and awards
Sales force	
Sales and distribution	Psychic income and financial income

new users to join the club, as opposed to short-term tactical sales boosts. Whether planned on a one-off tactical basis or on a more structured strategic approach basis, the sales promotion can have an impact on the brand or organization's overall image (eg Hoover). Corporate image is central to the longer-term strategic communications of the organization. Tracking studies (or continual market research) can monitor changes in specific aspects or dimensions of an organization's corporate or specific brand image.

Some organizations see promotions as only a short-term tactical tool to support what they call the more strategic communication tools such as advertising. Realistically, however, it is not always possible to achieve strategic goals if the client does not want them in the first place. Roger Hyslop (1989), Chairman and Founder of the Triangle Group, gives an example of a retailer who says: 'I don't need this promotion to add to my brand image, otherwise I wouldn't be spending millions on television. What I need is to bring 50,000 people in to see my store opening.' The difficulty is compounded by the fact that strategic promotions may sometimes not generate maximum customer response in the immediate short term. Should the longer-term image-building capability of a sales promotion be forfeited for the shorter-term tactical 'trial sales'

Strategic impact of sales promotions

'Years ago, Heinz used to say that they saw more far-reaching effects on image dimensions of their tracking studies from their sales promotion schemes than they ever saw resulting from advertising campaigns.'

Castling (1989)

TABLE 16.2   Linking the objective to the mechanics: how they match up

Objectives	Immediate free offers	Delayed free offers	Immediate price offers	Delayed price offers	Finance offers	Competitions	Games and draws	Charitable offers	Self-liquidators	Profit-making promotions
Increasing volume	9	7	9	7	5	1	3	5	2	1
Increasing trial	9	7	9	2	9	2	7	7	2	1
Increasing repeat purchase	2	9	2	9	5	3	2	7	3	3
Increasing loyalty	1	9	0	7	3	3	1	7	3	3
Widening usage	9	5	5	2	3	1	5	5	1	1
Creating interest	3	3	3	2	2	5	9	8	8	8
Creating awareness	3	3	3	1	1	5	9	8	8	8
Deflecting attention from price	9	7	0	7	7	3	5	5	2	2
Gaining intermediary support	9	5	9	5	9	3	7	5	1	1
Gaining display	9	5	9	5	9	3	7	5	1	1

Each square is filled with a rating from 0 (not well matched) to 10 (very well matched). Use it as a ready reckoner for linking your objective to the mechanics available

SOURCE: J Cummins (2003)

objective? Cummins (2003) explains why a strategic approach is preferred:

1 It enables one offer to build on the previous one, and to establish a continuity of communication.

2 It makes it possible to communicate image and functional values, so promotions work harder.

3 It can produce considerable savings in time and money.

4 It enables offers to be fully integrated into the other activities in the marketing programme (eg linking with advertising and PR).

5 It facilitates a better approach to joint promotions (see above).

A strategic approach does not exclude the use of tactical promotions, since it can provide a framework within which shorter-term tactics can be determined. In this way a sales promotion strategy makes the tactical planning easier and more productive.

How to develop a strategic approach

1 Identify what customers (and prospects) really want (in terms of promotions).

2 Identify the long-term strategic marketing and communications objectives.

3 Create guidelines for each product or service, showing the style of sales promotion that is most appropriate to the brand's long-term health. Ensure that this style contributes towards the strategic marketing goals (as opposed to sometimes going in the opposite direction).

4 Determine exactly how much of the total marketing communications budget is available for sales promotions.

5 Ensure that there is support and commitment from senior management (eg the marketing director) so that sufficient management expertise and funds are available for the promotions to be professionally carried out.

6 Develop a method of evaluation so that longer-term performance can be measured against longer-term objectives. Ideally, this might then be compared to other types of marketing expenditure. Agencies and consultancies can review the effectiveness of their activities at the end of the year. Some agencies and consultancies are then asked 'Which communications tool is more effective and why?'

7 Develop a promotions file that compiles ideas and costs throughout the year. These can then be reviewed closer to the time of planning.

8 Plan and forecast the sales promotions' results. This is obviously difficult to do, particularly the first time. Usually a best, worst and medium range of forecasts help to build some kind of management control and criteria for success or failure.

Tactics – the short-term tactical approach

The general short-term, 'immediate action', tactical nature of sales promotion contrasts with the longer-term image and brand-building capability of advertising. This need not be the case, because sales promotions can be planned on a strategic level. But, first, why is there a tendency towards short-termism?

Perhaps the short-term focus is a result of:

1 management pressure to boost quarterly sales, which therefore encourages the use of quick-response sales promotions;

2 shortening product life cycles, which demand quick sales results;

3 increased competition and increased new product introductions, which increase the need for tactical defensive sales promotions;

4 the speedy response required to handle business problems when they arise;

5 full-service agencies trying to sell the client additional services such as sales promotion on an ad hoc, 'add-on' tactical basis.

Action

This is where attention to detail and proper processes and resources are required to ensure the smooth running of any sales promotion. The choice of promotional tool can be directly affected by the availability of resources. The three key resources, men/women, money and minutes (the 3Ms), are tied up with a promotion. Careful contingency planning should cater for an unexpectedly large response. Insurance can help here, because things do go wrong and costs can rapidly escalate (see 'Disaster promotions' above). Although creating a promotion is exciting, finishing it is dull and boring, yet this is the mark of a true professional.

Cut-off dates, logistical arrangements (returning unused stocks) and even announcing the end of the promotion cost time and money. Shell wanted to avoid the flush of irritation that would undoubtedly rise up if its customers failed to cash in their carefully collected gift tokens before they expired and became worthless, so it advertised the end of the promotion.

Checklist

Here is a checklist covering some key sales promotions details:

1 Does the promotion exploit key strengths and unique selling propositions (USPs)?

2 Is it a franchise-building promotion? Does the gift, incentive or premium relate to or enhance your product or service or the organization's image? Does it carry a selling message or at least a subtle reminder of some selling message? Unrelated premiums, contests, refunds or price discounts do not reinforce the brand or enhance corporate values.

3 What can go wrong? Contingency planning, crisis management and insurance are worth considering.

4 Has the promotion got legal clearance? Should it be checked with the Committee of Advertising Practice (CAP) sales promotions department?

5 Will the promotion generate only a temporary gain while customers stock up and do not repurchase for twice the normal period? (See Figure 16.1.) Will existing or old stocks (not carrying the promotion) waste?

6 Does the promotion need advertising and PR support? How can it be spread into social media networks? Is it newsworthy (ie can the PR people get some media coverage anyway)? In B2C markets, will the retail trade demand some above-the-line support? A great promotion will die on its feet if no one knows about it.

7 What other communications tools are required – new packaging, point-of-sale materials, new literature or contract field sales teams? Are these in the budget (time and money restrictions)?

8 Is there an administrative burden created by new order forms, coupons, judging, choosing winners, dispatching gifts, etc? Or will this all be handled by an external agency?

9 Is there a cut-off date, and is it clearly stated when the offer closes? Is there a sell-off time, based on an estimate of how long it will take to use up the stock of incentives or gifts? Has the lead time (the period required to set up the whole sales promotion through to launch date) been established?

10 Is the sales promotion going to be costly? Does it fit the budget available? Is it cost-effective? Can it be measured?

Control and measurement

Control, measurement and monitoring form the loop in the management system. How can the success or otherwise of the promotion be measured? The number of respondents, redemptions and increased sales are all relatively easy to calculate, but these are only the surface figures. They may be hiding the fact that many of the responders are the wrong people (promiscuous nomads), or existing customers who simply buy twice as much this week (stocking up) but do not buy next week. In fact, it may be that less than one-quarter of the respondents actually represent new business.

The promotion may have worked well in one respect but failed in another. The purpose of measurement and monitoring is twofold: 1) to control current campaigns; and 2) to improve future campaigns by learning about what did and did not work with the current campaign. Each promotion has to work successfully across a number of communications stepping stones for it to succeed. As Holloway (1989b) puts it:

> It has to be: seen, interesting, understood, believed, relevant and compatible, persuasive, and produce the desired response among the right target audience... to be seen may require the promotion to be in pack, on pack, off pack, POS etc) while the design of the visual elements has to cut through the clutter as many on-pack flashed offers are often never 'seen' by the target market. The middle criteria of communication effectiveness relate to the nature of the offer, the platform involved and the visual/copy elements of the promotion. Persuasion and response are dependent on the combination of all of these variables. There are few promotions that emerge from pre- or post-testing which don't leave considerable room for improvement somewhere in the mix of essential ingredients.

Here are three case studies that demonstrate the diverse nature of using social media both to spread a message and to engage stakeholders at the highest level – collaborative co-creation. Effectively, these three sales promotions use social media platforms to create user-generated content across three art forms: digital art, rap (poetry and music) and film soundtrack. (Additional social media case studies can be found in Chapter 21.)

CASE STUDY 16.1   The V&A digital art promotion

Situation

On 8 December 2009, the Victoria and Albert museum (the V&A) opened Decode: Digital Design Sensations. Decode showcased the latest developments in digital and interactive art and design from around the world. The V&A required an online and offline marketing plan to promote the exhibition over a four-month period.

Objectives

- To raise awareness of Decode: Digital Design Sensations at the V&A.

- To increase footfall and drive at least 40,000 visitors to the exhibition.

- To inspire people to get involved.

- To create a cultural buzz around digital art.

Strategy

The central aim was to activate a predominantly young, tech-savvy, male audience with a campaign idea that was in line with the core values inherent in digital art – openness, fluidity, collaboration and playfulness. The idea was to create a truly open-source participative campaign that would not just promote the exhibition but also enhance and extend it. By tapping into the natural creativity of its audience, the campaign would inspire and enlist them to help market and promote Decode through both online and offline channels.

Tactics

Karsten Schmidt, one of the world's most respected digital artists, worked with digital agency Saint to create a generative piece of art for exclusive use on the exhibition website. Schmidt's work was to be made open-source and available for 'recoding' (user modification). Recode Decode was born.

Via the Recode Decode microsite, visitors were invited to download, modify and submit their own creative interpretation of the work. These user-generated 'Recodes' were then showcased on the Decode website, and the best 'Recoded' works were used as part of the marketing and promotion of the exhibition across the London Underground and within online banner adverts.

In addition to this, Saint created an augmented reality (AR) platform for people to get an advanced look at Karsten Schmidt's work. The AR marker was included on all printed material and e-newsletters to encourage people to visit the website and find out about Recode Decode. The exhibition was also promoted via a dedicated Twitter hashtag discussion.

To ensure maximum exposure, the team worked with a third-party seeding agency to target online influencers within the world of digital art (see the box below). They were enlisted to blog about and share Recode within their core networks. This created organic word-of-mouth growth. In addition, the V&A ran a bloggers' event giving them an exclusive preview of the exhibition.

Control

Exhibition attendance completely exceeded the client's expectations, achieving 88,000 visits, more than double the original target. The Recode application was downloaded over 3,500 times in the first three months of the campaign, demonstrating an eagerness from the audience to get involved directly. Fifty-four 'Recoded' entries were chosen for display on the website, of which three were selected to be used to market the exhibition.

Social media successes included:

- 157 blog mentions;

- 69 news mentions;

- 942 tweets;

- 23 message board posts.

Men/women

Saint developed the project entirely in-house, using a core creative team (a creative director and creatives), a planner, an information architect, two designers, a symphony programmer, an action scripter, and a question-and-answer team for testing. Saint invited people to test, review and feed back on the various elements of the campaign – website usability, augmented reality performance, etc).

Money

The total cost for the campaign was £40,000, which included creative development, building, testing and all media costs (including printing).

Minutes

Saint pitched for the V&A work in August 2009. The website went live in October (four weeks' development), and the exhibition ran from November 2009 until April 2010.

Identifying opinion formers

Media partner Agenda 21 uses its own bespoke tool to identify opinion formers online. It tracks a number of related keywords within the blogosphere, eg 'digital', 'art', 'V&A' and 'museum', as well as the names of the artists, the names of the art on show, etc. Agenda 21 starts to follow bloggers who regularly post articles that feature one or more of these keywords, and it determines how big their blog audience is and how active (comments). With this information, Agenda 21 is able to identify who the real opinion formers are – the 100 bloggers it invited to attend the preview at the V&A, and the 300 bloggers it wanted to drive to the website.

Influencer engagement comprised two phases: 1) One hundred influencers in the London and Greater London area were identified and invited to a preview of the event in early December. This was to encourage excitement and coverage of the event within their online communities. 2) Three hundred influencers, including the hundred above, were invited to visit the Decode Recode site and to download the piece of code submitted by Karsten Schmidt for the chance to have their artwork displayed on the London Underground as part of the V&A's above-the-line promotional activity.

CASE STUDY 16.2   Rap anti-knife campaign

Situation

Saint and youth marketing agency Uproar run the 'It doesn't have to happen' Bebo community platform on behalf of the Home Office. The platform is part of the Home Office's three-year campaign to reduce knife crime amongst young people. Over the past two years the community has grown exponentially, and there are now over 11,500 active followers who support the message 'Carry a knife and lose your life'. The Bebo page is updated each month with fresh and

unique content. Through the page, members get positive alternatives to knife culture, which helps to effect positive change. However, the community wants to keep growing and reduce knife crime.

To ensure credibility, young people were enlisted to guest-edit the 'It doesn't have to happen' community page on a month-by-month basis. By working closely with the community, the guest editors are often able to spot trends and advise on how to develop the page to ensure that 'It doesn't have to happen' remains authentic. In the summer of 2009 a guest editor noted that many of the comments, blog entries and written content submissions by the community were uploaded in the form of lyrics and poems. The opportunity to tap into the creative and musical talent that existed within the community was recognized immediately, and the team started to consider how, through music, it could get the members to publicly pledge their support of the anti-knife crime message.

Objectives

- Connect with hard-to-reach youth audiences.

- Empower young people and give them a safe space to have a say around the issue of knife crime.

- Inspire young people to get involved in the campaign.

- Reach a Bebo profile member target of 20,000.

Strategy

The strategy was cognizant of the sensitivity of talking to the core audience – 10- to 17-year-olds who could be persuaded to reject knife carrying with a strong and credible message – through user-generated poetry and music (rap).

The three rules of engagement were:

1 Be credible.

2 Be relevant.

3 Invite participation.

Tactics

In September 2009, Freestyle King was launched – a competition to engage young musical talent by encouraging them to create their own lyrical rejection of knife carrying. The competition offered young people the chance to show off their freestyle rap skills in a series of knockout online battles. Freestyle King carries the strapline 'Drop Lyrics. Drop Knives'. It offers entrants the opportunity to build a personal profile, including their MC name, a tagline, and what part of the UK they represent. Entrants are then able to record their anti-knife crime video 'spits' to a selection of free beats.

FIGURE 16.2   'It doesn't have to happen'

Eight competitors were picked by a judging panel and appeared in a two-round battle on the site. The competition was then opened up to public vote, and the 'It doesn't have to happen' community along with the contestants themselves were challenged to share their favourite entry (and the 'It doesn't have to happen' message) across their personal network of friends – the core and hard-to-reach youth audiences.

After one week of voting, a winner – 'Lil Dreads' – was crowned Freestyle King by the community, and was awarded £200 in music vouchers.

Action

The MC battles were hosted on the Bebo social networking site, as it allowed the team to entertain the audience within the home of the campaign. In addition to this, the message was extended via a seeding strategy, engaging users across the web and driving them to the destination site. Seeding involved working with the youth task force on networks like Bebo, Facebook and Myspace to spread news of the campaign across their core network of friends.

The campaign idea revolved around the production of a piece of Flash content in which visitors could watch and vote on MC battles. The battles themselves had been contributed by the community following promotion on the 'It doesn't have to happen' homepage.

Control

The Bebo profile member target is 20,000, to be achieved at the end of year 3. With a current active community at over 11,500, the campaign is on target. Already a total of over 20,000 battles have been played, and the average visitor dwell time was over eight minutes.

Evidence of the effectiveness of Freestyle King included the Freestyle King winner, 'Lil Dreads', being awarded a gold Blue Peter badge by Chipmunk at the BBC 1Xtra awards (alongside Gary Barlow, Jenson Button and Usain Bolt) for his contribution to the campaign against knives.

In addition to this, 'Lil Dreads' took part in a 15-minute radio interview on BBC Solent, where he performed a live rap, and his story (and the campaign story) was featured in the *Dorset Echo* and covered on many youth-orientated

FIGURE 16.3   Freestyle King results

blogs and websites online. The editorial and media value of this coverage alone more than paid for the total cost of the campaign.

Men/women

Saint developed the project entirely in-house, using a core creative team (a creative director and creatives), a planner, an information architect, two designers, a database programmer, an action scripter, and a QA team for testing.

Money

The total cost for the campaign was £21,950, which included creative development, build, testing and seeding.

Minutes

Saint was briefed by the Home Office in the second quarter of 2009, with the campaign running from 2 to 18 September 2009. The original Bebo platform took just days to set up and launch. However, content and modules were added over time as the community grew. It has been running for over two years, and new features are still added every month (such as Freestyle King) to ensure that the community remains active.

Seeding

Seeding involved working with Saint's youth task force on networks like Bebo, Facebook and Myspace to spread news of the campaign across their core network of friends. Uproar, a youth consulting and marketing agency (**http://www.uproaruk.com/**), is in regular contact with a youth task force (15 young teenagers) who have been involved in the campaign from the very beginning. Each has been directly affected by knife crime. These young people guest-edit the Bebo profile, and work with the team to ensure the campaign always remains relevant. With the launch of Freestyle King, these young people were asked to post information about the campaign in their status updated on various social networks, and to e-mail it to friends, family and networks.

For the Home Office anti-knife crime campaign, Uproar helped Saint to identify young people of influence online. It works closely with these young people to guest-edit and manage the 'It doesn't have to happen' network. The young people are encouraged to spread word of the campaign and various bits of activity that happens around it. They also feed back insight – current and popular trends, etc that lead to mini-campaigns such as Freestyle King.

CASE STUDY 16.3   Muzu.TV film soundtrack promotion

Situation background

Muzu.TV is a vast free online music video service that churns out videos by artist, random selection or jukebox (selected by others). It is fully social media enabled. Growth has come purely from social media, as it does not advertise. In fact, its success comes from a combination of factors, including always high-added-value events, and promotions (exclusive videos and competitions) for its stakeholders. Muzu.TV has been using win–win social media multiplier campaigns built around simple sales promotions concepts such as exclusive tickets to see artists perform in an intimate studio environment plus an exclusive video feed of the private gig for a national daily's website, in return for editorial coverage promoting the competition prize.

FIGURE 16.4   Muzu.TV focuses on music videos

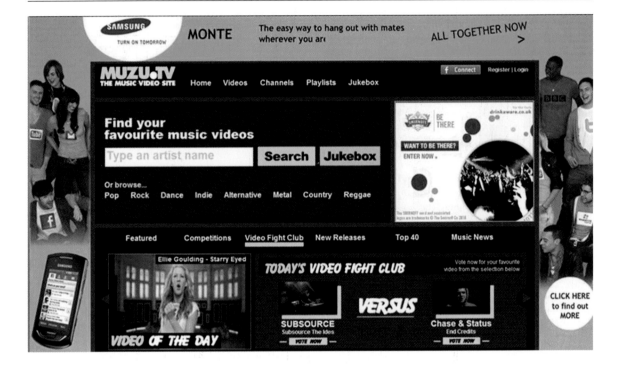

See Case study 14.2 for more examples of Muzu.TV's musicians' intimate performances for fans.

Objectives

Muzu.TV constantly seeks new sales promotion and PR concepts to raise its profile but also help bands boost their profile and fans get closer to the performer they love.

Strategy

The strategy is to create a new user-generated social media concept for movies that mashes music and video together in a unique manner that delivers huge added value for all stakeholders (musicians, songwriters, movie makers, Muzu.TV audiences and, last but not least, Muzu.TV), and to create a real soundtrack for a real movie. The winning track will be used in the movie. The process is:

- Watch 10 clips from an independent movie (which is currently in the editing stage).
- Select a scene from 10 scenes from the movie.

- Write a song or select one from your own repertoire.
- Attach the soundtrack to the movie clip.
- Upload the song to a particular movie clip.

A new feature for the Muzu.TV music-loving audience will be to see dramatic music clips. Movie makers will benefit from the buzz built around a movie, through new ways to raise their profile and create buzz. New ways to source a soundtrack for a movie will lead to financial savings. There will be new ways to promote singer-songwriters.

Tactics

The concept will be promoted through Muzu.TV, the usual social media channels, news releases and partners' social media channels and news releases. In addition, Muzu.TV can invite songwriters (from a songwriters' database of 400,000 songwriters). This creates opportunities for un-signed musicians to get a position in the charts (with a track in the movie getting additional airtime and additional sales). Artists can also boost their own 'likers' and friends and generate traffic for their own websites.

Action

The judging criteria combine scores from social media popularity ratings and a panel of judges from the music and film industry, including the head of sync publishing at EMI and the lead actor/singer and guitarist from the Oscar-winning musical film *Once*.

Control

BuzzRadar will monitor the social buzz (using its own proprietary tool originally created to measure Red Bull's social media performance).

The Buzz Chart measures the activity relating to a band across the internet and over a range of social media to work out the buzz around a band. This includes:

- the number of views on a page;
- the rating on the band page;
- the comments on the band page;

- tweets sent on Twitter that mention your Twitter ID eg @yourband;
- page views on Myspace;
- number of plays on a Myspace music player;
- number of fans on Facebook;
- number of plays and shares a video has had on Facebook.

Note that number of views is an insufficient criterion, as some people write scripts that keep viewing the video without anyone watching it but keeping the 'views' score high. Hence a number of variables are factored in.

And the winner gets...

The real songwriter's prize is getting the music in a movie, and also getting a 'sync deal' (the artist gets a percentage royalty every time the movie is shown or played).

Advantages and disadvantages

Here are some of the advantages and disadvantages to consider when deciding whether to increase or reduce this communications tool.

Advantages

Sales promotions are useful when trying to close the sale or push the customer through the last stage of the buying process. They can also help to keep a relationship alive with existing customers by rewarding their loyalty. Sales promotions can support the brand and customer relations. They can be developed strategically to strengthen relationships over time.

Disadvantages

Promotions require other tools to promote them, eg advertising, PR, direct mail or social media announcing the promotion. What can go wrong will go wrong, hence the need for insurance. Some promotions actually damage the brand. Promotions can be expensive to set up, procure, administer and wind down, although third parties are generally contracted to do so. On a CPT basis, promotions are expensive, although they can prove to be more cost-effective on a cost-per-order (CPO) basis.

Key points from Chapter 16

- Sales promotions can be used strategically rather than simply as short-term tactical tools.
- Sales promotions must integrate with other elements of the marketing mix.

- Attention to detail is required, as sales promotions can go horribly wrong.
- There is room for enhanced creativity, as social media has opened up a vast range of collaborative opportunities.

References and further reading

Bird, D (1990) No mileage in frequency marketing, *Marketing*, 10 October, p 12

Bird, J (1997) How to keep them faithful the world over, *Precision Marketing*, 26 May

Bond, C (1991) Marriages of some convenience, *Marketing*, 10 October, pp 23–26

Britt, B (1990) Coke's magic spells trouble, *Marketing*, 31 May

Castling, J (1989) Buying strategic sales promotion, *Sales Promotion*, July, p 11

Chapman, N (1985) Cadburys pays up in Typhoo game, *Marketing Week*, 17 May

Cummins, J (2003) *Sales Promotion: How to create and implement campaigns that really work*, 3rd edn, Kogan Page, London

Douglas, T (1987) *The Complete Guide to Advertising*, Pan Macmillan, London

Ehrenberg, A, Hammond, K and Godheart, G (1991) *The After-Effects of Large Consumer Promotions*, London Business School, London

Farrell, J (1989) Which countries allow which promotions?, *Marketing Week*, 16 June, pp 75–77

Hollinger, P (1996) Electronic age raises ghost of Green Shield stamps, *Financial Times*, 9–10 November

Holloway, P (1989a) Can research really help?, *Sales Promotion*, July, pp 12, 13

Holloway, P (1989b) Getting it right in the 90s, *Sales Promotion*, February, pp 23, 24

Hyslop, R (1989) Round table discussion, *Sales Promotion*, July, p 14

Kotler, P (2000) *Marketing Management: Analysis, planning, implementation and control*, millennium edn, Prentice Hall, Englewood Cliffs, NJ

Marketing Breakthroughs (1991) Polish give-aways struggle to reach target, December

Smith, D (2008) Google, 10 years in: Big, friendly giant or a greedy Goliath?, *Observer*, 17 August

Smith, P R and Chaffey, D (2001) *eMarketing eXcellence*, 2nd edn, Butterworth-Heinemann, Oxford

Zeisser, M (2010) Unlocking the elusive potential of social networks, *McKinsey Quarterly*, member edn, June

Further information

British Promotional Merchandise Association (BPMA)
52–53 Russell Square
London WC1B 4HP
Tel: +44 (0)20 7631 6960
Fax: +44 (0)20 7631 6944
www.bpma.co.uk

Institute of Promotional Marketing Ltd (ISPM)
70 Margaret Street
London W1W 8SS
Tel: +44 (0)20 7291 7730
Fax: +44 (0)20 7291 7731
www.theipm.org.uk

Marketing Communications Consultants Association (MCCA)
4 New Quebec Street
London
Tel: +44 (0)20 7535 3550
Fax: +44 (0)20 7535 3551
www.mcca.org.uk

Promota UK (Promotional Merchandise Trade Association)
Concorde House
Trinity Park
Solihull
Birmingham B37 7UQ
Tel: +44 (0)8453 714335
Fax: +44 (0)8453 714336
www.promota.co.uk

17
Direct mail – online and offline

LEARNING OBJECTIVES

By the end of this chapter you will be able to:

- Be aware of the changing trends in direct mail and opt-in e-mail
- Integrate direct mail (snail mail) and opt-in e-mail into both acquisition and retention communications campaigns
- Understand the advantages and disadvantages of both types of direct mail compared to other communication tools
- Appreciate the importance of integrating all direct mail as part of an integrated communications campaign or part of a contact strategy

Introduction to direct mail (and e-mail)

Direct marketing includes any marketing communications tools that interact directly with customers. This includes direct response advertising, telemarketing and direct mail (including e-mail). This chapter explores direct mail and opt-in e-mail. See Chapter 3 for more on contact strategies, data mining and profiling.

The growth of direct marketing, in general, and direct mail, in particular, has been fuelled by:

- tailor-made technology;
- profiling technology;
- the list explosion;
- integrated marketing;
- the constant search for cost-effectiveness.

Tailor-made technology

Online newsletters and e-mails as well as offline newsletters, newspapers and letters can be personalized by name and also by relevant needs, eg many years ago the US *Farmer's Journal*'s 825,000 circulation received a tailor-made magazine with a minimum of 2,000 and a maximum of 8,896 different editions per issue. Essentially, the pig farmer's edition would not carry features or advertisements about cereal farming, etc. Farmers prefer their magazine to carry relevant material. The advertisers like it, because it offers better targeting. The magazine saves money on paper and post. The environmentalists might prefer it too. One day everyone might have their own personalized magazine. Personalized interactive TV programmes are already running in Spain and France, while the internet provides personalized newspapers, and tailored online newsletters are common.

Profiling technology

Basic technology allows different mailing lists and databases to be added together and even superimposed on each other. Lists can be merged, and any overlap or duplications can be deduplicated ('deduped'). Geodemographics mix geographical location, type of neighbourhood and demographic

FIGURE 17.1   Any product, service or communication can be tailored specifically for a customer

Reproduced from P R Smith, *Marketing CD 2: Segmentation, positioning and the marketing mix*

data such as age, income and family life cycle. Other fields or layers of data can be added. Everyone fits into a cluster, eg from the keying of an address

They know you better than you do

An investigative journalist decided that he wanted to find out about himself, as he was soon moving to south-east San Francisco. Having keyed in his new address, he was told by the database company that he was classified as a 'young influential'. He was moving into a 'thirty-something childbearing neighbourhood'. It also told him that 'he may still be in a town house or a row house and may not have graduated to the detached single home but they were definitely starting to have children, making the transition from a couple-orientated lifestyle to a family-orientated lifestyle'. Furthermore, the 'young influentials' typically were aged 20–35, had a median income of $39,500, enjoyed jogging, travelling, new wave music and investing, read magazines like *Rudder*, *Scientific American* and *Town and Country*, and liked to eat yogurt, wholemeal bread and Mexican food and drink low-fat milk. This profile almost exactly matched the journalist's profile. That was over 20 years ago. Contextual advertising (Chapter 13) is even more interesting.

the database identifies the neighbourhood's cluster type or profile. This geodemographic typecasting uses shorthand names to identify cluster types. For example, a US database company classifies people with mature families living in affluent suburbs as 'pools and patios', whereas poorer rural areas are called 'shotguns and pickups'. People living there may have aspirations to move towards 'golf clubs and Volvos'.

It is said that demographics say 'You are where you live' (meaning your neighbourhood is a good indicator of your lifestyle and the kinds of products you are likely to buy) and psychographic databases say 'You are what you do' (meaning your behaviour patterns and buying preferences can be estimated from collected data on your (or similar people's) lifestyle, eg whether you are likely to own an iPod. **In the UK, geodemographic packages such as ACORN, Pinpoint, Mosaic and SuperProfile are easily cross-referenced with media usage, product usage and lifestyle statements.** Contextual layers can be added according to online behaviour on a specific site (see Chapter 11 on digital body language for more).

If you run up a bad debt...

'… the computer will know about it, if you subscribe to a dubious magazine, forget to return library books or collect parking tickets, everyone with access to a computer will know about it!' This light-hearted suggestion was made in an article in *Marketing Week* (3 December 1982), but try to hire a TV if you have a county court judgment against you: the retailer will find out through the online database of the United Protection of Traders Association.

The list explosion

The third factor fuelling the growth of direct marketing is the proliferation of lists or databases available both online and offline. The only restriction is imagination, or one's ability to define a target market or customer profile in a range of different ways. For example, home decorators could be redefined as 'home movers'. The million or so UK home movers could then be reduced to those moving into certain geographic locations or even neighbourhood areas,

which might indicate their propensity to undertake the decorating themselves (as opposed to hiring someone to do it for them). A list, or a section of the list, can be hired or bought, and tested and/or refined by using certain software packages. It is important to select and check lists carefully, since the quality of many of the UK's 'cold' lists can be a problem, although data integrity is now much improved, especially with newer lifestyle databases.

The diversity of the lists available is intriguing and sometimes bewildering. The lists range from 'cynical humorous intellectuals' (18,000 *Punch* magazine subscribers) to 'slimming pill buyers who read the *Sun*' to 'young mothers' to 'fork-lift truck buyers'. Just about anything can be targeted. Even lists of 'right-wing, money-orientated gamblers who are influenced by advertising, react to new ideas and have disposable income' can be created (eg the original list

---

What profile do you want to target?

Here is a small selection of lists that could be relevant for the three types of target customers shown below:

- *Prominent people:* Rolls-Royce owners, Lamborghini and Jaguar owners, UK millionaires, rich ladies, tennis court owners, private plane owners, racehorse owners, greyhound owners and even cat owners.

- *Entertainment seekers:* theatre goers, Shaftesbury Theatre goers, club goers.

- *Improvers:* named clergy, buyers of self-improvement books, house improvers, house movers, and even a list of owners of Black & Decker drills.

There are many other unusual lists that can fit target customer profiles like a glove (the skill is matching the two): people who have aerial photos of their homes, personalized car number plate owners, buyers of military prints and memorabilia, tall ladies, people in prisons, borstals and detention centres, women executives, hypochondriacs, management consultants, librarians, educational children's book buyers and so on. And, of course, the electoral roll is also publicly available.

of 3 million British Gas shareholders was available from the British Investor Database).

It is worth phoning list brokers and list owners to request a catalogue of lists (consumer or business-to-business) and spending an hour browsing. A compiled list is collected from public records, directories, trade show registrations, etc. According to *World List News*, a mail-responsive list can produce a 300 per cent increase in response over a compiled list. The best list is an organization's own house list of customers, enquirers, visitors, employees, shareholders, etc.

Integrated systems

Direct marketing can, and should, integrate with other communications tools. It can link different direct marketing tools to create a more cost-effective method of marketing communications. Depending on the quality of the lead, the lead can be followed up by mailing a brochure, or hot prospects might be telephoned to set up an appointment or to invite them to an event.

The lead generation might be created in the first place by a direct mail offer that invites readers, viewers or listeners to send in for a free gift. Some marketers maintain that 45 per cent of business enquirers will buy within 12 months. The challenge then lies in identifying the hottest prospects and directing the sales force to the 1 out of every 2.2 enquirers who will buy within the 12 months, and then to follow up the other leads over time.

Identifying the hottest prospects or 'screening' can be carried out by following up with an outbound telephone interview to determine the prospect's status. Alternatively, the analysis can be carried out directly from the coupon if it was designed to capture the required detailed information. The outbound phone call can screen and ultimately fix an appointment for the sales or progress to the next appropriate stage in the buying process. Alternatively, an inbound phone catering for an 0800 or freephone number can accommodate enquiries generated from either a direct response advertisement or a mailshot.

This is only the start. **After the initial sale, database marketing can help to keep in touch with customers as they move towards a repeat purchase.** Conservative estimates suggest that it is five times easier to sell to an existing customer than to a new one.

Cost-effectiveness per order

Ideally, costs should be measured against results, not simply outputs. The cost of testing say a telesales campaign (1,000 names at roughly £10 per call) might be, say, £10,000, but the result might be 2 per cent success or 20 new customers. The cost per order or cost per customer in this case is calculated as £500. How does this compare with the current cost per new customer generated by other marketing techniques, such as direct mail, exhibitions, advertising or even the field sales team? The results, and costs, may vary if, for example, the telesales team is focused only on appointment setting and the field sales team handles the rest. This may result in, say, 15 per cent appointments (150); the sales team then convert, say, 30 per cent of these into 45 new customers. The telesales cost of £10,000 is added to the field sales cost of, say, £8,550. Then £18,550 divided by 45 gives a cost per new customer of £412. Alternatively, say a mailshot to 1,000 people costs £2,000 and 1 per cent convert to a sale, that cost per order is only £200 (£2,000 cost divided by 10 orders).

The lifetime value of the customer can then be calculated by multiplying the average value of expected orders per annum by the number of years the customer will exist. The cost per order of subsequent orders will be significantly less than the cost of the initial order because, as already mentioned, estimates suggest that it is at least five times cheaper and easier to sell to an existing customer than to a prospect.

Telesales can be used to support a sales force by servicing accounts over the phone instead of having a sales rep visit every month. Telesales can also be used to generate or even screen leads. At a cost of anywhere between £7 and £70 per appointment set up, a telesales campaign can release the salesperson from prospecting and even administration into doing what most reps are best at, face-to-face selling. Some estimates show that salespeople spend less than 20 per cent of their time actually selling; the rest is prospecting, travelling, form filling, etc. The average cost of a single sales visit of £150 can be reduced if salespeople are released from other duties and therefore make more visits. Some telesales campaigns link in with computer models that select the optimum call plan to minimize travel time. All of these activities, including order fulfilment, can be handled by an outside agency if needed.

Not surprisingly, TV ads and mailshots can link together both activity-wise and image-wise. Drayton Bird's *Commonsense Direct Marketing* (2000) revealed that awareness for a particular airline's TV ad four months after screening was 50 per cent higher among those who had received a mailshot that featured a scene from the TV ad than among a similar panel who had not received the mailshot. **The database can also be used to research the impact of, say, a TV advertisement or a sponsorship package among different types of audiences.**

A challenging data-mining brief

Find meaningful patterns in the data, target potential consumers, retain existing consumers more effectively, predict who would buy certain products, anticipate the volume of high sales of specific high-margin products and discover and capitalize on opportunities for cross-couponing.

Opt-in e-mail and mobile messaging

Opt-in e-mail is a useful online communications tool primarily for customer retention programmes rather than customer acquisition programmes. Despite this (and falling e-mail opening rates), some organizations buy huge databases of 'opt-in' e-mail addresses, personalize a relevant offer and, despite the very small percentage response rates, still find it works for mass markets. However, opt-in e-mail campaigns are best used as part of a contact strategy for prospects who have enquired or customers who have bought. The contact strategy can include e-mail, snail mail, telemarketing and personal visits. The mailings (online or offline) can be short messages or letters, newsletters, vouchers or full brochures (or links to a website section: video, e-book or web pages).

Although it is similar to direct mail, e-mail is most widely used for direct response (as opposed to brand building or brand awareness), although e-newsletters in particular can also support brand awareness. E-mail enables a targeted, and personalized, message to be pushed out to customers to inform and remind. They will, at worst, see the subject line within their e-mail inbox, even if only to delete it. Contrast this with the web, which is a pull medium where customers will visit your site only if there is a reason to do so. Nevertheless, unsolicited e-mail (spam) is illegal in B2C markets and damaging to a brand.

Opt-in is the key to successful e-mail marketing, whether B2C or B2B. E-mailing only those who have opted in is simply best practice. Before starting an e-mail dialogue with customers, companies must ask them to provide their e-mail addresses. Privacy law in many countries requires customers to proactively opt in by checking a box (showing consent in some way). In the UK it is all right to e-mail prospects either if they have been customers or if they have made enquiries and have given their e-mail address. With every subsequent e-mail, however, marketers must offer customers an easy way to opt out at any time.

Opt-in e-mail

'E-mail is an effective push online communications method. It is essential that e-mail is opt-in, otherwise it is illegal spam. Consider options for customer acquisition including cold e-mail, co-branded e-mails and placements in third-party e-mails. For house list e-mails, experiment with achieving the correct frequency, or give customers the choice. Consider automated event triggered e-mails. Work hard on e-mail design and maintaining up-to-date lists. Stay within the law.'

Chaffey and Smith (2008)

Success factors

Regardless of the type of e-mail, the direct mail variables have an even bigger impact on response rates. Once again, relevancy prevails.

Offer and creative execution

If the offer, or fundamental proposition, is not relevant it will not get a response. If the subject line in the e-mail is not deemed relevant it will not even get opened.

Continual customer research helps to keep offers relevant. The creative execution can vary. The key part is, as mentioned, a subject headline that catches attention and interest. Once opened, the e-mail has to be very short (it should have links to further information such as see, try and buy. Layout, colour and image need careful attention, as they affect the perception of the creative message, which itself has to be carefully crafted (in fact usually a series of messages has to be crafted as part of a contact strategy). **The incentive should become a strong call to action**: to act now and not wait until later. Split testing and multivariate testing help identify what works best before rolling out the mailing. One final check for branding is to ask: 'Are the creative content and copy consistent with the brand?'

The e-mail copy should:

- grab attention in the subject line and in the first sentence;
- be brief and relevant to the target segment (use links to the website for more information);
- be personalized – not 'Dear Valued Customer' but 'Dear Ms Smith';
- have a clear call to action at the start and end of the message;
- provide an opt-out or 'unsubscribe' option by law;
- contain full address and contact details;
- operate within legal and ethical constraints for a country;
- send out multipart or MIME messages that display HTML or text according to the capability of the recipients' e-mail readers. Offer a choice of HTML or text to match users' preferences.

Timing

E-mail response rates vary according to the time of day, week, month and year. External events also affect response rates, as themes can match topical events. Some organizations find that Friday afternoon e-mails don't work whereas Tuesday mornings do. Many organizations note what particular time works best for maximum opening rates. And, as with any mailing online or offline, split tests before the campaign roll-out help, and careful monitoring thereafter is required.

Targeting

In list or database selection, the variable that has the highest impact on success or failure is targeting: matching the right profile of customer with the right offer (see Chapter 2 on the magic marketing formula). The higher the relevance to the target market, the higher the response. This can be continually refined, as customer profiling can be continually improved as more data are captured over time and preferences are identified.

Response mechanism

Have a relevant landing page (or microsite). Do not send customers to a general home page where they have to start searching for the e-mail offer. Some e-mails when clicked through for the offer present an online form to profile the customer. Simplifying the form can have a dramatic impact, as can varying landing pages to boost sales.

Testing: split testing and multivariate testing

A/B testing allows marketers to test different headlines, different offers, different photographs and even different background colours to see which perform the best. From the creation of two versions of one variable (say two different headlines), A/B tests reveal which works better. **Multivariate testing is a process that tests more than one component, effectively testing numerous A/B tests at the same time.** By analysing different test results, marketers can spot which variables consistently deliver the best results.

MAD contact strategy

MAD (**www.mad.co.uk**) is a marketing-specific portal accessed through online subscriptions. It offers a trial one-month subscription to its service. During this period, a series of e-mails is used to help convert the prospect to a full subscription. E-mails are sent out at approximately 3, 10, 25 and 28 days to encourage a subscription before the trial lapses.

Chaffey and Smith (2008)

Customer retention

As mentioned, e-mail marketing is best for customer retention, as part of an ongoing contact strategy to keep in touch with customers and deliver them relevant updates, offers, tips and advice. It also provides a response mechanism for customers to air their views and give valuable feedback. Every contact creates an opportunity to continuously add data to the customer profile. It is therefore important that marketing integrates with the rest of the organization's operations, particularly if there was a sudden surge in responses but there was no system in place to manage responses (whether asking a question, making a complaint, looking for advice or trying to buy the product or service). Any glitches in the system can damage the customer relations that have been built up over time. **Well-managed systems test campaigns before roll-out and build in the facility of continual customer profiling to identify which customers are likely to want which products or services.** (See the grandfather clock story in Chapter 3, 'Profiling' on page 71.)

Customer acquisition

For those companies that use opt-in e-mail for customer acquisition, there are three main options for customer acquisition programmes as highlighted in *eMarketing eXcellence* (Chaffey and Smith, 2008):

- *Cold e-mail campaign.* In this case, the recipient receives an opt-in e-mail from an organization that has rented an e-mail list from a consumer e-mail list provider such as Experian (**www.experian.com**), Claritas (**www.claritas.com**) or IPT Limited (**www.myoffers.co.uk**), a business e-mail list provider such as Mardev (**www.mardev.com**) or Corpdata (**www.corpdata.com**), or trade publishers or event providers such as VNU. Although the recipients have agreed to receive offers by e-mail, the e-mail is effectively cold. For example, a credit card provider could send a cold e-mail to a list member who is not currently their member. It is important to use some form of 'statement of origination', as otherwise the message may be considered spam. Cold e-mails tend to have a higher cost per acquisition (CPA) than other forms of online marketing, but different lists should still be evaluated.

- *Co-branded e-mail.* Here, recipients receive an e-mail with an offer from a company with which they have a reasonably strong affinity. For example, the same credit card company could partner with a mobile service provider such as Vodafone and send out the offer to their customers who have opted in to receive e-mails from third parties. Although this can be considered a form of cold e-mail, it is warmer, since there is a stronger relationship with one of the brands, and the subject line and creative will refer to both brands. Co-branded e-mails tend to be more responsive than cold e-mails to rented lists, since the relationship exists and fewer offers tend to be given.

- *Third-party e-newsletter.* In this visitor acquisition option, a company publicizes itself in a third-party e-newsletter. This could be in the form of an ad, sponsorship or PR (editorial) that links through to a destination site. These placements may be set up as part of an interactive advertising ad buy, since many e-newsletters also have permanent versions on the website. Since e-newsletter recipients tend to engage with them by scanning the headlines or reading them if they have time, e-newsletter placements can be relatively cost-effective.

Mobile messaging

Whether text messages, vouchers, downloadable podcasts, video clips or photos, mobile messaging is going to get bigger. (Location-based advertising is covered in Chapter 13). Suffice to say here that special offers made only to the relevant target market as they pass by a relevant venue will work, at least in the short term. Longer-term success will be determined by how well the industry regulates itself and the need for privacy (which is an issue that will continue to grow in importance also). If too many location-based mobile messages appear and customers' inboxes become cluttered with too many commercial messages, customers will bar such messages and may also take legal action.

Managing a direct mail campaign

Whether an organization is planning an advertising campaign or a direct mail campaign, a similarly disciplined approach should be taken, ie researching the situation, message development (creative mailing), media planning (list selection and timing), testing and monitoring, etc.

A direct mail campaign can be planned in the same way as an advertising campaign, ie by using SOSTAC® + 3Ms (see Chapter 10). However, six factors – timing, list selection, creative mailings, budgeting, operational implications and testing – will be examined in more detail using the SOSTAC® structure.

Situation analysis

The usual product interrogation, trend identification and soliciting customer feedback help build a bigger picture as to where the brand is.

Objectives

Crystal-clear objectives can eventually be broken down to ensure that everyone knows where the brand is going. Ideally, marketing communications objectives should be numerical for sales, enquiries and even brand awareness.

Strategy

Use STP (from the STOP & SIT components of strategy discussed in Chapter 10). Segmentation creates customer profiles from the database (or just select profiles from a mailing list). Target or select the best profiles. Positioning ensures the message is right.

List selection is the most important stage in the whole direct marketing process. Sixty per cent of any project's time should be spent on list selection. 'There's no point fishing in the pool if the pool ain't got any fish.' Here are some questions that should be asked before using a list:

1 Where do the names come from (eg compiled, previous mail responsive, subscription lists, etc)?

2 When was the list built?

3 How often is it cleaned (updated)? Is it Mailing Preference Service (MPS) cleaned?

4 When was the list last used (and by whom) and what was the percentage of gone-aways (redundant names or addresses that the post office return to the sender)? Are there any known results or any references from past users?

5 What is the rebate per gone-away that is returned to the list owner for future cleaning?

6 What proportion of the target's total universe does the list represent, eg does the 1 million list of home movers represent all the home movers, or half, or what?

7 What selections are available (eg geographic split, job title, etc)? Are there any additional costs?

8 What net names percentage is quoted (ie net usable names after deduping with other lists)?

9 Are there any rental restrictions (minimum quantities, competitive products subject to the list owner's approval, etc)?

10 Assuming the list has an appropriate profile (similar to your specified target market), clarify whether:
    – it has named individuals as opposed to job titles or 'the occupier';
    – it is in an appropriate format, ie labels, disk, etc; if disk, check that the disk format suits the letter shop's requirements;
    – it is postcoded (for post office mailsort discounts).

11 How much does it cost? What is the lead time from order to delivery?

If the list is hired, permission is usually given for one use only. Sleeper names are planted in the list to ensure that it is not used more than once (the sleepers immediately notify the list owner if they receive two mailings). Hiring charges vary from £50 to £350 per thousand. Many lists are not available for purchase, but those that are available are often priced at least four times higher than the rental price.

Tactics: creative mailings

Opportunities for creativity abound. Most mail competes with bills and statements. Many of the top creative people still feel television advertising is more glamorous, so perhaps most mailings are restrained either by the people who create them or by the managers who commission them. Here are some odd exceptions:

- A plastic green cucumber was mailed by the Direct Mail Sales Bureau to all UK media buyers to raise awareness of the direct mail option.

- The Prince's Trust, when targeting company chairmen, mailed a box containing a ceramic bowl created by one of the businesses the Trust had supported (the bowl provided a gift for the chairmen's secretaries, to encourage them to pass on the pack; it also brought the achievements of the Trust to life for the chairmen).

- A briefcase was mailed to car distributors. When opened, the briefcase resembled a car dashboard complete with audio system and car phone. The recipient inserted a CD and lifted the phone to hear a sales pitch about why that particular car phone was outstanding. The briefcase further doubled as a point-of-sale item for the distributor.

- The mailing piece and the incentive can affect the budget significantly. Not all creative mailings need anything other than a few clever words. A recent mailing simply said 'Good morning'. This generated a lot of interest, anticipation and eagerness to get the next mailing in the sequence.

Action

Integrated systems

If carefully thought out, the operational requirements clarify how the campaign will actually work. For example, what happens to the information that is collected during a telephone conversation? How do the sales representatives' diaries get updated, and who monitors representatives' availability? Research by Euro RSCG Direct found 'an irresponsible use of response-handling mechanisms', with only a 70 per cent chance of respondents receiving information. The majority of this 70 per cent were never contacted again. Only 5 per cent ever received a follow-up telephone call. Is there a plan or system that ensures follow-up? Who controls and delivers stocks of goods or stocks of brochures? How and when are invoices generated?

Marketing is the last bastion of under-automation, whereas manufacturing and production have generally been automated to the point where labour costs account for only 8–12 per cent of production costs. Sales and marketing costs can account for between 15 and 35 per cent of costs. Automation can deliver both cost savings and increased effectiveness of marketing and sales follow-through. Hybrid systems help salespeople by reminding them which customers need attention this month, next month and so on. Enquiries generated through an array of marketing efforts are all dealt with (a brochure is dispatched along with a letter; telesales follow up for an appointment; an appointment is made for the salesperson). Nothing slips through the system. No enquiries are lost. All are followed up. The system has to accommodate returned goods and cancelled orders. Up-front investment in an integrated system is falling as more and more sales-tracking software packages come on to the marketplace.

A strain on your office?

'Even if the response is fairly modest it can still be a strain on your office resources. Could your telephone system handle thousands of calls in an hour? Could your staff still treat customers with enthusiasm at the end of a whole day of frantic answering? Do you have space for sackfuls of mail? Do you have time to answer every reply quickly? If not, a specialist fulfilment company can help.'

Royal Mail (2001)

Timing

The mailing schedule illustrated in Figure 17.2 shows why a minimum of 12 weeks, preferably six months, is needed to set up a direct marketing campaign that feeds into a database system from scratch. As Bird (2000) says, 'the faster you need something done the more likely there will be mistakes. The answer is either give more time, or pay a great deal more money.' Deciding whether the campaign should be multi-stage (generate enquiries, screening, follow-up phone calls and sales visits, etc) or single-stage (straight order), multimedia or single media, and so on, is arguably less important than determining strategically how each mailing forms part of an overall campaign that develops a cumulative effect. One-off large mailings should gradually be replaced by smaller, more frequent mailings as the database identifies what is needed by whom and when. Many direct mail agencies can develop a campaign in four to six weeks, but ideally the campaign should be researched and planned strategically, and with a greater emphasis on creativity, to achieve 'cut-through'; the ideal lead time is 17 weeks.

Timing also refers to identifying when a target market buys and how often. Markets are constantly moving. Buyers drift in and out at different stages. Some markets are seasonal, and others again have peaks and troughs on different days of the week. Are target respondents more receptive to a mailshot that lands on a Friday morning or a Monday morning?

The development and scheduling of the campaign are shown in Figure 17.2. Essentially they follow the normal advertising campaign development sequence: brief, concept development, research artwork, production and roll-out (note that research can be supplemented by continual testing).

As in advertising, a creative brief is followed by concepts that are subsequently approved, amended, researched and eventually developed into final copy and design. This is turned into artwork that is checked, proofed and eventually turned into final approved artwork that goes to the printer. Prior to this (or sometimes simultaneously) a list brief is agreed. This defines the target market. Lists are carefully researched and checked.

A list proposal is subsequently approved for ordering (purchase or hire). The letter shop puts the required letter into the system ready for laser printing on to personalized letters. Proof letters are checked and approved while the lists are prepared, merged and purged (duplicate names withdrawn). The printer dispatches the brochure to the letter shop, which then presses the button. The letters are lasered, folded, collated and inserted with the brochure or mailing piece into lasered (or window) envelopes (sometimes pre-printed with teaser messages or images) and posted. Then a dreadful

quietness descends as the bags of mail are driven off into the sunset and the long wait begins. Pre-mailshot tension can run riot, with nightmares about postal strikes, redundant lists, a printing error, a wrong expiry date or, worse still, a nil response level.

Good planning ensures that the best lists are used (perhaps based on test results), print, proofs, dates, etc are checked, and acceptable results are projected. Even in a situation where a lot of variables are unknown, careful planning can reduce the chance of failure.

Control

Budgeting 'money'

One way of budgeting is by asking: 'How much can the organization afford to spend to recruit a new customer? How much is a new customer worth or what is the allowable cost per customer? What is the customer's lifetime value?' Then multiply this by the number of customers required and, bingo, a budget emerges. Another way to build a budget or at least a ballpark cost figure is to calculate 50p per shot. Thus if an organization is running a 20,000 mailshot, then ballpark costs to cover everything (design, artwork, print, list, letter shop, insertion or collation incentive, envelope and postage) would be £10,000; a 500,000 mailshot would enjoy economies of scale and cost less than £250,000.

Cost per thousand
This translates into £500 per thousand contacts, compared with:

Telesales (at, say, £10)	£10,000
Door-to-door drop	£250
Inserts (including print)	£100
Magazine ads	£50
Web balance ads	£30
National press	£10
TV ads	£5

Cost per response and cost per order give the bottom line of success or failure. Percentage response levels vary from 0.5 per cent to 5 per cent, although there are many examples now of much higher rates – as high as 60 per cent – especially when targeting existing customers with strong creative combined with highly relevant incentives. (Note that enquiries,

FIGURE 17.2   Example of a mailing schedule

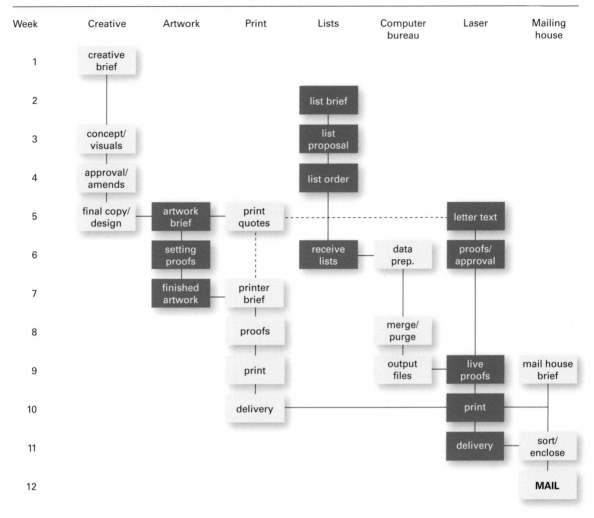

Notes: 1 Print includes letters, brochures, envelopes.
2 If large mail quantity mail house need more notice.
3 If envelopes special their make-up requires longer lead time.

SOURCE: Institute of Direct Marketing

as opposed to orders, are easier to get and therefore pull higher response levels.)

How much would you spend on winning a customer? What kind of incentive would you offer a customer to take action and place an order? Here are a few examples: $50 Amazon voucher; Alliance & Leicester (bank) £50 (to open an account); Virgin £400 (free laptop to selected customers); FedEx £1,000 (free PC); Streamline.com $1,000 (free fridge-freezer).

The direct mail budgeting worksheet shown in Figure 17.3 helps to identify and control costs.

Test, test, test

One of the advantages of direct marketing is the ability to test, retest, change, monitor and learn what works best. Everything can be tested, including the colour of the signature. A white envelope will do better than a manila envelope, and a brightly

FIGURE 17.3   Direct mail budgeting worksheet

CAMPAIGN TITLE: Est   Actual
BUDGET: PROMOTION DATE:
TARGET: MAIL QUANTITY

		Estimated Costs	Actual Costs	Invoice Y/N	Comments
1 ORIGINATION	– Copywriting/Design – Artwork Production				
2 DATABASE LIST PREPARATION	– List Rental – Data Preparation – Merge/Purge – Mailsort				
3 LASER PRINTING	– Text Setting – Printing				
4 PRINT PRODUCTION	– Letterhead – Continuation sheet – Brochure – Flyer – Order Form – Other				
5 ENVELOPES	– Outer – Reply				
6 LETTERSHOP	– Folding – Collating – Enclosing				
7 POSTAGE	– Postage – (Discount)				
8 MISC.	– Couriers etc				
9 TOTAL COSTS					
10 COST PER 1000 MAILED = (Total Cost/Qty. mailed) × 1,000					
11 COST PER RESPONSE = Total Cost/No. of Responses					
12 COST PER SALE = Total Cost/No. of Sales					
13 TOTAL REVENUE					
14 REVENUE TO COST = Revenue/Total Cost					

SOURCE: Institute of Direct Marketing

coloured envelope will do better than a white one (but will it damage the long-term corporate image?). If 10 per cent of a direct marketing budget is allocated to continual testing, then response levels will be continually higher.

Drayton Bird (2000) tested 12 different 'appropriate' lists, three different prices, two different ways to pay, different times for the mailings, alternative ways of responding and several creative approaches. He found that the best combination of all these factors produced a result 58 times better than the worst combination. By identifying the best and worst responses for each variable, the maximum response variation (difference between best and worst) was found. Table 17.1 shows the results.

TABLE 17.1   The impact of different direct-mail variables on response levels

Variable	Different response between worst and best
List	× 6.0
Offer	× 3.0
Timing	× 2.0
Creative	× 1.35
Response	× 1.2

Ideally, everything should be tested in isolation to give more realistic results. There are sometimes so many combinations that testing might appear endless. However, the big variables (those likely to have a significant impact on the bottom line) should be tested. Work down the list, but stop when the cost of testing outweighs the benefits. As mentioned, direct mail lends itself to testing. It allows the marketing manager to become more scientific and more precise – basically a better manager. Testing the colour of a signature may yield only one-twentieth of 1 per cent difference in response, but even so it still generates increased revenues, so it is worth testing everything.

The Eskimo story

Two Eskimos break a hole in the ice and drop their fishing line in. After some time a deep voice booms out slowly: 'There ain't no fish down there.' The two shocked Eskimos quickly pull up their line and wander off further down the ice, break another hole and drop their line in. The same voice eventually booms out the same message, upon which the younger Eskimo braces himself and shouts back 'Who is it that speaks to us?' A deathly silence follows. Eventually, the voice booms out: 'The ice rink manager'.

Why fish in the wrong pond? If there ain't no fish in the pond, don't fish there. Spend time researching lists and databases.

Advantages of direct mail over advertising or sales management

There has always been some debate over whether to allocate direct mail more of the communications budget than perhaps advertising or the sales force itself. Therefore the advantages and disadvantages are considered in some detail here.

If the targeting is right, direct marketing can deliver a cost-effective customer acquisition (or retention) programme. It can also open up a new distribution channel offering delivery from the supplier to the customer directly. This can save money by saving margins previously given to distributors or retailers, but it can also damage relations with distributors if they feel the direct marketing competes with them. Direct mail can, on the other hand, work with them by referring enquiries to or generating leads for distributors, or simply expanding the market.

1 *Targeting* – isolate and talk to tight, well-defined target markets, eg 'slimming pill buyers who read the *Sun*'. Tight targets exclude waste associated with promoting to a mass audience.

2 *Cost-effective* – although initially there is a higher cost per thousand contacted, the cost per enquiry or order can be substantially lower, particularly with repeat sales.

3 *Control and accountability* – there are easy-to-measure, immediate results as the responses come in. This facilitates continuous improvement and clearer direction for future activities.

4 *Fast response within a few days* – it is easy to see if a mailshot or opt-in e-mail campaign has worked.

5 *Opportunity to test* – and retest – any variable, eg prices, promotions, timing, lists and even the colour of a signature and/or the colour of the envelope (split mailings – 50 per cent blue and 50 per cent black).

6 *International* – can offer an alternative route for new market entry. Direct contact by mail or telephone may be cheaper and faster than a personal visit at the early stages of the buying cycle.

7 *Opportunity to build a database* – and win repeat sales by developing a personalized or individual dialogue and ultimately a continuous relationship with the customer base. A database also facilitates the testing and researching of the impact of, say, TV advertisements on different segments.

8 *Tailored messages* – customers with different needs or even different levels of loyalty can receive separate offers, eg brand-loyal customers can receive offers different from brand switchers.

9 *Long-term customers* – the opportunity of developing long-term active relationships with customers through the database.

10 *Building customer profiles* by collecting information about reactions to advertisements, promotions, mailshots and even reasons for buying or not buying, segmenting customers into clusters, generating leads, qualifying leads, selling, and giving customer service.

CASE STUDY 17.1   Acronis automated marketing campaign

Situation

Acronis is a software company that helps small to medium businesses manage their back-up and disaster recovery operations. The automated marketing agency CleverTouch launched a campaign entitled 'Digital assets' in the UK, which targeted senior IT contacts in organizations of up to 500 employees.

Objective

The objective was to target new customers in the UK with the aim of achieving about 65 attendees per webinar for real educational engagement. From these attendees, an estimated 10–20 opportunities per event would evolve with an average value of typically £5,000, ie £50,000–£100,000 revenue generated from each event.

Strategy

CleverTouch marketing deployed a strategy intended to in-form identified organizations' IT managers about the latest practices in storage, back-up and recovery whilst meeting the objective to confirm that any existing contact still existed and was relevant. The focus was on helping prospects along their buying cycle or journey of under-standing and not purely selling to them or securing a sales appointment.

Tactics

Acronis commissioned market research to identify the key pain points for IT managers implementing storage back-up and disaster recovery solutions. The results were presented in an Acronis white paper, which became the call to action for the first e-mail, an Acronis white paper entitled 'Digital assets research findings: Unveiling backup and recovery practices across Europe'.

- *Stage 1:* E-mail 1 was sent to 24,000 contacts. It had a secondary purpose of cleansing the database of contacts that were no longer in the role or relevant. The initial e-mail was resent to all those who had not clicked through or registered whose e-mail address was still valid (*c.* 21,500). Duplicates were suppressed at all stages.

FIGURE 17.4   The amount of time IT managers could lose in the event of data loss (e-mail 1 with 'Digital assets research findings' attachment)

THROW AWAY EVERYTHING YOU DID YESTERDAY THEN TELL YOUR WHOLE COMPANY TO DO THE SAME.

Dear Phil Crawley,

Recent research indicates that a massive two thirds (63%) of IT managers would take a day or more to recover their company's data in the event of system downtime, leading to lost revenue, lost productivity and huge frustration of both employees and customers.

If you're not backing up regularly, one minor disaster could mean that everything everyone in your organisation did yesterday, the day before and last week...could be lost.

Read the Digital Assets Research Findings: Unveiling Backup & Recovery Practices across Europe.

✓ What you fear most about system failure

✓ How confident you are that you could recover in the event of a disaster

✓ How quickly you could recover

✓ How stressful data loss is in comparison to other events

☟ <u>Download the Acronis complimentary White Paper 'Digital Assets Research Findings: Unveiling Backup & Recovery Practices Across Europe'</u>

Best Regards,
Acronis Team

Get your Free Research Findings!

DOWNLOAD NOW

Acronis® Digital Assets Research Findings:

Unveiling Backup & Recovery Practices across Europe

March 2010

Acronis. Move. Manage. Maintain. Seamlessly.

FIGURE 17.5   A guide to back-up and recovery for small and medium businesses (e-mail 2 with 'SMB guide to backup and recovery' attachment)

) Acronis®

THROW AWAY EVERYTHING
YOU DID YESTERDAY
THEN TELL YOUR WHOLE COMPANY TO DO THE SAME.

Dear **Phil Crawley,**

It really doesn't matter what causes your systems to fail, the result is the same: weeks or even months' worth of work, gone. Cost of retrieval, including lost productivity, is huge. At Acronis we understand that backup and recovery may not always be at the top of your agenda, that's why we've gathered these tips & tricks to help you.

Read our SMB Blueprint Guide to quickly assess your business' approach to disaster recovery.

✓ Simple tips to implement an effective backup and recovery strategy

✓ Best practice advice on the areas of your business which should be protected

✓ Learn more about the true cost of downtime

<u>**Download Acronis complimentary 'SMB Blue Print Guide to Backup & Recovery'**</u>

Best Regards,
Acronis Team

Get your Free Blue Print Guide!

DOWNLOAD NOW

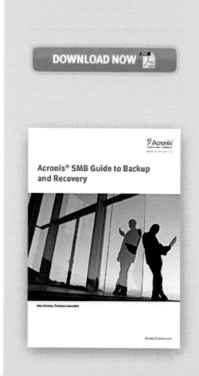

Acronis® SMB Guide to Backup and Recovery

Acronis. Move. Manage. Maintain. Seamlessly.

FIGURE 17.6   Invitation to a webinar exploring the challenges and pitfalls of protecting virtual server environments (e-mail 3)

Join us for an exclusive webinar to gain actionable insight from **Lauren Whitehouse**, Senior Analyst, Enterprise Strategy Group, about the challenges and common pitfalls of protecting virtual server environments. **Michael Lee**, Acronis Principal Solutions Architect, will demonstrate the award-winning Acronis® Backup & Recovery™ 10 solution.

We will address such questions as; are you encountering stumbling blocks as you deploy virtual machines? Are you looking for better ways to protect data and mission-critical applications as virtual machine counts increase? Are you re-evaluating best practices to secure data across physical and virtual environments?

Topics we will cover:

- ✓ How to optimise virtual machine backup and recovery

- ✓ How to gain efficiency of a unified approach to protecting physical and virtual machines

Webinar Details: Thursday June 3rd, 2:00 - 3:00 PM London Time
Duration 45 mins.

Don't miss out register now!

Best Regards,
Acronis Team

Register now for our exclusive webinar!

"Virtualisation is about more than deploying virtual machines"

Date:
Thursday, June 3rd

Time:
2:00 - 3:00 PM, London Time

Presenters:

Lauren Whitehouse,
Senior Analyst
Enterprise Strategy Group

Michael Lee,
Principal Solutions Architect
Acronis, Inc

Acronis. Move. Manage. Maintain. Seamlessly.

FIGURE 17.7   Contact workflow strategy

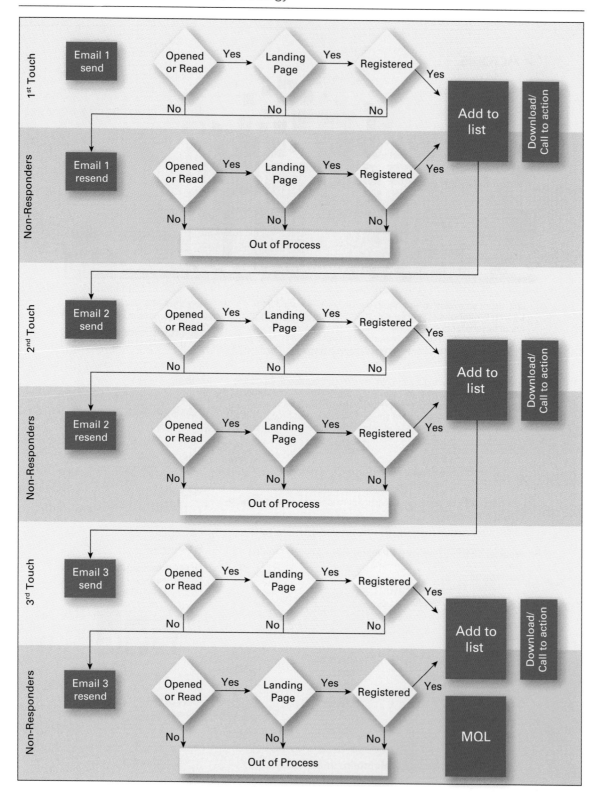

- *Stage 2:* E-mail 2 was sent to those who had opened the initial e-mail with an invitation to download an Acronis blueprint in back-up and disaster recovery. The blueprint e-mail was resent to those who had not opened it and whose e-mail address was still valid (*c.* 2,125). Simply put, this e-mail was sent to everyone who downloaded 'Digital assets research findings'.

- *Stage 3:* E-mail 3 was sent to respondees of the first two e-mails inviting them to attend a market-research-led webinar – again highlighting the findings from the market research conducted and linking the findings into Acronis best practice (*c.* 4,600). Simply put, this e-mail was sent to everyone who downloaded e-mail 1 or 2.

- *Stage 4:* Throughout the campaign a link was included that enabled the recipient to forward the e-mail to a friend, providing Acronis with the possibility to acquire relevant contacts for this and further campaigns.

- *Stage 5:* Marketing engagement was used to follow up on those contacts who registered and attended and those who registered but did not attend the webinar, to identify any immediate sales opportunities. The qualified sales leads were passed to the Acronis sales team for closure (80 leads).

Action

The campaign ran across a five-week time frame, with typically five working days between e-mail distributions. This meant that contacts who were out of the office for a week would not miss the follow-up e-mail. When resending an e-mail the identical e-mail was sent with a different subject line. Recipients' e-mail addresses that were no longer valid (hard bounce) were removed from the contact database.

Marketing automation technology increased efficiencies in the whole process and workflow and reduced costs (see Figure 17.7).

Control

The goal was to get 65 attendees to a webinar (based on previous history and experience). The result was over 140 attendees, with 10 immediate opportunities (worth over approximately £50,000 in year 1) and one initial sale of £10,000. As a result of the campaign's success, the same process was applied to a secondary campaign within a three-week time frame. This second campaign had equally successful results, with again over 140 contacts in attendance.

As a result of the success, the campaign has now expanded to other languages and regions within Europe. To supplement the campaign with additional coverage, a channel partner version was developed, which was used by Acronis channel partners to enhance their marketing activities.

The key to this campaign was to nurture the prospects through the campaign and create a pool of engaged contacts to be used in future, more targeted campaigns, eg direct mail. This method of continued, ongoing activity aimed at educating and engaging contacts is far more beneficial than a single campaign that is executed in isolation.

Men/women, minutes and money

This campaign required an estimated 10 days from Acronis and an estimated 5 days from CleverTouch. The campaign was a digital multi-step campaign, with each step requiring ever increasing degrees of commitment and engagement on both sides. The campaign took eight weeks to research and plan and was rolled out in eight weeks. The budget for this campaign, including imagery and CleverTouch's development, build and delivery time, was estimated at £25,000. Currently the ROI is 4:1, and it is expected to peak at 10:1.

Advantages and disadvantages

Here are some of the advantages and disadvantages to consider when deciding whether to increase or reduce this communications tool.

Advantages

Direct mail can be tightly targeted (as can opt-in e-mail). Although the cost per thousand (CPT) for direct mail is high, the cost per order (CPO) can be a lot lower than for other communications tools. It can also be used for customer retention and nurturing customers over their lifetime. Direct mail is arguably better for customer retention than for customer acquisition. Ideally, direct mail (and opt-in e-mail) should be integrated into an overall contact strategy that is tailored according to the customers' preferences. This achieves high levels of satisfaction, because the mailings are always totally relevant to the customers' needs (remember the magic marketing formula). A well-targeted mailing in a jiffy bag or gift wrapped, with an attractive incentive inside, can generate unexpectedly high response rates, trigger word of mouth and sometimes generate publicity in the press.

Disadvantages

In addition to sometimes upsetting intermediaries (through selling directly to customers), direct marketing has a problem with its image. Direct mail has connotations of 'junk mail' and is therefore vulnerable to criticism from environmental pressure groups. Opt-in e-mail has connotations of spam. Although research shows that a large majority prefer to receive direct mail, there is a percentage who consider it to be an intrusion or invasion of their privacy. Online, an unsolicited e-mail is considered even more unacceptable – a breach of netiquette (net etiquette) and therefore spam. In consumer markets this is now against the law. It is not surprising that spammers get 'flamed' by angry customers who send abusive messages back, sometimes repeatedly and sometimes with a mailbomb (a massive file) that may effectively close down the spammer's system. Database maintenance is also critical (and costs resources). This is an increasing problem, as e-mail lists are offered at very cheap prices, eg \$35 per million (compared to £200 per thousand 'snail mail' addresses). The initial customer acquisition costs in snail mail can be high (subsequent transactions are much cheaper). Direct marketing has a high CPT compared to advertising. An average response of 1 per cent suggests, by definition, that 99 per cent of mailings get chucked in the bin. Poorly targeted mailings might one day be considered a threat to trees and the environment. There can also be a heavy investment cost in developing a database. Direct marketing can prove to be expensive for a one-off sale. Used effectively to develop repeat sales, gain 'lifetime value' and nurture relationships, it can prove extremely profitable. Finally, there is the risk involved with any marketing communications activity. A bad mailing, for example, can not only lose money but reduce sales and damage the company's corporate image. In fact a spam mailing would be considered irresponsible by any well-run company.

Key points from Chapter 17

- Direct mail and opt-in e-mail can be used to generate new business. Opt-in e-mail can, ideally, be used for customer retention (or as part of a CRM contact strategy) rather than just for customer acquisition.
- Direct mail is highly targetable and relatively easy to test and control.
- The systems and database behind any campaign must be fully integrated into the campaign or ongoing contact strategy.
- Organizations that ignore direct marketing and database techniques will suffer a competitive disadvantage.

References and further reading

Bird, D (2000) *Commonsense Direct Marketing*, 4th edn, Kogan Page, London

Brann, C (1984) *Cost-Effective Direct Marketing: By mail, telephone and direct response advertising*, Collectors' Books, Cirencester

Chaffey, D and Smith, P R (2008) *eMarketing eXcellence*, Butterworth-Heinemann, Oxford

Considine, R and Raphel, M (1987) *The Great Brain Robbery*, The Great Brain Robbery, Pasadena, CA

Exhibition Venues Association (2000) *UK Exhibition Facts*, Vol. 12, Exhibition Venues Association, Mayfield, East Sussex

Howard, M (1989) Telephone marketing vs direct sales force costs, Commissioned by Datapoint (UK) Ltd, London

McCorkell, G (1997) *Direct and Database Marketing*, Kogan Page, London

Moriarty, R and Moran, U (1990) Managing hybrid systems, *Harvard Business Review*, November–December

Moriarty, R and Swartz, G (1989) Automation to boost sales and marketing, *Harvard Business Review*, January–February

Royal Mail (2001) *Getting More from Integrated Marketing and Making Direct Mail Work for You*, MBO, London

Schlosser, J (2003) Looking for intelligence in ice cream, *Fortune*, 17 March

Stevens, M (1991) *The Handbook of Telemarketing*, Kogan Page, London

Tapp, A (2001) *Principles of Direct and Database Marketing*, 2nd edn, Financial Times/Prentice Hall, Englewood Cliffs, NJ

Toffler, A (1980) *The Third Wave*, Collins, London

Watson, J (1989) The direct marketing guide, *Marketing Magazine*, 9 February

Worcester, R (2002) Customers: Handle with care, *Purple Issue*, 30 October

Further information

Direct Marketing Association
DMA House
70 Margaret Street
London W1W 8SS
Tel: +44 (0)20 7291 3300
Fax: +44 (0)20 7323 4426
www.dma.org.uk

Federation of European Direct Marketing (FEDMA)
Avenue de Tervuren 439
B-1150 Brussels
Belgium
Tel: +32 (0)2 77 899 28
www.fedma.org

Institute of Direct Marketing (IDM)
1 Park Road
Teddington
Middlesex TW11 OAR
Tel: +44 (0)20 8977 5705
Fax: +44 (0)20 8943 2535
www.theidm.com

Mailing Preference Service (MPS)
DMA House
70 Margaret Street
London W1W 8SS
Tel: +44 (0)20 7291 3310
Fax: +44 (0)20 7323 4226
www.mpsonline.org.uk

Office of the Data Protection Registrar
Wycliffe House
Water Lane
Wilmslow
Cheshire SK9 5AF
Tel: +44 (0)303 123 1113
Fax: +44 (0)1625 524510
www.dataprotection.gov.uk

18
Exhibitions – online and offline

LEARNING OBJECTIVES

By the end of this chapter you will be able to:

- Discuss an exhibition strategy
- Help to plan an exhibition
- Understand how measuring exhibitions and events is important
- Appreciate how exhibitions can be part of a contact strategy

Introduction

Imagine bringing a whole market together, under one roof, for a few days. An exciting idea? An explosive concept? It happens all the time. Exhibitions are unique in that they are the only medium that brings the whole market together – buyers, sellers and competitors – all under one roof for a few days. Products and services can be seen, demonstrated or tested, and face-to-face contact can be made with a large number of relevant decision makers in a short period of time. Relationships can be strengthened and opportunities seized if planned carefully. Exhibitions are a powerful MarComms tool, but they require detailed planning whether offline, online or in virtual worlds (see page 259). The same rules apply – thorough planning and training is required.

Managing exhibitions

Exhibitions offer an array of opportunities, problems and challenges to the keen marketing manager. They can be leveraged to the maximum effect by integrating them with other communications tools and developing a longer-term perspective incorporating an overall exhibition strategy. Detailed exhibition planning skills require the manager to work through the following:

- Situation – to exhibit or not to exhibit?
- Objectives – prioritize exhibition objectives.
- Strategy – develop an exhibition strategy including:
  - selecting the right shows;
  - agreeing a design strategy.
- Tactics – determine pre-show promotional tactics.
- Action – train exhibition staff:
  - finalize the exhibition operational (daily action) plan;
  - ensure follow-up;
- Control – evaluate post-show.

Situation – to exhibit or not to exhibit?

Many marketers find exhibitions to be very expensive investments in terms of money required for renting the space, building a stand, promoting it, entertaining customers, travel and accommodation. They also find it expensive in terms of human resources and time required. Sometimes it's disproportionate in terms of return on investment, and marketers have to make tough decisions as to whether to continue attending all the usual exhibitions and conferences, particularly if customers are migrating online and doing business online instead of visiting trade shows. For the marketer who wants to attend some exhibitions, whether online or offline, here are the stages of planning that will help to boost return on investment, save time and, ideally, reduce workload through better planning.

Objectives – prioritize exhibition objectives

If you don't know where you are going, how do you know when you have arrived? How do you know if it is a good show or a waste of time and money? How do you know if you have had a good day or a bad day? How can you achieve if you don't know what you are trying to achieve? Clearly defined objectives are required to focus the effort. Typically, enquiries and orders can be easily quantified and broken into daily (or even hourly) objectives. A sweepstake among staff (guessing the numbers of enquiries and orders) can help to focus everyone's attention. Although exhibitions are hard work, they are dynamic in the variety of objectives they provide:

- Sell – generate sales and enquiries from new and existing customers, agents and distributors.
- Launch new products.
- Maintain a presence in the market.
- Press coverage – internal (newsletter) and external PR opportunities.
- Reinforce relationships with customers, distributors and agents through hospitality

and introductions to senior managers and directors. Taking care of customers at exhibitions can be part of a contact strategy (including e-mails, snail mail, telemarketing, sales team visits, etc).

- Support local distributors and agents by exhibiting.
- Market research – customers, non-customers and distributors.
- Test new ideas – product testing and informal creative discussions.
- Competitor analysis and intelligence gathering.
- Staff motivation – some exhibitions can be the focal point of the year. They allow staff to come to the show or exhibition and feel a certain amount of pride in their organization.
- Meet new staff or potential recruits.

Strategy

Develop an exhibition strategy

Ideally, exhibitions should not be used as a one-off, ad hoc activity. They can be used more effectively when: 1) they are viewed as a possible series of exhibitions; 2) they are integrated carefully with other communications tools; 3) they are selected and planned well in advance; and 4) their effectiveness is constantly measured. An exhibition strategy summarizes the frequency and types of show selected (eg national, international, real or virtual; see 'Selection checklist' below). Perhaps different segments of the market are served by different exhibitions, different product or service sectors, different geographical regions and different buying cycles (eg Christmas products have exhibitions in January for the coming Christmas season). Considering the bigger picture requires a knowledge of what exhibitions are available, suitable and affordable. This means continually collecting exhibition brochures and keeping them safely in an exhibition file for regular review.

An exhibition strategy can also give guidance about the kind of integrated marketing support provided and the total level of spending. Remember that the cost of hiring space at an exhibition is often only a small proportion of the total exhibition costs (between 20 and 25 per cent; see 'Costs' below).

Select the right shows

As with advertising or any marketing activity, exhibitions need careful targeting. There is an increasing number of exhibitions available, usually more than an organization can attend. Some are better than others. All of them have sales staff dedicated to promoting and selling their exhibition space. The exhibitor must choose carefully. The skill in selection is somewhat similar to that of the media planner (who must choose which media and specific media vehicles, except that media planners have access to considerably more audited information; see Chapter 7, 'Media selection'). There are various listings giving a diary of exhibitions and events for up to two years in advance.

Selection checklist

1 *Type of exhibition.* Local, national or international; vertical (tight focus of interest for buyers or sellers) or horizontal (wide range of interest for buyers or sellers); general public; trade events; private events; symposia or conferences where a limited amount of exhibiting facilities are available.

2 *Target audience.* Type and number of visitors; audited figures should be made available, eg Audit Bureau of Circulations (ABC) figures are approved by the Association of Event Organisers (AEO) (the use of ABC figures is also a compulsory requirement of membership of the AEO, largely because ABC's figures are reproducible for checking and testing).

3 *Timing.* Does it meet buyers' purchasing patterns and can the organization prepare for it in time? For example, foreign shows may need to be planned 18 months in advance.

4 *Facilities.* Any limitations or constraints; how the organizers intend to promote the event; supporting contact events, eg dinners, award ceremonies, seminars, breakfast receptions, etc.

5 *Costs.* Compare 'cost of space' and 'size of audience' ratios between different exhibitions. The space cost is useful for comparison, but it represents only a small proportion of the total cost of exhibiting.

The cost of the stand design is generally excluded if the exhibitor already owns a mobile stand unit, but miscellaneous items (see Figure 18.1) rapidly cause costs to escalate.

6 *Previous success.* How long has the show been running? Has it been a success previously? Is it enjoying year-on-year growth? Are there any customer (exhibitor) testimonials or references available?

7 *Endorsements.* What official bodies are supporting it? There are independent surveys that list visitor numbers, visitor quality, sales enquiries and a summary of exhibitors' results (see 'Evaluate post-show' below).

Agree a design strategy

The stand design is a key factor in the overall exhibition strategy. It should present the right corporate image (see Chapters 14 and 21), announce the product or service, visualize benefits (arising from the product or service), attract interest and look aesthetically pleasing while providing for other functions such as display, demonstration, discussion, hospitality and storage (of spare samples, literature, coats, etc). **Identifying measurable exhibition success criteria** such as sales or orders, number of enquiries, cost per enquiry, cost per order, qualified contact names for a database, visitors' recall or level of awareness of the particular organization's stand, key messages intended by the stand, etc helps to guide the overall design of the exhibition stand.

A visitor may have less than three seconds to scan and decide whether to enter a particular stand instead of one of the many others competing for that same visitor's attention. Buyers have only a limited amount of time to visit a limited number of stands (the US Center for Exhibition Research suggests that the average visitor attending a show barely calls on 13 stands, regardless of the size of the exhibition). Buyers have to choose quickly whether to enter or not. Many exhibitions provide a computer printout of the exhibitors that fall into a particular category of suppliers of interest to a particular visitor. The printout usually includes a map identifying the location of the specific organizations listed in the category. This means that buyers can pause and decide what route they will take and which stands they will visit before entering the main exhibition hall. Despite a pre-planned schedule of visits, a busy buyer can still be attracted by an excellent stand design or promotional stunt to an unplanned visit. However, a stunt can also attract time-wasting, stand-congesting, non-target market visitors. Some stunts have been found to deter senior decision makers, who may feel that stunts are aimed at lower-level visitors.

The 'three-second' test

When you next visit an exhibition look around you and see how many (if any) stands clearly tell you what they offer. How many exhibition stands actually explain what business the exhibitors are in? Do any of them explain benefits? How many stand designs actually help you within three to five seconds before you pass by?

It is surprising to observe the number of organizations that promote their name first and foremost, perhaps followed by a product name, and somewhere, almost hidden, the product and product features are displayed. Product benefits (what buyers really seek) cannot be seen easily. Most buyers have to make the psychological leap and commit themselves by walking on to a stand to engage in discussion that may eventually reveal the hidden product benefits. Larger organizations may feel that they have too many products to highlight any one individually, or that their name is associated with the product area so strongly that all visitors (including those from overseas?) actually look for the company name since they already know the exhibitor's business. Perhaps some exhibitors do not want to reveal their benefits to the competition too readily. Perhaps others simply don't ask their stand designers to consider this issue.

The design should be consistent with the organization's corporate identity guidelines (the design manual specifies the logo style, typefaces, and primary and secondary colours). **The stand design should attract visitors and facilitate a simple selling sequence of attracting a visitor,** providing a comfortable space and facilities to demonstrate products, and fostering an environment for detailed discussion and negotiations if appropriate.

The design brief for an exhibition stand can use the basic SOSTAC® + 3Ms discussed in Chapter 10. Essentially the designer needs to know: who the target audience is; in what kinds of exhibitions the stand might appear; the locations and preferred stand locations (within the exhibition); stand size and function (display, demonstration, hospitality area, access and service facilities required); and whether the stand needs to be reusable. Information on competitors and their stands is also useful. Additional information such as the design manual and the dimensions of any display items is also important. The success criteria must be listed and objectives prioritized, eg presenting an image, attracting new business, meeting old customers, launching a new product, etc. The designer also needs to know the overall exhibition strategy (discussed above). Tactical information is sometimes included. This includes any promotional ideas, specific numbers of staff and visitors on the stand at any one time, whether any promotional off-stand activities will be attracting visitors on to the stand, whether the stand will be used for photo opportunities, and what kinds of electronic gadgetry (data projectors, laptops, sound, etc), products and sales literature need to be displayed. **The designer also needs to know about the 3Ms, the three key resources of men/women, money (budget) and minutes (time).**

The whole exhibition design should focus on key, measurable objectives (are all the elements linked up to and consistent with the overall exhibition strategy, etc?). Sound, sight, space and even smell can be used creatively by a designer (there are, however, likely to be some constraints imposed by the organizers). Good designers exploit both two-dimensional design (eg graphics) and three-dimensional design (eg the use of space).

Tactics – determine pre-show promotional tactics

To maximize effectiveness, exhibitors do not depend on stand design alone to attract visitors. Careful pre-show promotions can ensure a steady flow of visitors on to a stand. Direct mail, linked with an incentive or sales promotion, free tickets, inserts, advertising, publicity, etc, basically attempts to get visitors to decide to visit a particular stand before they arrive at the exhibition in the first place. Given

that the average visitor visits only 13 stands, it is important to get on to the appropriate target visitor's 'must visit' list. Pre-show marketing helps to identify who to expect and who to chase up. It also provides a fresh opportunity to talk to customers and prospects on the back of the urgency and excitement created by the show.

Given that exhibiting is a resource-consuming activity, pre-show activity aims to maximize the effectiveness of the investment. Some types of show, such as conferences and seminars, are almost totally dependent on pre-event activity, as attendees will not walk in off the street. Advertising and editorial opportunities range from the usual trade, professional and domestic press, local and regional media, and transport (taxis, trains, buses and stations) through to the exhibition catalogue itself. Sponsorship of guides, maps, promotions, teaser promotions, free gifts and competitions can all be offered to the target visitor through advertising, editorial, inserts, mailings and even telemarketing. Good exhibition planning can integrate with other communication activities at an early stage. This means that the costs of sales promotions and incentives can be reduced significantly by increasing the organization's buying power when sourcing many different sales promotion gifts simultaneously. Delivery and invoicing can also be staggered or delayed so that cash flow bottlenecks do not occur. It might be possible to run a joint promotion with a non-competing exhibitor so that your product or service (or even just the incentive) is combined with someone else's to promote both sites as 'must see' sites.

In summary, pre-show promotional activity can involve:

- snail mail invitations (with an incentive?);
- e-marketing invitations and reminders;
- telesales key customers or prospects;
- press activities;
- sales force briefing (to invite their customers);
- company calendars, diaries, etc, which can include dates of key exhibitions;
- sponsored activities;
- perimeter advertising (around the venue);
- press advertising (trade magazines);
- joint promotions.

Action

Train exhibition staff

After all the hard pre-show work, when a stunning stand has been created, the promotion has been publicized and a good flow of traffic on to the stand has been generated, what a shame it is to lose business through staff who don't know exactly how to deal with people. Staffing an exhibition stand is hard work. The day becomes even longer when staff have no goals, no targets and no exhibition training. The team needs to be briefed about why the organization is exhibiting (including specific objectives broken down into daily objectives). **Exhibition training helps staff to know: how to physically stand (the importance of body language); how to approach** a visitor (never with a closed question such as 'May I help you?' – try open-ended questions like 'What caught your eye?'); **what kind of information should be gleaned from visitors** (see the box below); **when a senior manager should be called over; how to demonstrate** (product knowledge and skills); **how to close a sale; and how to present records.** It is possible to practise before the show starts each day (or during quiet moments).

Finalize the exhibition action plan

Everything, from staffing to samples and sales promotions, has to be meticulously planned. Never underestimate the importance of attention to detail. Even contingencies should be allowed for. Exhibitions are hard work. A staffing roster schedules staff so that they can have a break and a chance to look around the exhibition (and report back on their observations). More importantly, the roster ensures that the stand is never understaffed or overstaffed with inexperienced staff. How many visitors are expected? How many staff will be required? How many junior and senior staff? Who staffs the stand and when? Comfortable shoes, regular breaks and solid rest between exhibition days are also essential. Individual performance on the stand can be measured against preset criteria (number and quality of enquiries, etc).

The 'What can go wrong will go wrong' law runs rampant in exhibitions. Contingency planning reduces risks, but inevitably something unforeseen still occurs. The author has had two such experiences, both of which happened at international shows: the first was in Birmingham, where a new electrical product set itself on fire while being exhibited; the second was in New York, where the freight company lost all the samples and display units. Other exhibition nightmares include a stand

---

Six essential questions for qualifying a prospect

1 'Thanks for stopping. How are you familiar with...?' or 'What attracted you to our display?' or 'What do you see that you like?' (This gives the history of the prospective buyer and tells you where to start selling.)

2 'What's your situation now?' (This tells you if the prospective buyer actually has a real live need.)

3 'What would you like to achieve [or change]?' (This further defines the prospective buyer's application of your product.)

4 'What are your concerns as to budget?' (This tells you if the prospective buyer has the money.)

5 'How does your timetable look on all of this?' (This gives you the prospective buyer's timetable for buying or acting.)

6 'How would you like to proceed from here?' (This lets the prospective buyer take over.)

Engebretson (2000)

Small exhibitors can be beautiful

NCH Action for Children charity had to break through the clutter with a small 2- by 2-metre stand. Its stunning backlit graphic of children's faces, supporting the 'All Children Dream' theme, did the trick. The stand staff were fully trained in exhibition techniques and fully briefed to communicate key messages and collect key information. They fulfilled their 'key contacts hit list', snapped publicity photos with visiting MPs and shone out from the heaving masses.

FIGURE 18.1   This checklist needs to be checked at the end of each day so that everything is in place for the next day

Daily checklist

Appointments diary

Visitors book

Enquiries log/Lead form

Brochures

Badges

Business cards

Samples

Spare parts

Scissors, Sellotape, penknife

Press packs

Give-aways (pens, notepads, etc)

Fish bowl (drop card in for free entry to prize draw)

Ashtrays

Water

Clean glasses

Flowers

Insurance

First aid kit (incl. aspirins)

that was built upside down (because the architect read the plans upside down) and neighbouring stands encroaching on each other's area (sometimes by accident).

Ensure follow-up

The exhibition is not an end in itself, although by the end of the show the exhausted staff probably feel as though it is. Careful follow-up work must start almost immediately. This is where the organization can earn its return from the exhibition. Leads, enquiries, quotations, sales and after-sales discussions need to be followed up in a professional manner. This requires a follow-up meeting where all the staff go through the cards they collected, the people they talked to and the projects or jobs that were discussed. This prevents the duplication, contradiction and conflict that can arise where two people from the same prospect organization have asked two different members of staff for a quotation for the same job, or where two different enquiries have emerged for the same job from two different prospects. Worse still are unfulfilled enquiries. How many times have you left an enquiry with exhibitors never to hear from them again? Lack of post-show follow-up makes all the previous exhibition efforts a waste of time.

The manager can determine who follows up what, with a report-back meeting date set to see what sales are actually generated. More detailed evaluation of the true exhibition results can be carried out so that future efforts are improved. It is worth formalizing the evaluation process so that the trend, individual performance and competitor performance can all be measured.

80 per cent make the same old mistakes

'Every four or five years 80 per cent of companies exhibiting make the same old mistakes, because a new man has been appointed.'
                                    Harry McDermott, Exhibition Surveys

Control

Evaluate post-show

Post-show evaluation measures performance against the preset objectives. It also examines whether the objectives were realistic, whether the show was the right show, and what was good and what was bad about the organization's performance. A competitor's performance can also be evaluated to a certain degree. How can the performance be improved? Should the exhibition be run again next year? Was it value for money?

Some post-show questions

1 What percentage of the potential number of visitors to the whole exhibition (that fitted the target market profile) visited our stand?

2 What percentage stopped but did not visit our stand?

3 What percentage saw but did not stop at our stand?

4 How many leads or enquiries were created?

5 What was the cost per contact or visitor?

6 What percentage of contacts or visitors plan to buy the product or service?

7 What was the cost per 'serious' visitor?

8 What was the cost per order?

9 How effective was each staff member's performance? (According to Harry McDermott of Exhibition Surveys, 'Stand staff should indoctrinate every visitor they meet on a stand. When those visitors think of the types of product shown they should think of the exhibitor. Research can get visitors to rate individual staff because the visitors' comments can be linked back to the stand record of contacts.')

10 Did we overspend or underspend (too large or too small a stand, or too many or too few staff)?

Exhibition value analysis

Exhibition value analysis is a type of survey that includes both a multi-client survey and a confidential private survey so that comparisons can be made between the performance of the client company and that of its competitors. The survey covers visitor potential, the percentage that saw, stopped or visited a particular stand, visitors' perceptions, intentions to buy, and the stand's strengths and weaknesses based on a sample of known visitors to it (supplied by the company). Some research findings suggest that companies do not attend trade exhibitions to sell, but rather to build corporate and brand awareness.

Costs

Exhibition costs need to be looked at carefully. Various sources suggest that the cost of hiring the exhibition space represents as little as one-fifth of the total costs of exhibiting. This obviously depends on whether the cost of the stand design is included, whether there is much integrated promotional activity and whether the opportunity cost of taking members of the sales team 'off the road' are included. The most important thing is to be consistent, so that year-on-year comparisons can be made. Cost per enquiry, cost per order, percentage of sales, return on investment (ROI) and experimental non-attendance are now considered. Note that, in the ROI calculation, costs are treated as an investment (as opposed to an expenditure), which, technically speaking, is not correct.

Cost per enquiry   Cost per enquiry can range from £25 to £500. However, the bottom line for many organizations is still 'How much business did it generate?'

$$\frac{\text{Total exhibition costs}}{\text{Number of serious enquiries}} = \text{Cost per enquiry}$$

Cost per order   Total exhibition costs can be divided by the number of orders taken to find the cost per order. There are some difficulties here, however. First, there is the timescale (some orders instigated by contact at a trade show or exhibition can take several months or longer to be finally confirmed). Second, the regular orders (which would have been brought in by the normal sales force visits anyway) should, ideally, be separated from those incremental orders generated solely by attending the show. Third, there is a school of thought that suggests that exhibitions do not generate sales; they only allow the exhibitor to meet a useful target market, but whether the target market buys depends on a number of factors totally divorced from the show (eg the product, competitors' products, and prices). An average of averages shows a cost per order in UK and overseas exhibitions of £75 and £125 respectively (EIF, 2002). This ignores both the size of the orders and their profitability. The size of the orders could be expressed as a percentage figure in the same way as a marketing communications budget is sometimes expressed, ie marketing expenses as a percentage of sales. In this case, exhibition costs as a percentage of sales generated can be calculated as:

$$\frac{\text{Total exhibition costs}}{\text{Number of orders}} = \text{Cost per order}$$

Percentage of sales

The difficulty here lies in isolating the sales generated exclusively through the exhibition, ie ignoring sales that would have been taken by the sales force regardless of the exhibition. Nevertheless, the cost of taking the same number of enquiries or sales by routine sales visits should be compared to the costs of enquiries or sales taken during the exhibition.

Return on investment

The long-term profitability of the sales is probably the most important of all the criteria. This is difficult to calculate, because the lifetime value of a customer is often difficult to calculate, particularly in industrial markets. However, the short-term ROI can be calculated by dividing the profit or contribution made from the orders by the total cost of the exhibition.

For example, if the orders taken during a show amounted to £200,000 and the total cost of or investment in the exhibition was £20,000, the calculation would be as follows:

Sales	£200,000
Less cost of sales (say 50 per cent)	£100,000
Contribution	£100,000
Less cost/investment in the exhibition	£20,000
Return or profit on the investment	£80,000
This can then be expressed in percentage terms	$\frac{£80,000}{£20,000} = 400$ per cent

The real ROI should in fact only be calculated from additional or new sales that were generated by the exhibition. Say the exhibition generated only five new customers, who in total bought £50,000 worth. The real ROI (on new business) would be 25 per cent. The word 'investment' is a bit misleading, since if the exhibition stand cannot be used again it is not an investment but an expense. If the exhibition produced only one new customer, who bought £10,000 worth, then the ROI would be negative.

Press coverage

One simple gauge is to collect the press clippings from the show. How important publicity and press coverage are as exhibition objectives determines how important this criterion is. See Chapter 14, 'Control – measuring media relations' for more on evaluating press coverage.

Experimental non-attendance

Some organizations decide to stop exhibiting and use the opportunity to measure the impact of non-attendance on their sales and on their competitors' exhibition results.

The many other functions exhibitions provide are not included in the costs or revenues used in the previous calculations. Other, non-selling exhibition activities such as maintaining a presence, projecting an image, entertaining customers, marketing research, competitor analysis and product testing all, in a sense, save costs that would have been incurred if they were commissioned outside the exhibition. Arguably, these 'saved costs' could be subtracted from the other costs in these calculations. Real costs can certainly be saved by careful coordination throughout the whole exhibition planning cycle.

12 reasons for poor performance

James Dudley (1990) highlighted research findings indicating the 12 main reasons for poor performance. How much has changed?

1 Inadequate statements of purpose and objectives – nobody quite knows what they are supposed to do.
2 Poor-quality visitors.
3 Bad location of the stand.
4 Ineffective quality and design of the stand.
5 Undistinguished performance of personnel running the stand, because of poor selection, training, motivation or management.
6 Lack of follow-up of leads and enquiries.
7 Ignoring the competition and letting them steal your prospective visitors.
8 Poor recognition of company by buyers.
9 Poor corporate identity, leading to low recall of the stand by visitors.
10 Breakdown in organization and control, leading to last-minute panics, such as an unfinished stand on the opening day of the show or late arrival of literature, give-aways and so on.
11 Inadequate arrangements made for staff working on the stand, such as locating their accommodation too far from the event, failing to obtain car park permits or not organizing meal vouchers.
12 Inadequate control of costs and budgets, leading to over-expenditure and consequently a poor return on investment.

CASE STUDY 18.1   Sedgwick at RIMS Monte Carlo

This case study demonstrates the kind of detailed and integrated planning required to run a successful exhibition.

Situation

With 60 European offices, Sedgwick is the largest European-based insurance broker and risk management consultancy (and ranked third in the world). Although Sedgwick is well respected, the similarity of competitor products and services makes professionalism, quality and expertise vital in adding value to the 'invisible' service. The credibility of the whole company is largely dependent on the credibility of the sales and support staff. Exhibitions provide a platform for staff visibility and customer contact. The Risk and Insurance Management Society (RIMS) Monte Carlo is a focal point for the European risk and insurance market. It takes place every two years and consists of a three-day, high-level conference and exhibition that attracts all major companies and buyers in the sector. It is therefore essential for Sedgwick to be there.

Target audience

The target audience is risk managers of medium-sized to large companies and managers responsible for buying insurance (finance directors, company secretaries and heads of administration) across Europe.

Objectives

The marketing objectives are:

- to introduce the new European client service network;
- to introduce several pan-European products (including the multilingual service and the eastern Europe network);
- to create an opportunity for cross-selling (new products to existing customers);
- to attract 100 visitors to the stand per day.

The communications objectives are:

- to reinforce Sedgwick's position as the foremost European-based broker with the best European network (including eastern Europe);
- to demonstrate true pan-European expertise (eg multilingualism);
- to project a visibly European image (and not UK dominated);
- to create a totally cohesive 'one company' (single European company) in a clear visual statement;
- to improve internal communications by creating a focal point for the meeting of staff from across the continent to break down barriers between divisions or trading companies.

Strategy

The above objectives would be achieved in a cost-competitive manner by developing an outstanding pan-European exhibition involving: a press conference and press lunch; senior speakers at the main conference dinner; hosting a major dinner; and an innovative exhibition crowd-pulling concept, all integrated into the creative theme 'One Europe, first in Europe'.

Stand design

The nature of the industry and the economic environment was such that lavishly designed stands could create a worry in the minds of clients that 'We are paying for all this.' For these reasons the stand looked smart, professional and European but was not a luxurious extravaganza. Visually, the stand took its style from the *ERA* magazine to create a cohesive look. All graphics were in French and English.

Tactics

Given that most of the RIMS exhibition visitors fell into the target group, it was essential to create a hub of activity around the Sedgwick stand. A new product demonstration was placed alongside a crowd-pulling cartoonist who sketched visitors on pre-printed, branded paper, giving full service and address details on the back. This allowed both client and prospect visitors to take away something that was personal to them but was also Sedgwick branded. The same artist drew European cameos of many countries for a competition. The production of Sedgwick's European magazine, *ERA 2* (published in six languages), was carefully planned so that it was available for the exhibition. The first article in *ERA 2* focused on Sedgwick's eastern European operations.

Action

The stand was staffed by an international team at all times.

Control

A post-exhibition meeting was held to arrange a follow-up schedule for all enquiries and to evaluate the overall exhibition performance. The new products and services helped to develop existing clients and attract new clients. One indicator of the stand's success was the front-page coverage of the stand and Sedgwick's keynote conference speaker in a magazine sponsored by a direct competitor. All stand members felt that the exhibition was a morale booster, and it helped them to feel more confident with their clients. The staff began to feel part of one European company. In fact, a subsequent pan-European slogan competition received 400 entries from company staff (nearly 20 per cent of the European workforce). Arguably, the winning slogan was born out of the new post-exhibition mood: 'One Europe, one broker. Sedgwick.'

Men/women

The entire project was planned by an in-house team with both international and exhibition expertise. Senior management support and commitment to the exhibition were evidenced by the constant presence and involvement of the managing director of the French operation (the local host). The UK-based European PR manager controlled the overall plan and execution.

Money

A basic 3- by 3-metre unit of exhibition floorspace costs between £3,000 and £9,000, depending on the exhibition. At RIMS, the 3- by 6-metre space (two units) cost £6,500. An additional £5,000 was budgeted for all other items, such as the cartoonist, contractor, transport, graphics and telephone lines. The high-quality, lightweight, flexible, re-usable exhibition kit was tailored for the RIMS exhibition and subsequently built into the 18 square metres of rented space. The standard shell scheme option was rejected ('too bland'), as was the purpose-built stand option ('too expensive', with a cost anywhere from £10,000 to £30,000).

The budget did not cover travel and accommodation, which, as is customary in a large organization, was paid for by each individual trading company.

Minutes

RIMS is a biennial event. Sedgwick's planning started 18 months in advance. Early commitment and good relationships with the exhibition organizers helped to secure the best stand location (and choice of halls), speaker opportunities and details of attendees, especially the press. Quarterly meetings were held with French colleagues. Planning meetings immediately before the exhibition were held on-site. Daily planning meetings for all staff members (around 70) were held early each morning to agree the day's strategy before the exhibition doors were opened to the public.

Advantages and disadvantages

Here are some of the advantages and disadvantages to consider when deciding whether to increase or reduce this communications tool.

Advantages

Exhibitions contain a whole market under one roof in an engaging environment where the message can be controlled: prospects, customers, distributors, competitors, the media and many more. While exhibitions do create a presence (or awareness in the mind of key customers), they do generate business. Orders can be taken (sales can be closed), and new customers can be introduced to the brand. Enquiries can be taken and customer needs explored in conversations that otherwise might be difficult to engage in.

Disadvantages

Many exhibitors are looking at the total cost of exhibitions (including pre-promotion, attendance, design and build, staff, sales promotions, gifts and 'freebies'. Some exhibition traffic is falling, and hence exhibitors see their costs rising. Lastly, exhibitions are hard work and require pre-show training and motivation, which are also time-consuming.

Key points from Chapter 18

- Exhibitions are hard work. They can work well for the exhibitor if they are planned and integrated with other marketing tools.
- Exhibitions can form part of a contact strategy.
- Exhibitions need visitors – pre-show promotion is critical.
- Every element of exhibition performance can be monitored and measured with a view to making improvements in the next exhibition.

References and further reading

Black, S (1989) *Exhibitions and Conferences from A to Z*, Modino Press, London

Cotterell, P (1992) *Exhibitions: An exhibitor's guide*, Hodder & Stoughton, London

Dudley, J W (1990) *Successful Exhibiting*, Kogan Page, London

Engebretson, D (2000) *Exhibiting in the USA* (video), Trade Partners UK, Department of Trade and Industry, produced in association with Multimedia Marketing.com, London

Exhibition Industry Federation (EIF) (2002) *The UK Exhibition Industry: The facts and how to exhibit*, EIF, London

Seekings, D (1996) *How to Organize Effective Conferences and Meetings*, Kogan Page, London

Talbot, J (1989) *How to Make Exhibitions Work for Your Business*, Daily Telegraph/Kogan Page, London

Further information

Association of Event Organisers
119 High Street
Berkhamsted
Hertfordshire HP4 2DJ
Tel: +44 (0)1442 285810
Fax: +44 (0)1442 875551
www.aeo.org.uk

British Exhibition Contractors Association
BECA House
Uplands Business Park
Blackhorse Lane
London E17 5QS
Tel: +44 (0)20 8523 5262
www.beca.org.uk

ESSA Event Supplier and Services Association Limited
119 High Street
Berkhamsted
Herts HP4 2DJ
Tel: 0845 122 1880
Fax: +44 (0)1442 875551
www.essa.uk.com

Society of Events Organisers
29A Market Square
Biggleswade
Bedfordshire SG18 8AQ
Tel: +44 (0)1767 316255
Fax: +44 (0)1767 316255
www.seoevent.co.uk

19
Merchandising and point of sale

LEARNING OBJECTIVES

By the end of this chapter you will be able to:

- Appreciate the impact of merchandising techniques
- Empathize with a retailer's strategies and merchandising policies
- Discuss retail strategies and how they incorporate store image, store layout, merchandise ranges, colour blocking, point-of-sale, promotions and a range of miscellaneous items
- Ensure that a culture of constant analysis and improvement is employed so that results can constantly be improved

Introduction

There was a time when below-the-line point-of-sale (POS) materials were considered relevant only to cosmetics, perfumery, confectionery and other impulse purchases. Today merchandising techniques apply to a broader spectrum of markets, from consumer to industrial. Although vast budgets can be spent above the line on advertising to gain the customer's attention or change an attitude, fewer resources are sometimes allocated to the crucial moment in the buying process – the point in the buying cycle where the customer is physically in front of the product or service and is about to make a decision as to whether to buy or pass by – the point-of-sale. Indeed, merchandising techniques have spilt over into websites where goods and services are displayed. In a sense, merchandising and point-of-sale are even more important in the online world. (See also Chapter 21.)

In-store drives awareness

'Over the past decade, the store has become the single leading driver of awareness of new package-goods products, significantly surpassing TV. While store shelves have traditionally been the place where marketers seal the deal – hitting consumers close to the purchase – their role in driving awareness has been growing, relative to other media. The store beat TV as an awareness driver by a 50% to 36% margin across the six countries – U.S., Canada, U.K., Germany, France and Italy – in 2008, the latest year for which Bases has released figures. That compares to a near tie only four years earlier, when the store barely edged out TV, 52% to 48%.'

Neff (2010)

Shopping for happiness

In the offline world, going shopping is claimed to be Britain's second most popular leisure activity after watching TV. This is also evident in the United States, where retail centres almost double as leisure centres. 'Mall walking' is a significant activity. In the north of England, customers are transported by the coachload to spend a day at one of Europe's largest retail centres, Gateshead's Metro Centre.

In many consumer markets the consumer's final decision to buy is often made inside, and not outside, the store. There is, however, some debate as to exactly what percentage of decisions are made inside the store. Although '70 per cent of decisions are made inside the store' appears to be used widely, Court *et al* (2009) suggests that these figures may vary according to sector. Neff (2010) suggests that retail stores have more impact than TV when generating awareness for new products.

Websites, mobile phones and apps may change these figures significantly, as all of these tools are vying for the consumer's attention and attempting to secure the decision making before point-of-sale can persuade or dissuade a customer. See how Dulux is actively shifting the decision from inside the store to outside the store (Chapter 4, 'The buying process' on Dulux). And mobile devices can influence a customer before, during and after a shopping trip.

Paperless couponing, special promotions, and information via SMS and location-based advertising are likely to have a significant impact on the customer decision journey.

Merchandising techniques such as display and store design are therefore vital communications tools that can guide a buyer towards making a purchase. They are often the last chance to communicate with the buyer. Merchandising does not apply just to the traditional retail outlets of supermarkets, garages and department stores, but also to DIY stores, brown-goods retailers (stereos and TVs), corner shops, office-equipment showrooms and cash-and-carry wholesalers.

The merchandising opportunity lies relatively untapped in industrial wholesale outlets such as electrical wholesalers and builders' suppliers, where a lot of merchandising tends to look dusty, dirty and uninteresting. There is room here for creative, intelligent and effective merchandising. It does require a delicate balance, since a hard-working electrician in search of some 2-core 3-millimetre cable might assume a distributor to be too expensive if it looked too glitzy and comfortable. On the other hand, merchandising here can provide customers with useful information, eg reminding the buyer about other relevant products and any special offers.

Distributor empathy required

Skilful supplier merchandising requires an ability to empathize with both the customer and the retailer/ wholesaler (distributor). Understanding customers is one thing. Understanding distributors and their perspectives, goals, strategies and tactics is another. It is easy to grasp the importance of maintaining the theme of an advertising campaign inside a store with carefully designed point-of-sale displays. It is not so easy to understand when, why and how a retailer will allow its space to be used for such in-store promotions and display, ie what its merchandising policies are and how to operate within that framework.

This 'distributor empathy' helps suppliers to make their product or service (and the relevant marketing communications) fit in with the retailer's plans. The retailer relationship is even more important in today's UK retail market, since market power has moved from the manufacturer into the hands of a few major retail chains. It is therefore necessary to understand the various distributor strategies and their approach to merchandising techniques.

Some retailers do not enter into any merchandising arrangements with suppliers, as the retailers prefer to control all aspects of product presentation centrally to ensure commonality and consistency in all their stores. This is managed by carefully supervised store personnel and/or a roving display management and merchandising team. This does not mean that the supplier can have no involvement in the merchandising. Many stores encourage proactive contributions from their suppliers. Some suppliers gain permission to use their own display teams to ensure that their particular products or services have optimum display on their allocated shelf at all times (see Case study 19.1).

Merchandising tools

In addition to store design, store layout, and merchandise ranges and policies, there are a number of in-store merchandising tools:

- leaflets and dispensers ('take one' boxes);
- stickers;
- posters;
- showcards and cardboard cut-outs;
- branded racks or display units;
- dump bins;
- three-dimensional:
  - injection-moulded characters (note that the toolmaking process required takes too long for some campaigns);
  - holograms;
  - free-standing floor displays;
- electronic gadgetry:
  - spotlighting systems;
  - video walls;
  - plasma screens;
  - illuminated display systems with fibre optics;
  - lenticular technology;
  - magic mirrors;
  - interactive POS systems, eg product advice systems, personal consultation systems, smart card POS suggested items;
- shelf space, eg number of facings, colour blocking (see page 420) and integrated pack design (how all the packs look beside each other on the shelf);
- shelf positioning (premium locations, cross-merchandising, etc);
- in-store sampling;
- window displays;
- digital imaging and web-based merchandising analysis tools.

These systems have been available for many years. One possible problem with high-tech POS is that customers end up admiring the POS material instead of buying the product. On the other hand, products can benefit from POS support, as many products can get lost, eg among the 25,000 lines of food that the average superstore displays. An innovative POS attracts attention – a key stage in the AIDA communication model (see Chapter 10). Although it is important to present fresh images to repeat-visit customers to maintain their interest and

The whispering windows

'Britain's high street took a step closer to the dystopian future of science fiction movies, with shop window advertisements that talk to passing shoppers. The new technology conjures up visions of scenes like that of the 2002 hit movie *Minority Report*, in which Tom Cruise's character is assailed by talking billboards that hail him by name and plug their products.

The whispering windows being installed by John Lewis aren't yet so advanced – but the company says it has already shown impressive results in trials. "After installing whispering windows into our storefront, the number of people who stopped to view our window displays increased by nearly 50 per cent", said Kevin Scully, the visual mechandising manager of the company's Peter Jones store in Sloane Square, west London, where testing has been carried out on the system since June.

The technology originated from sonar work developed for the US Navy and is being applied for John Lewis by Newlands Scientific, a spin-off company from Hull University. It effectively turns a shop window into a giant speaker, using vibrations through a "bug" attached to the window to project sound.

So far, John Lewis has used the device to project the sound of music playing on DVD players and high-end plasma television sets in its store window – although the developers boast that it can also be used to make dummies speak. The whispering window is able to monitor the level of external street noise and set its sound output just above the ambient level.'

Adams (2003)

Tomorrow's merchandising techniques yesterday

Over 15 years ago, Brian Oliver wrote in *Marketing* magazine:

> Imagine walking into a high street department store and being greeted by a three-dimensional lifelike copy of John McEnroe's head. As you walk past, it starts to move and even speaks to you… pointing out the features of a tennis racket suspended in mid-air in front of you with no apparent means of support. Then a giant pair of moving lips mounted on a glass display suddenly start talking to you, inviting you to try on the store's winter fashions without even undressing. All you have to do, say the lips, is stand in front of a 'magic mirror', select an item of clothing and, before you can say 'Bruce Oldfield', your reflection is wearing it. Today many websites engage customers by inviting them to upload their head and shoulders photographs (for trying on spectacles on an optician's website) or a full photograph for a boutique (to see what certain clothes look like on the customer).

Bumping into 3D images

'Today Reebok has developed 3D images that can be projected through a shop window and into the street. By means of "mirror technology" the 3D image literally hangs in space in front of pedestrians. More and more pedestrians will bump into 3D images like this as production costs fall.'

Marketing Business

loyalty, many retailers' obsession with product density and profit per square foot means that they instantly dismiss most of a supplier's branded merchandising tools. In fact the majority of stores do not have the flexibility or the luxury of space to dedicate to one-off 'stunts' with in-built novelty obsolescence.

Lenticular displays present more than one image, which changes and catches customers' eyes as they walk by. Power sneakers and smart shoes are capable of uploading advertisements as people walk by a store (like a sort of digital chewing gum). Location-based advertising and paperless coupons can be triggered by the actual location of a customer, so that, as customers walk through a shopping centre, their mobile rings, or a text message appears and mentions a relevant special offer in a store that is beside them at that precise moment. In-store screens and video terminals positioned at checkouts can transmit special relevant offers (based on previous purchase data) to customers as their store cards are swiped through the checkout. Finally, virtual reality can allow all of this (walking, browsing, examining, buying and prompting) without customers having to leaving their home or the safe confines of a local secure virtual hall or mall. And if you get bored you can nip over to the Louvre or to the cinema for a break without ever leaving your seat.

Retail strategies

Every retailer has its own marketing mix. This fits in with its retailing strategy, which should, in turn, exploit its source of competitive advantage (eg exclusive products, lower prices, location or image). A department store exploits location, its quality of service and its quality range of products. A small independent grocery cannot compete on product range or price but can compete on its convenient location, opening hours and friendly relationship or rapport. A takeaway restaurant may promote its unique home-delivery service. Competitive advantage is relative to competitors' unique selling propositions (USPs) and customer needs. A constant monitoring of the uncontrollable variables that affect markets reveals how competitive advantage can emerge or erode over relatively short periods of time. Merchandising strategies are also affected by corporate cultures. For example, some distributors and retailers are more profit orientated than turnover orientated. This, in turn, affects their pricing policies, promotion policies, merchandising policies and, in general, merchandising strategies.

The more common low-tech merchandising tools are now summarized and discussed under six key headings:

- store image (external and internal);
- store layout (customer traffic flows);
- merchandise ranges;
- colour blocking;
- point-of-sale displays and retail sales promotions;
- miscellaneous.

Store image

The human eye is more sensitive than is sometimes imagined. Clues about a shop are absorbed, often sometimes without our knowing it. Psychologists call these 'cue patterns'. They help shoppers to decide what kind of a shop it is before actually entering (if entering at all). The store's exterior offers an opportunity to communicate with customers, eg to invite them into the store or to reinforce a desired corporate image. Inside the shop the concept of the 'retail theatre' becomes evident. It has been suggested that a retail design concept lasts only three to five years, hence the need for the adaptable retail theatre that allows the store's interior layout and design to be changed easily. It is worth remembering that products, service and store design all contribute towards the overall store image, but if a customer has no prior experience of a particular store, or any word-of-mouth reference from peers, then the decision to enter or not to enter may be made solely from the store's visual image (or simply the way it looks). The store's exterior is a bundle of cues. Even the psychological barrier or obstacle, the door, is removed or minimized wherever possible, thereby facilitating an even easier store entry.

Store layout

Customer traffic flow can be directed around a store through detailed attention to layout. For example, 9 out of 10 people are right-handed and naturally prefer turning to the right, so most supermarkets have the primary doors on the left-hand side so the shopping is done to the right in a sort of clockwise manner. Flow-modelling time-lapse photos analyse which people go where in the store (and at what times, days, weeks or months). Further analysis reveals where the high-density areas are and whether they match the high-turnover areas. Customer movements can be predicted by model questions like 'If a customer were here (in the store), where would he or she go next?' This is important because, as a general rule, if the goods are in the wrong place they won't sell: 'out of sight, out of mind'. Primary and secondary visual points (as opposed to clutter) are used to pull the customer around the store or to 'shop the full shop' (visit every part of the store). Lighting, signage, photographs, software packages and even popular products like known value items

FIGURE 19.1   Optimum shelf stocking printout shown from two angles

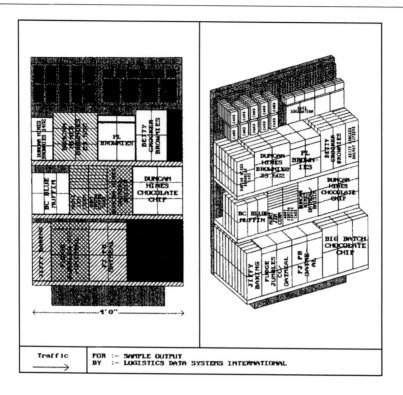

in a food supermarket help the customer to shop the full shop ('the more you see, the more you buy'). It is estimated that, out of the 25,000 food lines on display in a superstore, only approximately 250 are essential key value items such as tea, coffee, bread, etc.

Merchandise ranges

Once inside the store the customer is faced with a bundle of retail cues that are never neutral. Fruit or perfume is positioned at the front of a store (supermarket and department store respectively). This helps to create images and feelings of freshness and luxury respectively. Impulse products are placed at key positions. Cross-merchandising reminds the customer of related end-use products, which are carefully positioned beside each other, eg shirts and ties together, or pasta and pasta sauce. **The maxim 'Full shelves sell best'** is valid for FMCG retailers but not necessarily for some clothes boutiques. Although eye level is buy level, shelf positioning can reflect the current

product life cycle stage. The larger retail chains use merchandising display software packages to determine the right allocation of space to a particular product or brand. An 'optimum shelf layout' printout (see Figure 19.1) shows what mix and quantities of packs on a shelf maximize a store's objectives (eg maximize sales, minimize over- and understocking, maximize profitability). It presents a print-out of what the recommended shelf layout would look like. Some retailers like to have their own brands placed alongside the main brands, often on the left-hand side (since the Western eye reads from left to right and therefore spots the own brand first).

Colour blocking

A supermarket customer scans shelves at the rate of 4 feet per second from a distance of 8 feet away. Packaging, therefore, has to work very hard to attract the customer's eye. Retailers and packaging designers sometimes use colour blocking to attract attention by placing similarly coloured items close to each other to create a stronger shelf presence by means of a block of colour. Colour blocking can also link colours to product use associations, eg blue, green and white can be associated with stimulating and refreshing surf. This in turn might be built into the shower gel section.

Point-of-sale displays and retail sales promotions

This includes displays, sampling points, dump displays and so on. Many retailers will not allow suppliers this free space, since every square foot of retail generates a certain amount of revenue. In the appropriate store space, a retailer may allow the supplier the privilege of using extra space. Prime selling space can be bought by suppliers. A product's sales can be boosted depending on its location and shelf positioning. In-store sales promotion can tie in with advertising, cooperative advertising, publicity and perhaps even trade discounts and rebates. It should be designed to boost sales without creating any conflict with overall store image. Balance, proportion, lighting, colour and display units should be used to create the optimum impact on a consistent basis (perhaps across many hundreds of stores). Once the store grants permission, field marketing agencies can then provide merchandising teams to maintain proper POS displays or shelf facings.

Miscellaneous

In-store sound effects can be used to make announcements (eg to direct shoppers' attention to a special offer), to add atmosphere (crowd applause in sports shop video walls), to relax the buyer or to stimulate the buyer to move faster (eg varying the types of music) and so on. Some POS tools engage customers in a dialogue by asking questions.

Scents are also used inside a store to change shoppers' moods and buying behaviour. The Monell Chemical Senses Center in Philadelphia has found its pilot projects highlight how the use of smell affects sales. For example, certain scents (in this case, a fruity floral scent) caused casual shoppers at a jewellery store to linger longer. An individual's brainwaves and moods (eg relaxed and trusting) can be changed by extremely low levels of certain scents. In the UK one home furnishings retailer uses a bakery and café to entice customers into the store to buy non-food-related products, eg clothing and lighting.

In supermarkets it is interesting to note how odours are carefully managed, eg the smell from the fish counter is not as strong as the wafting smell of freshly baked bread at the bread counter. London-based DigiScents can create a particular atmosphere in a retail store or evoke associations in the customers' minds through a variety of dispersion techniques. This includes central ventilation systems to hand-held sprays, liquids, granules, gels or powder (or even pressure-sensitive micro-encapsulated strips). All of these can help to produce specific moods or simply neutralize unpleasant odours. Effectively they create an 'aromatic logo' by impregnating a product or a service environment or just corporate literature with an aroma.

Finally, 'mindshare' (discussed in Chapter 12) combined with merchandising techniques provides an extremely potent communications package as the store's sales staff, space and display promote a particular supplier's goods.

Measuring merchandising effectiveness

The bar code scanner at the checkout records what is being sold instantaneously. It can record the sales effect of allowing a product more shelf space, a different shelf location, special displays and so on. **Electronic point-of-sale (EPOS) scanners also measure sales responses to new advertising campaigns and price changes, as well as providing operational stock control data to central warehouses.** As suppliers and distributors work more closely together and become strategic partners, some suppliers are given access to a selection of EPOS data that measure sales results, store by store around the country, on a daily, weekly or even hourly basis.

This is similar to best practice web management, where the marketing team studies the analytics to see if there is any unusually busy activity on any particular product or service. Anything with a significant uplift in visits or sales can be highlighted on the home page to leverage the emerging popularity of the product or service. This gives the particular item an even bigger lift – until the next emerging popular item is identified and highlighted on the home page. Finding the most profitable mix of offers on the home page is similar to finding the most profitable mix of offers at key locations in-store. A constant process of analysis and improvement yields bigger and better results.

CASE STUDY 19.1   Thomson Tours

This case study demonstrates how vital merchandising is and how a field marketing agency manages the whole operation.

Situation

Major travel operator Thomson Tours enjoys a dominant market share and offers a wide range of long- and short-haul holidays to prospective customers via the travel agent in the competitive, and currently economically vulnerable, travel sector. 'Racking' (the display of a brochure in travel agents) is crucial to the success of all tour operators. Holidays are rarely booked without a comparison of the product offering from several competitors. Over 75 per cent of holidays are booked from a brochure that has been picked up and read. Few consumers ask counter staff for a brochure. It is therefore essential to ensure that the 30 different types of Thomson brochures are positioned in the right store, on the right shelf, at the right time of year. Stock of replacement supplies has to be ready so that the appropriate brochure is available at the point-of-sale at the right time. The several thousand travel agents mean that this is too big a requirement to be handled by Thomson's in-house marketing and sales team. Three thousand nominated UK travel agencies were targeted.

Objective

To ensure that the right brochures are available to the 3,000 nominated travel agents at all times.

Strategy

A comprehensive brochure management and merchandising support programme was developed and contracted out to the field marketing agency.

Tactics

- Stamping, racking and ordering brochures as required and where stocks allow. This includes use of BOBCAT – a computerized brochure-ordering system based on Psion technology developed by Thomson with CPM Field Marketing. The system allows the merchandiser to transmit daily via a handheld computer to the brochure distribution house, thereby ensuring a speedy, accurate and effective stock control and delivery system.

- Carrying out short sales presentations, highlighting key selling points to counter staff.

- Supporting brochure launches with additional tactical activity during key periods. Blitz operations such as these involve the team making 3,000 calls in two days, with the final results presented to Thomson three weeks later.

- Three thousand agents are visited, normally every two weeks.

Control

Thomson previously sent off batches of brochures to travel agents without really knowing which agents were running out, which agents placed them on which shelves and which agents had them thrown in a pile in the store room. The new merchandising system gives online data, which reduce wastage, as the team ensures the right brochures are on the right shelf at the right time. This has helped to increase sales by ensuring that the brochures are available at all the targeted agents. At the same time it has helped to reduce costs incurred by inappropriate print runs, unnecessary deliveries, etc.

Men/women

CPM allocated a team of 65 field staff, eight supervisors and one account manager to the ongoing field marketing activity. A team of 150 merchandisers and eight supervisors supports blitz operations at key times such as brochure launches. Both teams are headed by a national field manager who reports to Thomson's marketing department.

Money

Comprehensive field marketing activities range from £50,000 to £1,000,000 annually, depending on the size and scope of the operation.

Minutes

All field marketing staff attend a fortnightly half-day briefing. This is supplemented by six-monthly one-day sales conferences where major briefings and reviews are presented. The normal call cycle, which covers every one of the 3,000 travel agents, is two weeks. This means that every targeted travel agent gets visited and updated once a fortnight. Alternatively, a faster blitz can be completed within two days by using the extra 150 merchandisers.

Advantages and disadvantages

Here are some of the advantages and disadvantages to consider when deciding whether to increase or reduce this communications tool.

Advantages

Merchandising and point-of-sale are present at the point a customer makes a decision to buy, the very last opportunity to communicate with a customer before the decision is made. The message can be controlled, and it can range from ensuring customers are aware of the brand through to encouraging them to buy now. Special offers and sales promotions can be highlighted.

Disadvantages

Retail space is premium, and brands compete to get this space. It is therefore limited and expensive to secure this space. It is also expensive to create, deliver and install point-of-sale materials into the retail trade. Sales teams have to work hard and also try to motivate the busy retailer. Reverse logistics can be incurred at the end of a promotion if the POS has to be removed. Also the lead time has to include the retailer's time horizons as well as the time required to produce, deliver and install any POS.

Key points from Chapter 19

- Merchandising techniques not only offer a last chance to communicate with the buyer, but they can have a major impact on the customer's choice.
- Manufacturers need to empathize with their distributors' strategies and merchandising policies.
- Retail strategies incorporate store image, store layout, merchandise ranges, colour blocking, POS, promotions and a range of miscellaneous items.
- Constant analysis and improvement boost results.

References and further reading

Adams, R (2003) The whispering windows, *Guardian*, 8 August

Bryson York, E (2010) Shopping aisles at cutting edge of consumer research and tech, *Ad Age*, 15 March

Court, D *et al* (2009) The consumer decision journey, *McKinsey Quarterly*, Q3

Danger, P (1968) *Using Colour to Sell*, Gower, Aldershot

Engel, J, Warshaw, M and Kinnear, T (1991) *Promotional Strategy: Managing the marketing communications process*, 7th edn, Irwin, Homewood, IL

Erlichman, J (1992) How hidden persuasion makes shoppers spend, *Guardian*, 11 August

Neff, J (2010) This upfront, P&G may want to boost spend on Piggly Wiggly, *Ad Age*, 3 May

Further information

British Promotional Merchandise Association (BPMA)
52–53 Russell Square
London WC1B 4HP
Tel: +44 (0)20 7631 6960
Fax: +44 (0)20 7631 6944
www.bpma.co.uk

Institute of Promotional Marketing Ltd (IPM)
70 Margaret Street
London W1W 8SS
Tel: +44 (0)20 7291 7730
Fax: +44 (0)20 7291 7731
www.theipm.org.uk

Institute of Sales Promotion
Arena House
66–68 Pentonville Road
London N1 9HS
Tel: +44 (0)20 7837 5340
www.isp.org.uk

Marketing Communication Consultants Association (MCCA)
4 New Quebec Street
London W1H 7RF
Tel: +44 (0)20 7535 3550
Fax: +44 (0)20 7535 3551
www.mcca.org.uk

POPAI UK & Ireland Ltd (Point-of-Purchase Advertising International)
Highfields Farm
Huncote Road
Stoney Stanton
Leicestershire LE9 4DJ
Tel: +44 (0)1455 271856
Fax: +44 (0)1455 273918
www.popai.co.uk

20
Packaging

LEARNING OBJECTIVES

By the end of this chapter you will be able to:

- Understand the three functions of packaging and the importance of packaging at the point of sale
- Explain how packaging design can create competitive advantage
- Appreciate the six design variables
- Outline the stages in the packaging design process

Introduction

Once called 'the silent salesman', packaging has many purposes. It also presents opportunities to create competitive advantage and save money. Packaging designers work with six variables (shape, size, colour, graphics, materials and smell). Managing the packaging design process is similar in many ways to managing other marketing communications tools.

The importance of packaging

Since many sales assistants have been replaced by self-service systems, packaging today often has to act as a silent salesperson, helping customers by bringing a particular brand to their attention, highlighting unique selling propositions (USPs), giving friendly tips on usage and, ultimately, helping them to break through the misery of choice created by the increasingly vast range of seemingly similar brands. The plethora of 'me-toos' (similar products and brands) and the relentless fragmentation of markets mean that pack designs have to work very hard in these highly competitive, shorter life cycle markets of today.

The design of the pack can create competitive advantage by adding value, improving the product (eg improving the freshness or making it easier to pour, etc), developing stronger shelf presence, positioning a brand in a particular way, and creating or strengthening the brand's relationship with the buyer. **The pack should be what top designer Michael Peters calls 'a visual magnet' that entices the customer to purchase and, eventually, become loyal to a particular brand.** Packaging can also be an extraordinarily effective advertising medium, particularly in terms of cost and penetration, and reach or cover of a target audience. On the shelf and in the home it continues to work, day in, day out, for 52 weeks of the year. In some ways it is a free medium.

No single element of the communications mix comes under as much environmental scrutiny as packaging. In a sense, packaging will reduce as oversized cartons and unnecessary layers of packaging are stripped away by environmental pressures (and some cost pressures). Good pack design also pleases the distributor and retailer by helping to make distribution, warehousing and use of shelf space more efficient. In fact, many warehouses are becoming fully automated distribution centres, demanding packs of a size that suits the warehouse handling equipment. Good pack design also saves manufacturing costs.

Falling in love with a pack

Packaging facilitates choice. Choice is rarely made on a rational basis. In fact, the consumer is faced with several thousand packs screaming 'Buy me.' A well-designed pack offers relief from the misery of choice. Ernest Dichter (1964) suggested that 'this relief may be derived through being permitted to like a product, almost to love it indiscriminately and irrationally'. A well-designed pack can offer this permission and so assist in the choice.

The packaging opportunity

Packaging is an area of opportunity, as some sectors are laden with impenetrable packs, inadequate labelling and messy packets such as boxes of tea that leak leaf dust, sugar packs that spill sugar and bottles that dribble after pouring. In a market where pack design is weak, a new design can steal the advantage. It is worth remembering that, although pack design at worst is just a recognition symbol, at best it can offer so much more. As the cost of advertising rises, product life cycles shorten and hyper-competition becomes fiercer, marketers need to get more from their packaging. Creative packaging can create competitive advantage. Even dull and seemingly staid pack designs can be redesigned to create a competitive, cost-effective edge (see the box 'Creative industrial packaging can also gain competitive advantage' below).

The three basic functions of packaging

The three basic functions of packaging are to:

1 protect (and contain);

2 offer convenience;

3 communicate.

First and foremost, a pack must protect its contents during storage, transport and usage. Some packs have to protect the user from the contents (as in the case of children with weedkillers, medicine, chemicals, etc). Sadly, some packaging today must also protect the contents from tampering. Six people died in Chicago when Johnson & Johnson's Tylenol pain relievers were laced with cyanide. There is a market for tamper-proof packaging and tamper-evident packaging.

Second, the pack must offer convenience in pouring, squeezing, storing, stacking and consuming (in cars, in the garden, on the beach, in the home and, one day, in space). Sugar and milk have yet to be mastered in terms of truly convenient packaging. Even a minute improvement in convenience can create competitive advantage, as demonstrated by Schlitz beer's pop-top can, which helped to boost sales from 5.7 million in 1961 to 15.1 million in 1970. On the other hand, some pack designs are so poor that they cause their own problems. In 1985 the Norwegian company Elopak used TV advertising to try to explain how to open Elopak cartons.

Third, the pack must communicate. Before concentrating on the communications aspects of packaging, it is worth mentioning that all three packaging functions are interdependent. The first two, protection and convenience, both communicate indirectly. For example, if the product is damaged, tarnished or stale, then a negative image is what remains, despite advertising, publicity and sales promotions that claim otherwise. Equally, if the instructions for storage or pouring are not communicated clearly, then the pack loses its protective and convenience capabilities.

Some products prioritize some functions over others. Some design solutions (or redesigned packs) cannot optimize all three functions simultaneously because of constraints such as cost or overall pack size limitations. Trade-offs, or compromises, between functions will then occur. Surprisingly, some optimum functions can be forfeited for other reasons.

The communication functions of the pack

The communication function breaks down into several different sub-functions:

1 to grab the attention of the passing shopper;

2 to persuade and convince the viewer that the contents match the promise made by advertising or the pack itself (the pack should say 'Buy me');

3 to build brand personality and forge links with the buyer;

4 to build loyalty with a pack that:
   - looks nicer on the table;
   - is easy to find in the garden shed or in the warehouse;
   - is distinctive and easily recognizable in a shop carrying 9,000 separate items;
   - is easier to use than the competition's.

5 to instruct the user about how to use the product to optimum benefit;

6 to inform the user of mandatory requirements such as warnings, source of manufacture and/or ingredients (buyers tend to want more information today).

The silent salesperson

The pack is the last and sometimes the only opportunity to communicate with and sell to a customer. All the other elements of the communications mix can get lost in the competitive and noisy jungle of commercial messages where each appeals for your attention. The pack is the silent salesperson. Initially it has to shout boldly to grab attention and then fade into the background and let the product benefits come forward. A well-designed pack can stop customers dead in their tracks and invite them to have a look, pick it up and pause for a few valuable moments while they are engaged at the point-of-sale. It is here that the pack can develop a dialogue by attracting, intriguing, arousing unconscious aspirations, informing, reminding, involving, entertaining and, above all, persuading.

The pack can arouse or trigger stored images from a television advertisement that have been lying dormant in the memory bank either if the advertisement includes a 'pack shot' (close-up of the pack) or if the pack includes some of the images from the advertisement. The brand can reflect images and aspirations. The pack can help the customer to recall those aspirations and develop associations between the aspirations and the brand. The hand lifts the pack off the shelf, allowing the customer, his or her other aspirations and the brand to move closer together.

Packs like Heinz are sometimes called **'trigger packs'**, because there is little dialogue other than the announcement of a strong, confident tone. The pack design concentrates on being recognized through its unique visual identifiers, colours, keystone, name and lettering, while heavy advertising communicates the brand values and aspirations. It is interesting to see Campbell's Soups dispense with Andy Warhol's legendary red and white livery and replace it with another aspirational soup setting. The Campbell's graphics portray product values that are arguably less protectable from the inevitable 'me-toos' sometimes produced by the retail stores' own labels. The Heinz pack and image are unique and therefore more protectable (in terms of branding).

Overprotective packaging

There is a balance between protective packaging, sales, returns and overall costs incurred. Here are three examples from James Pilditch's outstanding book on packaging design, *The Silent Salesman* (1973). They demonstrate how overpackaging can be identified, reduced and subsequently used to boost sales and/or profits.

An electric light bulb company had a breakage rate so low that it prompted the question: were the bulbs overpackaged and too well protected? It subsequently reduced the grade of cardboard, and returns (of damaged bulbs) went up. The overall saving in packaging costs was greater than the increased costs of breakages and returns.

A detergent company used stronger boxes than its competitors. The distributors were aware of this and liked the better boxes, because they were able to put them on the bottom of the pile without their collapsing. The product was hidden at the bottom instead of being at eye level, which is the optimum 'buy level'. So the box weight was reduced. The boxes started to collapse and the detergent was soon freed from the bottom of the pile. Sales soon increased.

A London discount house was concerned over the lack of stealing. It thought, 'Maybe we make our goods too hard for people to get at', so the packs were redesigned.

The long-term commitment

The pack design needs to develop and change as markets constantly move away from existing products (and their packs). The pack may have to reflect changes in the customers' aspirations, incorporate demographic shifts such as an ageing population, exploit new technologically driven opportunities (such as microwaves, which require new food packaging) or simply highlight a new improvement in the product itself. There needs to be a constant review of customers and their perceptions, motivations and aspirations, and, of course, a constant review also of competitive packs. Sometimes customers simply get tired of a design.

One of the problems with packaging design is that it never shows up in a normal media budget. A major redesign involving a change of shape as well as a change in graphics can cost anywhere from £25,000 to £250,000 for the design stages. The tooling cost (the machine parts that the production line needs to produce the new pack shape) will probably double the cost. Packaging design is an evolutionary rather than revolutionary process. But not all designs involve three-dimensional changes; often it is simply a two-dimensional change of graphics. Sometimes this is so subtle (a 'design tweak') that the consumer is not even aware of the change, yet the new design will be working harder for the manufacturer. Look at the Heinz beans cans in Figure 20.1 and the subtle design tweak. Packaging design often does not sit comfortably in the marketing budget at all, but failure to get a pack

FIGURE 20.1　Spot the difference: subtle design tweaks increase shelf presence

right is tantamount to possibly wasting millions of pounds' worth of above-the-line advertising.

A constant design analysis looks at ways in which design can help to strengthen a brand's position. Heinz had maintained market share, but only at the expense of margin. Pack design gave it a lift. Turquoise is rarely associated with food except for Heinz. Subtle alterations have been made to make the product more appealing and give it a stronger image for the future. The Heinz lettering was changed from a thin typeface to a fuller, more generous style; the keystone was broadened and a white in-line used to sharpen its impact; the lettering of 'oven' and 'with tomato sauce' was changed from turquoise to gold; and the tone of the turquoise background was enriched to create added warmth.

It is possible, as Dichter (1964) suggests, to fall in love with a pack. It is also possible to form extremely strong trusting relationships with a pack, even for babies. The relationship-enhancing pack can also help to strengthen branding and even the corporate profile of the manufacturer or distributor that controls it. The next section of this chapter suggests how.

Would you pour a pile of white powder over your new baby?

'Would you have the confidence to pour an unknown pile of white powder over your new baby? 'Put the powder inside the pack called Johnson's, and emotions are immediately evoked of the caring mother–child relationship. You would certainly trust the product with your baby. You would not be willing to pay much, if anything, for the powder alone. You would be willing to pay a premium for a brand you trust and believe in.'

Lewis (1996)

Brands, packs and corporate identities

Some brands, and their packs, are inextricably linked with the corporation that owns or makes the brands (eg Heinz, Honda or BP). Others keep a lower profile with a more subtle form of corporate endorsement (like ICI's Crown Paints). Others still prefer to keep the freestanding brand or pack identity very separate from the corporation, which remains anonymously behind the scenes (eg After Eight chocolates and Nestlé). There are advantages and disadvantages to all three approaches. The corporate culture and diversity of products and markets can determine the specific approach. Packs can work in exactly the same way – linking the brand to the parent company. However, this may be restricted by the diversity of products and markets. For example, think of Esso ice cream, Lada airlines and Beecham's beer. If any of these products existed, the corporate link would not support the brand proposition; it would, arguably, detract from it.

The strengthening of the link between a company and its brands or packs can help the company by facilitating new product launches and brand stretching or brand extension (eg Heinz Weight Watchers). **It can also reinforce corporate presence** and, in turn, reassure different audiences, eg existing customers, new customers, investors and even employees. On the other hand, the link can create a design straitjacket that, as Lewis (1996) pointed out, 'inhibits the active development of sub-brands aimed at different target markets'. Since different target markets often require radically different images, these images may pull in different directions, thereby detracting from the consistency of the overall corporate identity and image. In addition, if a particular brand has a problem (such as product tampering or a faulty production batch), it is immediately associated with the parent company. This negative reflection can, if the link between brand and parent company is clearly established, affect all the other brands operating under the same corporate umbrella. As James Pilditch (1973) said, **'The pack can contribute to instant consumer recognition of the company or the brand.'** Now let us consider the other communication functions of the pack.

The designer's tools

The six variables or tools a designer can use are:

1 shape;

2 size;

3 colour;

4 graphics;

5 materials;

6 smell.

Shape

Some brands have such distinctive pack shapes that they are recognizable from the shape alone, eg Baileys, Mateus Rosé, Perrier and Jif Lemon. Other pack shapes communicate conscious and unconscious meanings.

Ask a group to draw the first image, abstract or otherwise, that comes into their minds when the word 'love' is mentioned. If they struggle with this, ask them to imagine they are a design consultancy whose job is to design a logo for a new political party called 'the Love Party'. After a minute ask them to do the same for 'hate'. (Close your eyes or make a doodle yourself before reading on.) Over 95 per cent of the drawings tend to conform to the same perceptions about shape. The love image usually has softer edges, curves and maybe heart shapes, while the hate image tends to have jagged edges and sharper shapes like swastikas and daggers. We may not consciously associate these meanings with shapes, but they are there. **During the Second World War, US paratroopers were tested to find whether they were shape orientated or colour orientated by being shown a film of abstract shapes and patterns.** The shapes moved from right to left and the colours moved from left to right. The paratroopers were then asked which way the design was moving. Shape-orientated men are supposed to be more intelligent, more stable and less emotional. The Thurstone test can be used for packaging design. It has revealed that younger children respond to colour more than form, while adults, and men in particular, react more to form.

Pilditch (1973) suggested that a rectangular box created images of sharpness, neatness and cleanliness, while a round box had associations of security, plentifulness and generosity. Go into a chemist's shop and observe the different packaging shapes used for adult and children's bubble baths. Some shapes give the product a value much greater than its contents. Shapes can also be masculine or feminine. Whisky bottles tend to be masculine in shape, while some perfume bottles are feminine.

Shape affects the protection and convenience functions in holding, pouring and storing. How a

FIGURE 20.2   This product can be recognized in the dark by feeling it

pack fits into the hand is part of the study of ergonomics. A well-designed pack fits the hand more comfortably and creates what Coca-Cola proudly calls 'in-hand embellishment' (it feels good in the hand). In 1910, part of the packaging design brief for the now famous Coca-Cola bottle read: 'We need a new bottle – a distinctive package that will help us fight substitution… we need a bottle which a person will recognize as a Coca-Cola bottle even when he feels it in the dark. The Coca-Cola bottle should be so shaped that, even if broken, a person could tell what it was.'

False ergonomics communicate unreal values to customers. For example, dimples (for fingers to grip) are sometimes placed down the side of a bottle, when in fact the bottle is rarely held by the two dimpled sides; instead, it is held by the two flat front and back sides of the pack. The subtle impression created by these false ergonomics is one of 'This pack looks slightly better or friendlier.' Customers do not consciously choose one brand instead of another. Ergonomics can help to express that one brand is nicer to use than another. Real ergonomics help the user to have a more pleasant experience with the pack and therefore encourage repeat purchasing.

Some shapes reinforce product values by designing product features into the pack, as with the honeycomb effect on the base of a honey jar or the dimpled plastic two-litre beer bottles associating the product with a dimpled beer mug. Other shapes reinforce brand values, eg the historic liqueur bottle designed in the shape of a monk. The ultimate brand shape is arguably Jif Lemon's lemon-shaped pack. The Law Lords granted Reckitt & Colman exclusive rights to this shape, ie only Jif can use this unique get-up or shape to package lemon juice.

Can manufacturers own monopoly rights to a pack shape? The test, it seems, is 'whether the shape serves mainly to distinguish a product from its rivals and whether a competitor using the shape is seeking to mislead purchasers' (Warden, 1990). There are an infinite number of shapes. Pack shape can form a valuable property of the brand. It can become part of the brand or become part of the brand equity.

Size

Size communicates. Would you give your loved one a perfume packed in a 2-litre bottle? The corollary, ie large pack communicates better quality, is true in product sectors such as breakfast cereals. Consumer perceptions about cornflakes have been found to change according to size of pack. Large cereal packs build feelings of plentiful, expansive, energy-giving food, whereas a smaller pack may make the cornflakes seem heavy, solid and no good. Size can be used to communicate in different ways. For example, a 33-centilitre bottle of premium beer cannot be fully poured into a half-pint glass. This forces the drinker, after filling a glass, to carry the bottle away from the bar and over to the table, where the unemptied bottle continues to work both as a badge and as an advertisement.

Different sizes are aimed at different segments, eg the family pack. Pack size can determine target markets, or is it that target markets can determine pack size? This may be similar to Ehrenberg's philosophy of marketing, which states that marketing means excluding many customers from a particular product (target marketing excludes the mass). Certain segments exclude certain sizes, as Coca-Cola discovered when it had to withdraw its 2-litre bottle from the Spanish market after discovering that few Spaniards owned large fridges. If the colour were changed, would the pack then fit the fridge? Warm colours like red and yellow seem to advance or make the pack appear larger, while cold colours like blue recede and make the pack appear smaller. Although a change of colour would not have saved Coca-Cola's large bottle in Spain, colour does communicate in many different ways.

Colour

Colour communicates. Albert Kner, former design chief of the Container Corporation of America, said 'Colour is the quickest path to the emotions.' Words have to be translated into images in the mind. These images, in turn, have to be assembled, organized and categorized to give them meaning. This may be followed by an emotional response, which may subsequently trigger a physical response. Colour skips all this and goes straight into the emotions, often creating a physiological response. Colour is physical. Russia's Pedagogical Institute has found that most people can feel colours. Eyeless sight or 'bio-introscopy' suggests that all one's skin has seeing power. Red, green and dark blue have been found to be sticky. This may have something to do with electromagnetic fields. There have been claims that the Chinese can teach children to see with their elbows. Many years ago the US Color Research Institute found that the colour of walls in an office could make people feel sleepy, excited or healthy. More recently, a British police force has experimented with pink cells for prisoners. Red increased blood pressure and pulse, while blue had the opposite effect.

The Lüscher colour test uses colour cards to analyse the reader's psychological, and specifically emotional, state. Green is 'the colour of the environment in Europe and a significant colour for all Muslims. It has religious significance in Malaysia and is popular in Mexico as a national colour' (Ronay, 2005).

Colour codes

Some product sectors, particularly food, appear to have colour codes. For example, within the carbonated drinks sector, red is cola and yellow is tonic. Freezer meat is red, fish is blue and anything low-calorie or diet is white. Pilditch (1973) has suggested that in the wake of health scares many of the world's cigarette packs now emphasize white: 'They hope white is associated with cleanliness and purity.'

Colours have meaning for people. Many people associate colours with images, eg 'garden fresh', 'mountain cool' or 'rugged manliness'. There was a group of people for whom 7UP's green bottle had almost medicinal links and therapeutic overtones: 'the thing to take when you had the flu and the doctor told you to take a lot of liquid'. Whether it is an annual report, a reception area, some sales literature or a piece of packaging, colour communicates.

This applies to products and services in both consumer and industrial markets.

Colour affects perception. This is probably best demonstrated by Ernest Dichter's research (1964) into how packaging colour affects people's perceptions of taste. Unknown to the respondent, the same coffee was put into four cups. One of four different-coloured coffee cans was placed beside each cup. Respondents were then asked to match the statements below with each cup tasted. The research revealed strong perceptions linked with specific colours:

- dark brown can: 73 per cent 'Too strong aroma or flavour';
- red can: 84 per cent 'Richer flavour or aroma';
- blue can: 79 per cent 'Milder flavour or aroma';
- yellow can: 87 per cent 'Too weak flavour or aroma'.

More recent research into packaging colour and perceptions of washing machine powder provided interesting results. The same powder was put into three different-coloured packs. The respondents tried them on delicate clothing for a few weeks and were then asked which was best for delicate clothing. Respondents thought the performance (of the same powder) was vastly different. Statements below demonstrate the striking finding:

- largely yellow pack: 'too strong', 'ruined clothes';
- largely blue pack: 'did not work', 'clothes were dirty looking';
- blue and yellow pack: 'fine', 'wonderful'.

This differs from previous US research reported by Terrell Williams (1982) that tested identical washing powders in three different-coloured boxes, yellow, blue and red. The yellow detergent was 'mild, too mild really'. The blue detergent was 'a good all-round laundry product'. The red detergent was 'good for stains and the like'.

Colours may not be international, since different colours have different meanings in different cultures. For example, white is life, purity and diet in the UK, but it means death in Japan. Softer pastel colours and brighter colours are perceived differently around the world. In China, bright colours symbolize quality. Scott entered the Taiwan market with its US blend of pastel-coloured toilet tissues; the launch flopped. Sales took off when it changed the colours to bright red, yellow and gold. Can you imagine UK toilets with bright red toilet paper? Pilditch (1973) remarked, 'Not only do simpler folk like stronger colours, but people who live under bright sun have different values from those whose outlook is dimmed, say, by England's "leaden" skies. Think of this when designing packs to sell to Italian wine-growers, or Glaswegian dockers.' This is important, because cross-border packaging may become more common than cross-border advertising.

The cost of colour

Four colours obviously cost more to print than two colours. Can one be economic with the use of colour, the number of colours and the kind of inks? Is single colour too downmarket? Are four colours really needed? Has anyone tested a change in colours?

Graphics

Graphics communicate on different levels. The two-dimensional design on a label can help to create and protect individuality and uniqueness, reinforce a brand name or image, help to reposition, increase shelf presence, etc. The use of graphics is arguably the easiest of the designer's tools to analyse, as marketing managers are reasonably design literate as far as graphics are concerned. A naked body on the label of a bottle of beer will attract attention. However, not every brand manager wants this kind of attention. Graphics can use other images to make a pack stand out from the crowd. In terms of branding, the visual image should be distinctive and should make the pack immediately and easily recognizable. Even an ordinary tin box can become a valued item once some attractive graphics have been applied. **Graphics add value by adding aesthetic quality.** This creates 'stay-after value', which allows the branding to keep working inside the home for many years, sometimes generations. Graphics are sometimes used as a kind of sales promotion by becoming a limited-edition or collector's item, as in the case of the Guinness centenary Christmas label.

Graphics can add value by offering, for example: additional features such as games (eg a box of matches with matchstick puzzles); intrigue; a room-enhancing, stimulating plaything rather than just a dull necessity (baby lotion with colourful children's toys); or quality associations with images of far-off places (coffee with palm trees).

Good graphics can create a mood or trigger lifestyle aspirations that reflect the often latent desires of the target market, eg a shampoo label showing an English country scene for one target market and a rugged desert for another aspiring lifestyle segment.

Attention to detail combined with an understanding of the cues and symbols that are relevant to a particular target market allow the designer to play with the unconscious meaning of symbols and images. In the case of a cooking fat, according to the psychologists, the positioning of a wooden spoon made it 'possible for the housewife to rehearse the use of the product while it was still on the shelf'. Pilditch (1973) explained that 'the spoon also served to inject the product with some of the reliability of grandmother's honest-to-goodness, my doesn't that smell good, old-fashioned kitchen'. In a separate piece of research the analysts turned to the number and layout of biscuits on a package. A picture showing biscuits scattered all over created psychological discomfort, or dissonance, because it suggested gaiety, disorganization, permissiveness and irresponsibility ('never know how many were eaten by the kids'). A different picture showing the biscuits in a neat line triggered associations with orderliness, parsimony, and fear of disrupting the line by taking a biscuit, which again resulted in unconscious psychological tension or discomfort. The third image of just a few biscuits on a plate cut out the chaos and the irresponsibility and invited the viewer to feel free to take a biscuit. The number of biscuits was, however, limited to demonstrate authority and control.

Graphics affect taste

In the same way as colour, graphics also affect taste perceptions. In fact, packaging designers can test different label graphics by asking focus groups or consumer panels to give their opinions on the taste of (unknown to them) the same product. The more elegant bottle will tend to have a refined taste, the macho label might have a stronger flavour, etc.

Graphics integrate with other packaging variables to create effective communications. Lewis (1996)

suggested that 'if the form [shape and size of the pack] makes the statement then the graphics should step back'. The Lewis Moberly consultancy worked on Yves Rocher aromatherapy oils and created a tactile experience prompted by graphics 'by running the typography [letters] right round the bottle to encourage the viewer to turn it, touch it and begin to experience the product through the pack'.

Many years ago Coca-Cola discovered that its dynamic white contour curve (the flowing white ribbon underlining the Coca-Cola and Coke logo) reminded observers of the famous profile of the hobble-skirted contour bottle.

The graphics should be developed only after some other key questions have been asked. These include: Does the pack use the logo effectively? Can the graphics make space for future on-pack promotions? Do the graphics leave space for international copy translation (usually requires more space than English)? Will the graphics lend themselves or at least link with point-of-sale materials? Are the graphic images unique and protectable, or can someone else design something similar, leaving customers confused and unaware of their own brand-switching decision?

The other pack functions are also helped by good graphics, eg a blend of visual and verbal instructions can make a product and pack much easier to use and store (convenience and protection).

Graphics can also indicate production processes or corporate caring values such as 'recycled' or 'free from animal testing'. There is some confusion currently because of the lack of central agreement on appropriate logos.

Finally, bar codes linked with electronic point-of-sale (EPOS) scanners at retail store checkouts help internal communications between the retailer

FIGURE 20.3   Bar codes provide useful marketing information

and supplier by updating stock levels, reorder information and other sales analysis (eg by product, by store, by day, etc).

Materials

Materials communicate. Certain materials, like glass or metal, have an intrinsic value. Glass still seems to be associated with higher quality. Many wine drinkers would be suspicious of a supposedly top-quality wine if it was presented to them in a plastic bottle. Nevertheless, the packaging of wine has gone through the most radical of shake-ups. Thirty years ago, if someone had forecast that people would soon be drinking wine out of cardboard boxes it is likely that the comment would have been taken as an insult – with hints of socially unacceptable behaviour. Yet today the wine box is arguably packaging's greatest innovation, with a nation happily drinking from cardboard boxes.

The materials used in packaging affect perceptions of product quality. A good example of this was discovered in the United States, where, ironically, the better product was perceived to be in the more difficult-to-open package. Crisps of equal freshness were packaged in wax paper bags and polyvinyl bags. The crisps in the polyvinyl bag were perceived (by 87 per cent) to be 'superior in taste and freshness' despite being more difficult to open.

Guinness found that packaging materials, and tins in particular, affected taste perceptions. There were comments like 'too gassy, it taints the flavour and it tastes of tin' (Nicholas, 1991). Pre-launch research of the Guinness draught can showed that in blind taste tests equal numbers preferred the pure draught Guinness and canned draught Guinness. Subsequent sight tests (showing the source, ie can or tap) revealed the hidden associations of tin cans: there was a 70:30 split in favour of the draught Guinness. Pretty Polly used tin as an innovative piece of packaging for its nylon tights.

Certain overseas markets have different packaging material expectations from what is considered to be the norm in the UK. For example, in Europe, meats, fruit, vegetables, pet foods and fruit juices are packed in glass. This means that if UK manufacturers want to enter these markets they will have to work with a new packaging medium, which may well be glass. In the UK, tin has an emotional quality. It can become even more emotional when

mixed with shape and colour, eg a red, heart-shaped tin box of chocolates for St Valentine's Day. Today tin box packs are used for boxer shorts and children's clothes as well as food.

Technological developments allow relatively sophisticated printing techniques to be used on almost any kind of surface, as demonstrated by the attractive graphics used on today's cardboard wine boxes and tin boxes.

Some packaging materials have to work very hard. For example, microwave packs have to be able to protect and store the food at temperatures below zero and then have to offer convenience cooking by being able to be put into the microwave at very high temperatures. Some packs are then used to eat out of. Self-heating and self-cooling cans offer new levels of convenience. Apart from the convenience and communications implications of packaging materials, the final materials choice is integrated with a host of other factors such as optimum size, weight, strength, cost and filling speed, together with other features such as colour, closure, secondary packaging, shelf life, barrier properties, tactile characteristics and shelf impact.

Finally, material is the variable that is affected directly by environmental pressure groups. New legislation is putting pressure on manufacturers and retailers to use more environmentally friendly packaging. The US garbologist now probes landfill sites to determine the state of decay of various materials. In Europe, Germany leads the way in environmental legislation. A company's overseas growth may be stifled by packaging and materials that do not meet legislative criteria. Despite the logistical nightmare, the refillable pack is here to stay. The environmental factor has a direct impact on packaging and, in particular, on packaging materials. Warner-Lambert is developing a new disposable plastic made almost entirely out of biodegradable starch derived from potatoes, corn, rice and wheat.

Smell

Smells can change shopping behaviour. In a Philadelphia jewellery store some years ago, casual shoppers lingered longer than usual because, claims the Monell Chemical Sense Center, scents change shoppers' moods. In this particular case it was a fruity floral scent. Mood-changing odours change people's brain patterns. The *Chicago Tribune* reported the renowned, neurological director of the Smell and Taste Treatment and Research Foundation in Chicago, Dr Alan Hursch, as saying, 'Eventually we will be able to influence in a much more powerful way. By making people more relaxed or more trusting you could sell them more.' Scented packaging is becoming more popular.

> ## Creative industrial packaging can also gain competitive advantage
>
> The design resource is not exclusively reserved for FMCG goods. There is always room for design, creativity and innovation in industrial markets. Electric cable manufacturer BICC used pack design to stand out from the competition in the commodity cable market and to offer USPs to a traditionally conservative market. It moved from the traditional reel of cable to a newly designed box of cable. This helped the electrical wholesaler by making stacking, storage and identifying (holes in the pack allowed the different colours of cable to be seen) a lot easier. The pack, however, was not allowed to look too upmarket, as the conservative buyers assumed it would be more expensive. Before phasing out the old cable packs (reels), they were used to advertise the imminent arrival of the new packs – the box of cable.

The packaging design process

Why redesign?

'If it ain't broke, don't fix it.' Perhaps, but some pack designs can become tired or dated, or the market simply moves away, making the pack's current position a liability. On the other hand, valuable brand equities or properties such as names and logos are assets worth maintaining. They may need 'tweaking' from time to time, but rarely need to be disposed of. Perhaps a creative brand manager and a professional printer can produce an updated or even new graphic design for a pack. Jan Hall, formerly of Coley Porter Bell, says this would be like 'putting together the Pope and a paint company

to paint the Sistine Chapel'. Alan Topalian (1984) suggested that the designer's interest (or input) into the pack increases progressively during the course of the product's life cycle (see Figure 20.4). In other words, the pack design has an increasingly important role as competition becomes more intense.

A packaging design brief

The SOS + 3Ms can be used as a checklist when writing a design brief, which can be modified for a packaging design brief.

Situation/background

- Company (history, production facilities).
- Product (range, features and benefits, material properties, eg liquids, gases, chemicals).
- Market (size, growth, competitive structure, positioning, specific requirements such as pallet configuration).
- Target markets: segments, targets, decision-making units – particularly tricky with gift products, eg at whom do you target the design, the giver or the receiver?
- Reason for design (eg pressure from retailers' own labels).
- Brand factors and personality, key design elements.
- Merchandising display opportunities.

Objectives

What packaging functions are prioritized (protection, convenience or communication)? If communication, state the objectives specifically, eg repositioning from what to what? Or is the new pack design primarily aimed at shouting louder or creating a stronger shelf presence, etc?

Strategy

How does the pack fit in with the rest of the communications mix (the communications objectives and mix)? The brief may also state whether the pack design is a low-risk design project (new unit load, new material, temporary sales promotion, secondary panel changes, new ingredients, etc) or a high-risk design project (new name, new colour, new image, new logo, new shape, etc).

FIGURE 20.4   How design attention shifts between content and presentation as a product progresses through its life cycle

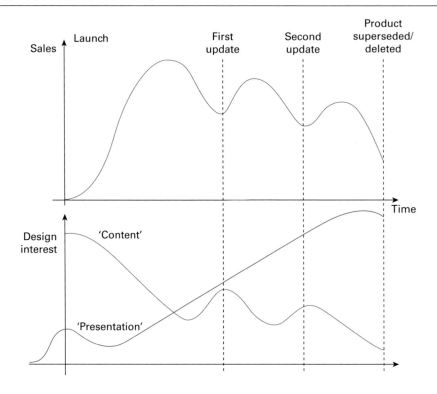

Tactics

Details are not always required here.

Men/women

These are the contact names for technical discussions (eg the production manager) and for marketing discussions. Clarify who makes the key decisions (who signs off or approves artwork, etc) and who can provide answers to miscellaneous questions. Provide the names of any other agencies that may be working on other marketing communications aspects, such as advertising and sales promotion.

Money

Money means the design fee, rejection fee (some designers charge a rejection fee for presenting ideas or concepts, even during a pitch), changeover costs

(this may incur capital expenditure if a change of shape requires a new machine tool) and, ideally, an indication of the maximum unit cost of the new pack (the designer will need to know the size of production runs, etc).

Minutes

This is the timescale. What are the launch deadlines? When must concepts be presented, agreed, re-searched, refined and approved? When must the final artwork be delivered? How long has been al-lowed for tooling (which can take up to 50 per cent of the total design time, eg three months)?

Measurement

What kind of research will be carried out to moni-tor the effectiveness of the new pack design?

FIGURE 20.5   The packaging design process

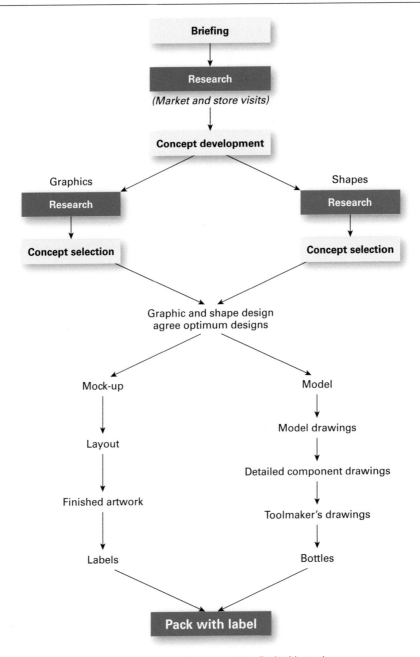

SOURCE: Adapted from the pack design management video *From Dream to Reality* (Smith, 1991)

Miscellaneous

Consider design constraints, eg size, shapes, colours, images or materials to be used or avoided because of technical, legislative and corporate restrictions on materials, warnings or warranties, and logos respectively.

The packaging design process

The brief may emerge after an initial review of the pack design. The designers (whether in-house or an external consultancy) often take the brief away, interpret it and rewrite it. Then they present this to the marketing team to ensure that everyone agrees with each other before embarking on any further creative work or research. This may be followed by further research, and eventually a range of concepts (two-dimensional labels and three-dimensional pack shapes, sizes and mechanisms) is developed for further research. This guides the selection of a concept for ultimate development into the new pack. Figure 20.5 shows the standard stages of a design project.

CASE STUDY 20.1   Brand range development in India

Situation

The background

During the winter months in northern and eastern India evening temperatures can drop down as low as 5 degrees. This causes dry skin conditions ranging from general dehydrated, chapped skin to more serious cracked skin. The market is flooded with manufacturers advertising skincare products that promise to 'keep skin healthy'.

In 1929 GD Pharmaceuticals based in Calcutta identified the need for an antiseptic ointment to combat dry skin problems. Boroline was launched. It was effectively the first brand in the antiseptic cream category. The consumer offer was a perfumed multi-purpose skin cream for cuts, burns, chapped skin, etc. The trusted Boroline brand achieved strong penetration in eastern Indian markets. Although Boroline had firmly established itself within the market, it had not capitalized on the huge potential opportunity of national penetration into India's giant marketplace of a population of one billion.

Boro Plus Antiseptic Cream was launched in 1982 to revolutionize the antiseptic cream market, and differentiate Boro Plus from Boroline through product formulation and branding. The name Boro Plus was created, as it was seen to convey a sense of added value. The herbal formulation combined with the Ayurvedic concept (an ancient Indian healthcare system that means 'the science of life') was marketed as a preventative, curative and healing ointment. Leading Ayurvedic authorities endorsed the brand.

- *Competition.* During the 1980s an established Indian manufacturer of beauty and healthcare products, Emami, saw the bigger market opportunity to introduce a low-end product into the mass market to directly compete with Boroline. The low-end segment had cold creams (for night use) and vanishing creams (for day use). The antiseptic cream category offered a multi-purpose product in a massive market – if positioned and marketed correctly.

- *Packaging.* Boroline packaging was perceived to be dull and old-fashioned: an earthy green pack that had not changed since its 1929 launch and was not seen as attractive. It lacked 'Pick me up' appeal. The new 1980s Boro Plus pack colours were purple and white and delivered brighter, fresher contemporary colours. These colours were also attention grabbing.

- *Advertising.* An advertising campaign created the category for a more youthful and aspirational quality by bringing in Bollywood celebrities to endorse the brand.

The challenge

Although Boro Plus had performed consistently since its successful 1980s launch, it was meeting increased competition, in particular from international brands entering the massive Indian domestic market. Over 20 years after Boro Plus's launch, Emami needed to do something because, firstly, being recognized as an antiseptic cream with a multi-purpose benefit restricted new product extensions and, secondly, there was an opportunity to create a range of skin care products for both domestic and export markets. Emami recruited a London design agency, Evolve Creative, to work on the new branding and packaging because of its track record of working with international beauty and healthcare companies. They work closely together today developing and tweaking designs to meet the continually changing market opportunities.

FIGURE 20.6 Repositioning from a traditional medical product to an aspirational beauty product

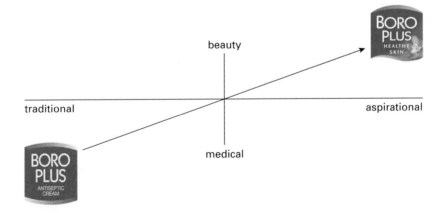

Market research conducted by Emami among retail outlets and users revealed one factor that went against Boroline, the oiliness of the product on the skin, which meant that during warmer months the use of the cream was uncomfortable on the skin due to the heat, and therefore larger purchases were seasonal, ie during the winter. This, in turn, restricted the multi-purpose proposition, so Emami decided to reposition the brand from a traditional medical product to an aspirational beauty product.

Objectives

- To create a new brand (identity and packaging design) for both Indian and export markets.

- To strengthen the brand's credibility as a skin care expert by simultaneously expanding the product range to meet new needs.

- To help boost sales by a minimum of 30 per cent.

Strategy

Reposition the conservative multi-purpose pharmaceutical product to an aspirational skincare brand bridging skin health and beauty, and expand the product range to fill identified needs.

Brand development

The brand repositioning was achieved by highlighting the product's natural herbal formulation and creating a softer and more distinctive logotype. The design also linked the product more directly with the media personality used for a testimonial in the launch TV and cinema campaign. The result was highly successful, and the year-on-year sales increased by 32 per cent.

New product extensions

Immediately following the approval of the relaunch pack design, work began on a series of product range extensions for both the domestic and the international market, which were test marketed and launched in India during 2007/08. These successfully positioned Boro Plus as a substantial and serious contender in the broader skin care market with the consumer promise of a full, natural skin care regime. Emami now work closely with Evolve design agency extending the range further. Market research has revealed that there was also a need for a low-unit product

FIGURE 20.7
Original logotype vs new identity

(LUP) in the antiseptic category. It showed a large number of women wanted to carry a tube of Boro Plus in their handbags, but couldn't because of its size. With this in mind, Emami launched the 8-gram variant priced at 5 rupees in 2002. The affordable price point has triggered impulse purchasing, which allows customers to trade up as they move up the ladder of loyalty.

Results

Boro Plus now successfully dominates the market with a 70 per cent market share. It continues to expand the range to fill identified gaps as they emerge from ongoing market research. The brand's now extensive range is being established in international markets, including Russia and Africa.

FIGURE 20.8

Boro Plus Antiseptic Cream packaging

FIGURE 20.9

Boro Plus Healthy Skin packaging

Men/women

The team consisted of three people (two designers and an account handler).

Money/budget

The budget for branding was £6,500, and for packaging £7,000.

Minutes/timescales

The lead time required to create, develop, test, refine and roll out the brand and the pack was three months for the brand and five months for the pack.

Advantages and disadvantages

Here are some of the advantages and disadvantages to consider when deciding whether to increase or reduce this communications tool.

Advantages

Packaging is the silent salesperson, catching customers' eyes, drawing them in and selling the finer detail as they digest the information. Like merchandising, it is often the last chance to communicate before the customer makes a decision. Packaging provides a platform where the exact message is controlled by the marketer (unlike PR and social media). It also carries the brand into the customers' homes or workplaces, so it keeps on working long after the sale. Great packaging stands out from the clutter and adds perceived value to a product. Within the retail environment, packaging can create or reinforce awareness as well as help to close the sale.

Disadvantages

Packaging requires long lead times and is expensive to change. The audience is obviously limited to retail traffic looking at the category. Wasteful packaging is not only an irritant for customers but also deemed to be un-environmental (in some markets this is a legal issue). If the pack is too trimmed or too light the product can get damaged.

Key points from Chapter 20

- Packaging has three functions: to protect, offer convenience and communicate.
- Packaging design presents an opportunity to create competitive advantage.
- The designer's six tools are shape, size, colour, graphics, materials and smell.
- All marketing is a series of processes, and packaging development is no different: there is a sequential method for managing the design process.

References and further reading

Bayley, S (1986) *Coke! Coca-Cola 1886–1986: Designing a megabrand*, Conran Foundation Boilerhouse Project, London

Dichter, E (1964) *Handbook of Consumer Motivations: The psychology of the world of objects*, McGraw-Hill, New York

Lewis, M (1996) in *Understanding Brands*, ed D Cowley, Kogan Page, London

Milton, H (1991) *Packaging Design*, Design Council, London

Nicholas, R (1991) Come home to a real beer, *Marketing Week*, 15 February

Opie, R (2001) *The Art of the Label*, Chartwell, London

Pilditch, J (1973) *The Silent Salesman*, 2nd edn, Business Books, London

Raeburn, O (2003) Design choice, *Marketing*, 8 May

Ronay, A (2005) Paint your brand, *The Marketer*, 15 September

Smith, P R (1991) *From Dream to Reality* (video), Media Services, London Metropolitan University, London

Southgate, P (1994) *Total Branding by Design*, Kogan Page, London

Topalian, A (1984) *Management of Design Projects*, Alto Design, London

Warden, J (1990) White paper gives shade to trademarks, *Marketing*, 27 September

Williams, T G (1982) *Consumer Behavior*, Research report, West Publishing, St Paul, MN

Further information

Chartered Society of Designers (CSD)
1 Cedar Court
Royal Oak Yard
Bermondsey Street
London SE1 3GA
Tel: +44 (0)20 7357 8088
www.csd.org.uk

Design Business Association
35–39 Old Street
London EC1V 9HX
Tel: +44 (0)20 7251 9229
Fax: +44 (0)20 7251 9221
www.dba.org.uk

Institute of Packaging
Sysonby Lodge
Nottingham Road
Melton Mowbray
Leicestershire LE13 0NU
Tel: +44 (0)1666 849705
Fax: +44 (0)1664 564164
www.iom3.org/packaging

21
Websites and social media

LEARNING OBJECTIVES

By the end of this chapter you will be able to:

- Ensure that the four key satisfaction factors are applied to your website
- Understand what increases the quality of the content on a website
- Understand what increases navigation's ease of use
- Convert visitors to customers and customers to lifetime customers
- Appreciate what makes social media successful
- Avoid the 10 common mistakes of social media

Successful websites

How to satisfy customers

The quality of the customer's experience, both online and offline, directly affects brand image (see Chapter 2). Poor product quality and sloppy service destroy brands more quickly than any large advertising budget can build them. Sloppy websites not only kill sales, but they can destroy a brand. Whether it's broken links, long registration forms or confusing order forms, error-laden websites all do serious damage. Web usability expert Jacob Nielsen identifies four basic website factors that keep visitors satisfied and coming back again and again: 1) high-quality content; 2) easy navigation; 3) quick downloading; and 4) updated information.

The last two factors are self-explanatory: sites that are slow to download (particularly on mobile handsets) will lose popularity, and sites that have out-of-date content will turn away visitors. This chapter concentrates on two of these factors: high-quality content and easy navigation. Marketers need to be familiar with various techniques to ensure they know how to use these factors properly. The chapter also explores 'sizzle' (exciting added-value content), customer engagement and customer conversion (from prospect to customer to lifetime customer), as well as the constant search for website improvement. The chapter then explores how to ensure social media actually win.

> In just a few seconds, sloppy websites destroy brands that took years to build.

Satisfying visitors key factor 1: high-quality content

In addition to the usual offline and online market research (see Chapter 6), which reveals what the target market wants to see on a website, marketers can also ensure that their site is even more relevant by using:

- scenario planning;
- personas;
- sizzle;
- customer engagement.

Scenario planning

It's all about relevance. Once a brand stops being relevant to a customer, the relationship dies. One tried-and-tested technique for ensuring relevance is scenario planning. Marketers take each target customer type and consider, in detail, the customers' situation, how they might use the product or service and the steps they would take when buying. A chocolate company might have some customers who want to buy a gift for a loved one, some customers who want chocolates for a dinner party, and other customers who are looking for chocolates for a wedding. By exploring what would be helpful to customers for each of these scenarios, marketers build sites that cater for each scenario, eg the wedding section might have ideas on wedding table layouts or love messages on chocolates, and the dinner party section might list ideas for dinner party games. **Scenario planning adds sizzle; because it is so relevant, customers love it.** A plumbing company might identify customers with emergencies (they need a big panel saying 'Emergency – call now 24/7' with a telephone number), while it should also have a section offering help and ideas for those who want to change a bathroom and those who want to redecorate a complete house. The ultimate example of scenario planning is so powerful that it delivered astonishing growth and created sustainable competitive advantage. This is National Semiconductor. Read on.

Personas

Personas also help decide what kind of content customers want. Essentially personas are 'thumbnail' descriptions of types of visitor. Advertising agencies used them for planning ads for many years, and now web designers find them helpful too.

Here is how Dulux use personas to create relevant and helpful websites. This case is adapted from Agency.com, which was available through the IAB (**www.iabuk.net**) and listed in Chaffey and Smith (2008).

The objectives of this project were to position Dulux.co.uk as 'the online destination for colour scheming and visualisation to help you achieve your individual style from the comfort of your home'. The objectives were to increase the number of unique visitors from 1 million to 3.5 million per annum and to drive 12 per cent of visitors to a desired outcome, eg ordering swatches.

Scenario planning that delivered massive success

National Semiconductor (NSC) supplies analogue and digital microchips that process sounds and images for mobiles and DVDs. Target decision makers are design engineers and corporate purchasing agents (they don't buy but they do specify what components they recommend at the beginning of new product development). This influences which components get bought later. The old website gave information about products.

The CEO one day challenged everyone and asked a great question: 'How can the website help engineers?' So a team launched a project to develop a deep understanding of engineers, including how they work (what their scenarios were). This helped them learn how engineers actually design components. This led them to consider creating online tools (on the website) to help engineers to do a better job (and save time).

They discovered that design engineers were under time pressure and realized that NSC could create easy-to-use tools that could speed the design process and save time, so they put a multifunctional team together (including marketing, application designers, web designers and engineers). They identified the design engineer's work process as follows:

1 Create a part.

2 Create a design.

3 Analyse the design (simulations).

4 Build a prototype.

NSC then created a web-based tool called 'web-bench', which helped engineers to complete the whole design process without special software. When engineers log on, they are prompted to specify overall parameters and key components. The web-bench auto-generates possible designs and complete technical specs, part lists, prices and cost benefit analysis. The engineer then refines the design. Next, the design engineer can run a real-time simulation (using sophisticated software that NSC had licensed).

An engineer can then easily alter the design many times and save iterations in 'My portfolio', with an e-mail link to colleagues so they can run and save simulations. Once the engineer agrees the final design, the system generates a bill of materials for the prototype, complete with NSC's components and all requirements from other manufacturers, with links to distributors and prices.

The result is that an engineer can do in two hours what previously took months. Not surprisingly, design engineers loved it. More than 20,000 power supplies were designed in this way in the first year of operation.

What next? The team went on to ask engineers about other activities with which they had difficulty. This revealed thermal simulations and circuitry, so new scenarios and applications were built for engineers who design wireless devices. By the end of the year NSC had 31,000 visitors on-site, generating approximately 3,000 orders or referrals every day. One particular order, from Nokia, was for an integrated socket for 40 million units.

Adapted from Seybold (2001)

The target audience covered the following:

- would-be adventurous 25–44 women, online;
- lack of confidence;
- gap between inspiration (TV, magazines, advertising) and lived experience (sheds, nervous discomfort);
- no guidance or reassurance is available currently on their journey;
- colours and colour combining are key;
- online is a well-used channel for help and guidance on other topics;
- 12-month decorating cycle;
- propensity to socialize;
- quality, technical innovation and scientific proficiency of Dulux is a given.

Examples of personas developed included:

- first-time buyer Penny Edwards, age 27, partner: Ben, location: North London, occupation: sales assistant;
- part-time mum Jane Lawrence, age 37, husband: Joe, location: Manchester, occupation: part-time PR consultant;

Guidelines for using personas and scenarios to improve website design

These are some guidelines and ideas on what can be included when developing a persona. Start or end with giving your persona a name. The detailed stages are:

1 Build personal attributes into personas:

   – demographic: age, gender, education, occupation and, for B2B, company size and position in buying unit;

   – psychographic: goals, tasks and motivation;

   – webographics: web experience (months), usage location (home or work), usage platform (dial-up, broadband), usage frequency and favourite sites.

2 Remember that personas are only models of characteristics and the environment:

   – design targets;

   – stereotypes;

   – three or four usually enough to improve general usability, but more are needed for specific behaviours;

   – choose one primary persona who, if satisfied, means others are likely to be satisfied.

3 Different scenarios can be developed for each persona as explained further below. Write three or four, for example:

   – information-seeking scenario (leads to site registration);

   – purchase scenario: new customer (leads to sale);

   – purchase scenario: existing customer (leads to sale).

After developing specific personas, a primary (most common) persona and a secondary persona can be identified. Other personas (complementary personas), although less common, may, if catered for on the site, generate extra revenues and can sometimes help marketers to think 'outside the box'.

Chaffey and Smith (2008)

● single mum Rachel Wilson, age 40, location: Reading, occupation: business analyst.

Each persona may have a different way of deciding on which paint to buy (and ultimately interacting with the brand). Penny summarized her situation: 'I've got loads of ideas and enthusiasm. I just don't know where to start.' Customer journeys are worked out for different scenarios and personas, and the final website design reflects this by helping different types of customers through their buying journey. See **www.dulux.co.uk**.

So personas help to tighten the content to match customer needs and ultimately help ensure high-quality content. Now consider the exciting part of adding some sizzle to a website.

Sizzle

The internet offers new opportunities to invigorate and add excitement to the brand, add some sizzle, add extra value (or 'added value'), extend the

experience and enhance the image. Ask yourself 'What experience could a website deliver that would be truly unique and representative of the brand?' Ask also 'How can my website help my customers [or other stakeholders – see "Scenario planning" above]?' or 'How can my website add value that is so exciting that it sizzles?'

Here are some creative ideas for sizzle. London's millennium wheel could offer a special virtual version of the tourist experience to those who have taken the actual tour. BBC TV shows could add a webcam into the green room where their celebrities congregate. Football clubs could add a webcam to their training ground or dressing rooms on certain days. A camera company could help users to learn how to take a great photograph by simulating taking photographs with different settings and allowing the user to compare and contrast the results (and also give tips on how to maintain the camera and invite users to send their best photos in to a competition). A travel company could give customers a 'virtual friend' that advises on 'things you might like to do' in each city (determined by the customers' interests).

Drinks brand Bacardi sizzles online by maintaining the club scene atmosphere with its online value proposition including a pulsating beat, BAT radio (the logo contains a bat), video clips and cocktail recipes. Food websites offer printable recipes, video demonstrations and discussion forums, as well as 'Ask the expert' sessions. Chocolate companies generate ideas for using the chocolates creatively in desserts, dinner party games and designs for table layouts. One site that gives excellent service online is the UK Patent Office's trademark division, which allows visitors to search by name, design and date for similar or the same trademarks. Its integrated system ensures Patent Office staff are available to talk customers through any of the processes. It also gives visitors access to their own archived applications – all with the click of a button. A complicated and sometimes dull process has been made surprisingly user-friendly.

A more exciting brand perhaps is Harley-Davidson. Its motorcycle website offers web visitors a virtual ride and lets them actually see the same view a Harley driver enjoys, cruising through the countryside. This extra sizzle can enhance the brand in a way that can only be done online. Some sizzle is very simple but adds excitement and positive experiences to the brand. Now consider, arguably, another type of sizzle – customer engagement.

Customer engagement

Scenario planning, personas and sizzle should ensure reasonably high-quality content that customers are interested in. If the site content reflects the customers' interests, then the magic marketing formula is activated (identify needs, reflect them and satisfy them). This will bring visitors back to the site and boost results. Another approach is customer engagement, which means getting the visitor interacting, or engaging, with the site. The ultimate engagement is where customers create user-generated content (UGC). This collaborative co-creation is discussed fully in Chapter 1, 'The ladder of engagement'.

Some forms of customer engagement are so absorbing that they sizzle. One classic piece of engagement, discussed in Chapter 1, is threadless.com, where users send in their designs for T-shirts and

all users vote for the best designs, which are then printed and sold online. This is UGC selling back to itself. These customers are highly engaged customers, as they are heavily involved with the brand – even creating some of its products. All brands have opportunities to extend the brand experience online by layering in new and exciting ways of engaging customers.

As customers move from giving a rating to a review to a discussion to collaborative co-creation, whether co-creating an ad, product or service, their level of engagement increases. UGC is a form of sizzle if it gets customers pouring their creative energies into a brand's website. This is collaborative co-creation, and it produces content. Some content will be better than other content, so a voting mechanism and/or a judging mechanism can be used to ensure that high-quality content receives prominence.

In summary, customer engagement, creating sizzle, developing personas and scenario planning combine to ensure a website contains high-quality content that is very relevant to customers, thereby exploiting the magic marketing formula (identify, reflect and deliver).

Now consider the second satisfaction factor – easy navigation.

Satisfying visitors key factor 2: navigation

Good websites are also carefully designed in terms of both form and function. Form means the way a site looks, ie the aesthetics, which includes layout, graphics, colour and typography. Function is interaction, integration, navigation and structure. Navigation and even the layout of each page require expert advice and careful attention. Navigation is a critical aspect, as it determines how users can move around a site using menus, hyperlinks and signposts or panels.

Different visitors search in different ways. They use different keywords, headings and links. Placing an order should never be more than three clicks away. Remember, some people are ready to buy right now, others want to try it first and others again want more information. Telephone numbers and contact details should always be readily accessible. Site structure should be simple, consistent and well signposted in order to create flow.

Navigation rules

The overall navigation structure should clearly demonstrate how content is grouped and how different pages relate to others. Without a planned structure, a site can soon end up as a 'spaghetti site'. At worst, this leaves visitors angry and frustrated. At best, it leaves them dazed, disorientated, confused and frustrated. If there is no natural flow, visitors may leave for ever.

Navigation requires careful consideration and eventual usability testing. This can be done on paper with mock-up screen grabs rather than on a fully developed site. Many navigation issues can be spotted before the site gets fully developed. Here are three navigation rules from *eMarketing eXcellence* (Chaffey and Smith, 2008):

1 *Keep it simple.* Do not have too many buttons. Psychologists who have analysed the behaviour of computer users in labs say the magic number is seven (or fewer). Any more than seven and the user will find it difficult to choose. You can use nesting or pop-up menus to avoid the need for too many menus or too many menu items. Simplicity is necessary to avoid confusing the user.

2 *Be consistent.* Consistency is helpful, since you want to avoid users seeing different menus and page layouts as they move around the site. For example, the menu structures for customer support should be similar to those for browsing product information.

3 *Signposts.* There should be signposts to help visitors by telling them where they are within the website and what else they might like to see.

Cater for customers at different stages of the buying process. Some want to see more information, some want to try a sample, and some want to buy right now. So 'See', 'Try' and 'Buy' options can help (see below). These can be presented in different formats, particularly when catering for customers who prefer to receive information in different formats, eg video (demonstration), text (often a PDF article) or actually speaking to a human (call-back technology). Clearly label the different folders or directories on the site so they act as a reference point for describing particular types of content on the site (Chaffey and Smith, 2008).

Top tasks

Another aspect of navigation is identifying the main tasks that visitors want to do when on a website. The website design is consequently driven by these kinds of tasks. Although identifying the top tasks is important, it is ignored by many sites, particularly when different departments want to get some prominence on the home page. This is another form of scope creep (see Chapter 3, 'Beware of scope creep'). Here is Gerry McGovern (2010b) explaining how identifying top tasks can reveal insights that directly affect customer conversion rates, enquiries and, ultimately, sales:

> Another legal and medical publisher spent a long time trying to figure out what its customers' top tasks were. One area in which they publish is family law. After much discussion it dawned on them that there are really only two tasks that matter: getting married and getting divorced. If you went to their current website these tasks would have been very hard to find amidst all the clutter.
>
> Have you heard of website creep? The new website launches and the top tasks are fairly visible. But there is an immediate and relentless pressure from the tiny tasks within the organization.
>
> They all want to be on the homepage. They all want to be a news item or an ad. They want more links. And they will press and press the web team to give them these things. Little by little the tiny tasks clutter the homepage, the other major pages, the navigation and the search. And of course once these tiny tasks are published there is absolutely no incentive to review or remove them. Thus as the website gets old it gets worse. What is the classic solution? A redesign.

Raving alcoholics and web redesign

'A classic web redesign is like taking a raving alcoholic and sending them to rehab for a month. (Giving a website to a marketer or communicator is like giving a pub to an alcoholic.) They come out looking clean and redesigned. However, the underlying problems have not been addressed so six months later you're back in the same mess.'

McGovern (2010b)

How to convert visitors to customers

In the offline world, many salespeople avoid asking for the sale or 'closing the sale', perhaps because of an unconscious fear of failure or possibly poor training. Whatever the reason, all the hard work of finding a prospect, getting an appointment, preparing, presenting, and handling objections is wasted if the salesperson does not ask for the business. The same applies online. Getting traffic to a website is one thing. The probability of a visitor actually buying increases if the following variables are in place:

- a call to action (with a strong incentive);
- 'See', 'Try' and 'Buy' options;
- price lining;
- simplified processes;
- reduced customer anxiety;
- a contact strategy and digital body language;
- relevant landing pages.

A call to action

Whether it is 'Register now' for an e-newsletter or 'Buy now', the call to action can be enhanced by adding an incentive to act now. Effective incentives include gifts, free products, reduced prices or anything that might nudge a prospect into taking action immediately as opposed to delaying a decision. A limited number of gifts or products may also act as an incentive to 'decide now'. (See Chapter 16 for more on sales promotions.) **Well-targeted incentives do not have to cost very much but do have to be of value to the target market.** Often these knowledge assets are content that the organization has already created for some other purpose. It effectively costs nothing to give it away as an incentive. Whatever the incentive, the calls to action should be visible across the site, as visitors land on different pages. Note that some countries do not allow free gifts and incentives. If targeting certain export countries, check first with UK Trade & Investment or the equivalent export bodies to see what is permissible. Finally, ensure customers are reassured by all the credibility factors, including money-back guarantees, customer ratings, reviews and endorsements, privacy policy, reassurance about security and full contact details including postal address and customer services (ideally via phone, e-mail and text or chat).

'See', 'Try' and 'Buy' options

In the same way that an offline retail clothes store tries to let customers see its best clothes and then encourages customers to try them on in the hope of making a sale, websites can also accommodate the three stages of 'See it', 'Try it' and 'Buy it'. It can happen all in one go if online customers can try it there online immediately or try it for a period of time, followed by prompts to buy it (contact strategy). In the offline clothes retailing example, companies all know that getting customers to engage and try the clothes increases the chance of making a sale. The same applies online, although it may take a little longer. A key point to remember here is that some visitors have found exactly what they want and are ready to buy right now, while other visitors want to trial it, and others again are interested but want to see more about the product first. The site should accommodate all three types of visitor by offering all three options.

Price lining

Price lining effectively means having a range of prices so that anyone with any budget can always buy something, even if it is a sample unit or a small version. A range of sizes allows for a range of price points, which guarantees that anyone with any money can at least be in a position to buy something. Not having enough money or budget is no longer a barrier. A variation of this theme of having something for every budget is rental or leasing, eg some organizations partner with leasing companies that effectively give the customer a choice of paying a large capital sum or paying a smaller weekly or monthly amount.

Simplified processes

All interactions should be easy, particularly form filling. Some marketers get greedy for data and think that, if customers are prepared to register for a newsletter or white paper or even buy a product, the marketers can collect a lot of data from the customers (and maybe eventually do some really useful customer profiling or customer analyses). This is a mistake. Generally, visitors do not like having to register for anything, so if they do have to register make it easy for them by having only a few questions initially. More information can be collected later. If one of the top customer tasks is to download a white paper or register for a newsletter, make it easy for the busy visitor. Make the form short. Do not create barriers with forms.

Here is Gerry McGovern (2010a) with some stunning results that demonstrate how form filling can affect sales directly and indirectly.

Keep it simple. Keep it short. Visitors are under time pressure. Having seen the huge success of keeping things simple, HSBC wanted to see where else it could apply these insights. It decided to tackle travel insurance. Two per cent of travel insurance applications were coming through the web channel; it wanted to double that, so it improved the application form. It took only two weeks to redesign the website application form into a single one-page form. As McGovern (2010a) says: 'It took 4 months to get the compliance and legal department to sign off on the change, because they didn't like the simple approach – it lacked the detail they were used to. So how did that go? HSBC now receives more than 75 per cent of their applications for travel insurance online.'

Big forms kill customers

Some years ago, HSBC Hong Kong had what they thought was a reasonably straightforward mortgage inquiry form. It had 17 fields requesting:

- Property information (address, price)
- Applicant information (name, occupation)
- Loan information (amount, repayment period, etc.)

They were getting 2 enquiries a week through the form. They felt that they could do better. They turned to Brett King, a friend of mine, who has just published an excellent book called *Bank 2.0*. Brett and his team convinced them to radically simplify the form.

They reduced the number of fields from 17 to 3: Name, E-mail and Phone number. The simplification process met some resistance. People said that the old form gathered data that integrated well into the internal system. People felt that the new form would encourage frivolous enquiries from the likes of Donald Duck and Arnold Schwarzenegger.

'They finally launched the new form. There was no publicity or special promotion, so the basic number of visitors to the mortgage pages remained the same. However, enquiries jumped from 2 per week to 180 per week. And yes, they did indeed get mortgage requests from Arnie. Despite such frivolous enquiries, new mortgage business directly connected with the new, simpler online form reached $20 million in the first quarter after its release. With the old form they were doing less than $1 million a quarter.'

McGovern (2010a)

Tesco's usability tests focus on tiny details, which integrate offline and online

"Little tiny things make a big difference to the customer experience, and Tesco is unbelievably good at creating that differentiation," says Catriona Campbell, director at Foviance. When Tesco was developing Tesco Direct, Foviance was tasked with getting real customers to test the site.

"We used eye-tracking, so we literally tracked where their eyes were going on the catalogue and on the web, and we could see that some of the creative in the catalogue wasn't transferring to the web," she says. The usability innovations that came out of the research were not huge, but they made a big difference, she says.

"It was things like putting the catalogue page number into the website, so you could search for something you had seen in the catalogue. Customers also wanted to see the Tesco Value 'stickers' throughout the website and the catalogue as well, the way they do in store. It doesn't make it easier to read, but they just wanted to see that big red splodge."

The point, says Campbell, is that true usability depends less on creative ideas that spring from nowhere than it does on asking the audience. "A lot of the things that came out of the research you couldn't have come up with in isolation," she says. "The creative had to go hand in hand with research into real-life situations, and the beauty is in combining the skills of researchers with those of the designers to get that creative idea out that really makes a difference."

'"Little tiny things make a big difference to the customer experience, and Tesco is unbelievably good at creating that differentiation," says Catriona Campbell.'

Woods (2007)

The ultimate way to check to see if the website is easy to use is to carry out usability testing. Here, customers matching the target market profile are given sets of tasks to complete.

Reduced customer anxiety

Customers are nervous about giving their personal data and their money to someone they don't know, often thousands of miles away. They are also nervous about clicking a link that might take them somewhere irrelevant or aggravating, thereby wasting their third key resource – time. A typo-free professionally designed site is essential. An uncluttered design gives a reassuring sense of order amidst a chaotic world. Customer endorsements and a list of high-profile customers reassure customers, as do trusted internet infrastructure services like VeriSign, membership of professional bodies, and awards won. The 'About us' section should show photographs of real staff, contact details and, ideally, a photograph of a real building with a full address. Finally, at both 'Add to shopping basket' and the checkout it is worth reminding customers about money-back guarantees, whether the item is in stock and any express shipping options. Let customers know how quickly it can be received and what the next steps are. Buyer anxiety must be dispelled at every opportunity.

A contact strategy

Visitors can be converted to customers even after they have left the website if, firstly, the organization has captured the prospect's e-mail address and name and, secondly, the organization follows up with a structured contact strategy. Each contact (e-mail, letter or phone call) usually contains an incentivized call to action. See Tesco's simple e-mail contact strategies for customers at different stages in the buying process in Chapter 3. There is usually a different sequence of contacts depending on whether customers registered for an e-mail newsletter, made an enquiry, took a trial or actually made a purchase. Making a purchase is just the start of what it is hoped is a lifetime relationship.

Advanced marketers watch website visitors' behaviour (or digital body language) to determine what, if any, contact is most helpful. This could be a pop-up message on a website, an offer of a phone call or a visit from a sales rep. A series of three visits online could trigger an alert to a sales rep (with the relevant prospect data) followed by a courtesy sales call. An alternative contact strategy would be where

each prospect who engages with the brand through search, advertising, webinars or white papers is subsequently entered into a 'nurturing campaign' that combines direct mail and e-mail to strengthen the brand's proposition. Three visits trigger an attractive incentive-based offer to meet with a consultant.

> ### Excellent contact strategies vary according to the prospects' preferences in media type, frequency and style
>
> Some prospects want information via RSS feeds into their RSS readers; others prefer e-mail, direct mail, podcasts, trade shows or industry analyst reports. Some want quarterly, monthly or weekly contact. The more engaged customers tend to be more comfortable with increased frequency of contact. The prospects' progression though the sales cycle can be identified by profiling both the communication frequency and any responses. If open rates start dropping, prospects are either under time pressure or losing interest and therefore it may be worth reconsidering the contact strategy for them. Again all this can be managed by a set of rules that trigger various contact strategies and particular propositions and offers. Some prospects prefer rich graphical communication, while others just want the basic information in a text or e-mail.

Digital body language and joined-up marketing

B2B buyers today can do a lot of their procurement online without ever seeing a sales representative. They can compile a list of potential suppliers, brief them and subsequently analyse the best solution – all without the a salesperson's visit, effectively squeezing the sales rep out of the equation. Many professional buyers meet fewer salespeople today, as they can complete a lot of the procurement process online. So, despite not being able to watch buyers' body language during a sales pitch, top marketers still know how to read (and use) their prospect buyers' digital body language. Marketers watch website visitors and know which prospects are at what stages, and almost what their thought processes are as they move through their buying stages. Marketers can give relevant information at the right time and ultimately help prospects to buy (either online or offline with a salesperson) without ever seeing the buyer physically. It combines digital body language with joined-up marketing.

Visitors can be scored according to their digital body language – how many visits to a particular section, how long spent on various pages, and what was downloaded, as these activities give an indication of how interested a visitor is in a product or service. Equally if several visitors from the same organization start spending time on a site, it may be an indicator that a prospect is warming up.

Expert marketers define what level of interest (or online activity) identifies a quality lead, where in the buying cycle the prospect is and when to bring a salesperson into a deal and when not to. Sales and marketing managers get to know which buyers are actively engaged in a buying process and which are not. Subtle digital buying signals are recognized. If digital body language is objectively scored and suddenly changes, this can indicate that the prospect has moved to a different phase in the buying process. It is the classic prospect entering the sales funnel and being helped through the sales process with highly relevant information and offers.

Relevant landing pages

When prospects click on a PPC adword or a hyperlink, they expect to land on a page that contains relevant information. They do not expect to land on a home page and have to start drilling down to find the relevant information, so make sure the visitors get to the relevant page with just one click. The more relevant the page the more closely it reflects the user's needs and ergo the more likely the visitor is to buy. Some sites serve personalized web pages that effectively remember the customer's preferences and therefore serve even more relevant content. Another approach is to create a microsite of tailored content to match a sales promotion or an ad campaign. See Case study 21.1. Yet another approach is to create many variations of the same page, some with different offers, some with different images and some with different words, to see which page is the most relevant to customers by monitoring which test page converts the most prospects into customers. This is not as expensive as it sounds, as in the second case the marketing team can create these page variations themselves and test them themselves. First, see how some brands build tailor-made microsites dedicated to a relevant theme.

CASE STUDY 21.1   Times Online microsite – Brian Clough, *The Damned United*

Situation analysis

Digital agency Moonshine Media was asked by Times Online to create an engaging showcase to celebrate the colourful life and times of Brian Clough, one of England's most controversial and outspoken football managers.

Objectives

The ultimate objective for the website was to help promote *The Damned United* film, an adaption of David Peace's bestselling novel *The Damned Utd* about Clough's stormy 44-day tenure as manager of Leeds United.

Strategy

The website was designed to focus on Clough's career as opposed to his personal life, which was why the inspiration for the website layout was derived from an interest in card collecting, as well as showing a clean and text-minimalist look.

Tactics

The site provided links to an archive of information including video, images and articles. The website ultimately displayed an interactive timeline, 'Clough in the rough', and aggregated video as well as images. The *Sunday Times* archive content highlighted the key events in Clough's career, enabling readers to explore and navigate through the most memorable moments in Old Big 'Ead's life.

Action

See Figure 21.1.

FIGURE 21.1 Times Online microsite timetable

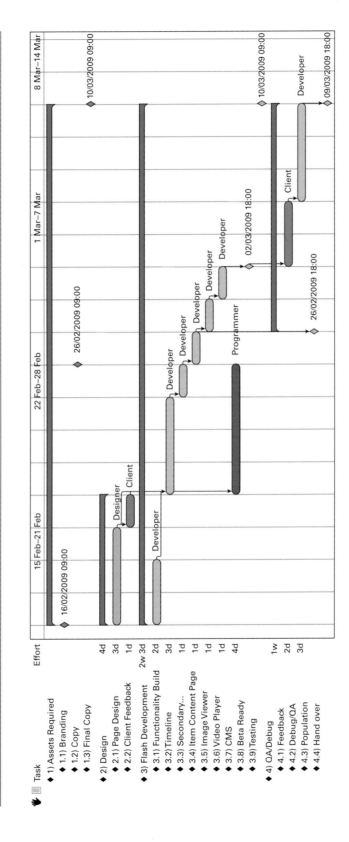

Control/results

Feedback from Times Online praised the website for having a 'slick and exciting design which showed off our content in a fresh and dynamic manner'. The project was completed with Times Online feeling 'confident' that the application would engage and entertain its readers.

Men/women

A research team involving five individuals from Times Online worked for a month before the project started in order to collect all the information with which to populate the site.

They went through archives from newspapers, looked through interviews, and bought very limited film footage. Moonshine Media was given the content and populated the site with everything that was supplied.

Money

Times Online had a budget of £13,000 for the microsite (no retainer, pay by results).

Minutes

From start to finish took 30 days.

Do not forget internal communications – 10 per cent of the budget

Flawless execution of marketing campaigns and simple tools like websites is not as common as it should be. In fact some years ago a US book by Bossidy and Charan (2002) claimed that execution was the last bastion of competitive advantage, ie being able to execute plans better than your competitors created competitive advantage. One aspect that is critical to flawless execution of marketing communications is internal marketing, which means communicating to your team, colleagues, staff and other departments within your organization. Figures vary, but many well-run organizations allocate a minimum of 10 per cent of their resources to communicating internally.

CASE STUDY 21.2   American Greetings e-cards – the LiveBall system

Situation analysis

American Greetings has the largest collection of electronic greetings on the web, including cards available at AmericanGreetings.com through AG Interactive, Inc, the company's online division. AG Interactive funnelled online traffic to the **www.americangreetings.com** home page, or a single multivariate testing (MVT)-optimized landing page. The marketing team decided they needed to launch an aggressive landing page testing in order to lift visitor conversion rates from an average of 1.47 per cent to 2.01 per cent.

Objectives

The goal was to convert traffic using online registration for a free trial subscription (which later converted to a paid subscription on AmericanGreetings.com); however, one landing page was not converting enough of the total traffic. Implementing testing on one landing page was slow, with a multi-month feedback loop to the marketing team. Experimentation with alternative design and content was even slower.

Strategy

To lift conversions, the marketing team decided to create and test several different context-specific landing pages for each keyword: e-cards, free e-cards, birthday, create and print, and international. They determined they needed to experiment broadly with content and layout, test results and view analysis in real time to find which landing pages worked best. Their new strategy was based around a system (Ion's LiveBall) where the marketers could change the offers, propositions and even pictures directly without needing developers and designers to code and create new pages for them.

Tactics

American Greetings adopted LiveBall in order to increase agility, speed to market, and specificity and ultimately to improve conversion performance to lower cost per customer acquisition. Ion worked closely with the AG Interactive marketing manager to launch and test alternative landing experiences that were specific to marketing segments and traffic sources.

Action

Within the first three months of testing with LiveBall, American Greetings moved from a single, optimized land-ing page to over 40 unique landing pages, each context-specific to its source of traffic. Three entirely different design formats were tested with 12 different price points across 200 different audience segments. By speaking to each segment, American Greetings was able to increase conversions despite an economic fallout that actually reduced the flow of traffic.

Customers looking for e-cards search using different phrases. Tests revealed which landing page performed best for each key phrase. Once these 'champion' landing pages were identified, all traffic from a particular ad word was directed to that champion page. Consider three search phrases: 'e-cards', 'birthdays' and 'create and print' (your own card). Each phrase is linked to a specific landing page that reflects the phrase. Each landing page has several versions tested before the marketing team selects the 'optimum' landing page for each key phrase. This is the magic marketing formula at work.

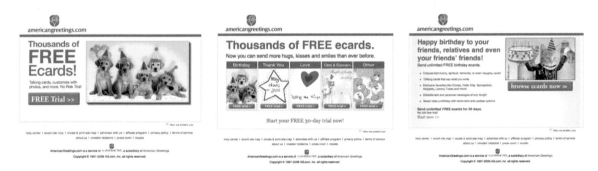

The key phrase 'e-cards' was tested against many different landing pages before choosing the landing page called 'Browse with Flash' (on the right hand side). This was the champion page (which made the most sales).

The key phrase 'birthdays' was tested against many different landing pages to see which page converted the most visitors into customers. The landing page called 'Browse with Flash' (in the middle) was the champion (ie it sold the most cards).

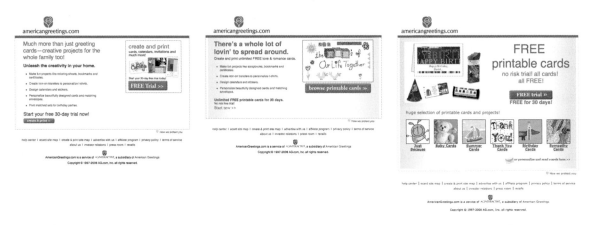

Many different landing pages were tested for the key phrase 'Create and Print'. The 'general' landing page (on the left hand side) converted higher than the other family focused themes.

Control

Each unique landing page format was customized and matched with the PPC ad that was sending it traffic. The testing resulted in an almost immediate 30 per cent increase in conversion and a subsequent 20 per cent decrease in cost per acquisition (which is a net benefit that included the added expenses associated with Ion's LiveBall platform and conversion optimization services). E-cards run 13 or 14 tests simultaneously at any one time and get quick, actionable learning.

Over the first five months using LiveBall, the American Greetings online marketing team created over 700 unique landing pages, which were tested across hundreds of unique traffic sources. The real-time testing and analytics in LiveBall ensured that traffic arrived at the best-performing landing page for each traffic source. As soon as American

Greetings got statistical significance on a test, they drove traffic immediately to the champion landing page in real time. On Mother's Day alone this resulted in $45,000 in incremental revenue. That's revenue that would have been lost without LiveBall's actionable, real-time approach.

New tests are always in the works at American Greetings. The conversion goal for 2010 was over 40 per cent higher than for 2009, and another 33 per cent lift was targeted for 2011 over 2010. American Greetings uses Ion's Live-Ball platform to drive real business ROI at scale. Smaller-percentage improvements on the top-line sales figures have a big impact on the bottom-line profit figures. LiveBall gives fast speed to market and learning. It's a visual tool that lets marketers focus on what's working to improve results.

World-class marketers constantly try to optimize and improve their marketing performances, and American Greetings is a good example. Testing multiple landing pages is one of many ways to boost the conversion of visitors to customers. Marketing professionals now need to convert existing customers to lifetime, repeat-purchasing customers. Here's how.

Convert customers into lifetime customers

It has been suggested that the second visit to a website is the beginning of a relationship. Today marketers ask themselves whether they are giving customers enough reasons to come back and visit the site for a second time. It is a great question. Honest answers will improve the website. On the assumption that the site works and customers have bought once, how do marketers convert those same customers into lifetime customers. How do marketers keep the relationship alive? Answer: the same way anyone keeps a relationship alive and well – by listening to them, understanding their needs, speaking to them regularly, always giving them good value (never breaking the promise) and occasionally giving them a nice surprise. What does that mean? It means marketers must deliver the quality the brand promises, have a contact strategy, respond to the customers – their questions, queries, worries, complaints or suggestions – and reward them occasionally. Part of the contact strategy includes acknowledging the order, confirming delivery dates, and following up with a satisfaction survey. Ongoing tailored special offers and reminders should help to keep the relationship alive.

Now that successful websites have been explored, consider successful social media: the key factors and the errors to avoid.

Successful social media

As mentioned in Chapter 1, social media is 'the biggest change since the industrial revolution'. Both Chapter 1 and all the other chapters refer to social media and how to integrate it into a wide range of campaigns. Chapter 16 specifically includes three social media campaigns that involve collaborative co-creation of digital art, music and poetry (rap) and movie soundtracks. This is exciting UGC and is at the top level of the ladder of engagement (Chapter 1). Chapter 13 discusses **UGC campaigns** that generate long-form ads, some of which have been broadcast as movies. As businesses scramble to jump on the social media bandwagon, it is now worth exploring how to integrate social media into business systems, how **social media optimization (SMO) is the new search engine optimization (SEO)**, and how to avoid the 10 most common social media mistakes.

10 steps to integrate social media into the business

Here are 10 steps towards integrating social media into business processes so that it becomes a normal process required to run a business. There is some overlap with the three-step approach to

blogging: lurk (listen and learn); participate (post a comment); blog (write your own blog posts).

The steps below are more detailed ones for integrating all social media processes. This was adapted from Brian Solis (2010), who suggests we are witnessing 'the transformation of business acumen while also shifting the culture and the communication that embraces an inward and outward flow for listening, interacting, learning, and adapting... it is listening that sets the stage for intelligent participation'. Solis sees the better organizations evolving their social media usage: 'The next stage of Social Media Marketing will mature from one of listening and unguided participation to one of strategic observation, analysis and informed engagement.' So here is an adaptation of Brian Solis's 10 steps:

1   *Listen.* Staff members are allocated certain groups and communities. They search for the use of certain brands, people and key phrases and use listening tools such as Google Alerts, Twitter Search, Radian6, and PR Newswire's Social Media Metrics in addition to monitoring their own allocated communities. Log hot topics (generate a lot of comments) as well as the number of positive and negative mentions (sentiment). Listen for heated topics packed with emotion that could go viral.

2   *Create a presence.* Create a presence on the usual social networks, including Twitter and possibly Facebook (the fan pages), YouTube and Flickr. This is not strategic engagement, just experimental at this stage, 'resembling chatter or traditional broadcasting of messages'.

3   *Join the conversation.* Take the plunge, join some relevant conversations, and announce activities, events and competitions on your own pages or tweets. If in another community's discussion, add these announcements to the conversation only if they are relevant and useful. Keep a watch on the number or amount of friends, fans, followers, conversations, sentiment, mentions, traffic and reach.

4   *Identify communities, burning issues and opinion formers.* Moving beyond just listening to observing where the really significant conversations are, the types of

responses and the language that is used can reveal burning issues, pain points, new ideas and a lot more valuable intelligence. Businesses do not have to be everywhere to create a presence, just where relevant conversations are occurring with significant audiences or influencers.

5 *Content strategy*. As the needs of relevant communities and opinion formers emerge, an organization can begin to define what kind of content, questions, challenges and collaborative co-creation it would be good to feed into these communities. This is the shift from ad hoc communications to a more carefully planned communications agenda. It means strategically defining the topics, questions, issues, worries and anxieties that a relevant community has that can be answered by the organization and its teams of experts. It is driven partly by the overall positioning the brand wants to achieve and partly by the market itself.

6 *Social media guidelines*. These guidelines are issued to everyone in the organization and particularly to those who blog, tweet or participate in discussions, or create videos, graphics or anything else that may be posted to social communities. The guidelines spell out the desired positioning of the brand, key phrases with which the brand wants to be associated, typical hot issues in which the organization has expertise, and possible links to some of the brand's own popular pages, specific landing pages, articles, PowerPoint slide shows or videos. The guidelines can also include other brand guidelines covering tone of voice, use of logos and straplines, etc.

7 *Grow the community*. A community does not grow simply by establishing a blog, a Facebook fan page, a group or 'any old online profile'. A presence on these social media platforms is not enough. High-quality content that encourages members to share and engage with each other is required. Community members are also required, as are opinion formers. At this stage the brand must reach out and invite ideal participants and potential advocates to join the community. It is a significant task inviting and encouraging members to join a new

social media community. This takes time and is part of an ongoing process.

8 *Socialization of the team*. The organization's own team has to believe in the power of social media, and needs to research and explore various social media platforms in search of useful information, whether for their personal hobbies or ultimately the business. Staff have got to get used to the sharing and collaborating potential of social media. The listening and conversing stages are only as effective as their ability to inspire transformation. Interdepartmental cooperation (sharing) is required. All staff are brand ambassadors and members of the social team. Social marketing integrates with CRM systems, as questions may need to be answered by the team. In fact any external-facing department will have to be socially mobilized. Internal social champions must be identified and encouraged to collaborate.

9 *Socialization of business processes and workflow*. Monitoring discussions, discovering great resources, participating in conversations, blogging and encouraging UGC all require staff time and also processes that ensure conversations are fulfilled and intelligence is collected, shared and used to make better decisions and ultimately run a better organization. New workflows require the reorganization of teams and processes. Organizations will have to manage the social workflow. The ability to learn and adapt determines organizations' future survival.

10 *Measure and report*. So that marketing can stop being referred to as the 'colouring department' (see Chapter 1), marketers must be able to evaluate the value of social media marketing (as well as all aspects of marketing) and present this to the board. For each social media tool, it is possible to quantify and compare ROI, cost per thousand, cost per enquiry, cost per order and cost per customer acquired across all other marketing communications tools, online and offline, inbound and outbound. The difficult bit is measuring the impact of social media on the brand value, which can now be included as an asset on the balance sheet.

Social media optimization – SMO is the new SEO

Search engine optimization means optimizing a website so that it gets found by search engines and appears high up in the **search engine results page (SERPs)**. A lot of effort goes into SEO but, as more and more searches being carried out start within social media platforms, it follows that social media platforms or, more specifically, the social media content needs to be optimized also. Social media content, otherwise known as social media objects, includes videos, photographs, blog posts, articles, white papers and even comments, status updates and wall posts. **SMO boosts the findability** and, consequently, the visibility of content created for social media.

> 'Social media is becoming a core product research channel', with social networks accounting for 18 per cent of where all searches begin.
>
> Gibs (2009)

When searching the combined universe of traditional websites and the new social media platforms, the same principles apply to SMO as SEO, and that is to use keywords and key phrases, titles, descriptions, tags and links:

- *Keywords and key phrases.* Use keywords or key phrases: the headlines, tags and descriptions. The first step here is building a key phrase list or inventory of words and phrases that the target market would use when searching for an organization's product or service. This requires marketers' empathy – the ability to think like their customers and list the words and phrases customers would use. Marketers also look at their own web analytics to see which words bring them the most traffic. They watch competitor sites to see what words and phrases they use. Their sales teams ask customers what phrases they use when searching. And the marketers use tools to generate keywords and compare popular ones with the same phrases used on other websites. Once equipped with key

phrases for different products or services, marketers can then add them into the content as well as the headlines, tags and descriptions.

- *Titles.* These should include key phrases to attract searchers. It is worth trying to squeeze a keyword or phrase into a headline, rather than using sophisticated alliteration or intriguing wording.

- *Descriptions.* The same applies here. Key phrases should be included. In fact at least three can be inserted, but be careful to weave them in so that they sound sensible and not like contrived keyword manipulation.

- *Tags.* These are keywords that help to further categorize social media objects. Tags should include keywords that are relevant to the social media object.

- *Links.* As with SEO, links have the most impact on findability and visibility. Links drive traffic directly, as a link posted on Twitter or on a wall can boost traffic directly. They also tell a search engine that this object has some authority (as links equate to authority, particularly if the link is from a venerable institute or a popular site). This pushes it up the rankings, and it consequently appears higher in search results.

10 common social media mistakes

Here are 10 common social media mistakes highlighted by *Econsultancy*'s Patricia Robles (2010):

Many businesses are increasingly comfortable with social media, and many more have decided that social media is far too important not to experiment with. But the growing level of maturity in the world of social media doesn't mean that mistakes are uncommon. To the contrary: many businesses make the same mistakes over and over again. Here are 10 of the most common:

1 *Overfollowing.* Social media is called 'social' media for a reason, but there's nothing 'social' about following an ungodly number of users, especially in a short amount of time. Success with social media is just like marketing, sales and PR: results are achieved one victory at a time.

2 *Using every tool available*. Getting social media 'right' is harder than it looks. One of the things that's required: focus. But it's hard to focus when you try to build a presence on every popular social media website. Which is why companies should resist the urge to get involved with all the new and shiny toys and instead focus on the social media platforms that are most likely to be a good fit.

3 *Falling off the wagon*. A social media effort is easy to start, but it can be a challenge to keep going. In short, social media is a journey, not a destination. Businesses that aren't prepared for the long haul are far more likely to give up. That's not a good thing because social media is a party and the other partygoers (your customers, competitors, etc.) are likely to notice if you pass out.

4 *Not training employees*. Social media may look easy, but it really isn't. How your employees behave can have a big impact on your company's social media reputation. For companies that are actively involved with social media, setting expectations and creating policies for employees is the best way to ensure that they help your reputation, not hurt it.

5 *Letting the new kid or a low-level employee manage your profiles*. Who should be in charge of your social media endeavors? The young employee who joined Facebook back in 2004 and who has 5,000 followers on Twitter might seem like a good choice, but chances are he or she isn't. Your social media presence is far too valuable to leave in the hands of somebody who is new, inexperienced, lacks detailed knowledge about the company or isn't heavily invested in the company's success. Putting it in the hands of anyone else can quickly lead to disaster.

6 *Pretending that social media is free*. Signing up for a Twitter account and Facebook Page, for instance, may not cost any money, but managing them (and managing them well) doesn't magically happen without an investment that can be quantified in dollars and cents. Social media will always require somebody's time and may require that certain corporate resources be allocated differently. Businesses can't ignore these costs when planning their social media strategies and evaluating what they're delivering.

7 *Publishing first, thinking later*. In the world of social media, everything you say can and will be held against you. Unfortunately, the real-time nature of many social media websites encourages a 'publish first, think later' dynamic. Companies have far too much to lose, however, and need to ensure that what's being published is accurate, honest and in line with the company's values. Sometimes, it's better not to publish.

8 *Ignoring metrics*. When it comes to social media, companies need to be comfortable experimenting. But experimentation doesn't mean that companies shouldn't define the metrics by which progress and success can be measured. Measurement is just as important with social media as it is with any other business effort.

9 *Assuming ROI isn't possible to calculate*. The three letters R-O-I often make social media proponents cringe and social media skeptics grin. Many companies buy into the notion that social media is really, really important, but a lot of them also buy into the notion that social media's value can't reasonably be calculated in terms of ROI. That's a mistake because for all of social media's virtues, any effort made by a business eventually has to produce tangible value that can be correlated the bottom line.

10 *Expecting the world*. Social media can do many great things for businesses, but it has its limitations. For instance, it isn't necessarily going to drive sales, increase brand loyalty or create buzz – especially overnight. Getting the most out of social media requires healthy, not unrealistic, expectations.

So these are the classic social media errors to avoid. CEOs are right to be cautious and right to demand more systematic and measured approaches to social media. However, the benefits of social media must not be ignored in deepening brand relationships, listening to stakeholders, and spreading awareness and presence, as well as generating enquiries, leads and sales. Here are a few anecdotal statistics that demonstrate some of the growing benefits of doing business online:

- Offline TV ads' reducing effectiveness: only 18 per cent of traditional TV campaigns generate a positive ROI.

- Increasing internet: internet usage, over the last seven years, has increased 70 per cent

CEO's cynicism of social media –
mash me up?

'What's it going to be tomorrow – scan my body into a mash-up simulator to create a hologram so I can telepresence myself into sales calls in Madrid via FourSquare using Flickr? All I know is that I've spent a *lot* of time and money on a series of disjointed initiatives and campaigns and so far *none* have performed as advertised… so far nobody in my organization has stepped forward with a cerebral, strategic, multi-generational, integrated, systematic, and sustainable methodology and roadmap for synergistically capitalizing on this medium over the long haul.'

Byron, Kievman and Schrum (2010)

- Increased sales: Naked Pizza set a one-day sales record using social media with 68 per cent of its sales coming via Twitter and 85 per cent of its new customers.
- Increased sales: Dell has already made over $7 million in sales via Twitter.
- Increased conversions: software company Genius.com reports that 24 per cent of social media leads convert to sales opportunities.
- Increased awareness: 37 per cent of Generation Y heard about the Ford Fiesta via social media before its launch in the United States, and currently 25 per cent of Ford's marketing budget is spent on digital or social media.
- A Wetpaint/Altimeter Group study found that companies that widely engage in social media surpass their peers in both revenue and profit.

Byron, Kievman and Schrum (2010), whose sources include: meyersreport.com, lenovosocial.com, George Wright of Blendtec, Mashable.com, econsultancy.com and businessweek.com

per annum. Spending for digital advertising in 2010 will be more than $25 billion and surpass print advertising spending (for ever).

- Increasing social media: 71 per cent of companies plan to increase investments in social media by an average of 40 per cent.
- Reduced costs: Lenovo has experienced a 20 per cent reduction in activity to its call centre since it launched its community website for customers.
- Increased sales: Blendtec quintupled sales with its 'Will it blend?' series on YouTube.

Two case studies follow that show creative social media in action. Social media can generate an ongoing systematic dialogue with stakeholders (rather than a one-off campaign). These social media campaigns are a starting point to create dialogue, interaction and UGC, which boost engagement and embed key messages.

CASE STUDY 21.3   Using social media (and UGC movies) to help 11- to 15-year-olds to stop smoking

Situation

Although the proportion of young people aged 11–15 who smoke had fallen over the previous 10 years, in 2008 it was reported that by age 15 the proportion who reported smoking at least once a week had approximately risen to one in seven (14 per cent). Smoking is the main cause of preventable morbidity and premature death in England. The Deborah Hutton Campaign is working in harmony with existing government and charitable initiatives to reduce the prevalence of smoking among young people.

Objectives

Change agency ICE has worked with the Deborah Hutton Campaign on a pilot, Cut Films, a film-making competition which took place across 10 schools and a youth club nationwide. The challenge was to develop a creative concept that

FIGURE 21.2   Cut Films – 'film page' containing multiscreen grabs

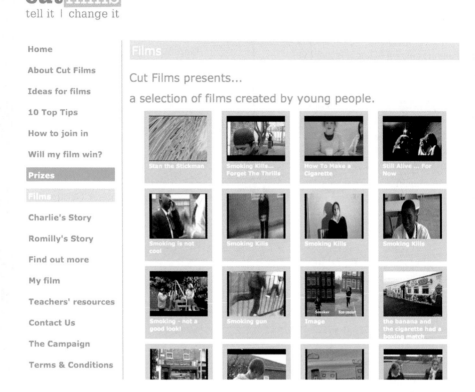

would positively resonate with and inspire young people, so the campaign grew through genuine enthusiasm, supported by schools and young people across the country. Ultimately, the project aimed to engender 1,000 films, generating a change in the attitudes of young people towards smoking and a reduction in the number of young people smoking.

Strategy

Cut Films used the creative film-making process, combined with the use of social media, to influence 11- to 15-year-olds. It attracted young people and encouraged them to share their own personal messages and creative work by using the relational nature of social media. This enabled users to forward films and messages, in order to create a snowball campaign that aimed to influence the cultural attitudes of young people towards smoking. The power of the campaign lay in the use of social media as part of a peer-to-peer approach engaging young people

through the creative attraction of film and new media technologies.

Tactics

The campaign set up a presence for Cut Films on a range of social media sites. Films were uploaded to YouTube and then 'pinged' across to pages on Facebook and Twitter. The campaign also promoted its presence among key stakeholders.

Action

The Cut Films competition was managed by the campaign director, who supported schools and youth clubs throughout the process. However, the main way of managing the results was through the 'My film' document that young people used to help them plan, reflect on and evaluate the process of producing a film, and reflect on the content they discovered throughout the process.

FIGURE 21.3   'Smoking is not cool' on YouTube

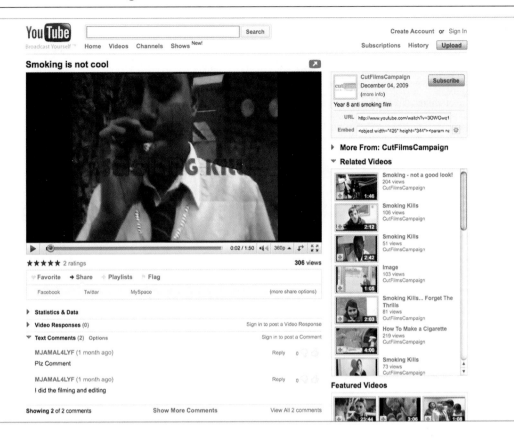

All films were submitted to the Cut Films website, moderated and uploaded to YouTube. There is an ongoing effort to introduce the campaign to schools, as well as constant communication with key stakeholders, including:

- the Department of Health;

- the head of features, ITV;

- key academic health promotion specialists;

- the head of public health sciences at the University of Edinburgh;

- schools and youth clubs;

- regional and local tobacco leads within local NHS services.

Control

Cut Films fed into health and citizenship issues within the PSHE curriculum, and this was underpinned with social marketing or social change principles from the National Social Marketing Centre. This provided rigorous evaluation and evidence for the campaign's long-term impact.

Underpinning every aspect of the project, ICE's social marketing division provided key insight focusing on re-aligning concepts of normal behaviour and identifying film topics that would inspire as well as nudge young people and their communities towards a move in behaviour. They also created an evaluation framework and focus groups to inform the roll-out and evaluation of the campaign nationally.

Men/women

The campaign director is the only full-time member of staff. She is supported at board level and is also working alongside social marketing company ICE, which as part of the pilot has provided free access to expertise in web development, design, social marketing and PR.

Money

ICE provided its expertise for the pilot free of charge, as a contribution to this charitable initiative.

Minutes

- Cut Films' pilot: June 2009 to March 2010.

- Website and resources designed: August to September 2009.

- Film deadline: December 2009.

- Awards ceremony: March 2010.

- National roll-out of campaign: September 2010 onwards.

See the Deborah Hutton Campaign website (**www. deborahhuttoncampaign.org**) and the Cut Films website (**www.cutfilms.org**).

CASE STUDY 21.4   Minime – a new social networking app to reduce cancer from sun bed abuse

Situation

A report published in 2009 by Cancer Research UK revealed that 20 per cent of young people in Liverpool aged 11–16 had used a sun bed. This compares to 6 per cent nationally. The World Health Organization has classified sun beds

FIGURE 21.4   Minime log-on

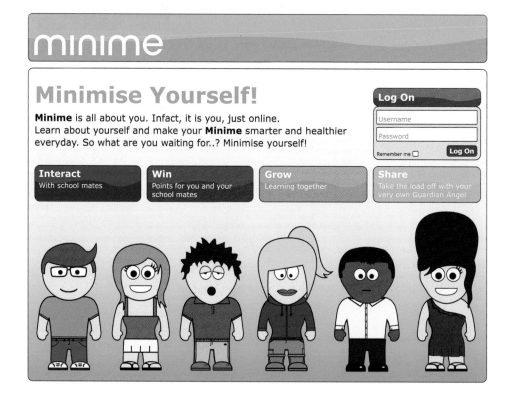

as carcinogenic, meaning they cause cancer and are as dangerous as cigarettes. Change agency ICE worked with Merseyside and Cheshire Cancer Network on an innovative social marketing approach to tackle the issues surrounding sun beds and sun exposure risks to young people.

Objectives

The underlying objective of this campaign was to engage with 11- to 16-year-olds and their parents across Merseyside and Cheshire about the dangers of sun exposure and sun bed use. The longer-term behavioural goal was to develop a targeted programme of education for children and young adults that would positively shift young people's behaviours more in line with the national average. There was great potential to reach seldom heard audience groups to discourage risky health behaviours.

Strategy

ICE harnessed social media for social good by developing a cutting-edge integrated Web 2.0 campaign, tailored to the needs of the target group. Built on robust research, insight and consultation, Minime is a social networking web application that works in a similar way to social media such as Facebook and Myspace.

Using the insights gathered, the company worked in partnership with Mersey and Cheshire Cancer Network to develop a social networking web application. A crucial part of developing this e-learning tool was tested with the target 11–16 age group to evaluate whether the message positively resonated with them and would move young people towards positive, long-term behaviour change. The rapid growth of social networking holds massive untapped potential for reaching out to hard-to-reach groups.

FIGURE 21.5   Minime question

FIGURE 21.6   Minime home page

Tactics

This project saw the development of new, interactive software that allowed students to create virtual personas of themselves. Minime is a discrete, managed system and can be safely used by schools, clubs and community organizations. Students can 'chat' to each other, scenarios will 'pop up', or users can specifically choose to take sun-related quizzes. Students can accumulate points by answering quiz questions and tackling real-life scenarios. They can then use their points to purchase 'stuff' for their character, including clothing, accessories and other possessions.

The principles are to: educate; create discussion, debate and opinions; and encourage each young person to make an informed choice about sun bathing and sun beds.

Action

This is a pilot project. ICE hosts the system, and there is a network administrator within each school, who sets and configures the system at a school level; the administrator can then monitor the content. ICE can target and filter quizzes, based on a user's profile. This interactive tool can also be linked to real-world performance in areas such as school attendance, and lesson plans are currently being developed to enable teachers to integrate this e-tool into PSHE lessons.

Control

Use of the system can be monitored on a daily basis; weekly reports can also be generated to show when students are using and accessing their account and how they are accumulating points.

The baseline data will help inform the next stage of the project and track the usability of the software. It is envisaged that this innovative e-learning tool will eventually be used in a range of educational settings to tackle other targeted health- or social-related issues, such as alcohol, smoking and drugs.

Men/women

Merseyside and Cheshire Cancer Network is working with two project managers and a web developer from ICE, with support from the PR team to build awareness in local schools and nationally. The project has also involved the buy-in of pilot schools, including headteachers, PSHE teachers and the young people themselves.

Money

ICE developed this campaign in conjunction with the National Cancer Action Team and other stakeholders. There have been financial contributions from Merseyside and Cheshire Cancer Network and ICE. The plan is to roll out a hosted version of the system, which a range of organizations can use.

Minutes

The pilot project involved an initial intensive development period for ICE (project management team and web development), including intensive research and scoping, over a 10-month period.

See also Case studies 16.1, 16.2 and 16.3.

Advantages and disadvantages

Here are some of the advantages and disadvantages to consider when deciding whether to increase or reduce this communications tool.

Advantages

Websites can help to establish the credibility of a brand, engage customers in a unique way and convert them into lifetime customers and brand advocates. Combine this with social media platforms, and the combination can be used to move customers up the ladder of engagement and spread the word. The website is a controlled environment (assuming it is moderated). Added value can be given to the site continually, so social media can help to create awareness and engage customers all the way through a purchase and becoming an advocate. While the website is generally not a tool for building awareness, it is a tool for nurturing awareness into relationships. Social media, on the other hand, can create awareness, change attitudes and help to convert prospects to customers and customers into lifetime customers.

Disadvantages

Websites are totally dependent on traffic. No traffic makes a website useless. Investment is required for, first, traffic-building campaigns and, second, maintenance of the site with fresh content. Equally, social media requires a continued feed of fresh content (as well as resources to respond to discussions). This can be resource hungry (SMO is the new SEO), and as yet there are few models to indicate the optimum resource allocation here. The usual issues of servers crashing, security hackers, scams and spammers jeopardizing the control of the message are challenges, and constant vigilance is required. Equally, conversations across the full social media spectrum need to be monitored and tracked continually. Scope creep can mess up a website, as can poor content management, eg out-of-date content left online. Maintenance is essential.

Conclusion

There are four key satisfaction factors for websites: high-quality content; easy navigation; fast downloads; and updated content. High-quality content is more likely with some scenario planning, persona development, creative sizzle and customer engagement. The second factor, navigation, requires careful planning, including navigation rules and identifying the top tasks. Then comes the challenge of customer conversion (from prospect or visitor to customer). The probability of success increases with: a strong call to action; 'See', 'Try' and 'Buy'; price lining; simplified processes; reduced customer anxiety; a contact strategy and digital body language; and relevant landing pages. The chapter also focuses on successful social media, which require high-quality content, suitably optimized and spread across various social networks. The chapter explores how to integrate social media into business systems, optimize social media and, finally, avoid the 10 most common social media mistakes.

Key points from Chapter 21

- There are four key satisfaction factors for websites: high-quality content, easy navigation, fast downloads and updated content.

- High-quality content is more likely with some scenario planning, persona development, creative sizzle and customer engagement.

- Navigation requires careful planning, including navigation rules and identifying the top tasks.

- Customer conversion increases with: a strong call to action; 'See', 'Try' and 'Buy'; price lining; simplified processes; reduced customer anxiety; a contact strategy and digital body language; and relevant landing pages.

- Successful social media requires high-quality content, suitably optimized and spread across various social networks.

- Social media must be integrated into business systems and databases.

- SMO is the new SEO – social media must be optimized.

- The 10 most common social media mistakes can be avoided with common sense.

References and further reading

Bossidy, L and Charan, R (2002) *Execution: The discipline of getting things done*, Soundview Executive Books, Concordville, PA

Byron, D, Kievman, N and Schrum, R (2010) Why executives hate social media: An executive's guide to social media, *Deming Hill*

Chaffey, D and Smith, P R (2008) *eMarketing eXcellence*, Butterworth-Heinemann, Oxford

Gibs, J (2009) Social media: The next great gateway for content discovery?, *Nielsen Wire*, 5 October

McGovern, G (2010a) The customer is a stranger, *New Thinking*, 7 June

McGovern, G (2010b) Web manager: Top tasks versus tiny tasks, *New Thinking*, 28 June

Robles, P (2010) 10 common social media mistakes, *Econsultancy*, 31 March

Sexton, J (2010) Dispelling buyer anxiety and replacing it with buyer confidence, *Web Marketing Today*, 3 August

Seybold, P (2001) Get inside the lives of your customers, *Harvard Business Review*, May

Solis, B (2010) The 10 stages of social media integration in business, *BrianSolis.com*, 22 January

Surowiecki, J (2005) *The Wisdom of Crowds*, Anchor Books, New York

Woods, A (2007) The Revolution usability report: Creativity – looks aren't everything, *Revolution magazine.com*, 4 December

Woods, S (2009) *Digital Body Language*, New Year Publishing, Danville, CA

Further information

Advance Positions
www.advancepositions.com

Advertising Standards Authority (ASA)
2 Torrington Place
London WC1E 7HW
Tel: +44 (0)20 7580 5555
www.asa.org.uk

Business Link
Tel: 0845 600 9006
www.businesslink.gov.uk

Cloudmark Europe Ltd (anti-spam software)
Garrick House
26–27 Southampton Street
London WC2E 7RS
Tel: +44 (0)20 7100 5224
www.cloudmark.com

Committee of Advertising Practice (CAP)
Mid City Place
71 High Holborn
London WC1V 6QT
Tel: +44 (0)20 7492 2100
www.cap.org.uk

Google Business Solutions
www.google.co.uk/services/

Office of the Data Protection Registrar
Wycliffe House
Water Lane
Wilmslow
Cheshire SK9 5AF
Tel: +44 (0)30 3123 1113
Fax: +44 (0)1625 524510
www.dataprotection.gov.uk

Rivergold Associates Ltd (t/a Wordtracker)
Unit 11–12 Apollo Studios
Charlton King's Road
London NW5 2SB
Tel: +44 (0)33 3200 4555
Fax: +44 (0)20 7424 8844
www.wordtracker.com

INDEX

NB: page numbers in *italic* indicate figures or tables